Churches of Ethiopia. The Monastery di Nārgā Śellāsē

Mario Di Salvo

Churches of Ethiopia

The Monastery of Nārgā Śellāsē

with texts by
Stanislaw Chojnacki
Osvaldo Raineri

Graphic Design
Marcello Francone

Editorial Coordination
Giovanni Keller

Layout
Evelina Laviano

Translations
Nicholas Holland Brendan
Maria Luisa Sala

First published in Italy in 1999 by
Skira Editore S.p.A.
Palazzo Casati Stampa
via Torino 61
20123 Milano
Italy

Printed and bound in Italy.
First edition

ISBN 88-8118-529-6

Distributed in North America and Latin America by Abbeville Publishing Group, 22 Cortlandt Street, New York, NY 10007, USA.
Distributed elsewhere in the world by Thames and Hudson Ltd., 181a High Holborn, London WC1V 7QX, United Kingdom.

Acknowledgements

I would like to express my deep gratitude to His Holiness Abuna Pawlos, Patriarch of Ethiopia, whose high benediction has accompanied our work.
I thank all those who have given their valuable support and contributed to the birth of this undertaking:
Ato Jarra Ḫayle Māryām, of the Ethiopian Ministry of Cultural Heritage
Ato Ghenna Desta, essential and substantial collaborator,
Ato Mezemir Abiy, of the West Gojjam Culture, Tourism and Information Department,
Mamher Gabra Māryām, abbot of Nārgā Śellāsē's monastery
Heartfelt thanks are due to all those who, in various capacities, have given their necessary contribution to the successful outcome of the expedition to Nārgā.

Mario Di Salvo

Photographic references

G. Rovelli and U. Ambrogio, Studio Aleph: 1, 12, 111, 112, 113, 114, 117, 120, 125, 126, 132, 137, 138, 139, 140, 142, 143, 144, 145, 147, 149, 152, 153, 154, 155, 156, 157, 158, 159, 161, 162, 163, 164, 165, 166, 167, 168, 169, 170, 171, 172, 173, 174, 175, 176, 177, 178, 179, 180, 181, 182, 183, 184, 185, 186, 187, 188, 189, 190, 191, 192, 193, 194, 195, 196, 197, 198, 199, 200, 201, 202, 203, 204, 205, 206, 207, 208, 209, 210, 211, 212, 213, 214, 215, 216, 217, 218
M. Baccaglini: 10, 39, 40, 43, 44, 64, 68, 103, 150
S. Chojnacki: 11, 17, 18
M. Di Salvo: 2, 3, 5, 6, 7, 8, 13, 14, 15, 16, 19, 20, 21, 22, 24, 28, 32, 34, 37, 41, 45, 63, 73, 88, 93, 99, 100, 101, 105, 106, 107, 109, 115, 118, 119, 121, 122, 123, 124, 127, 131, 148, 151
W. Krafft: 141
A. Pozzi: 42, 81, 82, 83, 92, 102, 133, 134, 135, 136, 146

Everywhere, in every epoch, man has felt the desire to honour his Creator and he expressed this feeling by transposing it into often sublime works of art: this happened also in the heart of Africa, in hidden and secluded places, such as the area of Lake Tana, in Ethiopia.

Ethiopian orthodox Christians have been praising God for centuries, with a passion which is reflected in long religious ceremonies, suggestive processions, the coloured figures of the maqdas*, the splendour of the crosses and the illuminations of ancient sacred manuscripts.*

Anyone who has been to Ethiopia knows that there the general atmosphere is not so strange for western eyes as it could be in other far-away places, probably because of the deep sense of Christian faith easily perceivable everywhere.

Probably, it is exactly this comforting sense of pertenance which inspires in the traveller a strong desire for a better understanding, for joining in.

The genesis of this book has its own little story: during a journey to Ethiopia with friends—also officials of the Carlo Leone Montandon Foundation—, on the shores of Lake Tana we were stunned by the unexpected, incredible paintings of a church with a thatched roof, hidden in the greenery, the first of a series of similarly stupefying examples. The impression they made on us did not diminish with time: on the contrary, we have wondered what we could actually do in order to make these treasures better known.

Thus was born the idea of this book, of which the architect Mario Di Salvo is the main promoter and author.

The carrying out of a thorough survey of all or even of just a part of the huge number of churches of the Lake Tana area is certainly to be hoped for. However, it would be a huge task and we therefore decided to confine this study to only one church, to describe it exhaustively and to present it within a general study.

The problem of which church to choose, amongst the many available for study, has been easily solved thanks to the authoritative advice of the renowned expert on Ethiopian culture, Professor Stanislaw Chojnacki, to whom we are very grateful.

The photographic work and the survey of the Nārgā Śellāsē monastery has been neither easy nor simple: we had to organize an expedition to an islet inhabited only by a few monks, some priests and their families, with no electricity, no running water apart from that of the lake and where there were no lodgings; a place where the lifestyle is altogether different from that to which we are accustomed, both in the spiritual and practical sense. We had to organise some sort of accomodation, under these rough circumstances, for a number of people—photographers, architects, engineers, specialized workers and somebody to take care of them all—, twelve people in all from Italy plus some Ethiopian

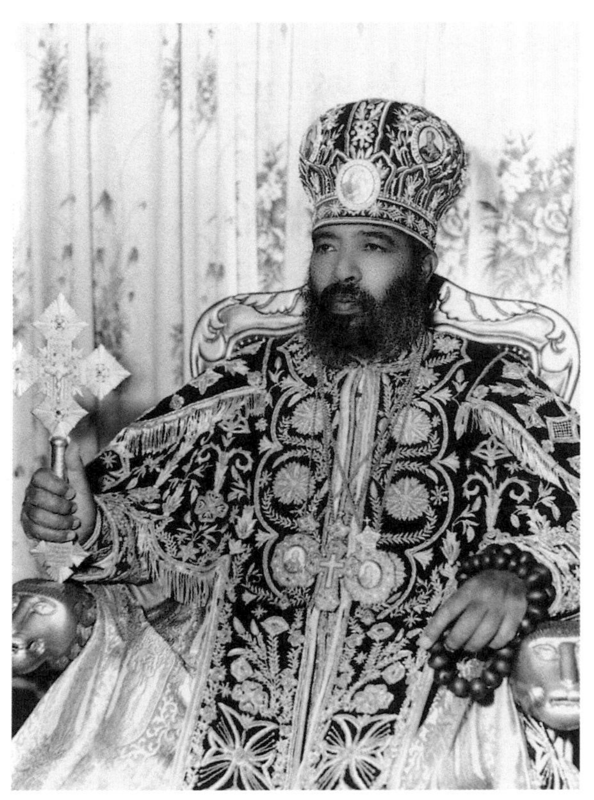

His Holiness Abuna Pawlos,
Patriarch of Ethiopia and eč̣agē
of the see of St. Tekle Haymānot.

friends whose valuable and necessary collaboration made this whole enterprise possible. Perhaps if we had known in advance that that year the rainy season was going to be exceptionally long, bringing each night flooding, heavy showers and formidable storms; that the tents were going to suddenly collapse in the middle of the night, battered down by the torrential rain; that many of us were going to sleep under the external portico of the church, with the perplexed consent of the priests and monks, who every morning at five, psalmodizing, jumped over the pallets to get into the church for morning mass; that the generator which had been transported there at great pains was going to break down, risking the failure of the whole operation..., if we had known all this in advance, probably the book on Nārgā Śellāsē would not yet exist.

But luckily we had no foreknowledge of these events and in the end those involved in this enterprise would not have exchanged for anything the pleasure of the morning sun, drying up everything in an instant; the silent and participating activity of the workers who every morning arrived on their tānqwā *from the near isle of Dek and every night lapped in the darkness towards distant huts; the vigilant, curious and increasingly more convinced presence of the monks; the evening splashes into the thick and warm water of the lake to get rid of tiredness and sweat; the tasty lunches and dinners invented in improbable conditions, eaten sitting all together on the steps of the quay, bathed in the twilight; the experience of life, friendship, tolerance, sharing: this adventure, which will remain indelible in the hearts and the minds of all of us.*

The directors of the Carlo Leone Montandon Foundation are therefore very happy and proud to offer both the occasional reader and the scholar an appropriate instrument for approaching such a distant world, with the hope that it becomes an enrichment and a source for further curiosity.

The Foundation also hopes that the work carried out with such passion and love by the whole team and those responsible for the work at the publishers, Skira, contributes to giving rise to initiatives aimed at increasing our knowledge of the countless treasures, both artistic and cultural, of the wonderful land of Ethiopia and to their conservation for future generations.

Mariena Mondelli Montandon
President of the Carlo Leone Montandon Foundation

Contents

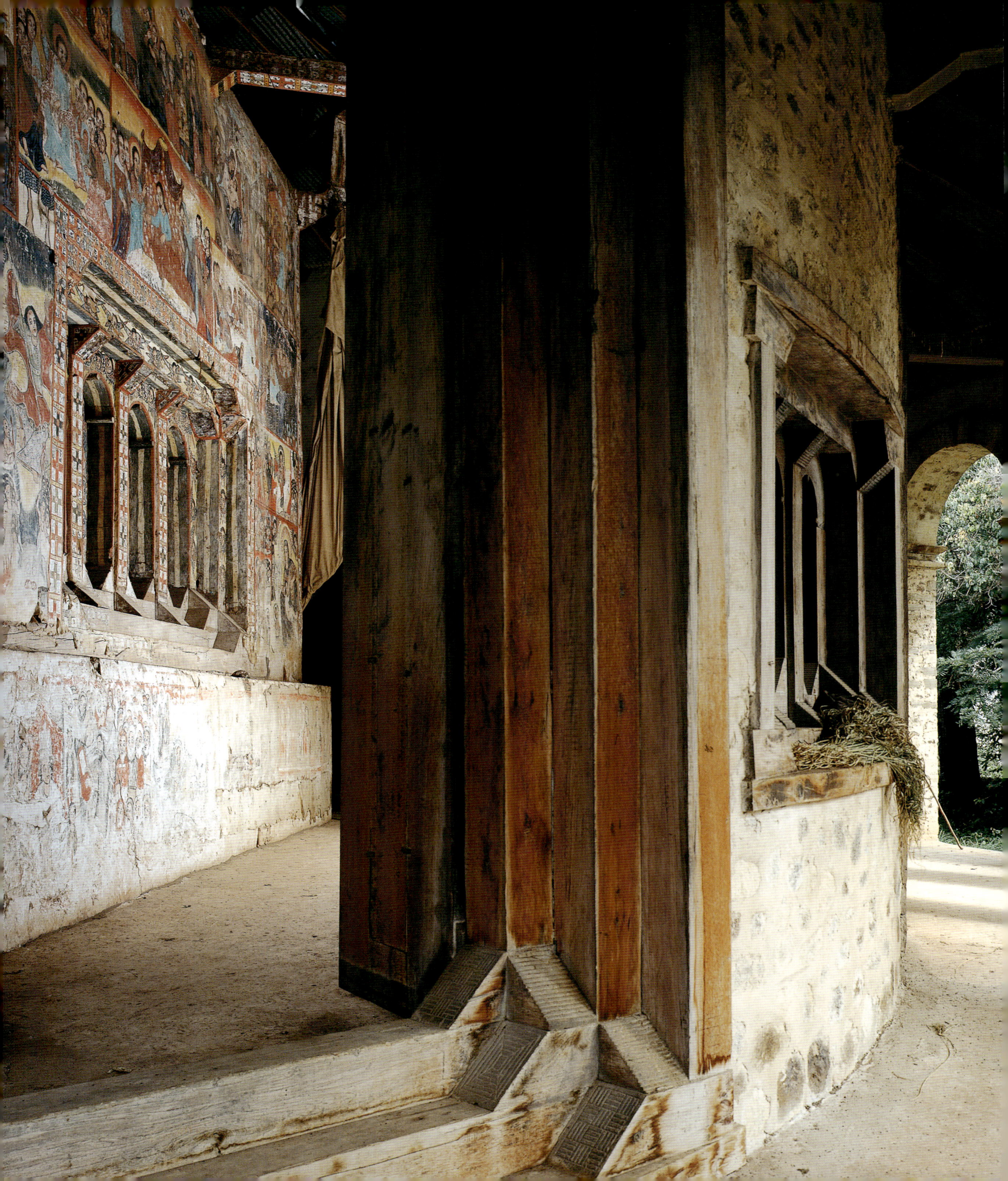

Preface

Stanislaw Chojnacki

This important publication is the result of an auspicious encounter between the architect Mario Di Salvo, Director of the Foundation Carlo Leone Montandon and myself at an exhibition of Ethiopian art held in Rome, in October 1996. On that occasion, Di Salvo expressed the intention of the Foundation to "undertake something relating to the churches on the islands of Lake Tana." My immediate response was to put forward the suggestion of a publication on the wall paintings at Nārgā Śellāsē, one of the churches of the Dek group of islands on the lake.

One year later, Di Salvo informed me that the Foundation had decided to take up my suggestion and that after obtaining official permission, the project was proceeding well; with the photography already finished, the measurements of the buildings recorded and all related drawings completed. Di Salvo also invited me to assume an active role in the preparation of the text. This was most gratifying, but prior obligations unfortunately prevented me from active participation. I did, however, assure him that I would be available for consultation and that I would be honoured to write a preface to this publication.

Although the inception of the Nārgā Śellāsē project was the result of a chance meeting, its successful outcome would never have been realised without the involvement of the foundress of the Carlo Leone Montandon Foundation. Her firm belief in the bond of brotherhood linking all people, coupled with a strong commitment to human culture and its interrelationships have combined to make this project a reality. This humanistic philosophy was the legacy of her Swiss father, Dott. Carlo Leone Montandon, in whose name the Foundation was incorporated. It is expressed, as well, in the charter of the Foundation, which directs its assistance to cultural and educational activities both in Switzerland and abroad, as well as supporting research in various disciplines, including art history.

In turning its attention to Ethiopia's artistic heritage, the Foundation Carlo Leone Montandon, seated in Switzerland, but with strong ties to Italy, is not only helping to strengthen the bonds of friendship between these two countries and Ethiopia, but has become the vehicle for expanding an awareness of Ethiopia's rich cultural history. Moreover, in sponsoring the publication of this work on the architecture and paintings of Nārgā Śellāsē Church—the epitome of Ethiopia's artistic creativity—the Foundation is maintaining the long-standing tradition of Italian scholarly interest in Ethiopia, while, at the same time fulfilling the expectations of scholars and others with an interest in Ethiopian art and culture throughout the world.

1. Various rings of walls adorned with paintings surround Nārgā Śellāsē sanctuary.

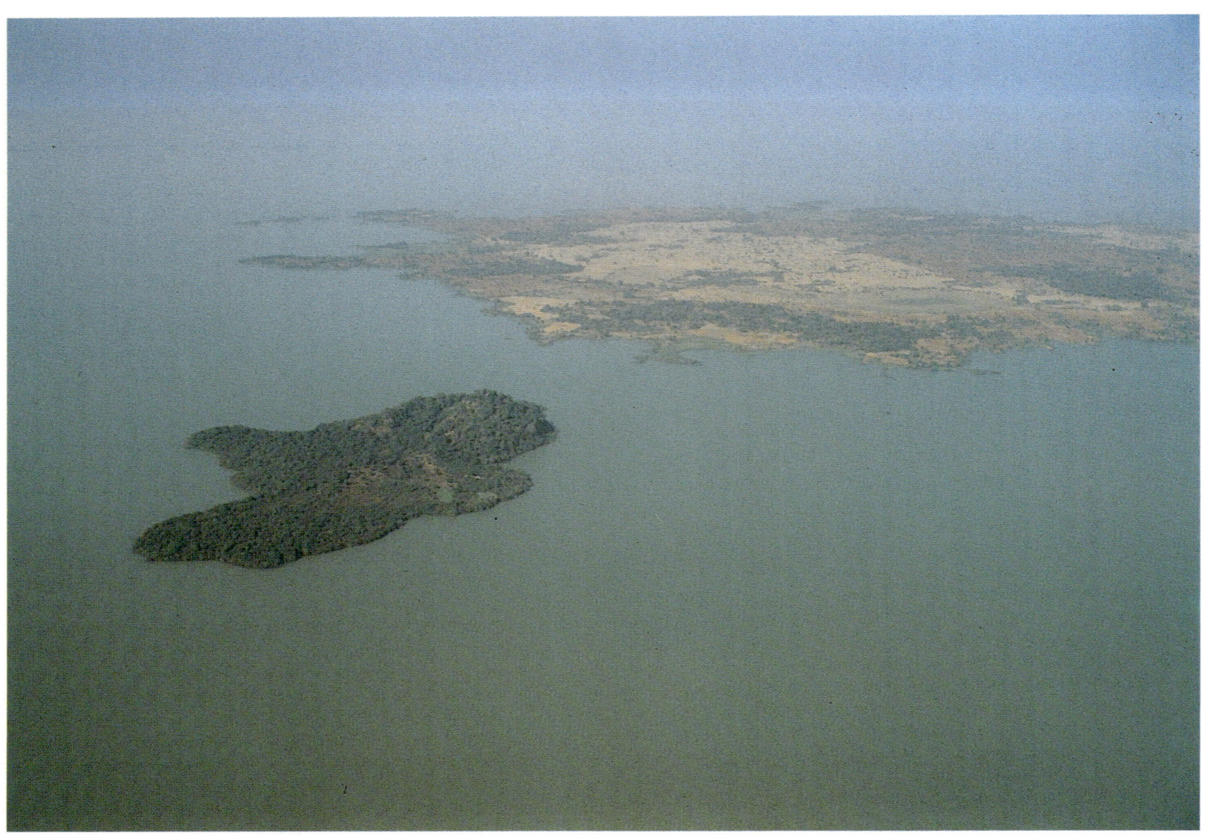

2. The flat island of Dek frays into small islets, on one of which stands the monastery of Nārgā Śellāsē. On the islet in front, is the ancient convent of Dāgā Esṭifanos.

Until the latter part of the 20th century, the unique art of Christian Ethiopia remained virtually unknown beyond its borders. This was due, in part, to Ethiopia's geographic location. Situated high on an East African plateau, for centuries its people remained essentially removed from the currents of world history. Yet, despite their relative isolation, over the years Ethiopian artists have produced a prodigious body of manuscript miniatures, church murals and religious icons. In the context of art history these works have provided us with a wealth of new and uncharted territory.

Initially, however, a series of questions must be raised. What are the elements that combine to define the art of Ethiopia ? What is its significance in the history of art in general, and what is its specific significance, in the context of Christian art in Africa?

There are three key elements which have led to the marked singularity of Ethiopia's artistic expression. The first is the indomitable spirit of the people of Ethiopia, who have succeeded in preserving their independence for the last two thousand years. As a result, they have been free to develop as a unique cultural and artistic entity.

Of equal importance is the role of the Ethiopian Orthodox church, which, since its inception, has served as the wellspring of Ethiopia's religious art. The advent of Christianity in the 4th century marked the beginnings of the tradition of religious painting in Ethiopia—a tradition which continues to this day. The pervasive spirit of Ethiopian painting is largely derived from its interpretations of the art of Eastern Christianity; expressing in an Ethiopian context a fervent confirmation of the Christian faith. Painting, as an act of piety, reflects another world, acting as an intermediary between the realms of the spiritual and the terrestrial to express the inexpressible in visible form.

The third element in the development of Ethiopia's artistic singularity is the fact that it has taken root, grown and flourished on African soil. By the same token the art of Ethiopia differs significantly from the art which is currently referred to as African, i.e. the art of the indigenous people of Western, Central, and Southern Africa. By virtue of tradition, the main idiom of expression here has been sculpture, whereas,

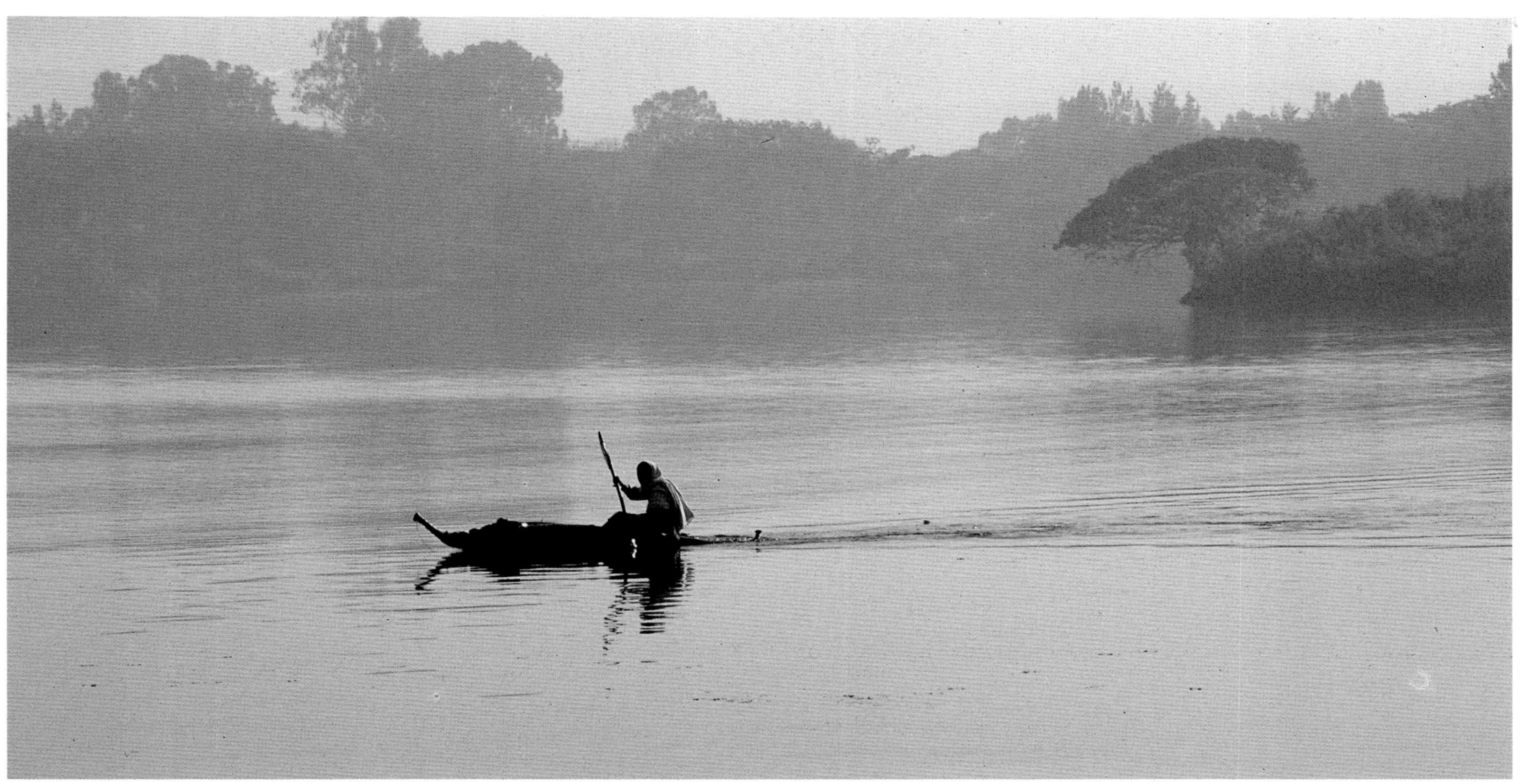

3. On a *tānkuā*, the papyrus boat typical of Lake Tana.

from the outset, Ethiopian artistic creativity has been almost entirely defined by its paintings. Together these three elements have worked to generate a distinctive artistic phenomenon.

From the standpoint of its evolution, however, changing styles in Ethiopian traditional art cannot be considered comparable to stylistic changes in Western art. The underlying principles of Ethiopian painting always remain the same due to its didactic and devotional character. Its purpose is to depict in colour the narrative of the Gospels, to portray hallowed personages in forms that are intelligible to believers, and to render votive prayers more effective by expressing requests through the creation of painted images.

By virtue of its geographic situation, Ethiopian art belongs to Africa, yet its development over many centuries is interwoven with the introduction of models borrowed from Eastern as well as Western Christian art. It has absorbed, as well, the impact of Islamic culture and art and responded to influences emanating from the vast area of the Indian Ocean. In short, Ethiopian painters faithfully reproduced what they regarded as the most significant iconographic characteristics of these external models while at the same time incorporating stylistic elements derived from African art forms.

The convergence of these influences occured intermittently and at certain times simultaneously. The strength of Ethiopian attachment to the iconographic tradition of both Eastern and Western Christian art is evidenced by its sustained existence in Ethiopia. Ethiopian paintings—even relatively modern ones—often reflect, with simple fidelity, archaic types of iconographic art forrns, that have long since been lost to the cultures of their origin. For example, images of the Virgin Mary, separated by three centuries, have been reproduced with an iconographic accuracy that is nothing short of remarkable.

A particularly fascinating aspect of Ethiopian art is its adherence to the expression of an objective truth independent of time and space. Subjects are depicted in what are considered their real and immutable form. At the height of its stylistic perfection, Ethiopian art renounces the illusion of volume, depth and perspective. The paintings are conceptual and composed of a series of 'image-signs' according to spiritual considerations. Their image-signs arranged on a flat surface are meant to give the impression of a concept or a narration. Human figures, the epitome of Ethiopian art, are characterised by non-realistic head and body proportions and generally static poses.

Church decorations represent what is possibly the richest and yet the least studied element of Ethiopian art. They serve as a dramatic illustration of the development of many centuries.

Illuminated manuscripts also constitute a highly significant portion of Ethiopia's artistic heritage. In Ethiopia, the ancient art of producing illustrated books on parchment is a tradition that has continued for centuries. In the light of the antiquity of their origins, these manuscripts are of exceptional artistic and cultural value.

The existence of a wealth of paintings on wood, on the other hand, is a comparatively recent discovery. Icons preserved in churches and monasteries over the course of centuries have gradually come to light; substantially broadening our knowledge of Ethiopian art and revealing a new dimension of Christian art in Africa. However, unlike other centres of Eastern Christianity such as Russia or Greece, the practice of keeping icons in people's homes was never established. Even today, the icons believed to have been painted by St. Luke are carried by priests in procession only during annual feasts or in times of war or drought.

For several centuries privately commissioned icons were offered to churches in order to ensure the salvation of the donor's soul. These votive donations were attested to by the solemn formulae inscribed on the icons. Until the 18th century, the actual figures of the donors seldom appeared; however, as the century advanced, Ethiopian rulers developed a desire to be depicted together with the sacred image of the Virgin or Christ or possibly that of a favourite saint. This innovation was emulated, in turn, by the nobility and clergy, and in the course of the last two centuries, donor figures became a permanent feature of Ethiopian religious art.

The essential attributes of the supplicant figures and their importance are indicated symbolically through size, positioning and pose; each determining relative stature and rank. In general, donors are shown at the bottom of the work and are depicted either prostrate or standing to the side. Since Ethiopian artists did not attempt to individualise physiognomy, the inscription simply provides a possible indication of the donor's identity. On the other hand, individual artists faithfully reproduced costumes, ornaments, weapons and other accessories. Although usually in simplified form, these details are true reflections of historical conditions and are also significant indications of the subject's social status and distinction.

The themes and forms of religious paintings in Ethiopia have been handed down from one generation of monastic or clerical painters to another; the masters passing on to their students the various themes and forms in strict accordance to local tradition. This accounts for the remarkable continuity that has been maintained for centuries virtually impervious to change as it applies to symbolic meaning and form, yet not without a degree of flexibility. The timeless practice of copying, coupled with the simultaneous process of adaptation is integral to artistic endeavour in Ethiopia. As a result, a powerful stylistic transmutation of external models, has come to uniquely characterise the creative expression of Ethiopia's artists throughout its extensive history.

Within this context, for what reasons was Nārgā Śellāsē chosen as the subject of this study from among the dozens of churches of Lake Tana? In my view, there are four basic reasons for this choice; the first being the lake itself, with its particular fascination and mystique. In addition, it is clear that Nārgā Śellāsē is an exceptional architectural complex, including its enclosure and tower, and various outbuildings as well as the church itself. Moreover, the quality of the wall paintings and their place in the history of Ethiopian art are reflections of the ideas and artistic tastes of its 18th century

4. The Lake Tana region: (from DAINELLI 1938).

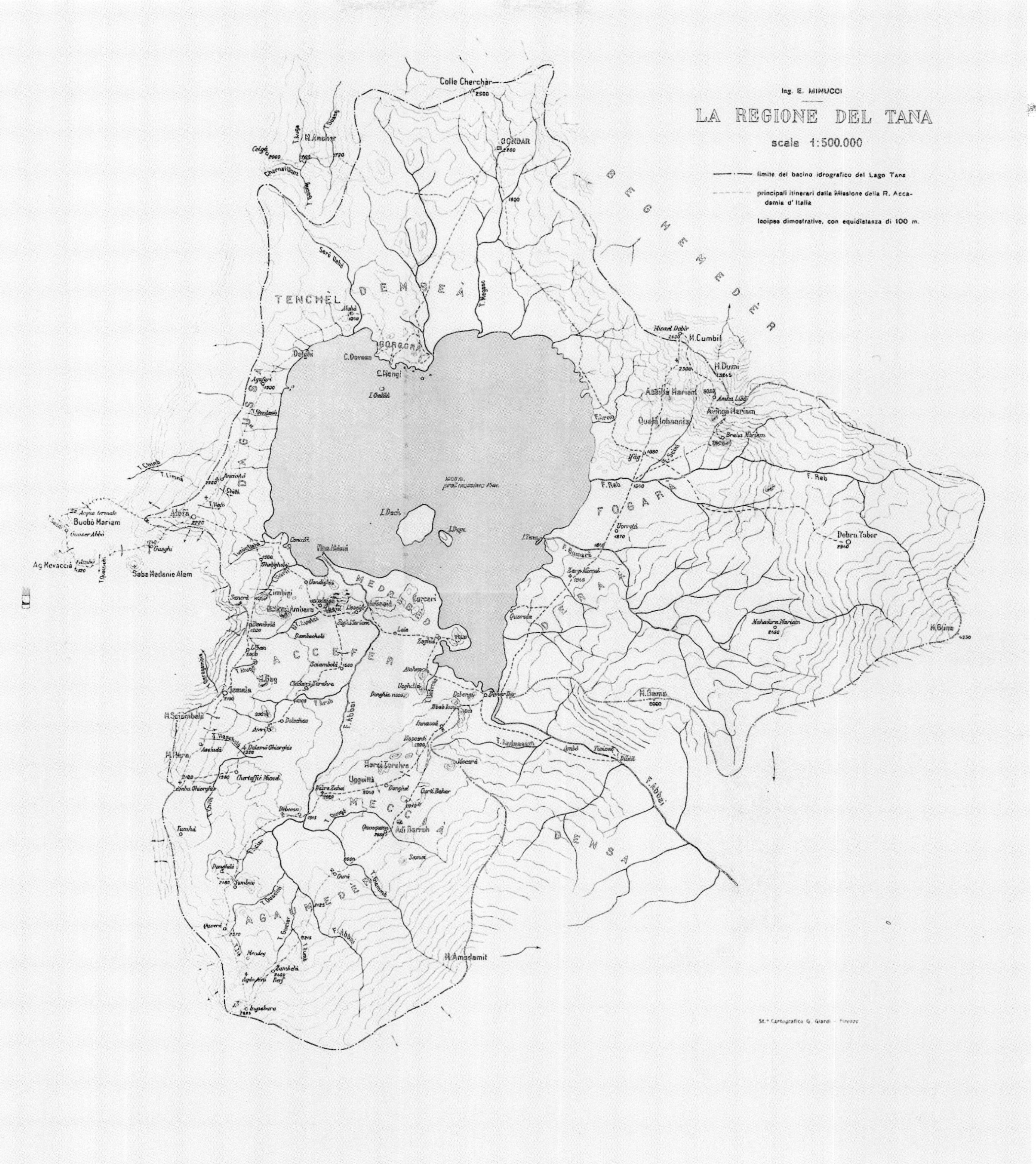

Ing. E. MINUCCI
LA REGIONE DEL TANA
scala 1:500.000
limite del bacino idrografico del Lago Tana
principali itinerari della Missione della R. Accademia d' Italia
Isoipse dimostrative, con equidistanza di 100 m.
Colle Cherchar
GONDAR
BEGHEMEDER
TENCHEL
DEMBEA
GORGORA
M. Cumbil
M. Dumi
Assilla Mariam
Quora Iohannis
FOGARA
F. Reb
Debra Tabor
DAGUSSA
Buobò Mariam
Ag. Mevaccià
Saba Madanie Alem
Zimbiri
MEDREBAHD
ACCEFER
F. Abbai
M. Sciambela
Ugguittà
MECCIA
Adi Darrah
DENSA
M. Gama
T. Andassam
AGAU MEDER
M. Amadamit
St.° Cartografico G. Giardi - Firenze

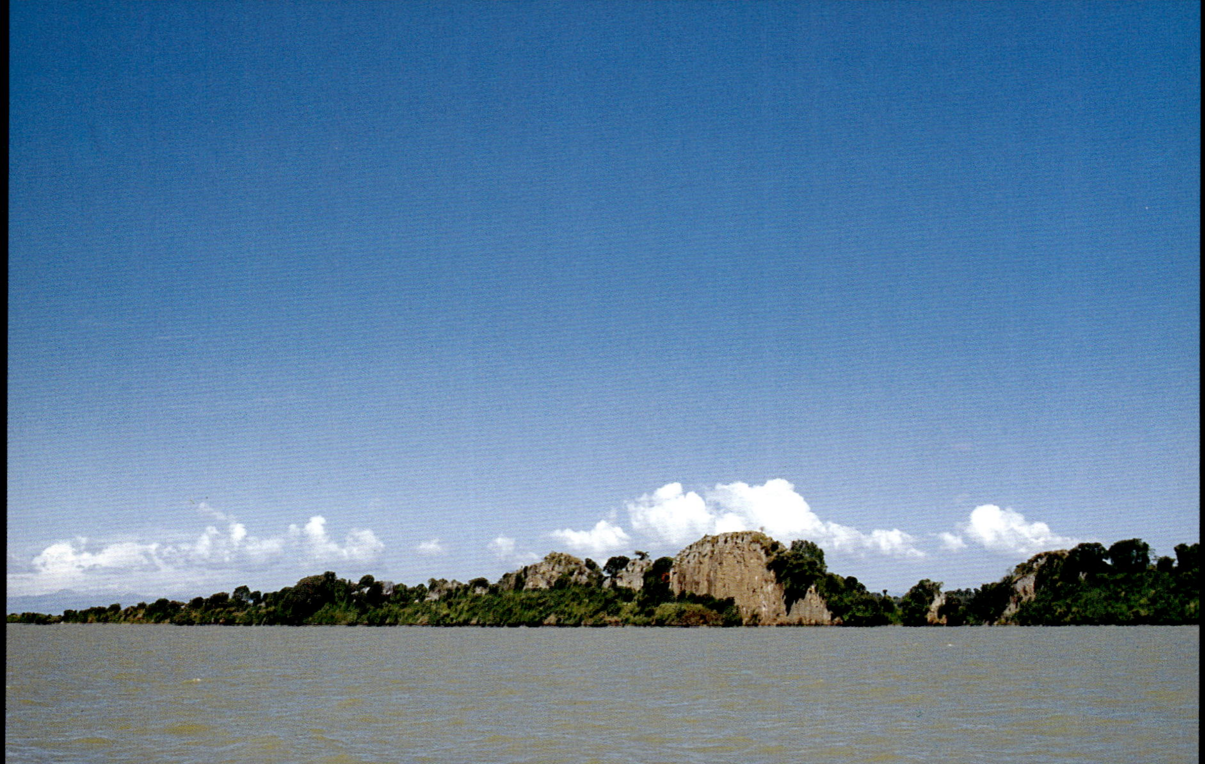

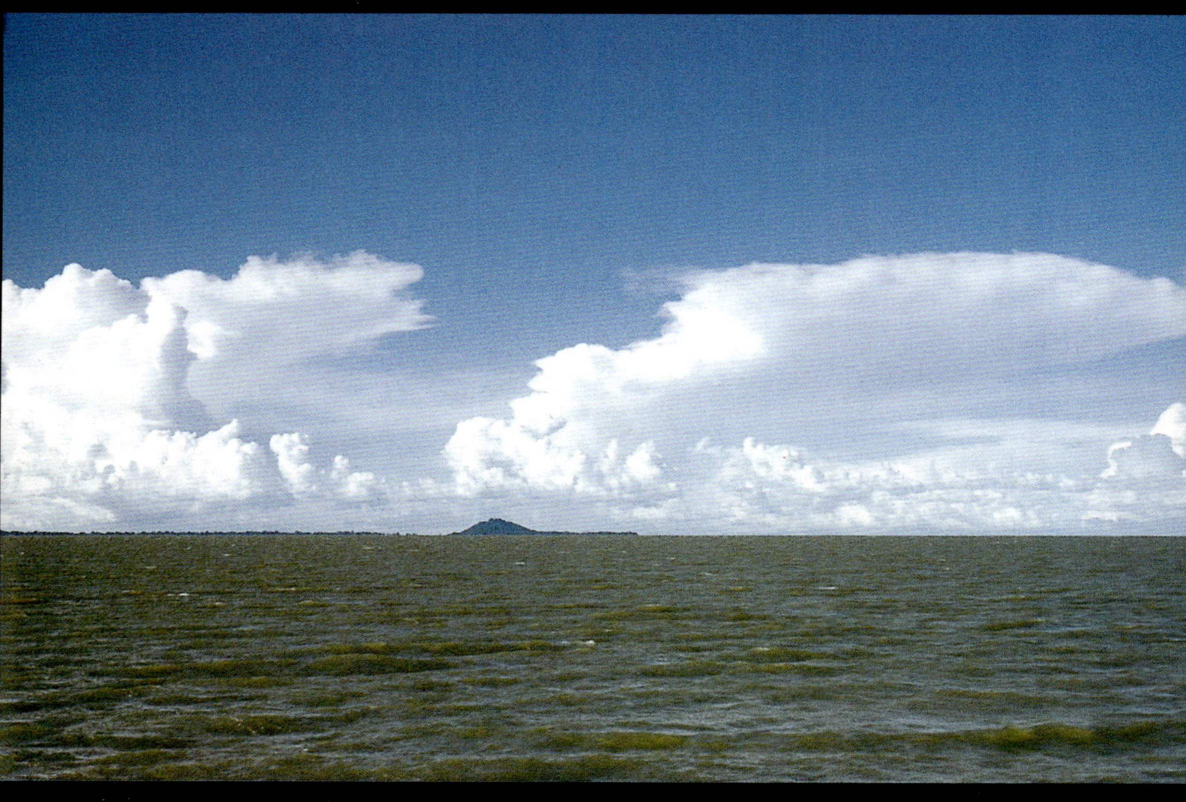

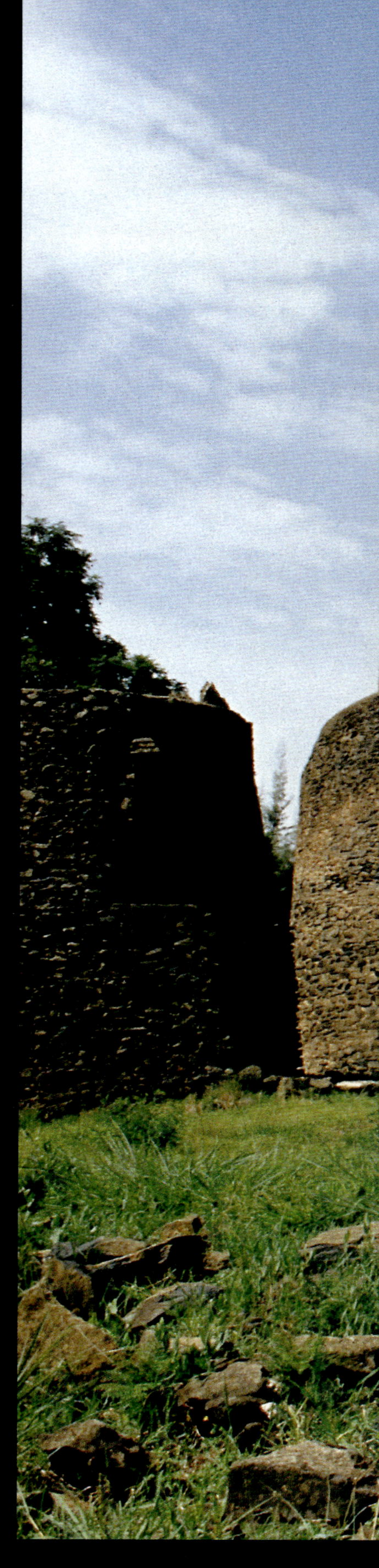

5-6. The impending rocky spur of Ṭānā Qirqos and the pointed top of the islet of Dāgā Esṭifanos, in the middle of Lake Tana, are the lake's main visual reference points. On both of them stand ancient monasteries.

7. The castle of Iyāsu I (1730-1755) and that of Fāsiladas (1632-1667) in Gondar.

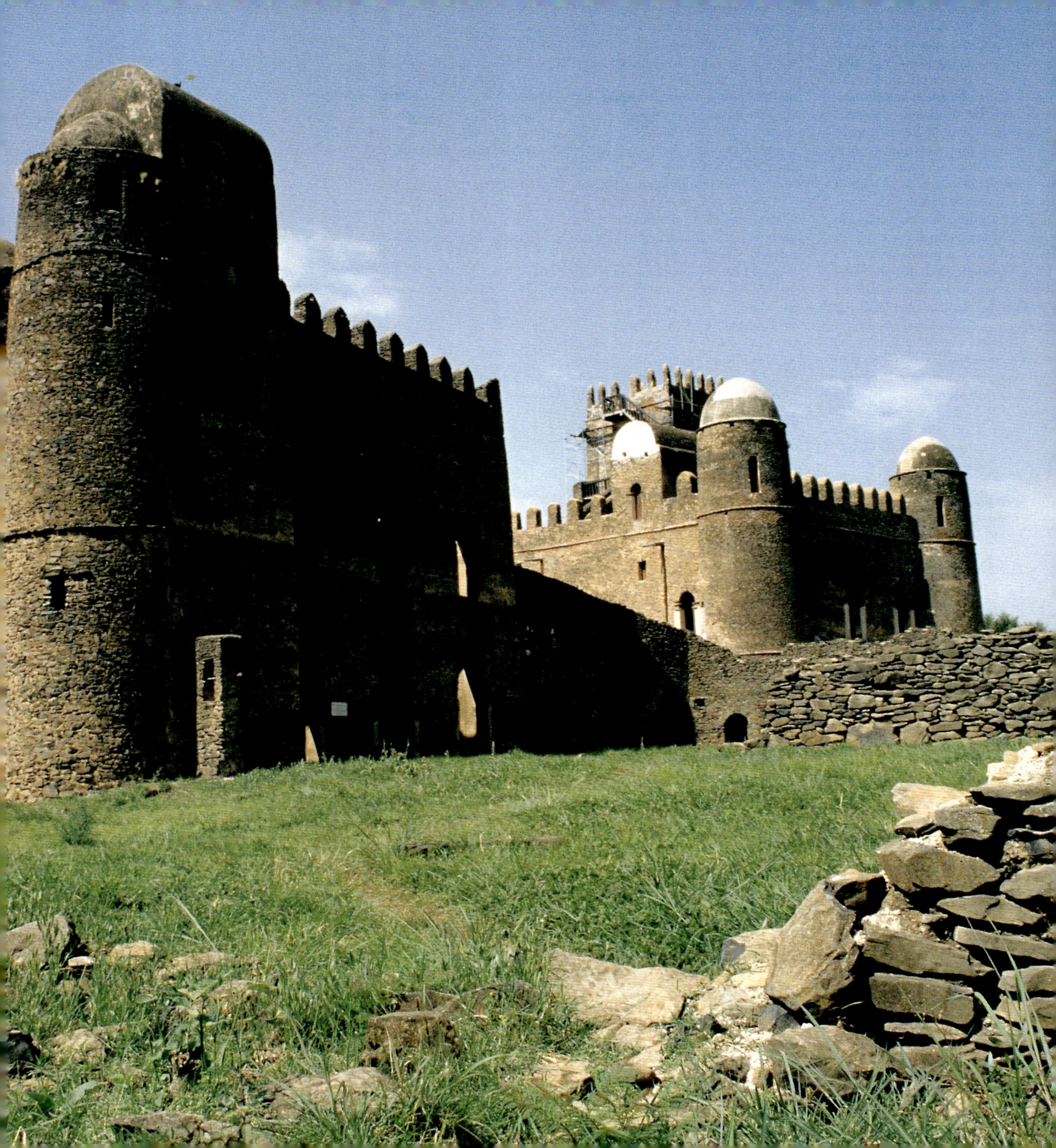

foundress, Empress Mentewwāb. Moreover, the extraordinarily compelling personality of this remarkable woman must also be taken into account.

Lake Tana was known to ancient geographers for its life-giving soil brought to Egypt with the waters of the Blue Nile. The lake, eighty kilometres long and sixty kilometres in width, is shallow and framed by sinuous shores covered with lush vegetation. It is dotted with roughly forty islands, of which close to twenty are said to have had churches and monasteries situated on them. The islands lie close to the shores of the lake, except for one central cluster. It is here that the tiny island of Nārgā is situated. The water is usually calm in the mornings, with waves forming in the afternoon wind. In the past, there was a great quantity of fish of different kinds, and many hippopotami, however only a specific group of people, the Wayto, hunted these creatures and ate their flesh. The local inhabitants still traverse the lake in slender papyrus boats, called *tānquā*, just as the ancient Egyptians poled them up and down the Nile. It could well be said that on Lake Tana, a sense of the remote past belongs to the present.

In the history of the lake itself, there are two periods of great significance. The first was characterised by monastic settlements originating in the 13th century. The possibility exists that there were, in fact, earlier settlements, since local tradition attributes the existence of the monasteries to Aksumite kings. In the interval, however, a number of these early monasteries have disappeared without a trace. During the next two centuries, settlement of the islands developed more fully, as hermits and monks sought seclusion and a degree of security from the pagan inhabitants dwelling on the shores of the lake. These settlements became the seat of local Christianisation and of missionary work. The most important of these was Ṭānā Qirqos, which became a centre of Christian learning. Under the aegis of King Amda Ṣeyon, it also received the benefit of his generous sponsorship. In the 15th century, the Monastery of Esṭifanos (St. Stephen) on Dāgā Island in the middle of the lake, was favoured by Ethiopian royalty and two of its kings are buried there. This period is also renowned for the important churches erected on the islands, while the monasteries were the source of the copious production of manuscripts and flourishing artistic creativity.

In the 16th century, however, conditions changed radically in the course of a turbulent period of Moslem and Oromo invasions. The islands became a refuge for monks and also depositories for objects salvaged from burned churches on the mainland. The most noteworthy change, however, was the northward movement of the Empire's political power. In the late 16th and early 17th century, the once ubiquitous Ethiopian kings began building their residences to the east and north of Lake Tana; the lake itself becoming the focal point of this relocation. King Sarṣa Dengel consolidated his control over the north, building a royal castle at Guzārā in a mountainous area overlooking the north-eastern shore of the lake. Its imposing ruins still exist providing evidence of the trend towards the establishment of permanent residences.

In time, Sarṣa Dengel's successors moved even closer to the lake. At Gorgorā, Emperor Susenyos had a huge stone church and palace erected on the peninsula. Susenyos also had another palace constructed at Danqaz, north of Gorgorā, and nearby were his leisure residence and gardens. During the same period, the monasteries on the lake became the centre of Ethiopian Church opposition to the missionary work of Jesuit priests, who were active in Ethiopia at that time.

During the reign of Fāsiladas, the successor to Susenyos, the city of Gondar was established and became the capital of Ethiopia. The founding of Gondar did not, however, diminish the importance of Lake Tana and the surrounding areas; as each Emperor in turn developed a predilection to a particular island or area close to the lake. Yoḥannes, who succeeded Fāsiladas, maintained his favourite residence at Yebaba, some thirty kilometres south of the lake, where he constructed a stone palace in a

8. The castle of Guzārā, near Lake Tana, which was erected by Emperor Sarṣa Dengel (1563-1597).

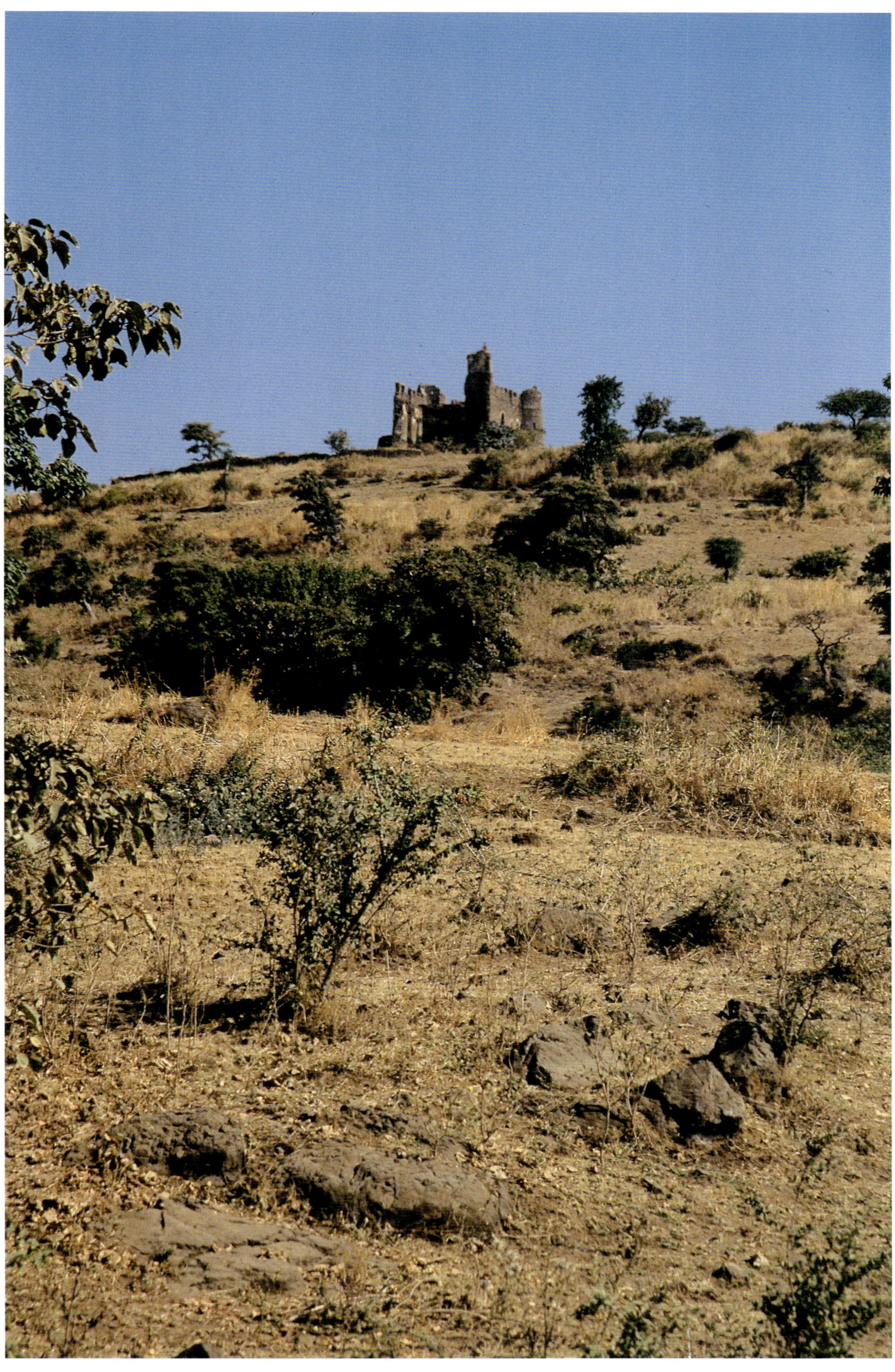

vast area surrounded by high walls with towers and arched gates. He returned to Yebaba for the Lenten season almost every year, and towards the end of his reign, remained for longer periods. In Yebaba, it is also recorded that Yoḥannes held an important council to settle ecumenical disputes, however the proceedings were interrupted by his sudden death. Although, unlike his successors, Yoḥannes did not frequent the islands of the lake, his final wish was to be buried on the island of Mesraha, where his mother, children and relatives were already interred.

Although he also enjoyed Yebaba, Iyāsu I, the successor to Yoḥannes, developed a strong attachment to the lake and its monasteries. Shortly after his accession to the throne, he toured all the island monasteries in order to receive the monks' blessing. On this occasion, a remarkable occurrence is purported to have taken place. According to his chronicler, Iyāsu, along with his horse and mule, was being taken across the lake in a *tānquā*, which is, by definition, a fragile means of transportation. Grass had been laid over the papyrus reeds to make its surface sufficiently firm for the horse and the mule to stand on during the crossing. Presumably the animals instinctively understood their precarious situation since neither one attempted to move or to eat the grass, with the result that the king's potentially dangerous voyage ended without mishap and this, in turn, came to be regarded locally as a miraculous feat.

Iyāsu became a frequent visitor to the islands, returning to Ṭānā Qirqos for the feast of St.Cyriacus, to Meṣelē Fāsiladas for the feast of St. Basilides and for another complete tour of the monasteries. Time and again, he returned for his annual Lenten retreat to Guangut Island, also known as Caqla Manzo. The emperor's close bond with the lake and its monasteries was sealed with the construction of a splendid church dedicated to St. Gabriel in 1686 on the island of Kebrān. When his queen, Walatta Ṣeyon, died, he buried her on the island of Mesraha.

Towards the end of Iyāsu's life, the lake was destined to play a tragic role. In 1705, while Iyāsu was away on a military expedition, the high officials of Gondar announced his deposition. Initially Iyāsu endeavoured to regain the throne, but illness prevented him from continuing the struggle and he retreated to Dek Island. His partisans attempted to restore him to power, however Talcla Haymānot, his son and successor, sent his uncles to Caqla Manzo, where Iyāsu was in temporary residence, and here they killed him. Priests later buried the emperor's body near that of his queen on the island of Mesraha.

Another of Iyāsu's sons, Emperor Bakāffā, inherited his father's love of the lake and chose Birgidā Island as his preferred location. In 1725, he travelled there twice to mourn the death of his mother. At a later date, he returned again to supervise the construction of a two masted sailing vessel measuring approximately ten meters in length. This was a notable event described in detail by his chronicler. The boat was constructed by two Egyptian experts aided by Ethiopian craftsmen, all of whom were generously supplied by Bakāffā with food and drink. Whether or not their efforts were crowned with success or Bakāffā ever sailed on his boat, the mere record of its existence is an indication of his keen interest in Lake Tana.

In the subsequent construction of a church on the island of Nārgā, Empress Mentewwāb, followed the traditionally close connection between the Gondar monarchs and Lake Tana. It is possible that she also had a personal affinity for the lake, since she had grown up in the highlands overlooking it.

Among the great women in Ethiopia's history, in many respects Empress Mentewwāb is regarded as exceptional. Over a span of thirty years she distinguished herself as a de facto ruler, not only during the reign of her son, but also during a portion of the reign of her grandson. Even in her old age when, after a largely self-imposed exile, she returned once more to Gondar, she was reputedly accepted with enthusiasm as the embodiment of imperial power. In a sense it is ironic that, although Empress

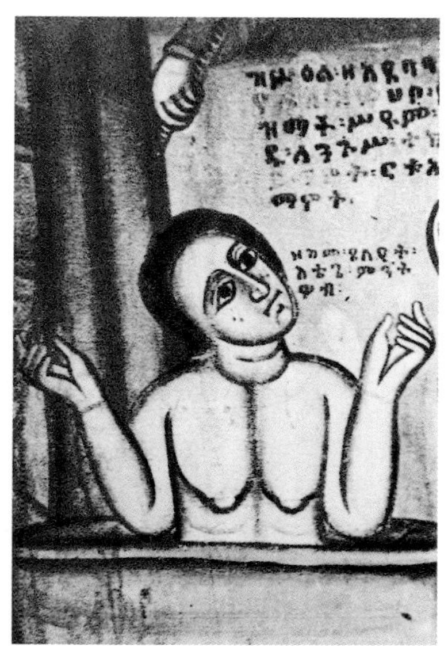

9. A painting in the church of Addebabai Jesus portrays Empress Mentewwāb bathing: (from MONTI DELLA CORTE).

Mentewwāb is mentioned in numerous publications, her own life story remains virtually unrecorded. The royal chronicle of her son Iyāsu II, written under her supervision, is, in effect, her only official history; however the account of Remedius Prutky, a Franciscan missionary who visited Ethiopia in 1752 and who met both the Queen and her son, is probably a more reliable source. The narrative of Scottish explorer James Bruce, who personally met and spoke with her in her old age, is written in a somewhat unconstrained manner. Although all three accounts are in general agreement on most points, they differ significantly in certain areas.

Originally Emperor Bakāffā had only one wife, Awāldā-Negeśt, who died within a few days of their marriage. At the time, it was an established custom for Ethiopian rulers to have relations with many women, and all male offspring of these liasons were accorded equal rights to the throne—a fact which greatly scandalised Father Prutky. The most illustrious of Bakāffā's female companions was Wallata Giyorgis or Mentewwāb, meaning literally "How beautiful she is!". Eventually she became Empress, bearing the royal name of Berhan Mogasa, and in time, her son succeeded her as Emperor Iyāsu II. Mentewwāb was born into a noble family in upper Qwarā, west of Lake Tana. It is said that Bakāffā learned of her beauty and sent a trusted equerry to the girl's grandmother, Yolyana, a woman of intelligence and wit. An agreement was quickly concluded with the words, "May the wish of God be fulfilled", and Mentewwāb was dispatched to the court. Finding the girl "without defect", Emperor Bakāffā immediately invited her to his table. They feasted together and in due course, he "knew her as Adam knew Eve and found her to be a virgin" and she conceived forthwith. These details are all faithfully reported in her son Iyāsu II's chronicle, in order to ensure his right to the throne. In Bakāffā's chronicle, however, there is no mention of Mentewwāb nor any reference to the above story.

Later developments suggest that Mentewwāb was not only exceptionally beautiful, but was also a clever and ambitious woman. Indeed, she defined herself as a woman by nature, but with the qualities of the most valiant of men. Her royal son, Iyāsu, following the rule of succession, was destined to be confined to the royal prison at Mount Wahni, awaiting his election as king by the high officials of the court. Instead, with Bakāffā's tacit agreement and the consent of certain friendly dignitaries, Mentewwāb kept Iyāsu in a distant province, while maintaining the official pretence that he was at Wahni. According to the chronicle, Mentewwāb acted openly on her son's behalf, although Prutky writes that all this was accomplished in the greatest of secrecy. Indeed, under the circumstances, this appears to be a more plausible account. During the remainder of Bakāffā's reign, Mentewwāb was actively building political support, and bringing members of her family into the court of Gondar. Here again, accounts of what occurred following the death of Bakāffā differ substantially.

According to the chronicle, Iyāsu, then only seven years of age, was crowned as the uncontested Emperor. Shortly thereafter Mentewwāb was crowned Empress at the express wish of her young son. On the other hand, Prutky relates that Bakāffā's death was concealed for an entire year, during which time Iyāsu was brought secretly to Gondar and arms were stockpiled in the castle. Once Mentewwāb's preparations were complete, the election of her son was announced, however, most of the high officials, including the Abuna of the Ethiopian Church and the Ecege of the monks rose up in rebellion. Surrounded by her enemies and cut off from supplies of food and water, Mentewwāb, along with Iyāsu and a small group of loyal followers, warded off a series of attacks on the royal castle for eight days, and were only saved by the timely arrival of a friend and ally from Gojjam with his troops. The short-lived rebellion had failed and Mentewwāb's position was never again challenged.

Jealously guarding her power, she was later instrumental in separating her son, Iyāsu, from his first wife. Having displayed a tendency for independence, the wife in question was summari-

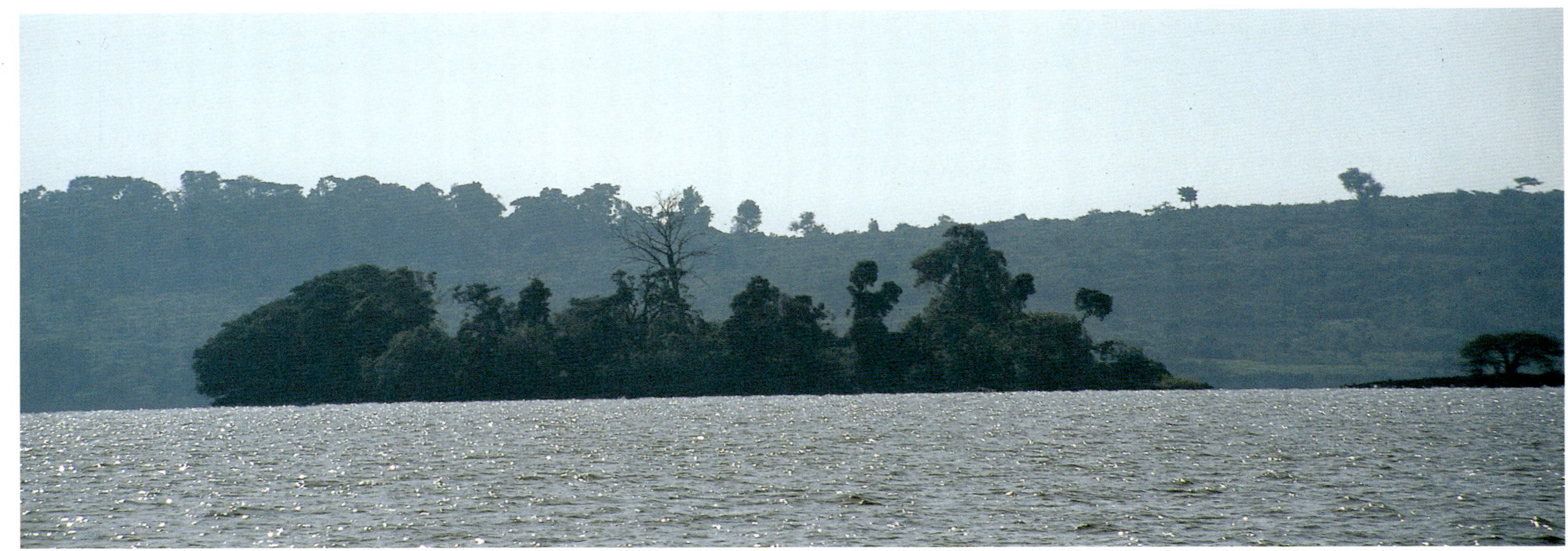

10. On Lake Tana nature is still uncontaminated.

ly dispatched with her two sons to Wahni. Mentewwāb then proceeded to arrange Iyāsu's second marriage to an Oromo princess by whom Iyāsu had a son, Iyo'as. It was an ill-fated political alliance that led to considerable dissension and eventually contributed to the fall of the Gondar monarchy.

On the other hand, Mentewwāb was largely successful in her policies relating to the church. On the whole, her long rule was essentially a period of peace within her immediate realm, although the degree of control over the distant provinces of the Empire diminished radically as a result. In her old age, at the time of her encounter with James Bruce, she was living out her last days in her palace at Qusqwam, watching the gradual disintegration of the Empire and the humiliation of her family until her death sometime after 1771.

A short and regrettably incomplete passage on f. 140 in the chronicle of Iyāsu II is of particular importance in this regard. It says that on the 15th of *magābit* (March 1748) Queen Wallata Giyorgis (Mentewwāb) left Gondar, and passed through Camara, where she was received by her mother, Princess Enkoye. She continued her journey, resting in various places and finally arrived at Dek Island on Lake Tana. Her goal was to see the superb house which *daggazmāc* Benyām had built for her and to find a suitable site for the construction of a church. She then visited Dāgā Esṭifanos and was ceremoniously received by the clergy. On the 14th of *miyāzyā*, the Queen returned to Gondar resting in the same stopping places, with the entire journey lasting one month. There is, however, no further mention of the above church in the chronicle.

What, then, can be concluded from this scant information? It is certainly clear that the Queen had a strong attachment to Lake Tana and the islands around Dek in particular, since she wished to have a house built there. Indeed, she made a long and tiring journey there, which included crossing the lake to view the fulfilment of her wishes. It is also evident that she had a particular interest in the construction of a church on one of the islands. Which one, in fact, became the island of her choice? In all probability it was Nārgā, the island lying closest to both Dek and Dāgā, which must surely have enchanted the Queen in much the same way as it captivates visitors today.

This passage in the chronicle provides confirmation of the local tradition that the Nārgā Church was founded by Mentewwāb. It also strengthens the belief that the figure depicted in the wall painting beneath the image of Mary is a portrait of the foundress herself. This is further confirmed by the inscribed portrayal of Walatta Giyorgis (Mentewwāb) in the miniature on f. 134r of the *Acts of St. George*, Brit. Lib. Or. 715. The location for the church was obviously decided upon during Mentewwāb's visit to Nārgā and its construction was begun shortly thereafter. Given the difficulties involved in transporting material from the mainland and bringing master craftsmen from Gondar, the construction could well have taken several years. The few inscriptions on the wall paintings in Nārgā Śellāsē unfortunately provide no indication. However, the two processional crosses given to the church bearing incised portraits of Walatta Giyorgis and Iyāsu, suggest that the construction and the paintings were completed and the church dedicated to the Holy Trinity before Iyāsu's death in the 1755.

An enlightened and benevolent ruler, Mentewwāb actively encouraged artistic creativity and personally advised specific artists. The churches and palaces she built all mirror her sense of tasteful individuality. In Gondar itself, she constructed a church dedicated to Abuna Ewostatewos. Her most notable building project, however, is the complex of pavilions and the church dedicated to Our Lady Mary at Qusqwam, which were erected on a hill close to Gondar, between the early 1730s and 1740. Built at great expense as her private residence, these buildings are now only impressive ruins. Fortunately, the church and buildings at Nārgā survived in better condition and provide a fascinating example of the Empress's aesthetic sensibilities. In its setting and architecture it is probably without equal among Lake Tana's many monastic buildings.

In Ethiopian history, the era of Mentewwāb is marked by its great artistic creativity. The pictorial art of the time is known as the Qwarā style, named after the region of the Empress' s origin. It is, therefore, of particular significance that Mario Di Salvo and his group of experts have done justice to Nārgā Śellāsē church, a pearl of the Qwarā style, in preparing the text and photographs for publication in such an accomplished manner. And Skira Press is also to be commended for the production of this exceptionally fine publication. Thanks to the fortitude, knowledge and cultural insight of all those involved, there now exists a comprehensive record of the architectural setting of Nārgā in its various forms, of the paintings and carvings and other decorations, as well as of the objects which the Queen, her son, and others donated to the church.

In my estimation, the most admirable aspect of this achievement is the keen attention of Di Salvo to the manner in which the church was built. Due to his excellent comparative study of selected Lake Tana churches and others in the surrounding area, the evolution of the round churches in Ethiopia becomes greatly illuminated. He presents the fundamental question of why and how this type of church came into being, and the related architectural concepts. Not satisfied with the apparent external similarity between the round churches and peasants' huts, Di Salvo has meticulously investigated the internal structure of the church. He envisages the evolution not from the round external wall, but from the rectangle of the sanctuary, which is dictated by liturgical requirements and from the structural imperative of providing an adequate cover based on the most logical solution. This necessitated constructing the round form, or tambour, resting on the walls of the rectangular sanctuary, which in turn supports the conical roof. This combination of two geometric forms, the square and the circle, is highly ingenious, and represents the architectural principle on which the Ethiopian round church is based.

I now turn to the wall paintings of Nārgā Śelāsē, so striking in their freshness, with the minor exception of those on the plinth, which have been damaged through carelessness. The photographers have worked most effectively under extremely difficult conditions and the resulting reproductions demonstrate their considerable capabilities. Painted by court artists, these wall murals are the best of their kind, and provide a fine example of the Qwarā school.

Although the Qwarā school belongs to the mainstream of the Second Gondar style and bears its major characteristics, it has its own distinctive features. The first of these is the quality of the colours. In general, the colours of 18th century Ethiopian paintings are deep, at times even

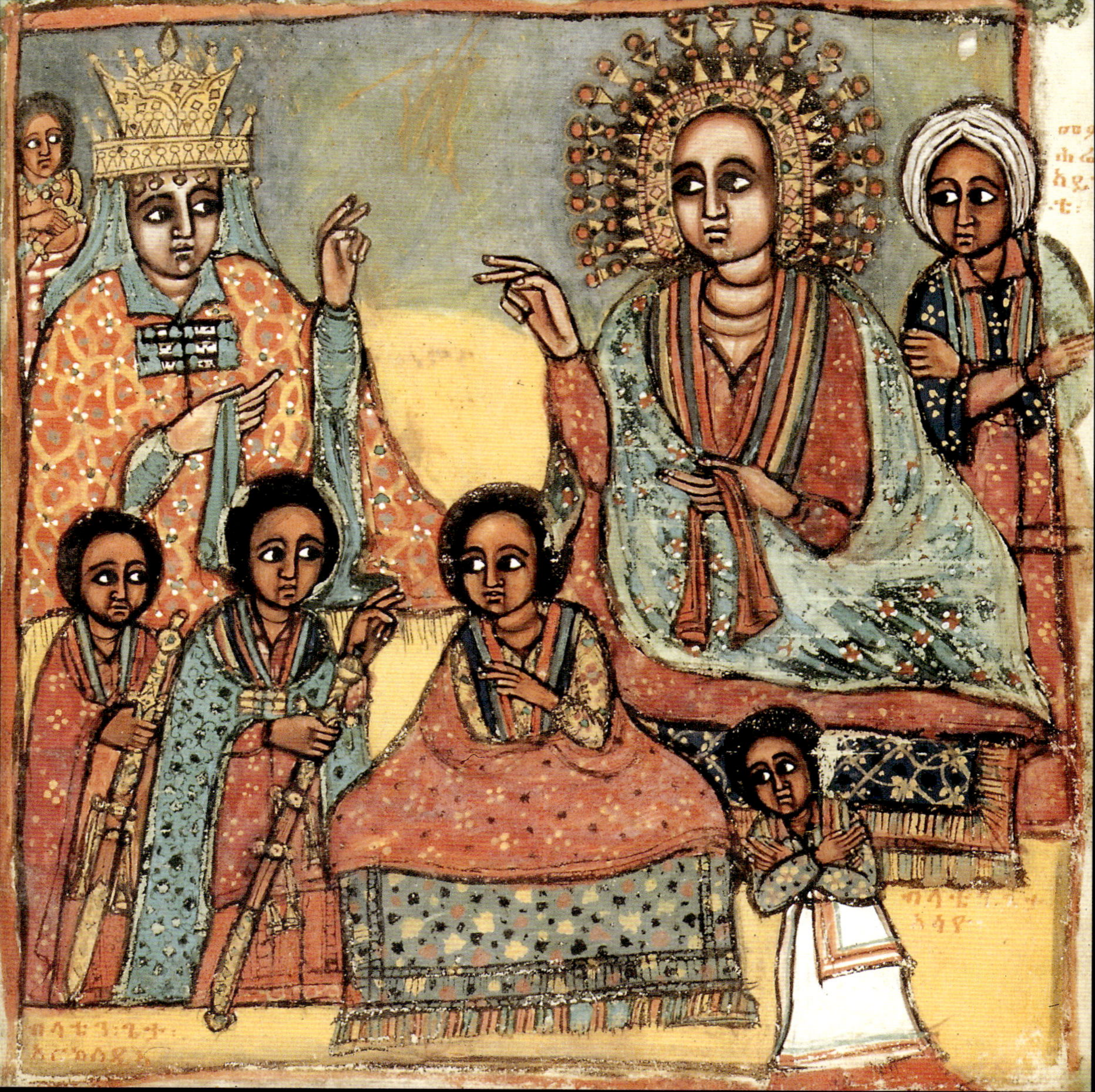

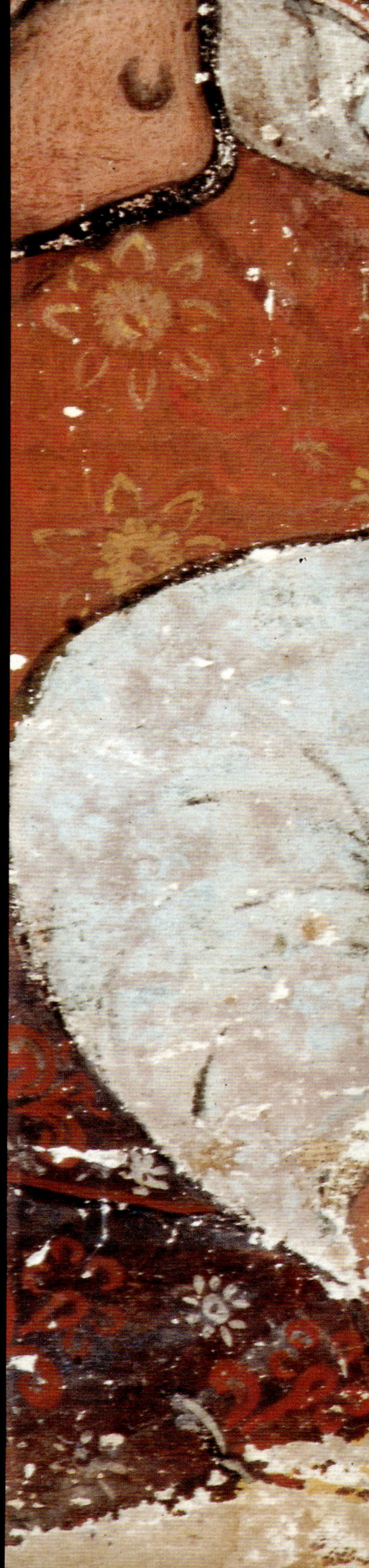

11. Queen Mentewwāb Walatta Giyorgis with her son Iyāsu II, portrayed in a royal pose with an illuminated manuscript dating from the 18th century.

12. Queen Mentewwāb, prostrate in an act of submission, portrayed at the feet of the Virgin on the west wall of the *maqdas* in Nārgā Śellāsē church.

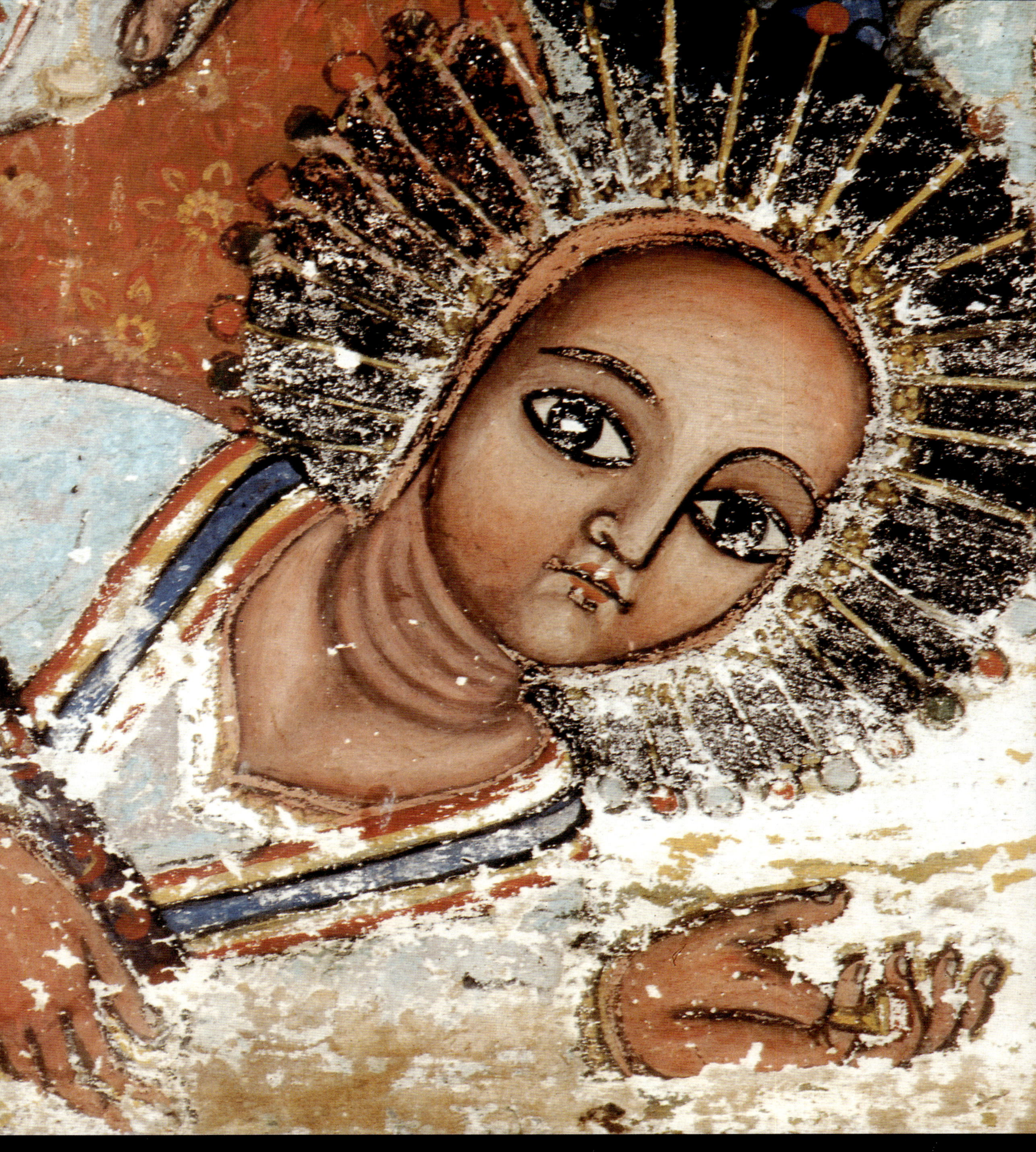

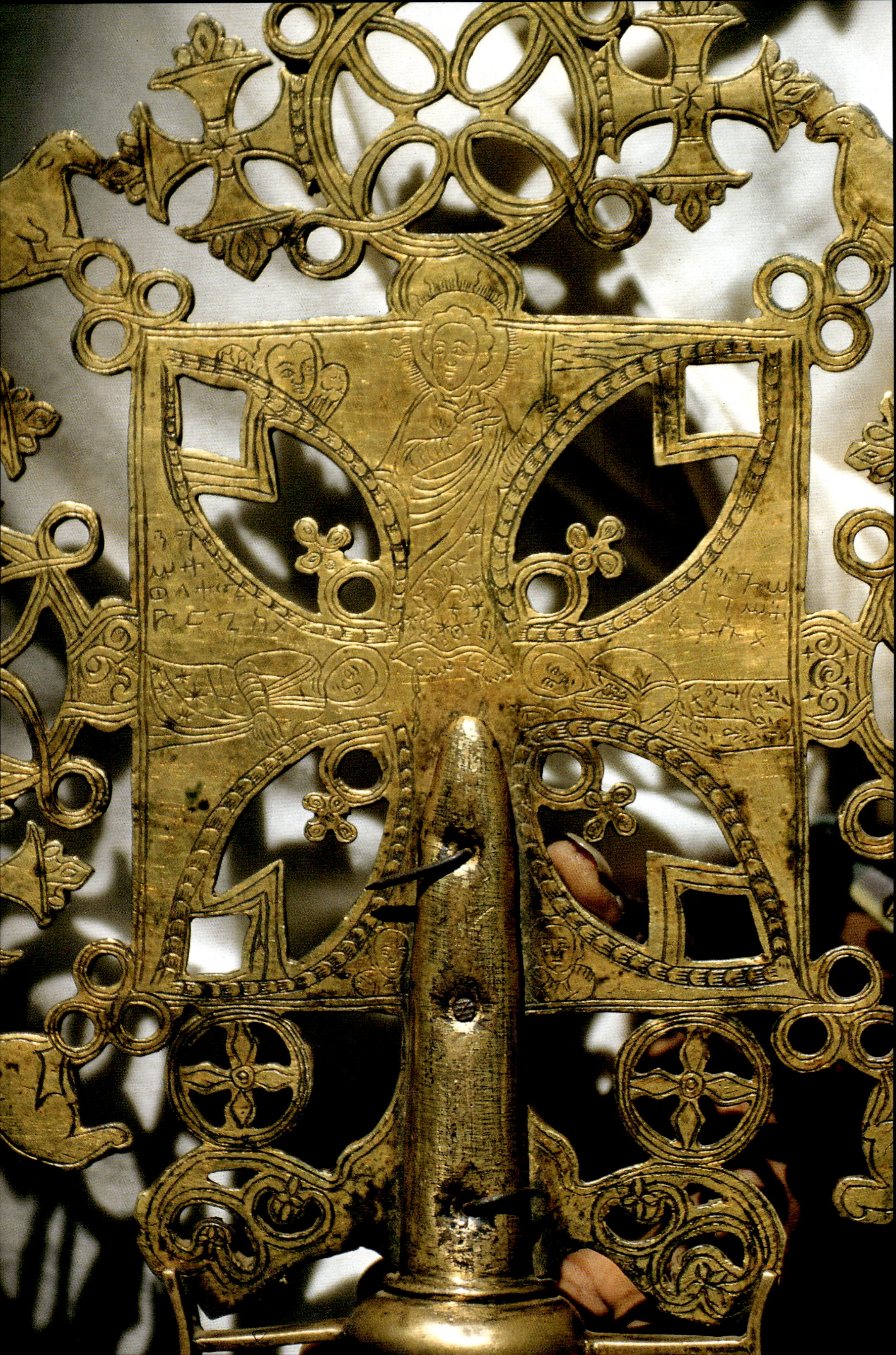

13-14. Processional bronze cross of the church of Nārgā Śellāsē (18th century). On the left is portrayed Queen Walatta Giyorgis, Daughter of Saint George (as Mentewwāb was addressed) and on the right her son, King Iyāsu II. They are both prostrate at the feet of the resurrected Christ.

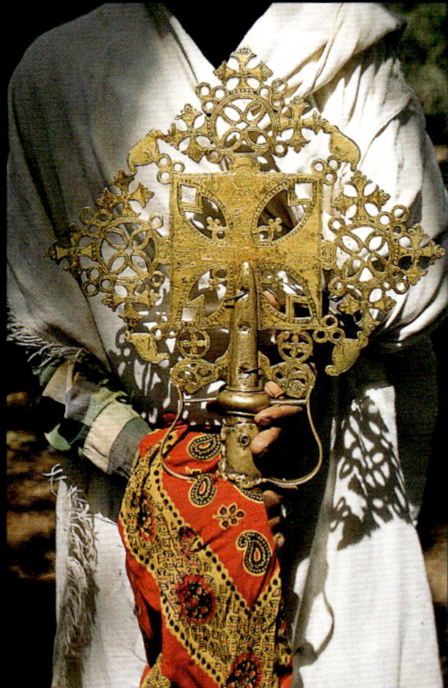

15-16. Large silver portable cross with 18th century gold-leaf work from Nārgā Śellāsē church, with ring attached to the scroll on which are engraved under a representation of the Holy Trinity, the prostrate figures of *neguś negeśt* Adyām Sagad *seltān* Iyāsu, on the left, and his mother, Queen Walatta Giyorgis (Mentewwāb).

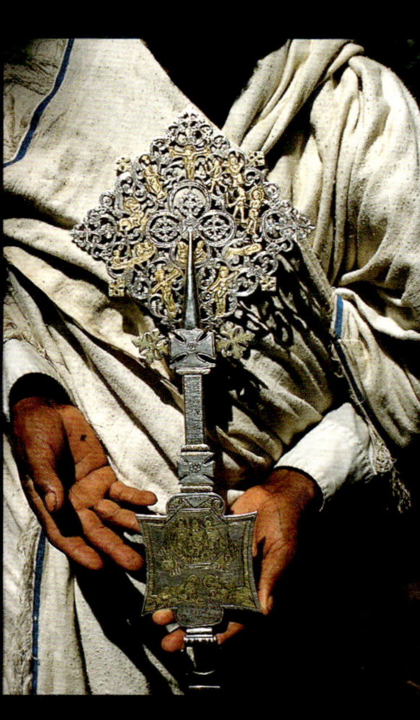

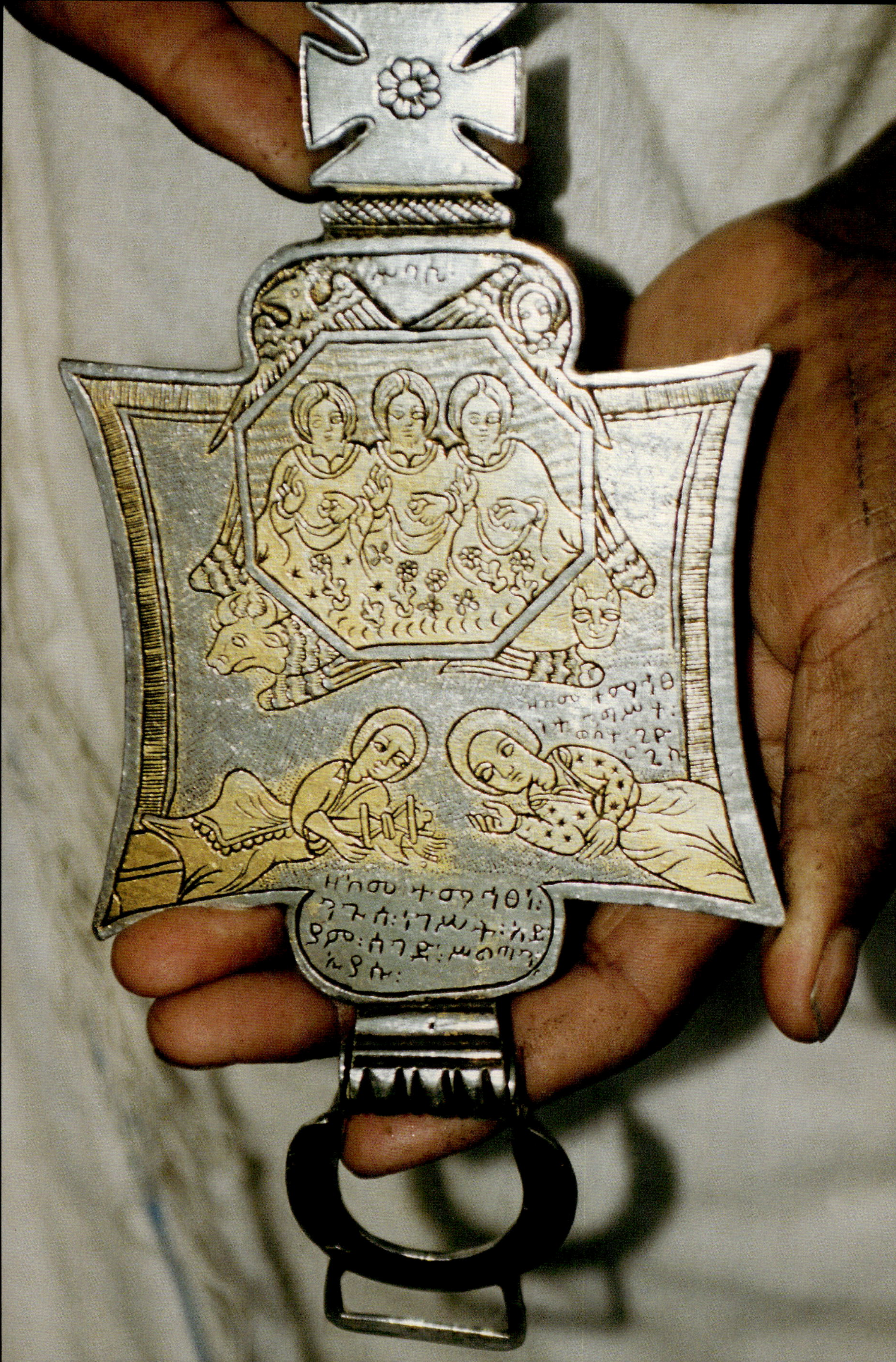

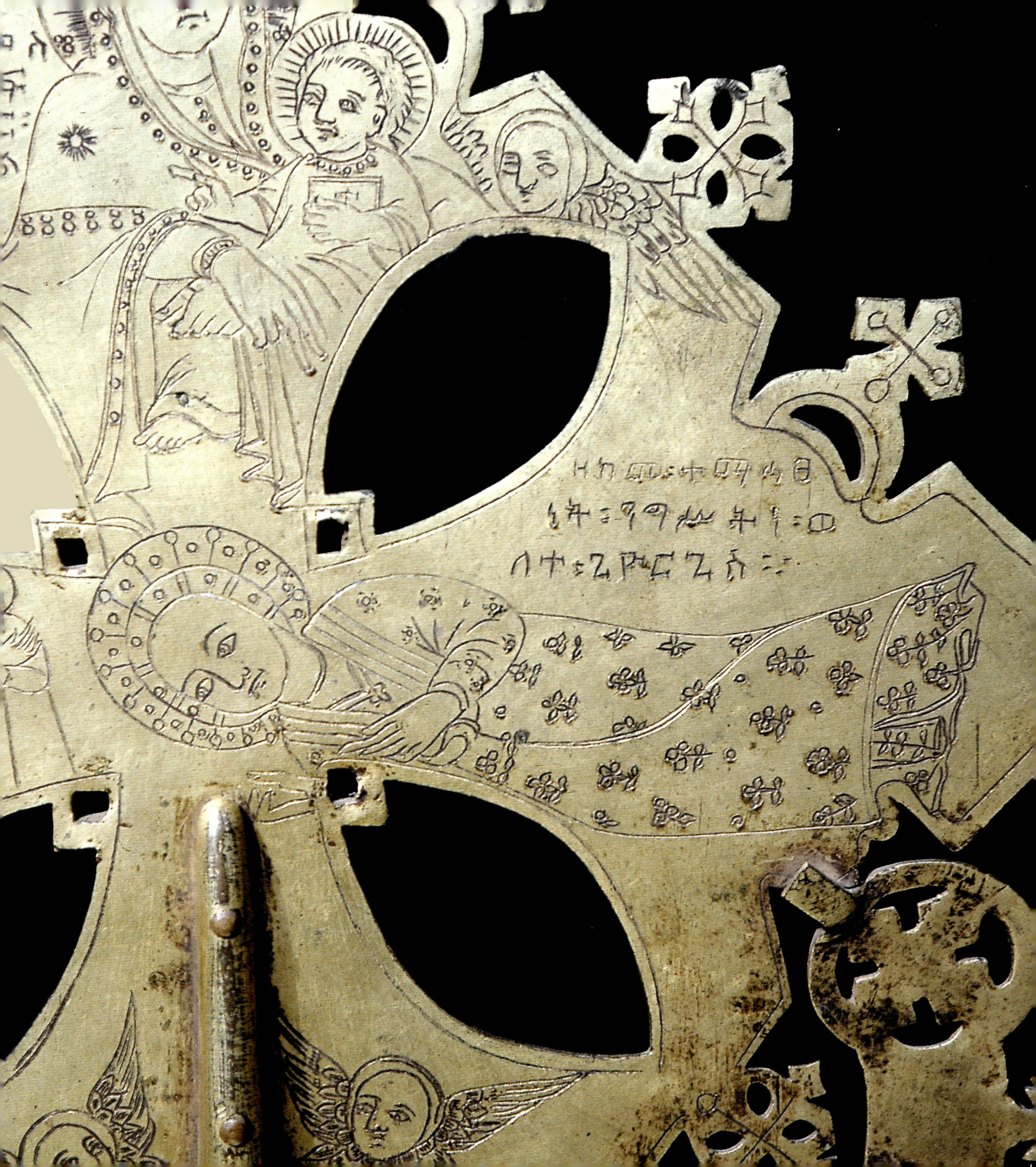

19. An 18th century Nārgā Śellāsē illuminated manuscript portrays Queen Walatta Giyorgis (Mentewwāb).

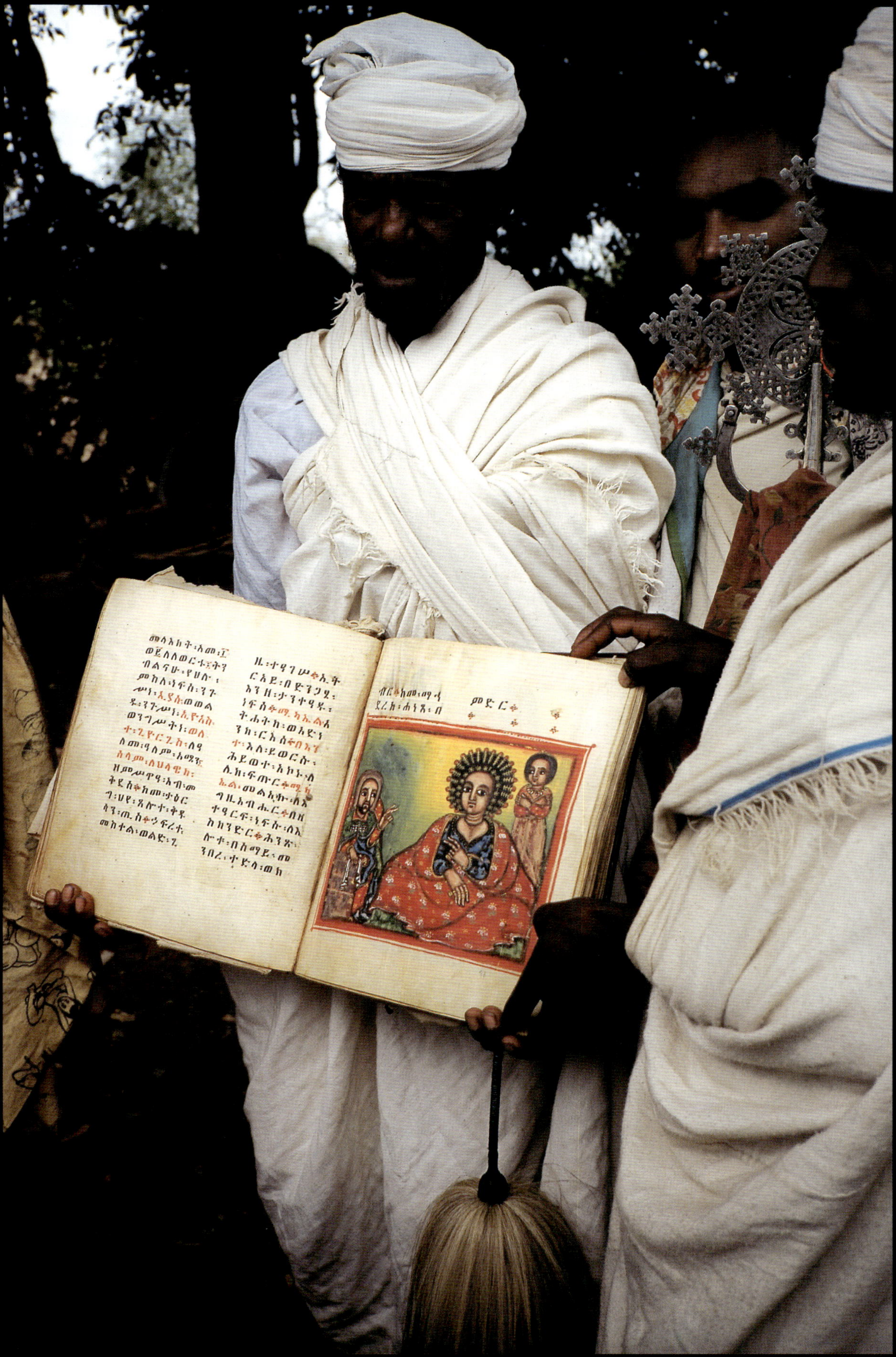

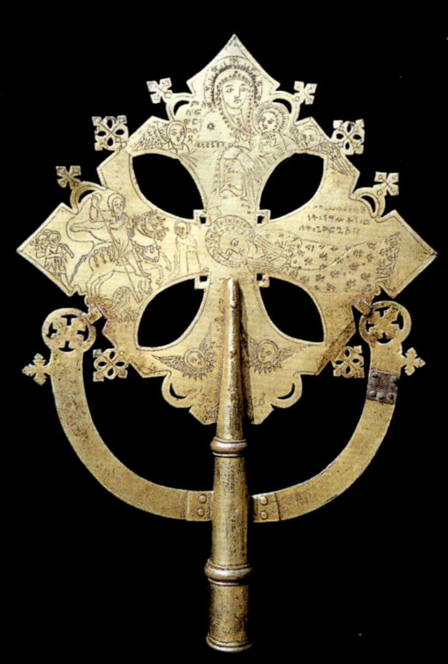

17-18. An 18th century processional bronze cross (bottom). Queen Walatta Giyorgis prostrate at the Virgin's feet, detail (left).

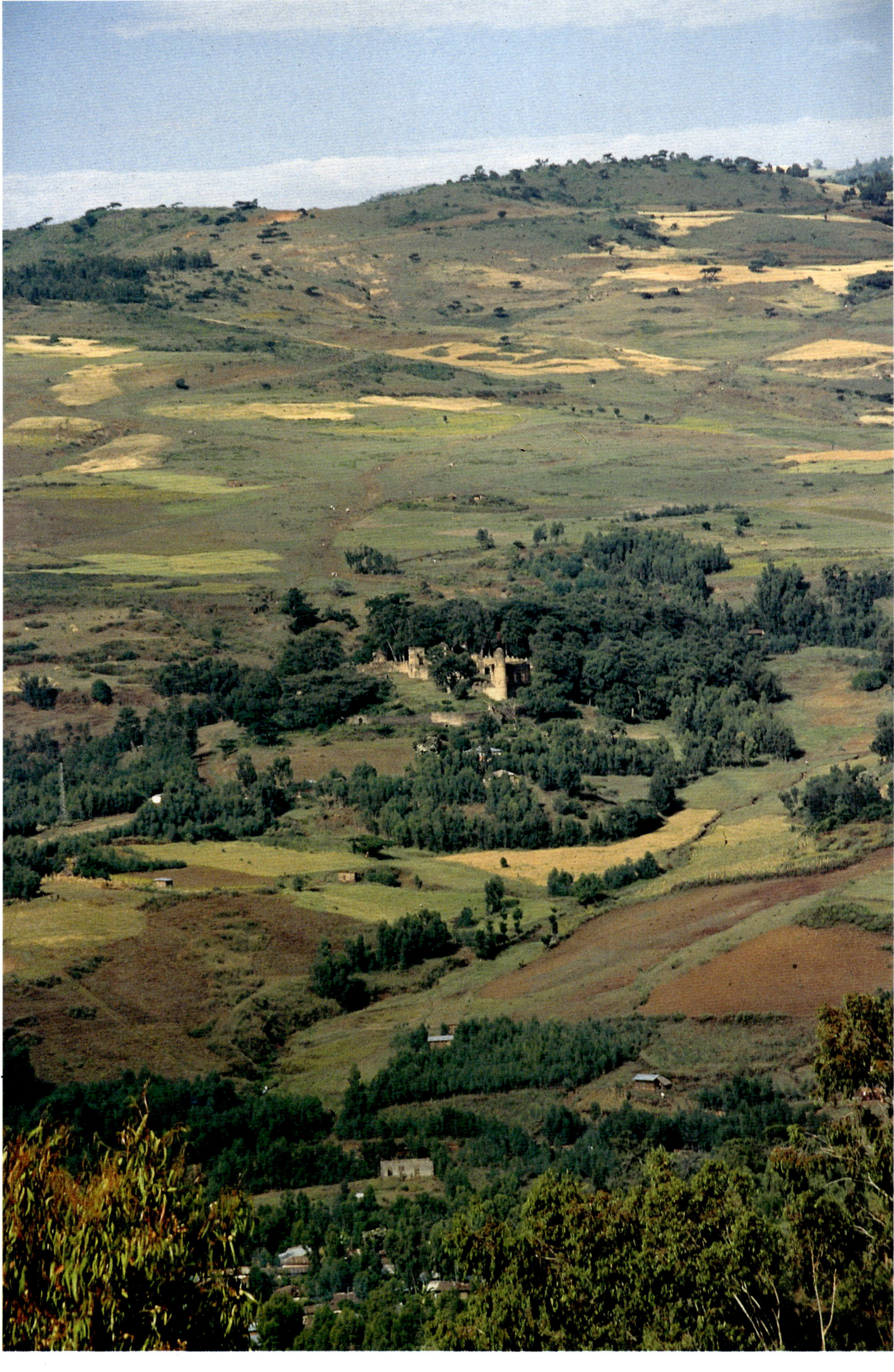

20. Queen Mentewwāb's residence at Qusqwām, near Gondar.

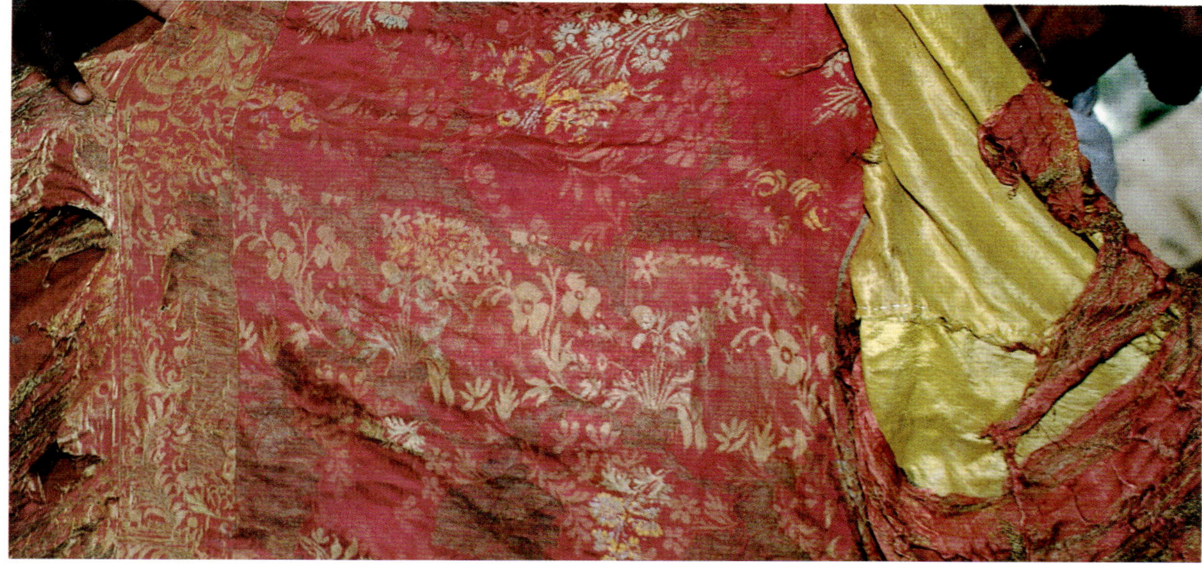

21. Remnants of Iyāsu II's precious cape (18th century), which is kept in Nārgā Śellāsē church.

sombre, while those of the Qwarā school are clear and at times intense, displaying various hues of red, orange and brown. The use of Green Earth pigment (*terre-verte*) of a distinctive bluish shade is also characteristic of the school. A second feature is the rounded youthful faces, even of those figures representing old men with grey hair, moustaches and beards, such as the Holy Trinity.

The school's third distinguishing feature is the fully developed, indeed abandonedly joyous decorative quality inherent in these paintings. The subjects are attired in beautifully patterned textiles, carefully copied brocades, and other precious materials. Characteristically, not only the Virgin and Child are sumptuously dressed, but also the Trinity, aswell as Christ, the Apostles, the Prophets in the Transfiguration, and Adam in the scene of Eve's creation. Together these three features demonstrate the artistic proficiency of the Qwarā painters in producing a delicate effect similar to that of European paintings during the Rococo period. In turn, these three features qualify the Qwarā school for a special place in the history of Ethiopian art.

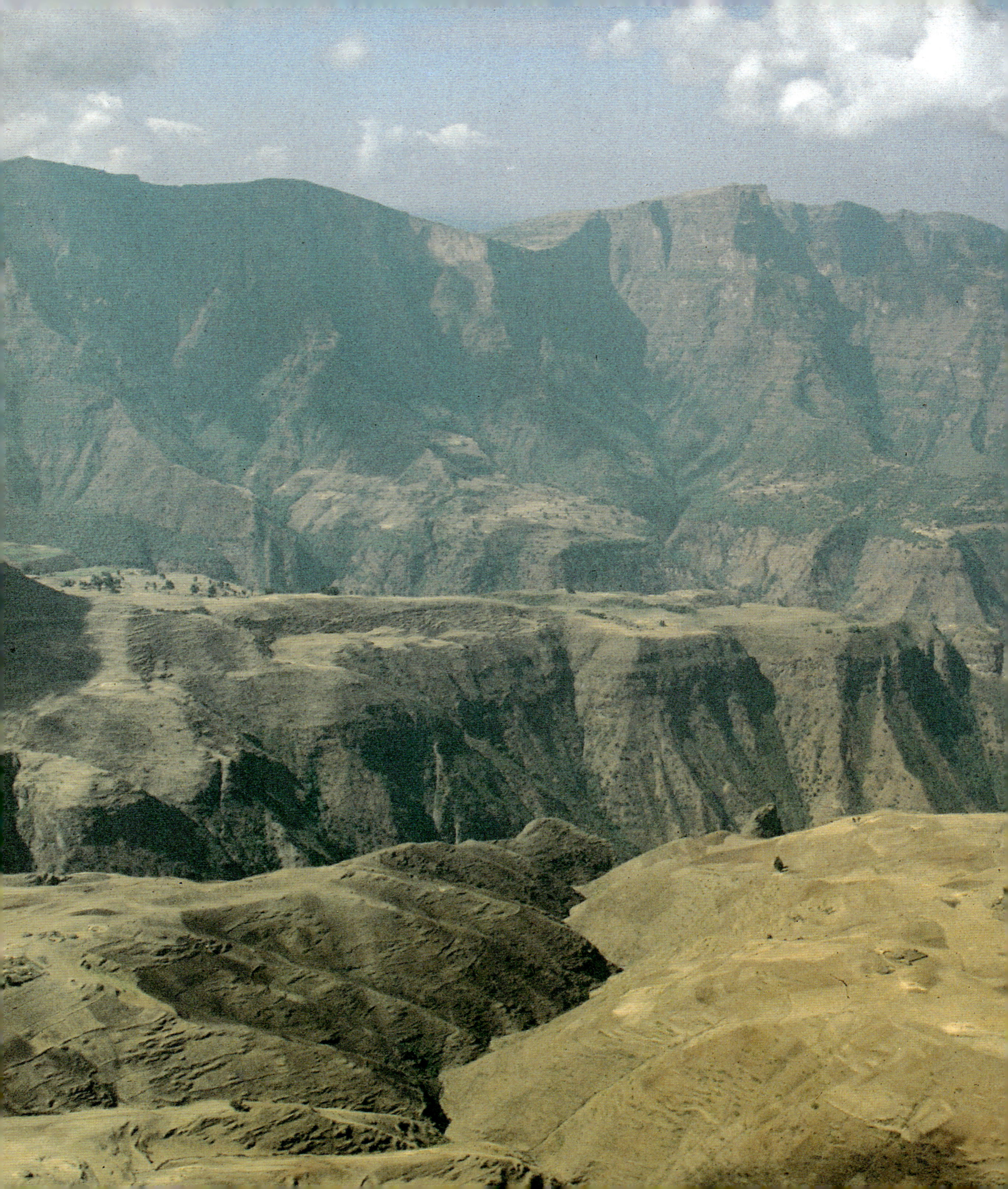

Ethiopia, History and Geography. From Aksum to Lake Tana

22. Typical plateau landscape.

Ethiopia's backbone is formed by a mountainous ridge, a natural route, which in time has generated a series of stable settlements, each progressively taking control of the surrounding areas. To begin with, in the northern territory of Tigrē, the fabulous Aksum kingdom stretched from the heights to the Red Sea coast. Then, in the southern Lāstā region, an area populated by the Agaw, the mystical Lalibela; in the middle, the Amhara kingdom, with its imperial capital, Gondar, from whose heights can be seen the mists of lake Tana; finally, in the southern area of the Shoa region, the *novum et novissimus* emblematic flower of Addis Ababa (fig. 23).
The country therefore extends from the north southward, along the watershed between the Red Sea and the territory crossed by the Nile. It is a sort of obligatory way, up on the ridges of the powerful mountains which, in the east, are impending over the desolate landscape of the desert-like Dancalian low-land plains, whilst in the west they slope towards the Sudanese plains, down to the Nile. Rivers and streams run between steep eroded crevices, sometimes very rapidly, almost sinking through. Consequently, to cover a small distance, as the crow flies, one has to face the obstacle of great differences in height, and this requires time and effort. A well-informed Italian traveller of the 19th century wrote: "Abyssinia must be considered from a viewpoint different to that appliable to all other countries, that is, whilst in any other region, from the medium level at which one walks, one can admire the chain of mountains, here one must take as a medium level the plateau itself, and admire the gorges and valleys opening up underneath it" (VIGONI, p. 168). Therefore, much easier travelling routes run on the sloping crests of the mountains, between one depression and another (fig. 32).
Thus, a natural morphology can be discerned, tracing on the territory a gigantic "comb-shaped" system, its jagged peaks facing westward, linked to the vertical axis of the Ethiopian ridge. Due to this particular orographical configuration, the different regions of the country have often been isolated on the various secondary ridges—the prongs of the comb—which depart, in the north, in the middle and in the south, from the main ridge, distinct and protected from one another, with obvious ethnical and historical implications.
An area crossed by routes and punctuated with villages is never determined casually, as both routes and settlements obey conditions determined by the natural morphology of the territory. Without bearing in mind this concept one gains the wrong image of Ethiopia, perceiving it as an aggregation of different realities separated purely by chance. Instead, this is far from the truth: people have been conditioned by the place where they lived and viceversa, up to the

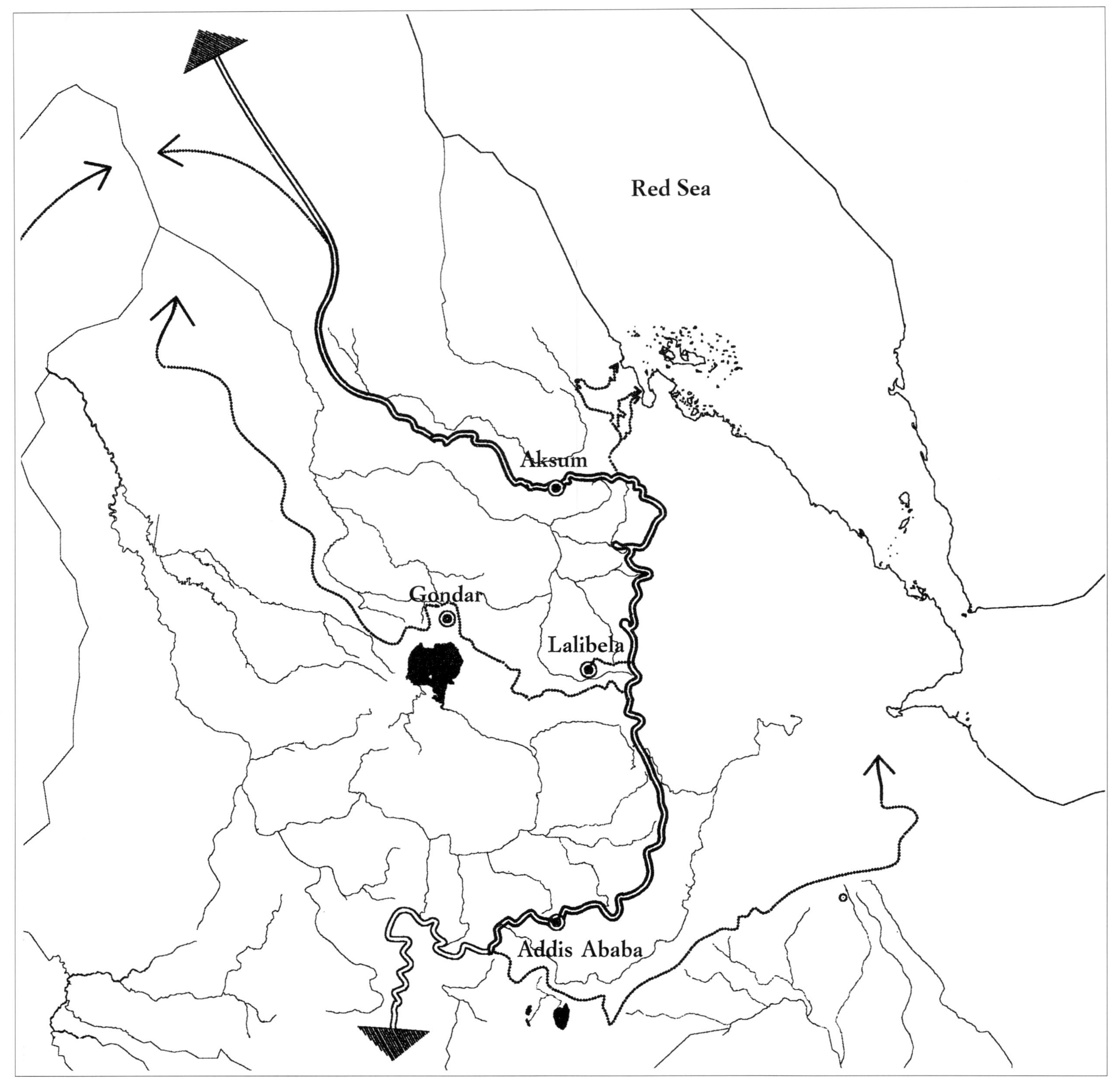

23. Along the main ridge of the plateau, and leading off it, the most representative settlements in Ethiopian history developed: first, in the north, the fabulous Aksum kingdom, then in the south the mystical Lalibela, then mid-way along it Gondar, the Imperial capital; finally, at the far south, Addis Ababa, the 'new flower' of contemporary Ethiopia.

25. Through natural routes, the Aksumite-Nubian region is connected to the southern end of the Gulf of Guinea and to Central-South Africa.

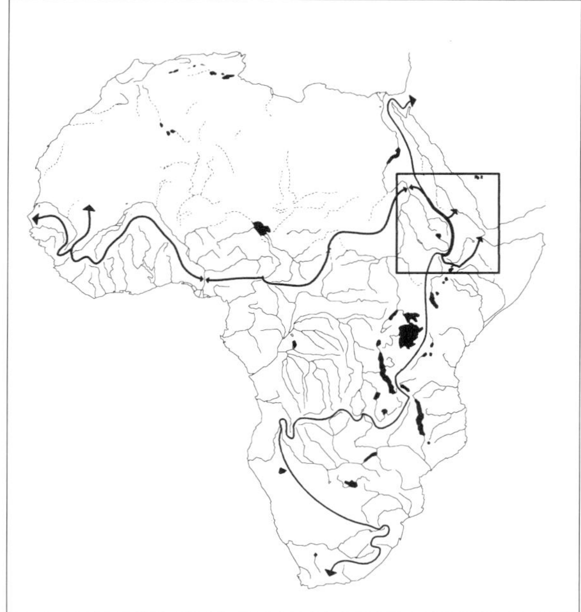

26. Ethiopia is a natural link not only between the Mediterranean basin and the Red Sea, but also with the Indian Ocean and beyond.
1- The Mediterranean basin
2- The Red Sea basin
3- The Indian Ocean basin
4- Central African basin

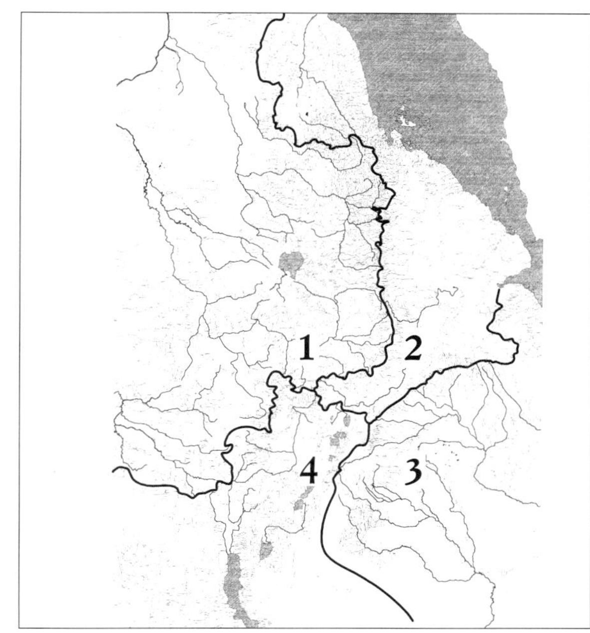

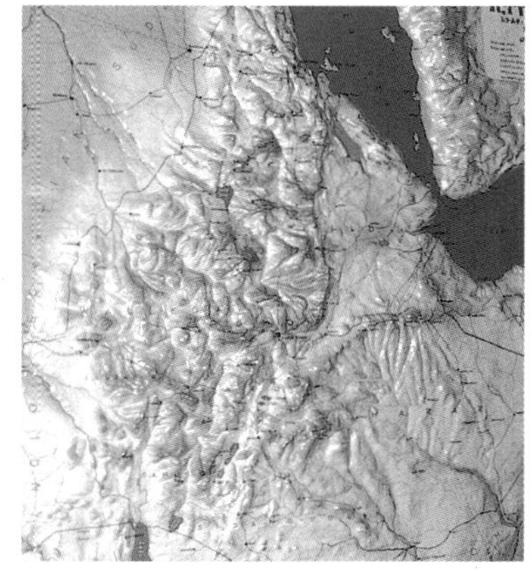

24. Orography of Ethiopia.

point that both people and place have acquired similar characteristics, peculiar and identifying, in a sort of reciprocal exchange.

In Ethiopia, so close to the equator, settlements are generally located between 1,500 and 2,000 metres above sea level, in correspondance with the area known as *wayna dāgā*. Above 2,500 metres there is the region known as *dāgā*, crossed by routes but not ideal for settlements because of its cold weather. Under 1,500 metres there is the *qwallā*, where the heat and the high level of humidity create a habitat unfavourable to man, and more apt to nomadic types of settlements. The layout of the country was therefore organized through a succession of structures (routes, settlements, productive areas) which were functional to the characteristics of the territory.

This network of connections and links allowed any area of settlement or transit—either a village, a city or a region—to take on and play a 'hinge' rôle in relation to the surrounding territory, which was stronger where this surrounding territory brought in a conspicuos contribution in values and interests.

The whole of the Ethiopian ridge was—and still is—a place having the function of a 'hinge' not only between the Mediterranean basin and the Red Sea, but also with the Indian Ocean and beyond. In fact, when in the south the Ethiopian ridge dips to go round the basin of the Awash River, it crosses the long and deep fissure of the lake region (the mythical Omo), splitting up towards the heart of Africa on one side, and on the other becoming linked to the eastern plateaux of the Horn of Africa (watershed between the Awash River in the north and the huge Juba and Webi Shebeli Rivers in the south, which run into the Indian Ocean) (fig. 26).

Its arrangement along a primary north-south axis is conferred on Ethiopia the rôle of a junction for those links which along the ridge always found the possibility of attachment, even a transversal one. Along the upper course of the Nile, in Nubia, and in the southern part of the Arabian peninsula, in the legendary kingdom of the Queen of Sheba, two great reference points, as far as commerce and administration were concerned, were transforming into market systems: on the Ethiopian plateau these two worlds met. That is how the history of Ethiopia began, with the passage from a subsistence economy to one of exchange.

The Sabean settlers, who came from the *Arabia Felix*, having traded along the coast, ended up at the foot of the Abyssinian plateau since the 6th century BC. They could not avoid relationships with the local Agaw population of inner Ethiopia, who lived in rooted, well-defined and developed settlements.

Here, probably, there was some need to put an

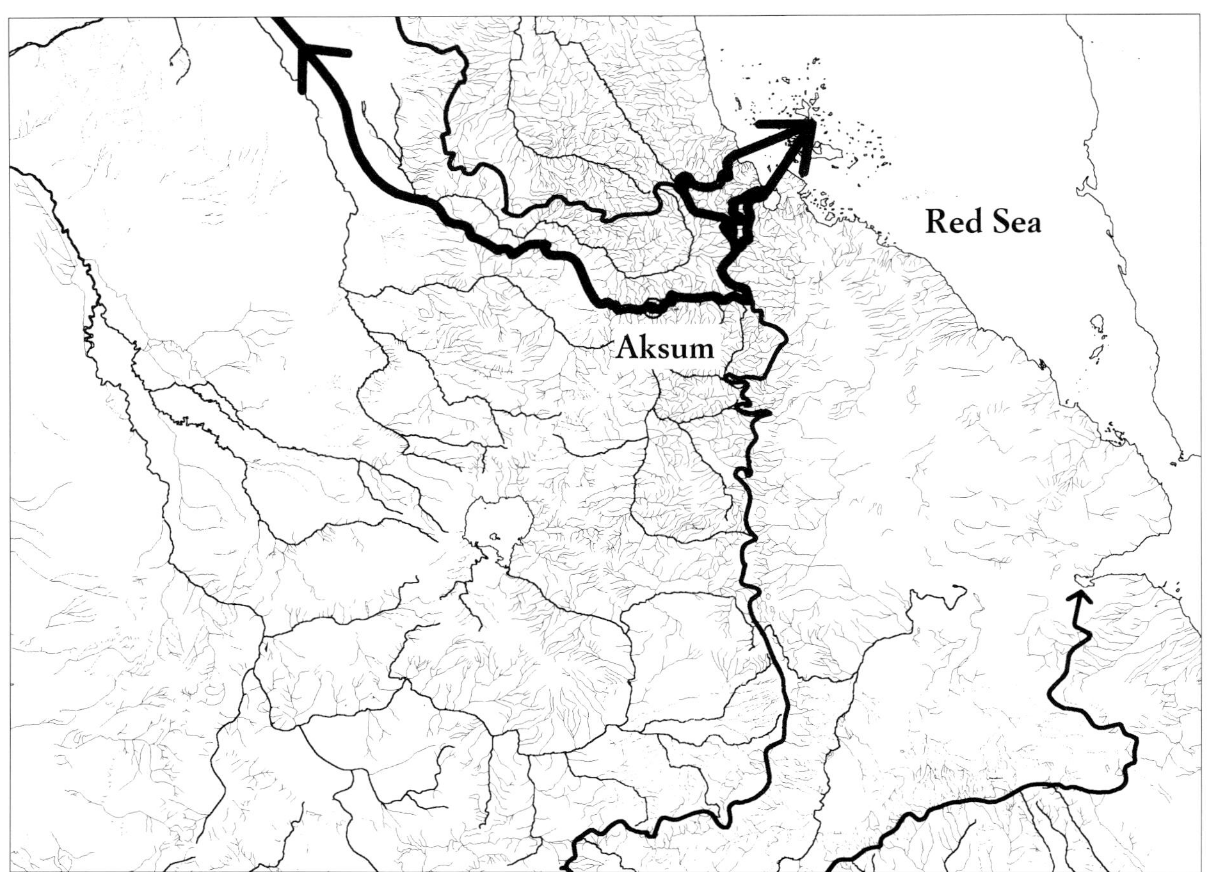

27. The city of Aksum was equidistant from the Sabean kingdoms of the *Arabia felix*, beyond the Red Sea, and the Nubian kingdoms which developed along the Upper Nile.

end to a conflict between the coast and the interior which the Greek colonies in the Mediterranean had previously experienced. On the Ethiopian plateau a new political unity emerged; it developed in a position equidistant from the Sabean kingdom in southern Arabia and the Nubian kingdom of Napata, precisely on the route which naturally connects them—between Mareb and Takkaze—, facing the gulf of Zula, where the Sabeans had founded the emporium of Adulis, to the east, and the open Nubian plains to the west (fig. 27).

The territorial system thus taking form was vast and particularly rich in opportunities and further connections. It was in fact coupled with the northern side of the Ethiopian ridge, but also with a sort of ending of the east-west mid-African ridge which, enclosed between the basins of Lake Chad and the Congo River, connected the Nubian region with the western extremity of the Gulf of Guinea through a simple fording of the mouth of the Niger (fig. 28). The Arabian peninsula maintained direct contacts with the mid and far east. The economical centres placed within this territorial system were able to act as a filter on what converged in the Mediterranean, through the Nile, the Red Sea and the caravan routes of Arabia, as well as in the opposite direction.

From 750 BC and for a whole century, a Nubian dynasty, the 25th, known as Ethiopian, reigned over Egypt. Along the upper valley of the Nile, between Egypt and the Abyssinian plateau, the region of Cush preserved this civilization throughout the centuries during which Egypt fell under other foreign influences (Assyrian, Persian, Greek, Roman). As a consequence of the recurrent incursions of the enemy, the capital town of the Nubian reign was moved even further south, from Napata to Meroe.

The kingdom of Cush fell in the 4th century AD, after that Ēzānā, Aksum's first Christian king, sacked Meroe and took direct control over it. Eastward, King Aphilas, his predecessor, as early as the 3rd century AD, had already added to the royal protocol the titles of 'King of Sheba,

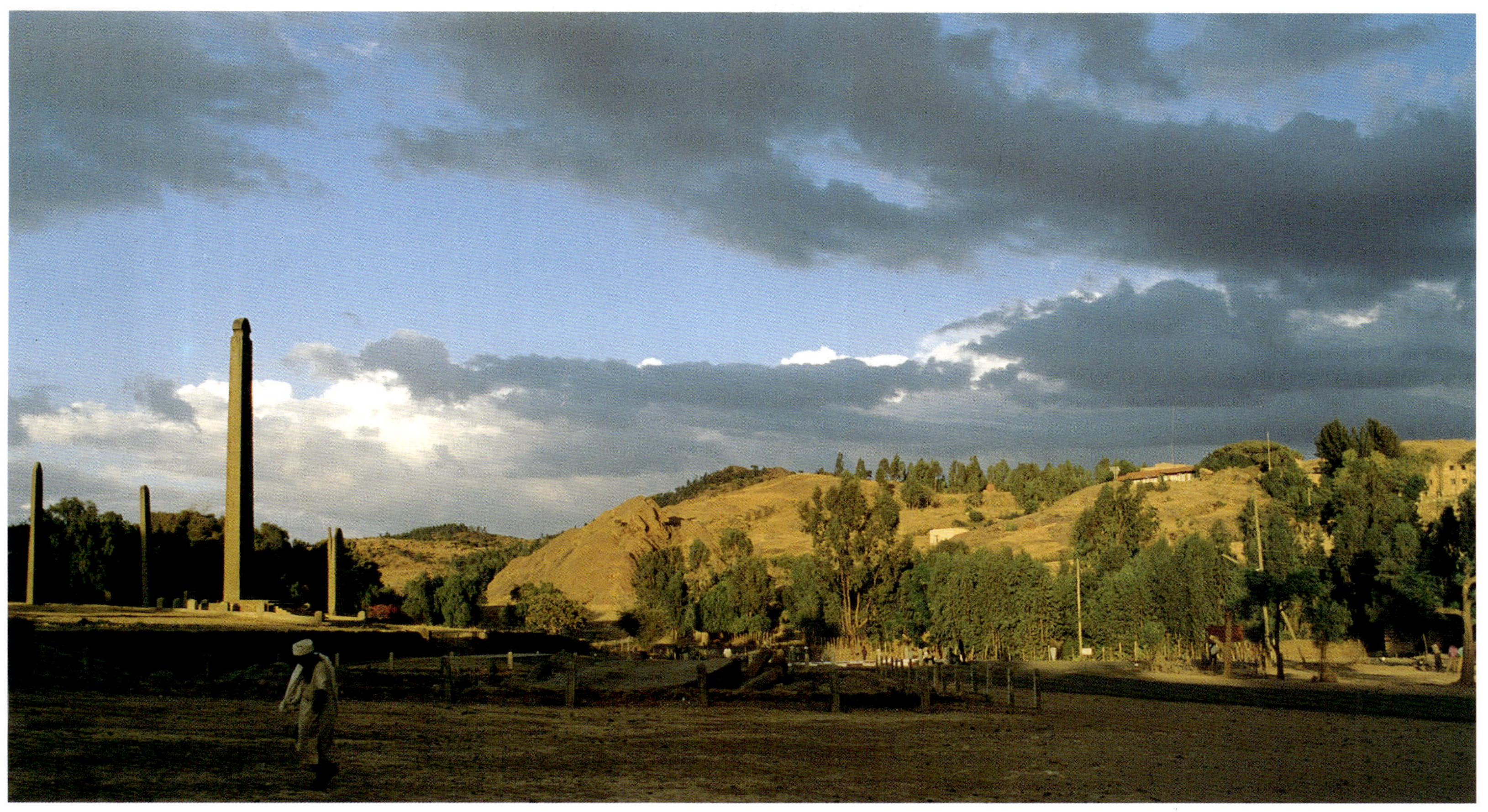

28. The esplanade of the obelisks at Aksum.

of the Himyarites and of Raydan', which is to say, the whole of the *Arabia Felix*. The weakening of both the centres of power of which Aksum was the territorial 'hinge' induced the Aksumite *neguś* to take over their rôle, thus taking advantage of the previously acquired importance.

During the 6th century the Aksumite king, Kālēb, occupied the Sabean capital, Ṣānā—today in Yemen—, which had a strategical relevance to the caravan trades with the Orient. This conquest was propelled also by Byzantium, since the extension of the Sassanid dominion to the Red Sea was prejudicial to the interests of the Mediterranean world and to those of Aksum itself, on which relied the only strategical commercial route not controlled by the Sassanids. The occupation of Arabia by the Aksumites lasted only a few decades: in 570 Cosroe I chased them out of Yemen and, 50 years later, the Sassanids drew a barrier between the East and the West, the North and the South, by annexing also Egypt. The position of the Aksumite kingdom was consequently unbalanced and, when political and historical factors caused the crisis which deprived Aksum of its long-standinging strategic rôle as a territorial 'hinge', its decline began.

No territorial entity can live outside its environment, as it always relies on external relationships: it is therefore subject to the vital laws of development and decay, which are a consequence of a change in the overall situation. The network of routes and communications which, during a given period, is established and which reflects the geographical conformation of the place, down the centuries consequently undergoes alterations in the hierarchical relationship of the centres which were thus alligned. In Ethiopia the economical reference points, the seat of the administration and, therefore, their influence on the social structure changed, as if they were the parts of a nervous system where the demands of a whole territory had long been represented, adopted and adapted.

Besides the Persian factor, there came the Islamic expansion, both on the Arabian peninsula

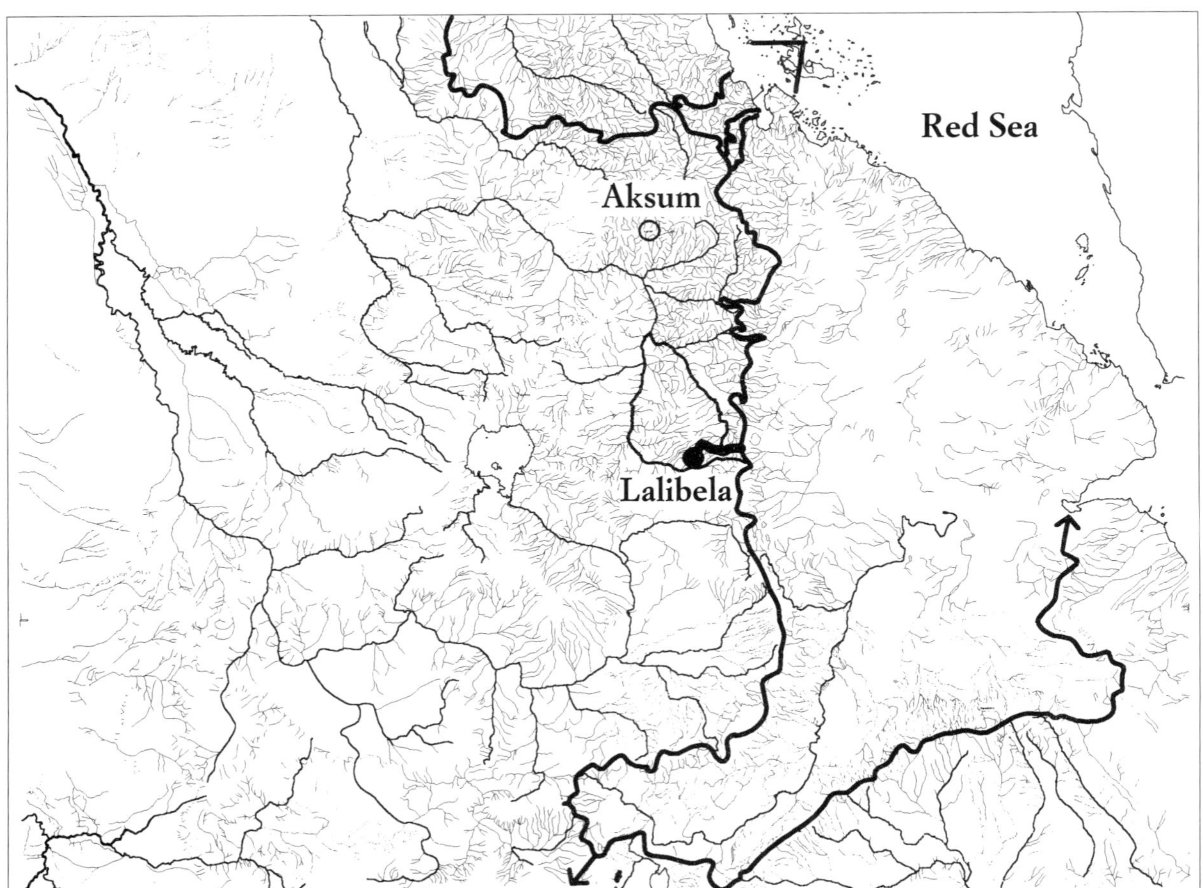

29. Lalibela, capital of the Zāgwē dynasty, in Lāstā, a region linked to the the middle of the Ethiopian ridge on a promontory between two rushing streams which flow into the Takkaze.

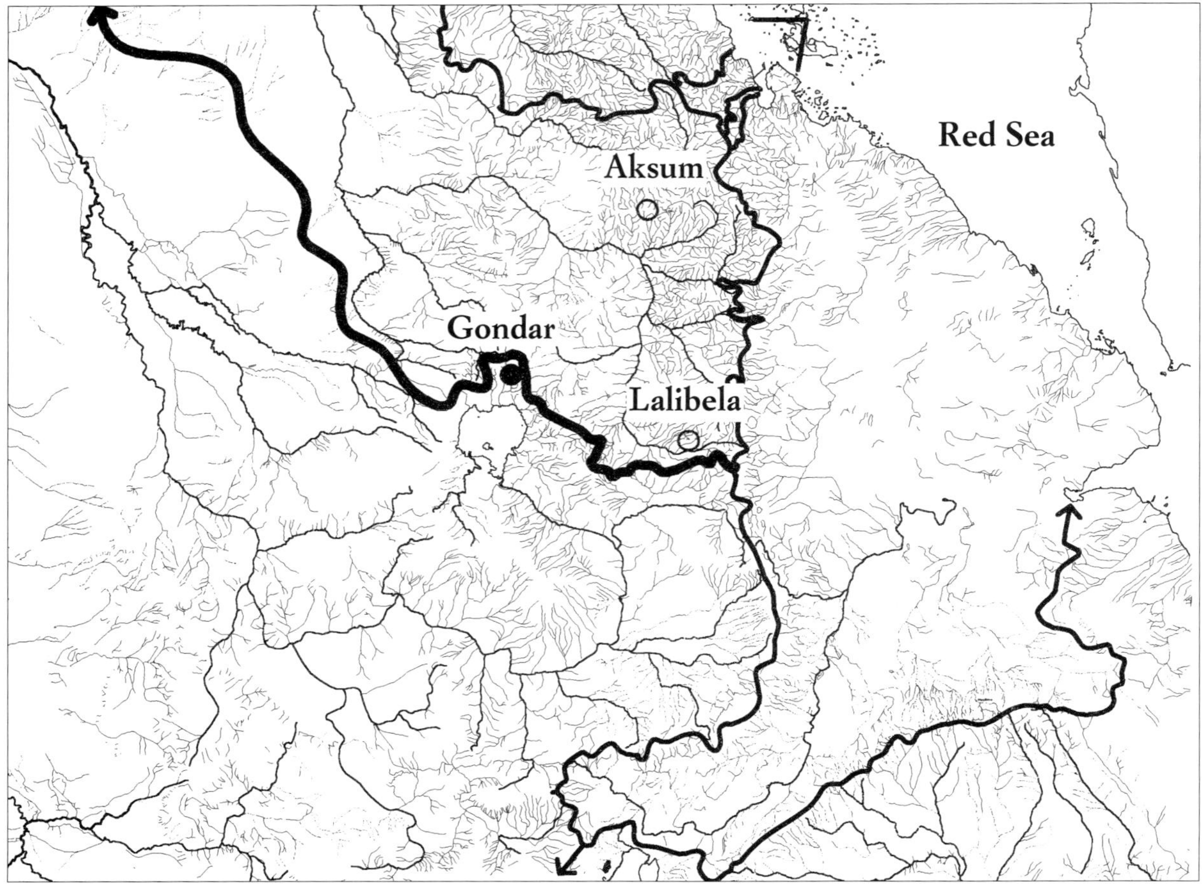

30. Gondar, the imperial capital, founded in the 17th century near Lake Tana, is equidistant from the Ethiopian ridge and the Sudanese plain, it reproduced, further south, the same territorial structure as the Aksumite kingdom.

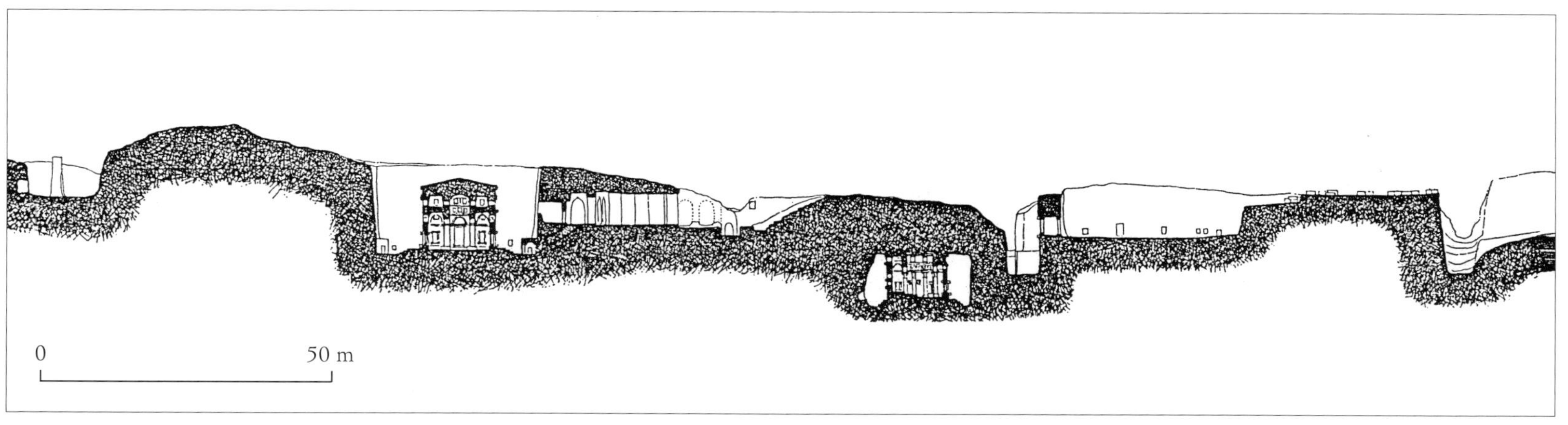

31. The monolithic churches of Lalibela, cut into stone: (section) (BIANCHI BARRIVIERA, tav. 23).

(628) and in Egypt (642) and the Persian-Arabian colonization included the coasts of eastern Africa, thus taking control over trade between the Mediterranean and the Red Sea and between the East and the West (Yemen and the Nile Valley).

Islam installed itself just outside Ethiopia, whose strategic rôle was progressively eroded, as it became almost a frontier, a boundary, a borderline between two worlds, two religions, with more limited importance. The relationships and the balance on which the Christian kingdom of Aksum had based its fortune changed for ever and, from the 7th century onward, Ethiopia's conctacts with the external world had to be filtered through the diaphragm no longer—or not just—of Alexandrian language and culture (of which the marvellous Aksumite coins had been a faithful reflection), but also through Arabian language and culture.

The Christian monarchy, repositary of the sacredness of Ethiopian royalty, thus retreated from the coasts of the Red Sea and from the Nubian planes, withdrawing evermore into the heart of the Abyssinian plateau. Unyet, notwithstanding the decline of its political rôle, it was the only force capable of preserving a native culture against the invasions of previous subjects, now rebellious, such as the assault which the terrible Yodit, a pagan queen, launched at the very heart of the Aksumite empire in 980. The kingdom underwent heavy raids and sacks, which weakened the population's resistance and the authority of the dynasty in power was eclipsed. The sudden weakness of the central power caused a mutation towards fractioned forms of government, which in turn allowed the easy eruption of a series of internal fights responsible for the true, if not the formal, division of the empire and the definitive decline of Aksum as a capital city.

The new millenium, with the rise to power of the Zāgwē dynasty of the Agaw tribes, was marked by the passage from a prosperous trading economy to forms of almost mere survival. The north-south ridge of the Abyssinian plateau, once the commercial opportunities with the Mediterranean were lost, naturally became the main axis of a system more open to connections with the southern regions, easier to reach. The Ethiopian civilization secluded itself on the headlands radiating from this ridge, a refuge erected by nature against any incursion. However, it retained its ability to control the surrounding territories thanks to its being physically linked with the ridge itself, which conferred on it a strategical connecting function.

The headlands are naturally defended by sheer drops on all sides except one, thus allowing a way of access which is generally quite narrow and consequently easy to control and to fortify. Once more, the fact that Lalibela, the capital town of the new Zāgwē dynasty, is located in Lāstā, is by no means casual: the region is, in fact, thinly linked to the Ethiopian ridge and is located on a promontory between two steeply descending streams which flow together into the Takkaze (fig. 29).

This may seem an involution similar to the so-called 'dark centuries' of the European Middle

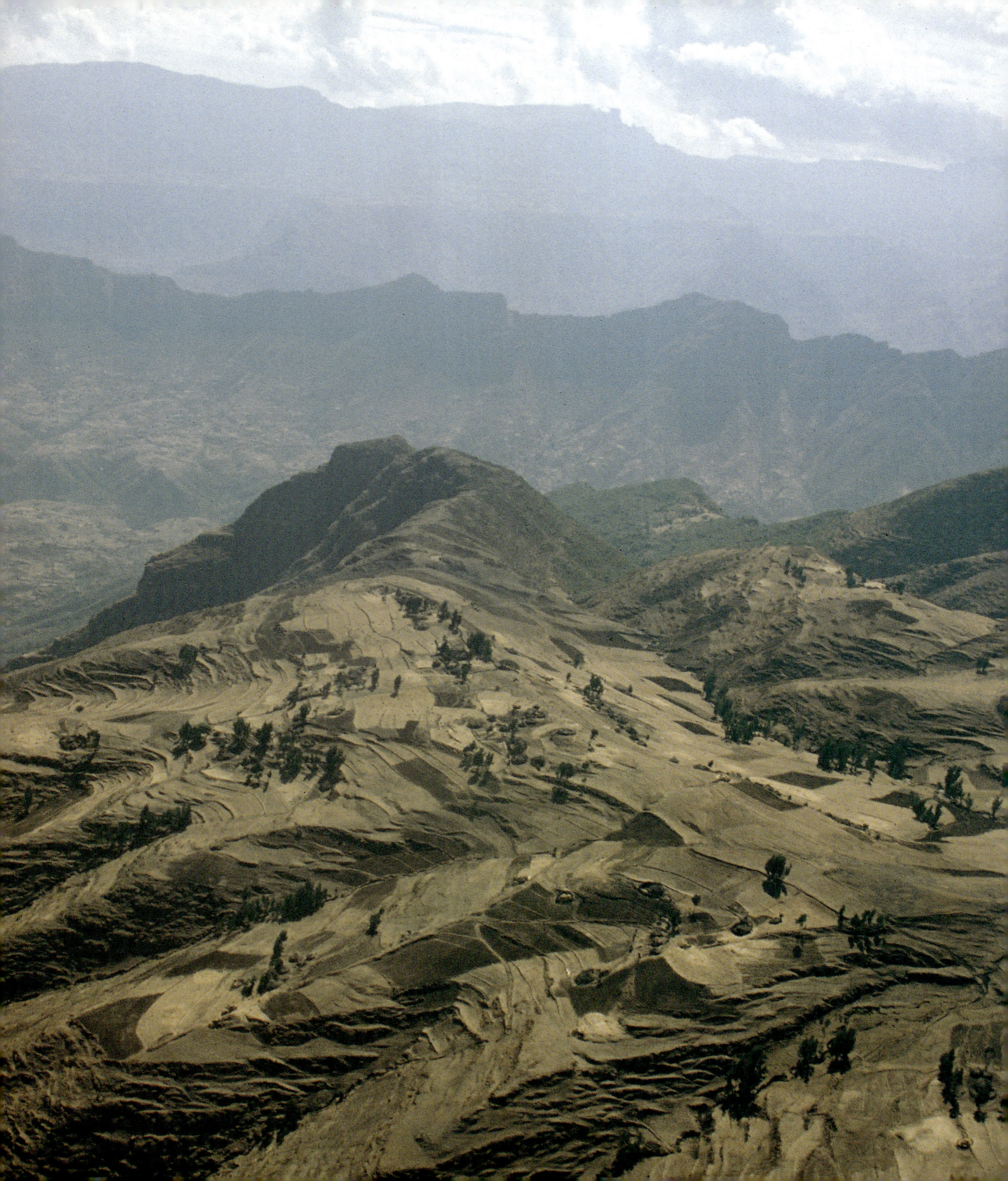

32. A ridge line on the plateau.

Ages; instead, as in Europe, it was a period "quand les cathédrales étaient blanches" (paraphrasing the title of a well-known book by Le Corbusier). In Ethiopia, this was the wonderful age of Lālibelā and of its incredible complex of monolithic churches, 'embedded' in the Ethiopian territory as the very identity of its civilization, spritual seat of the whole community. "Hic domus, haec patria est" (Verg., *Aen.* 7,122), here is home, this is the country, land/home of the ancestors, the fulcrum of an identity which, especially in certain historical periods, enriched its roots and its fruits.

One way or another, external contacts were always maintained. Following an explicit concession by the khalif, in 1187 the Ethiopians acquired those real rights which they still possess in Jerusalem and in Bethlehem. These rights were also based on ancient pious customs, since, as far back as 385 St. Jerome, in the 46th letter of his collection, wrote: "What shall I say, then, about the Armenians, the Persians, the people of India and Ethiopia and of near Egypt, so rich in monks, about Pontus, Cappadocia, Syria, Mesopotamia and all the people from the East who flock to these places?".

In 1268, with the restoration of the dynasty which had originally reigned over Aksum (called Solomonid because of its claimed ascendancy) by the *neguś* Yekuno Amlāk, the concept of sedentary sovereignity—that is, established in a capital town which served as a crucial reference point both in a functional and territorial sense—was overturned in favour of an itinerant, almost nomadic form both of the sovereign and of all his apparata: the court was where the sovereign was, founded on his personal prestige. "Il Prete Ianni —Prester John, the mythical king of Ethiopia— non ha luogo determinato dove di continuo egli stia, ma va sempre vagando ora ad una parte ora all'altra, e sempre in tende armate alla campagna, delle quali fra buone e triste nel suo campo possono essere da 5 o seimila, e fra genti a cavallo e mule da 50 e piú mila."[1] (ALVAREZ, p. 358).

The *Kebra Nagaśt*, or 'Glory of the King', fundamental codex of Ethiopian political structures which was written in the first decades of the 14th century, leads us to consider a vital reaction of the country against the Islamic world as the vector of the political and military renaissance of the empire. Here we find the first official definition of the Solomonid myth with the legend of the Queen of Sheba, as a passage of Solomon's royal power to the Ethiopian reigning dynasty, together with the apocalyptic vision of an end of the world when Ethiopia will reign over the whole of the world. Such a vision was the direct consequence of this claimed Solomonian ascendancy: if the only legitimate power was the Solomonian one, then Ethiopia was undoubtedly the country which had supremacy over all others.

This sort of mysticism of power, this peculiar sense of the state, has always been the vital guideline of any expression of the Ethiopian spirit. The preservation of the country's unity and its definitive insertion within Christianity are due to it. Both the people and the king found in religion the sense of each of their acts and the consacration of their history. In 1325 the great king Amda Ṣeyon, "Column of Zion", even threatened the sultan of Egypt that he would divert the course of the Nile, if the persecutions against the Ethiopian pilgrims on their way to the Saint Sepulchre, in Jerusalem, did not cease. The *neguś*, the king, who moved along the Ethiopian ridge, while exercising his authority, could never ignore the local powers, capable of great upheavals in the general balance of the state. Consequently, the administration was reformed in a centralizing sense, in order to better control the strong power of the peripheral provinces.

The rise of some relevant Muslim sultanates in the south-east of the Horn of Africa, which were the fulcrum of sea trade with the Arabs, the Persians and the Far East, but subjected to the Solomonids, led to an incessant series of fights for the control of those accesses to the sea where the great majority of trade was carried out by the Muslim merchants. The Arabic historian al-Maqrīzī wrote in 1434-1435: each of these regions are "controlled by a king; but over all the

[1] "Prester John does not live in a given place, but goes, vagrant, from one place to another, always in tents which can amount, counting the ones in good condition and those in a bad state, to five or six thousand, plus a court of horsemen and men mounted on mules of fifty thousand or more."

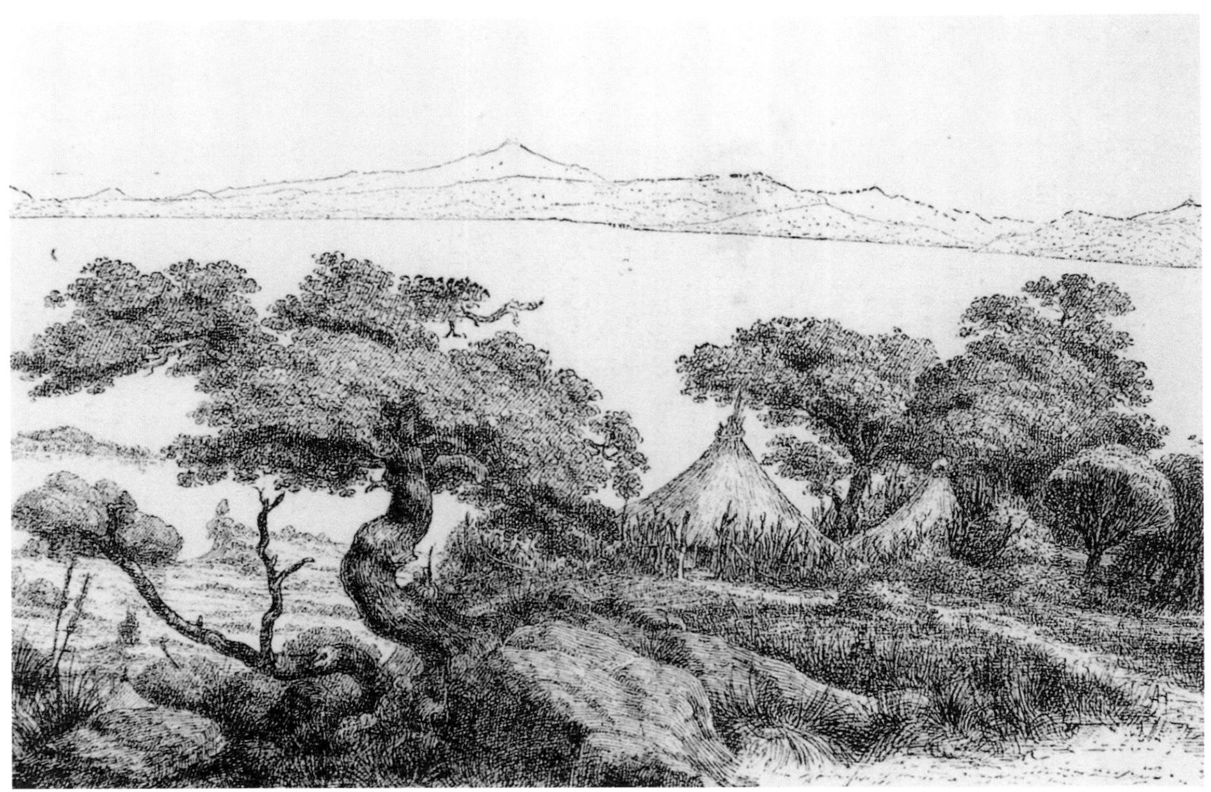

33. On the shores of Lake Tana: (RAFFRAY 1900, p. 9).

kings, the *Hati* reigns", that is, the *Aṣē*, the Christian emperor, who reigned over tens of sovereigns and governors of provinces, from whom he received an annual tribute. The same historian also pointed out the usage of Ethiopian language—the *ge'ez*—and the fact that different dialects in the region all used Ethiopian writing (DORESSE, p. 194). A century earlier, at the time of *neguś* Amda Ṣeyon, Ibn Fadl Allah al 'Omari wrote that the islamic provinces payed to the Christian emperor "a fixed annual tribute, consisting of silk and linen fabrics, imported from Egypt, Yemen and Iraq" (DORESSE, p. 196).

In an epoch when all other countries had become mono-religious, in the Horn of Africa Christians and Muslims lived together in the most Islamic provinces, vassals of the emperor, although Amda Ṣeyon had to fight repeated and successful campaigns in order to preserve the acceptance of his sovereignty. The new Solomonid dynasty then moved its political activity towards the south, always by travelling along the main route, which was the ridge commanding the Dankali depression.

The territory lying in the middle of that ridge, between the rivers Takkaze and Abbāy—inhabited by Amharic populations and open westward on the Nubian planes over Metemma—therefore assumed a strategical rôle with more decisive control and power of intervention in the north of the country, but with an even stronger influence in the South (fig. 30).

Thus, from the end of 13th century onwards, a system is created according to a line of development which is absolutely parallel to that originally occupied by the Aksumite civilization, sharing the same connotations of a transversal ridge, but placed much further south, more internal, more protected by a series of inlets and at the same time, more central to the places where the new political and economical equilibrium had developed.

It is precisely in this area that there lies the vast Lake Tana, the largest among the Ethiopian lakes, located at 1,860 metres above sea level. The Abbāy River—that is, the Blue Nile—flows into it and immediately flows out, describing a great semicircle directed first southward, then westward, and finally flowing north-west into the White Nile. The Abbāy River leaves behind a water surface of almost 3,600 Km^2 at the heart of this new polarity which favours the Ahmarik regions, so far from the Aksumite areas and only peripherical during the time of Lalibela's prosperity.

Many hermitages in the area claim to have been founded in this period. In fact, taking into account the habit of actually instituting religious communities right on the edges of pagan, or anyway non-Christian, areas, the fact that churches and convents on the islands of Lake Tana can be dated to the reign of Amda Ṣeyon (1313-1343) is not at all surprising. Such are Birgidā Māryām (ANNEQUIN 1975, p. 94), in the north part of the lake, or Dabra Māryām (ANNEQUIN 1975, p. 88), on a small isle near the present town of Bāḥer Dār where, according to a legend, the thaumaturge Bishop Tādēwos arrived without getting his feet wet. Monks and hermits arrived there in great number, such as the Tigrin monk Yāfqeranna Egzi, who chose the islet of Meṣelē Fāsiladas as his residence (ANNEQUIN 1976, p. 89). Abbā Za-Yoḥannes instead came from Shoa, installed himself at Kebrān Gabre'ēl (ANNEQUIN 1975, pp. 11-114), from where he committed himself to evangelizing the district, above all towards the peninsula of Ṣegē (ANNEQUIN 1975, pp. 106-108). The monk Batra Māryām went to live on this peninsula in the mid-14th century having been led to do so by the monks already settled in Dāgā Esṭifanos (ANNEQUIN 1975, pp. 102-105). He stayed for more than twenty-three years, during which time he was able to build the church of St. George. The writings of this period mention another five churches on the great island of Dek, the most important of which was Arsimā Samā'et (ANNEQUIN 1975, pp.96-97), now reduced to the state of a precious relic of itself. Also datable to the beginning of the 14th century seems to be the church on the islet of Rēmā Medḫānē 'Ālam (ANNEQUIN 1975, pp. 88-89), a clump of trees emerging from the lake, amongst the others not far from the shore. It is a landscape made of trees and birds, birds and trees in and on the water, which is surrounded by pleasant slopes and by fertile plains bordered by papyrus and punctuated by crosses (figs. 34-35). Around Lake Tana and on its islands a sort of 'holy land' was created, where emperors chose to be buried.

The itinerant *neguś* moved up and down the Ethiopian ridge throughout the 15th century: they fought against the Falashas (Ethiopian Jews, of mysterious origins) and in 1415 they conquered Zeila, in the south, on the Indian Ocean; in 1438 they conquered Massawa and the Dahlak Islands in the north; in 1443-45 they defeated the Muslim sultanates of the south in the Shoa region and on the left bank of the Awash River; again, in 1457 they had to organize another military expedition against Massawa and the Dahlaks. In 1494 the *neguś* Eskender died during a raid on the Dankali salt plain. In Venice, in 1459 Fra Mauro, in his world map, wrote above Mogadishu: "This extremely fertile region was reconquered by the great king of Abyssinia in about 1430".

These events, which in Ethiopian history took a secular dimension, stopped *pro fanum*, before the temple, before the secluded hermitages on the islands of Lake Tana , or on its shores: they almost pertained—and they still do—to a different spatial and temporal order. Here time is that of liturgy, a time revolving on itself, almost a projection on the plane of a point which follows an ascending spiral: the projection is a circle, in which no point is either the beginning or the end.

On the contrary, in a temporal, profane, historical dimension, the beginning is unexpectedly, violently realistic, such is our certainty of the abyss of the end, the eruption of the unexpected, the risk of the becoming.

For the whole of the 15th century Ethiopia almost imposed on itself an opening up to the Christian world, through continuous, harrassing conctacts and legations: to Venice, in 1402 and 1429; to Rome in 1404; to Alfonse of Aragon and to the Duke of Berry in 1428. And the list continues: in 1441 a small Ethiopian delegation took part in the Council of Florence, organized by Pope Eugene IV for the union of the different churches; in 1450 an Ethiopian delegation arrived in Naples and met Alfonse the Magnanimous, King of Aragon, Naples and Sicily, who despatched to Ethiopia craftworks and artisans (MILANESI, p. 44); in 1480 Nicolò Brancaleon and in 1482 Gerolamo Bicini, both Venetian painters, arrived in Ethiopia; finally, in 1487 João II, King of Portugal, sent Pero da Covilhão to gather precise information about Ethiopia, where he was detained.

However, the turning point in the history of Ethiopia took place at the end of the 15th century, with the Portuguese circumnavigation of the Cape of Good Hope: Vasco de Gama crossed the Indian Ocean and reached India, thus suddenly rendering obsolete ancient and traditional commercial routes. Immediately the Portuguese aimed, by building a series of fortresses both on the islands and the coasts, at controlling the Indian Ocean in its three main sections: the African coast, rich in gold; the Indian coast, from whence came pepper, and the Red Sea, that is, the access which had to be closed in order to gain exclusive control over the trading routes and divert them elsewhere. The Indian and Indonesian spices were paid for with gold and silver, with fabrics and Venetian glass: they arrived in Europe directly via the Indian Ocean, whereas before "obliged halting places had been Malacca, Calicut, Aden or Mecca, Alexandria and, in Europe, especially Venice. At each stop the merchandise changed hands and there was a consequent rise in the price of these already expensive goods. Portugal was the first country to reach the areas where the spices were produced and import them directly from there into Europe, substituting the mediation of the Islamic traders with its own, less costly and, above all, Christian merchants" (MILANESI, p. 48).

For the whole of the 16th century, whilst the Portuguese monopoly of the commercial routes circumnavigating Africa withstood the increasingly stronger competition of the Dutch and the English, the international situation led to heavy consequences throughout the whole of Ethiopia. Francisco de Almeida, the Portuguese governor of India, started relentless attacks on all commercial ships which, sailing on the route from India to the Red Sea, did not have a Portuguese safe-conduct. In 1506, still with the purpose of blocking the Red Sea, the Portuguese occupied the isle of Socotra and in 1508 they conquered Ormuz, so that they could control also the access to the Persian Gulf. Moreover, in the same year Alfonse de Albuquerque solicited an alliance with the Christian 'Prester John' against the Egyptians and the Yemenites, both Muslim, who up to that time had been the undisputed and necessary masters of the accesses to and the routes through the Red Sea.

The Portuguese king "relied on the alliance with an army which he considered seasoned (in fact, many Abyssinian slaves were valiant, special troops in the armies of various eastern monarchs) and with a country very rich in crops and livestock, which was to supply meat for the soldiers and leather for the military equipment" (MILANESI, p. 49).

The Egyptian Mamluks built a fleet which in 1509 faced the Portuguese at the mouth of the Red Sea, but was defeated. So, the attempt to get the Portuguese away from the Indian Ocean failed.

Also the Turks, from 1515 onwards reacted to the Portuguese block of the Red Sea by trying to conquer both Aden which dominated the Straits of Bāb el-Mandeb, and Zeila, on the opposite coast.

The Muslim sultanates on the coast of the Horn of Africa, previous vassals of the Emperor of Ethiopia, reacted to the new situation with repeated incursions into the heart of the Christian empire in Africa. In 1516 the twenty-year-old Lebna Dengel—who took the throne with the royal name of Dāwit II—had to face the Sultan of Adal. The first battles were won by the Christian king, who defeated the Muslim army and killed its commander, the terrible Mahfuz, Emir of Zeila.

The Turks took the situation in hand with the conquest of Egypt in 1517. In the same year a large Portuguese fleet left India heading for the Red Sea with the ambitious hope of dealing a mortal blow to the Islamic forces, by destroying Mecca and Ghedda. Instead, the Portuguese had to settle for the sack of Zeila and a first, un-

34-35. The landscape is rich in vegetation and birds.

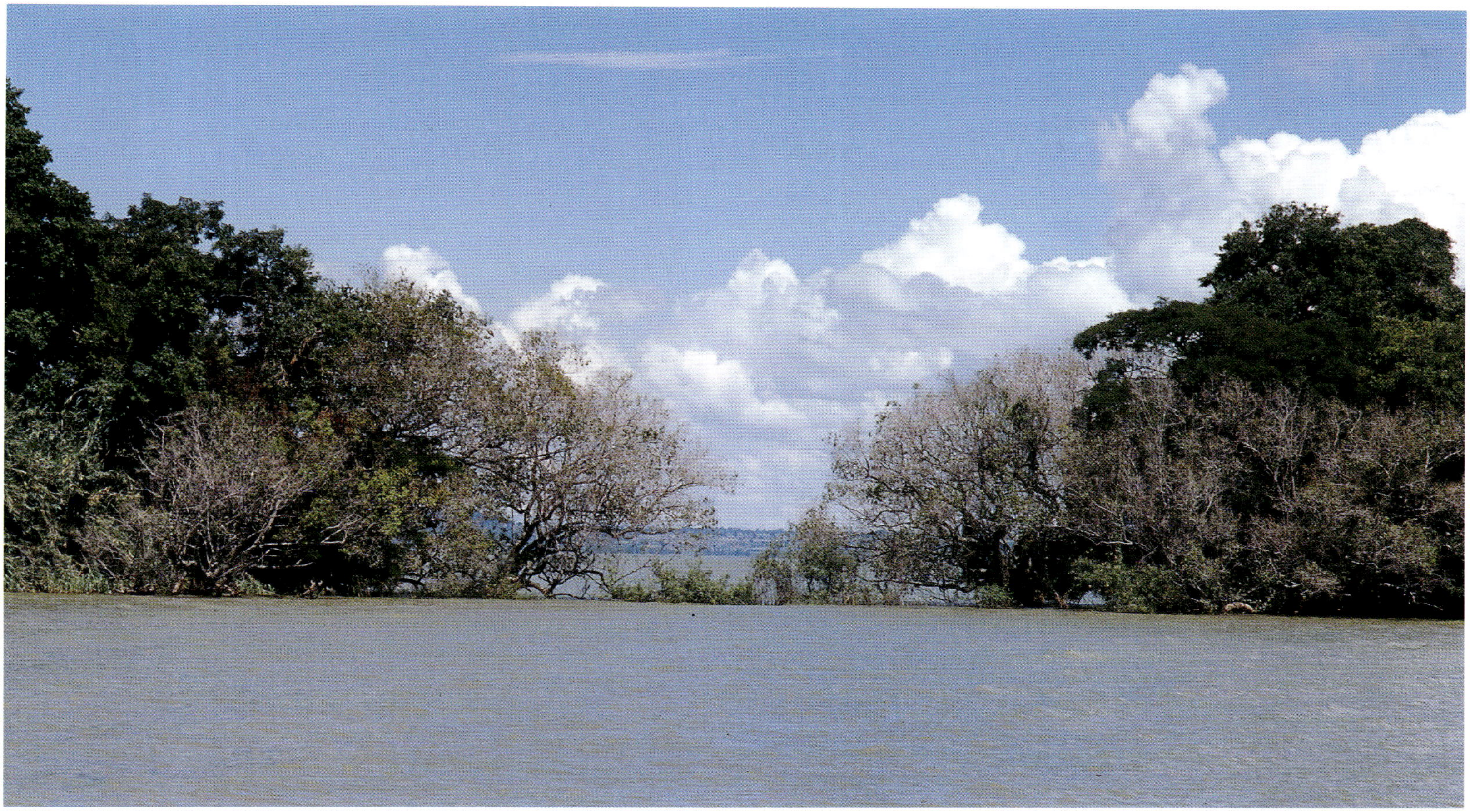

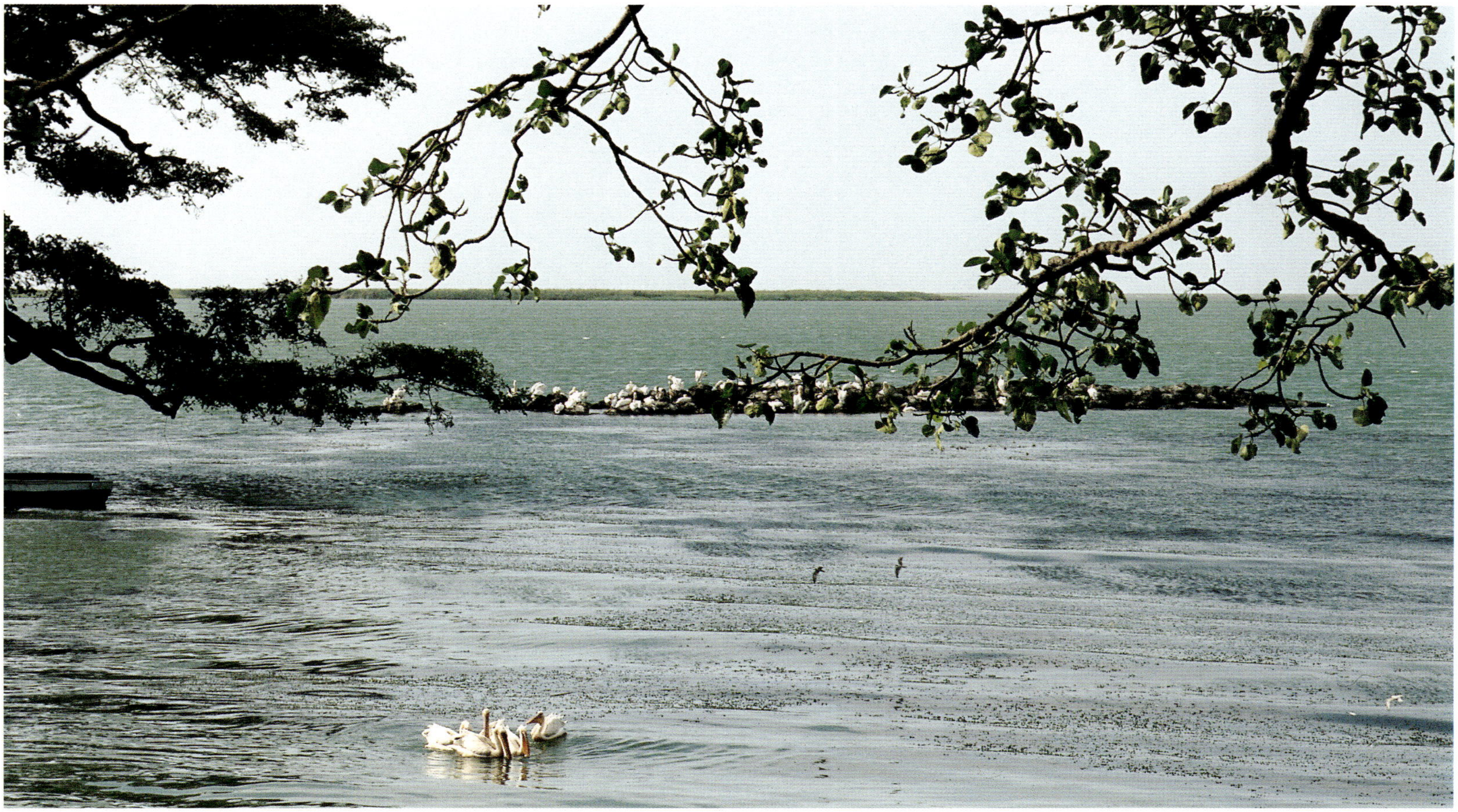

successful attempt at a landing in Ethiopia.
Three years later, in 1520, a Portuguese expedition under the command of Rodrigo da Lima finally managed to reach Ethiopia. Also present on this campaign was Francisco Alvarez, who wrote a chronicle of it (cf. ALVAREZ). Having landed in Massawa which was under the dominion Barnagassu or *bāḥer neguś*, King of the Sea, a vassal of the emperor of Ethiopia, the expedition climbed the Ethiopian ridge, crossed Tigrē, Lāstā, Amhara, and continued all the way up to the Shoa, where the *neguś* Lebna Dengel 'was lodged'. On the 8th of May, 1521 Dom Manuel, King of Portugal, wrote a letter to Pope Leon X to announce that he had finally been able to contact the mythical 'Prester John'. The Portuguese expedition left Ethiopia in 1526, not without arousing in the Muslim world well-founded worries about the potential risks implied in an alliance between the Portuguese and the Emperor of Ethiopia.

In the same year Abu-Bakr, Sultan of Adal, who had transferred his court to Harrar, was murdered by a young muslim leader who was soon to become famous: he would be called by his followers 'Lord and Master, Supreme Iman, Venerable Lordship, Emir of the Believers, Champion of the Faith, Marabut, Sultan Aḥmad ibn Ibrāḥim el-Ghazi (the Conqueror)' and 'Grañ', the 'Left-handed one' by the Ethiopian Christians.

Grañ's offensives, aimed at the devastation and submission of the greater part of the Christian kingdom started immediately, as early as 1527. The first—non-decisive—battle between Lebna Dengel and the Grañ took place in the Shoa region, right at the foot of a sacred mountain, Zeqwālā. Later on, repeatedly defeated, Lebna Dengel did not cease his desperate fight, day and night, reduced to a continuous movement war, escaping from one place to another, from one mountain to another, to prevent the Grañ from persuing him. In the meantime, the Portuguese kept reinforcing their strategical position on the eastern coast of Africa. Vincenzo Minuciano entitles one of his writings *Undertakings of the Great Turk against the Portuguese, both on the Sea and on the Land*, which testifies to the Turkish actions against the Portuguese presence in the Indian Ocean.

Within a general policy aimed at pushing back the growth of Portuguese influence by 'burning the earth' of their allies, in 1531 the Muslims, led by the Grañ, climbed the Harari ridge onto the Ethiopian highlands, where they first invaded the region at its entrance, Shoa, then later, in 1533, Amhara—including the region of Lake Tana—and Lāstā. Finally, in 1534 the tide of Muslims burst into Tigrē.

The island of Matraha (ANNEQUIN 1975, p. 92), which is the first to be encountered in Lake Tana when arriving from the east, still bears traces of the sackings carried out by the Grañ's hordes. Obviously the invaders did not reach all parts since other churches on the lake still house precious and ancient paintaings: perhaps they operated only in certain directions with their raids, offshoots along the main route. Sometimes, being peripheral is an advantage. Along the invaders' route, however, anything that could have happened, did happen.

The *neguś* Lebna Dengel, who was being hunted down, decided to ask the Portuguese for help. However, he did not get the chance to celebrate the foreign intervention he had sought so strongly: he died in 1540, at the age of only forty-four. The contingent of four hundred soldiers guided by Cristovão de Gama, son of the famous Vasco, armed with harquebuses and cannons, arrived in Ethiopia one year after his death. The Portuguese, united with the Ethiopian army, were not hesitant in their offensive against the Muslims, persuing it until, in 1543, the 'Left-Handed one' was defeated and killed at Zantara, in Dembea, not far from the shores of Lake Tana.

The rôle which the great Christian state of the Ethiopian plateau played with regard to the Indian Ocean was therefore limited: in fact, it could not offer any real support to the Portuguese in their fights—first against the Egyptians, then against the Turks—for supremacy on the sea and control over the commercial routes. Instead, it was the negus' who had to ask the Portuguese for help.

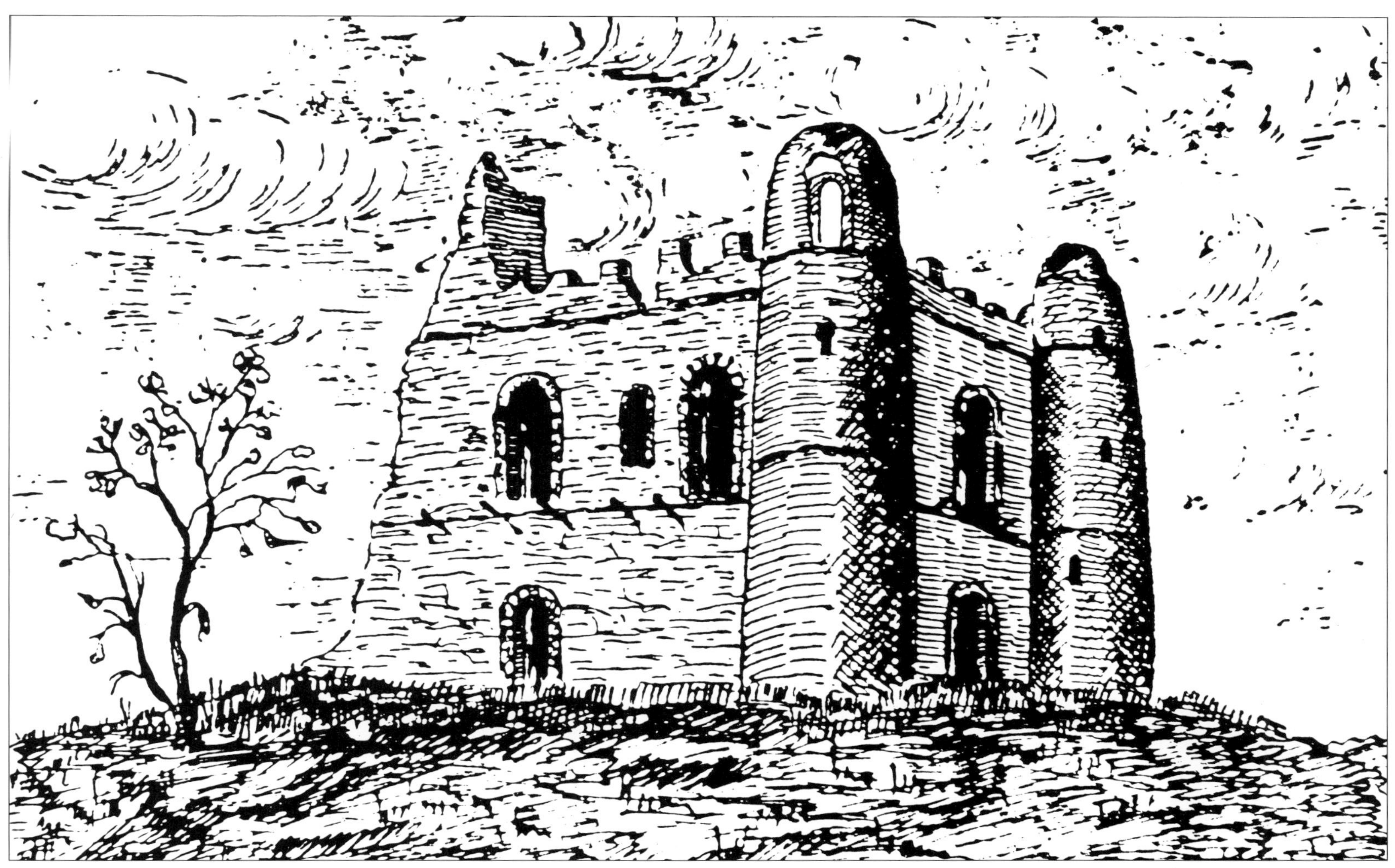

36. The castle of Guzārā, which was erected at the end of 16th century by *neguś* Sarṣa Dengel on a promontory from which one may gaze on the blue waters of Lake Tana: (MONTI DELLA CORTE, p. 110).

During the following sixteen years no Muslim dared to attack Ethiopia. However, it was only in 1578 that the Emperor Sarṣa Dengel, 'Bud of the Virgin', managed to stem rampant anarchy and the incursions from the south of the Oromo populations, which had assumed the character of a true mass immigration. More importantly, Sarṣa Dengel established new and different relationships with the Ottoman Empire, thus reducing the Ottomans' support of the various Muslim kingdoms on the coast of the Horn of Africa. Finally, there were the conditions necessary for the transformation of the 'itinerant' king into a 'sedentary' one, thus radically modifying the way in which sovereignity was organized since the fall of the Zāgwē dynasty in the 13th century. Sarṣa Dengel built himself a castle on the top of a rise from where the blue of Lake Tana can be admired, and there, in Guzārā (MONTI DELLA CORTE, p. 110; ANNEQUIN 1965, pp. 22-25), he established the capital city. Instead of sumptuous tents, there was a castle, a rectangular, two-storey brick building, with round towers bent forward on the corners, covered with cupolas in the shape of a sugarloaf, surrounded by a high wall with three doors and in a position which dominated the line of the ridge which crosses the Ahmaric region (fig. 36).

If the alliance of the Emperor of Ethiopia with the Portuguese proved to be a failure from the strategical point of view, the privileged contacts of the Portuguese with the Ethiopian court resulted in just as much of a disaster from the religious point of view, in their frustrated attempt to assimilate the Ethiopian Church into the demesne of Roman Catholicism.

During the 16th century many Jesuit missions managed to land on the coasts of the Red Sea and penetrate Ethiopia by breaking the block of the Eritrean coast, but the most relevant of these was the one guided by Pero Paez in 1603. Having landed in Massawa with five other mis-

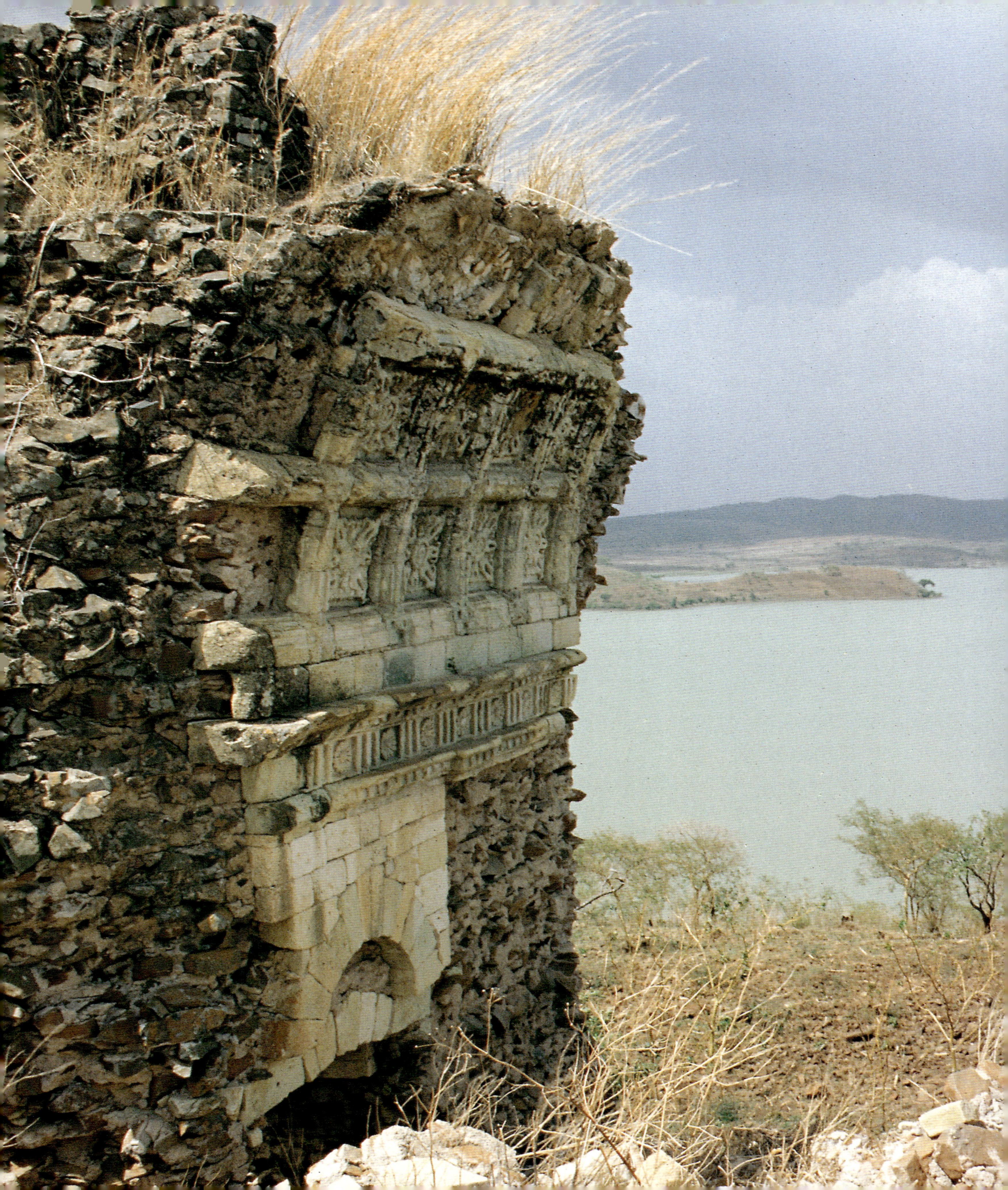

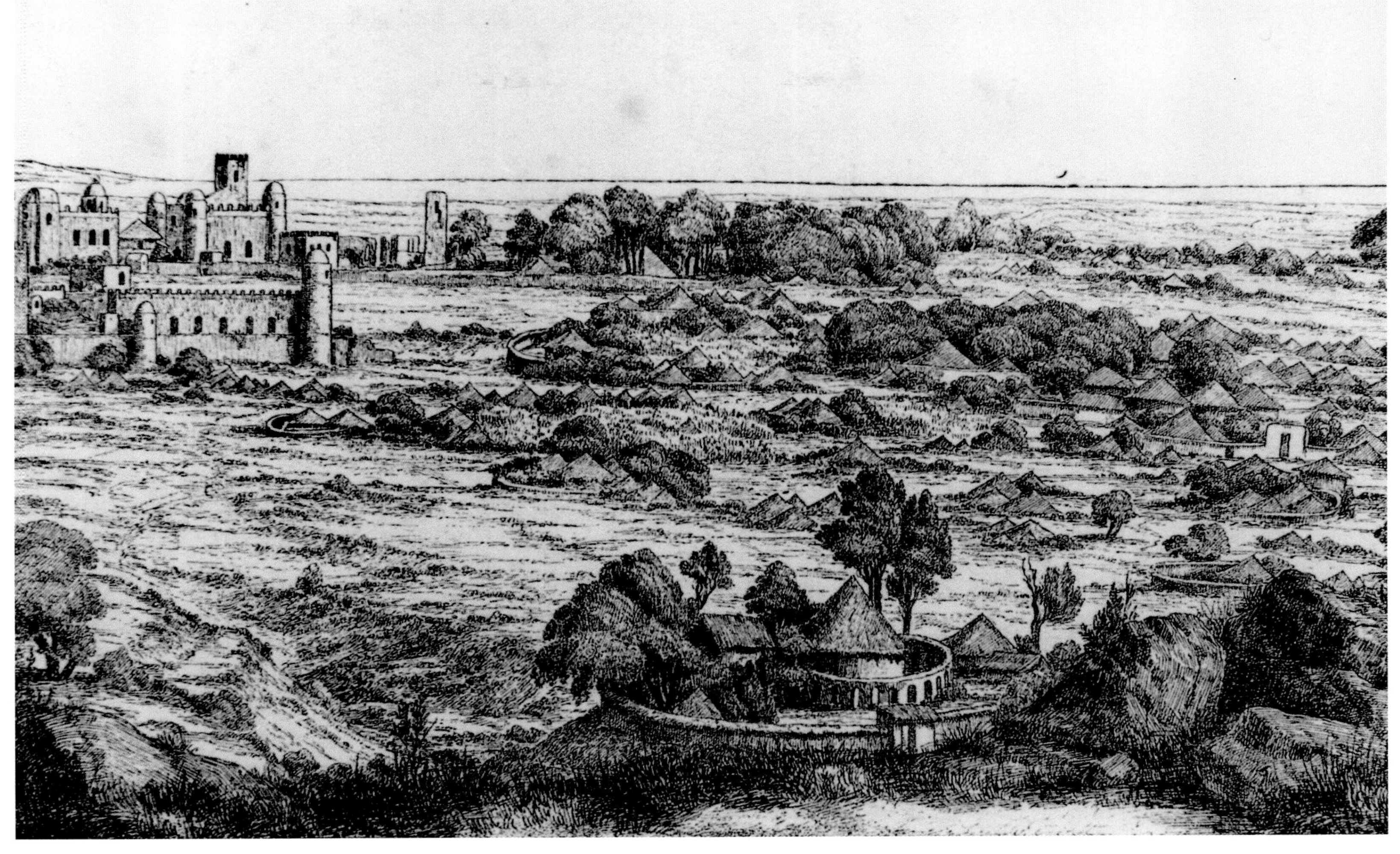

38. Castles and churches in Gondar, the new capital founded by Emperor Fāsiladas (1632-1667): (RAFFRAY 1900, p. 25)

37. Ruins of the majestic complex of Māryām Gemb, on the north shore of Lake Tana, which was completed by the Portuguese missionary Pero Paez in 1621.

sionaries, he arrived at court. Emperor Za-Dengel decided on obedience to the Roman Pope in exchange for soldiers to fight the Oromo and to protect himself, but Pero Paez's crucial encounter was the one with Susenyos, Za-Dengel's successor. He also lived in Guzārā and, full of admiration for the knowledge, the real and the exemplary morality of the Jesuit missionaries, he declared himself favourable to Catholicism, therefore rejecting the authority of the Church of Alexandria and accepting instead that of the Roman Pope.

For more than a decade Pero Paez devoted himself to the building of his residence, with a church, boarding-school and seminary attached, on the northern shore of Lake Tana, at Māryām Gemb, near Gorgorā, finishing it in 1621 (ANNEQUIN 1975, pp. 94-95). The building was erected on a rock which forms a promontory jutting far into the lake: it is a picturesque place, surrounded by water on all sides, except one (fig. 37). The view of the lake and the mountains is unbelievably magnificent: nature seems to have created a special place for quietness, meditation and well-being, to the point that the king decided to live there, in a sumptuous palace. Yet, neither the courtesans, nor the population accepted Susenyos' conversion and in the end, he had to admit that he had made a mistake. Thus, in 1632 he had to abdicate in favour of his son Fāsiladas, who expelled the foreign priests and transferred the capital to Gondar (fig. 38).

Transferred from Guzārā to Māryām Gemb and finally to Gondar—all places more or less close to Lake Tana—, the capital finally stabilized and the successive emperors competed in building palaces near to the original one erected by Fāsiladas: his son Yoḥannes built an elegant library and a pavillion used as a chancellery; then Iyāsu I, who reigned between the end of the 16th and the beginning of the 17th century,

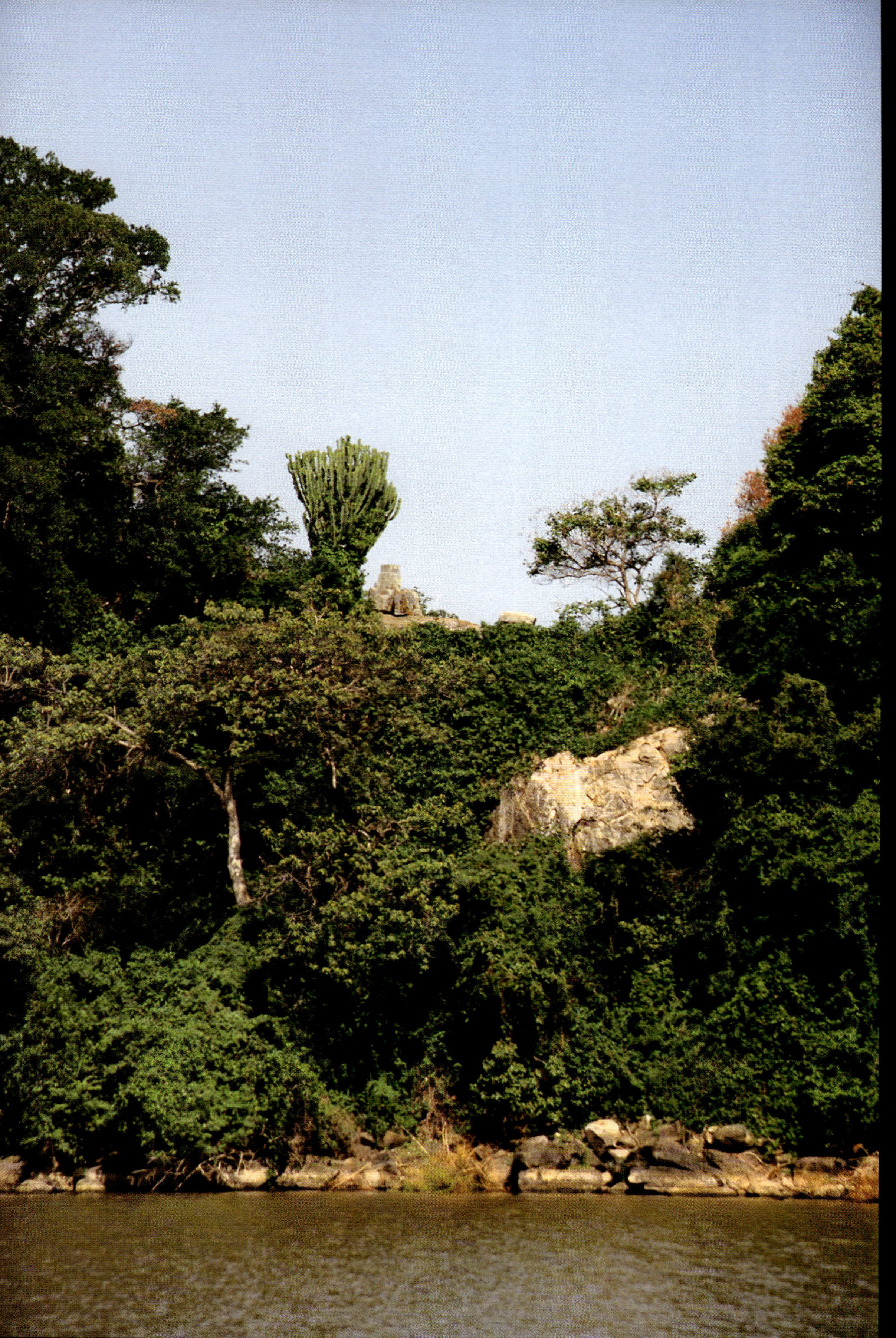

39-40. Even from a distance the hermitage at Ṭānā Qirqos may be discerned amongst the vegetation. Here, in a hollow, a group of standing stones are preserved whose form seems to be Aksumite. They are almost like fragments of ancient square pilasters with rounded edges and are widely considered to be the remnants of a pre-Christian altar because of the large crucibles (*coppelle*) carved in their tops.

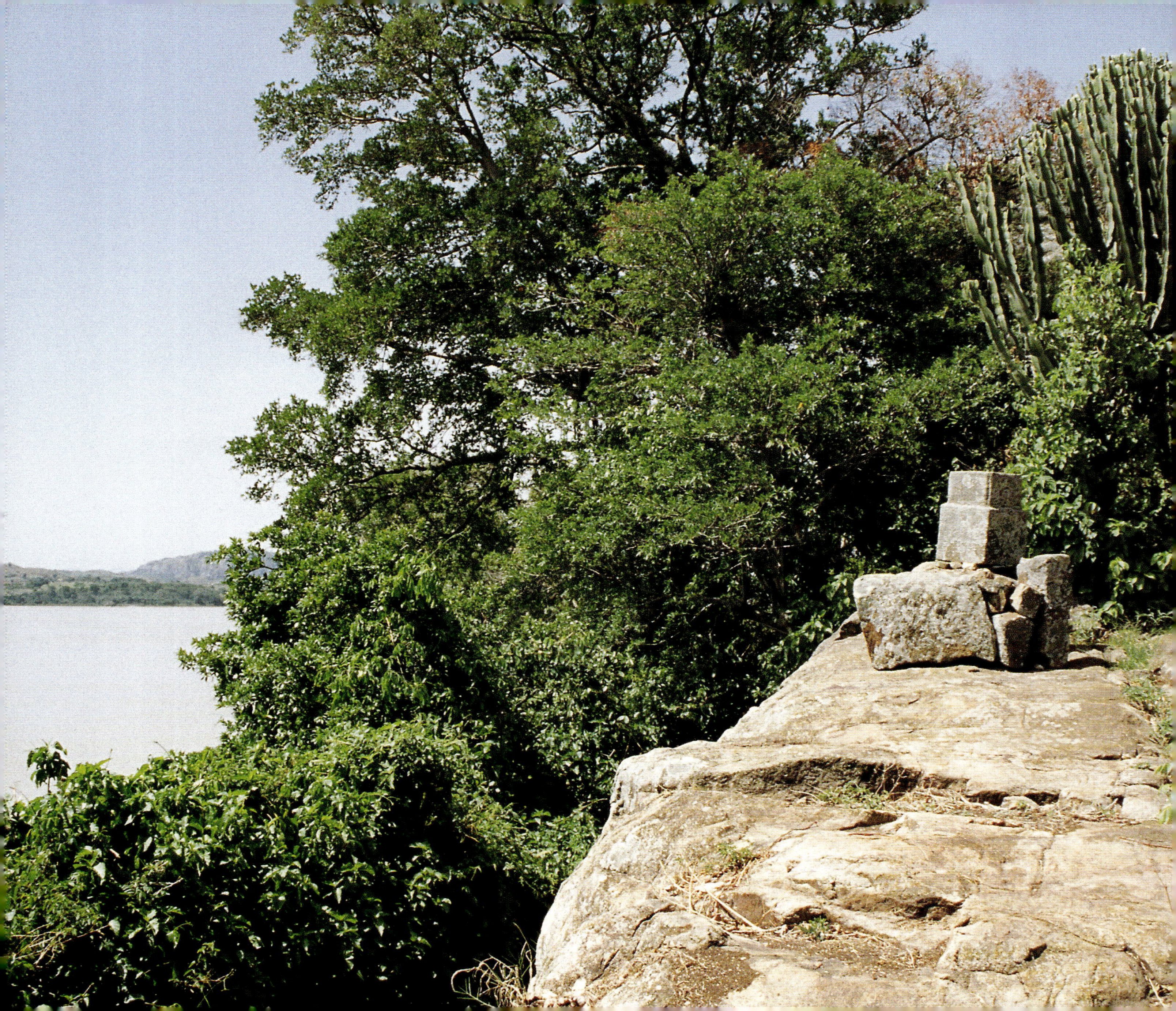

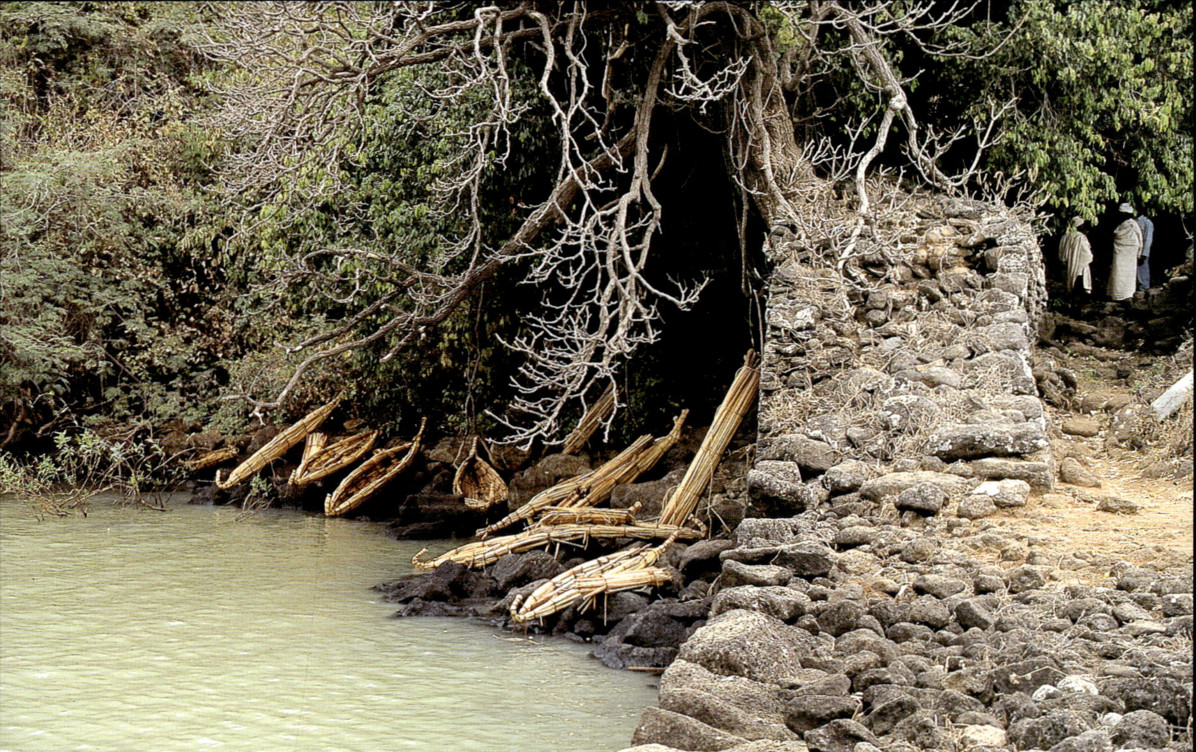

41. Remnants of the massive walls, two and half metres thick, flanking the short isthumus connecting the islet of Nārgā with the larger island of Dek.

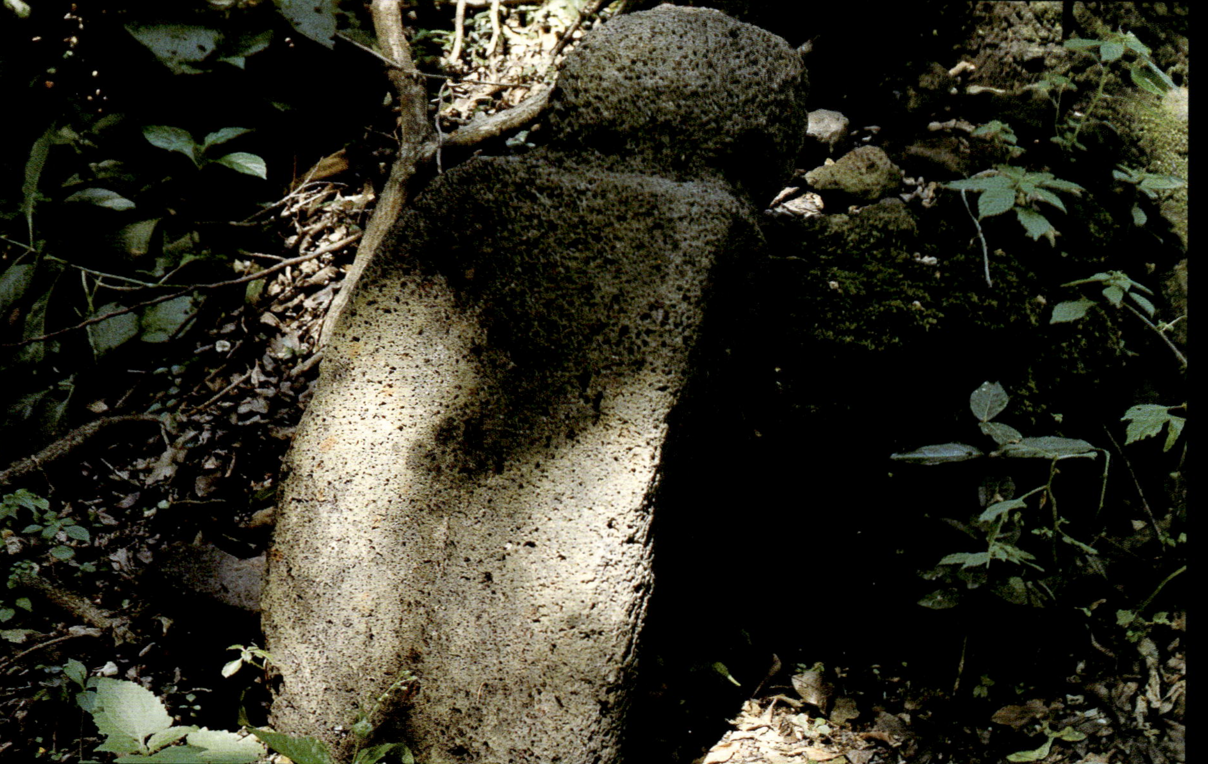

42. Anthropomorphic *betilus* (sacred stone) which is placed as a deterrent at the beginning of the short slope leading to Kebrān Gabre'ēl's monastery.

43. The islet of Dāgā Esṭifanos stands out, isolated and pointed: it is visible from everywhere and is an unmistakable reference point in the landscape, almost an *umbilicum* of the whole lake.

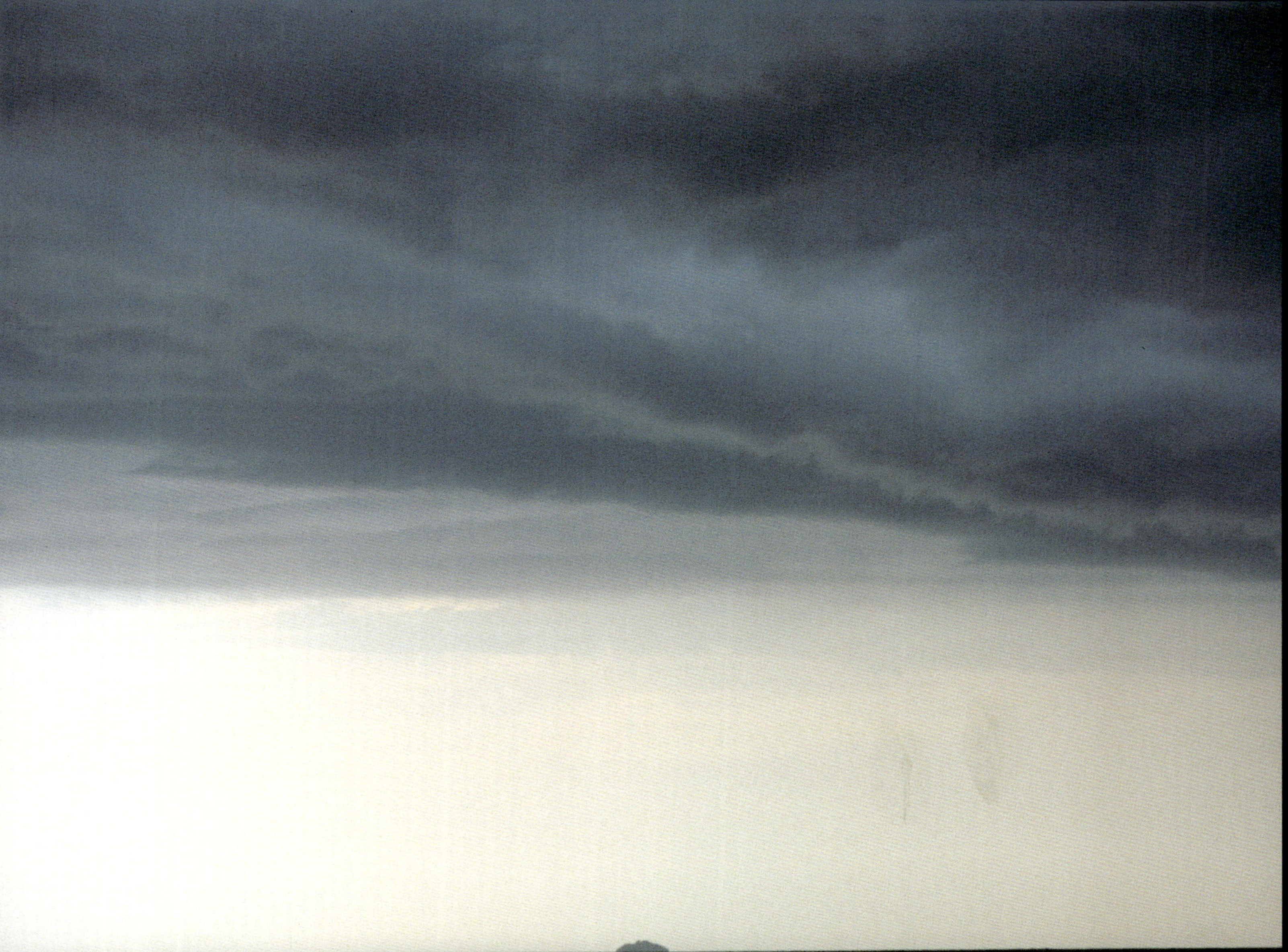

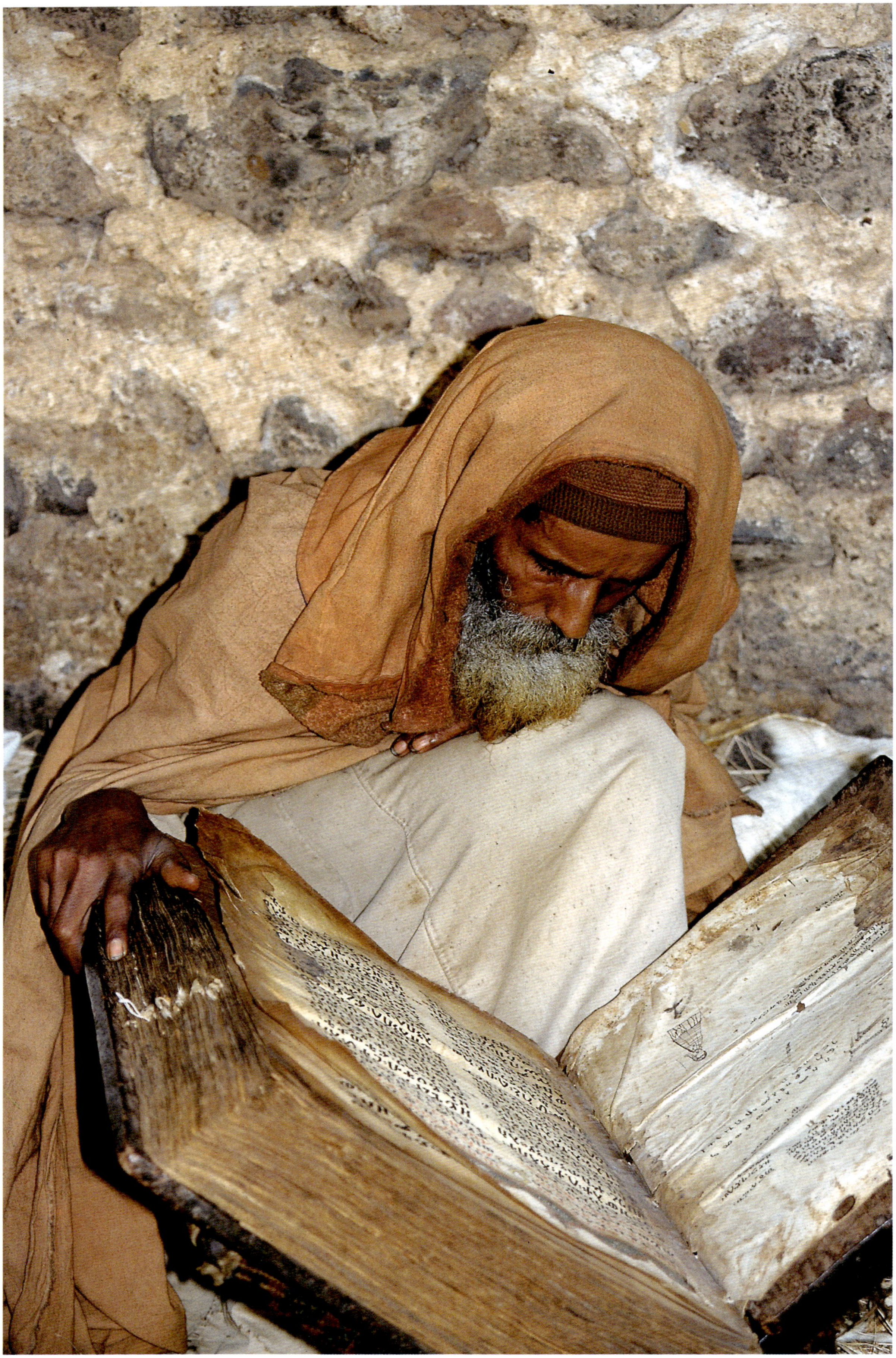

44. A priest absorbed in the study of one of the many manuscripts still kept in various hermitages.

then Bakāffā, Queen Mentewwāb, and her son Iyāsu II (MONTI DELLA CORTE).

It was under the reign of Iyāsu II that the choice of Gondar as a non-movable capital began to produce disastrous effects. The lack of the emperor's mobility and presence in the territory encouraged and caused breakaway tendencies: the Shoa region became almost independent, Tigrē fell under the dominion of a *rās*, Mikā'ēl, and Gojjam was in a condition of perpetual revolt.

On the other hand, for Lake Tana it was a period of great splendour. The emperors' devotion—once the expulsion, and often the martyrdom, of those who did not abjure Catholicism was completed—expressed itelf in their assiduity in paying homage to the sacredness of the place. Also, before and after military expeditions, they visited the place and brought rich gifts and apanages to this or that hermitage, according to their personal preference for this or that entitled saint. They contributed to their preservation or embellishment and founded new ones, chosing them as their burial places, but they also directly intervened to calm diatribes and doctrinal controversies which were reasons for dispute amongst the monks.

Thus Lake Tana became to an even greater extent one of the privileged places of Ethiopian spirituality.

The hermitage of Ṭānā Qirqos from which the lake derives its name (ANNEQUIN 1975, p. 90) is the most outstanding one, signalled by the crest of the vertical rock which stands out on the lake, amongst the greenery, well visible from far away. Preserved in this spot is a group of squared *betilos* (sacred stones) with rounded off edges, apparently of Aksumite shape (figs. 39-40).

Facing the hermitage is the islet of Dāgā Esṭifanos, isolated and with a pointed shape, visible from everywhere and an unmistakeable reference point in the landscape, almost an *umbilicum* of the whole lake. The islet presents the same type of rectangularly shaped church that we find in the hermitage of Ṭānā Qirqos, the only two of this type on the lake, whose typology is in all probability derived from that of the churches in the north, the area from which Christianity in Ethiopia first spread (fig. 43).

Adjacent to Dāgā, on the isle of Dek—so flat that, when one arrives there, it can be perceived, more than seen, due to the tops of the trees which seem to float on the water—there are walls from which no historical reference can be drawn (an archeological survey, if carried out, perhaps could shed some light) (fig. 41). In the same way, nothing is known about the anthropomorphic stele placed as a deterrent, at the beginning of the short slope leading to the church on the islet of Kebrān Gabre'ēl (fig. 42).

The signs testifying to the fact that the lake has been frequented since ancient times are therefore many, even if they appear under disguised forms. Just as myths do—quoting Mircea Eliade—, "they always tell a story of facts which really happened". On Lake Tana, the religious fervour which regained strength after the restoration of the Solomonid dynasty to the throne of Ethiopia, is also attested by the extremely precious relics, both from the artistic and historical point of view, still present in various hermitages. They have been saved by God's mercy only, surely not by the will of men: they survived, even if decimated, not only historical turmoils, but also carelesness and *cupiditas rerum novarum*.

In this land, so fertile in meditation and prayer, on an islet almost attached to the greater isle of Dek, Mentewwāb, wife of Emperor Bakāffā, and regent after the death of the Emperor, offered to God the church of Nārgā Śellāsē.

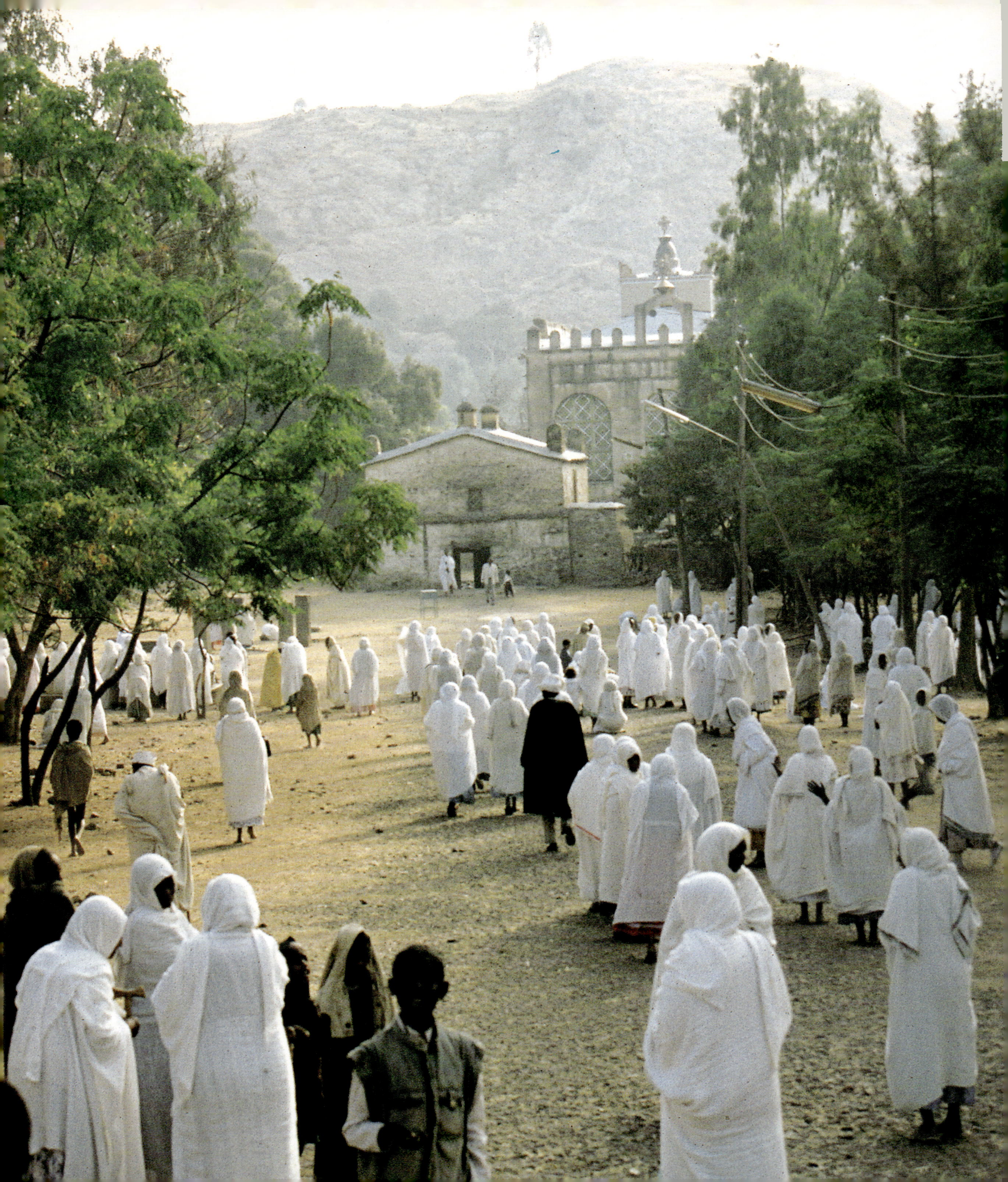

The Typology of Ethiopian Churches: From the Basilica to the Centrally Planned Churches, in Their Structural and Symbolic Aspects

45. In the early morning, believers go towards the church of Saint Mary of Zion, at Aksum.

Understanding Lake Tana requires the consideration of the great cultural heritage which is kept there: that of Christian Ethiopia. Unfortunately, a homogenous and finished documentary study of this artistic and cultural legacy is still lacking, notwithstanding the praise-worthy, qualified and thorough survey already carried out and the remarkable amount of information already gathered in many important sectors.

Even today, definite and documented dates or chronologies of ancient Ethiopian churches, are rarely, or only with difficulty, available: often, the only material for study is the local oral tradition, in which elements totally extraneous to historical logic prevail.

Verifiable data and dates would be of primary interest to the researcher and the art historian, who have to locate these works within a temporal and spatial frame and draw precise conclusions. Many questions remain to be answered.

Certainly, there are still unrecorded churches or—even if they have been recorded—those not carefully studied so that the necessary comparisons and synthesis are made possible. There is neither an exhaustive inventory of the widespread network, which includes less important work but is certainly a trait-d'union of the main artistic trends nor, above all, a register (with the exception of some buildings and rock-painting).

Once more, especially with regard to the architecture of Christian Ethiopia, new surveys, which are the necessary premise to any further analysis, are therefore the preliminary operation required in order to arrive at a systematic picture of their development.

The art of the multimillenial Ethiopian civilization, and in particular its architecture, obviously developed as a result of the opportunities and conditioning by historical events and by the nature of the territory. Similarities, but also important differences, can be drawn between buildings of the same period in the same place or, on the contrary, between buildings of different periods and in different places. A given building shows some characteristics which testify to its pertainance to a given type, but also other traits which cannot be considered typical, since they are its own, depending on various factors, included that precise localization in time and space which confers on it its historical value.

At the present stage, research is capable of pointing out directions for future investigations, whose results could even contrast with the present, temporarily, established convictions. Given these limitations—which one cannot avoid mentioning—a constant prudence is necessary, together with a benevolent indulgence by those who read about this subject for the first time, because of the frequent inexactitude and indetermination of the hypotheses and suggestions proposed hereafter.

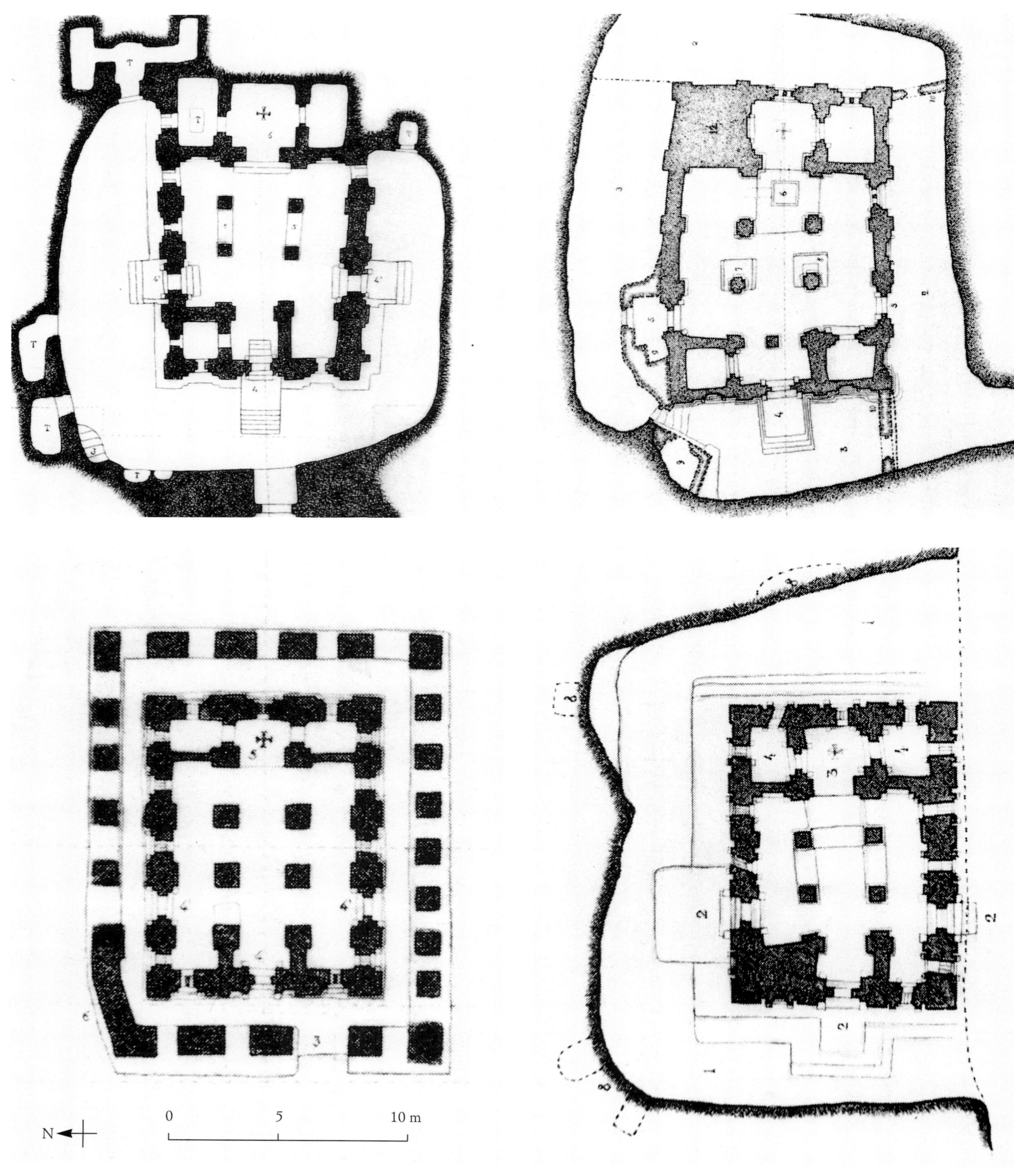
N
0
5
10 m

50. Plan of the monolithic church of Māryām at Lalibela: (BIANCHI BARRIVIERA, tav. 13).

51. Plan of the monolithic church of Emānu'ēl at Lalibela: (BIANCHI BARRIVIERA, tav. 39).

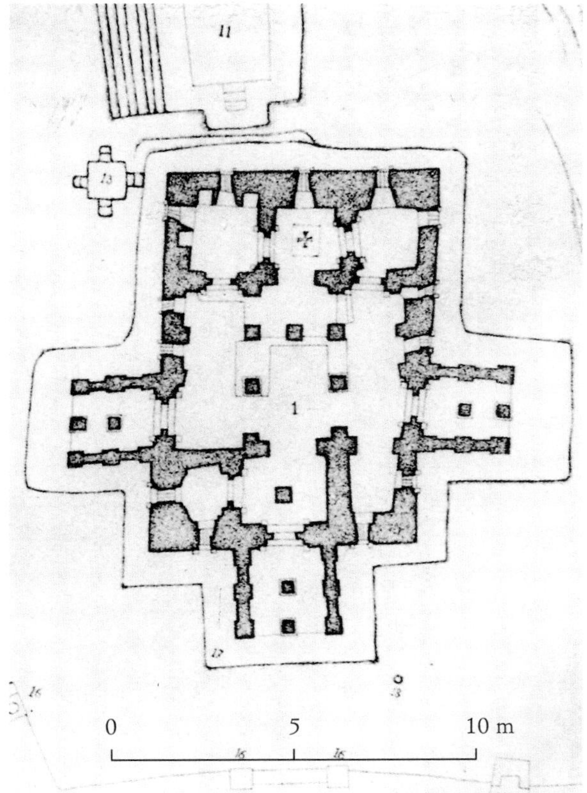

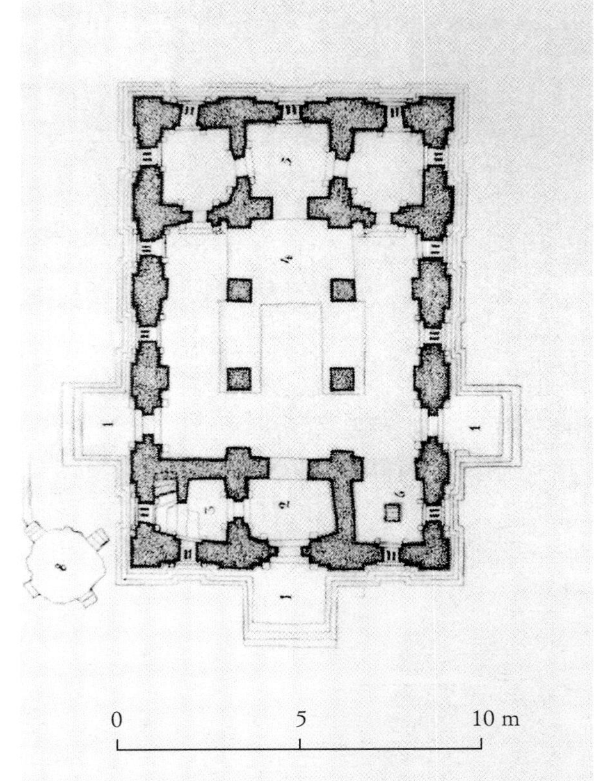

52. Transverse section of the monolithic church of Māryām at Lalibela. Situated over the aisles are the women's galleries. In the middle of the nave there is a full-lenght pier, which symbolically represents the *axis mundi*: (BIANCHI BARRIVIERA, tav. 14).

53. Transverse section of the monolithic church of Emānu'ēl at Lalibela: (BIANCHI BARRIVIERA, tav. 39)

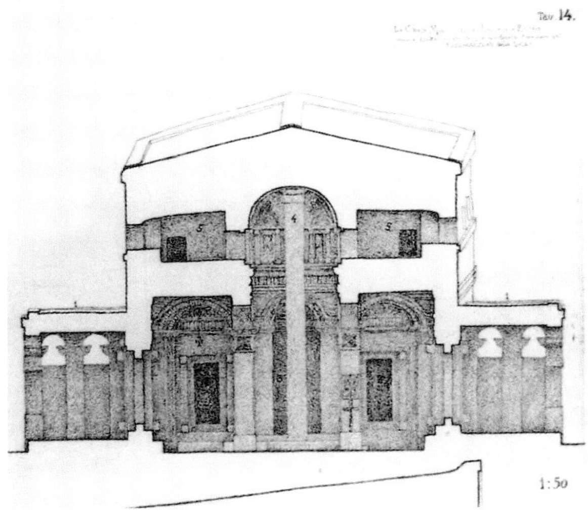

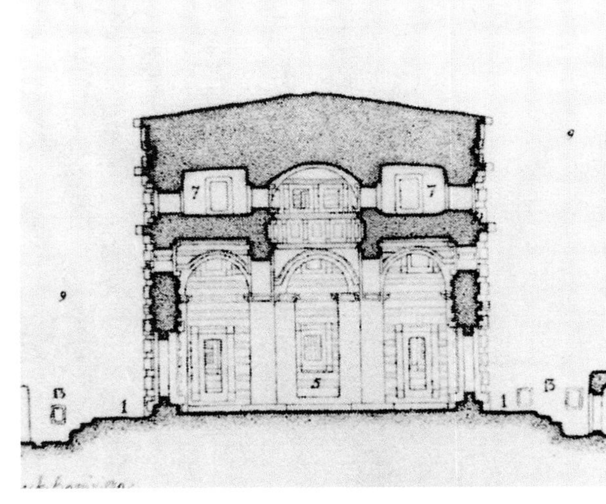

46. Plan of the monolithic church of Bilbalā Çerqos: (BIANCHI BARRIVIERA, tav. 46).

47. Plan of the monolithic church of Wuqro Masqāla Krestos: (BIANCHI BARRIVIERA, tav. 50).

48. Plan of the monolithic church of Gannata Māryām: (BIANCHI BARRIVIERA, tav. 52).

49. Plan of the monolithic church of Abbā Libānos: (BIANCHI BARRIVIERA, tav. 37).

The basilica type

Carlo Conti Rossini, the renowned expert on Ethiopian architecture, had already pointed out the peculiarities and specific characteristics of the basilical tradition when he schematized the different typologies of the old churches in Ethiopia (CONTI ROSSINI 1928, pp.232-234).

The most common typology which was officially present in the whole of the Christian world and conceived exclusively as a church was in fact the basilica, made of one covered, rectangular hall, subdivided lengthwise into aisles by columns or piers arranged in rows along many bays, starting from the narthex at the entrance all the way to the apse at the end.

The structure of the basilica spread also to Ethiopia: it is already traceable in some ruins of Aksumite churches, which show a high grade of specialization in the different usage of the various spaces devoted to religious ritual. The basilica type, however, was largely employed in northern Syria during the Paleo-Christian era, as well as in

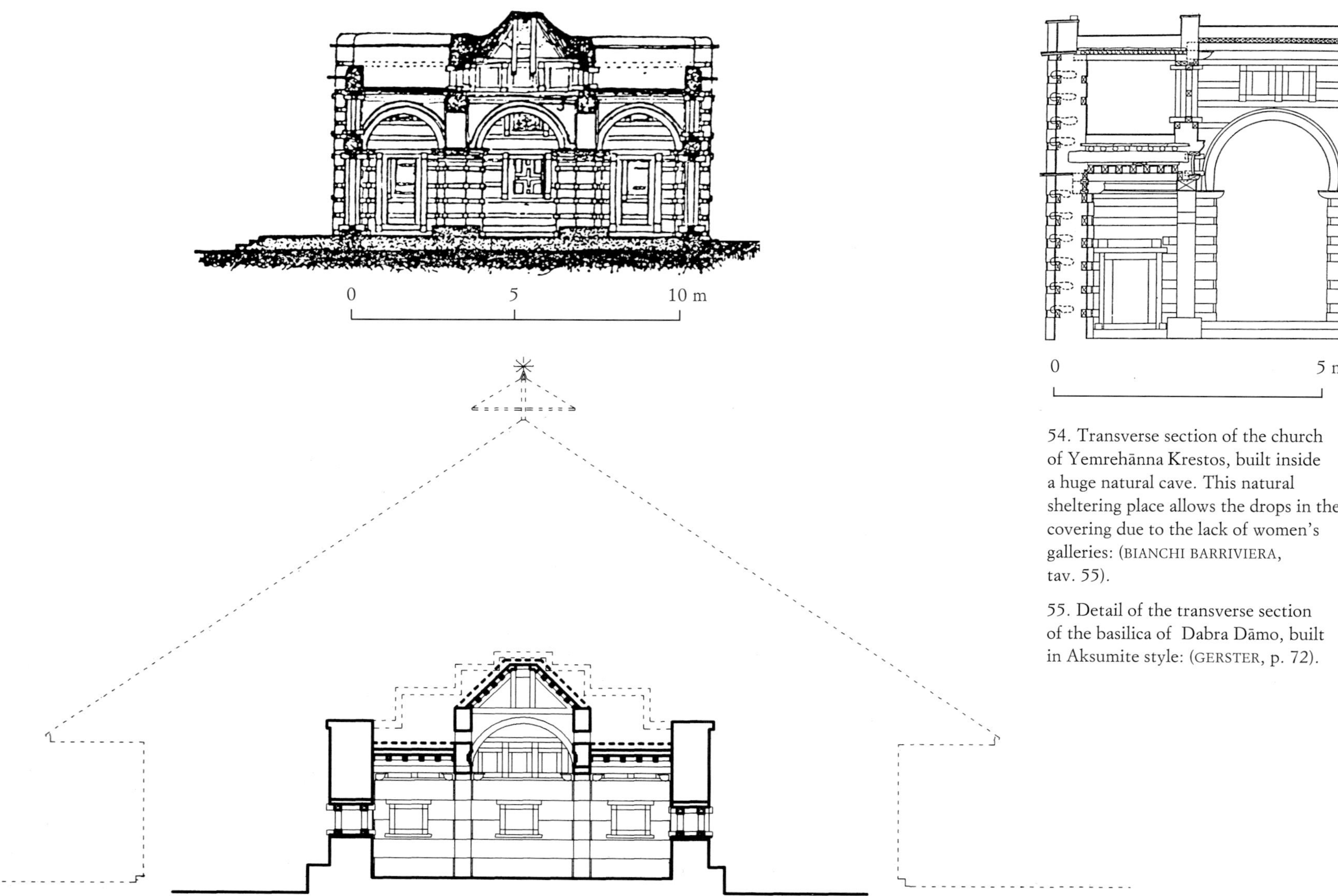

54. Transverse section of the church of Yemrehānna Krestos, built inside a huge natural cave. This natural sheltering place allows the drops in the covering due to the lack of women's galleries: (BIANCHI BARRIVIERA, tav. 55).

55. Detail of the transverse section of the basilica of Dabra Dāmo, built in Aksumite style: (GERSTER, p. 72).

56. Transverse section of the ancient church of Bētalehēm, in Gaynt, incorporated within a later conical covering (from Mezemir Abiy's reliefs).

the Nile Valley, so that: "Malgré l'influence syrienne qui se manifeste dans le basiliques d'Adoulis, Yeha e Melazo, il est donc permis de se demander si dès l'origine, cette influence ne s'est pas transmise per l'intermédiaire de l'église copte primitive. Les récits sur la conversion de l'Ethiopie donnent bien pour foundateurs de son église des Syriens, Edèse de Tyr et Frumence, mais celui-ci fut consacré éveque par le patriarche d'Alexandrie, Athanase" (DE CONTENSON 1961, p. 43).

Between the 12th and the 13th century, in the Lāstā region (above all in Lalibela and its environs), but also in Tigrē, the monolithic churches—so called because they were sculpted in only one block of mother rock—reproduced the partition of the actual buildings, even though with the changes imposed by the orographical system and by the different consistency of the material. The main typological characteristics remained the same, although they underwent a continuous process of transformation. Within these different conditions, often the building elements even assumed a merely allusive or ornamental role, thus surviving the loss of their original building functionality.

"...vi sono edifici di tal sorte che, secondo il mio giudico, nel mondo non credo si trovino altrettanti, li quali sono chiese tutte cavate in pera viva di monte tenero over tofo, molto ben lavorata."[1] (ALVAREZ, p. 177).

If what is built can be considered as the product of the relationship between a given natural environment and a given culture, then the presence

[1] "... there are buildings which, in my opinion, one cannot find elsewhere, such as the churches all sculpted into a real, tender stone, or rather tufa, very well carved."

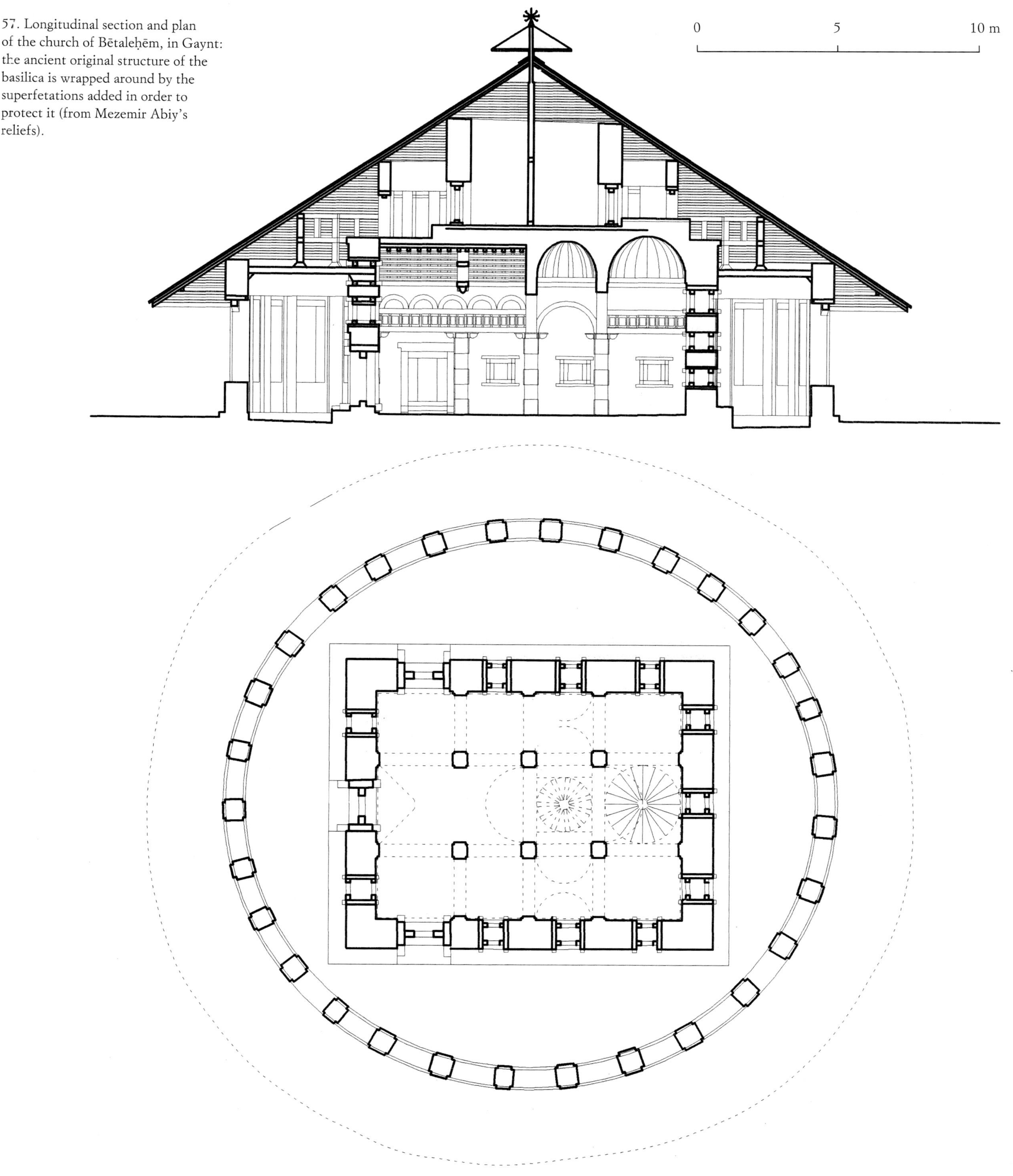

57. Longitudinal section and plan of the church of Bētaleḥēm, in Gaynt: the ancient original structure of the basilica is wrapped around by the superfetations added in order to protect it (from Mezemir Abiy's reliefs).

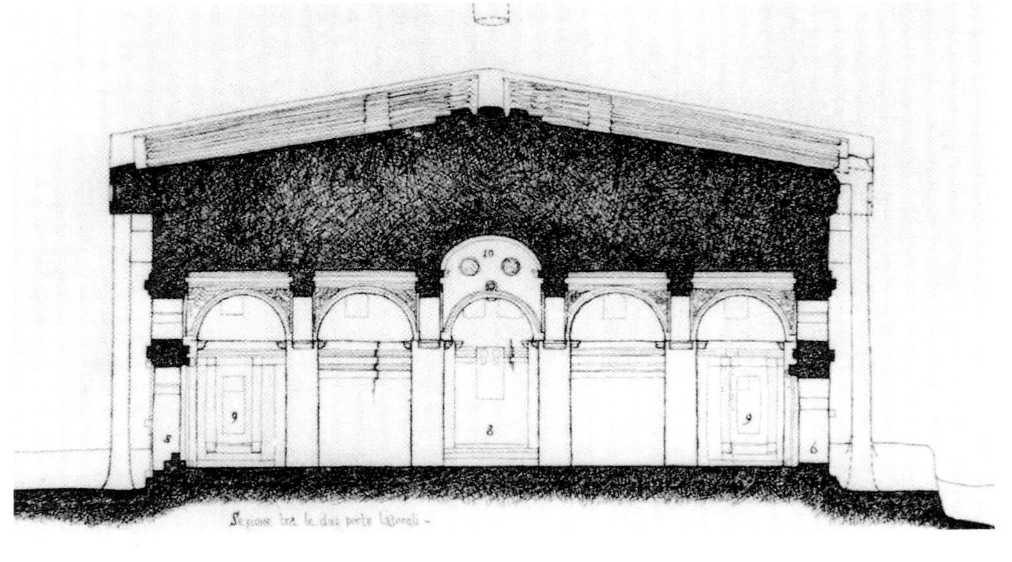

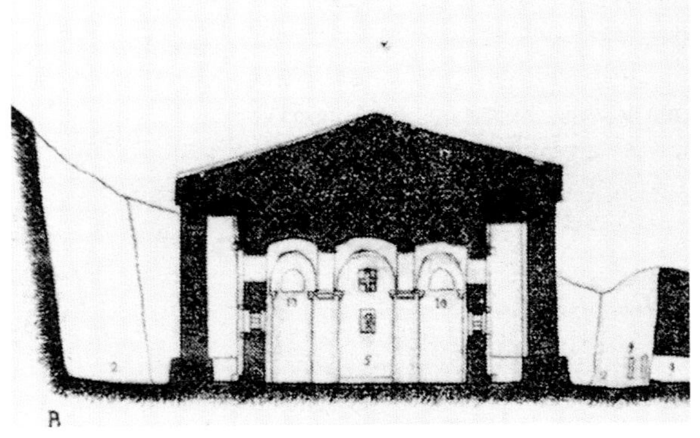

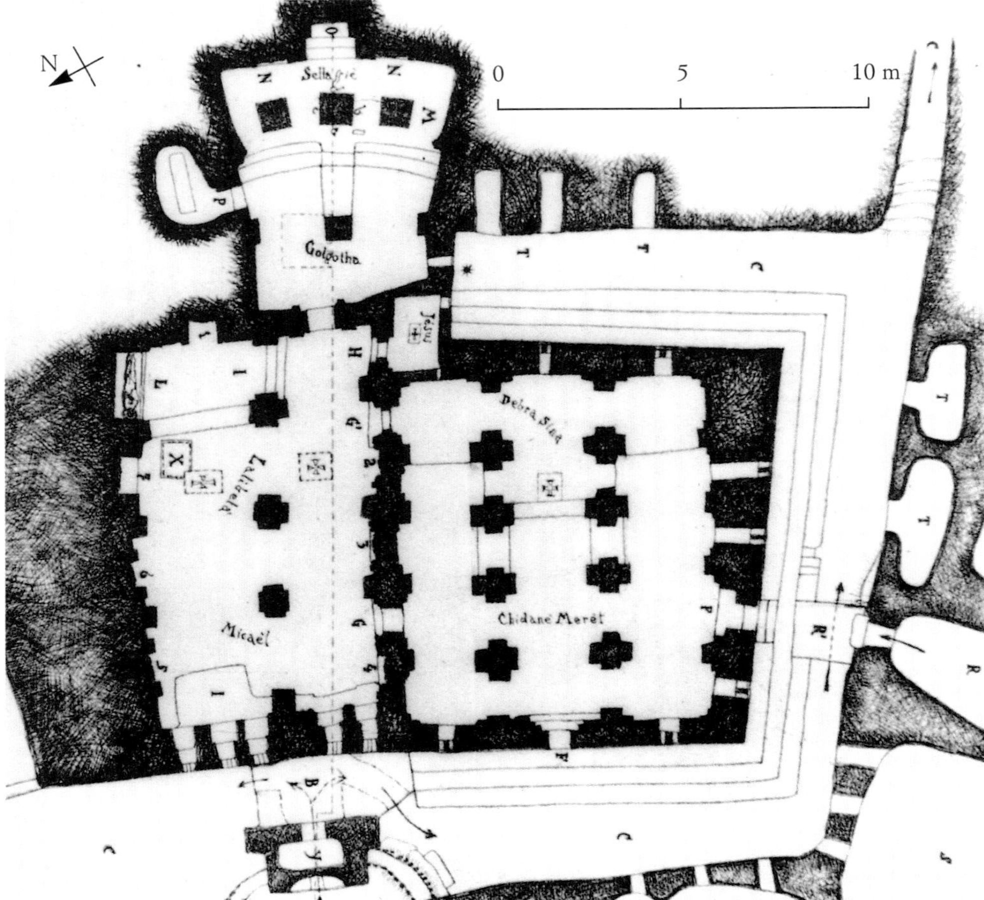

58. Transverse section of the monolithic church of Madhānē 'Ālam at Lalibela: (BIANCHI BARRIVIERA, tav. 20)

59. Transverse section of the monolithic church of Gannata Māryām: (BIANCHI BARRIVIERA, tav. 52).

60. Plan of the monolithic churches of Golgotā, Mikā'ēl and Śellāsē, examples of hypostyle structures which have simply been placed next to one another: (BIANCHI BARRIVIERA, tav. 8).

of numerous rupestral and underground churches in Ethiopia must be examined also from the historical point of view and building elements must be taken into account, besides the (unluckily, still quite unclear) concepts of the history of religion, which are certainly appliable to many civilizations in various parts of the world.

Monolithic churches survived the great destruction of the 16th century: their survival makes it possible to consider both their planimetry and the structural conception of their elevation. Thanks to these churches, it is therefore possible to verify how Aksumite architectural traditions have been transmitted at least down to the restoration of the Solomonid dynasty.

When considering only the main aspects, despite the great variety of forms, dimensions and modalities, the planimetrical arrangement of a great number of monolithic churches seems to be perfectly homologous.[2] (figs. 46-51) The individuated basilical shape is rigorously predetermined as the expression of a whole, organical in its reciprocal correspondance between spaces and their specific function. The tripartite system of the apses, facing eastward on the last bay, is counterbalanced on the west by a sort of narthex, similarly tripartite, where the main opening is the axial access to the church—which also has direct lateral entrances to the central hall, that is, to the actual basilica. Even dimensions are often the same: an average width of about 7 metres and a depth of about 14 metres.[3]

Only a few of these churches[4] show also in elevation the peculiar characteristics of the basilica type, such as the higher level of the nave in comparison to that of the aisles, in order to endow it with a direct source of light (figs. 52-53). A few ancient churches, extremely rare, allow the verification of the recurrence of the basilica type as it was elaborated in Ethiopia, both with a women's gallery (such as the very ancient church of Dabra Dāmo, built in the Aksum Paleo-Ethiopian style) (GERSTER, p. 71) (fig. 55) or without it (see the old church of Aramò (MORDINI, p. 39), and the churches of Makina Madhānē 'Ālam and Yemrehānna Krestos (fig. 54) (BIANCHI BARRIVIERA, p. 81; GERSTER, p. 109; SAUTER, n. 33), built under the vast vault of powerful caverns, or the church of Bētaleḥēm, in Gaynt (GERSTER, p. 137) which presents a much later addition of a conical thatched roof (figs. 56-57).

These elements thus testify to the survival of the typology of the basilica in Ethiopia—a trait which reveals common influences in the whole of the Christian world—, at least until the restoration of the Solomonid dynasty in the 13th century, if not even later.

The hypostyle type

Many other monolithic churches, whether rupestral or underground, although reproducing the typical basilica plan, correspond to a typology which can be more correctly identified as that of the hypostyle halls. In fact, they are characterized by a general equalness in height of the intrados of the covering in regard to the various aisles (even though in the church of Madhānē 'Ālam—BIANCHI BARRIVIERA, p. 61; GERSTER, p. 92; SAUTER, n. 35—, which is the major one and is in Lalibela, the nave is hierarchically differentiated by a lowered barrel vault, which is the only feature distinguishing it from the other aisles) (fig. 58).

The pilasters supporting the rock covering, even when they are organized in such a way to be oriented according to an apse system within the basilica-type structure, can determine a great variety of planimetrical arrangements, since they are constricted by the nature of the place where they are built and by the exigency of taking it into account (fig. 60).

Also for this typology references can be made to actual buildings where, because of the non-compatible distance of the outer walls, it is necessary to insert pilasters in the interior, in order to support the wooden framework of the covering. In fact, in some churches which Conti Rossini classified as basilica-type, specialists already pointed out the particularity that "very often, the total width of the three aisles is more or less equal to their length: [...] in a way that in the end they have a square structure, in the middle of which there are four columns which create a square concentric to the first one. It is a shape which other

[2] The churches of Abbā Libānos (BIANCHI BARRIVIERA, p. 49; GERSTER, p. 104; SAUTER, n. 46), Māryām (BIANCHI BARRIVIERA, p.41; GERSTER, p. 95; SAUTER, n. 36), Emānu'ēl (BIANCHI BARRIVIERA, p. 41; GERSTER, p. 95; SAUTER, n. 36), all in Lalibela, and those of Gannata Māryām (BIANCHI BARRIVIERA, p. 66; GERSTER, p. 115; SAUTER, n. 55), Bilbalā Čerqos (BIANCHI BARRIVIERA, p. 71; GERSTER, p. 119, SAUTER, n. 29), and Wuqro Maskāla Krestos in the surroundings (BIANCHI BARRIVIERA, p. 61).

[3] The network of the bays' division therefore corresponds to an average interaxis of about 2.5 metres: in fact, the very nature of the horizontal elements (pseudo-beams, pseudo-slabs) would hardly be compatible, in such a monolithic structure, to the covering of wider sources of light.

[4] Māryām: cfr. BIANCHI BARRIVIERA, p. 41; GERSTER, p. 95; SAUTER, n. 36 . Emmānu'ēl a Lalibela: cfr. BIANCHI BARRIVIERA, p. 41; GERSTER, p. 95; SAUTER, n. 36. See also note 2.

Aksumite buildings share" (MONNERET DE VILLARD 1935, p. 2). These are, in effect, spaces divided by columns which belong to and derive from the Aksumite tradition of hypostyle halls: consequently, their apparent subdivision into aisles does not justify their inclusion *ipso facto* into the basilica-type.

Tripartite alignment type, either with an axial or lateral entrance

Many experts have studied Ethiopian Christianity to establish whether a direct connection with the Old Testament can be found, or if its origin could be better explained by pointing out its common ground with the tradition of Oriental Christianity (which, anyway, comes from Judaism).

A cautious attitude suggests the avoidance of excessevely wide-ranging hypotheses. For example, it is certainly possible to observe that the tripartition of the sacred space in Ethiopian churches is a phenomenon shared by the whole of the Paleo-Christian enclave, but it should also be noted that the same tripartite plan characterized the Temple of Jerusalem, according to its description in the *Book of Kings*.

"Domus autem, quaem aedificabat rex Salomon Domino, habebat sexaginta cubitos in longitudine, et viginti cubitos in latitudine, et triginta cubitos in altitudine" (*Kings*, 3.vi.2). "Et porticus erat ante templum..." (*Kings*, 3.VI.3). "Oraculum autem in medio domus, in interiori parte fecerat, ut poneret ibi arcam foederis Domini" (*Kings*, 3.VI.19) (fig.61).

This description can be considered—in virtue of the sacre dress of the Book where it appears—as an *a priori* model for some later reproductions and modifications of the sacred building, even though it is difficult to isolate the basic building type from its historical context, just as it is not always easy to define the process which leads from the original prototype to the existing architecture.

Anyway, the tradition which endowed Ethiopian civilization with a fundamental substrata of great strength and prestige has always remained valid and unchanged: the consciousness that, with the transference of the Ark of the Covenant from Jerusalem to Aksum (the second Zion), Ethiopia had taken on Israel's inheritance. Thanks to the absolute certainty of being, since time immemorial, the Keepers of the Sacred Ark, the Ethiopians considered themselves the heirs of the Chosen People and the reigning dynasty which claimed a direct ascendancy from Solomon found its legitimation precisely in this certainty.

Aksum, the town from which Christianity first spread, became an unquestioned cultural and religious reference point, as it was the inheritor and the depositary of the Ark of the Covenant: according to the tradition, in fact, the Tablets of the Law which Jahveh gave to Moses are kept there, in the church of Saint Mary of Zion. All Ethiopian churches have copies of Moses' Tablets—the *tābots*—either in stone or in hard wood, which during the liturgy are put on the altar and solemny carried around in procession during the *ṭemqat* (Epiphany) or on other special religious feasts.

"Be the tābot of the sacrifice lit with candles and lamps, when the bishop consacrates it [...] be it signed with the sacred chrism [...] since it is the seal of God and it may become worth of the mysteries which are celebrated upon it [...] And the tābot be such that it can be moved from one place to another, like the stone of the Sons of Israel, which was carried from one place to another" (*FETḤA NAGAŚT*, p. 19).

What we are approaching here is a myth, that is, the narration of a sacred story—to use Mircea Eliade's definition—which brings the eruptions of the sacred or the supernatural back to the beginning of the world. In order to be fruitful, the myth must be reproposed according to a ritual, so that mythical time is almost re-actualized and incarnated into the present, thus making somehow contemporary and updated the evoked events, within a qualitatively different time, both primordial and unendingly recuperable at the same time.

A series of ancient Ethiopian churches seem to reproduce the typical Jerusalem model: a rectangular building made of three aligned rooms interconnected, the first of which (the *qenē māḫlēt*, 'chant of praise', where the *Dabtarā* chant the Divine

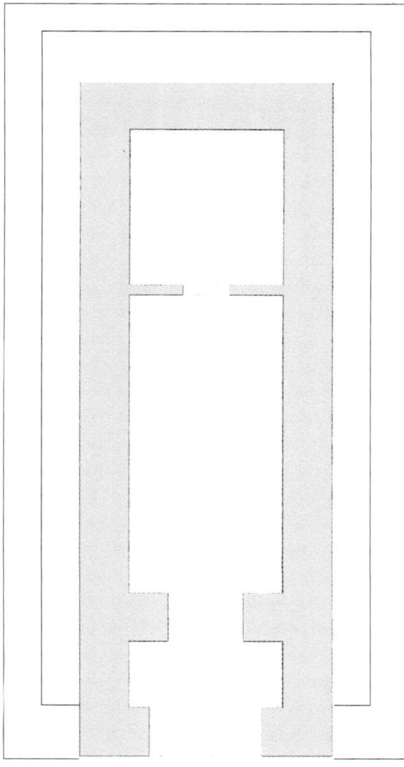

61. Reconstruction of the plan of the Temple of Jeusalem, made of three hierarchically arranged spaces, one after the other, with the tabernacle in the rear one.

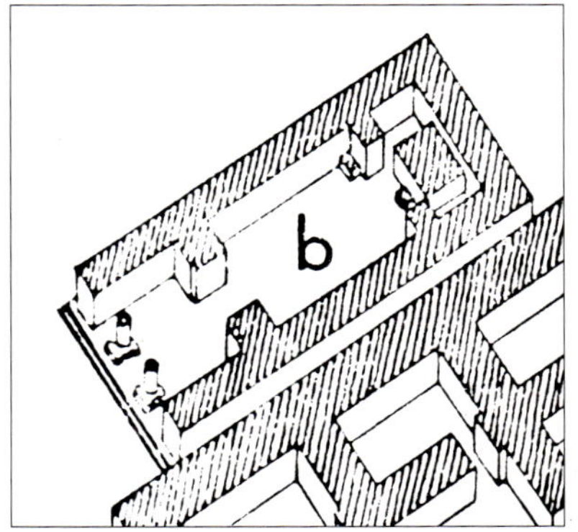

62. Axonometric view of the temple of Tell Taynat: (GARBINI, col. 582).

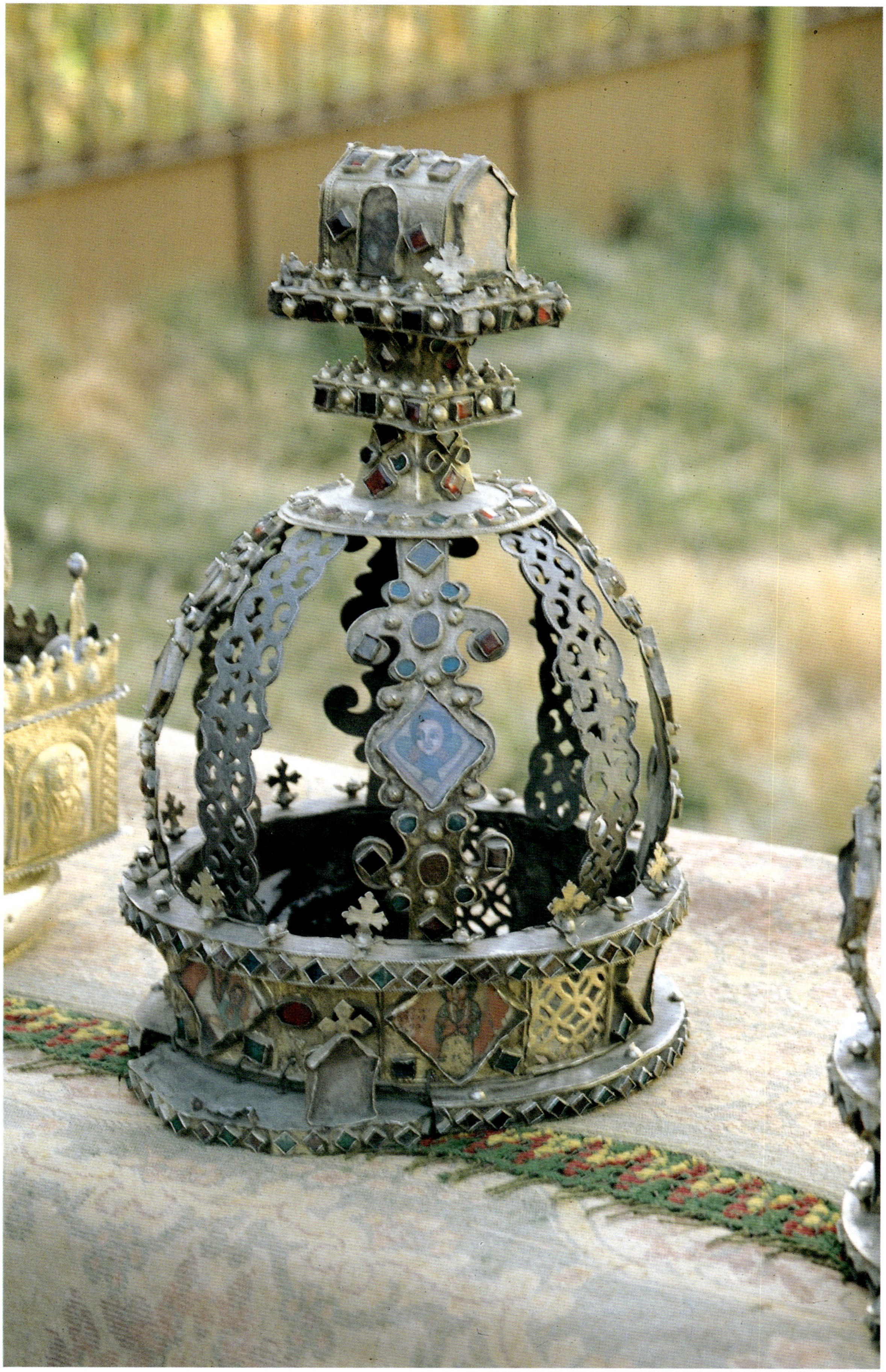

63. The Ark of the Covenant towers over the royal crown at Aksum.

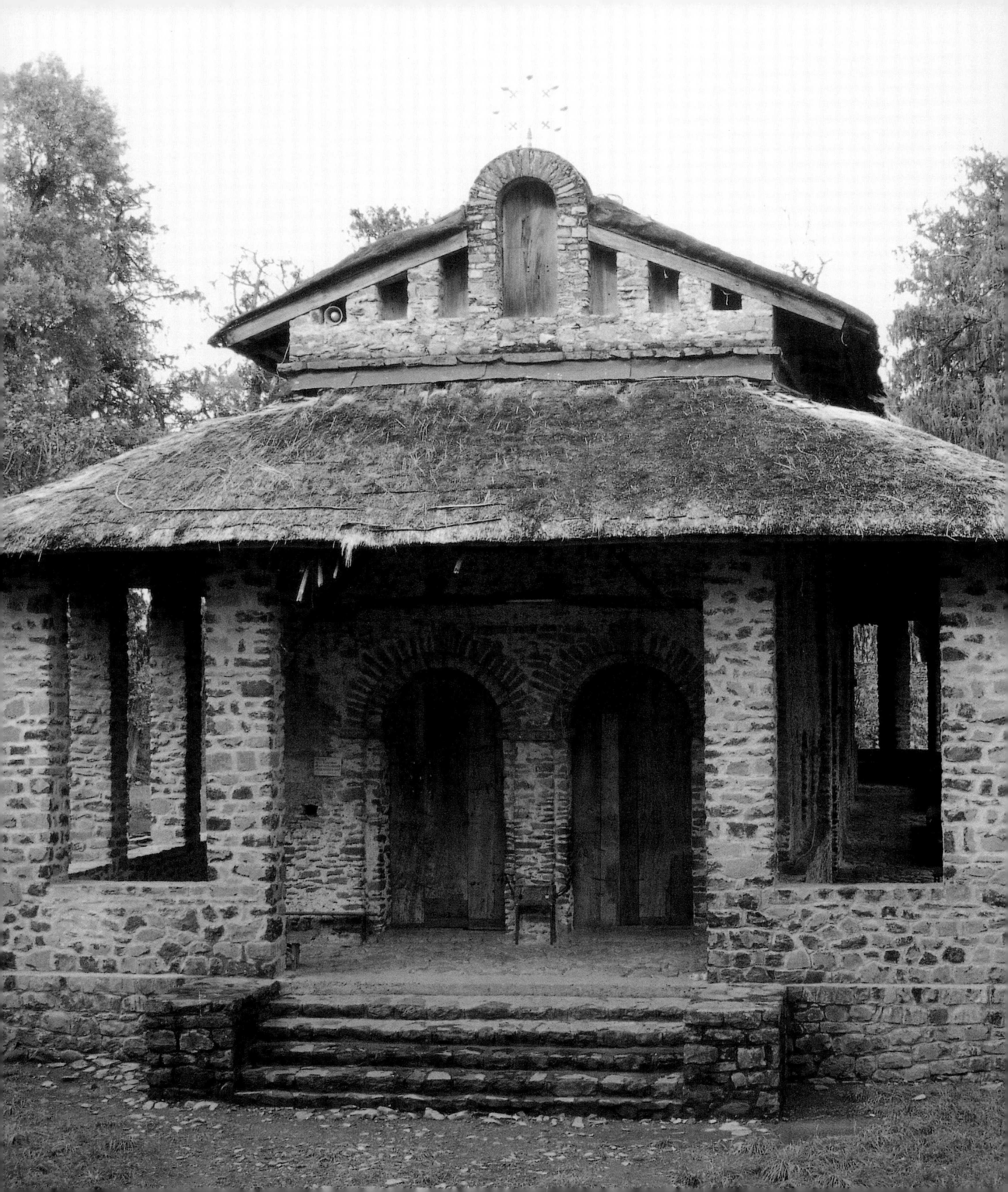

64. Façade of the church of Dabra Berhān Śellāsē at Gondar.

65. The church of Dabra Berhān Śellāsē at Gondar, built on a previous, important round-planned church at the beginning of the 19th century, reproduces the tripartite-alignment's planimetrical arrangement.

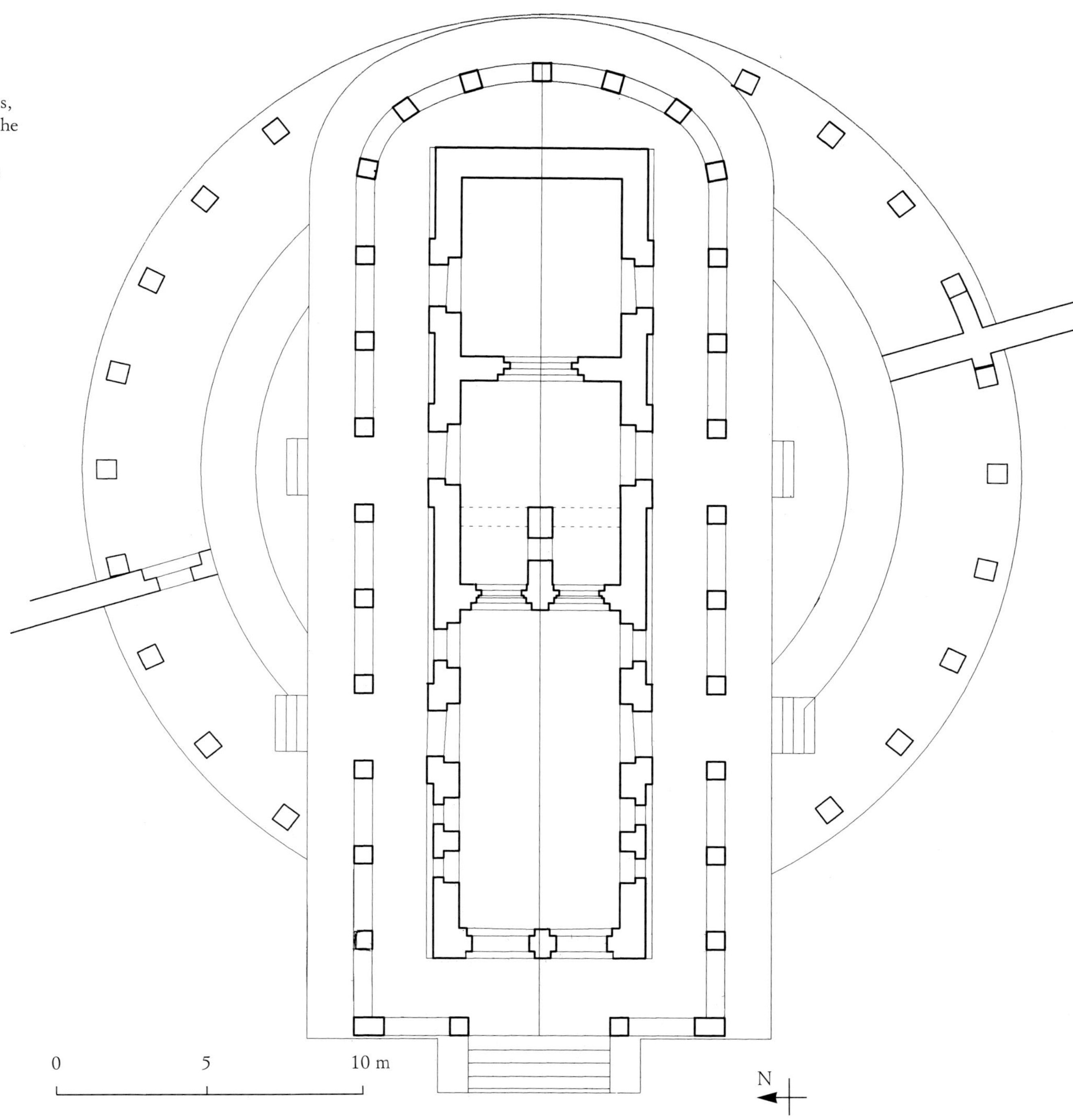

Office) is reserved for the chantors and the congregation, while the second (the *qeddest*, 'saint') is occupied by the non-officioting clergy and also destined for the giving of the Eucharist to the congregation. Finally, the third (the *maqdas*, the 'sanctuary') is the place where the liturgy is celebrated and whose access is reserved for the priests celebrating the office: *sancta sanctorum/qeddesta qeddusān*, since here is kept the *tābot*—which, as a single part instead of the whole, works as a ritual reproposition of the most important part of the Ark—, just as the Ark was kept in the *qodeš ḥaqqodašim* of the Temple of Solomon in Jerusalem.

However, in Ethiopian churches of various epochs and located in different places[5]—even though they obey the rule of the three aligned rooms arranged one after the other, which maintain the hierarchical arrangement of the functions expressed by their specific usage—other, apparently a-typical aspects appear. In fact, they present a structure where the *sancta sanctorum*

[5] These churches range from Saint Mary of Zion in Aksum (rebuilt after the Grañ's incursions) (*DAE* III, pp. 75-85) to the much later rectangular church of Dabra Berhān Śellāsē, in Gondar (rebuilt between 1815 and 1826 on the ruins of a previous round church) (ANNEQUIN 1976).

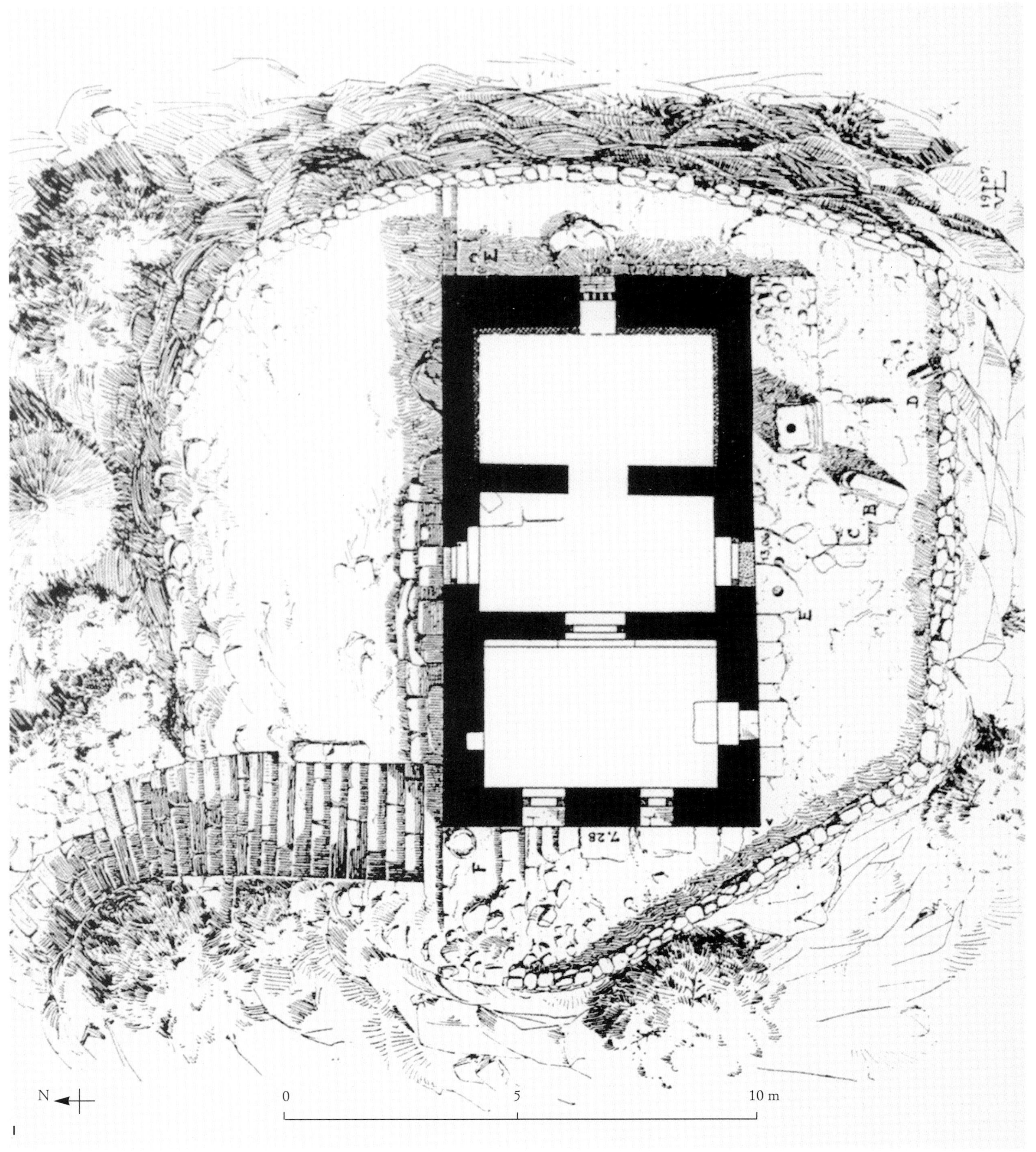
N
0
5
10 m
A
B
C
D
E
F

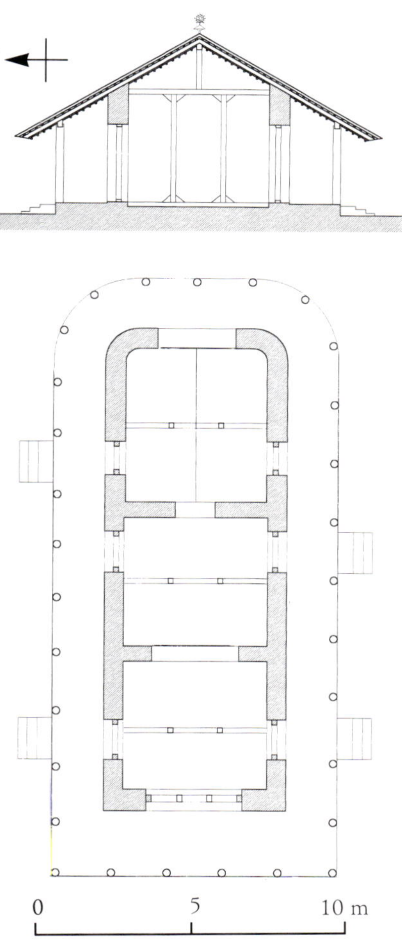

67. Plan and transverse section of the church of Dāgā Esṭifanos, on an islet in the middle of Lake Tana, rebuilt according to the old layout after the fire which destroyed it in the last century.

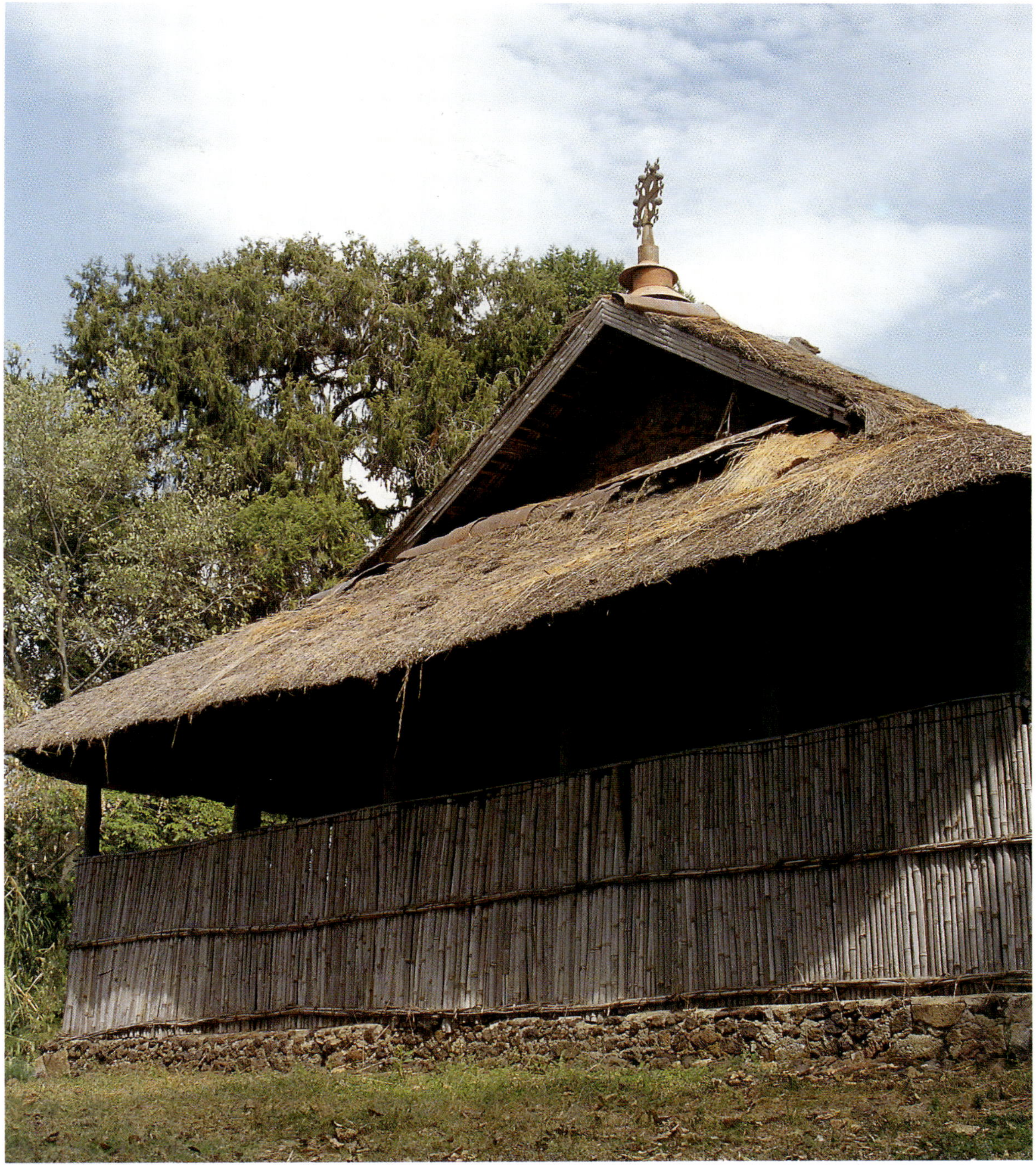

68. The church of Dāgā Estifānos.

(the *maqdas*) is facing eastward—*ex oriente lux*—thus reversing the Biblical model. However, a derivation of these churches from a basilical model cannot be suggested: rather, it is more plausible that the specialized tripartite function which characterized Judaic religious buildings could be easily transformed to suit a Christian background. The intentional usage of a model implies a way of proceeding which is a continuous overcoming of typological solutions previously attained.

The extremely similar churches of Ṭānā Qirqos (ANNEQUIN 1975, pp. 89-90) and Dāgā Esṭifanos (ANNEQUIN 1975, pp. 102-105) on lake Tana (certainly rebuilt, maybe with the original arrangement being kept), as well as the churches of Abbā Pantalēwon in Aksum (*DAE* III, pp. 70-71) and of Yehā (*DAE* III, pp. 72-74) (fig. 70), seem to have been influenced also by the so-called 'large room' typologies, which spread into Syria from the Sassanid area from the end of the 6th century onwards (fig. 70). According to this

66. Planimetry of the church of Abbā Pantalēwon, near Aksum: (*DAE* III, p. 71).

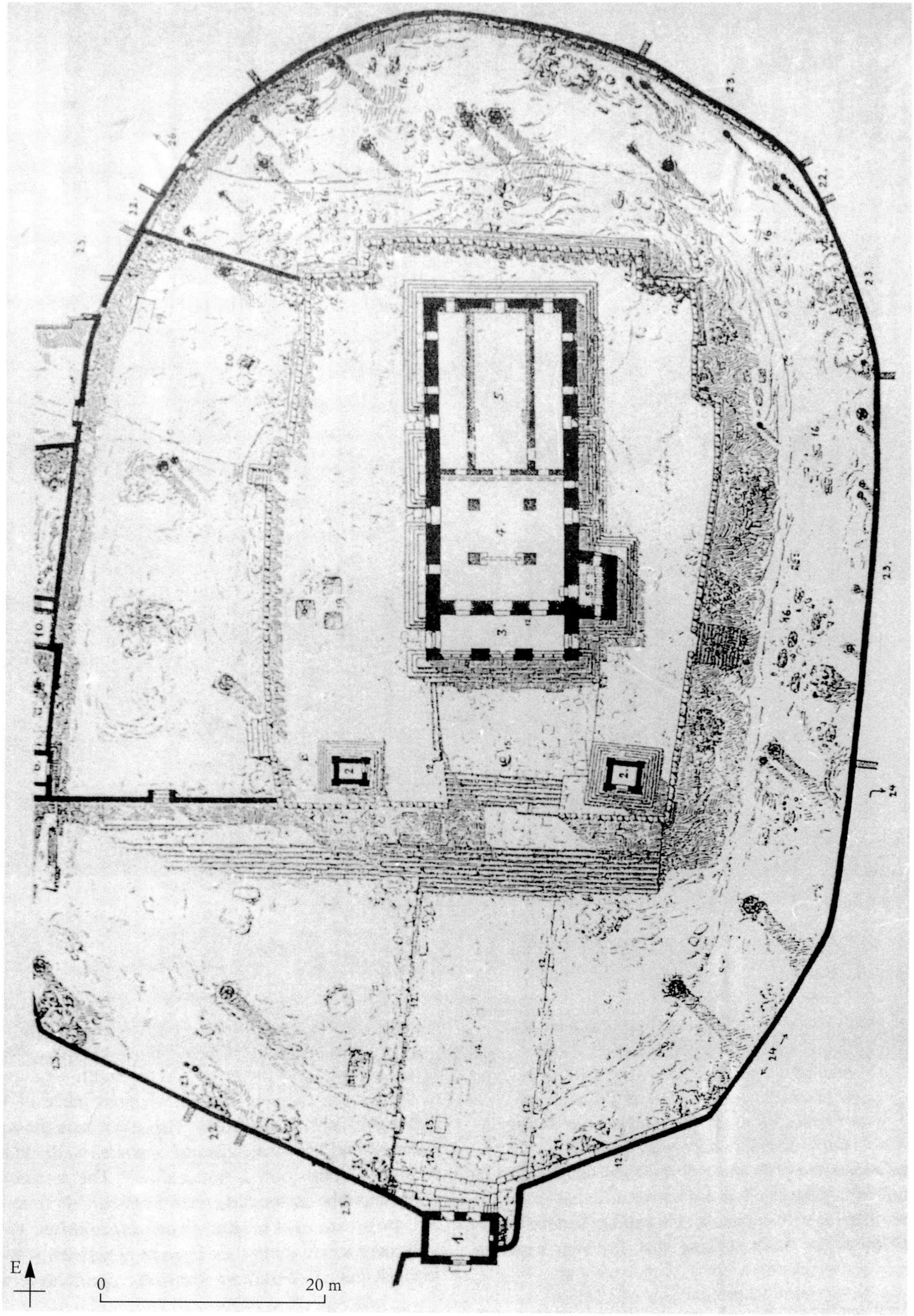

69. Overall planimetry of Saint Mary of Zion at Aksum, rebuilt after the Grañ's raids in the 16th century: (PHILLIPSON 1997, p. 173).

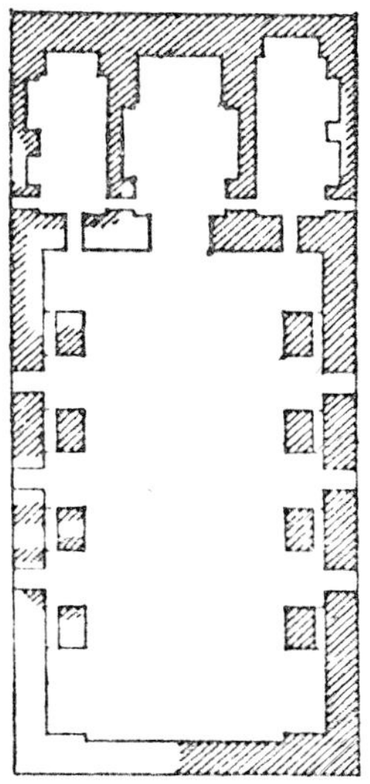

70. Plan of a Christian church of the Sassanid period at Ctesifonte: (SCERRATO, col. 226).

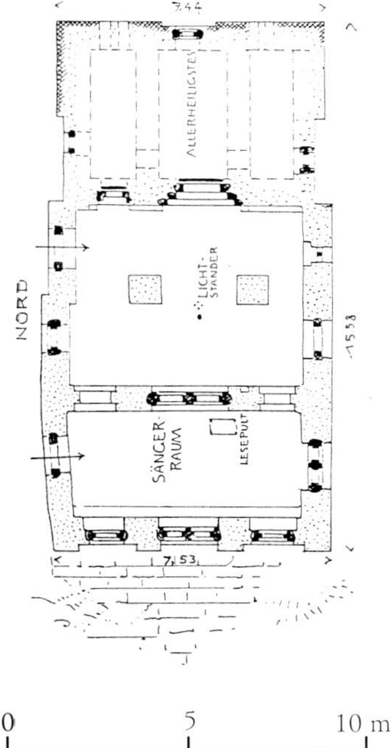

71. Plan of the ancient church of Yeḥā: (*DAE* III, p. 74).

type, the entrances inside the building open along the long side walls, instead of being arranged along the longitudinal axis on the side opposite the sanctuary. Actually, in the above-mentioned examples, the axiality of the tripartite alignment is contradicted exactly by the system of the entrances, which is here arranged perpendicularly and sideways to afford direct access to the *qenē māḥlēt* and the *qeddest*, and sometimes to the *maqdas* itself.

The church of Saint Mary of Zion in Aksum and that of Yehā show correspondances with the Sassanid 'large room' model also in the cut of the presbytery, which is tripartite in rectangular, long, intercommunicating rooms, which do not receive any light from the exterior. This structure seems to recall a functional specialization of the presbytery derived from examples of Sassanid churches which matured in a climate permeated by Nestorianism, rather than of basilicas, where however this structure was quite common since the paleo-Christian phase although with quite different dimensions.

Specialized buildings, churches included, derive their structural conception basically from the association or aggregation of basic cellas, thus resulting in spaces and bays which can be brought back to elementary modules (3 to 4 metres wide) or to their multiples. It is not casual that the transversal dimension of the above-mentioned churches with a tripartite alignment, either with an axial or a transversal entrance, is either 3-4 metres, 6-8 metres, 12-16 metres. Also fundamental to the final architectural result is the type of covering: either flat or with inclined layers. In the case of a flat covering and with rooms of a monocellular depth, that is, ranging from 3 to 4 metres, the wooden framework may be arranged lengthwise, but in the church of Yeḥā and even more in Saint Mary of Zion in Aksum, the rooms' depth is even greater, thus imposing on the interior break-line structures such as pilasters (for the greatest part with "console-like" capitals, which make the light of the bays even dimmer) or walls supporting the trussing which decorates the covering, changing the total distance between the external walls on many bays.

In this last type of church the tripartite scheme is organized in a short narthex (the *qenē māḥlēt*), followed by a hypostyle *qeddest*—the first with two, the second with four pilasters—which preceeds a deep *maqdas*, divided in three very long spaces by wall baffles.

Moreover, it has to be remarked that the main longitudinal bay (arranged along the alignment of the *qeddest* and of the *maqdas*) is wider than the lateral ones—a characteristic of the basilica type—not so much as a result of building exigencies, but rather to be functional to a hierarchical arrangement of the interior space. Still, once more the lateral position of the accesses contradicts this scheme, crossing a sense of space based on the longitudinal axiality of these buildings, which is somehow privileged in comparison to the alignment of the space.

In the case of double weathered coverings it is possible to cover bigger sources of light by using wooden trusses (whose tie beam is either supported by wooden walls as in Dāgā Esṭifanos (fig. 67) or free, completely open to the light, as in Dabra Behrān Śellāsē) (fig. 65). The length of the building—that is, of three canonical rooms—seems therefore free from a structural conditioning, since the breaking-lines or the trusses cannot be arranged according to a serial repetition.

The lapse of centuries—from the Aksumite phase to the modern age—which accompanies the typology of a tripartite alignment testifies anyway to the prestige which it always had, perhaps because of its Biblical references and consequently to its being deeply rooted in Ethiopian Christianity. In the complexity produced by an often spurious fusion of contrasting axialities, in order to pervene to a more precise definition, further studies will be necessary, ascertaining both its origins and the story of its evolution, also taking into account the survival of links with the Middle-Eastern traditions which in Ethiopia found a continuity of expression and their new homeland.

Centrally planned type

In Ethiopia, as in the rest of the Christian world, associated with the basilica-type churches, with a

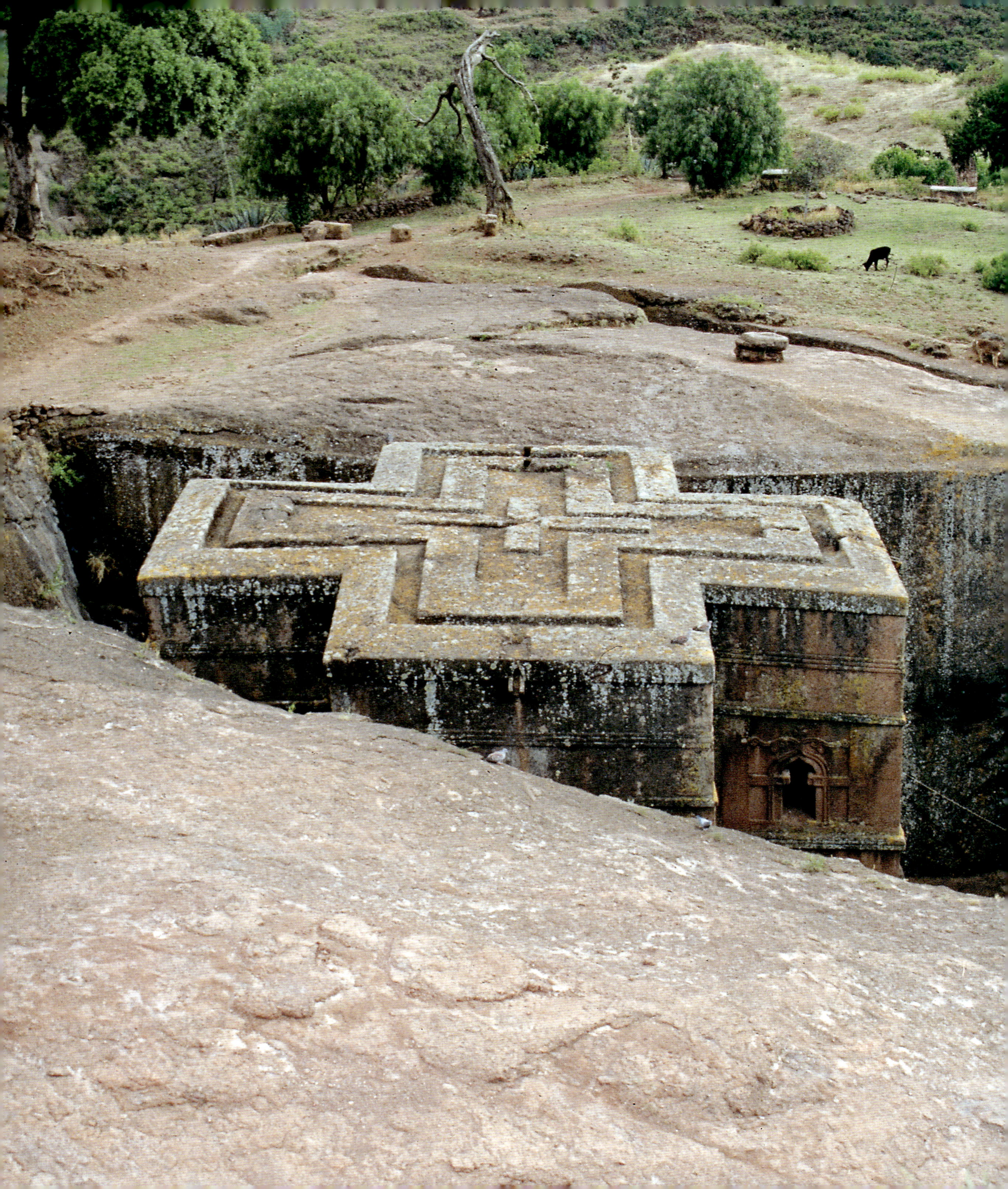

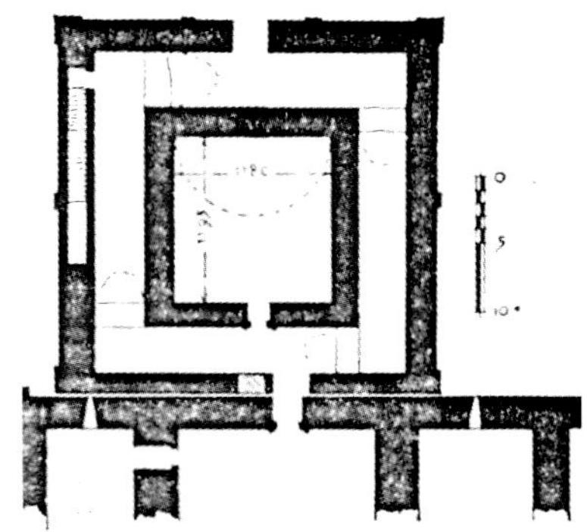

72. The sanctuary of Hatra, in the northern part of the Arabian peninsula: (MONNERET DE VILLARD, p. 29).

73. The Greek cross-planned monolithic church of Giyorgis at Lalibela.

longitudinal asset or with the tripartite alignment-type, either with an axial or a lateral access, is the centrally planned type. This definition applies to an arrangement built around a *fulcrum*—either real or virtual—gathered around the centre, with characteristics of verticality, around which a more or less complex radial symmetry develops.

Particularly developed in the East on the base of the Byzantine line of thought and of Greek philosophy, the central plan became very popular as a typology which in itself bears all the cosmological reflections, the point in which the whole of creation converges, the symbol of the One counterposed to the seriality of the becoming, and of a microcosm which is a mirror and almost the *simulacrum* of the macrocosm.

Scholars have debated at length on this subject: the *martyrium*, that is, the memorial to the sacrifice of a martyr, has been identified as one of the usages leading to the naissance of the centrally planned church type. Standing out amongst the churches of Ethiopia is the one at Gyiorgis in Lalibela which forms, in the earth and in the stone in which it is embedded, the shape of a Greek cross. It is worth mentioning that amongst the possible Christian prototypes is the *Anastasis*, which Constantine built in Jerusalem in the 4th century; a round planned building with the Sepulchre in the middle, where the sense of the *martyrium* is strong since Christ is the prototype of all the martyrs. In the Orient, to recall the Holy Sepulcre of Jerusalem the *sancta sanctorum* may have been placed at the centre of holy buildings.

Square centrally planned type

Ethiopian tradition also presents the type of a square church with the *maqdas* in the middle, surrounded by the *qeddest*, which therefore takes the aspect of an ambulachrum enclosing it on all sides. For this type scholars still have the problem of individuating its genesis.

The Southern-Arabic origin of the Ḥabashat could once more reinforce the hypothesis of a possible ascendancy from Arabic-Sassanid models, reproduced in a style adapted to Ethiopia. In the northern region of the Arabian Peninsula, in Hauran, among Hatra's ruins, a sanctuary has been discovered dedicated to a solar deity, made of a square cella placed in the middle of a square building (MONNERET DE VILLARD 1935, p. 5).

There is also a tradition according to which the Magi, on their way back to Persia, built a church in honour of the Virgin, which has been identified as the one still existing in the village of Haq, in Tur Abdin, a region of Syria. The church, socalled 'El-Adra', or 'of the Virgin', has a square shape and dates to the 6th century (SELIS, p. 151).

To try historicizing this typological model and fixing its synchronical and diachronical aspects, however, would not be a wise choice. Just as the presence of buildings dating to a certain epoch does not imply that their prototype dates to the same period: what is still exisiting today, or even merely known about, could be a reproduction of other ancient examples, still unknown or not carefully studied yet.

The process of typological evolution is, as usual, various, articulated and complex, since it is conditioned by structural connotations linked to the technological level of each culture, but also by its need to be functional to the purposes for which the building was designed (well known in this respect are the transitional phases from the pagan basilica to the Christian one, in different places and epochs). Nor should the level of self-sciouness implied by the presence of symbolic aspects be disregarded.

Neither is it surprising that there are churches which, in themselves, tend to a combined evaluation of different typologies, that is, to form spurious solutions which derive from a fusion of a longitudinal plan with a central one, such as can also be found in the Western tradition of Romanesque architecture.

Vigoni, an attentive Italian traveller of the 19th century, thus described the ancient church of Asmara—which no longer exists—, with the *maqdas* in the middle (*DAE* III, p. 67): "... there stands the rectangular church, low, with a flat roof, roughly built in wood and stone: on the front, the narrower shape of the building almost forms a peristyle walled in the intercolumns [...] From

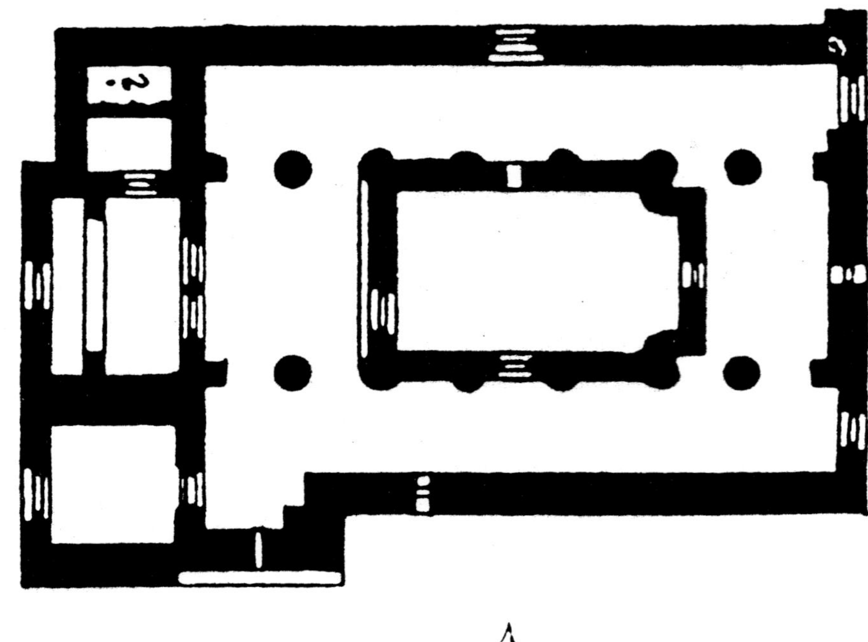

74. Plan of the ancient church at Asmara, which no longer exists. The structure was that of the basilica, obviously modified so that the sanctuary could be inserted in the middle of the nave: (*DAE* III, p. 67).

75. Plan and façade of Enda Qeddus Mika'ēl at Cieffā: (*DAE* III, p. 66).

76. Plan and façade of Enda Giyorgis at Fremona, near Adua, a Portuguese settlement in 16th century: (*DAE* III, p. 65).

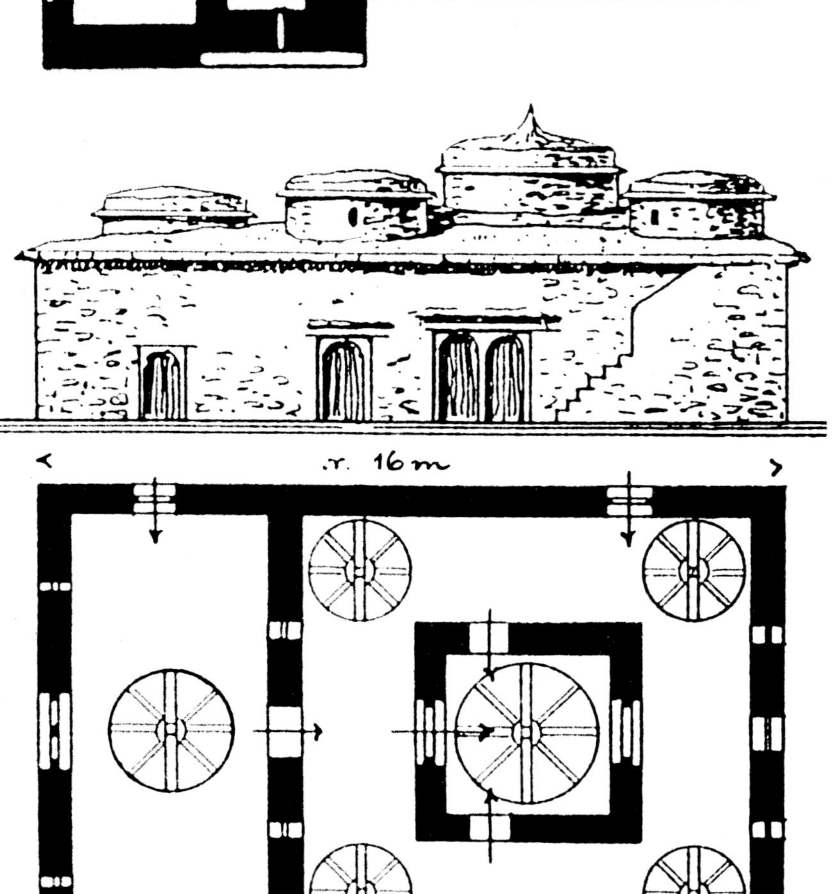

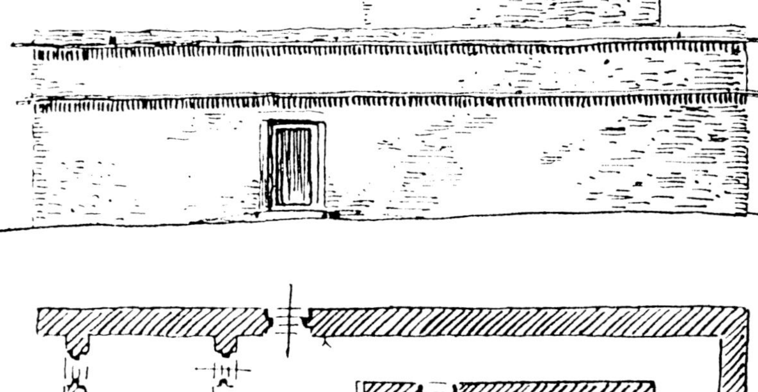

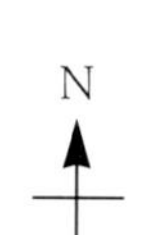

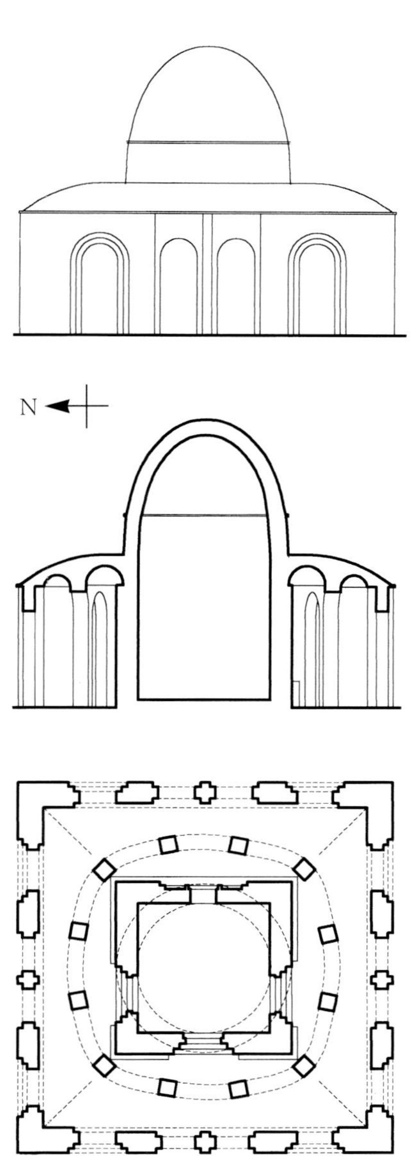

77. Façade, section and schematic plan, and of Qeddus Mika'ēl at Barié Gemb which, according to tradition, already existed at the beginning of the 16th century.

here one enters a larger space, divided by great piers into three aisles, of which the nave is enclosed by walls and reserved for reigious services, while the other ones are open to the audience ..." (VIGONI, p. 72). The spatial arrangement of the narthex and the subdivision into three aisles (the nave being higher than the aisles) correspond to the basilica-type, although it is evolved so as to conform to a typology which placed the *maqdas* at the centre of the hall, rather than in an apse at the end of the nave (fig. 74).

Other examples may instead hint at a typological syncretism, which developed also from the tripartite alignment churches with lateral entrances, in a period in which a different idea of liturgy determined the disappearance, in the area of the apse, of that functional arrangement which traditionally placed the *protesis* and the *diaconicon* close to the altar. As a result of this new, innovative arrangement of spaces, these two rooms, which were particularly long, seem to have been assimilated into the *qeddest*, which progressively evolves to become an ambulachrum surrounding, at the sides and rear, a sanctuary thus protruding from the walls. The arrangement of the openings of the *maqdas*, in the final form it acquired with time, could confirm this hypothesis—which is by itself good enough to explain its origin—, with the three canonical accesses, a frontal one and two advanced lateral ones, and with a window open to the east, which does not seem to be found in ancient examples of churches.

In the rectangularly planned church of Enda Qeddus Mikāʼēl at Cieffà (cf. DAE III, pp. 66-67; *Guida*, p. 297), near Maṭarā, the memory of the *qeddest* as an intermediate space between the narthex and the *sancta sanctorum* leads to the creation of an ambulachrum which is much larger in the front and surrounds the *maqdas* (fig. 75). This latter also has a rectangular shape and is divided into two parts: a front one, where there is the entrance, and a rear one, for the placement of the real sanctuary.

Such an arrangement is generally associated with a flat covering, in the cases where the wall of the *maqdas* is higher than the surrounding ambulachrum, even though without openings large enough to allow direct light. It is not casual that the ancient documented examples of this type are all located in northern Ethiopia, where the building typology of a covering made with horizontal wooden rafters is traditional, but where there are also to be found buildings with a double protective covering, such as the church of Abbā Libānos near Aksum (*DAE* III, pp. 67-69).

However, in the purest form of the centrally planned typology, perhaps also because of the already mentioned influence of cosmological thought on architecture, the *qeddest* and the *maqdas* take a perfectly square shape. The examples studied and catalogued up to now date from the 16th and 17th centuries: such are the churches of Enda Giyorgis at Fremona (*DAE* III, pp. 64-66) (fig. 76), of Qeddus Mikāʼēl at Barié Gemb, thirty-two kilometres from Gondar (MONTI DELLA CORTE, pp. 106-107; ANNEQUIN 1965, II) (fig. 77) and of Attatami Qeddus Mikāʼēl (MONTI DELLA CORTE, pp. 37-38) (fig. 78), within the capital's imperial walls. Once more, significant to the definition of this typology is the coincidence of measurements in these three churches, with the *qeddest* 14-15 metres each side and the *maqdas* in the middle, of 6-7 metres each side. However, each church shows distinctive traits: Enda Giyorgis at Fremona is preceded by a narthex which is as wide as the church, with a flat covering, from which stand out five symmetrical tambours (plus one on the narthex), the largest one of which is built on the square of the *maqdas* (an architectural solution certainly coherent with Byzantine prototypes). In the case of Qeddus Mikāʼēl at Barié Gemb interpretations of symbolic memory or of typological symbology cannot be avoided: here the *qeddest*, which is covered with a tunnel vault with variable light, is broken by the insertion of twelve pseudo-circular pillars, linked by round arches which, as far as statics is concerned, are absolutely non-functional, with a sugarloaf cupola over the *maqdas*. Finally, the church of Attatami Qeddus Mikāʼēl seems to have been conceived under a pyramidal covering, which reached to cover a *qenē māḫlēt*, which surrounded the *qeddest* on all sides, at whose corners stood four little towers.

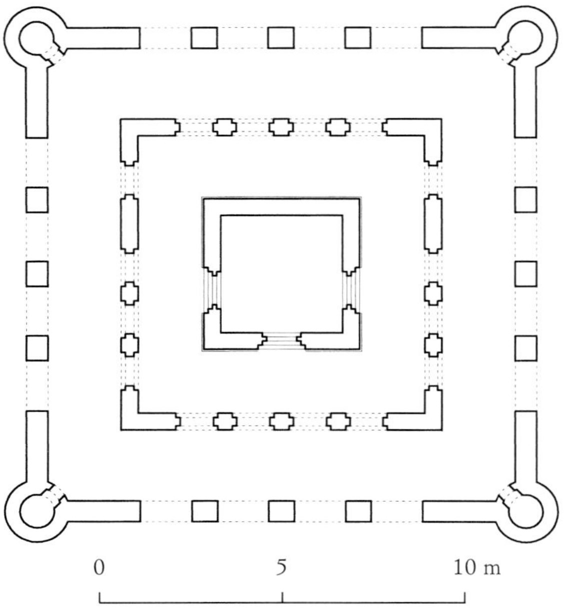

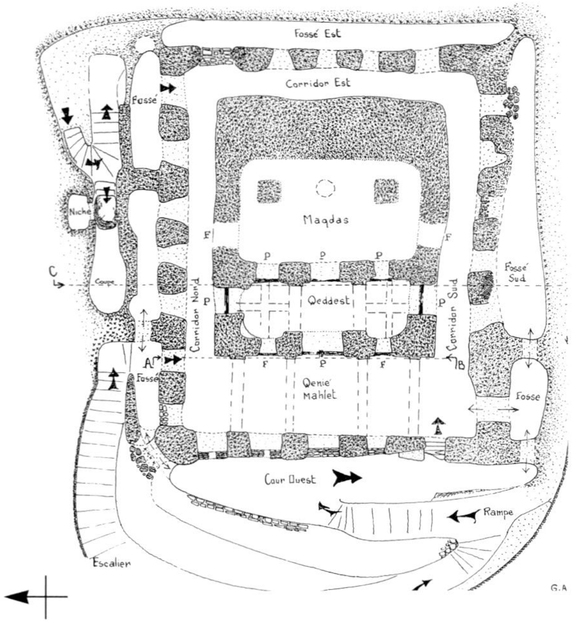

78. Schematic plan of Attatami Qeddus Mika'ēl, bult at the beginning of the 18th century within the enclosure of Gondar's castles.

79. Plan of Adādi Māryām, in Soddo, which is the most southerly monolithic church: (ANNEQUIN 1965, tav. XI).

There is even the monolithic version of the square centrally planned church, even though it is subject to the conditioning and the adaptation which in rupestral churches are due to the nature of the place: the church of Adadi Māryām (ANNEQUIN 1965, I) (fig. 79), perhaps the most southerly of monolithic churches, where the function of ambulachrum surrounding the *maqdas* is taken up by the gallery of the *qenē māḥlēt*, since the *qeddest* is not larger than the front of the *maqdas* itself.

Round centrally planned type

Ave perfect circle
Centre of our love
Circuit of pity
(Giovanni Pozzi, Church of Santa Maria degli Angeli, Monte Tamaro, Ticino, Switzerland)

The round centrally planned church type met in Ethiopia with great and ever increasing success, so much so that it became the distinctive trait of the Christian village because of the substantial level of reciprocal compatibility between the church and the environment, the product of the relationship between natural environment and human culture.
A widely diffused tradition, almost endemic, is the use of a round shape with a conical straw roof, similar to that of the *tucul*, the traditional aboriginal house. "In particular, among all buildings, the *house* is undoubtly the most representative object of material culture, for its double functional capacity of expressing both the private, 'internal', unifying world of family life and the public, 'external', aggregational world of social life [...] The problem of the covering, in the passage from the found shelter to the built hut, is contained in the difficulties arising when the underlying soil offers no support, a situation remedied by thickening the outer wall of the standing structure: the most common solution is that of using in the middle of the base circle the additional support of a pole, on which the sloping rafters somehow converge" (CATALDI, p. 13). The conical-cylindrical hut is characterized precisely by the insertion in the structure of elevational elements which allow a better usage of the interior and support the covering.
Basically, it is a *tucul*, however stylistically evolute, which seems almost to be elevated to the nobleness of a sanctuary: "... vous arriverez a une construction cylindrique, couverte d'un toit conique en chaume, que surmonte une croix grecque [...] La muraille est percée de plusieures portes en plein cintre e d'autant depetites fenêtres munies de leurs volets et de leurs châssis, grossièrement taillés avec la hache et l'herminette. Franchissant ce seuil, vous vous trouverez dans une galerie circulaire, ouverte a tous

les vents, et qui entoure une construction intérieure carrée. C'est l'église proprement dite, renfermant le tabernacle, que voile encore un immense rideau" (RAFFRAY 1876, p. 300).

The structure, evolving from the *tucul* to the church, inevitably undergoes a continuous series of modifications, conditioned by dimensional factors, which imply the variation of the spatial parameters, even if the main 'genetic' characteristics of the type remain unchanged.

In its more primitive form the *tucul* has a diameter of about 5 or 6 metres which works as a limit to the wooden framework which from the perimetral support is joined to the pole standing in the middle of the circle of the base. Even in the aboriginal house, when this type develops to take bigger dimensions, a surrogate structure can be found in the interior, generally a square planned one, which also takes the function of holding the network of rafters which support the covering. These structures also allow the supporting pole of the top of the conical covering to start not from the ground but from high up, so that the central part of the *tucul* can be used to its fullest, free from structural impediments. Through the dialectic relationship between body and structure emerges an ensemble where the potentialities of the square basic cell and the round one are added together; the first type is used for its simple functional usage of space, while the second is used as a natural support for the conical covering, which minimizes the problem of the drainage of rain from the roofing, reducing the ridge to only one point (the vertex of the cone), which is relatively easy to protect.

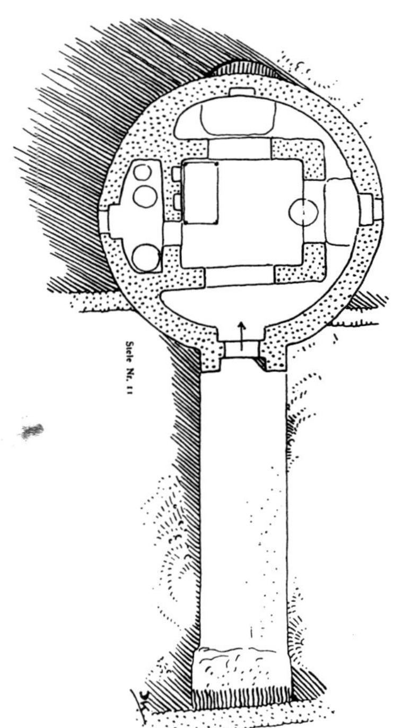

80. Plan of a tucul at Aksum: (FHILLIPSON 1997, p. 50).

The central area of the *tucul* is therefore used as a living-room area, while the space between the external round wall and the internal quadrangular one is devoted to specialized functions (the kitchen, the storage-room, etc.) A larger dimension allows, therefore, the distributional specialization of the inside, with either a division, or a hierarchical arrangement of different functions in particular areas, which is perfectly congruent with the structural arrangement (fig. 80).

In the church, the modifications, or changes connected with the need for adjustment to its own functional exigencies develop to form an ensemble of different structures—arranged according to a precise hierarchical order—, each one having a specific role, as though they were parts which collaborate to different aims and all working towards the creation of a whole.

Thus, on the central cube of the *maqdas*, which usually has sides of 6-8 metres, is superimposed a cylindrical tambour which forms a first supporting ring for the rafters which from the vertex radiate to the compass of the walls. The circle of the base of the tambour joins to the orthogonal angles of the square structure underneath through wood trusses arranged diagonally, or cut in a circular way.

The main pole supporting the vertex of the conical covering can consequently be organized on a beam placed at the same height as the cylindrical tambour—sometimes supported by walls—which crosses the *maqdas* up high, from side to side (fig. 81).

Around the *maqdas* there is the *qeddest*. It is delineated by a ring of walls, whose width is conditioned by the exigency of guaranteeing a congruous possibility of movement at the corners of the *maqdas*. Consequently, the distance between the tambour superimposed on the square of the *maqdas* and the perimetral wall of the *qeddest* is usually excessive and not-compatible with the bearing capacity of the wooden rafters—radially arranged in the covering—which rest upon it. Another, merely structural, ring must therefore be added, in order to break the excessive light of the bay (fig. 82).

Finally, the *qenē māḫlēt* is placed externally to the *qeddest* and is delineated by a series of walls arranged in a ring-shape which support the eave of the covering (fig. 83).

The difusion of this typology of religious building in Ethiopia is generally considered to have taken place after the Grañ's incursions, but its origin is much earlier, both because of its connections with the cylindrical-conical hut (which is 'endemic' in the region) and for the ancient examples still surviving, such as the ruins of the church of Enda Jesus in Aksum (*DAE* III, p. 62) (fig. 84), or the second church of Enda Çerqos in

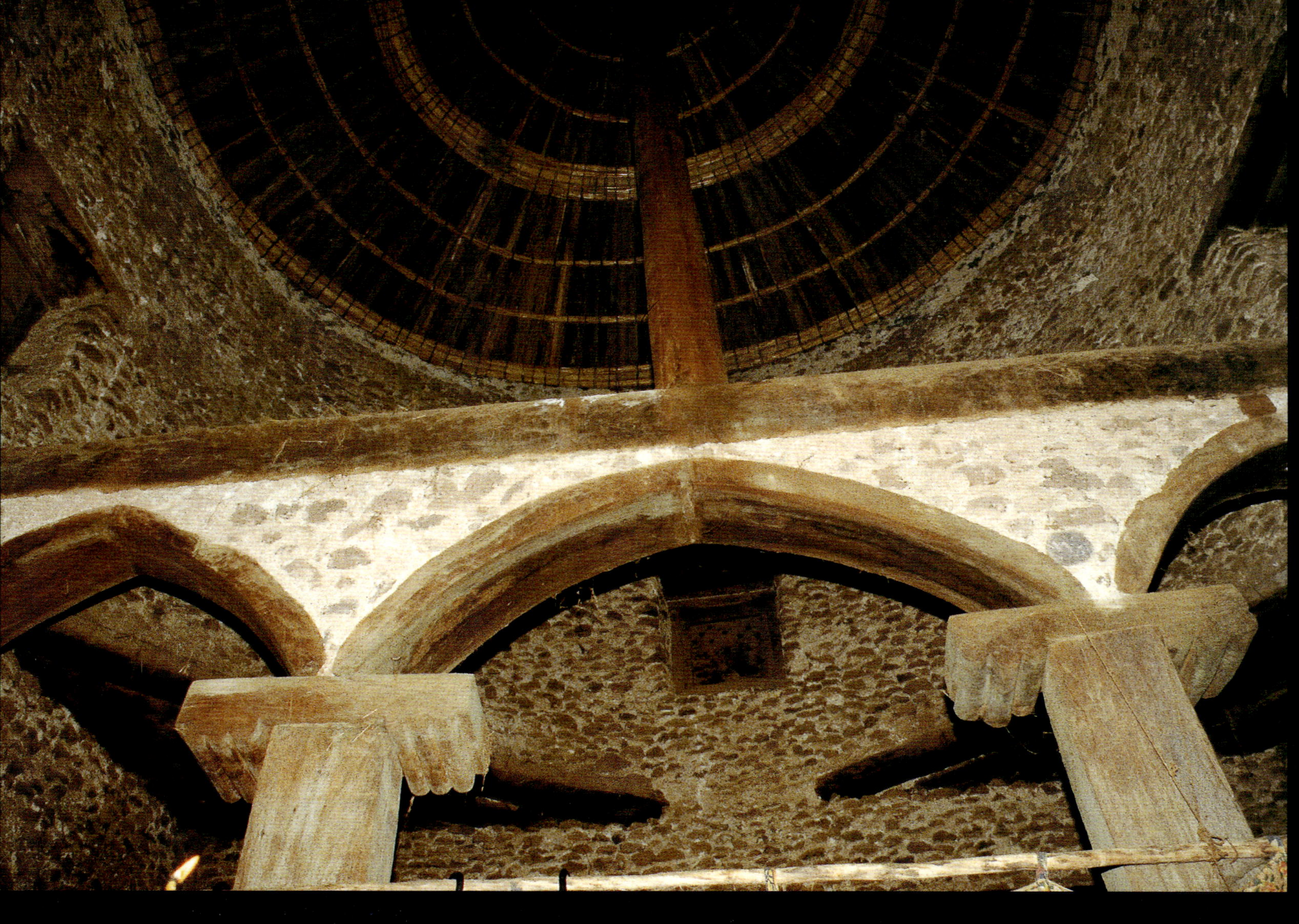

81. Kota Māryām on the island of Dek (second half of the 16th century). Interior of the *maqdas*, 'sanctuary', where the liturgy is celebrated and where only the offciating prests are allowed.

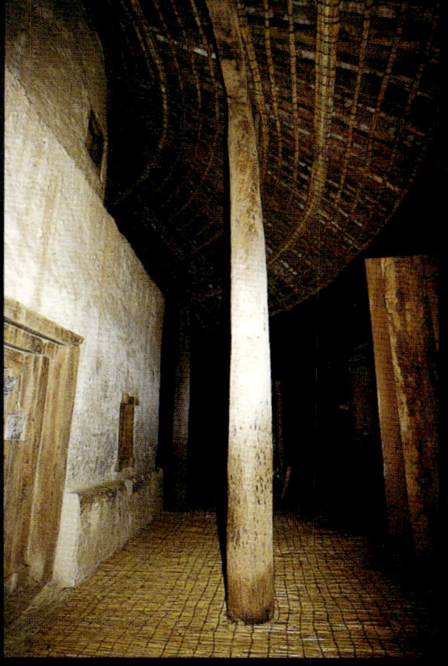

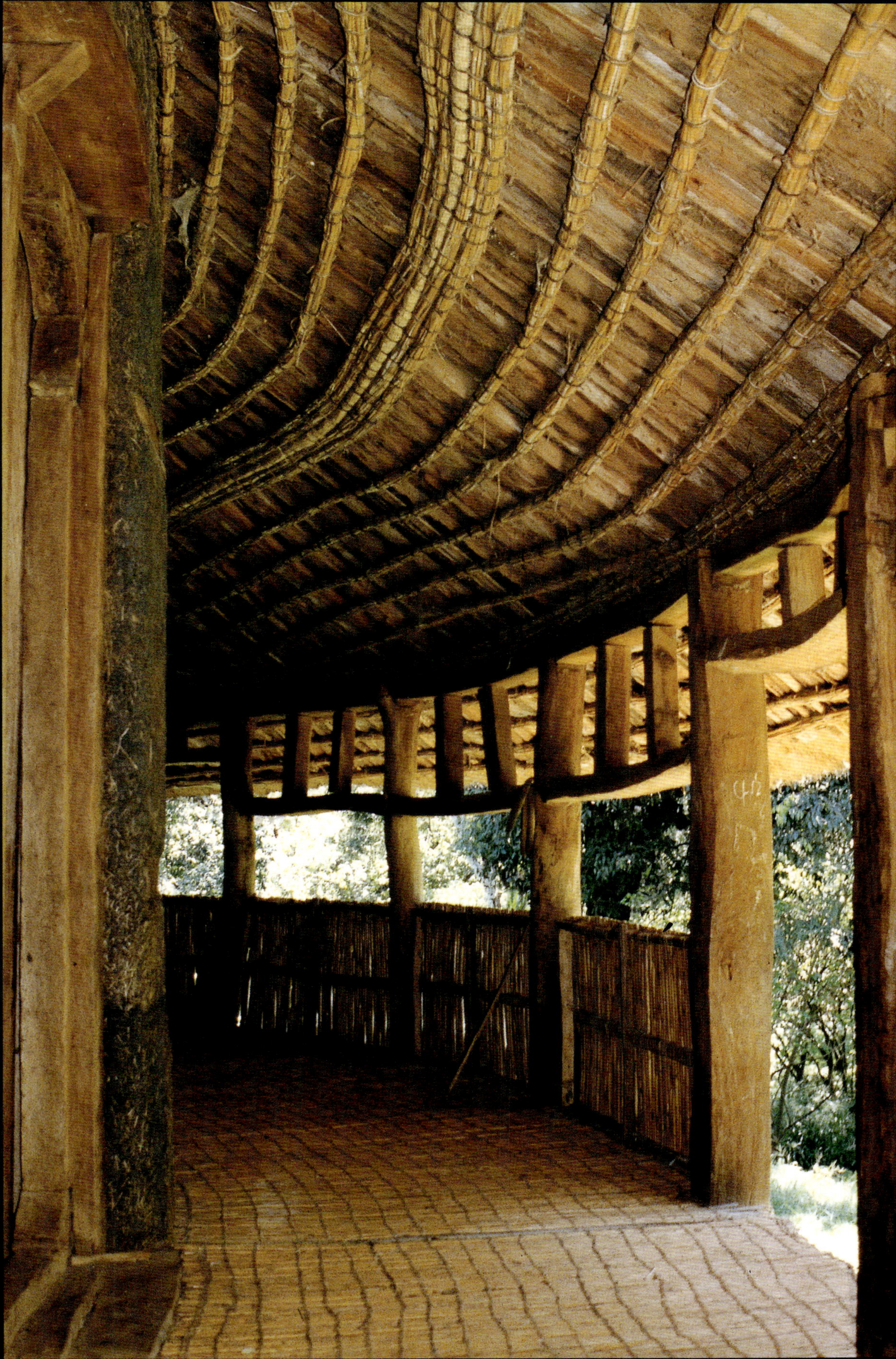

82. Kota Māryām on the island of Dek. The *qeddest*, 'saint': an inside gallery around the sanctuary used for the non-officiating clergy and for the distribution of the Eucharist to the believers.

83. Kota Māryām on the island of Dek. The *qenē māḥlēt*, 'chant of praise', an exterior portico where the *dabtara* chant the Divine Office and which is destined for the cantors and the congregation.

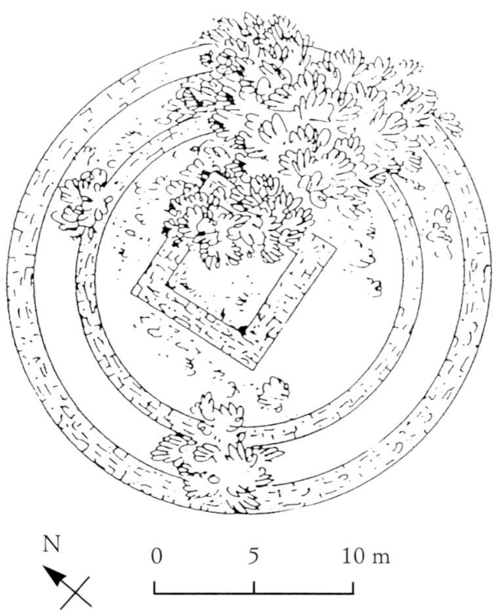

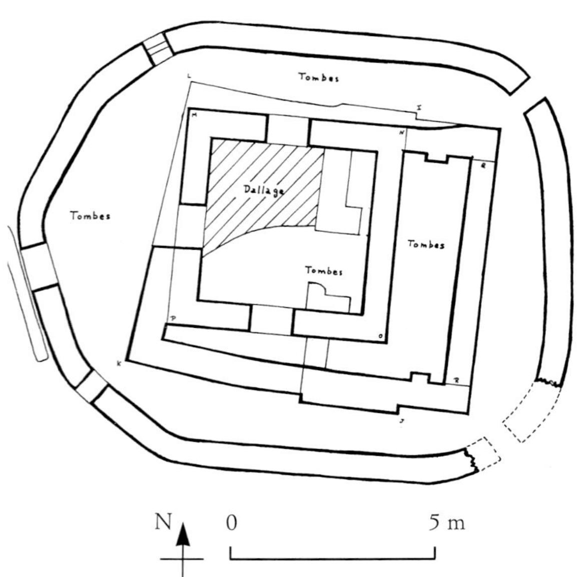

84. Plan of the ancient church of Enda Jesus at Aksum: (*DAE* III, p. 62).

85. Excavation relief of the second church of Enda Čerqos: (DE CONTENSON, tav. XXX).

the area of Ḥawlti Melāzo (DE CONTENSON, pp. 43-44) (fig. 85), including the churches of Sandābā Iyāsus and of Bētaleḥēm Dabra Tābor, whose foundation probably dates to the end of the 14th century and therefore pre-dates the Grañ's incursions.[6] The distribution within the territory of the above-mentioned examples seems to deny a limited southern origin for the type of round planned churches with the square of the *sancta sanctorum* in the middle. This current opinion may derive from the fact that the south of the country is, in fact, the area where nowadays the typology of the cylindrical-conical hut is more common.

From a survey of the ancient examples of round centrally planned churches the *maqdas* seems to have originally lacked the window oriented towards the east. This fact is evident even in the ruins of the church of Abbā Samuel at Azazo, which is presumibly datable to the beginning of the 16th century (fig. 86). Such a structuring of the opening of the *maqdas* could reinforce the hypothesis of its possible derivation—as the product of a typological evolution—from the presbytery of tripartite-allignment churches, where the main hall of the presbytery had only one front access and two connections with the lateral long spaces (later absorbed into the *qeddest* in square centrally planned churches).

In round centrally planned churches, apart from the walls of the *maqdas* and those surrounding the *qeddest*, all other structural elements are generally made of wood, from the antenna supporting the vertex of the covering, to the structural system inside the *qeddest*, made of a ring of poles joined at the top by a typical double-order scaffold of trusses (functional to their joining and to the support of the rafters of the covering). Also the perimetral structure of the *qenē māḫlēt* is generally made of wood, and it reproduces the arrangement of the inside frame of the *qeddest*.

On Lake Tana a similar arrangement—reproposed identically, notwithstanding the difference in dimensions—can be found for example in the churches of Kota Māryām on the isle of Dek (which dates to the 16th century) (fig. 89) and of Dabra Sinā, near Gorgorā, of the 17th century (ANNEQUIN 1975, pp. 92-93) (figs. 87-88).

The chronology of the churches having this structure can in fact be established starting from the 16th-17th century, even though sometimes their very typology and the fact that they keep much older objects, paintings and mass-books may testify to an earlier date.

In the case of the church of Kebrān Gabre'ēl, which dates to the 17th century and is located on the homonymous island in Lake Tana (ANNEQUIN 1975, pp. 111-114), its particularly conspicuous artistic wealth induced substitution—both in the perimeter of the *qeddest* and inside it—of the wooden structures with pilasters made of hewn stone, joined by arches to form the con-

[6] These two churches, of which a careful survey would be highly desirable, have been kindly mentioned to us by professor Stanislaw Chojnacki.

86. Abbā Samu'ēl at Azazo
(early 16th century?), reconstruction.

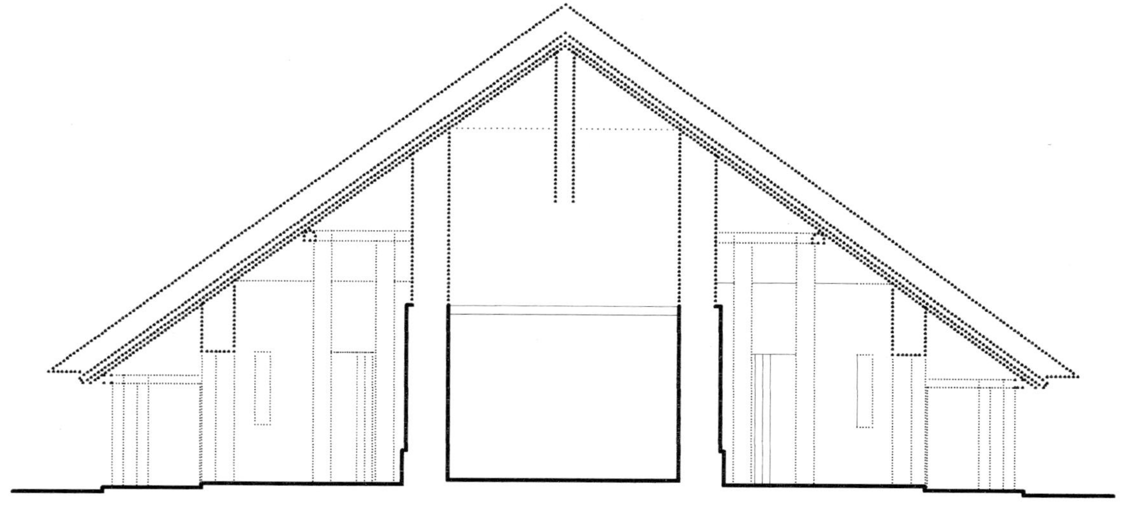

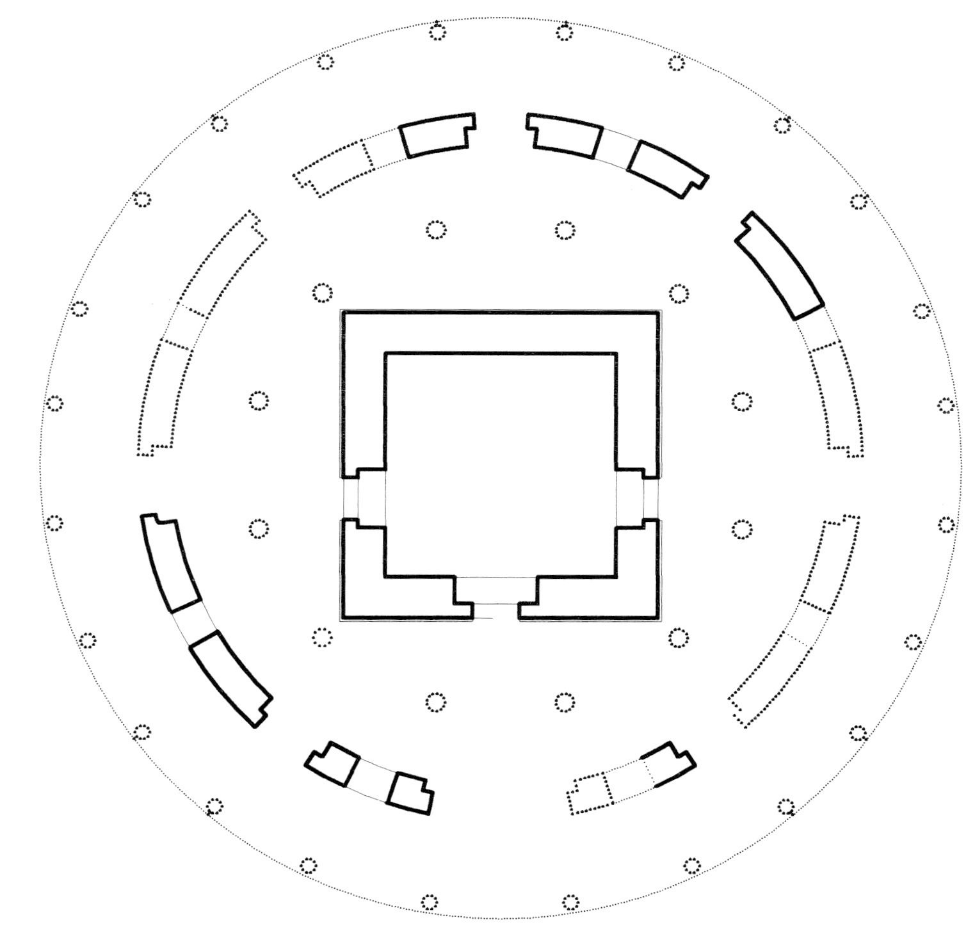

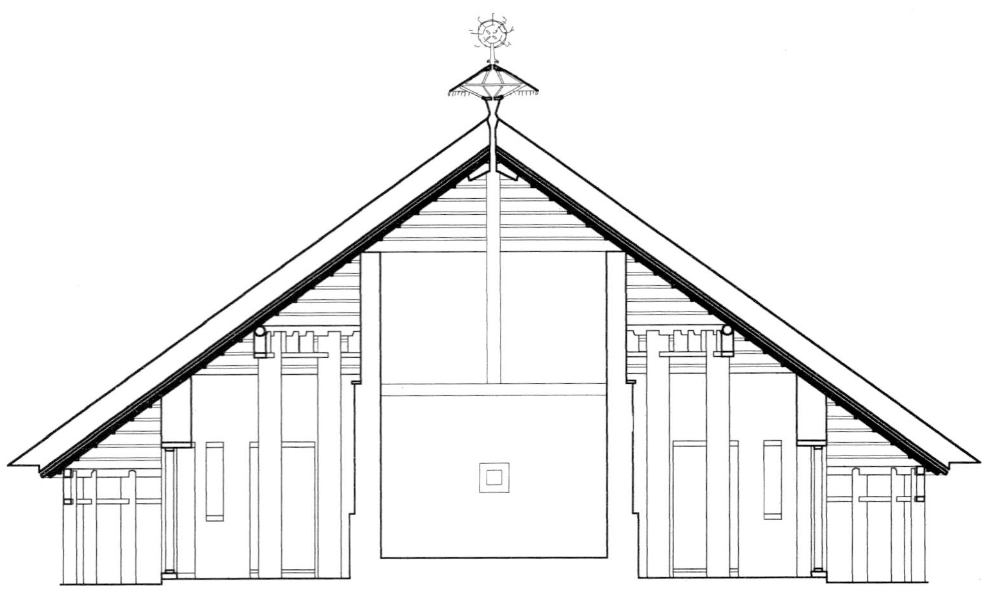

87. Schematic plan and section of Dabra Sinā at Gorgorā (17th century).

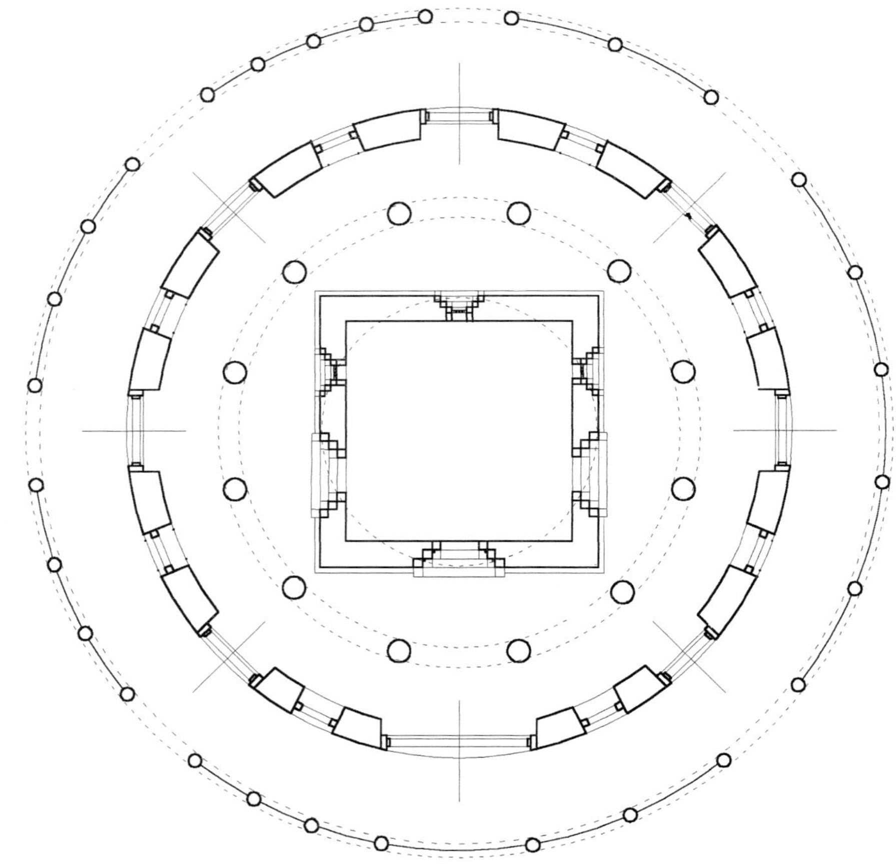

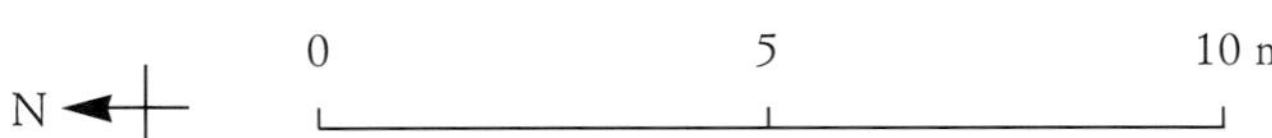

88. Dabra Sinā at Gorgorā, on Lake Tana.

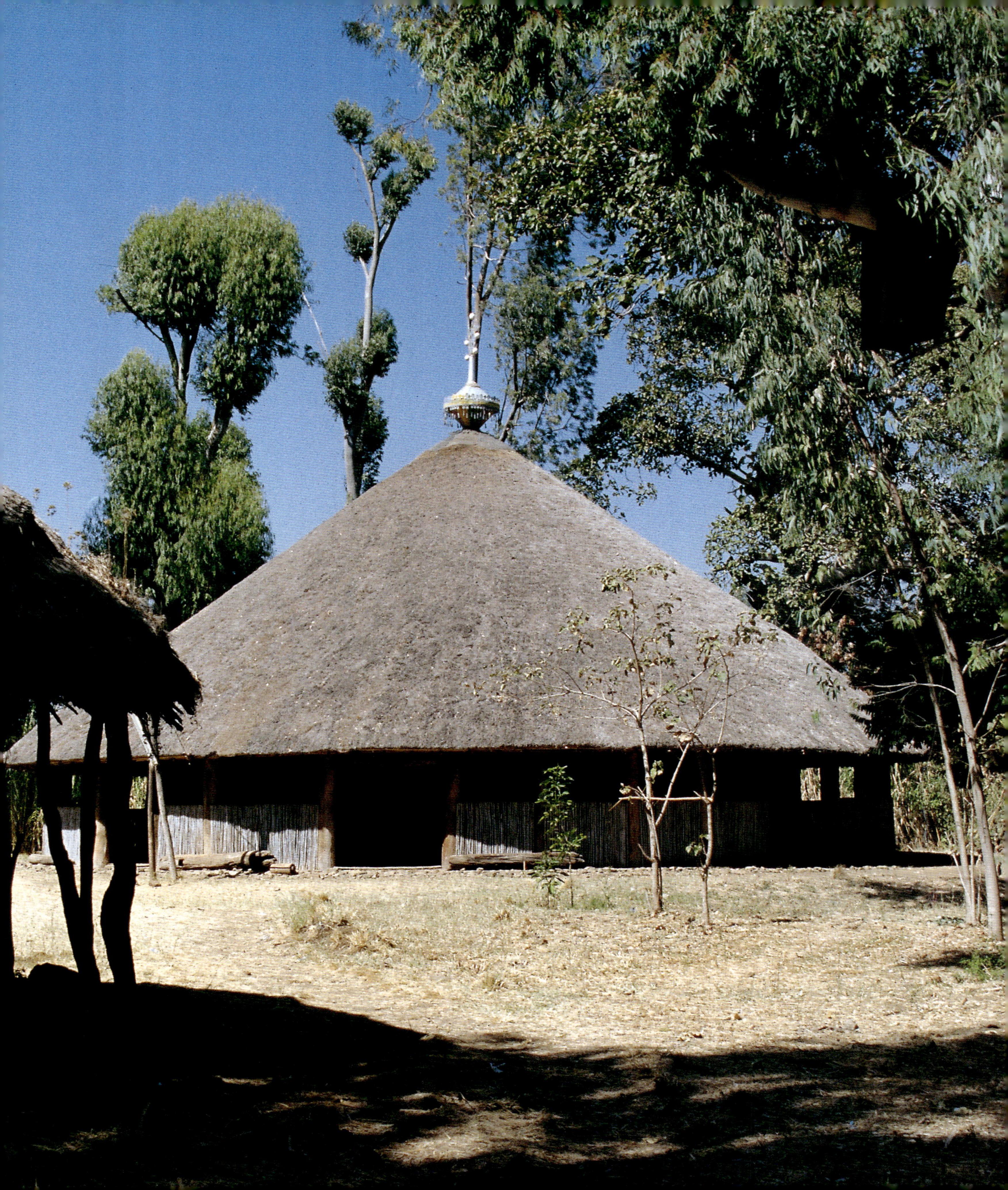

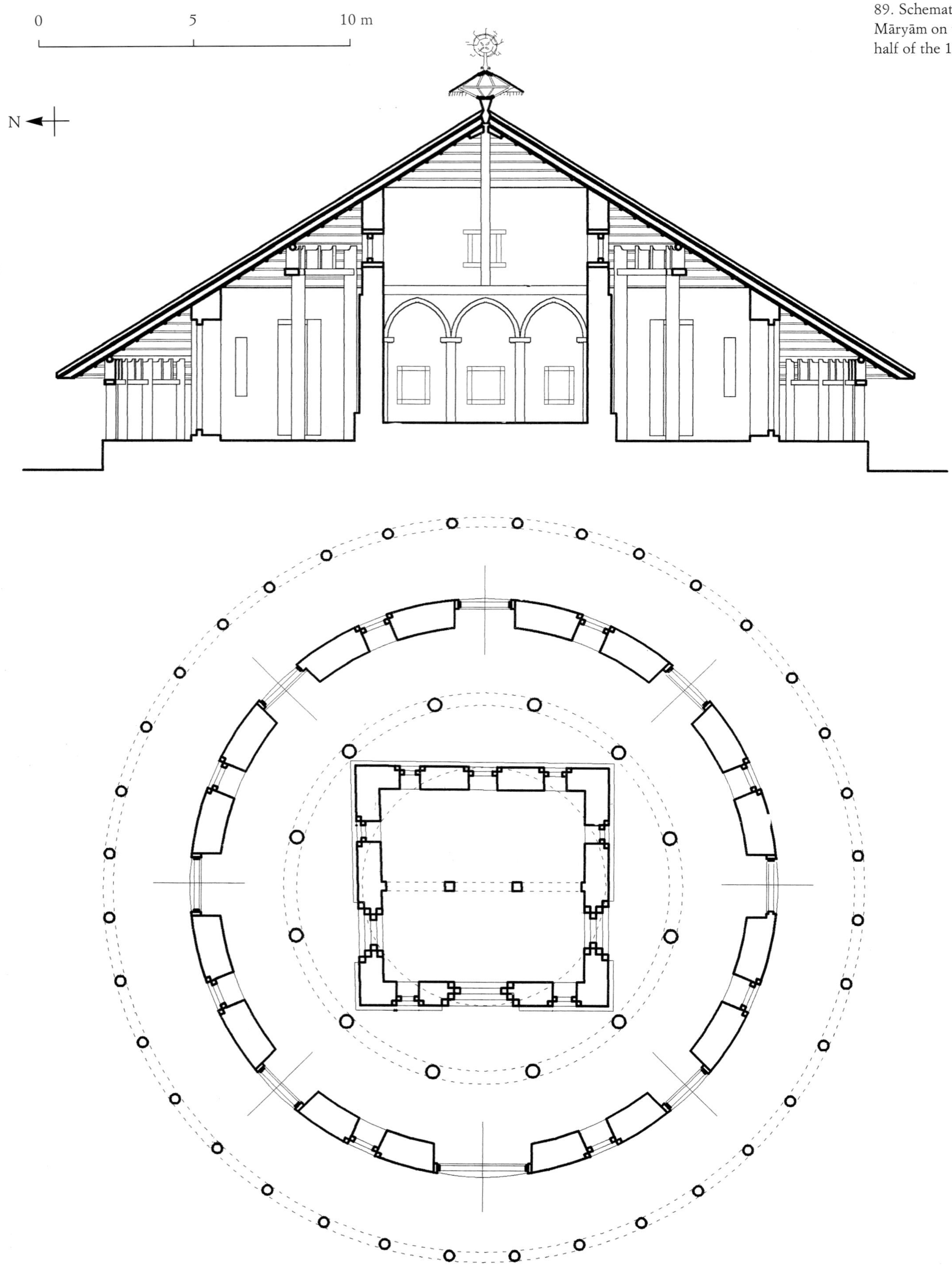

0 5 10 m

N

89. Schematic plan and section of Kota Māryām on the island of Dek (second half of the 16th century).

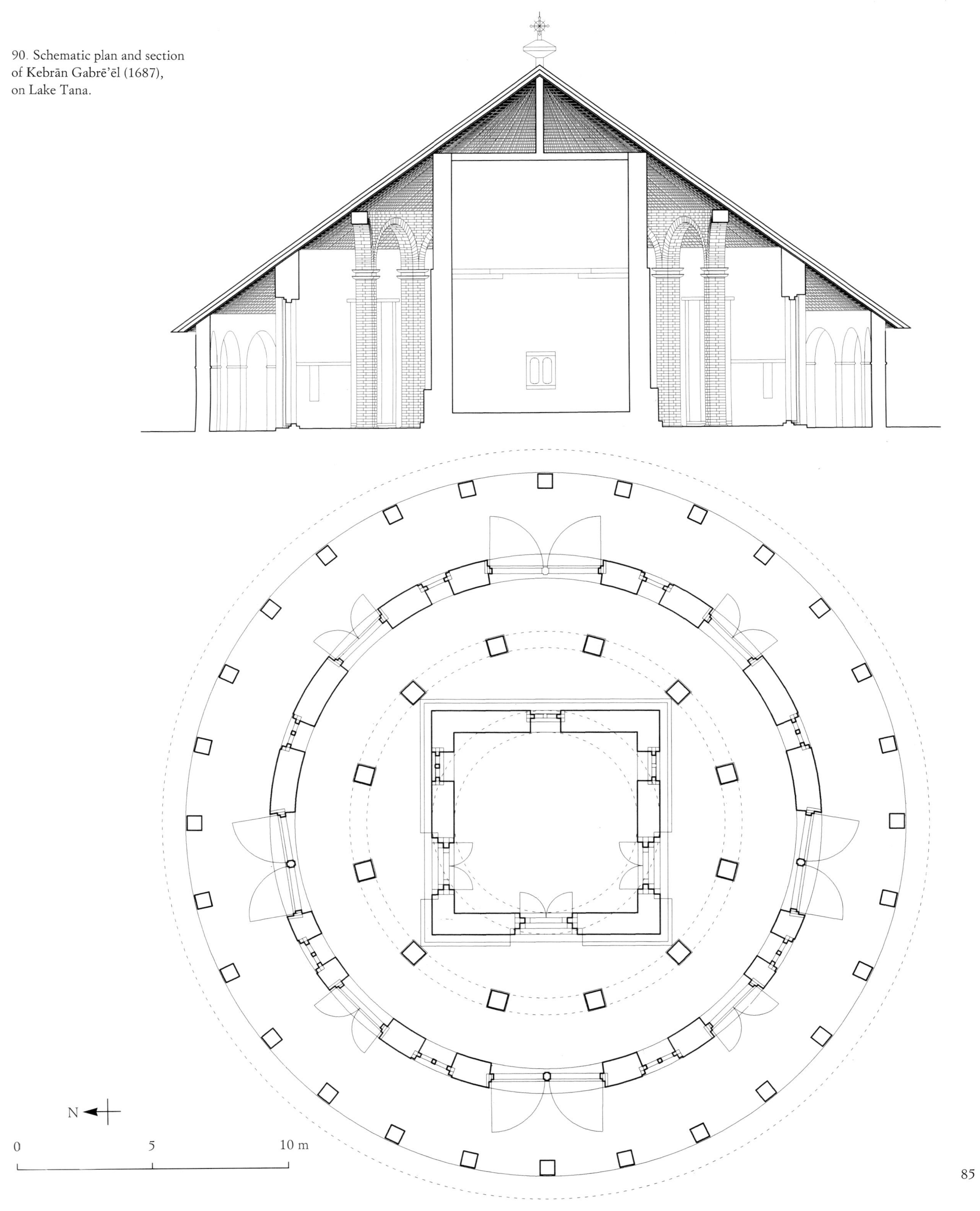

90. Schematic plan and section of Kebrān Gabrē'ēl (1687), on Lake Tana.

91. Axionometric sketch of Kebrān Gabrē'l, on Lake Tana.

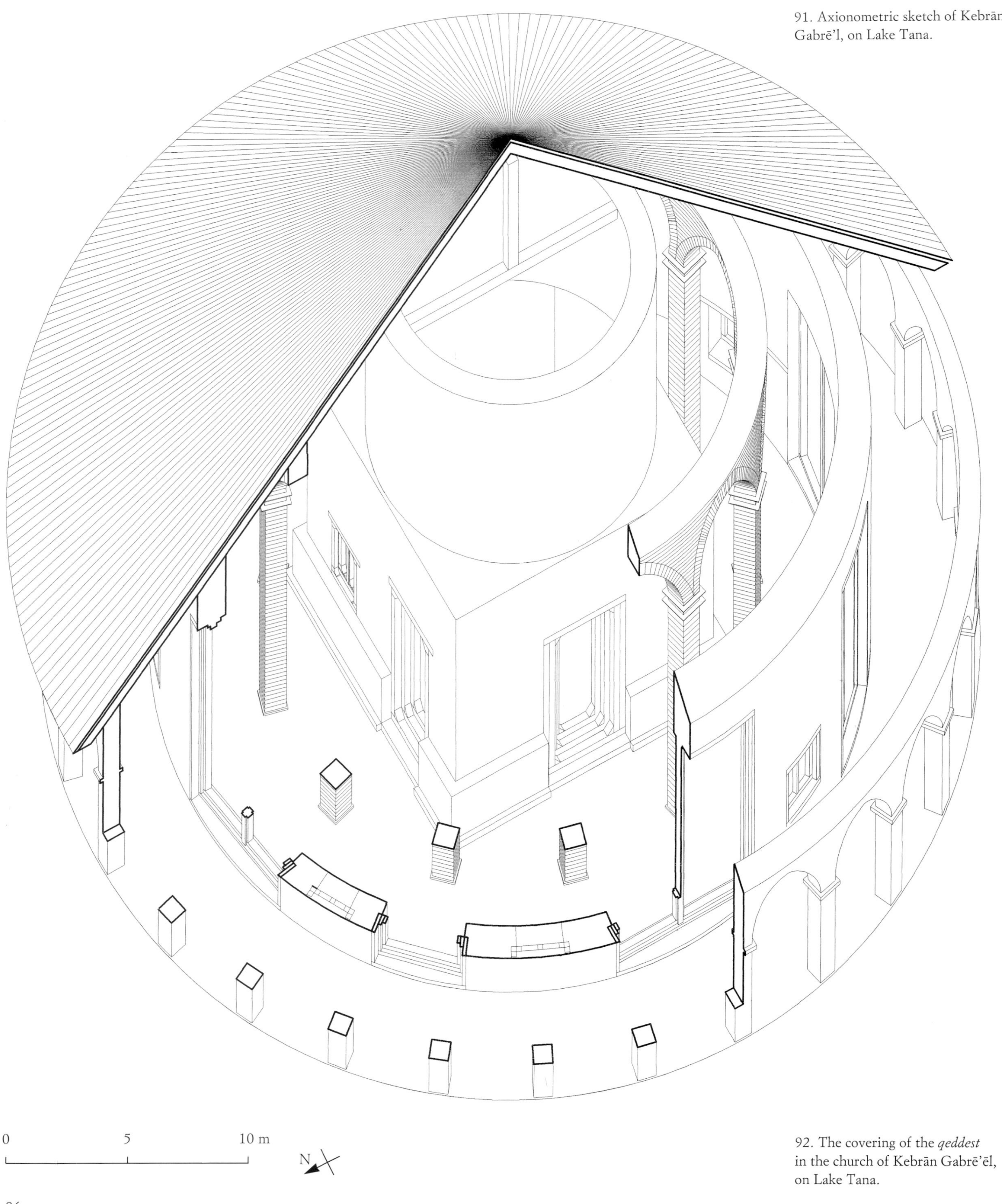

92. The covering of the *qeddest* in the church of Kebrān Gabrē'ēl, on Lake Tana.

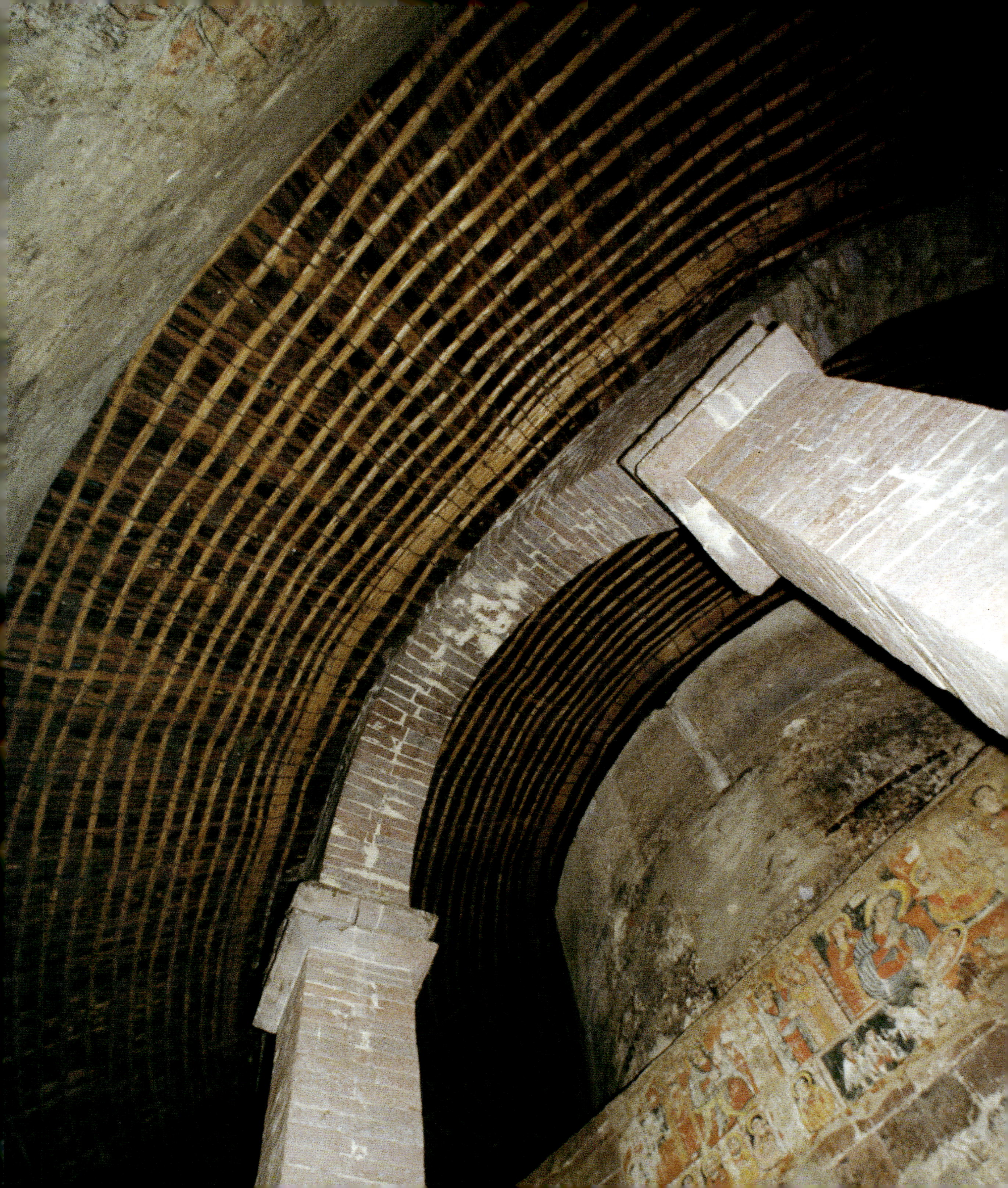

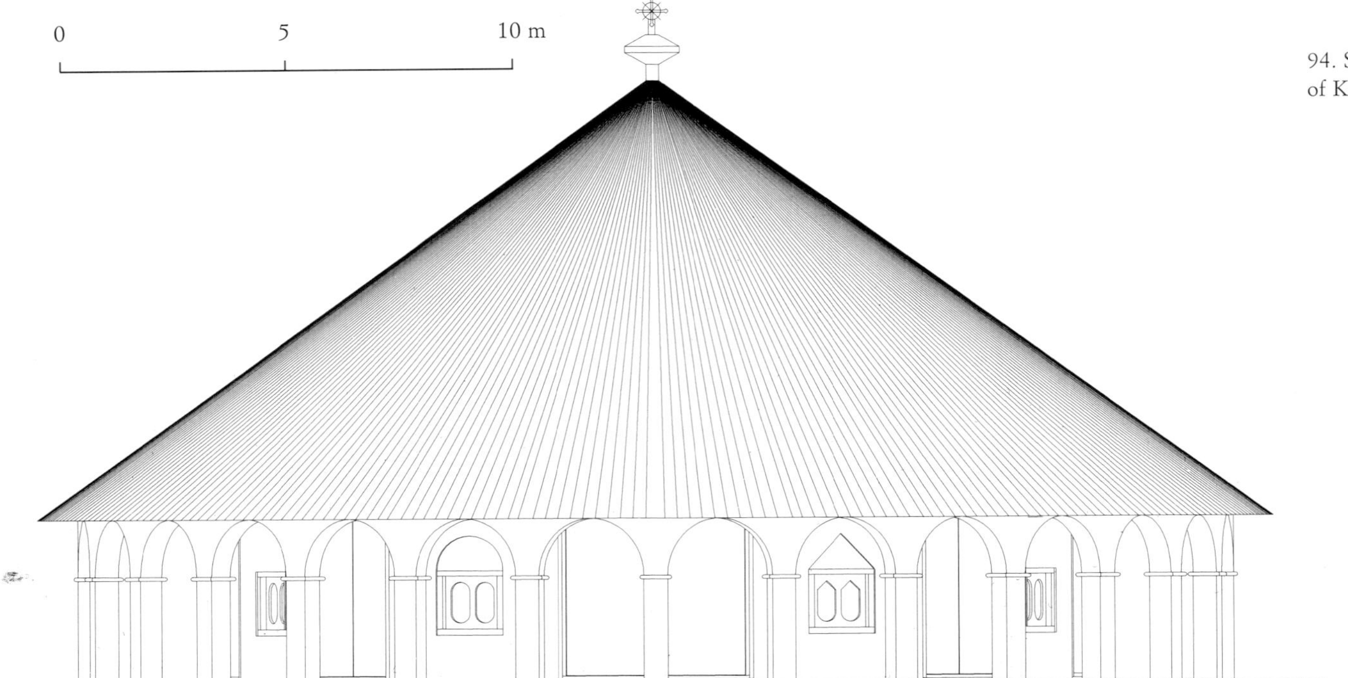

94. Sketch of the western façade of Kebrān Gabrē'ēl, on Lake Tana.

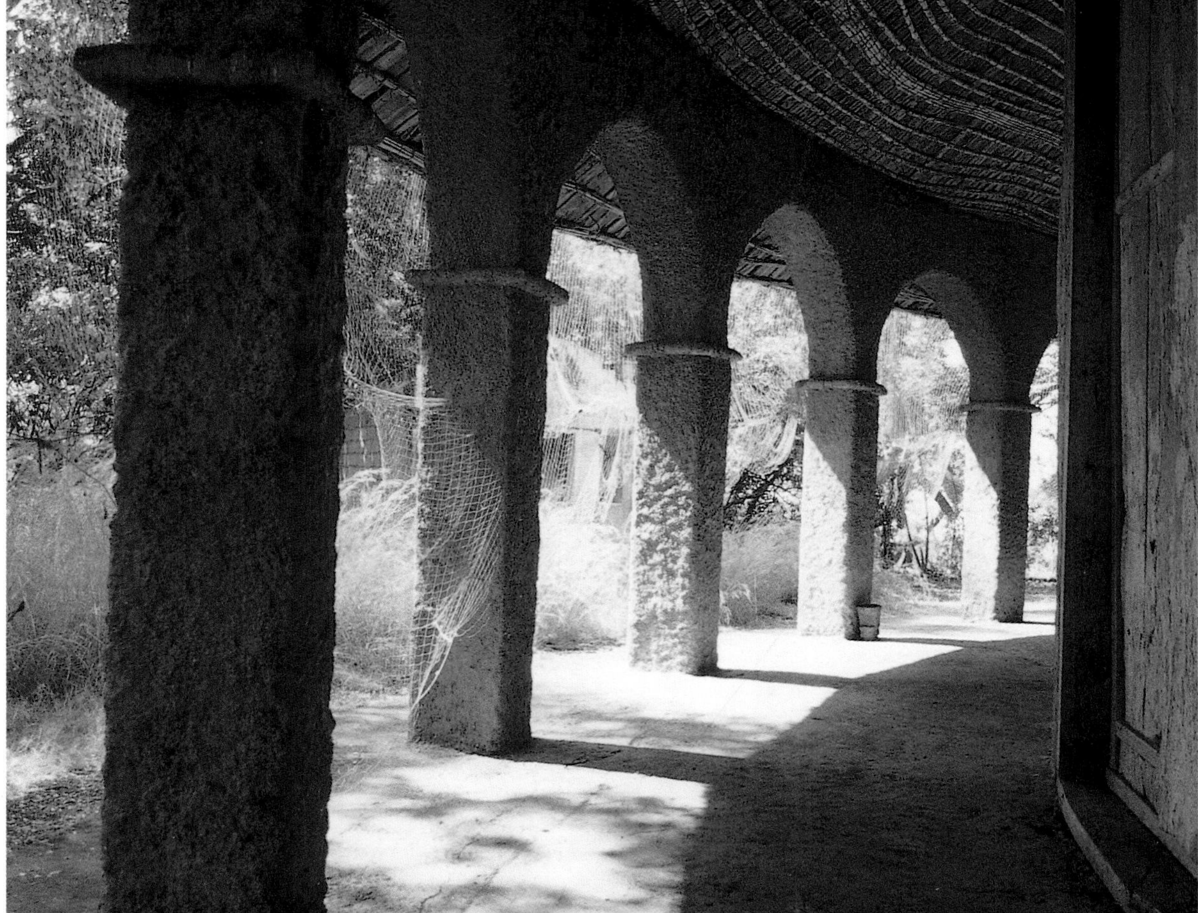

93. The external portico, *qenē māhlēt*, of Kebrān Gabrē'ēl, on Lake Tana.

95. Axionometric sketch of Kebrān Gabrē'ēl, on Lake Tana.
The sanctuary is encircled and protected by a series of annular curtains.

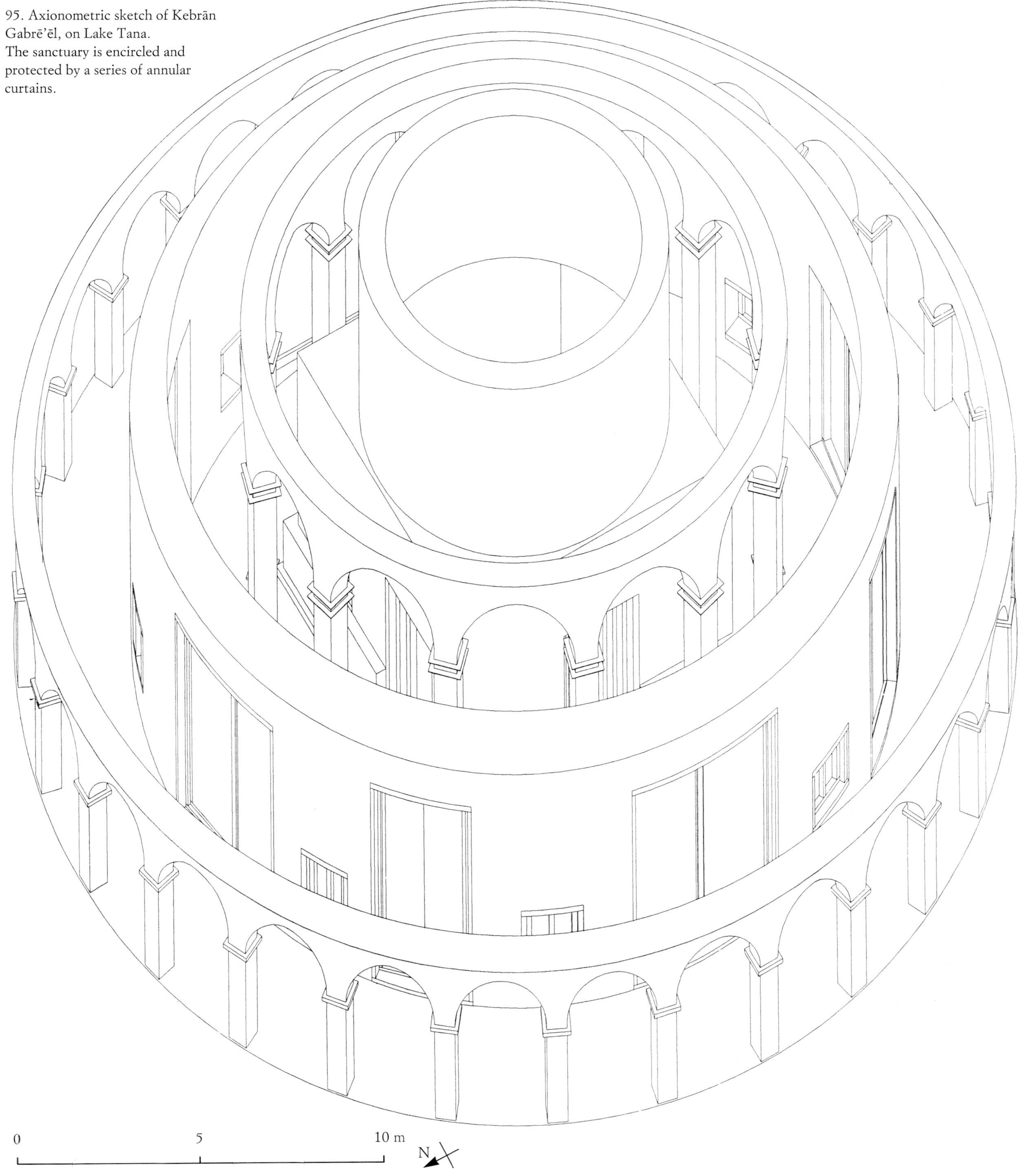

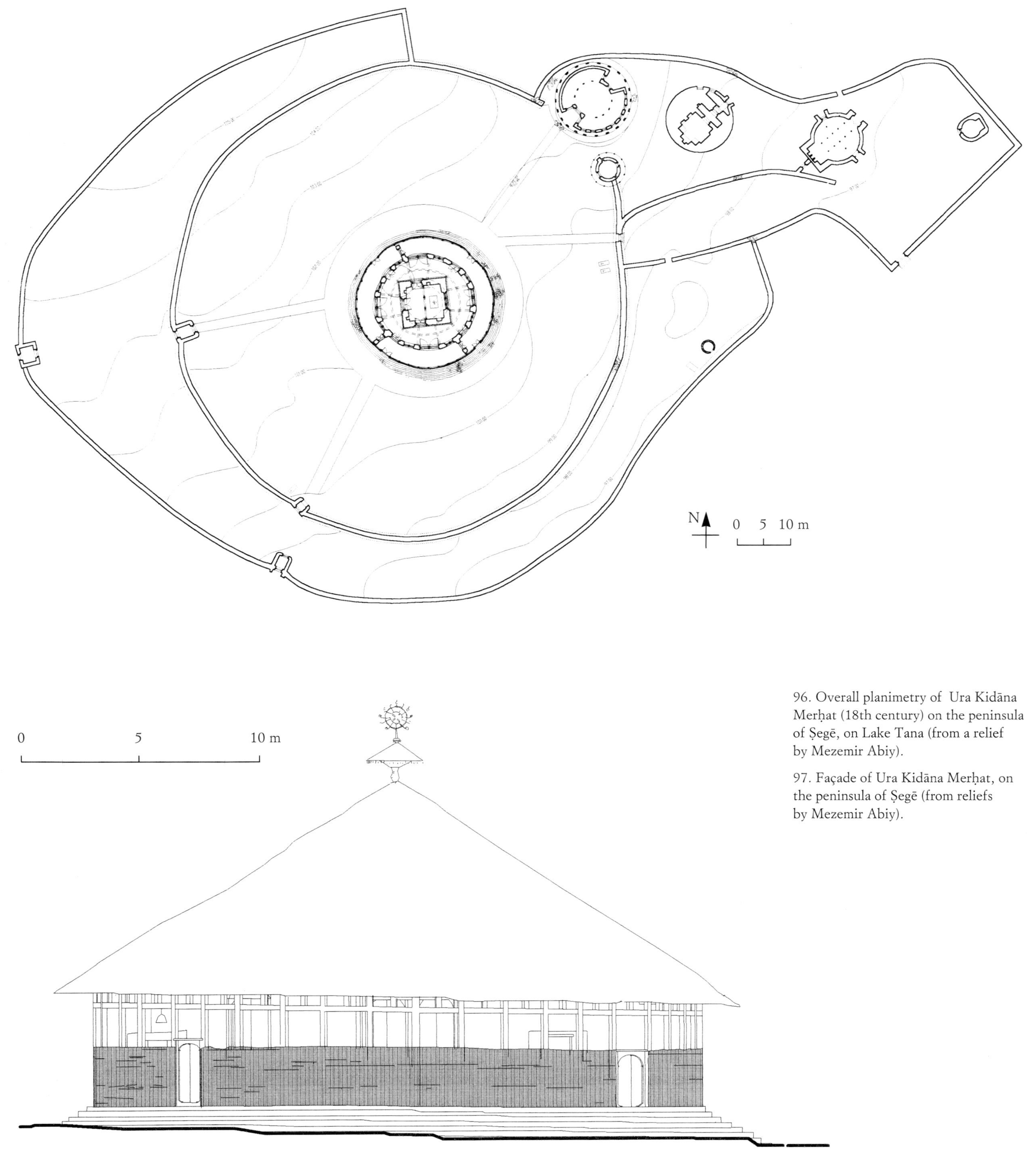

96. Overall planimetry of Ura Kidāna Merḥat (18th century) on the peninsula of Ṣegē, on Lake Tana (from a relief by Mezemir Abiy).

97. Façade of Ura Kidāna Merḥat, on the peninsula of Ṣegē (from reliefs by Mezemir Abiy).

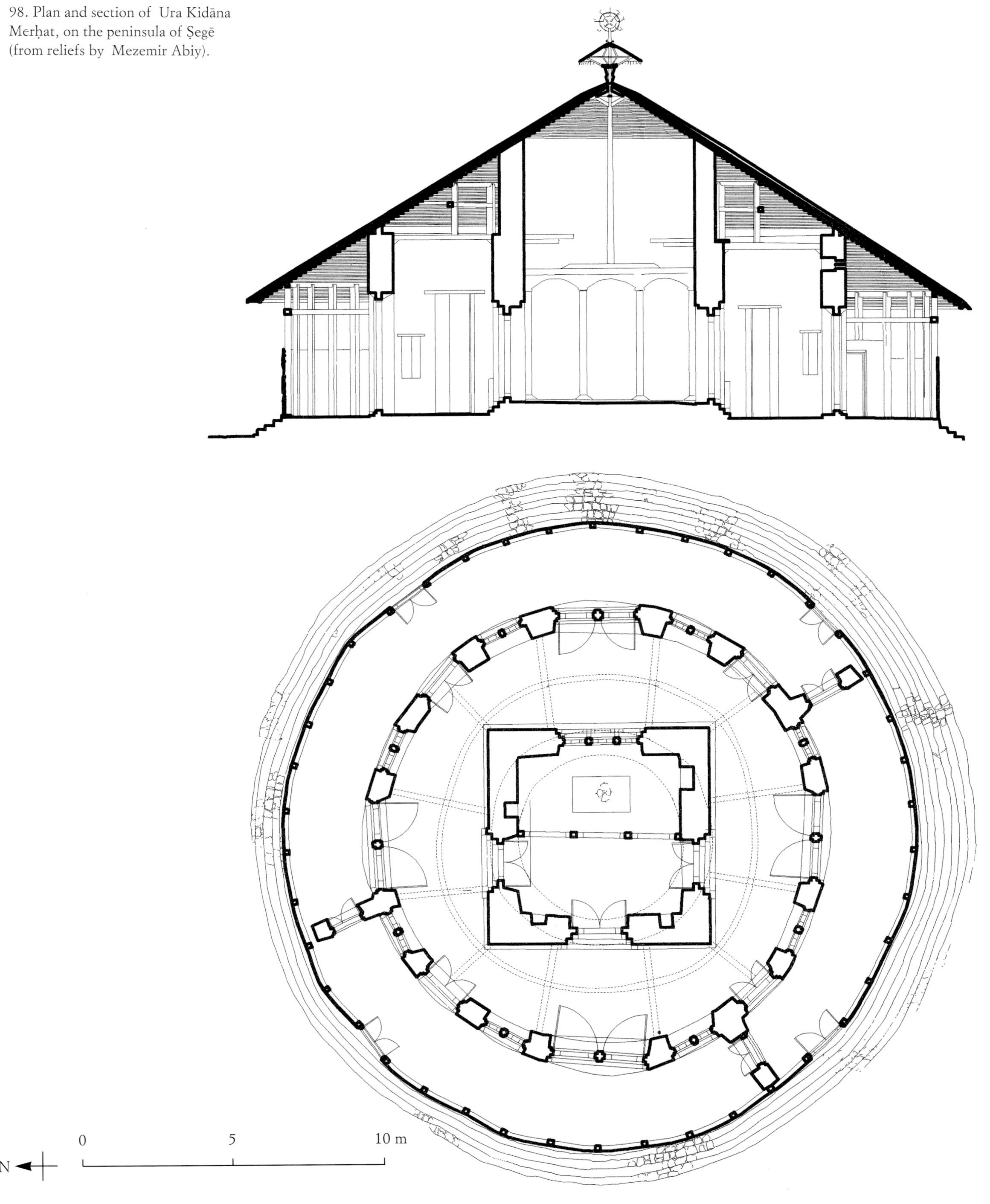

98. Plan and section of Ura Kidāna Merḥat, on the peninsula of Ṣegē (from reliefs by Mezemir Abiy).

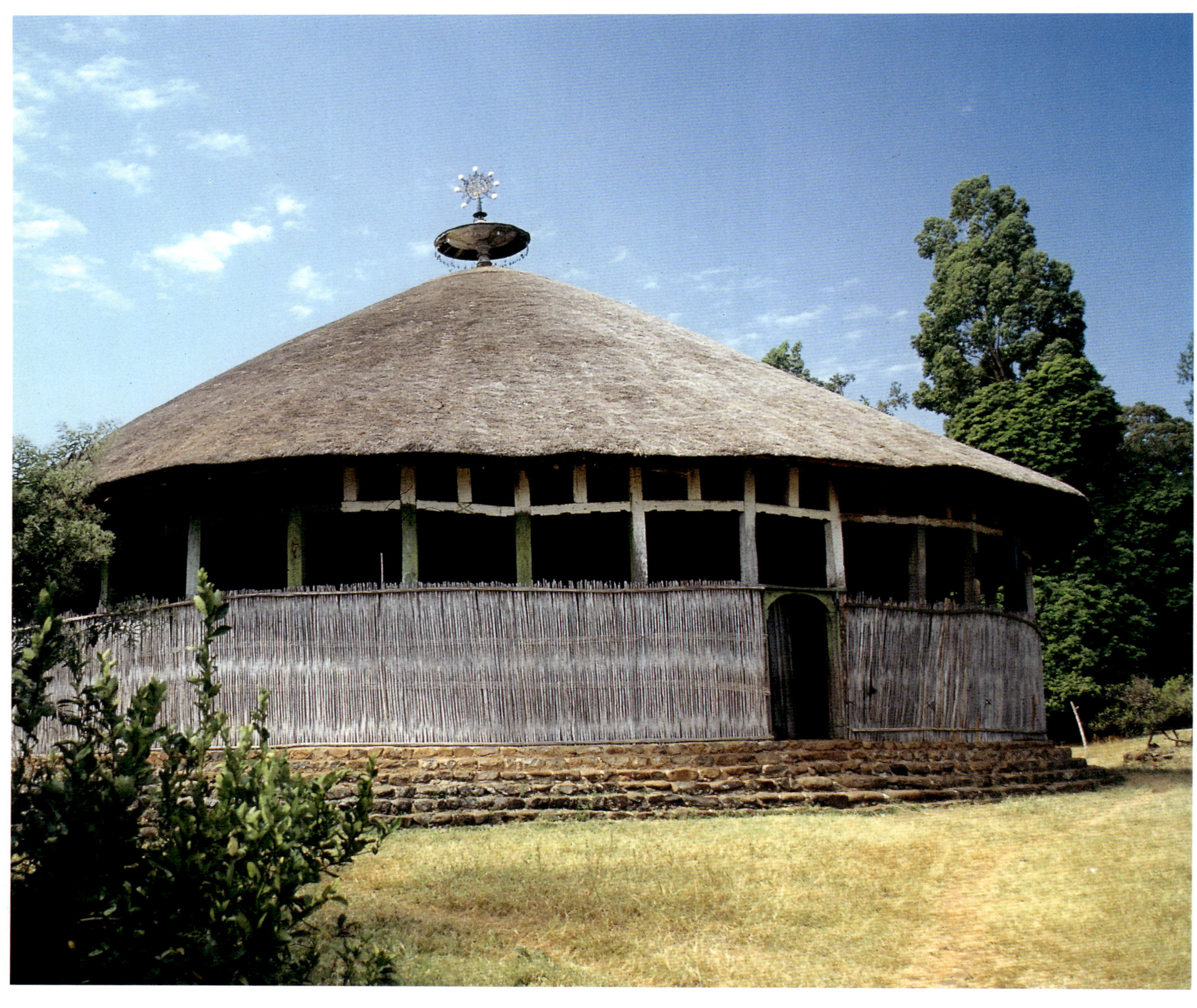

tinuous wall ring supporting the cone of the covering (figs. 90-95).

During the 18th century a relevant typological innovation intervened: the pilasters inside the *qeddest* were eliminated, thus freeing its floor surface of any obstacle to its full usage. In the same period, at the top of the cube of the *maqdas,* twelve radial trusses were introduced (one at each corner plus two at each side), attached on the side opposite to the wall of the *maqdas*, so as to support the rafters of the covering (fig. 101). This architectural solution is adopted also in the church of Nārgā Śellāsē (ANNEQUIN 1975, pp. 97-101), where the perimetral pilasters of the *qenē māḥlēt* are made of stone. On the other and, in the more recent church of Ura Kidāne Meḥrāt (ANNEQUIN 1975, pp. 107-110), as in many other churches, the frame of wooden perimetral walls is maintained (figs. 96-101).

As can be seen easily in the relief diagrams—the necessity for which must never be underestimated—the evolution of the type consists of the in-

99. Ura Kidāna Merḥat, on the peninsula of Ṣegē.

100. The *qeddest* of Ura Kidāna Merḥat, on the peninsula of Ṣegē.

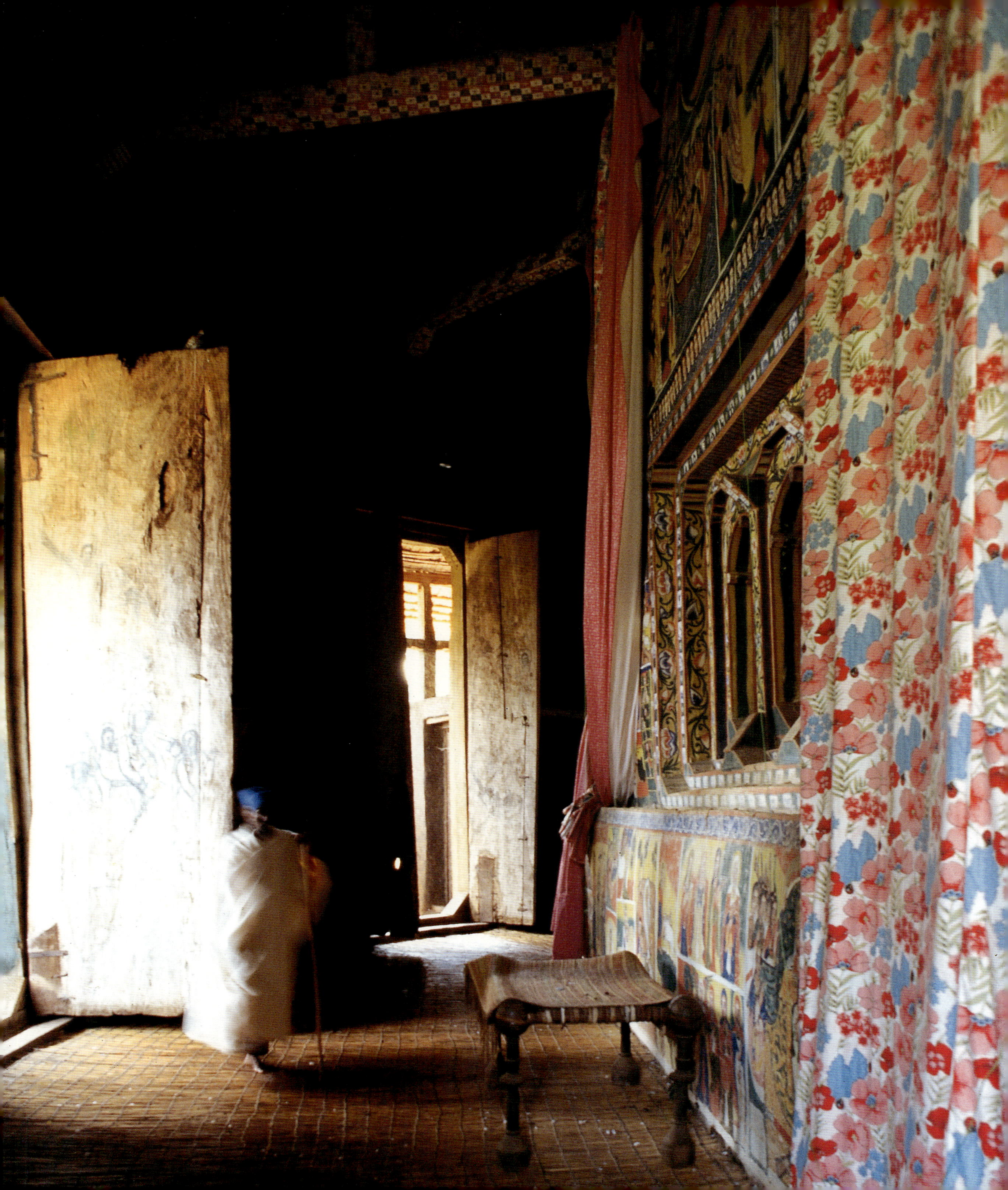

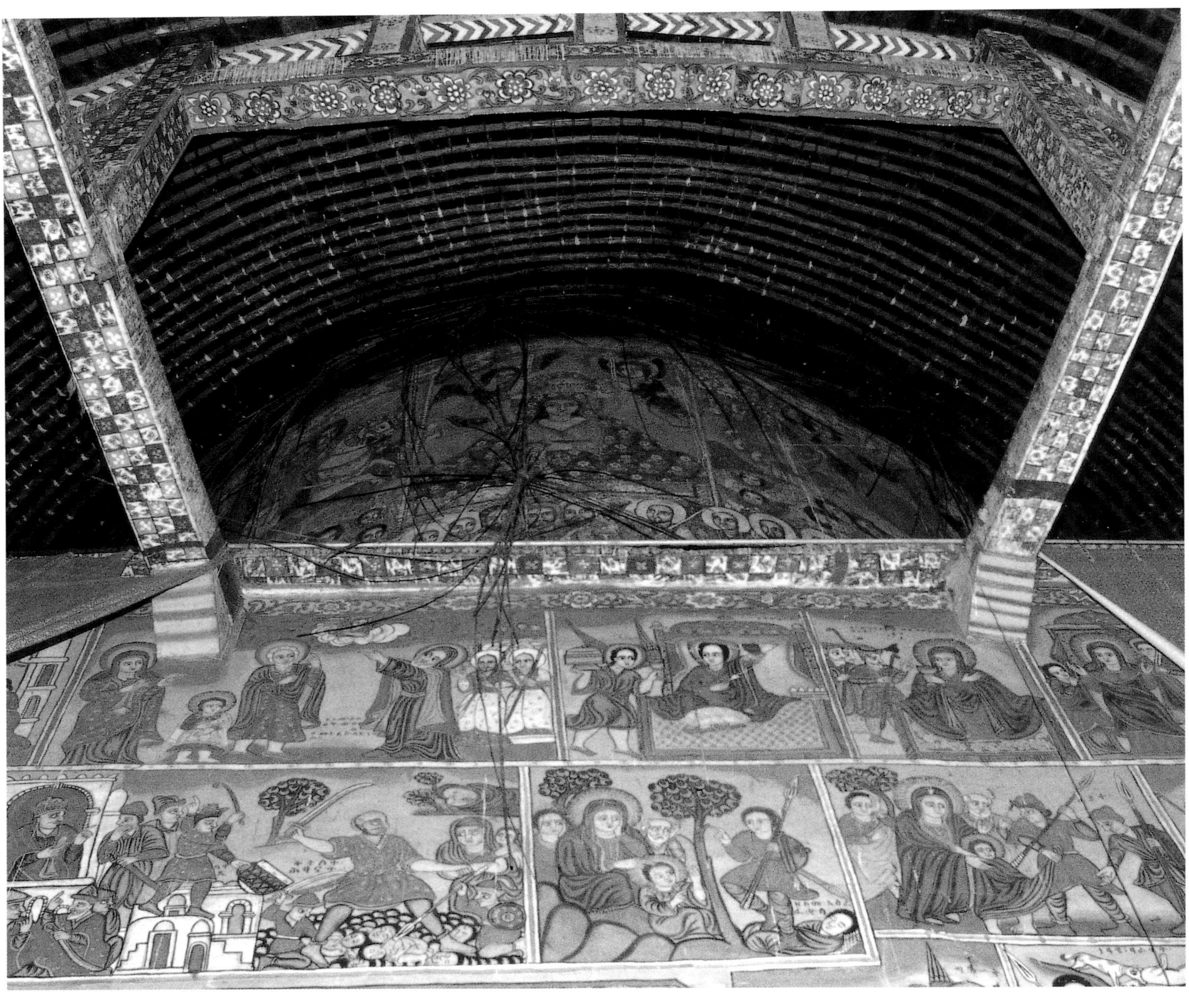

101. Typical trusses frame in the church of Ura Kidāna Merḥat, on the peninsula of Ṣegē.

troduction of this typical device, both structural and functional, inside the *qeddest*, but also by the progressively higher importance of the *maqdas*' and the *qeddest*'s openings, at the expense of the wall sections, increasingly lightened and reduced. This typological interpretation of Ethiopian round centrally planned churches may derive from ethnical, environmental and structural considerations, surely relevant and patent. However, the adherence has to be mentioned of this typology to the sacredness of the place and to symbolic suggestions which, without rejecting those etchnical, environmental and structural values, may even coincide with them in an organical adhesion to form a well-structured whole.

"Without doubt, in Ethiopia (and not only in Ethiopia) stricter rules for the strucural form have been used, while content and meaning are either no longer the same or not understandable any longer. But the profound religious spirit whch is shared by the great majority of Ethiopians cannot be underrated: it is a religiousness which is in many ways more linked to external forms than to internal ones, but without them becoming the final content, in a reality of everyday life according to which also exterior forms are assimilated and absorbed into that lifestyle" (GENSTER, p. 49).

Even without trying to force upon it ideas of a 'collective unconscious', in the plan of Abyssinian churches can be found "... important analogies with parallel solutions employed by currents of thought of other epochs and in other countries, [...] and it could not have been otherwise, since they are archetypes embedded in human soul and which therefore reappear, under different skies and in different periods, under a similar appearance" (TUCCI, p. 9).

As with the *mandala*—with which connections are only superficial—"... They have just elaborated in a more precise way a very ancient intuition, which with time became more definite, making good use, at least for the external plan, also of foreign conceptions" (TUCCI, p. 36).

"... The mandala [...] is much more than a simple sacred surface, which has to be kept pure for ritual and liturgical uses. In fact, it is rather a cosmogram, it is the whole universe in its essential scheme [...], a vital process developing from an essential principle which revolves around a central axis [...], the *axis mundi* on which rests the sky which is rooted in the mysterious underworld" (TUCCI, p. 37). The fact that also in Ethiopia this was the result of an intentional choice is proved also by the pilaster inside the nave of the church of Betra Māryām at Lalibela (fig. 52).

In a projection of the world, where the world is reduced to its essential scheme, "... the geometrical representation is that which associates circular forms with the sky and square ones with the earth [...]. In this regard, we should remember that the descending path of the cycle of the Manifestation [...] , a path which goes from its upper pole, the Sky, to its lower one, the Earth [...], has its origin in the least 'specified' of forms, the sphere, and ends up with the most 'definite' one, the cube [...] The Sky and the Earth, as is natural, are represented respectively by a circle and square within it [...] (GUÉNON, pp. 35-37), almost as in the *maqdas*.

Each church is a spiritual pole in itself. "For the Jews, this spiritual pole can be identified with the hill of Zion, which they call the 'Heart of the World', and which is shared by all the 'Holy Lands'. The tabernacle of the Holyness of *Jehovah*, the residence of the *Shekinah* is the Saint of Saints which is the heart of the temple, which is in turn in the centre of Zion (Jerusalem), just as the Holy Zion is in the middle of the Holy Land of Israel, which is again, in turn, the centre of the world" (GUÉNON, p. 65). For the Ethiopians, their land is the new Zion, and going backwards, from the tabernacle to the *maqdas*, to the Ark of the Covenant inside the tabernacle and, on the Ark, the *tābot*—the place where the *Shekinah* manifests itself between two *Kerubim*—, the centre of Ethiopian spirituality is incarnated in the incredible number of churches which punctuate the country.

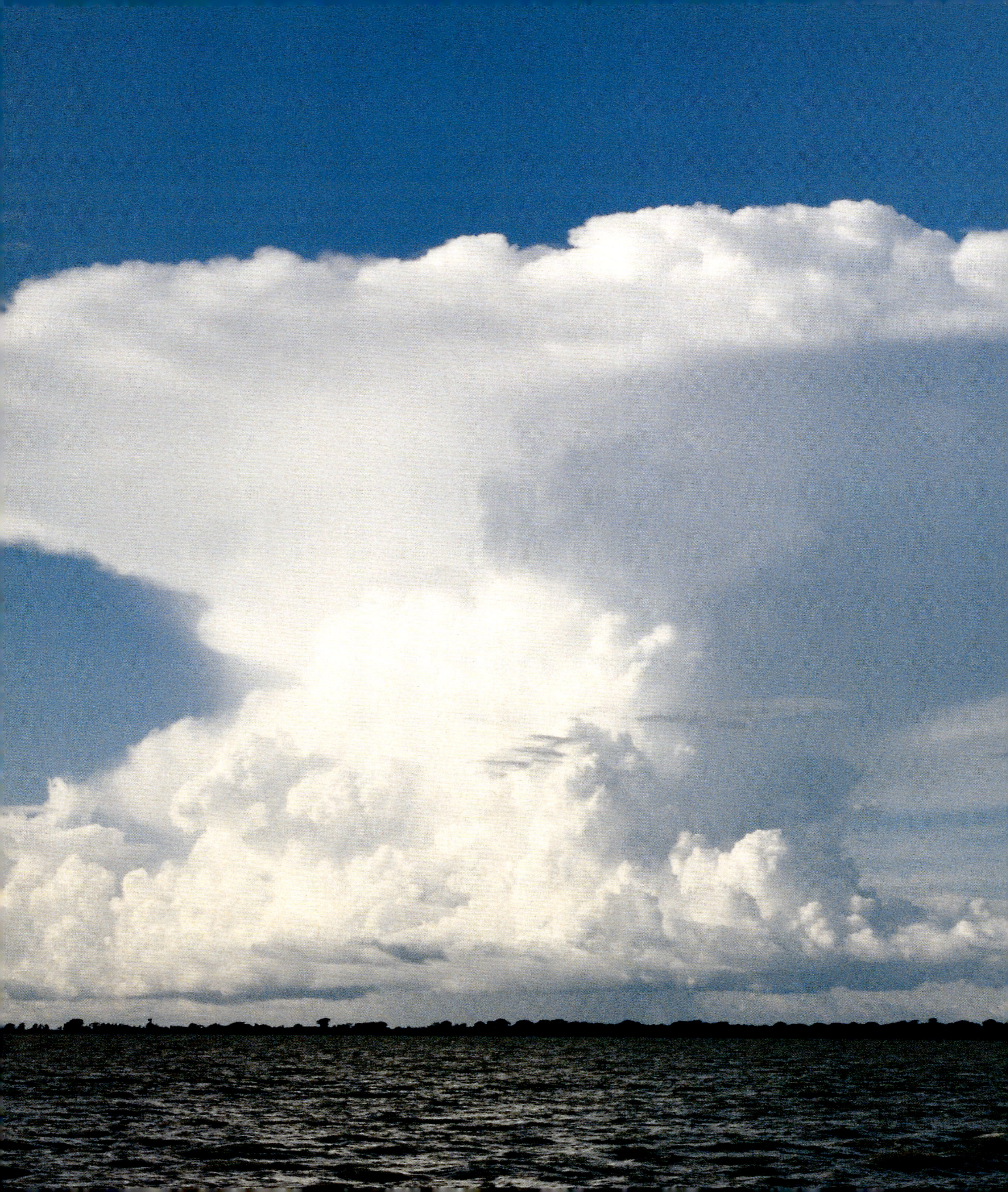

Nārgā Śellāsē. Typology, Structure and Style of a Monastery

On the 23rd March 1747 (the 15th *magābit* of the year of the world 7239, according to the Julian calendar) Mentewwāb, the Queen of Queens—in agreement with her son, Iyāsu II, the King of Kings—left Gondar heading southward to look for a place to build a sanctuary which would be a repayment to God for the favours she had received.

From far off she could already see Dāgā Esṭifanos (ANNEQUIN 1975, pp. 102-105), an isolated abrupt hill in the middle of Lake Tana, visible from all around (fig. 43). When she arrived at the lake-shore she saw beside the hill a large wedge shaped land mass. It was the flat island of Dek (ANNEQUIN 1975, p. 96).

In a few months time the rains would arrive to swell the small tributaries which form a sunburst pattern around the lake, raising its water level. But at the moment of her arrival Walatta Giyorgis, Daugther of Saint George—as Mentewwāb used to be called and devotedly signed herself—was able to float to the middle of the lake on a fragile *tānkuā*. She paid homage to the hermitage of Saint Stephen, having climbed to Dāgā's small summit and also visited the sacred tombs of the great emperors. She sailed round Dek which when seen from closer appeared less flat, especially to the west where some of the islets formed a fringe into the water with the lush vegetation of places unfrequented by men (fig. 103).

102. The island of Dek appears flat on the horizon.

Chronacles tell of how on Nārgā, one of these islets, a 'magnificent house' was already being built for the queen. An isthmus connecting the islet with Dek would soon be submerged by the rising water. From her palace in Gondar, on clear days, Mentewwāb would have been able to make out her 'magnificent house', in front of which, before reparting on 21st April of the same year, she ordered the construction of a church dedicated to the Holy Trinity. Thus to the ring of hermitages on the lake another was added, Nārgā Śellāsē, which was to become chief amongst them.

The lake was off the main transport routes which served Gondar, the imperial capital, and even more isolated was the group of little islands which were detached from the shore. Amongst the peninsulas only Gorgorā in the north—the largest—and Ṣegē in the south—the smallest—have monasteries. Religious settlements are also to be found in the territory near the lake, but it is on the islets that there exists a true detachment from the world. Only the papyrus *tānkwā* were able to land there, slipping between the hanging branches of the trees which lean over the water (fig. 105). Today there are also struggling boats for which in certain places cement and metal jetties project vulgarly into the water where time stands still in its age-old benevolence.

Notwithstanding this, Cyclopean walls defended the perimeter of Nārgā, unlike elsewhere on the lake where only the natural waterline or rock faces encircled the ground. Thus before the arrival of Mentewwāb (whilst probable, this interpretation could be confirmed only by adequate research, which unfortunately today is unlikely) (fig. 106).

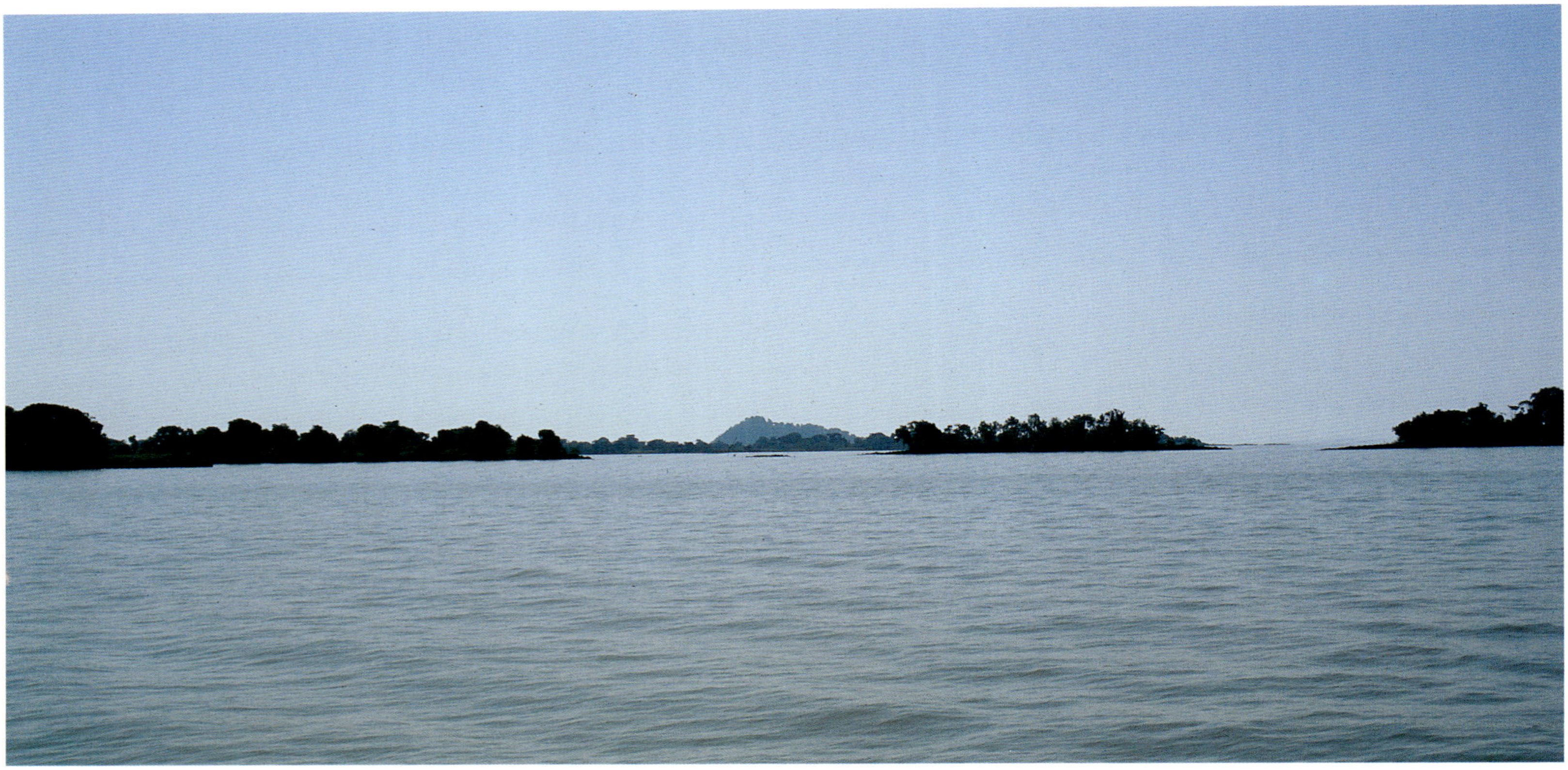

In order to prevent political conspiracies it was customary in Ethiopia to segregate anyone who, for different reasons and even legitimately, could claim any right to the highest positions: in such a way that they were almost reduced to the condition of exiles in their own cuntry. This seems to be the meaning of Ludolf's quotation: "omnes insulae lacus Tzanici, except Deka, monachorum sunt" (LUDOLF III, c. 3), since Dek not only did not belong to the monks, but "magnorum virorum exiliis famosa" (*ivi* I, c. 8), served as a deportation place (*ivi* II, c. 6). Whilst the above-mentioned certainly cannot be applied to the whole of the island, since the hypothetical non-existence of monasteries is contradicted by the presence of ancient religious buildings such as Kota Māryām, what Ludolf affirms fits in perfectly with the islet of Nārgā, which is a sort of annex of Dek.

The perimeter of the isle of Nārgā was therefore the first enclosure, for which the very water served as a screen. Two turrets watch over on it (with functions of entrance, defense, observation and signalling), which are inserted in such a way that they became an integral part of the walls jutting into the water: one, on the west side, served as a landing place, while the other, on the east side (fig. 109), was an opening onto the isthmus which links Nārgā with the bigger isle of Dek. The short pathway had already been organized for defending —flanked and protected by powerful dry walls— and ending at a round bridge-head attached to the first part of the major isle (fig. 107). There were therefore two accesses to the islet, one from the land and the other from the water, but within it, at the top of the hill another screen surrounded the sacred enclosure, interrupted by two similar and corresponding turrets, having once more the function of entrance, defense, observation and signalling post (fig. 108).

It is not uncommon to find a double circuit of walls surrounding the area at whose centre there is a church. Such is the case at the mainland church of Ura Kidāne Meḥrat on the peninsula of Ṣegē which juts into Lake Tana (fig. 96).

Finally, at the centre we find the church, at the heart of which there is the sacred *tābot*, encircled by the rings first of the *maqdas*, then the *qeddest*

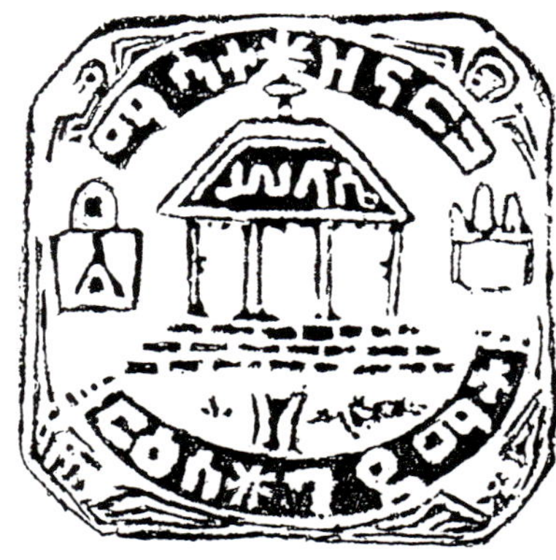

103. Small islets fringe the island of Dek.

104. Seal of the hermitage of Nārgā Śellāsē.

106. Dry walls run around the islet of Nārgā

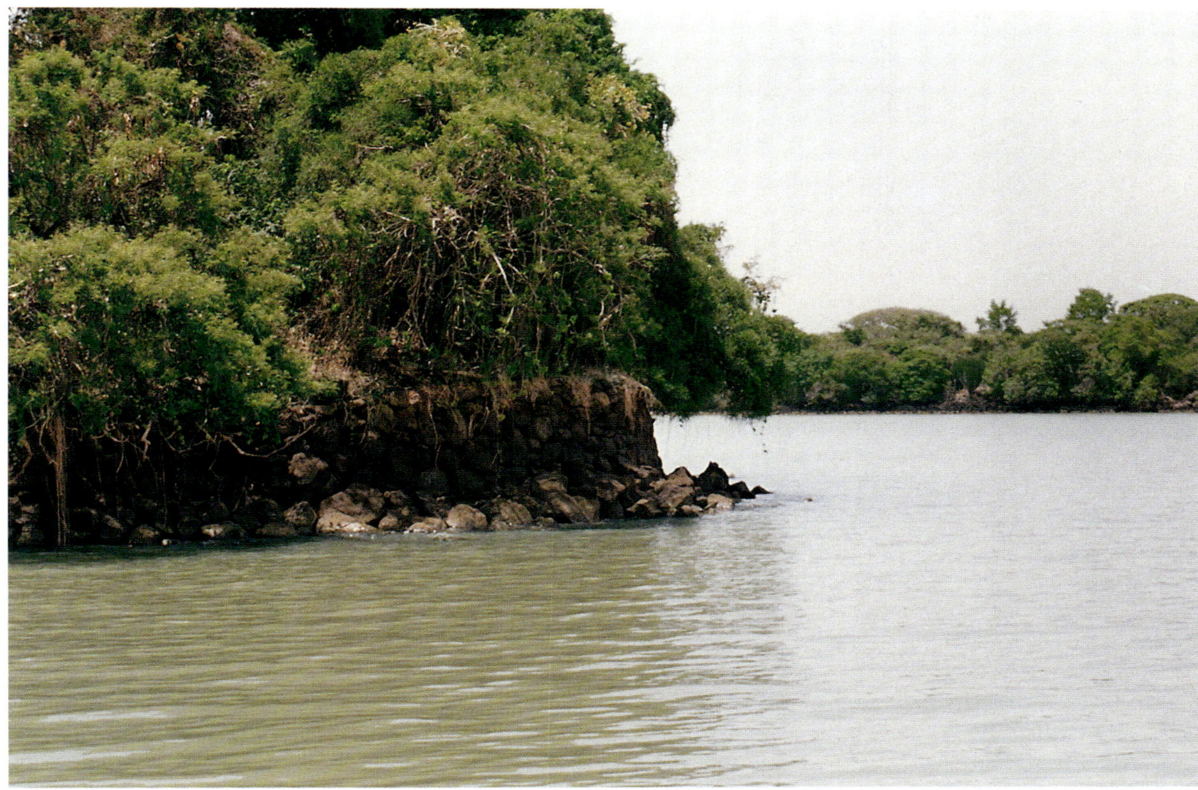

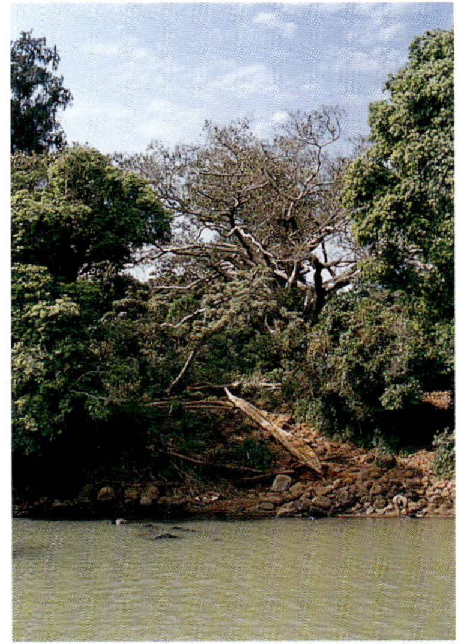

105. *Tānkwā*, papyrus boats typical of Lake Tana, moored under the leafy fronds of the trees hanging into the water.

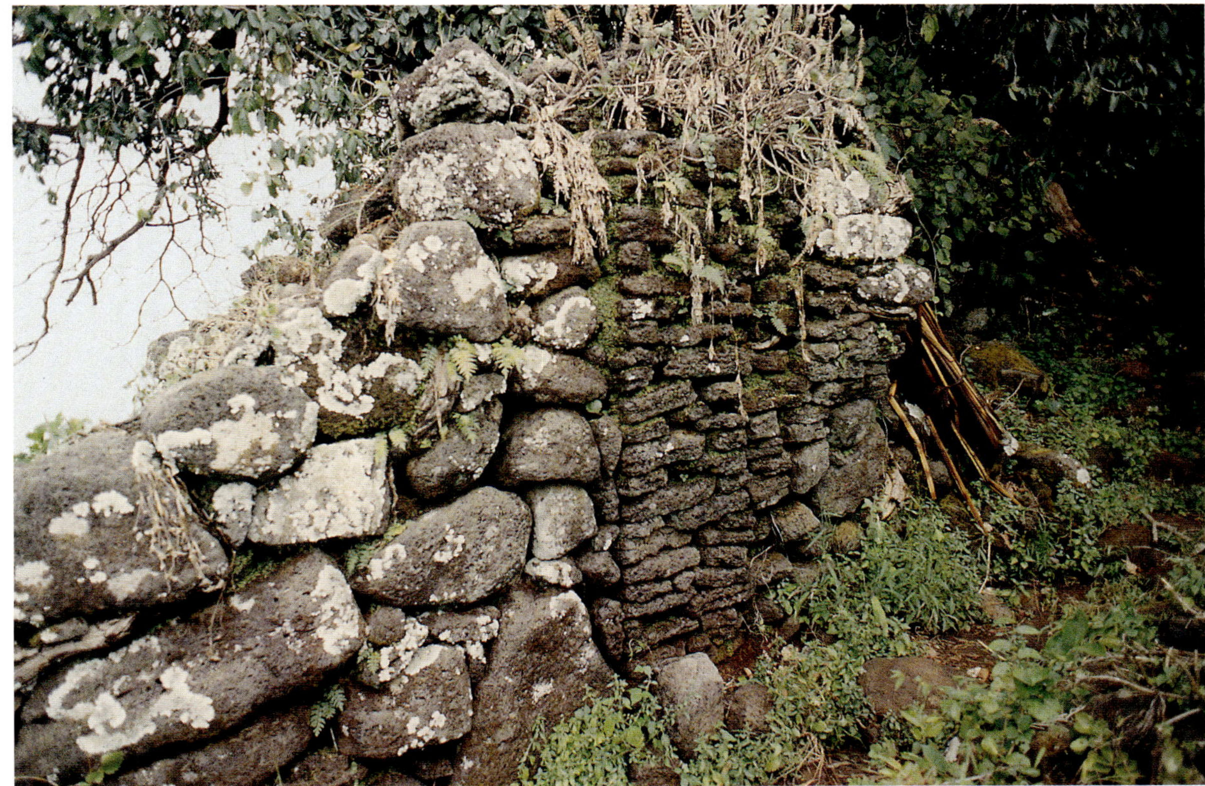

107. Structures defending the isthmus which connects the islet of Nārgā with the island of Dek.

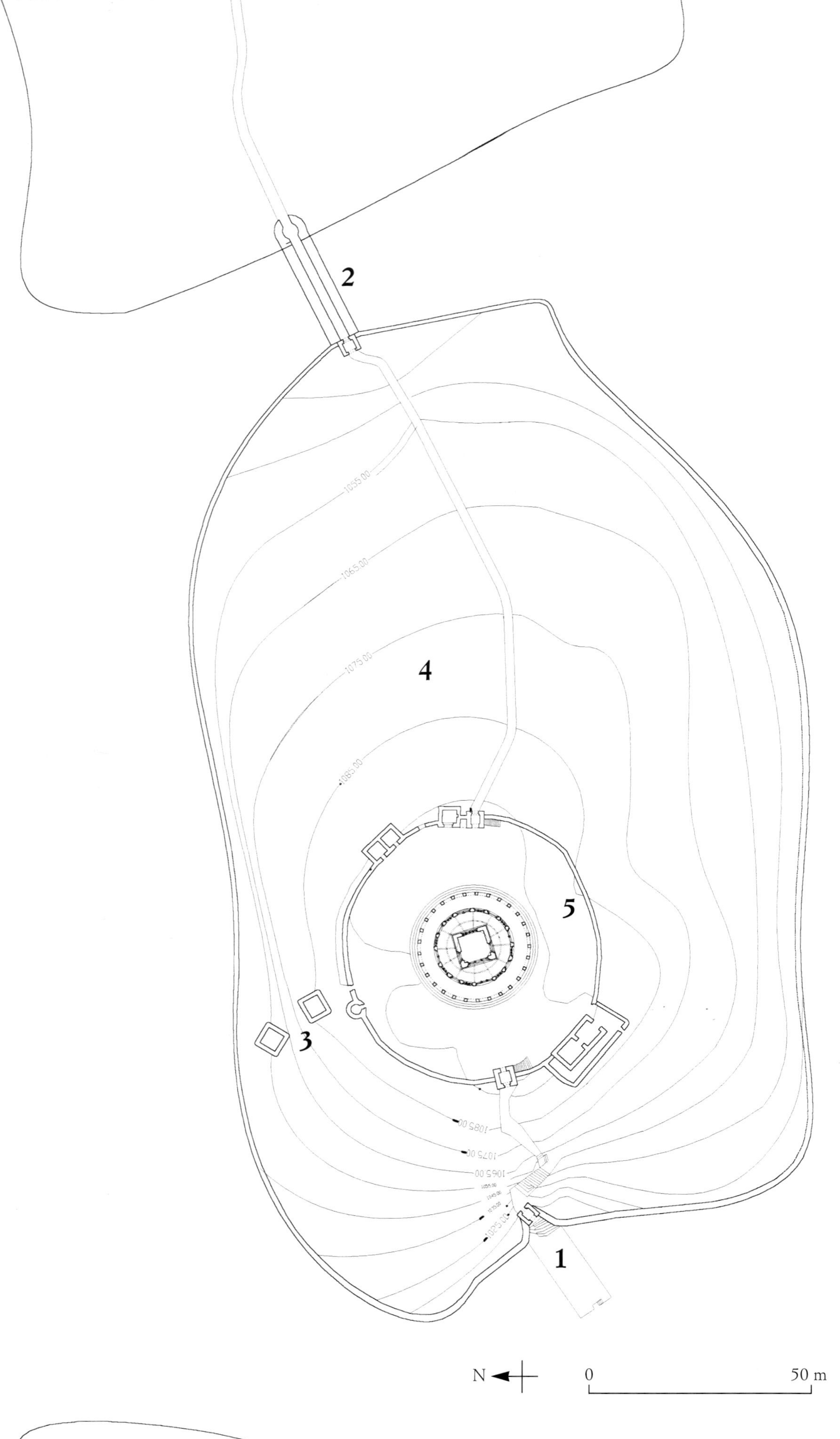

108. The islet of Nārgā.
1. Landing place
2. Isthmus connecting with the island of Dek
3. Ruins of dry walls
4. Monks' residences
5. The sacred enclosure
(from reliefs by Alberto Giussani and Giorgio Vassena)

109. The landing place on the islet of Nārgā is signalled from far away by a small tower built in pure Gondarian style.

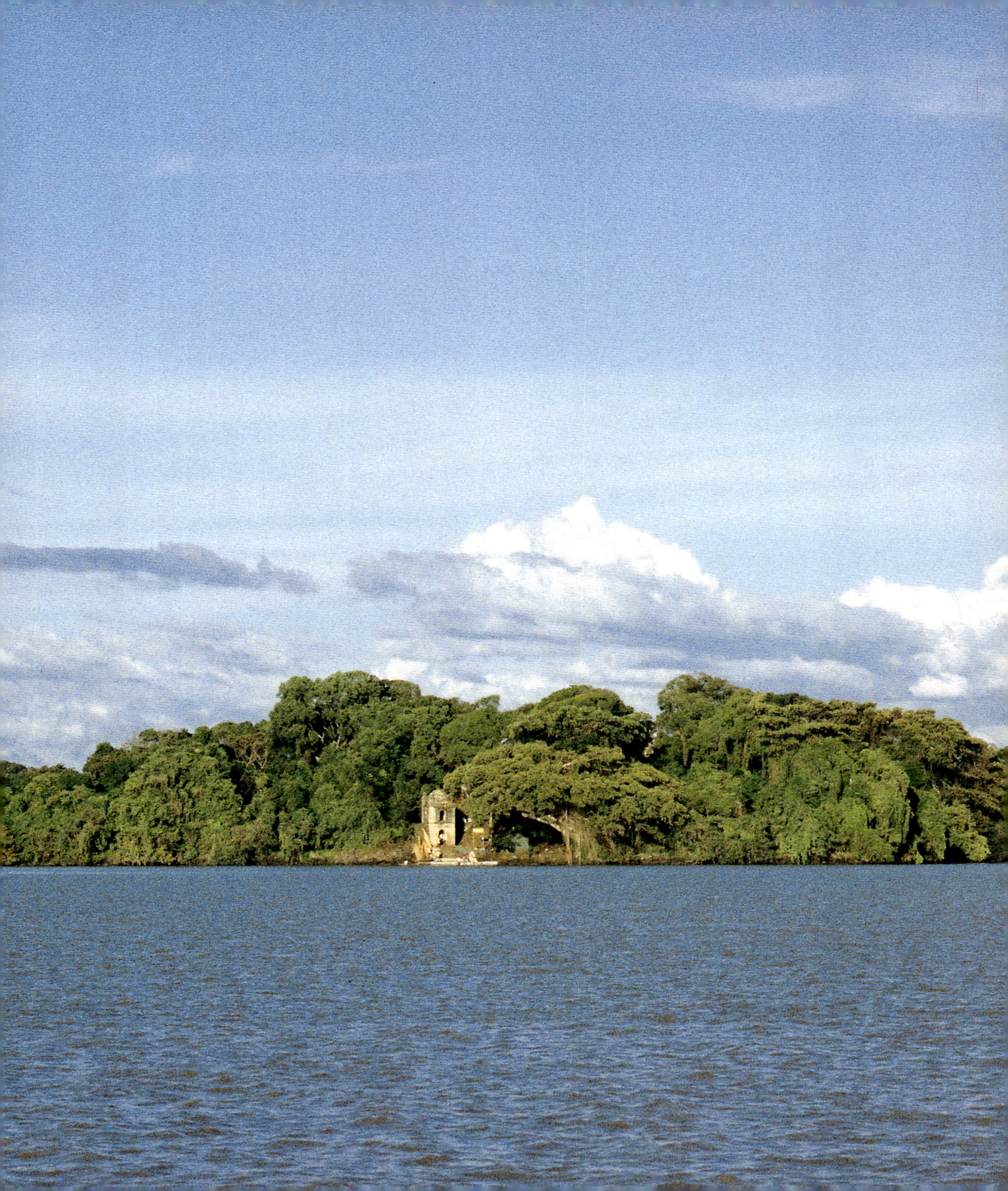

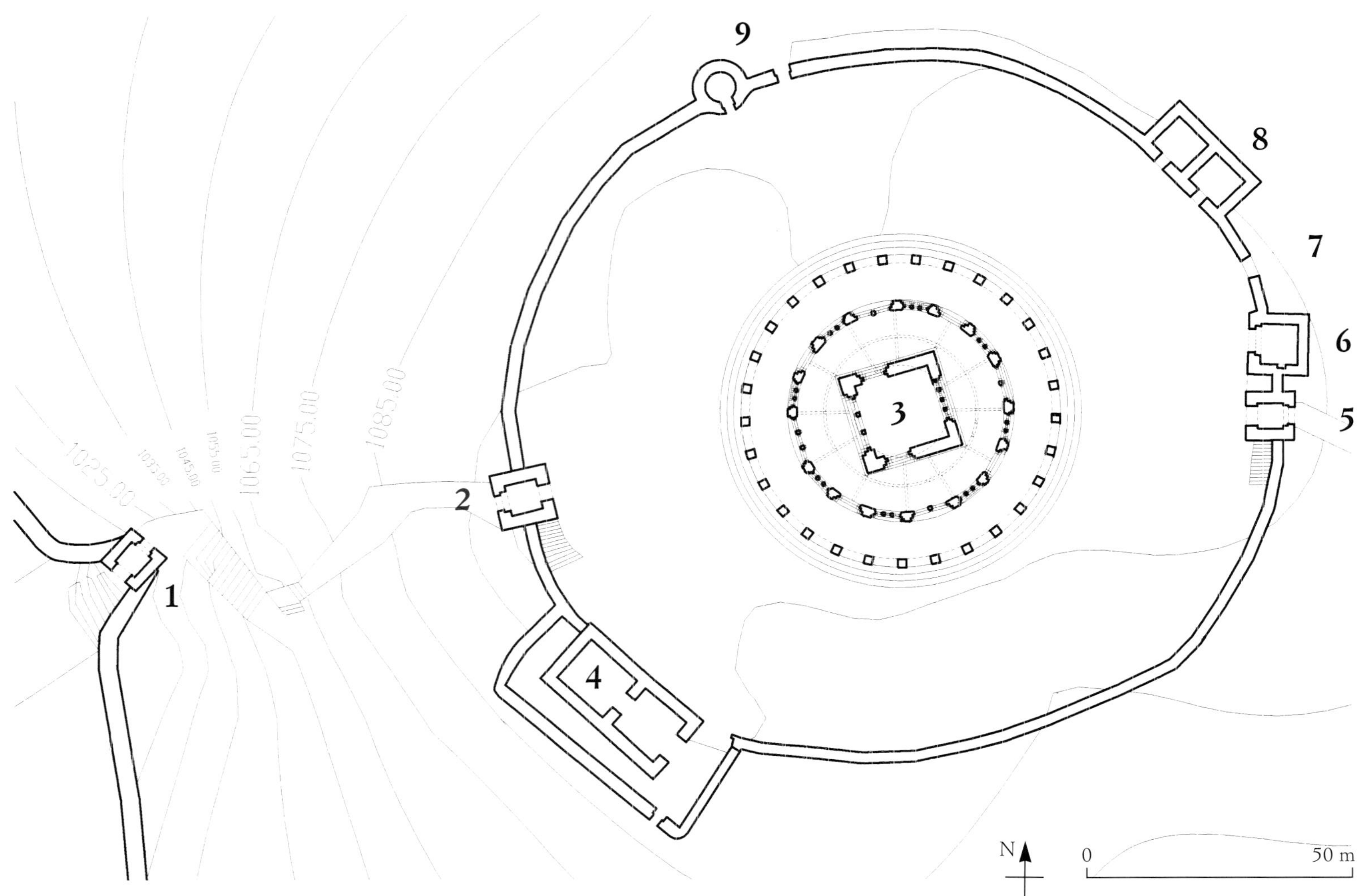

and the *qenē māḫlēt*, and finally by the perimeters of the sacred enclosure and of the second circuit of outside walls.

The theory of organisms requires that they are observed in their relationships: the *sancta sanctorum* must be considered in its space, within that which encloses it, as a sacred space which is part of a wide whole which, in turn, like any other organism, is a structure relating to an even wider space, to form a sort of geography of the sacred which spreads out on the territory and that, in Ethiopia, marks the landscape.

The sacred enclosure has always been the place of religious peace, of reflection; the outside space where one is made to feel the significance of the passing of time through its ambling perimeter, whose parts are never identical to each other, both for their positioning and their consequent luminosity, and because of the various buildings which are dotted along it.

It is an open space, a place of common joining, the point where more than elsewhere individuality is taken as the fundament of the whole community, a united plurality, multiform rather than dissimilar.

Moreover, as a place containing nature in itself, the sacred enclosure reproposes the Biblical theme of the garden: the garden of Eden, from which man from the beginning of his story has been cast out, but to which he always unconsciously aspires.

The Earthly Paradise, on the contrary, is a garden where God talks freely with Adam and Eve, in the brightness of the beginning, before sin created an abyss between man and his Creator: it is the sky on earth. Or, according to the 4th Book of Esdra (III, 6) it is the marvellous garden which was in heaven even before the world was created. Consequently, it has a round shape, and it is exactly like this that it is described according to the

110. Nārgā Śellāsē.
1. Small tower at the landing. 2. Small tower at the entrance to the sacred enclosure 3. The church 4. Queen Mentewwāb's residence, surrounded by a small circuit of walls directly connected both with the outside and with the inside of the sacred enclosure. 5. Small tower which leads to the isthmus connecting the islet with the island of Dek. 6. Room. 7. Cemetery. 8. *Bētaleḫēm*, where the bread and the wine for the Eucharist are prepared. 9. Small round tower flanked by an opening in the enclosure (from reliefs by Alberto Giussani and Giorgio Vassena).

111. Ruins of the small round tower inserted in the sacred enclosure.

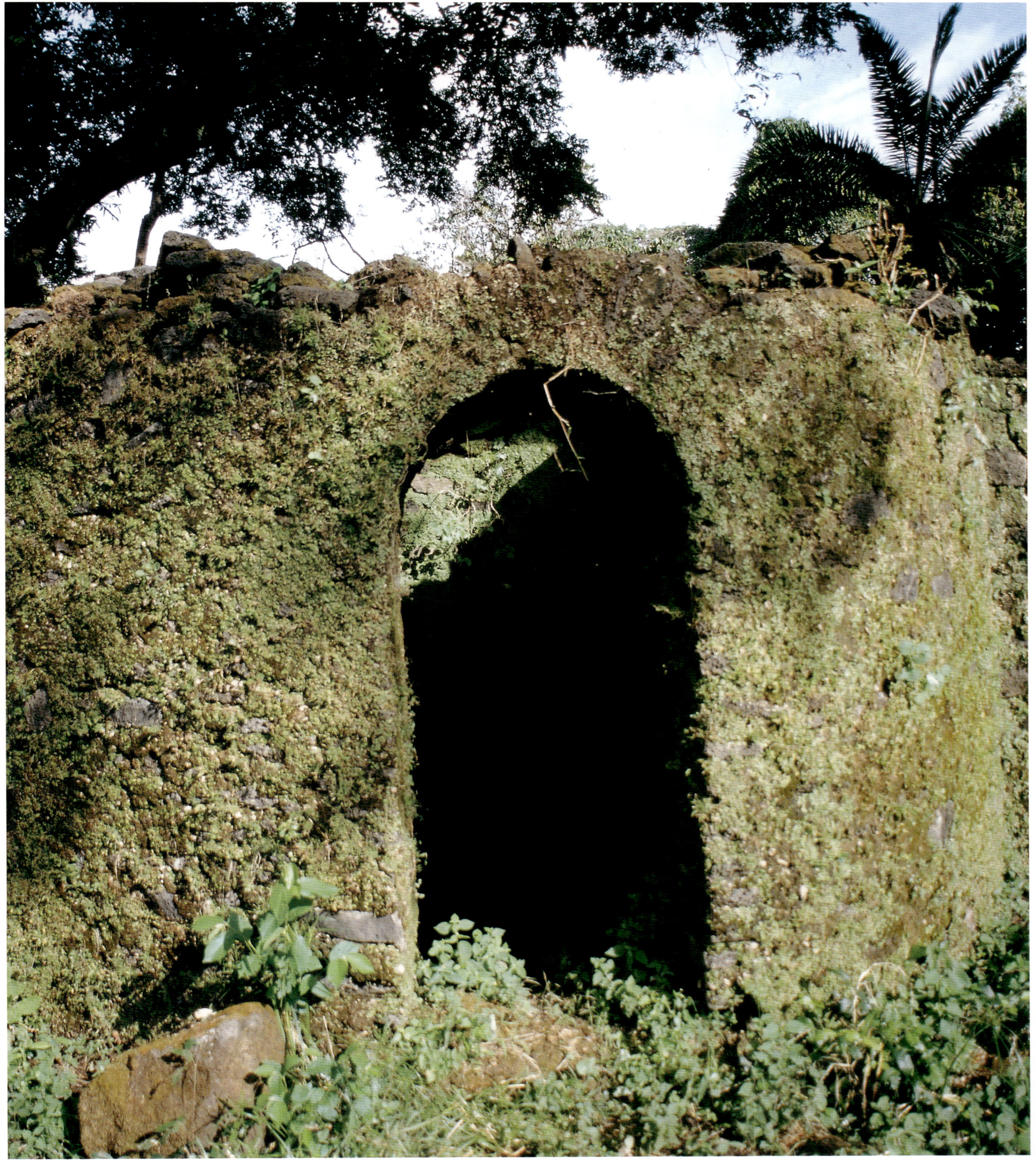

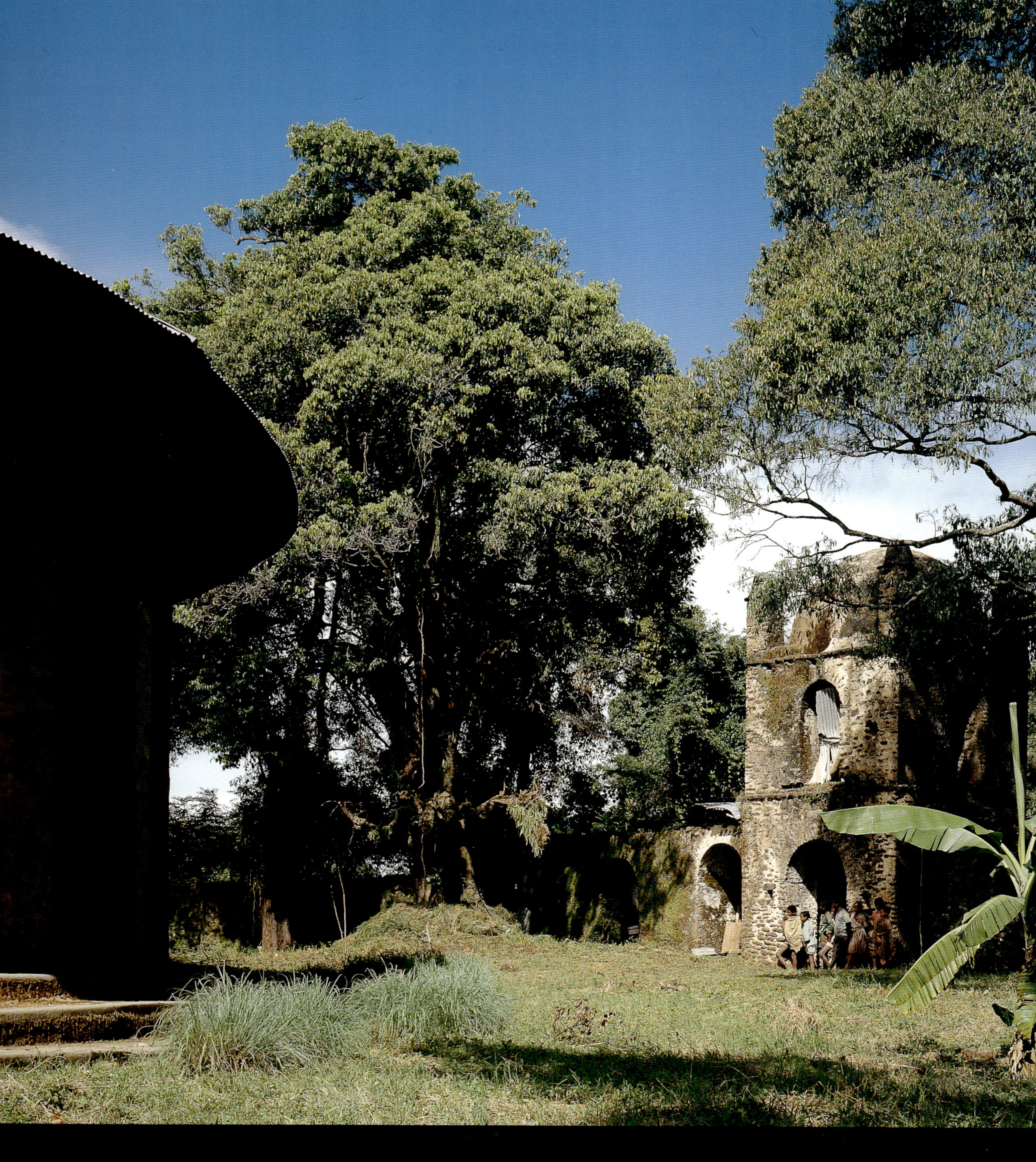

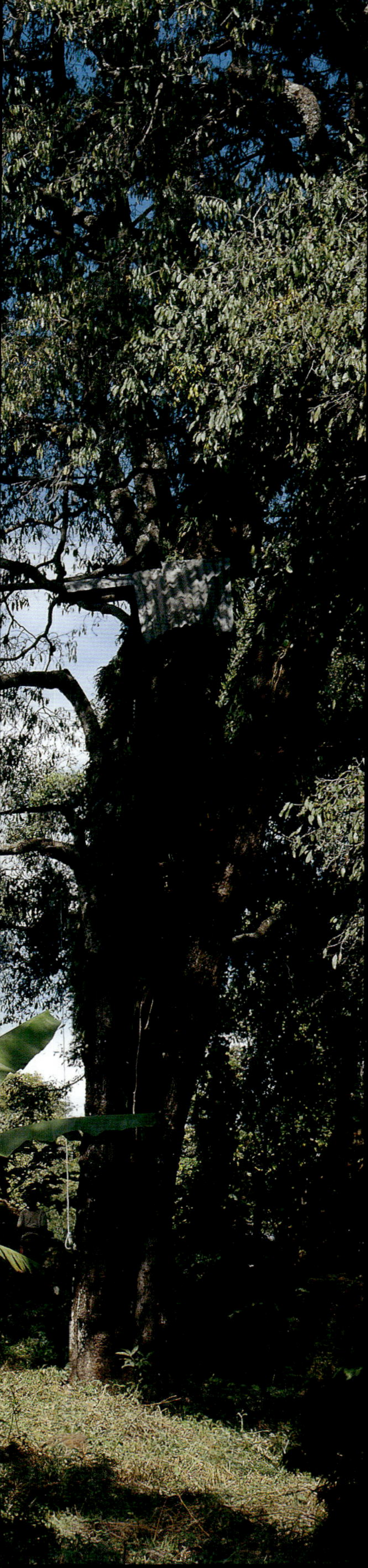

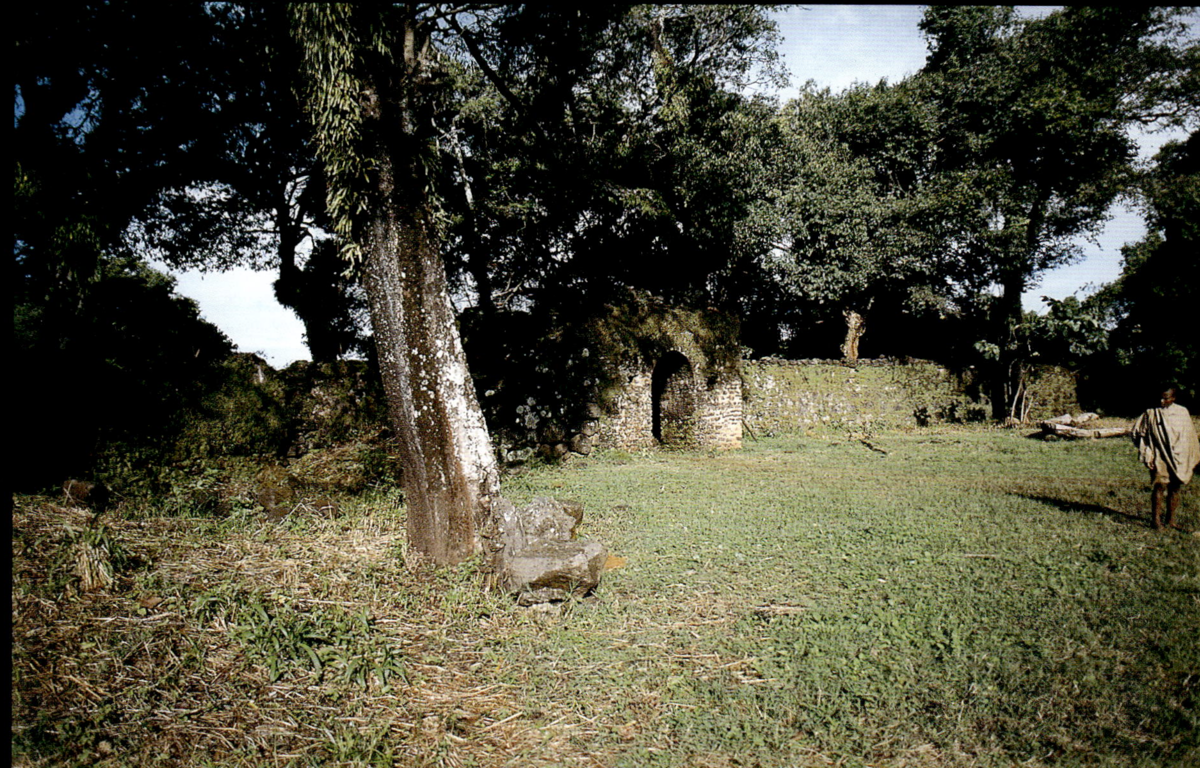

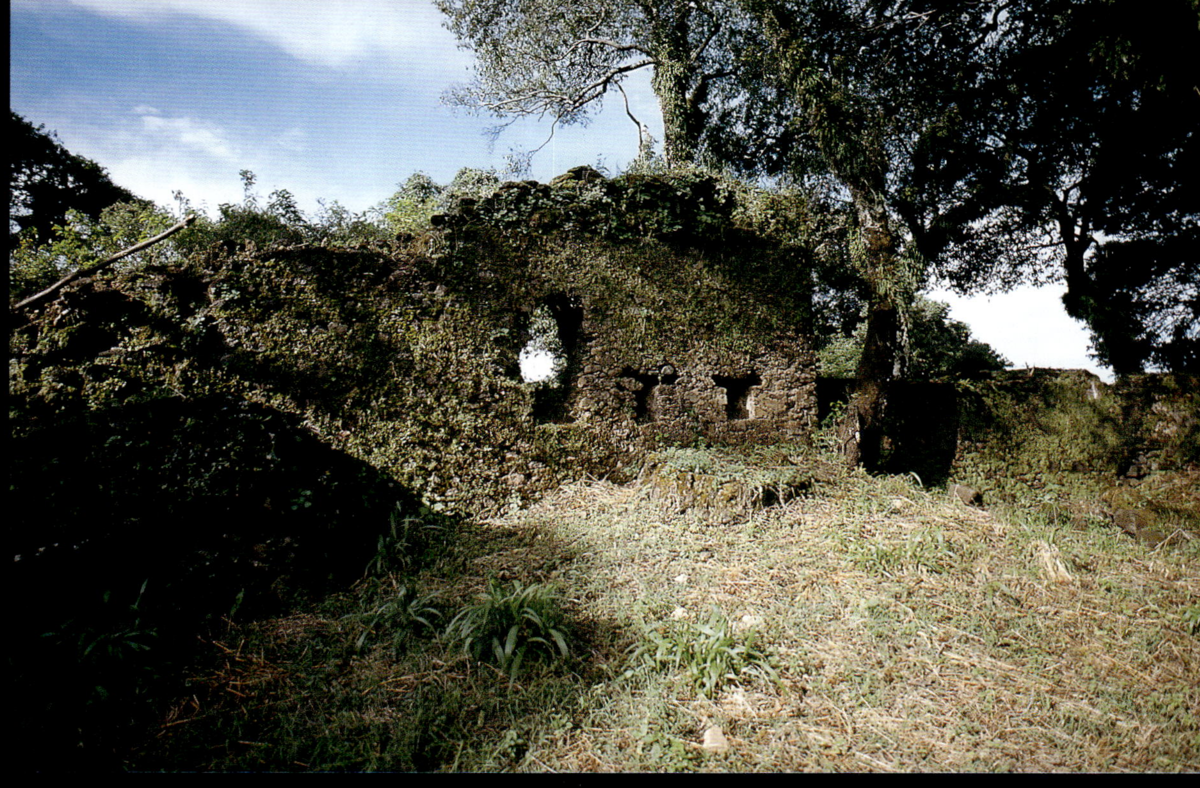

112. Interior of Nārgā Śellāsē's sacred enclosure.

113. Exterior of Nārgā Śellāsē's sacred enclosure.

114. Ruins of Queen Mentewwāb's 'magnificent house'.

most accepted tradition (DE CHAMPEAUX, p. 97, figs. 41, 42, 43).

The sacred enclosure, *hortus conclusus*, is closed to the external world: a place of this world, like the garden, but also a celestial, edenic one. The place where Queen Mentewwāb saw the earth but could also contemplate the sky, when she looked out of her 'magnificent house' (now completely destroyed) at Nārgā.

The house was encircled by a low wall with a direct access from the outside, but which also opened into the sacred enclosure. Only the basement survives, its walls perforated so that zebus' horns could be inserted at regular intervals and at the right hight for objects to hang from, according to the Abyssinian tradition (regardless of whether it was a storage-room or a treasure-room, the structure was the same). Inside the house, but also around it, there are the disordered relics left by the collapse of a massive structure in irregular hewn stones, bound with very strong mortar (figs. 113-114).

On the opposite part of the low wall, there is the *Bētaleḥēm*, the 'bread house', where the bread and the wine used in religious celebrations were prepared. On the right an opening leads to the cemetery with its numerous properly oriented tombs and, next to it, a space devoted—it is said—to the *memento* and to the spiritual retreat of each new *mamher* of the monastery. Then there is a small guardhouse and the small tower on the eastern side which leads, via a short path running beside the thicket where the houses of the monks are placed in small glades, to the isthmus.

On the north side, a small opening in the enclosure, beside the remains of a round turret—founded on a square perimeter which inclosed an underground cell (nowadays referred to as a prison)—leads to a rugged area on the lake-shore where there are the remains of two rooms quite roughly defined by dry-walls. The monks who live in Nārgā today are absolutely certain that these walls represent *quod superest* Mentewwāb's 'magnificent house', but it is impossible to trace in them any sign of previous magnificence.

In the *extra moenia* areas, outside the sacred enclosure, examinations of the ground could give precious and more precise information on the genesis of the area. In fact, a chronology of the architectural body can be given only for the church, in relation to the documented visit of Queen Mentewwāb, while at least three diachronical phases can be traced in the surviving structures. In fact, it is quite unlikely that the isle was colonized all in one operation, with the contemporary presence of craftsmen with different levels of dexterity who brought with them different styistical references, building typologies and technologies.

The powerfulness of the walls overlooking the lake and of the structure protecting the isthmus (which, anyway, do not hint at a priority in the building phase) is completely different to the building technique applied both to the towers and to the circuit of the sacred enclosure with its related buildings. These, in turn, differ from the particularly qualified and knowledgeable constructional awareness applied to the church, especially in the integration of the decorative apparatus.

Like other structures of the same type, whether contemporaneous, post-dating or pre-dating it, the sacred enclosure at Nārgā, with its buildings and its external turrets, corresponds to the typical canons of Gondar's architectural style, on a minor scale. These buildings have not yet been carefully examined, especially from the stylistical point of view, if we exclude the relevant study by Monti della Corte and other sporadic contributions.

The so-called Gondarian style reached its full maturity already in its first expressions, which date to the 16th century[1], and then spread throughout the following century and during the 18th century.

The walls, generally 'stone levelled' on the outside and plastered on the inside, are made of irregularly cut hewn stones, joined with mortar. They are arranged with a masterful insertion of horizontal wooden elements, such as trusses spreading the load and linking the walls and slabs intermediate to the construction. The wooden beams are made evident on the exterior by lines

[1] See the church of Qeddus Mikā'ēl at Māryām Gemb (fig. 77) and the castle of Guzārā (figs. 8 and 36).

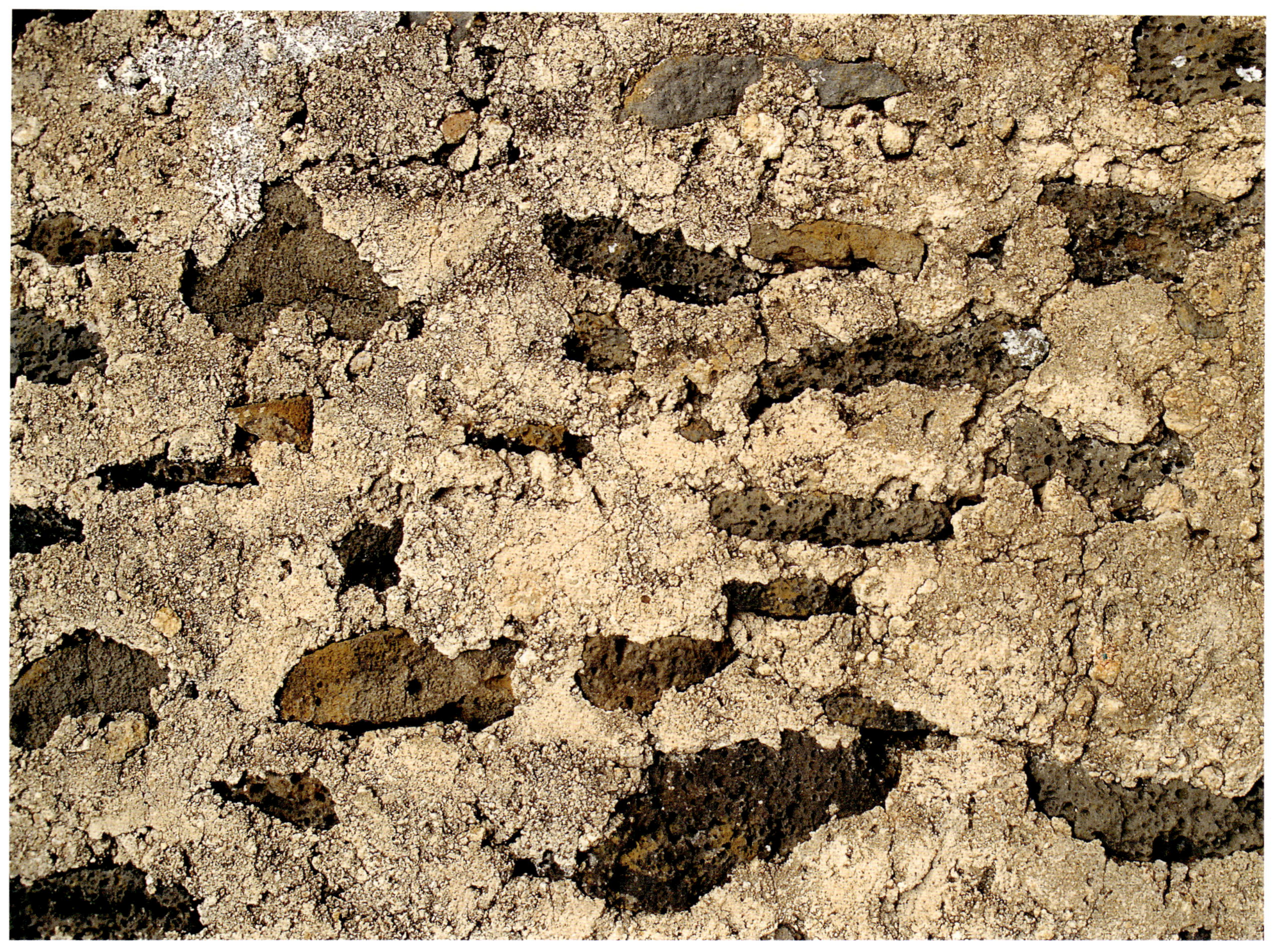

115. Smooth-stone wall typical of Gondarian architecture (detail of the small landing tower at Nārgā).

delineating the floors which were surely functional to the building sequence of the architectural body but also relevant to a proportionate definition of shapes. Also the projections supporting the balconies are made of wood, as well as all the flexional frameworks.

Often the buildings include angular turrets, but also square and round ones, covered with a cupola, and inserted within the perimeter of the outside walls of the churches. The coverings have barrel vaults and the halls present arched ribs, while the openings are finished with round-headed arches. Since the 16th century, in the most precious buildings, bands in shaped stone, mainly on a double line and with quite innovative mouldings in comparison to the classical ones, delineate the arches, working almost as capitals.

At Nārgā the typical turrets which mark the entrances on both the external and internal circuit of walls are square planned, well built in hewn stones bound together with very strong mortar and on the corners they take a more squared shape. Their dimensions are made obvious on the outside by cornices which mark the floors, at the level of the first floor and at that of the springer of the cupola above, with four angular pinnacles at the sides. At the junction between the circle of the springer of the cupola and the square of the base wooden trusses, either straight or appropriately curved, are arranged diagonally. Traces of

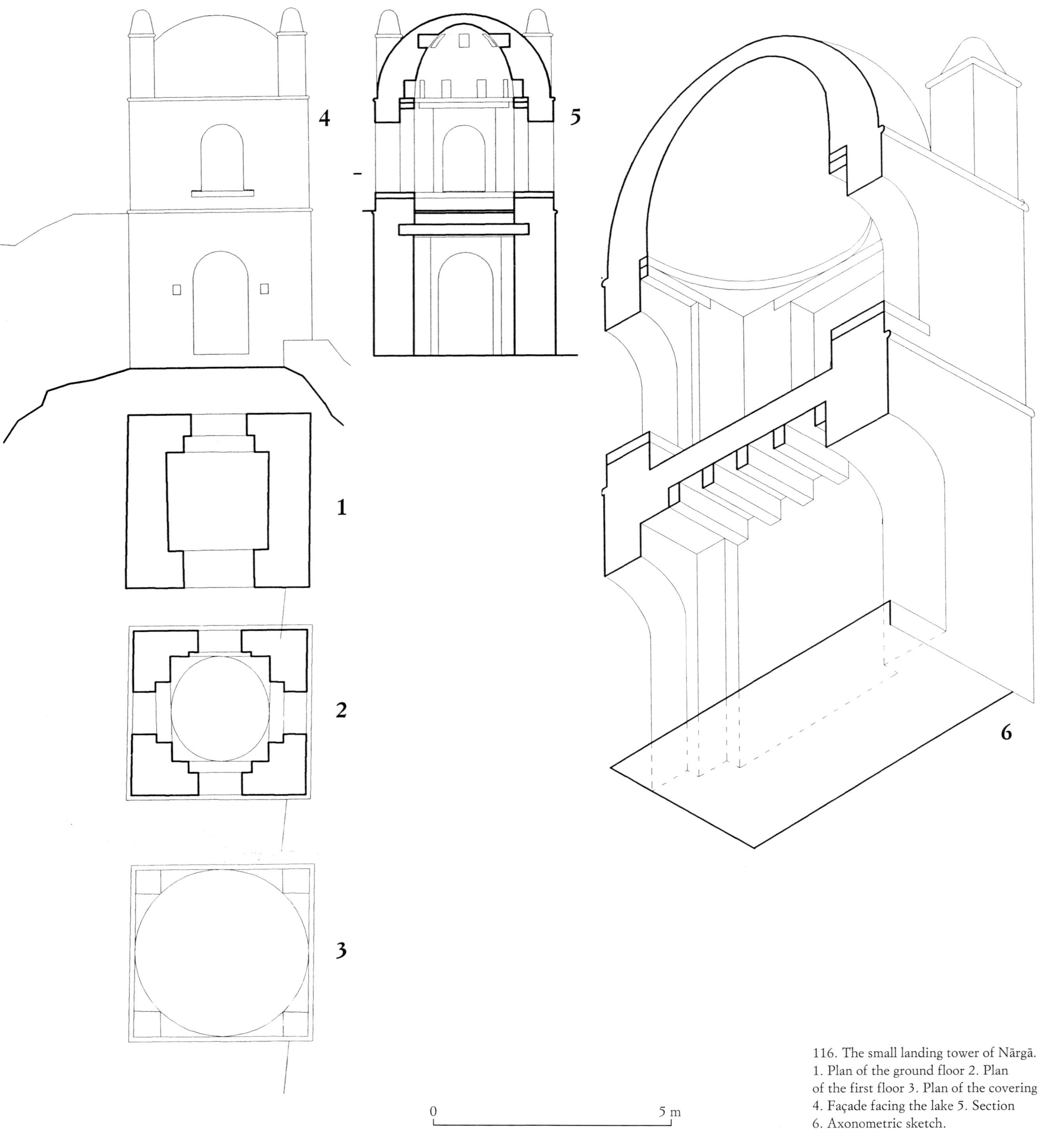

116. The small landing tower of Nārgā.
1. Plan of the ground floor 2. Plan of the first floor 3. Plan of the covering 4. Façade facing the lake 5. Section 6. Axonometric sketch.

117. The small landing tower of Nārgā. The concrete flight of steps is the result of the recent buiding of a pier.

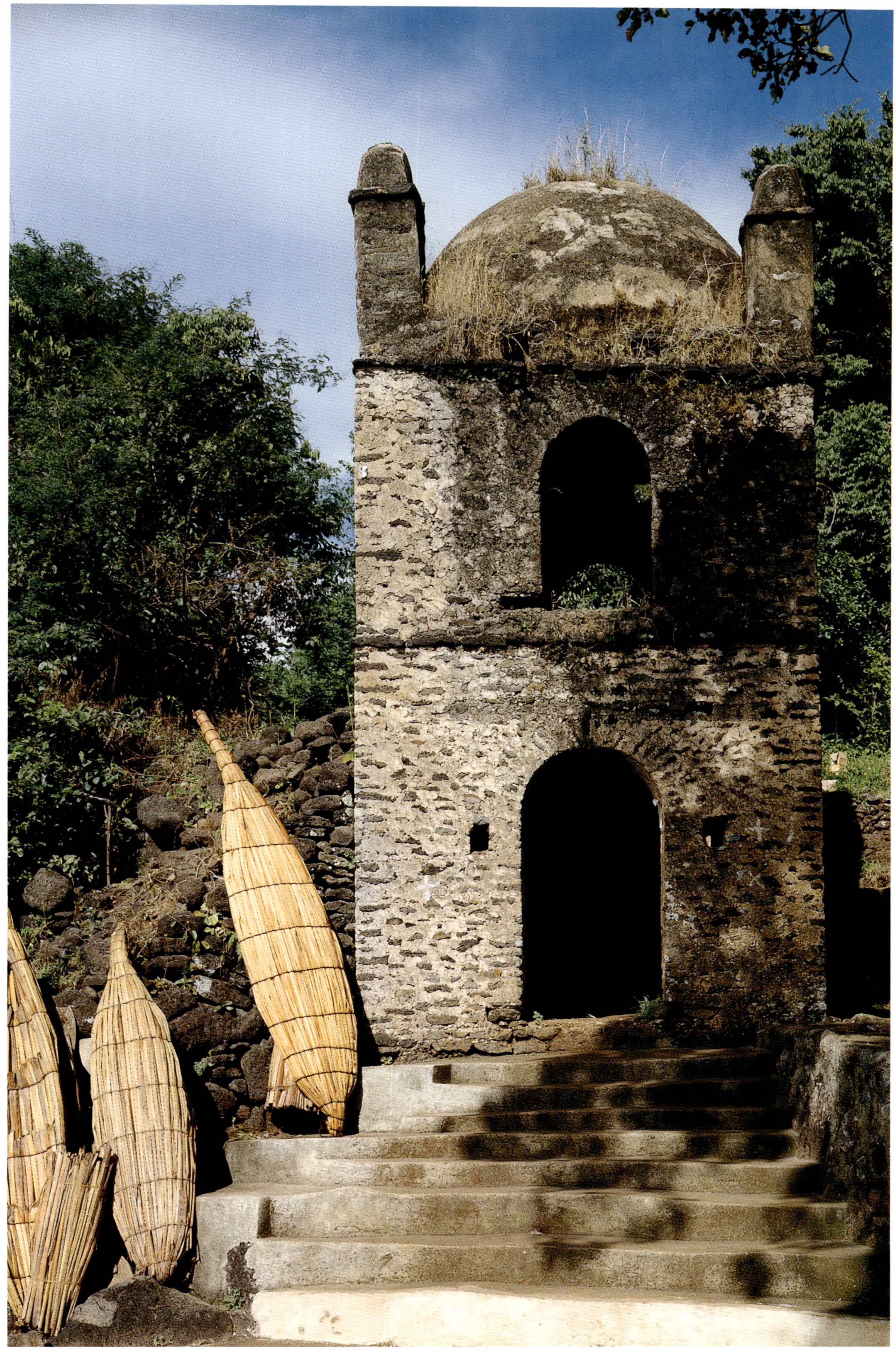

118. Interior of the external small tower guarding the isthumus connecting the islet with the island Dek.

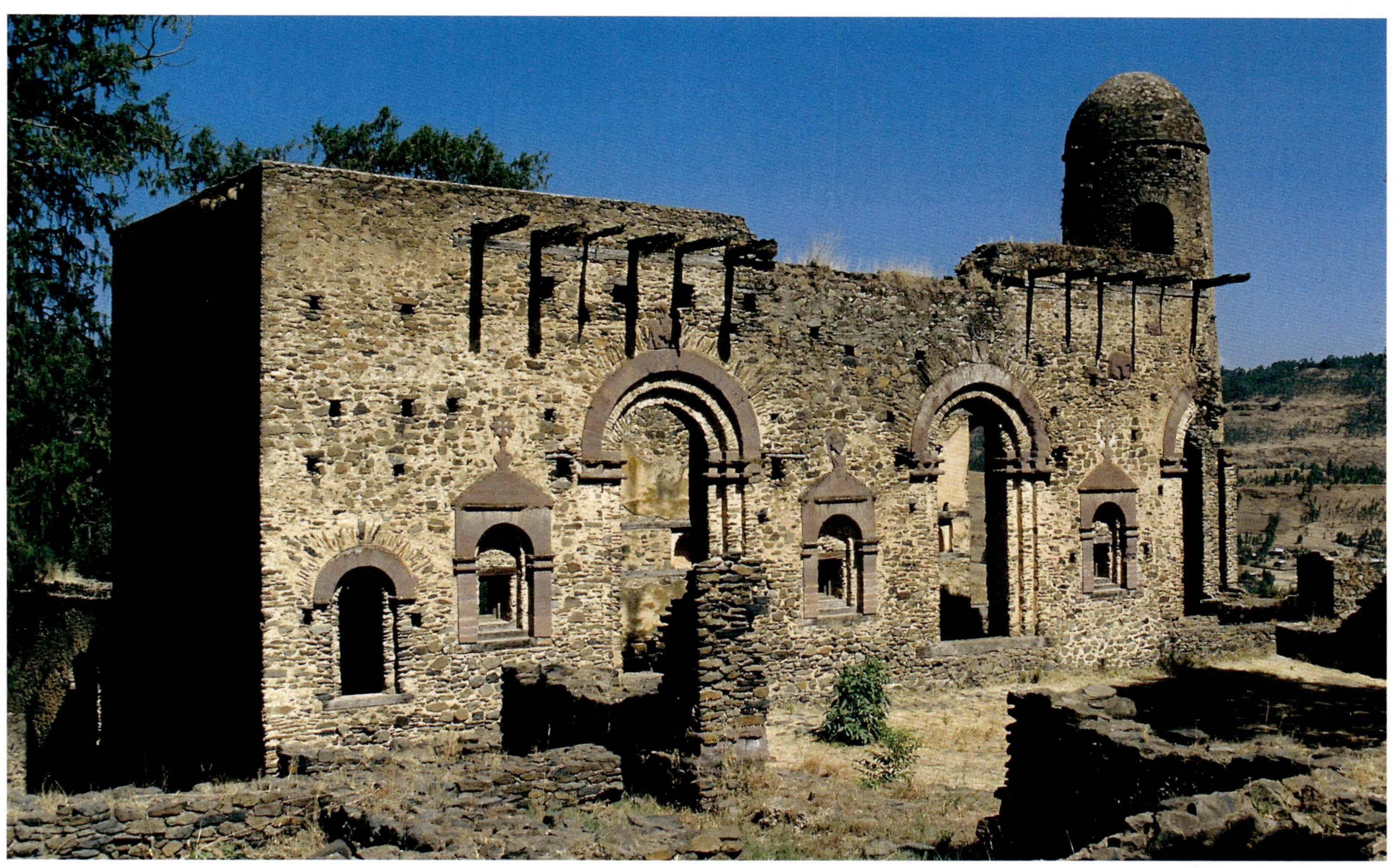

119. Queen Mentewwāb's Palace at Qusqwām near Gondar.

the use of centerings are obvious in the holes still remaining inside the cupolas, but also in the round-headed arched openings, whose hewn stones are typically sunburst arranged. On the ground floor of each turret there are two doors, one on the outside and one on the inside, on whose jambs can be seen complex articulations in the cross-section of the walls (they serve as the seat for closing-bars and peep-holes), obviously functional to an accurate system for guarding the entrances. The first floor was normally reached via staircases, joined to the inside of the circuit of walls and sometimes interrupted by provisional wooden steps which, if removed, could make climbing difficult. The first floor has openings on all sides and the smoke-stains on the intrados of the cupola could refer to a habit of lighting fires inside it, as a pure comfort to the sentinels, but perhaps also for signalling (figs. 116-117-118).

The architecture of the entrance turrets in the double compass of walls at Nārgā Śellāsē is unique amongst the monasteries around Lake Tana and confirms its reference to the noble city of Gondar. The little abbot's house which stands along the circuit of walls of the monastery of Dabra Ṣaḥāy at Qusqwām (MONTI DELLA CORTE, tab. XXVII), near Mentewwāb's residence, is very similar. However, other ascendancies can be mentioned, such as architectural styles typical of the Middle-East.

Also taking into account other characteristics, the Gondar style—so called because in the imperial capital, Gondar, we find the most massive examples of this style—testifies to a building and decorative wealth, perhaps similar to some other cultures, but certainly freely interpreted with original results. It is natural that the problem of the genesis of a style remains obscure whenever it appears *ex abrupto*, as a phenomenon of which the formative process is unknown. In Ethiopia

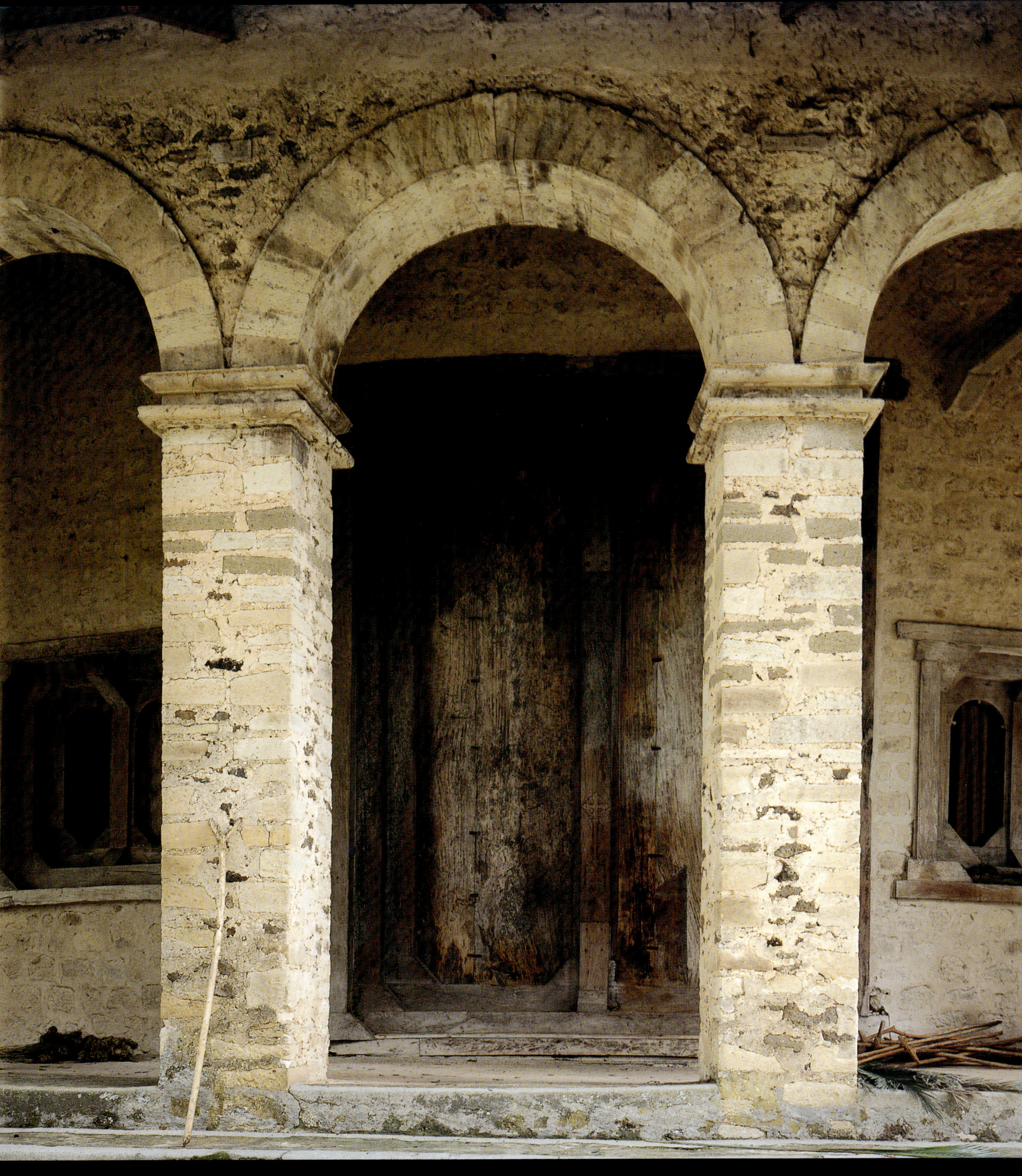

120. One of the bays of the outside portico of Nārgā Śellāsē.

121-123. Lozenge-shaped tile inside the *qenē māḥlēt*, the portico, of Nārgā Śellāsē.

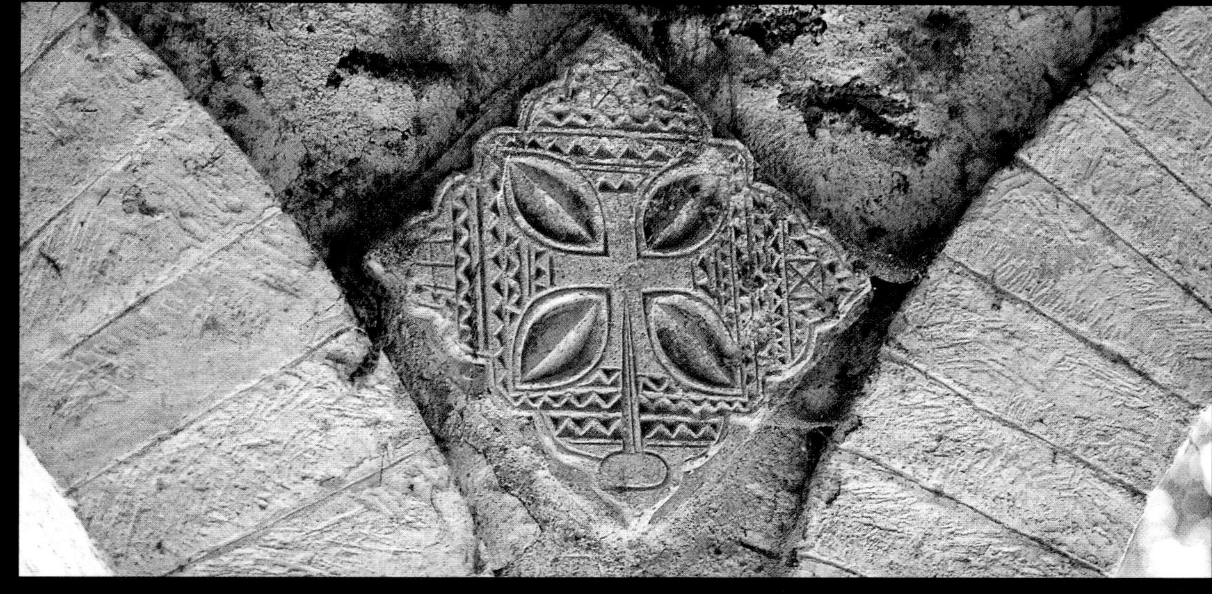

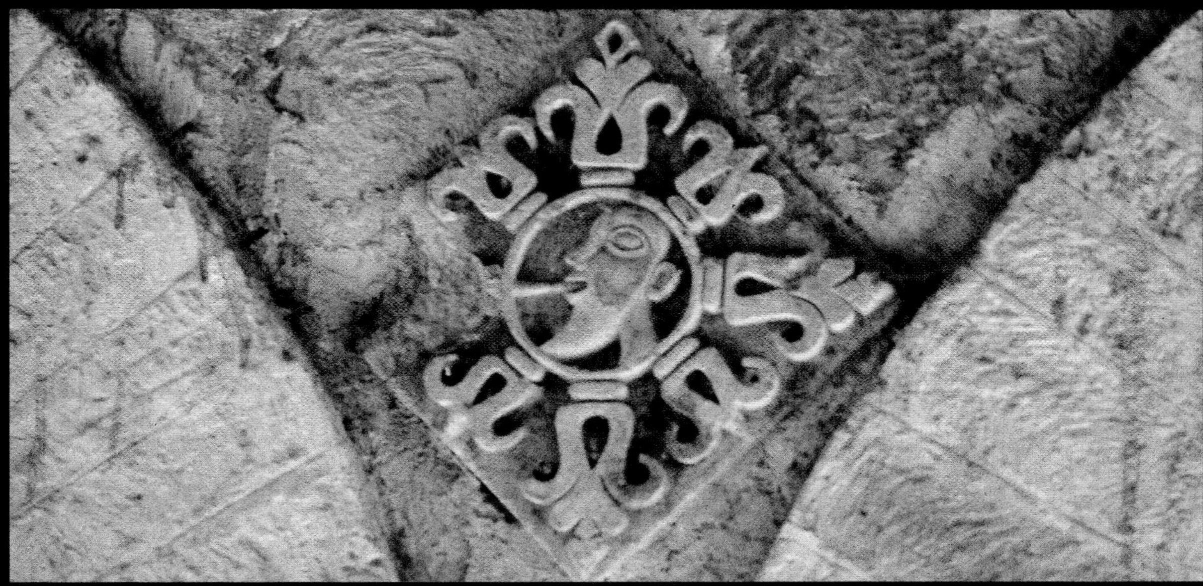

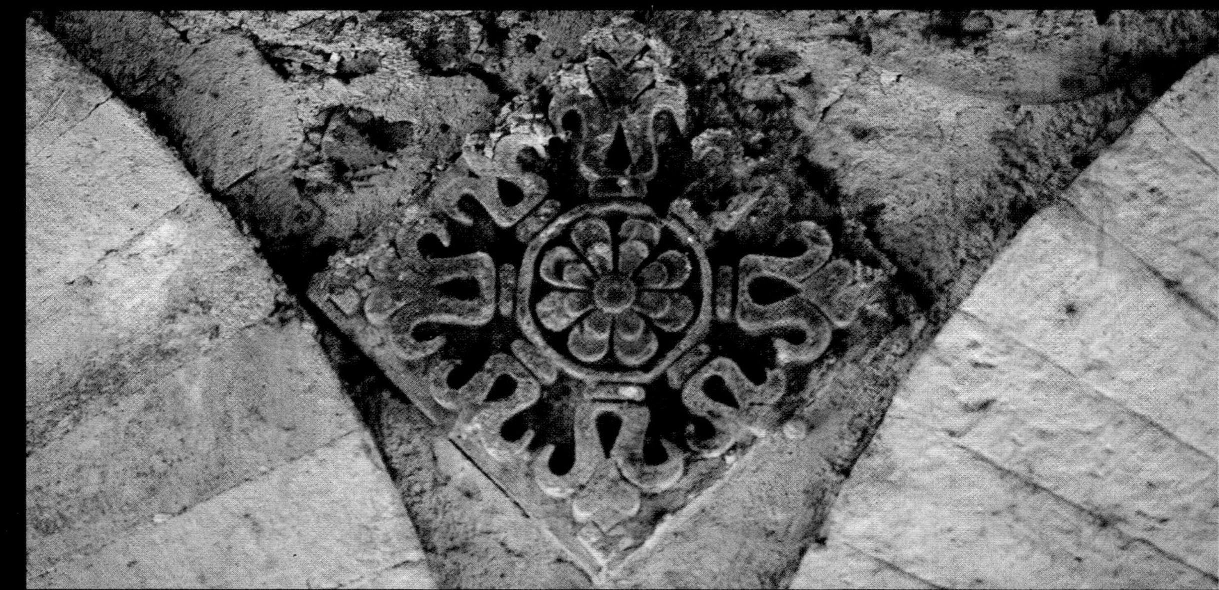

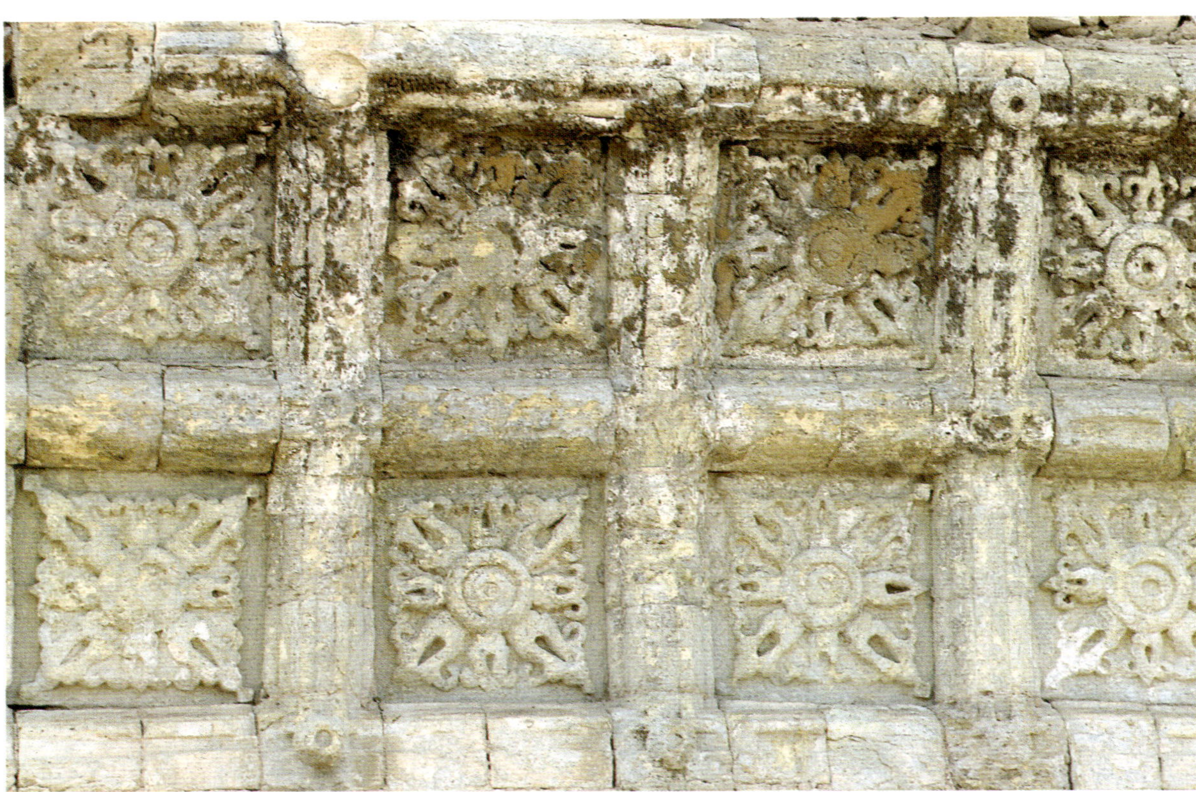

124. Decorations of the lacunars of the complex of Māryām Gemb (17th century).

125. The church of Nārgā Śellāsē.

we see the sudden appearance of a product, an already assessed style, endowed with its own peculiarities. It is therefore understandable that hypotheses of external contributions—generally and traditionally qualified as Portuguese—have been formulated. Accordingly, the foreigners would have brought a building technique and a typology with which they had obviously experimented extensively elsewhere. However, neither a stylistical nor a decorative reference to Portuguese architecture can be found, apart from a generical search for a certain chromatism which can sometimes be seen in the contrast between the stone bands contouring the openings and the wall from which they protrude. In fact, in some buildings of Gondar style, the purplish colour of the stone on the back wall accentuates a chromatism which also involves the jambs and the arches around the perfectly made openings in hewn stone which combine to form a sunburst decoration. The reference to Portuguese craftsmen could therefore be misleading, even though undoubtedly there must have been some form of external contribution, which is attested by the continuous and specific requests made in this regard to various European courts by the *neguś* in power. Still, it is a contribution which to date cannot be precisely identified, but rather just vaguely ascribed.

At Nārgā, even in the church, no reference to this type of chromatism appears along the walls or between the moulding of the capitals and the perfectly engraved arches which Queen Mentewwāb commissioned: all the ribs are made of the same type of stone. Yet, during the 18th century and precisely in the Queen's palaces of Gondar and Qusqwām (MONTI DELLA CORTE, pp. 35-37; 49-54) the pictorial character of the façades was accentuated by the application of prominent cornices in purple stone to doors and windows, which sometimes had a pseudo-tympanum shape and were crowned with cruciform motifs. Here and there, inserted in the walls, there are even purely decorative tiles in different colours, with a naturalistic theme, with a face and animals roughly sculpted in the stone (it would be better to say 'engraved', considering the quality of the sculpture).

Only inside the portico of the church of Nārgā Śellāsē arranged in a lozenge shape between the springers of the arches, three very well-made tiles were inserted (figs. 121-122-123). With the typi-

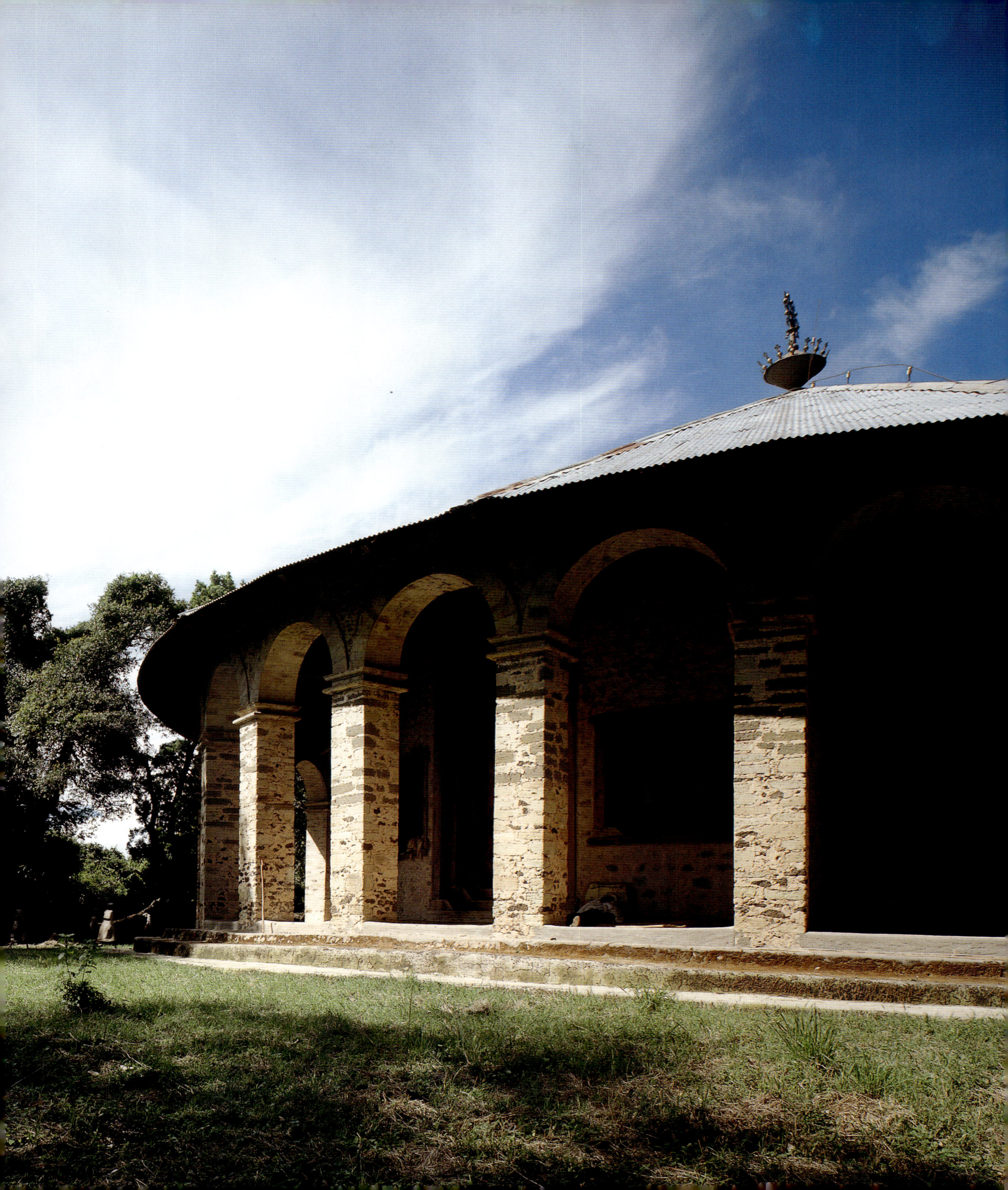

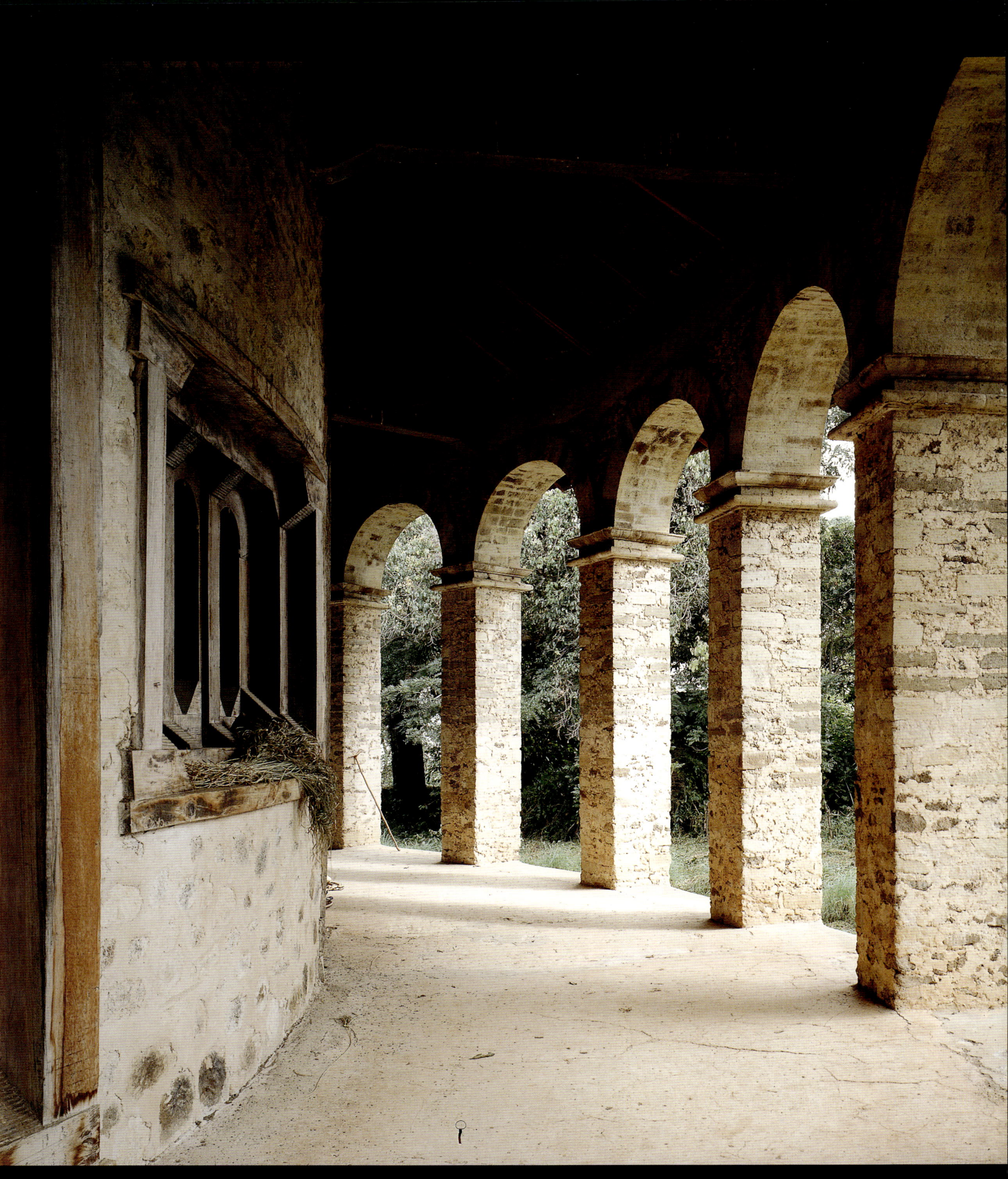

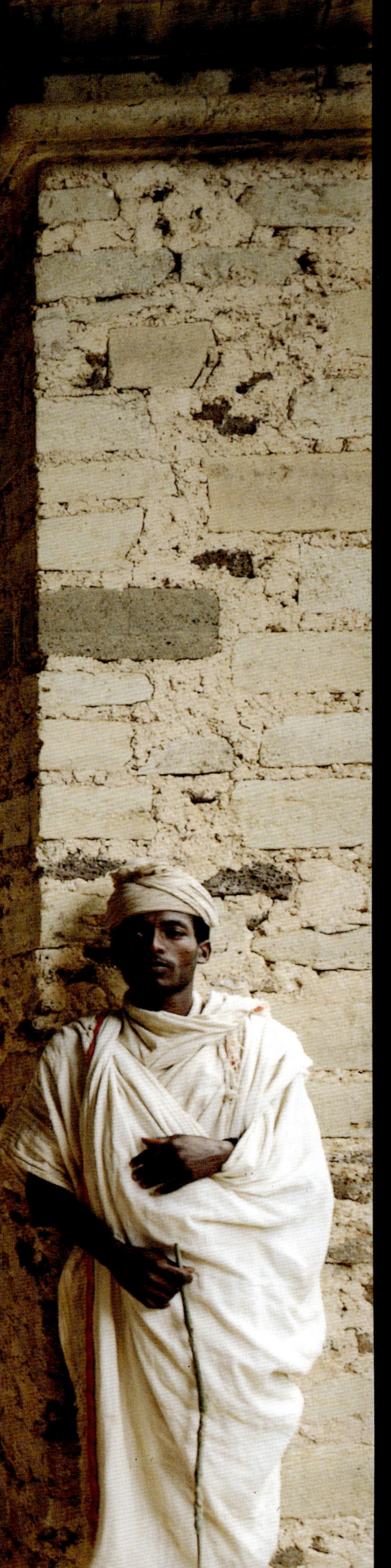

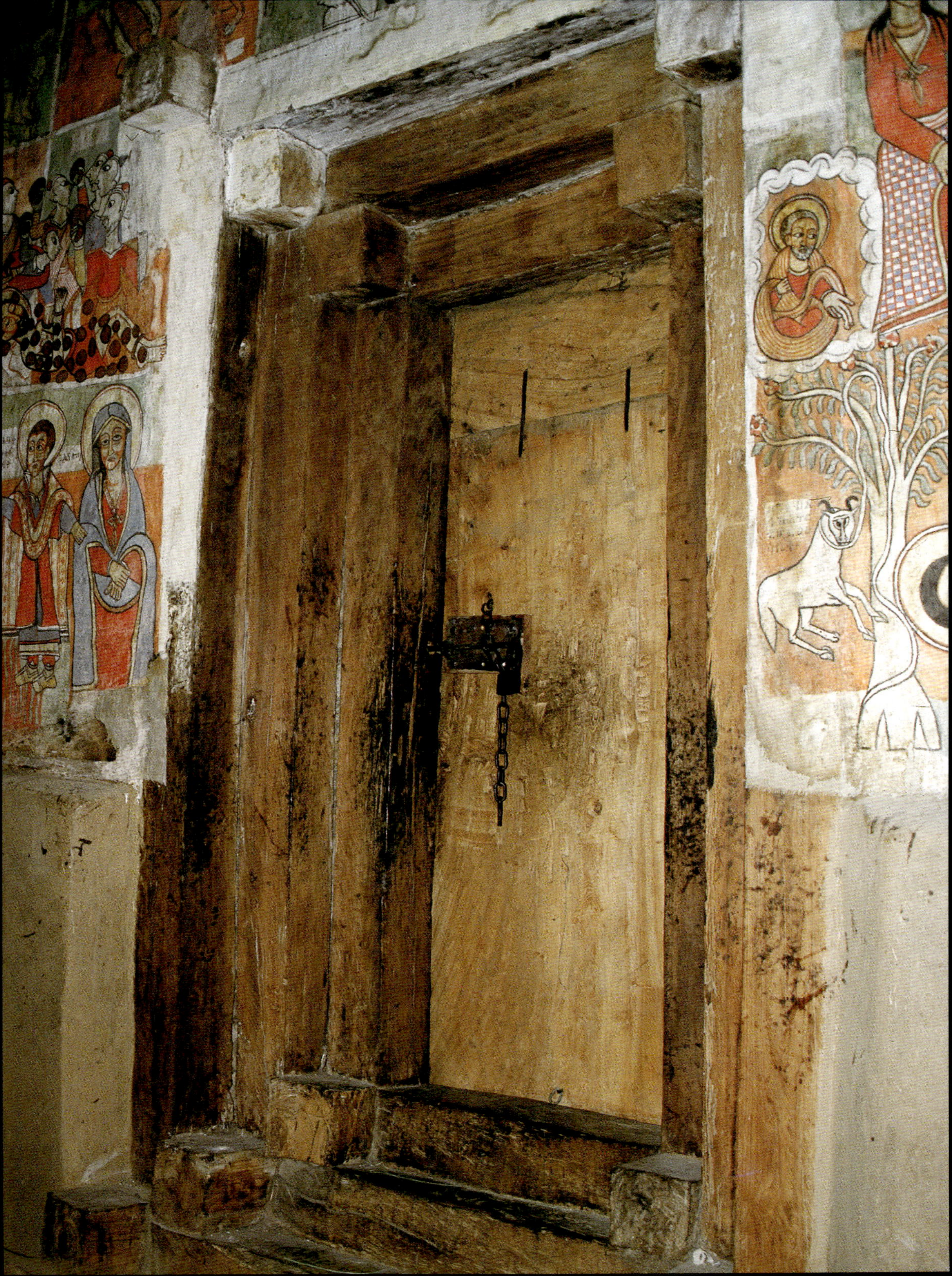

126. The *qenē māḫlēt*, the external portico destined for the cantors, of the church of Nārgā Śellāsē.

127. Side door of the *maqdas* of Dabra Sinā (first half of the 17th century)

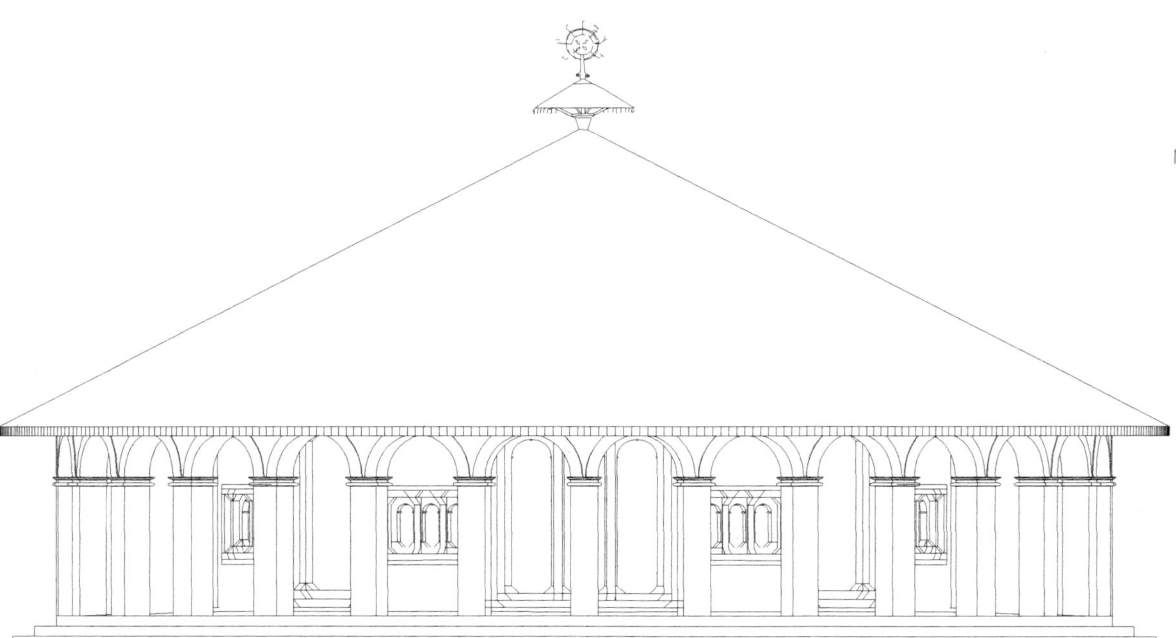

128. Western façade of the church of Nārgā Śellāsē (from reliefs by Alberto Giussani and Giorgio Vassena).

cal almost flat relief, they represent cruciform motifs, both geometrical (to recall the engraving technique of the traditional portable wooden crosses) and naturalistic (with stylized vegetable shapes). One of them even presents in the middle the bizarre profile of a bearded character which, with a sort of cigar in his mouth, seems to be smoking. Neither the technical nor the stylistical ascendancy of two out of these three tiles can in any way be ascribed to the decorative apparatus of Māryām Gemb (ANNEQUIN 1975, pp. 94-95), the great Jesuit complex on the peninsula of Gorgorā[2] which dates to more than one century earlier and where the Manueline Portuguese style was extensively employed.

The fact that at Nārgā, not even in the church, do we see in the treatment of the wall surfaces the pictorial sensitivity which instead seems to have spread, and almost to prevail, in the other buildings of Mentewwāb in Gondar, which date to the same period, cannot be ascribed to contingency (such as the type of material which could be found *in loco*), but rather to an excplicit and intentional choice by craftsmen endowed with a specific ability. On the same Lake Tana in fact there are also ancient churches, such as Kebrān Gabre'ēl, which dates to the 17th century, which show evident traces of the typical Gondarian chromatism.

Due to the scarcity of documentation and to the lack of its analysis, it is not anyway easy to define the stylistical references of spurious works in monuments which in many cases are the result of a sum of successive phases of interventions, such as integrations and rearrangements. As is natural, above all with religious architecture, some aspects establish themselves in a conservative way, the shape of the architectural body and the traditional solutions adopted become the very symbol and the image itself of the values of the Sacred. An example is given by the church of Qeddus Mikā'ēl at Barié Ghemb (ANNEQUIN 1965, pp. 17-22; MONTI DELLA CORTE, pp. 105-107), which represents a Gondarian version of the typology of centrally planned round churches. The fact that this church is an interpretation of an already established typology with different modalities and to fulfill other exigencies is attested by the clear architectural distorsions which can be seen in Qeddus Mikā'ēl, such as the use of the circuit of pilasters inside the *qeddest*, quite functional in the traditional structures with a conic roof, but almost gratuitous in a building with a vaulted covering as in this case (fig. 77).

As far as the treatment of the openings is concerned, different traditions met to create a typological evolution which produced quite innovative and original results. In Gondarian architec-

[2] Unluckily, its ruins in the last decades have deteriorated to the state of mere shapeless masses of worked hewn stones, while up to the thirties massive vaulted structures still faced the lake.

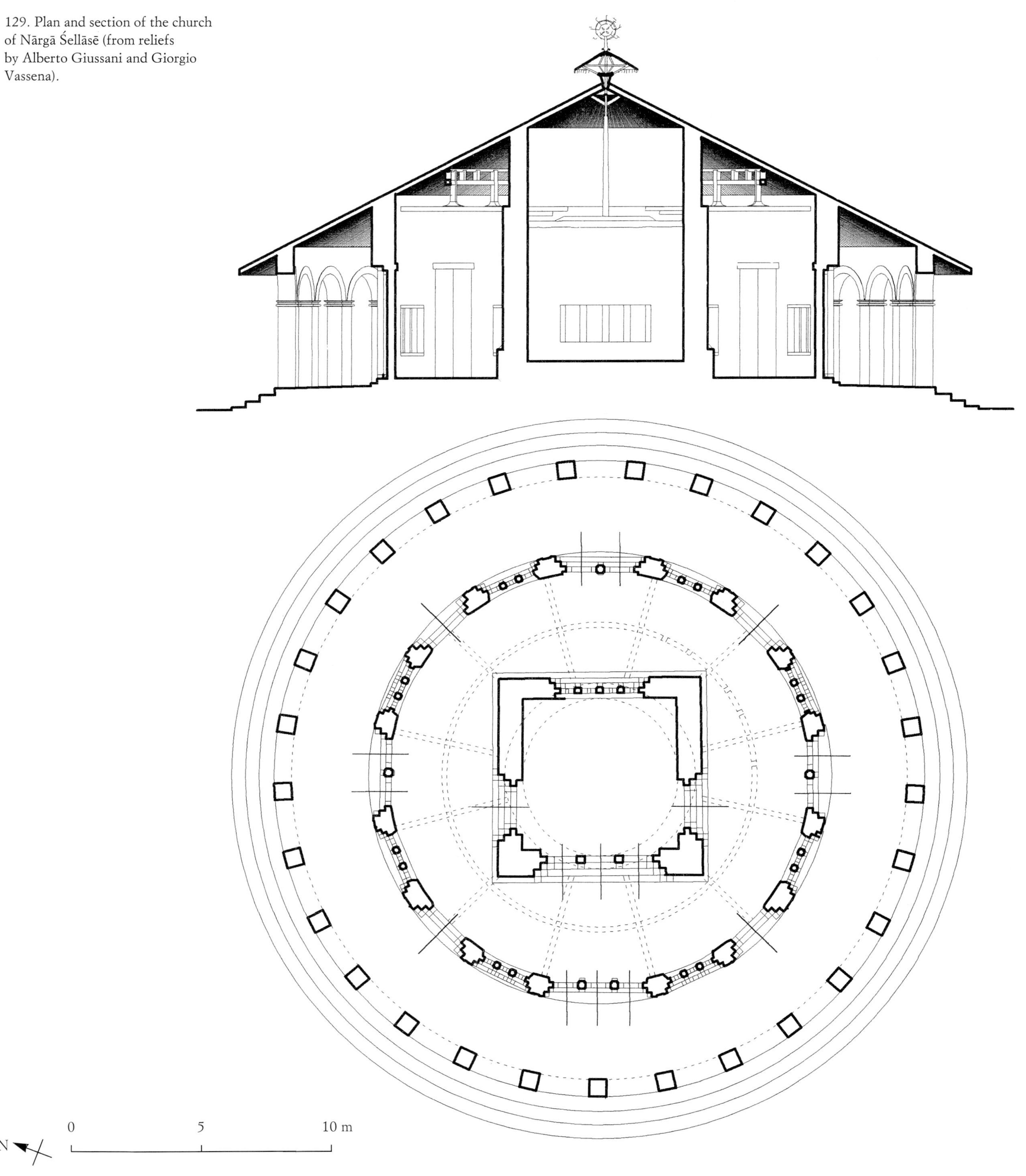

129. Plan and section of the church of Nārgā Śellāsē (from reliefs by Alberto Giussani and Giorgio Vassena).

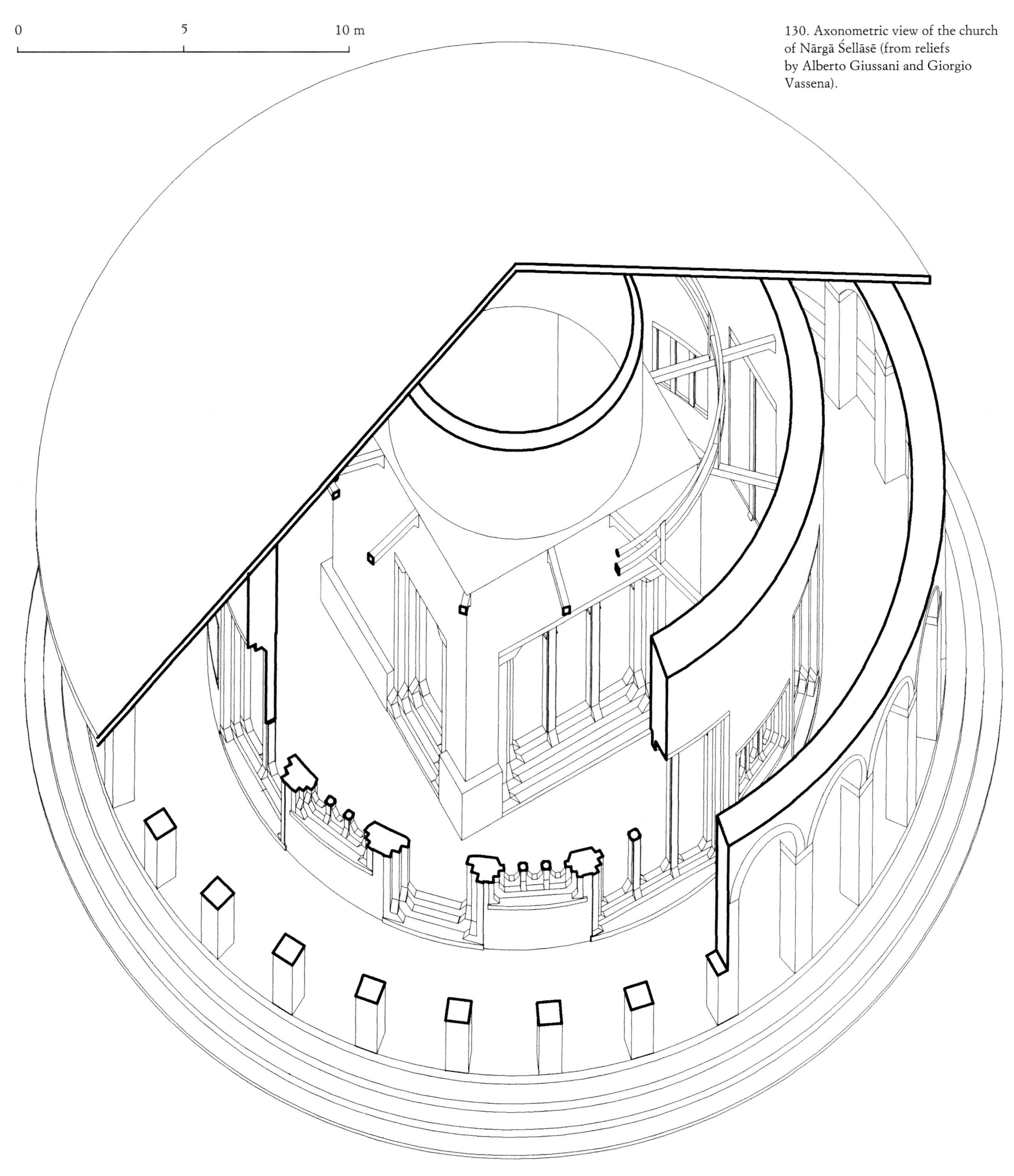

130. Axonometric view of the church of Nārgā Śellāsē (from reliefs by Alberto Giussani and Giorgio Vassena).

131. Detail of the side door of the *maqdas* of Kebrān Gabre'ēl (second half of the 17th century).

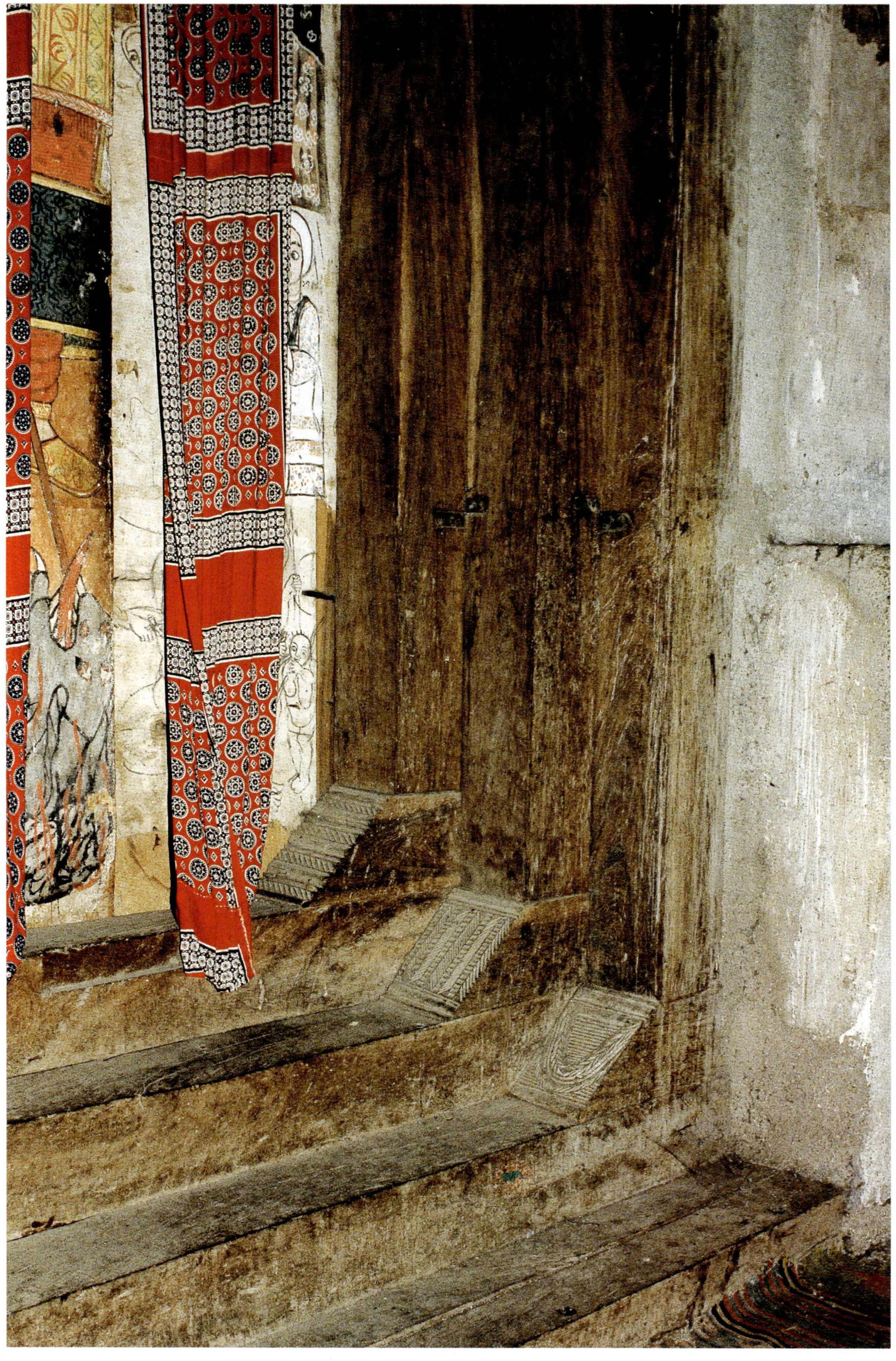

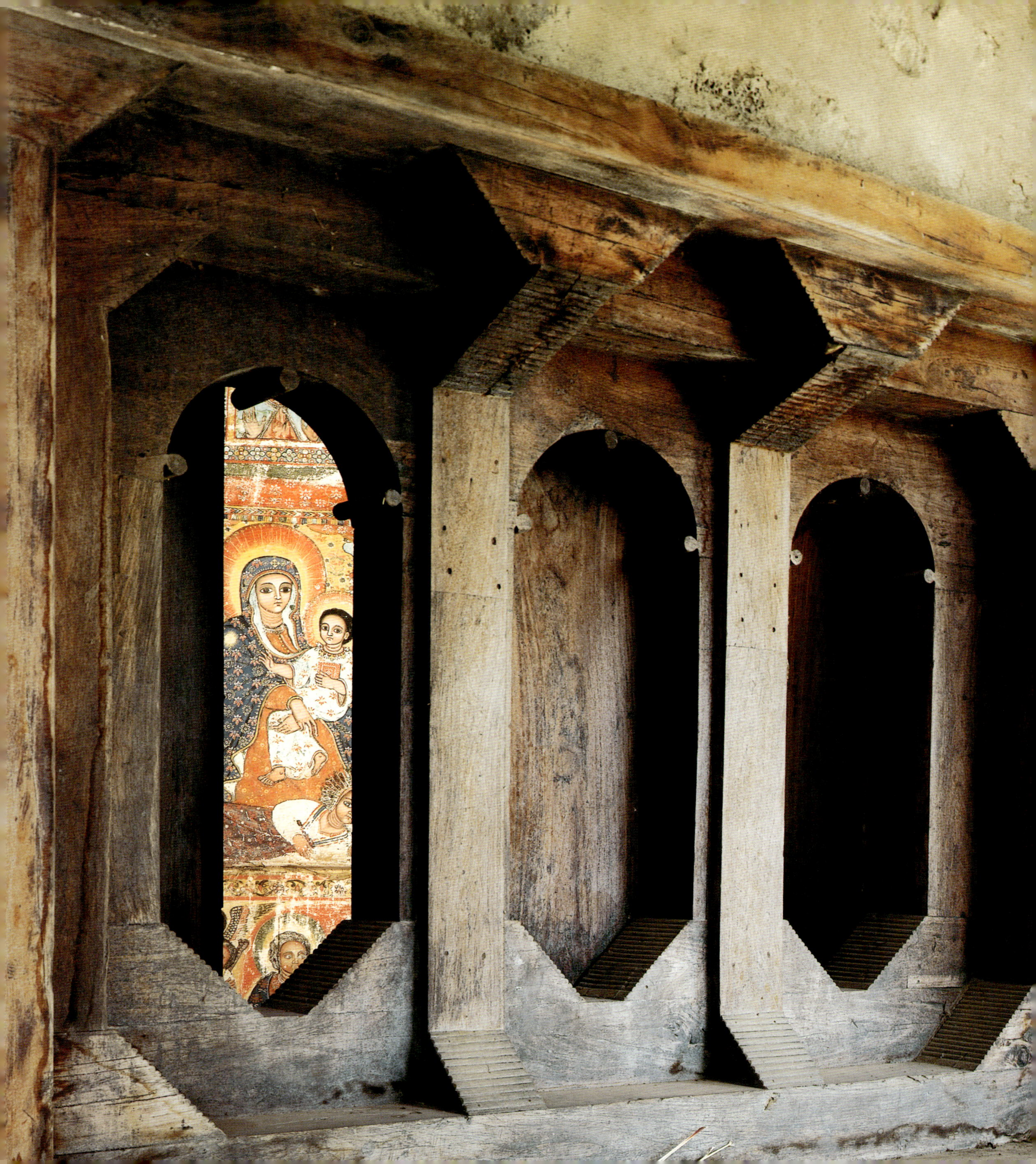

132. Triforate window of the *qenē māḥlēt* of the church of Nārgā Śellāsē.

133. Triforate window of the *qenē māḥlēt* of the church of Nārgā Śellāsē.

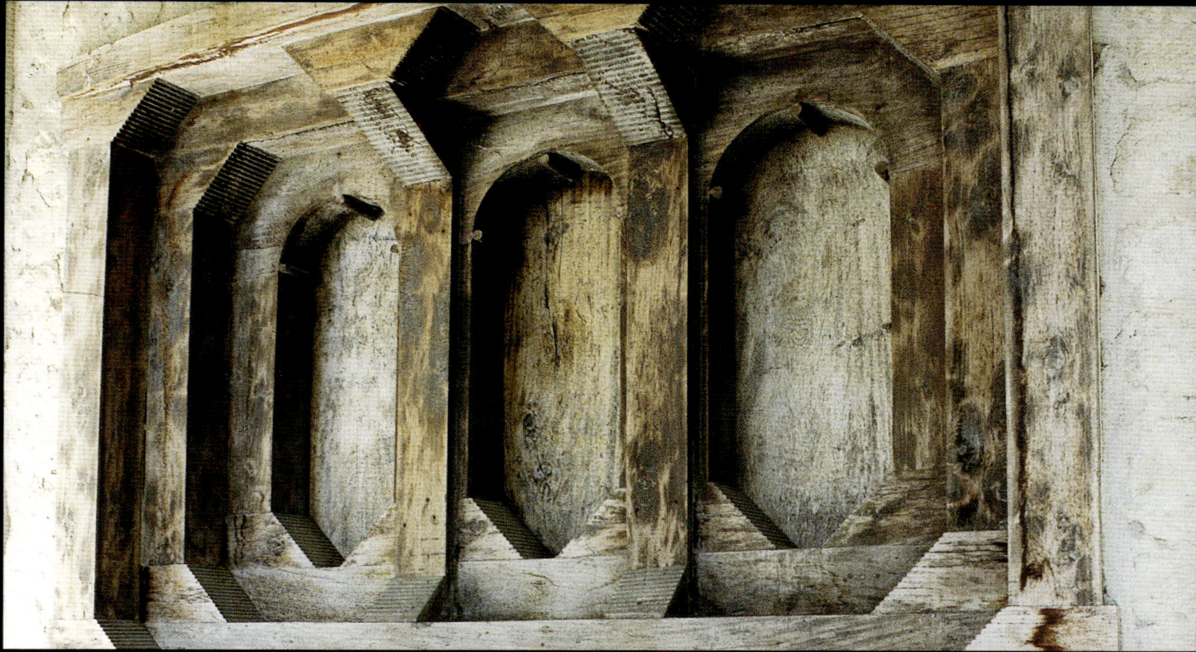

134. Triforate window of the *qenē māḥlēt* of the church of Nārgā Śellāsē.

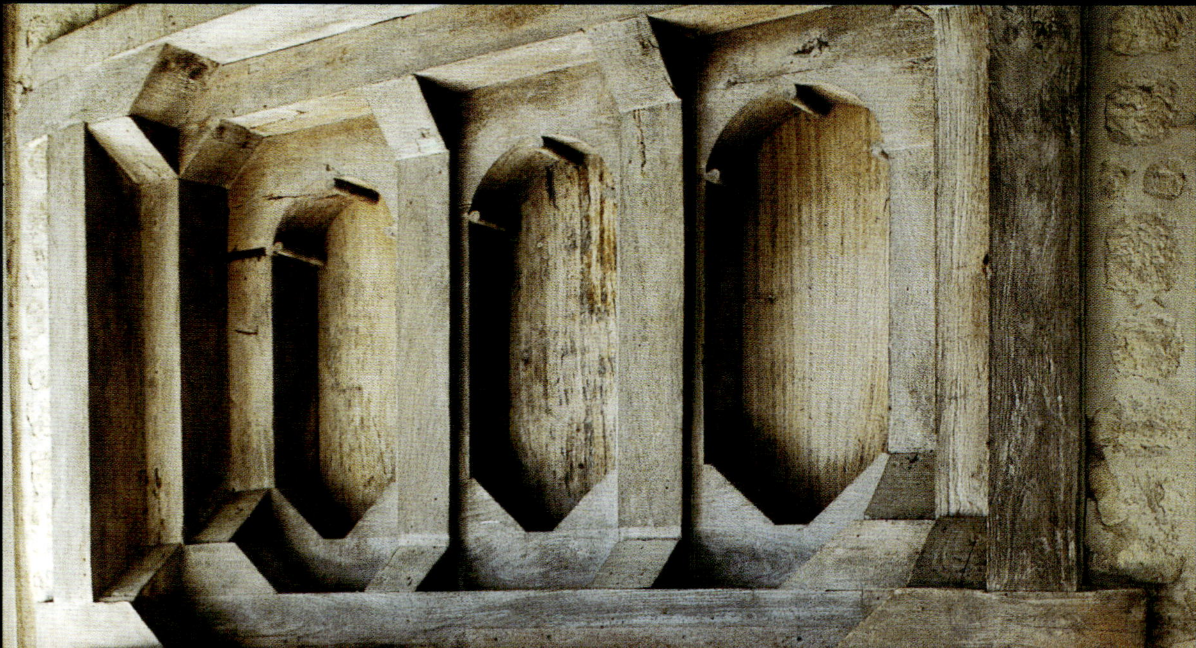

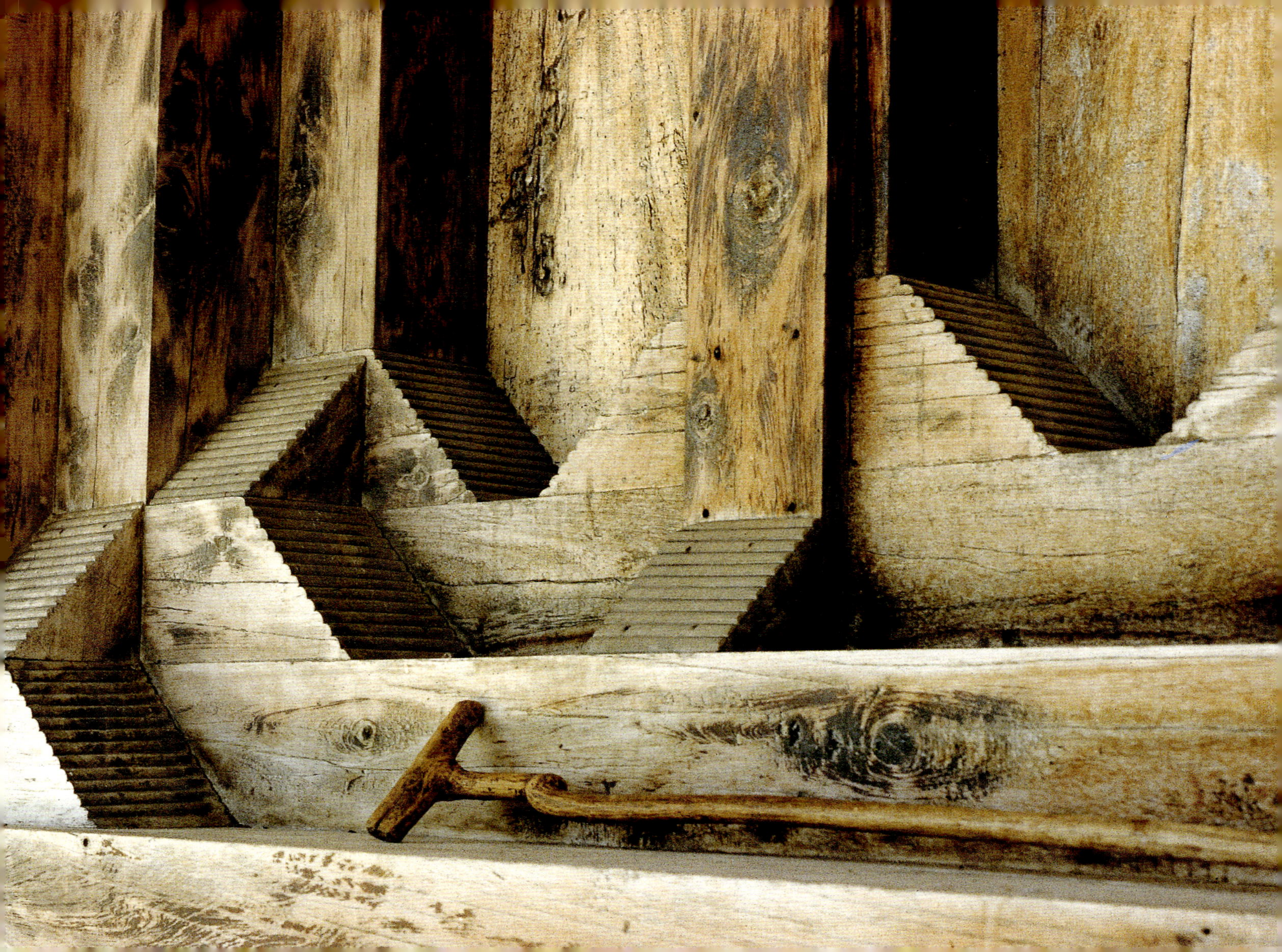

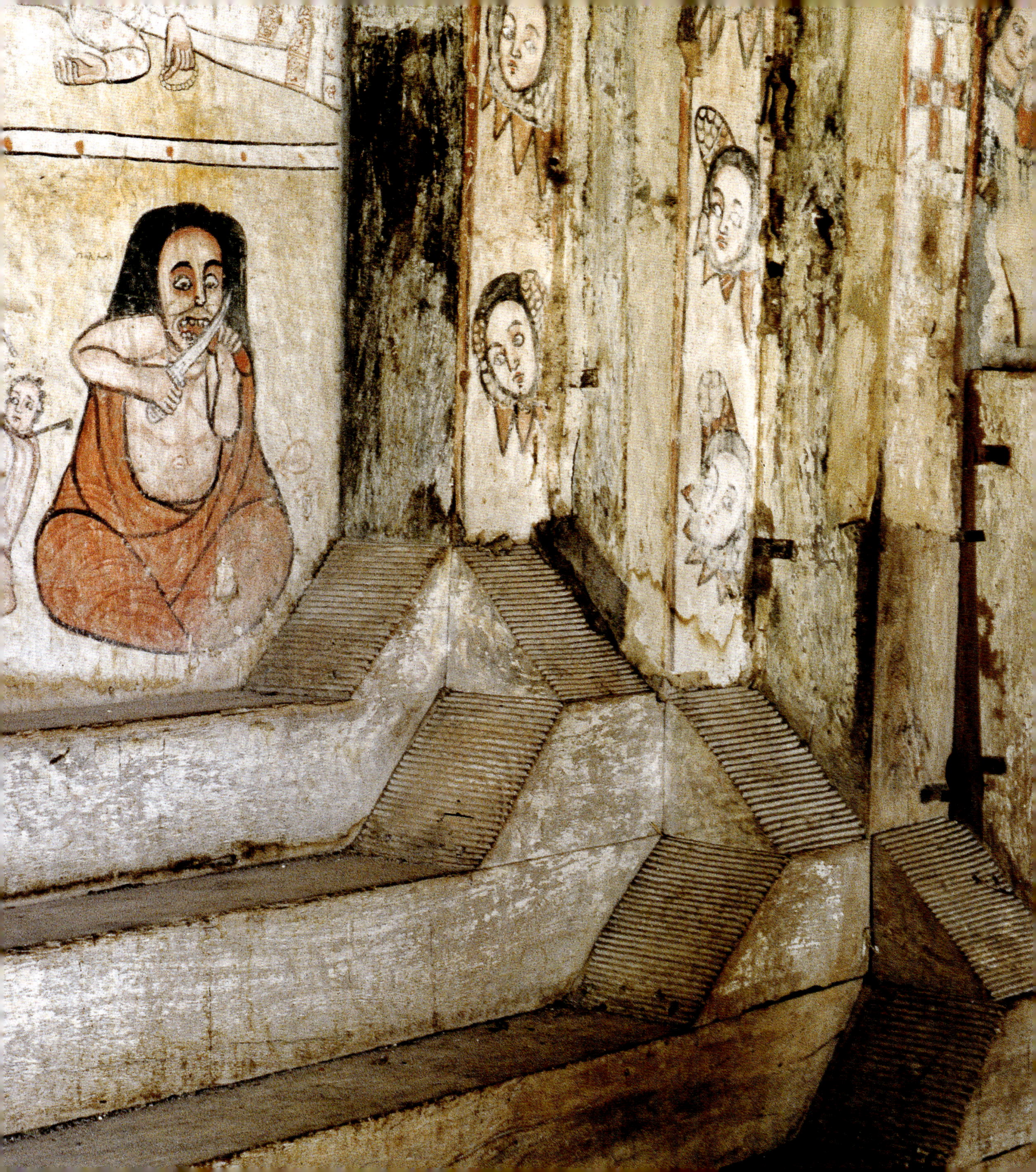

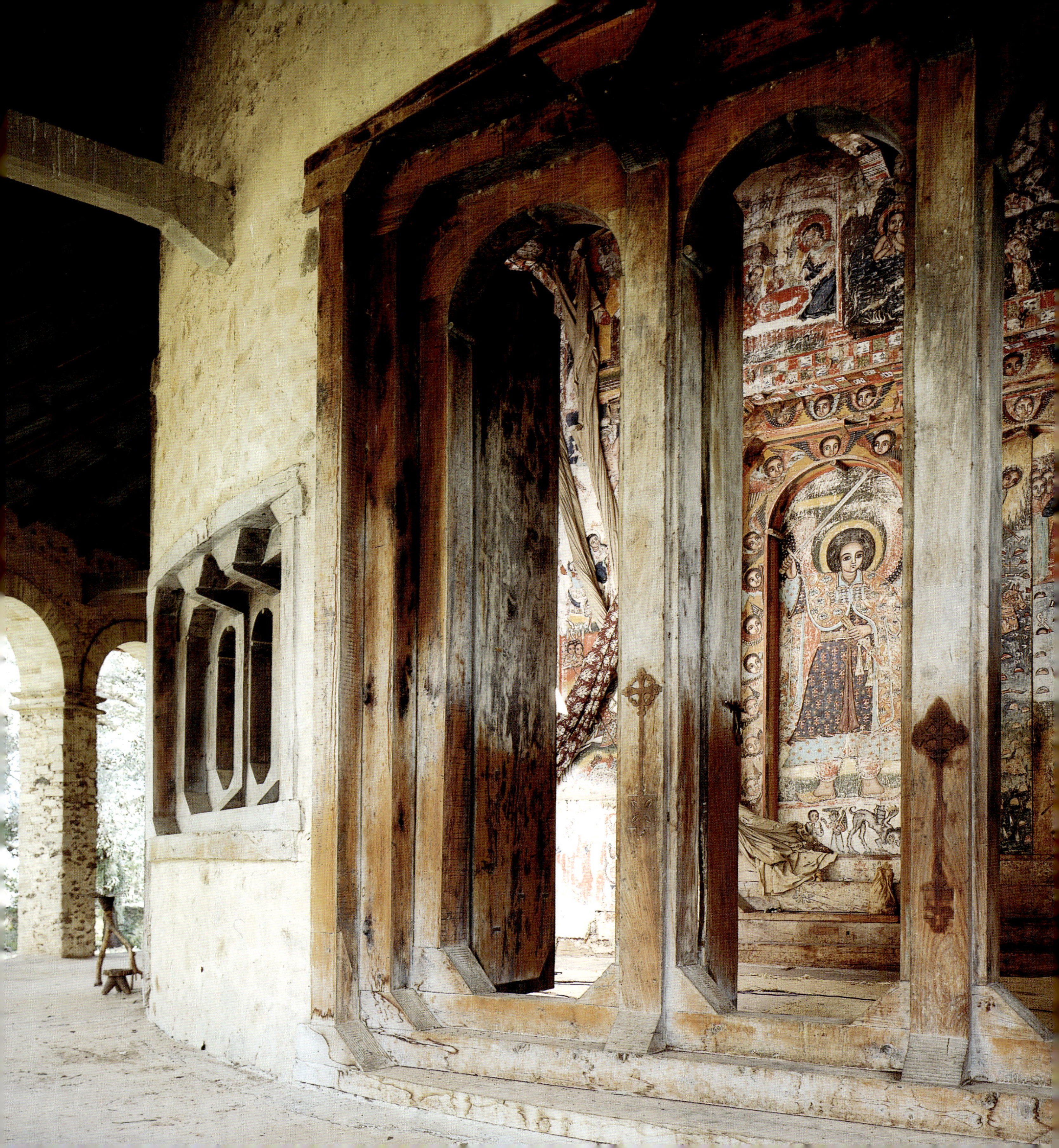

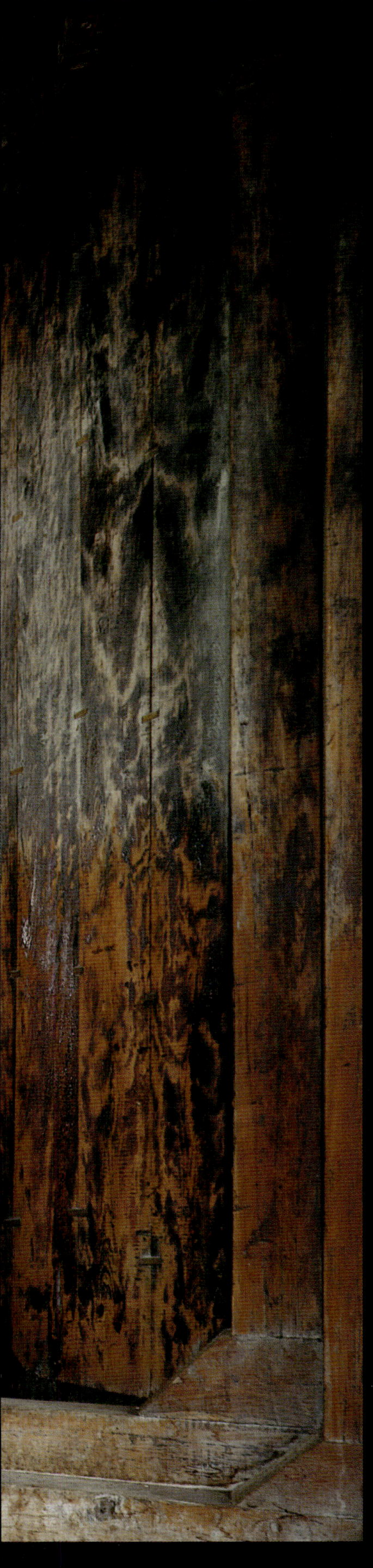

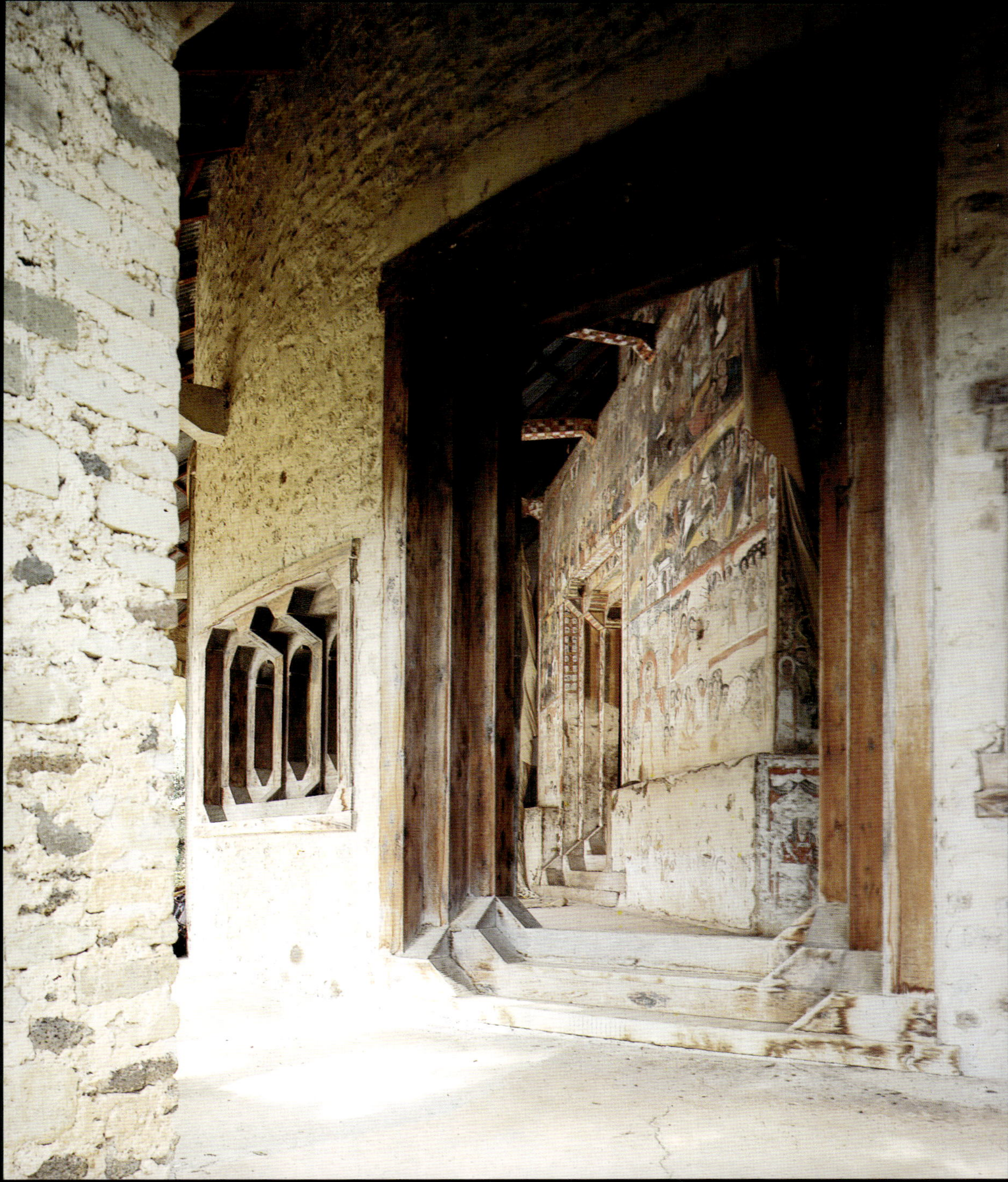

137. The large triforate door of access to the west side of the *qeddest* in the church of Nārgā Śellāsē. Inside, the painted wall of the *maqdas*, with its monumental entrance door.

138. Nārgā Śellāsē's church: through the door placed diagonally to the south side of the *maqdas* can be seen the decorated trusses placed radially, on which lay rafters supporting the covering

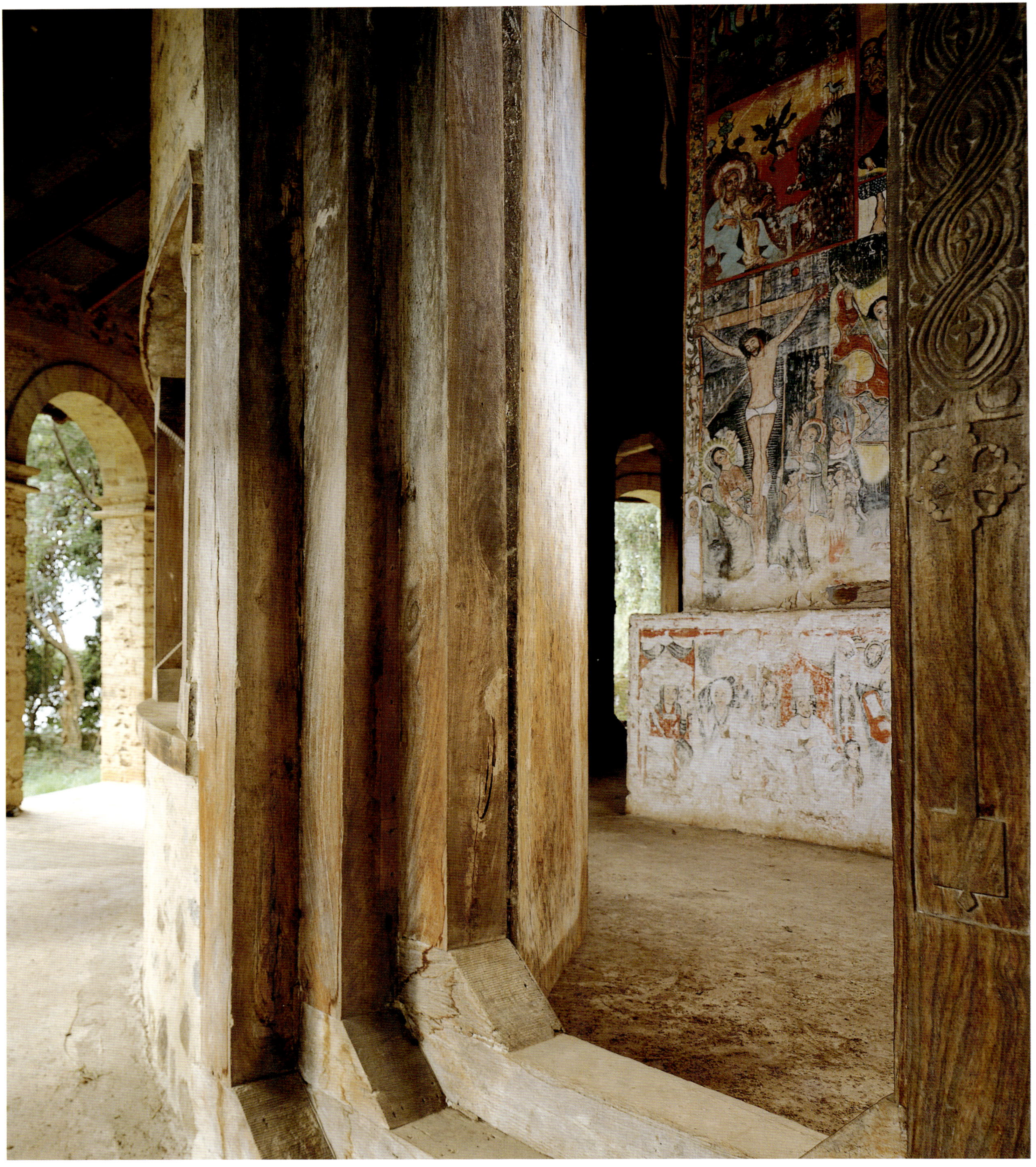

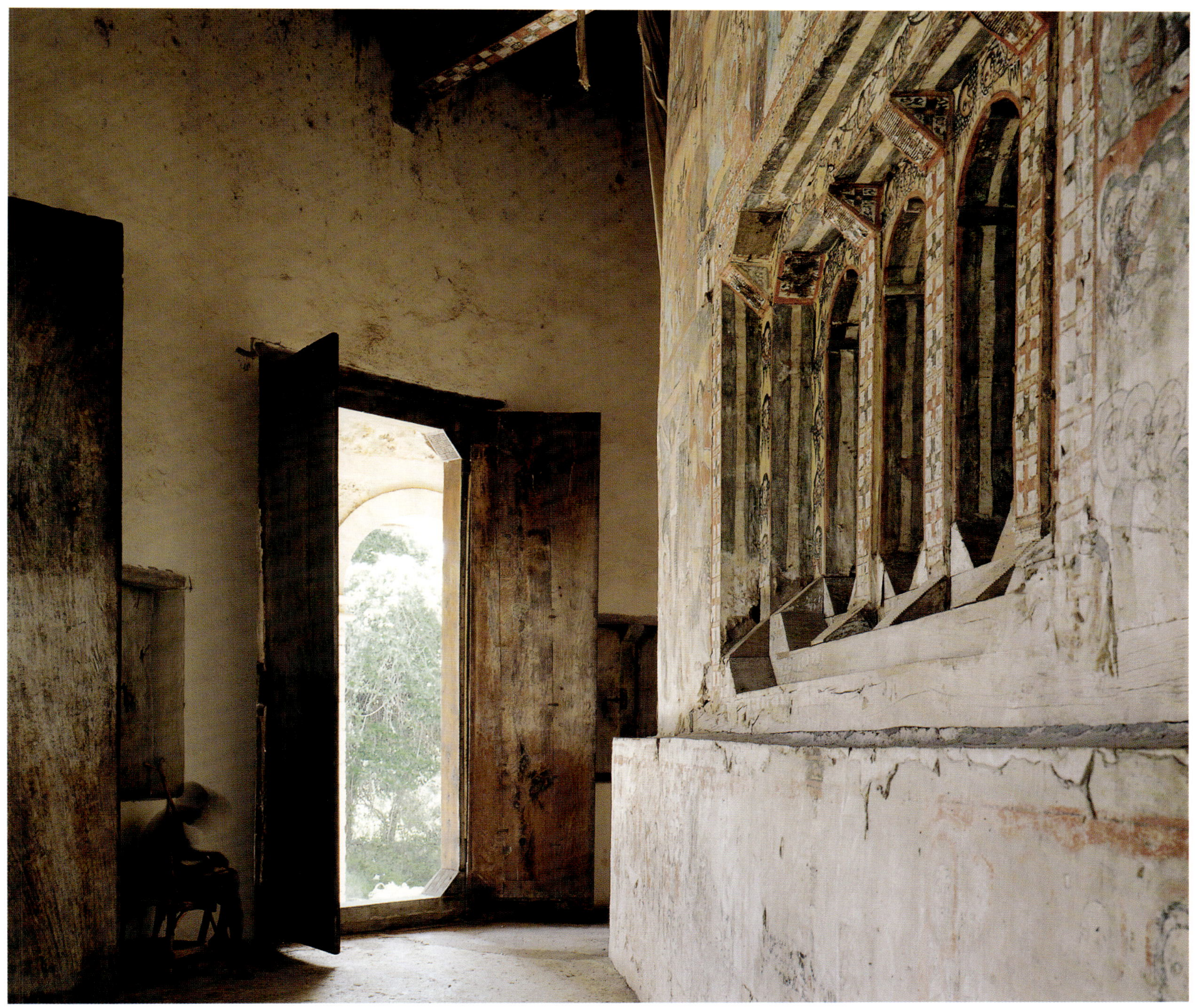

140. Nārgā Śellāsē's church: the east side of the *qeddest* of the church of Nārgā Śellāsē, with the quadriforate window painted on the corresponding side of the *maqdas*.

139. Nārgā Śellāsē's church: from the external portico, through the door which from the east side allows the entrance to the internal circuit, can be seen the Crucifixion painted on the east wall of the *maqdas*.

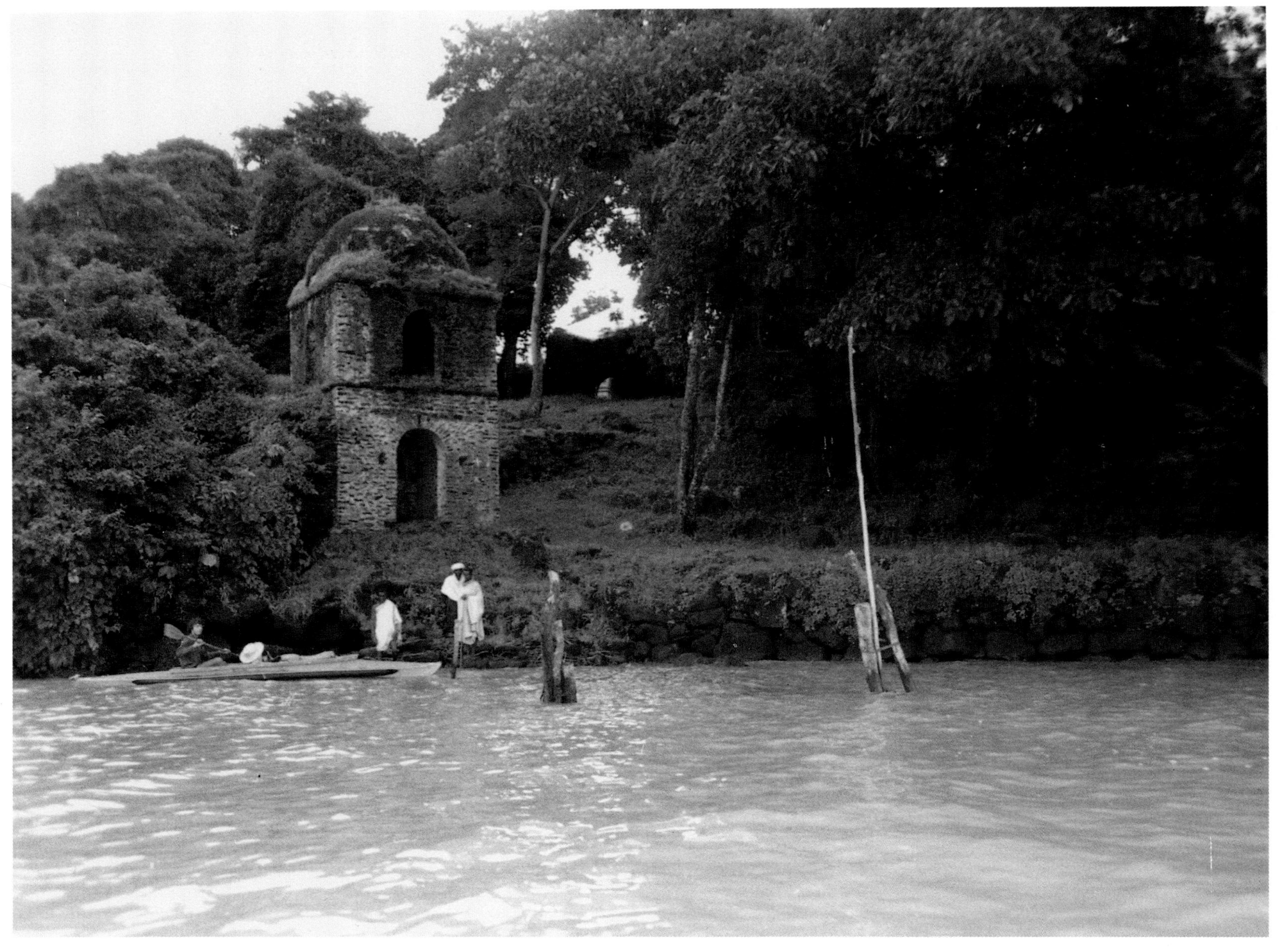

141. The way in which landing at Nārgā was achieved before the massive concrete pier was built.

ture doors and windows were surmounted by round headed arches whose fasciae gradually receded into the thickness of the wall. Examples can be found not only in secular architecture, but also in the doors of the *maqdas* of the church of Qeddus Mikā'ēl at Barié Ghemb. Abandoned in this church is the typology of paleo-Aksumite openings which survivied, before and up to the time when Gondar was the capital, in churches like Kota Māryām on the isle of Dek (fig. 130) and Dabra Sinā near Gorgorā: at the corners, wooden loops protruded to form the so-called 'monkeys' heads', which linked together the frames around doors and windows (and were placed both on the inside and the outside of the walls). From the 18th century onwards, these rigourously quadrangular openings became old-fashioned in the overall arrangement and in their articulation: the wooden frames kept the gradually receding implantation, while the linking-system based on 'monkeys' heads' was abandoned. In the corners of each frame, progressively receding, at the front and at the sides were introduced squares of counter-stays, linking and joining. Its figurative impact was quite powerful, since it created a perfect synthesis between shape, function and decoration because of the consequent sliding of planes joined in succession, in a non-schematical inventive and decorative application which was never merely repetitive (figs. 131-135). Only in the final recess, where the mouldings were, the arch motif, typical of Gondarian openings, was restored to use.

The use of this typology of doors and windows—whose genesis and references, until now, have been little studied by art historians—is redundant in the church of Nārgā Śellāsē.

The church stands atop the islet of Nārgā, and is one of the noblest and most representative examples of Ethiopian architecture as far as round centrally planned buildings are concerned. The church stands on a podium raised by three large steps and is delimitated by twenty-nine pilasters: on each of them, two pads of shaped stone work as the springers for a series of round headed arches—whose hewn stones, cut in a sunbeam shape, join perfectly—, raised on the ring supporting the covering of the eaves.

One passes from the circuit of the *qenē māḫlēt* to that of the *qeddest* through doors whose various shapes and widths alternate and whose veined darkness of natural wood stands out against the clear background wall. There is a set of eight doors hierarchically ordered, which for range of conception has no equals in any other church of Lake Tana: a wide triforate door on the west, three biforate doors in correspondance to the other cardinal points and four monoforate doors placed on the diagonals. Between each of them, eight triforate windows alternate, so that the circuit of walls which is placed as a filter between the *qenē māḫlēt* and the *qeddest* is much lightened in the supporting sections, already compressed and eroded by the openings.

Doors and windows, all made by carpenters, represent the richest and the most inventive and refined product which could have been realized for the joining of the progressive levels of in the thickness of the walls. In a composition of orthogonal and inclined elements the frames of the doors and windows are wind-braced always in a similar way from the conceptual point of view, even though different variations are offered.

The *maqdas*, which is built on another socle, opens at the west with a majestic triforate door, on the two sides with two monoforate doors which are not canonically centred on their respective walls, while at the east, above the socle, there is a wide quadrifora: the whole surface is covered with paintings, both on all sides and on the blind tambour crowning it.

From the springer of the tambour twelve trusses spread out sunburst, then they drive into the external wall of the *qeddest*. They support twelve rafters, all richly painted and decorated, which are joined at the top by a double crown of trusses which reduce the otherwise excessive light created between the tambour and the external wall of the *qeddest*.

Unluckily in the years immediately after the World War II Nārgā underwent a distasteful rearrangement: the intrusive insertion of tie-beams in reinforced concrete which, notwithstanding the use of profiles with pseudo-corbels, reveal their complete extraneousness to the stylistic coherence of the building.

Even the thatch roof has been replaced, as in many other churches, by sheets of corrugated iron, certainly less permeable to the rain but of a different quality, in every possible sense.

To commemorate this disastrous rearrangement, on a plaque placed in 1951 on one of the pilasters is written, in the beautiful characters of the Ethiopian alphabet: "The building of this church of Nārgā Śellāsē started at the beginning of the 18th century by Empress Mentewwāb. Since the roof, the *qeddest*, the *qenē māḫlēt* and six pilasters were damaged, in 1944,[3] in the 23rd year of his reign, Emperor Ḫayla Śellāsē I had them completely restored. The paintings, many of the doors and the windows belong to the ancient time."

Finally, in 1993 a wide and long pier, well smoothed with mortar, was built on the lakesense by the Office responsible for the Navigation on the lakes by the Ministry of Transport of the Amhara Government, thus covering up the old and certainly impractical landing place.

Finally in these last years qualified Ethiopian personnel carried out exemplary restorations[4]: a forthcoming restoration of the church of Nārgā Śellāsē, which will nullify the disfiguring effect of the previous restoration is therefore auspicable.

[3] The Ethiopian date refers to the Julian calendar.

[4] Such as, for example, that of the church of Kota Māryām on the isle of Dek, carried out under the direction of Ato Mezemir Abiy, of the Department of Culture of Bāḥer Dār, but others could also be mentioned.

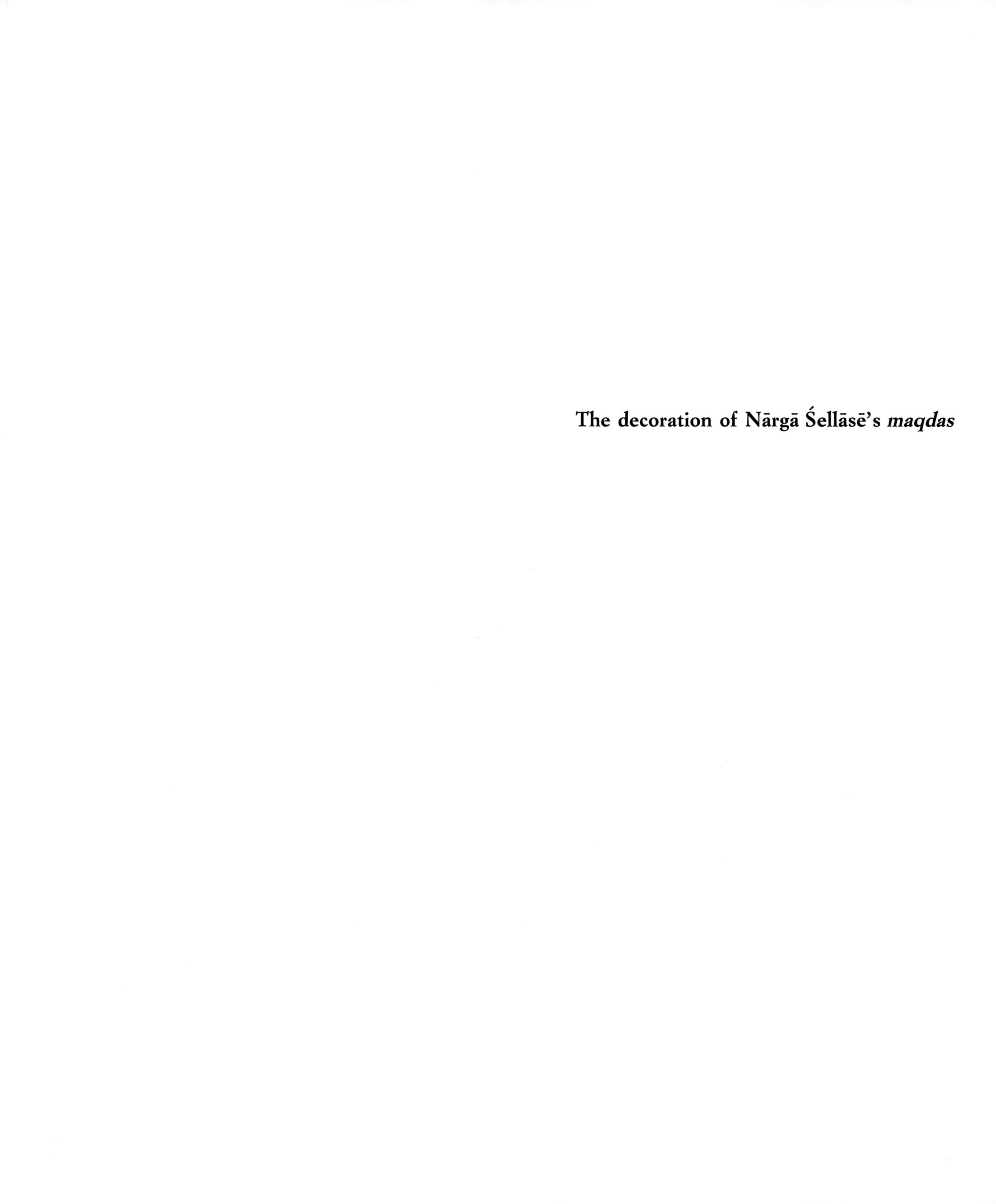

The decoration of Nārgā Śellāsē's *maqdas*

142. Nārgā Śellāsē: the east side of the *maqdas*.

143. Nārgā Śellāsē: the west side of the *maqdas*.

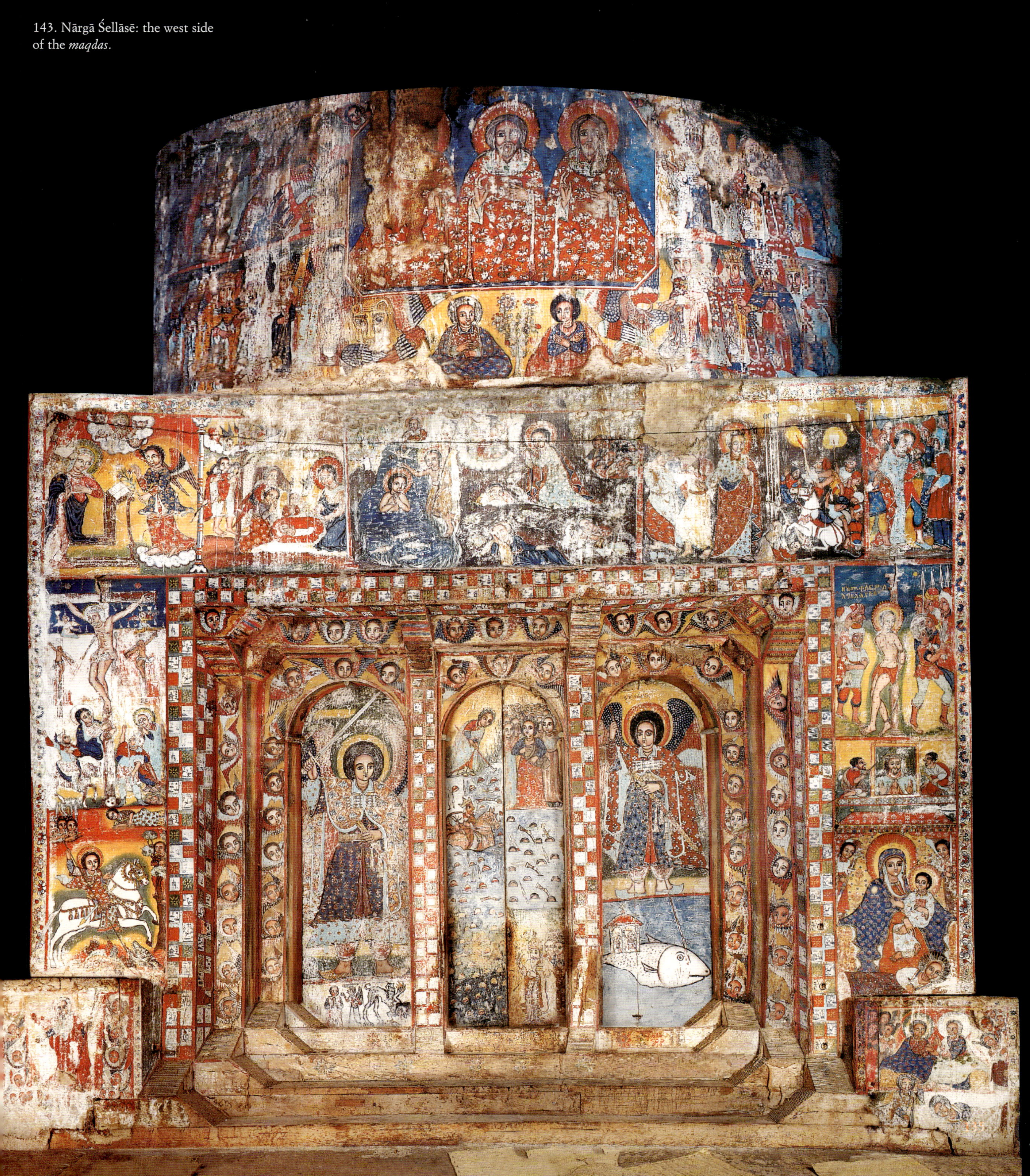

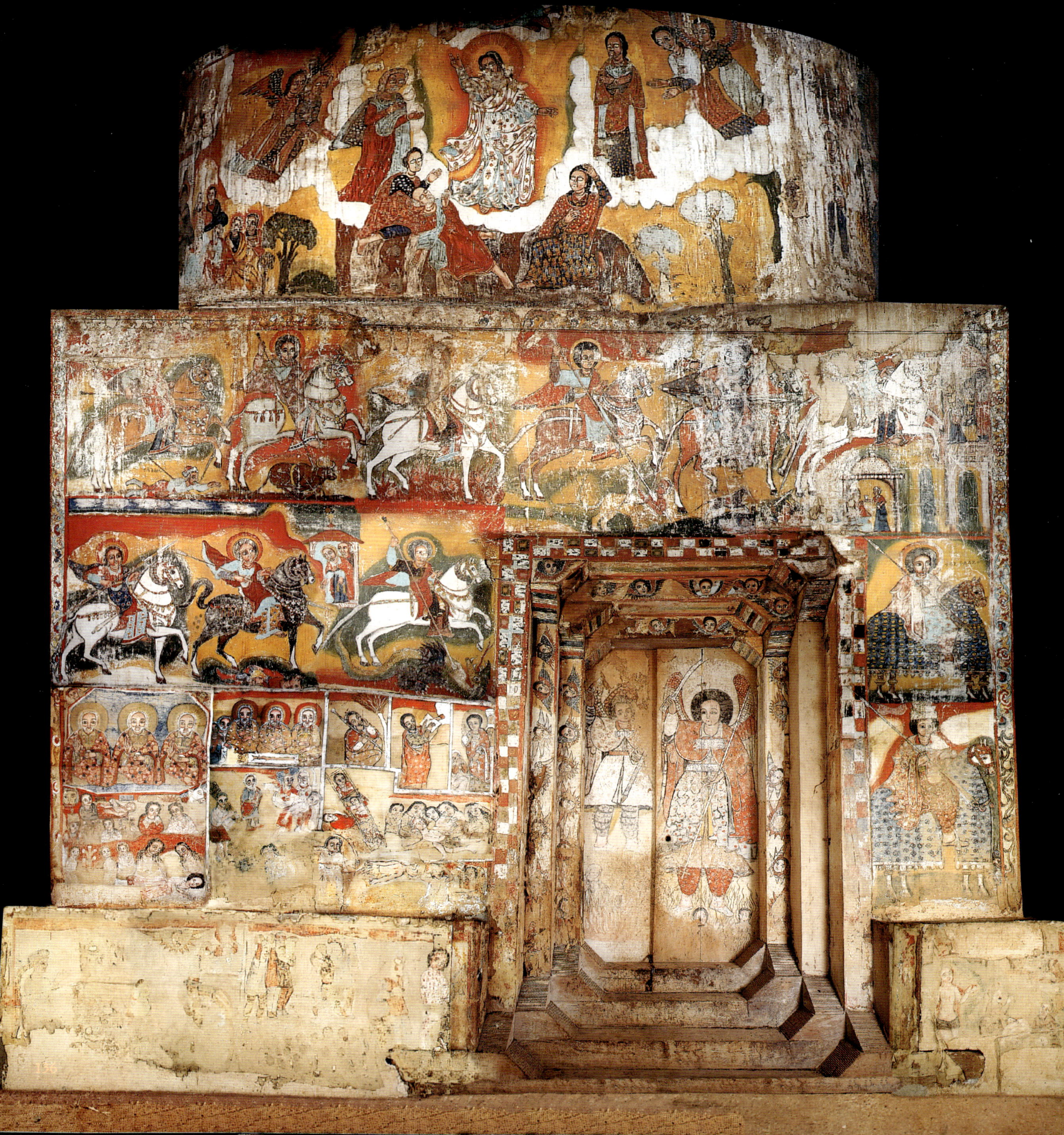

145. Nārgā Śellāsē: the south side of the *maqdas*.

The Cycle of Paintings

Ethiopia has many churches decorated with paintings, but at Nārgā Śellāsē, perhaps more then elsewhere, the way in which the subjects are chosen and arranged and above all their representation merit study both as a phenomenon of Ethiopian art and also in their relationship with art outside Ethiopia, Christian and non-Christian.

Even though the paintings date to a relatively recent period, astride the middle of the 18th century, a conspicuous part of the body of work has all but disappeared due to degradation by water and bird droppings. Others have been restored or substituted with later paintings (the paintings are easily removed from their support in order to be replaced by others).

In many cases art historians have been able to attribute a particular work to one period or another roughly by following comparative criteria in reference to stylistic characteristics of other paintings. In fact, apart from that on walls, Ethiopian painting has various methods of expression such as illuminated manuscripts and icons. Using these forms, experts have augmented the amount of material available for study, necessary in the formulation of a comparative overview. It is therefore possible to go back to their initial phases. The surviving examples make it possible to delineate the diachronical aspects of their stylistic evolution, as well as to establish a more precise chronology if, for examples, the works of art are linked to illuminated pages whose actual dating is more certain.

However, there are still many unresolved problems. But the complete catalogue of a cycle of paintings whose dating is certain, such as that of Nārgā Śellāsē—thanks to chronicles, allowing the scholar to individuate under what reign the body of work was completed—, offers an additional contribution to the comparative overall study, as far as recurrencies and novelties in style, up to a quite recent epoch.

The number of monuments whose history is recorded and which have been carefully examined is still quite limited. Additional systemic study of the mural cycles in the *maqdas* is necessary, at least in order to certify and document works of art, many of which unfortunately seem to be undergoing an unavoidable degradation.

Groups of artists whose formation took place at the Gondar school and later reached a more evolved level of artistic achievement must have had to follow well established rules as far as the choice, the distribution and the pose of the figures was concerned, as well as the way the drawing had to be made and colours added. An organization of art teaching and artistic practice similar to that of medieval "botteghe", where dexterity and technical skills were acquired by repetition during a long apprenticeship, seems highly plausible. The different tasks performed in the "bottega" must have been in accordance

146. 16th century paintings on the *maqdas* of Kota Māryām on the island of Dek.

with the skill acquired by each individual artist, following the stages on a real path of initiation. Travelling troops of painters carried their art to different regions, and following their route or the areas of their influence, using the as yet unstudied documentary evidence of the *maqdas* could be quite friuftful. Such research implies a general approach not confined to major works, but rather one willing to examine minor aspects from which they developed.

The history of Ethiopian painting "... is divided into two main periods; the medieval and the Gondarene. The important point is, of course, when the medieval period finished and the Gondarene started. Leroy proposed that the Moslem invasion under Aḥmad Grañ in the early 16th century should be considered as the dividing event" (CHOJNACKI, p. 23).

Without external influences which, as time passed, introduced some changes, the work of Gondarene painters probably woud have remained a genre entrenched in the reiteration of iconographic rules shared by the whole of Eastern Christianity.

"Dans les églises riches, le sanctuaire est souvent tapissé, du côté de la galerie, de fresques sur toile représentant les principale scénes du christianisme. Ces peintures sont curieuses à plus d'un titre; elles rappellent d'abord le style byzantin dont elles ont toute la roideur et tuote la naïveté. La perspective y est inconnu; le diable seul y est représenté sous les traits d'un nègre, tous les autres personnages ont la peau blanche et rouge; les coutumes, les étoffes, rappellent vaguement l'Inde et ses coutumes, ce qu'il faut, je pense, attribuer à l'intervention des Portugais..." (RAFFRAY 1876, p. 303).

In fact at the beginning of 18th century a new manner determined an evolution in the figurative style of Gondarene painters, both by accentuating the imitation of Western models and showing a stronger inclination towards oriental preciousness. The flat colours with a restricted range, the exaggerated outline, the number of figures and natural elements reduced to a minimum amount were replaced by modelling, a stronger attention to perspective, an enrichment of tones, a more naturalistic quality, patent even in the way shades were depicted. Also the Middle East and Far East—especially India, with the Portuguese colony of Goa—became another inspirational source in Ethiopian

147. Paintings dating to the second half of the 18th century on the *maqdas* of Kebrān Gabre'ēl on Lake Tana.

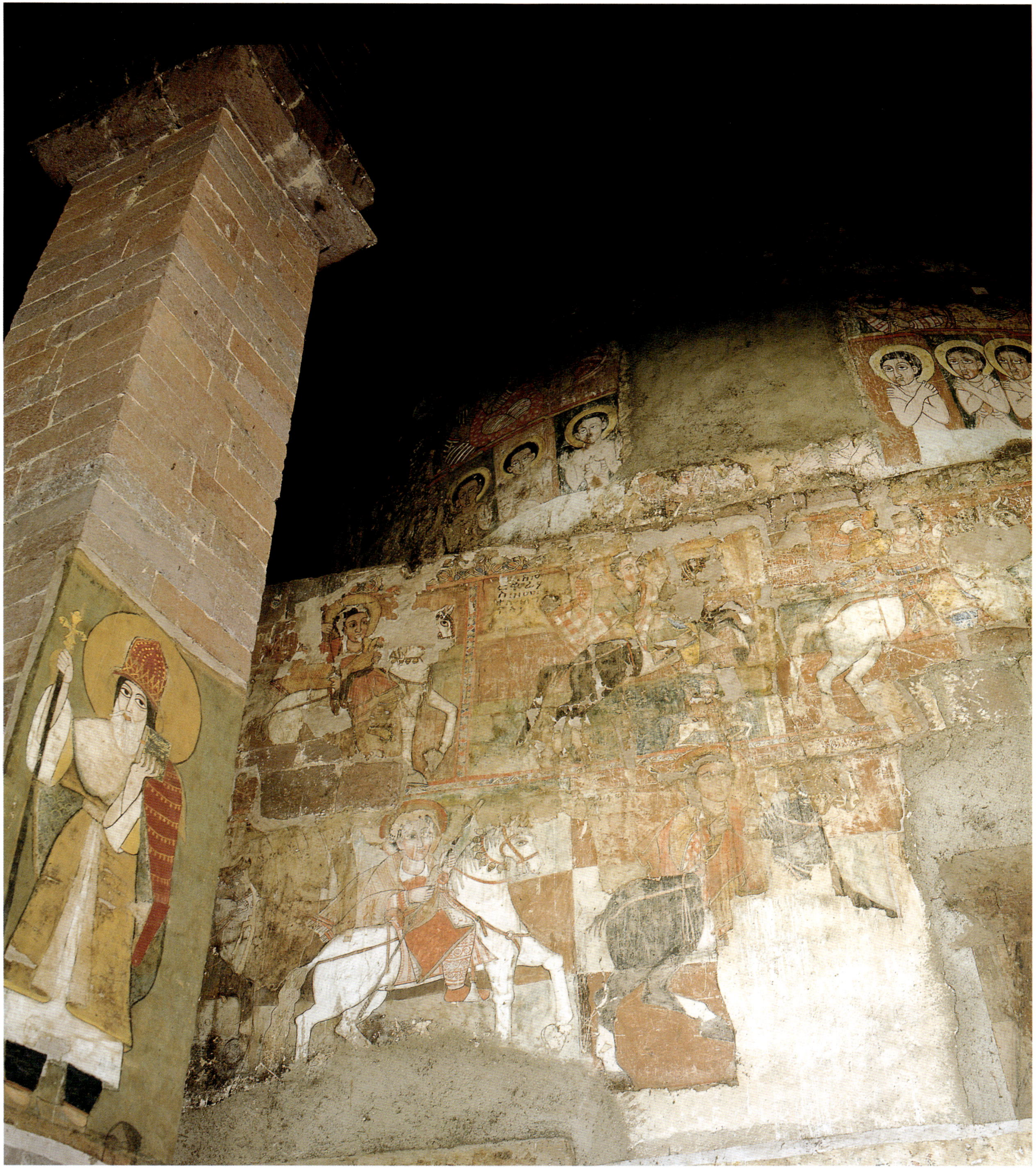

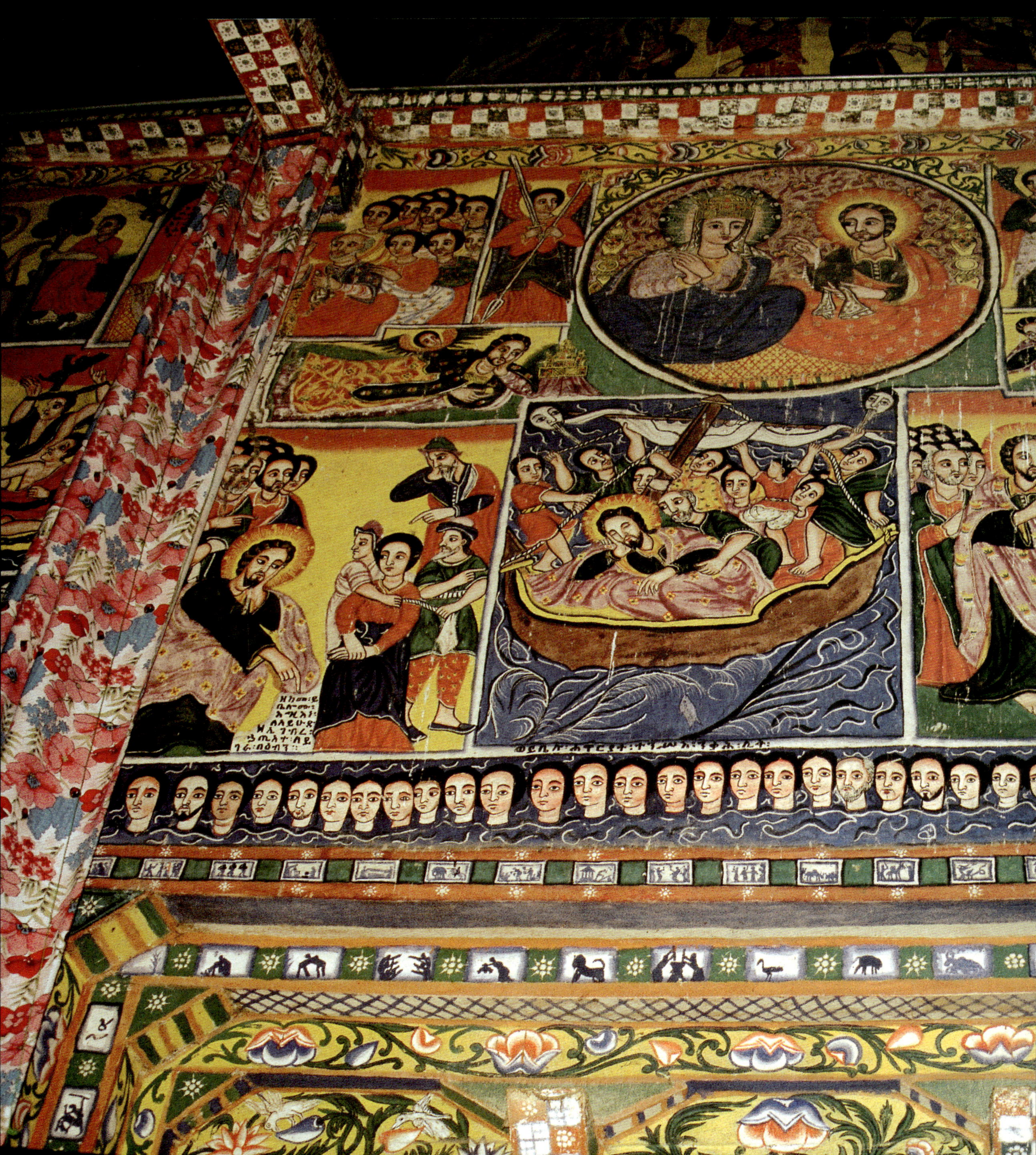

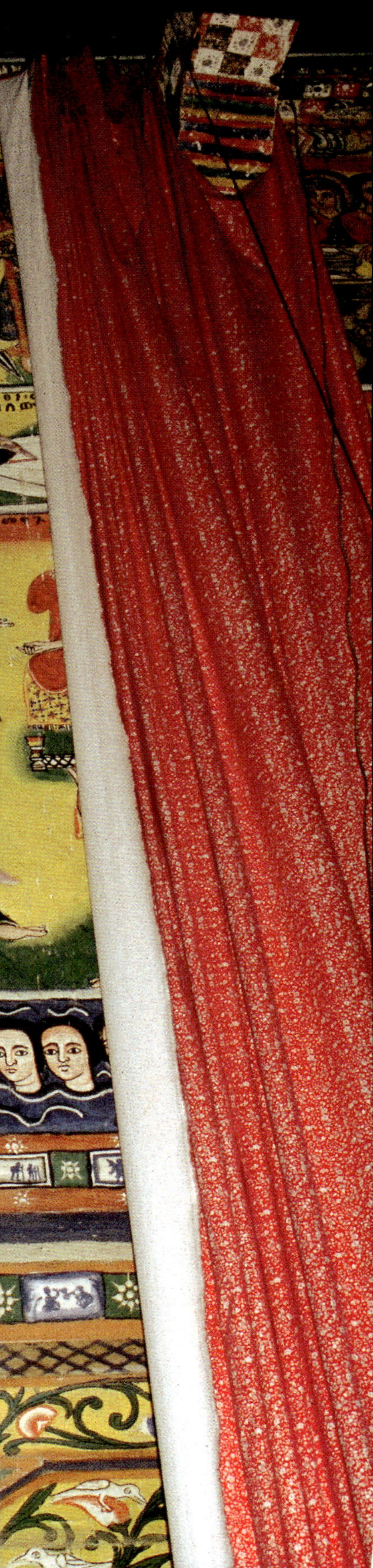

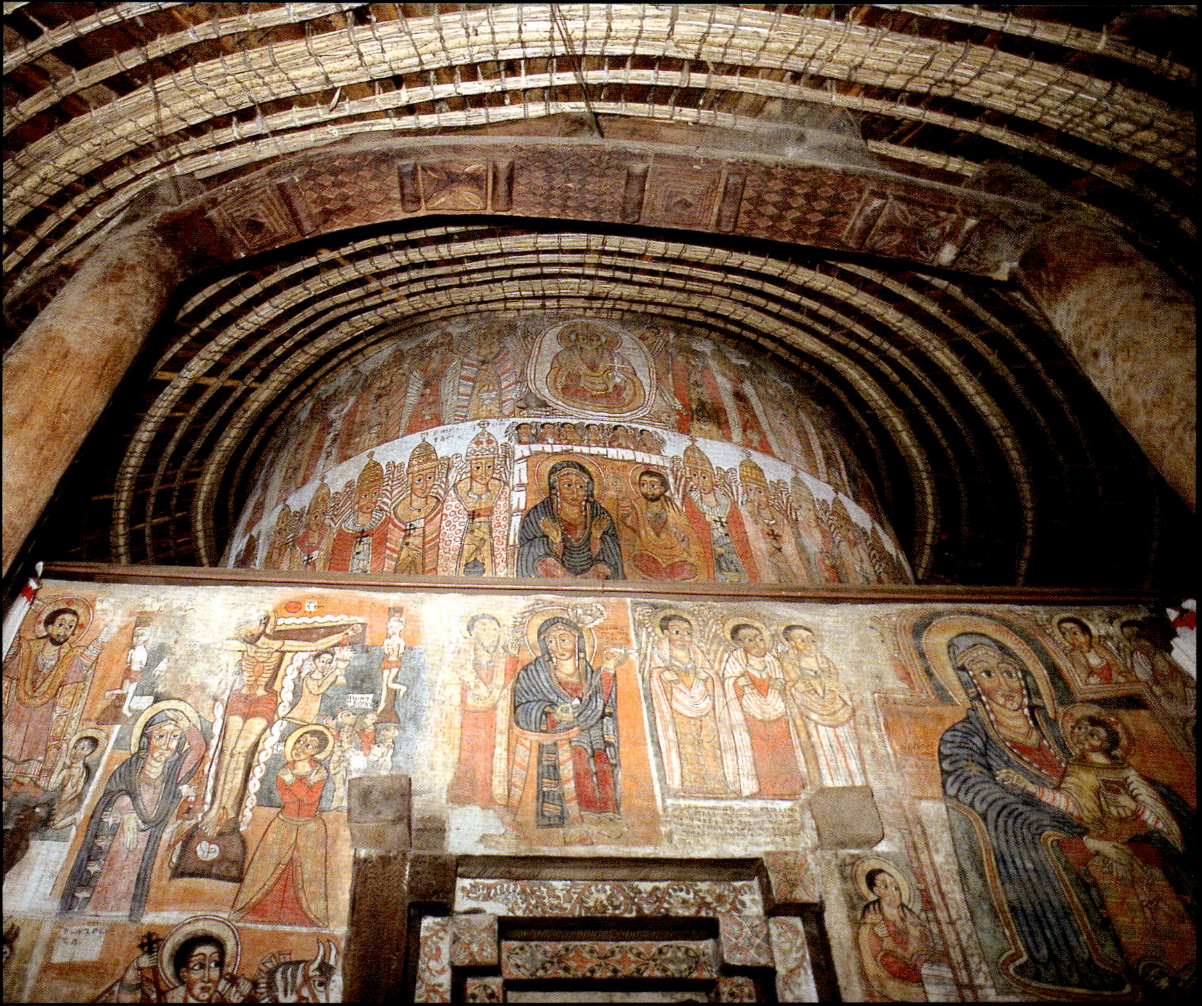

148. 19th century paintings on the *maqdas* of Ura Kidāna Merḥat on the peninsula of Ṣegē.

149. Paintings dating to the first half of the 17th century on the *maqdas* of Dabra Sinā, on the peninsula of Gorgorā.

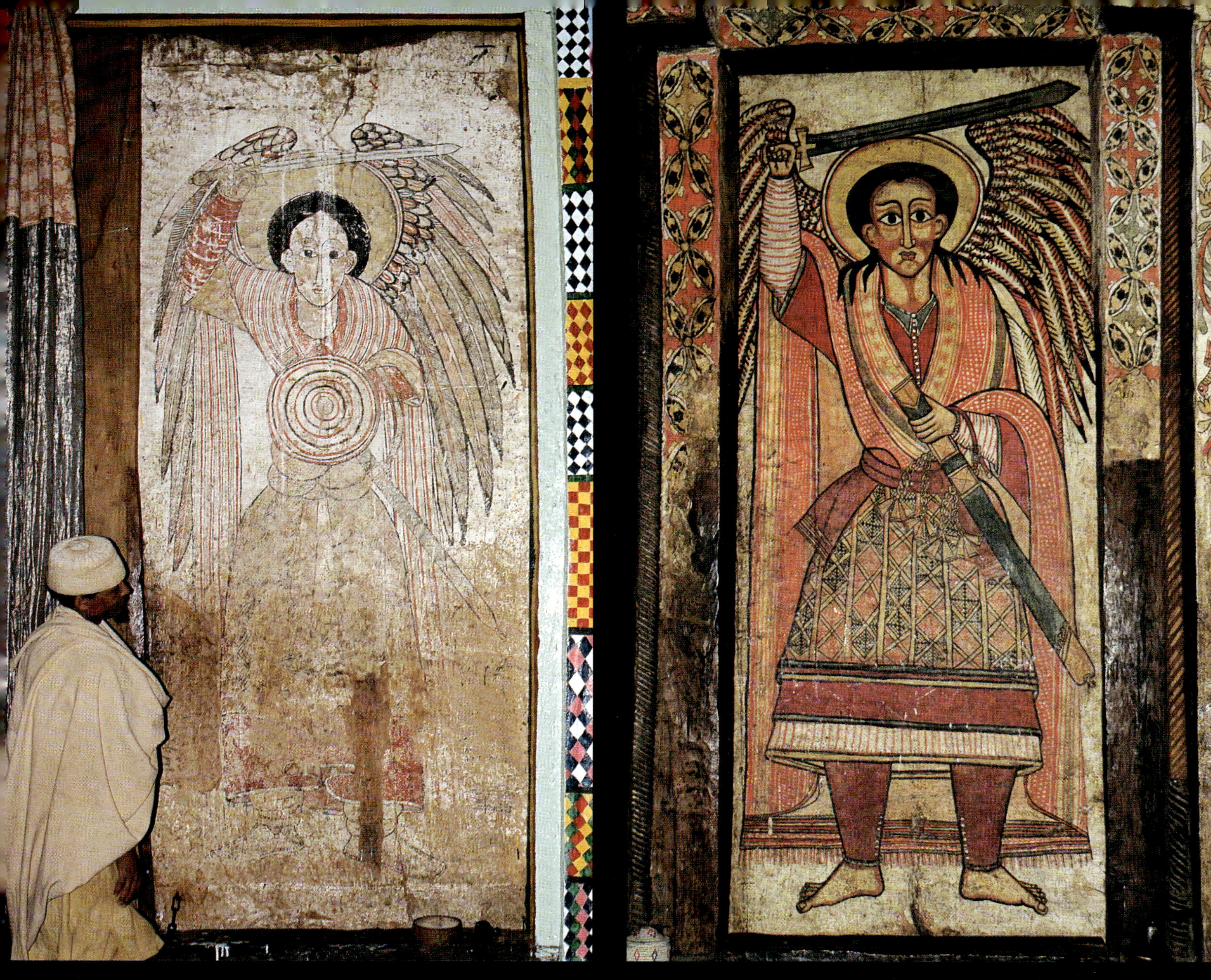

150. An Archangel, keeper of the door of the *maqdas* of Dāgā Estifanos

151. An Archangel, keeper of the west door of the *maqdas* of Dabra Sinā

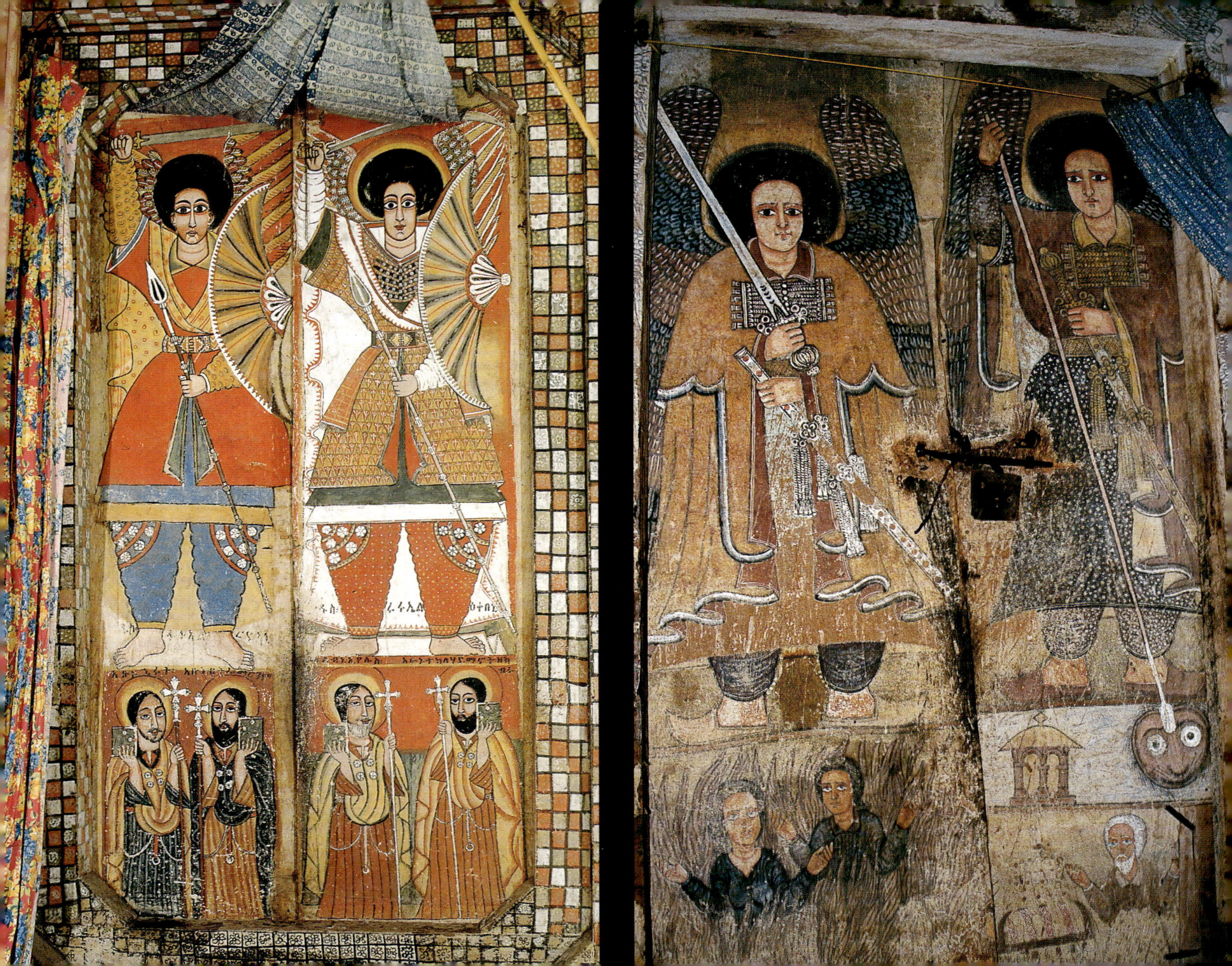

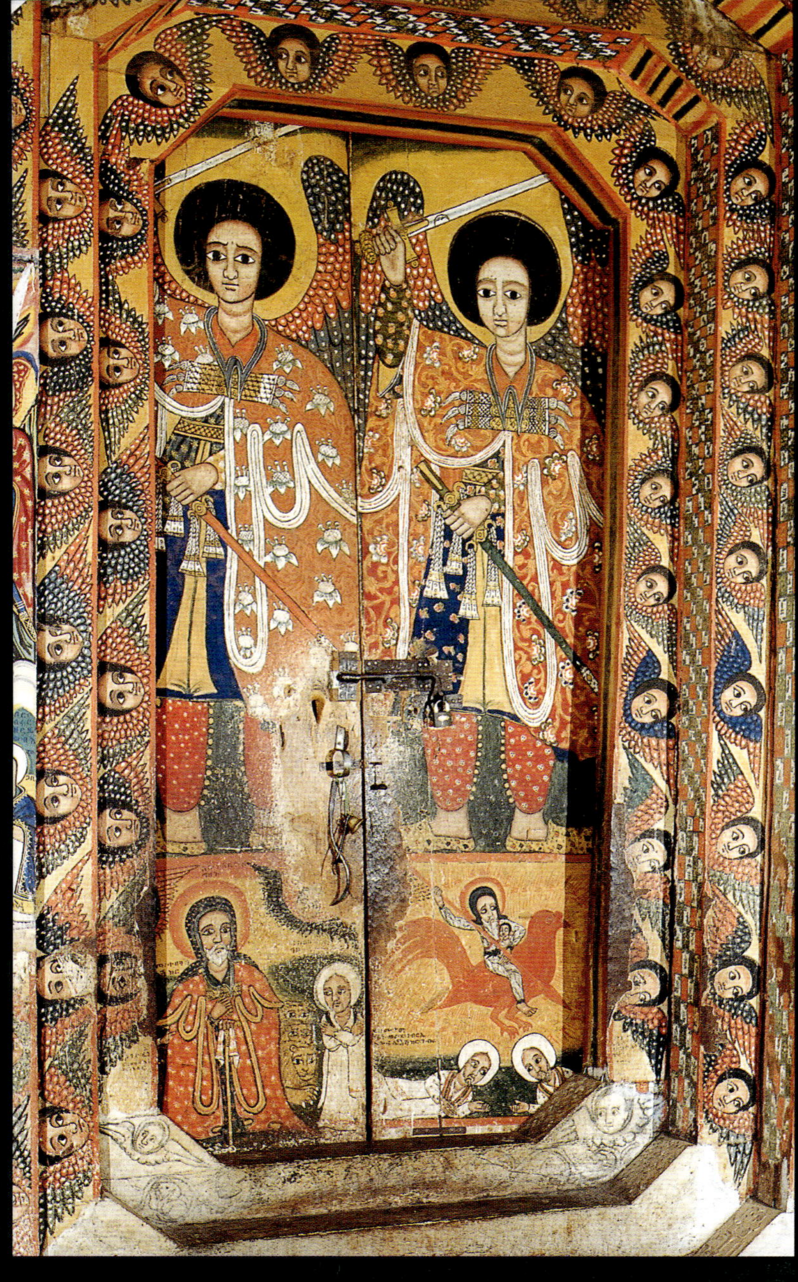

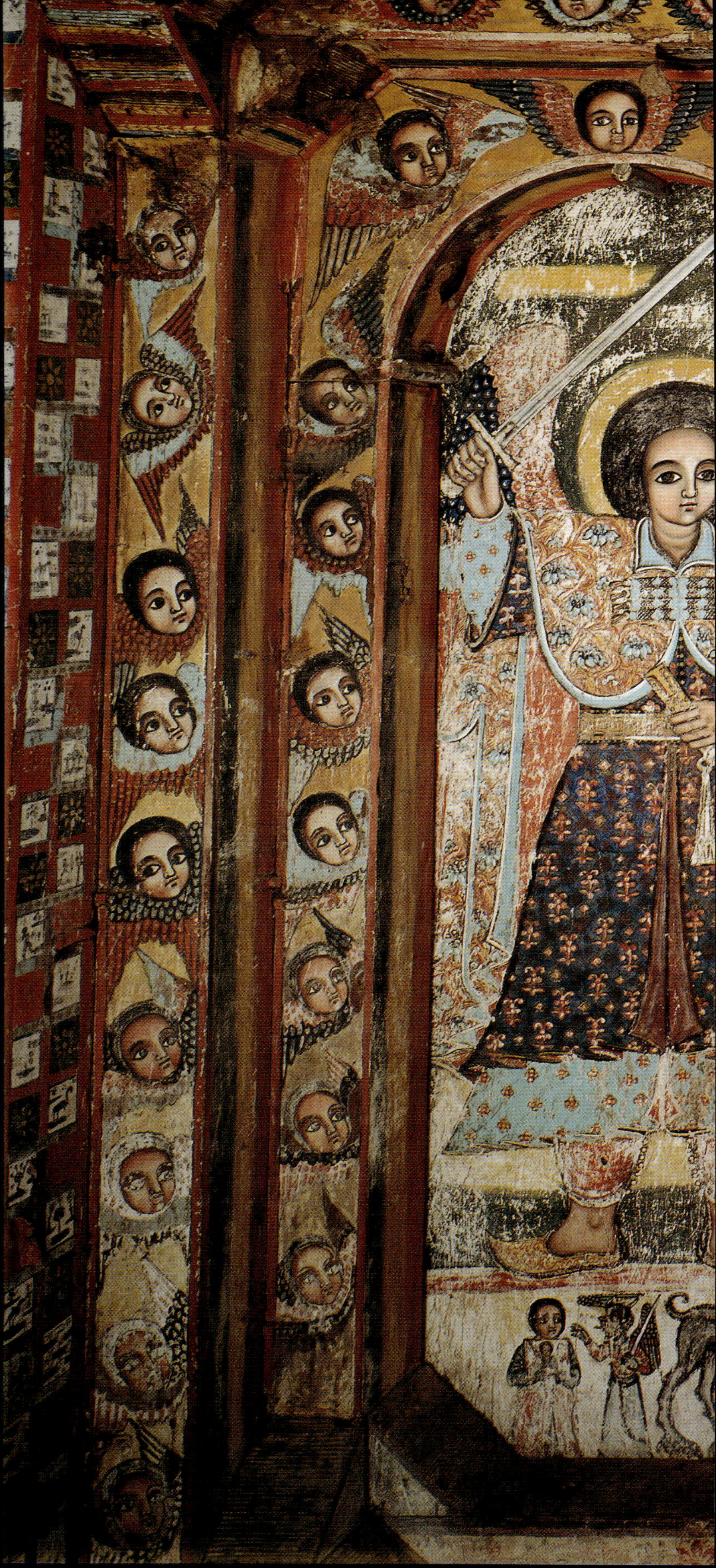

154. Archangels, keepers of the west door of the *maqdas* of Ura Kidāna Merḥat on the peninsula of Ṣegē.

155. Archangels, keepers of the west door of the *maqdas* of Nārgā Śellāsē.

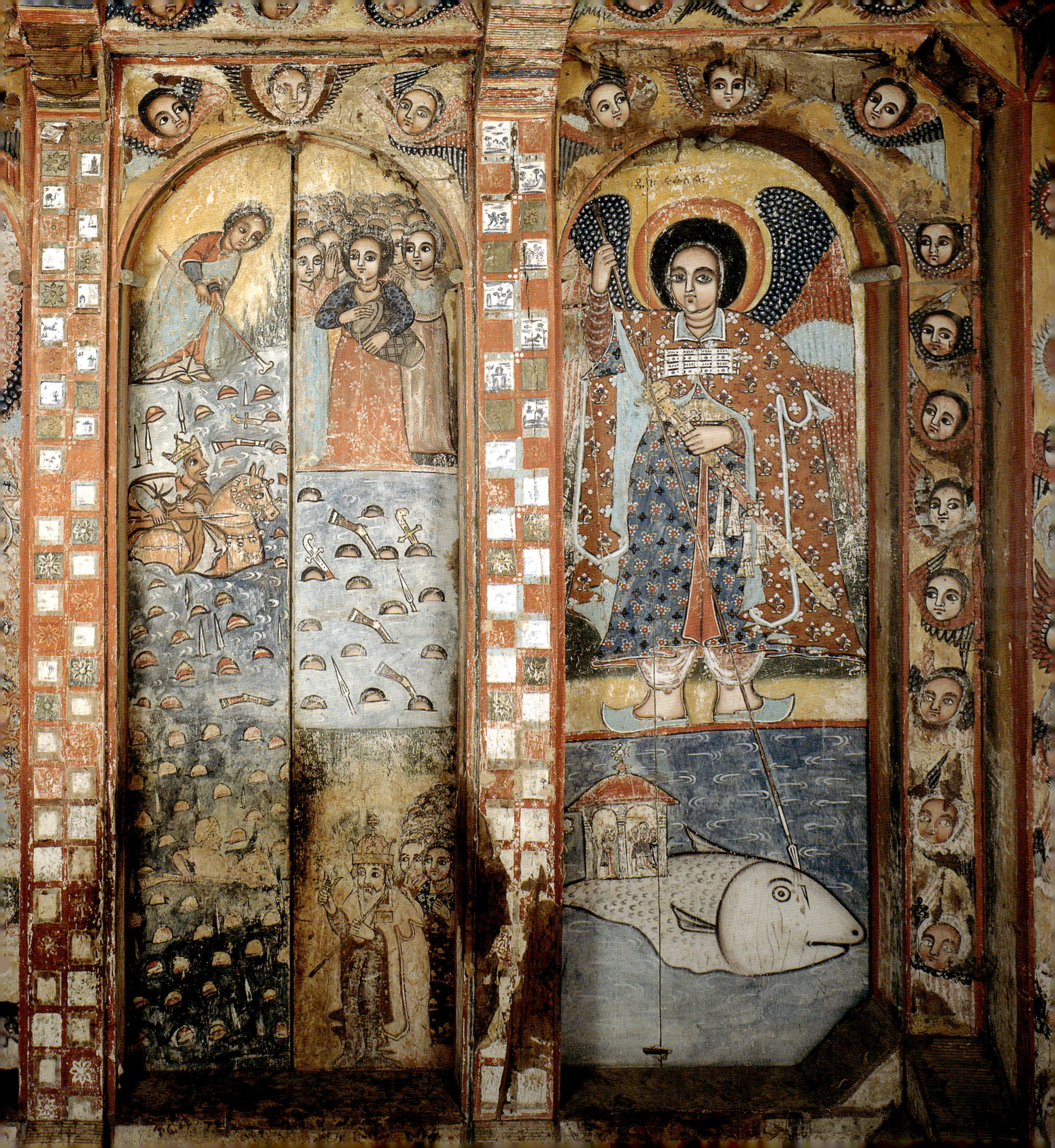

painting, even though at present it is not possible to trace definite references beyond appraisals of style.

It is difficult to imagine a round church, where the *maqdas*, the *sancta sanctorum* in the middle, is not covered with paintings from top to bottom: empty walls offered themselves to decoration and painting. Three doors open onto this area, oriented towards the cardinal points. Only facing east, towards the light, is there a window, while the doors are oriented towards everything which is outside, uncontrolled and always in turmoil. "Usually these doors are watched over by frightening-looking guardians: these scaring figures are therefore called the 'keepers of the doors'. They keep watch, armed and frightening [...] Who are these demons who can be seen at the edges of the mandala and who are almost always present also in those architectural mandalas, the temples? [...] in order to drive back the confusing swarm of that mysterious world from which the traps of the unexpected leap out, and to finally dominate it. Therefore these guardians do not only have a so-called defensive role, but also an offensive one. They are placed at the borders of conscience, just before the other realm, ready to enter it, after having taken [...] a shape which will make them adequate to the forces they have to face" (TUCCI, pp. 73-74).

The iconography of the archangels which guard the entrance doors to the *maqdas* is the same throughout the centuries, even though some accepted variations were inserted. An exemplification and a comparison may be useful, once the limits of our field of interest have been set, in order to trace the sylistic evolution of Ethiopian painting from the 16th to the 18th century.

In Dāgā Esṭifanos, on the front door of the *maqdas*—covered, in all the other parts, with contemporaneous paintings far more chromatically vulgar and totally out of place in such a context—the figure of an archangel has miraculously survived into our age. Standing, forward facing, he stares at the space before him with his large black eyes, his left arm holding in the middle of the painting a small round shield, while his right arm holds aloft a sword, which is as menacing as the uplifted wings crowning his aureole. The axis of the figure is linked to an asymmetry which runs diagonally from his raised arm down to the sheath of his sword, and which also concerns the folds of his cape covering a precious garment, with a geometrical pattern and tied at the waist with large twisted bands. Underneath, he wears a long-sleeved tunic down to his calf, closed at the front with a long line of buttons starting from the folds of a large collar. Still underneath, he wears trousers down to his sandals (fig. 150).

The linear style of the painting shows an exquisite sensitivity: the tracing of the plumes, the features of the face, the folds of the cape, the concentric circles of the shield. Everything—and not only the drawiing of the edges—is rendered through a coherent pictorial language which does not just delineate the painting of the background but rather involves its whole space. The strokes range from black, red, brown, ochre, to lighter tones which are better suited to the white of the background on which the drawing stands out, almost in transparency. This artistic choice is rooted in local tradition, since it derives from a centuries-old style typical of Ethiopian art which can also be found—although of a lower standard—elsewhere, such as in the paintings of the *maqdas* in the church of Kota Māryām, on the nearby island of Dek, dating to at least as far back as the 16th century (fig. 146).

The archangel painted on the similar one-leaf door of the *maqdas* in the church of Dabra Sinā, close to Gorgorā, of the first half of 17th century, reproposes the same iconography, with a variation: the shield—so effective in Dāgā Esṭifanos, there in the middle, exactly where a possible swordstroke might land—is no longer present. Still, the two paintings share the same static frontal pose of the figures and the same diagonal orientation which runs from the raised arm down to the sheath of the sword, which has been drawn and is held high, menacingly ready to strike. Shapes, always edged with thin lines, are here filled in with colours, and with the decorative patterns of the fabric, which are presented facing front, without following the even unlikely movement of the folds. The shading of the face is painted synthetically, even though anatomy is taken into account for a schematic specification. This stylistic choice can be found so much in the first phase of Gondarian painting that it can be considered a typical feature of this style all during 17th century. Also the falling of locks of black hair on the shoulders can be seen as a conscious naturalstic trait. The wings, no longer contained within the rectangular shape of the door-leaf, ideally reach beyond the avaliable surface, thus causing a lack of that perfect tension and formal definition which characterizes Dāgā Esṭifanos. Although this is obviously the reproposing of a model, the painting on the whole is less calligraphic, and concentrates more on the reproduction of the folds of the garments, while colours acquire a better consistency and become fuller thanks to the contrast with the white of the background surrounding the image (fig. 151).

In Kebrān Gabre'ēl (second half of 17th century), the depiction of the two archangels on the western door of the *maqdas* seems to revive a stronger tone of archaism, abstraction and stateliness. The usual frontal axis of the figure is, as always, associated with the dynamic layout of the composition: the disk of a round shield is painted in profile, so as to cover the left arm, holding an elegant, light and knotted spear which diagonally crosses the whole figure, pointing at the hilt of the uplifted, drawn sword. Clothing—in which is proclaimed an almost deformed geometry—includes trousers tight at the ankles, but ample at the knees, where the repeated horizontal bands in the edging seem to cut the figures in two. The upper part of the body rests on legs column-like in their strength, thus emphasizing the compositional layout already proposed in the portrayal of the guardian archangel in Dabra Sinā. Although it shows an obvious orientalizing of taste—which is underlined by the preciousness of the fabric, shown in all its exquisiteness without any consideration for a realistic rendering of the folds—the whole still belongs to the Ethiopian tradition of face depiction, with its typical still, huge pupils, with a bull-like neck and bushy head of hair, a trait of the local population. The linearity of the composition is no longer expressed just with the fluidity of features, lines or bands, but rather exalted in the arched, straight or undulating profiles of the background: the reds, the ochres, the browns, the black, the blue, create a brighter, richer and more precious range of colours, where the white itself loses its chacacteristics as background colour and becomes an integral part of the composition (fig. 152).

From the 18th century onwards, although the iconography of the winged figure, standing with feet apart and diagonally divided by the sheath of his sword which he holds with his right arm, remains constant, new elements appear, which more overtly recall foreign influences, such as that of Western painting (in the more realistic modelling, in the treatment of light and shadow) and of Eastern tradition from as far away as the Indian Ocean, Moghul's India—(especially in the refined quality of the decoration of clothes and accessories).

On the isle of Dek two archangels guard the *maqdas* of the church of Arsimā which sadly is crumbling. One of the figures, as at Kebrān Gabre'ēl, holds a spike, but here it is turned downwards, to stop a sea monster which challenges the stability of a church built on its back; the other holds, rather than brandishes, the sword, his arm resting on his chest. The faces are no longer facing front, but slightly three-quarters, with a thich head of hear, without a halo. The look is no longer terrifying and their clothing falls naturally and symmetrically, the long front hems of the *lembd* on top of a cloak with ample folds ending with a meander-like edging. The figures are painted on opaque backgrounds which have different tones, ranging from brown to grey. White marks the outline of the clothing and makes more precious the sword and the clasp of the *lembd*, and the vibrant wings. The rich pattern of the brocade, which is no longer schematically geometrical, follows the folds, presenting just a slight variation in tone.

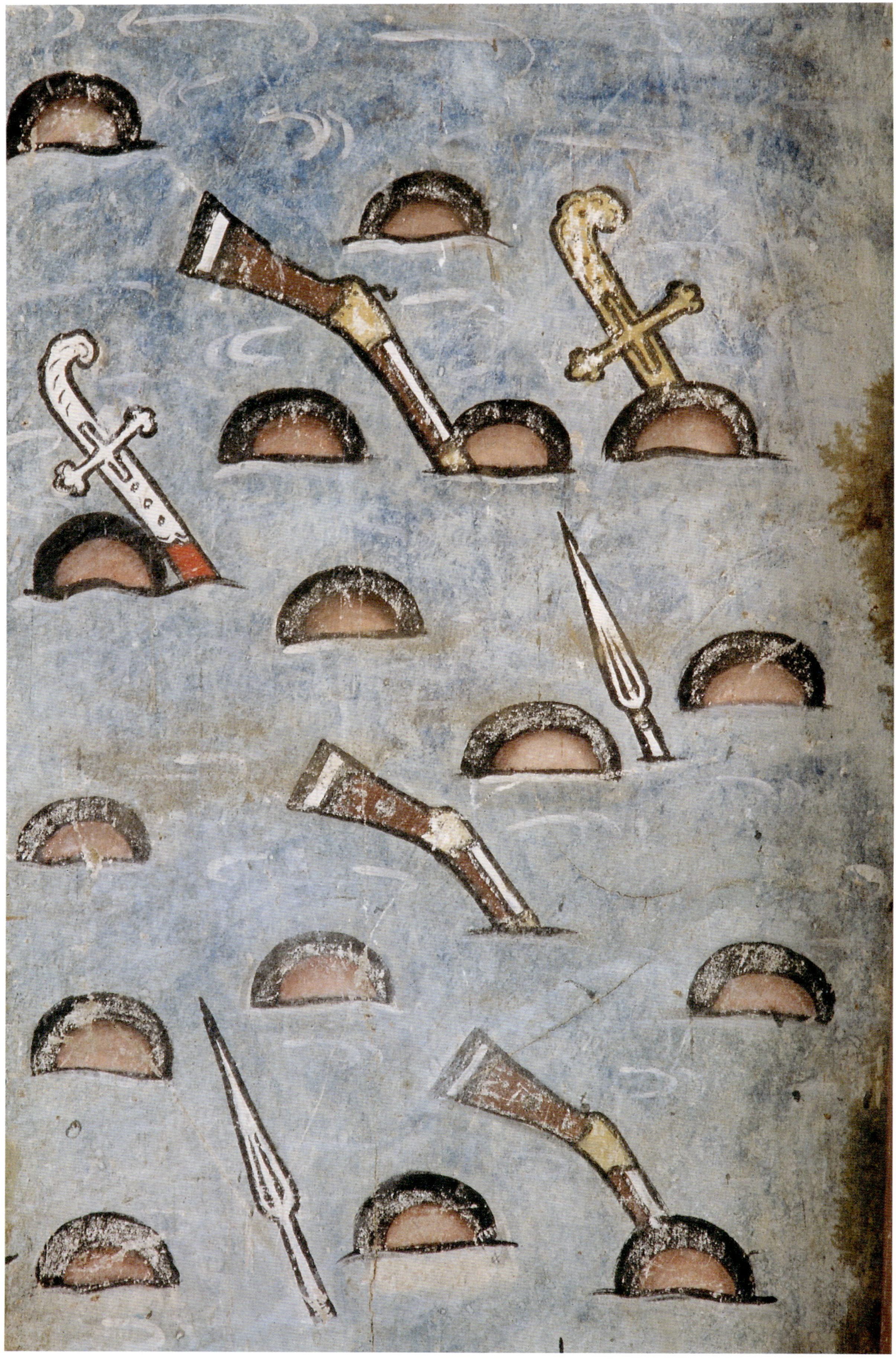

156. The Pharaoh's soldiers swept away by the Red Sea
(detail of the central leaf of the west door of the *maqdas* of the church of Nārgā Śellāsē).

157. The sea monster on which a church was built is stopped by the spear of the Archangel Gabriel (detail of the right leaf of the west door of the *maqdas* of the church of Nārgā Śellāsē).

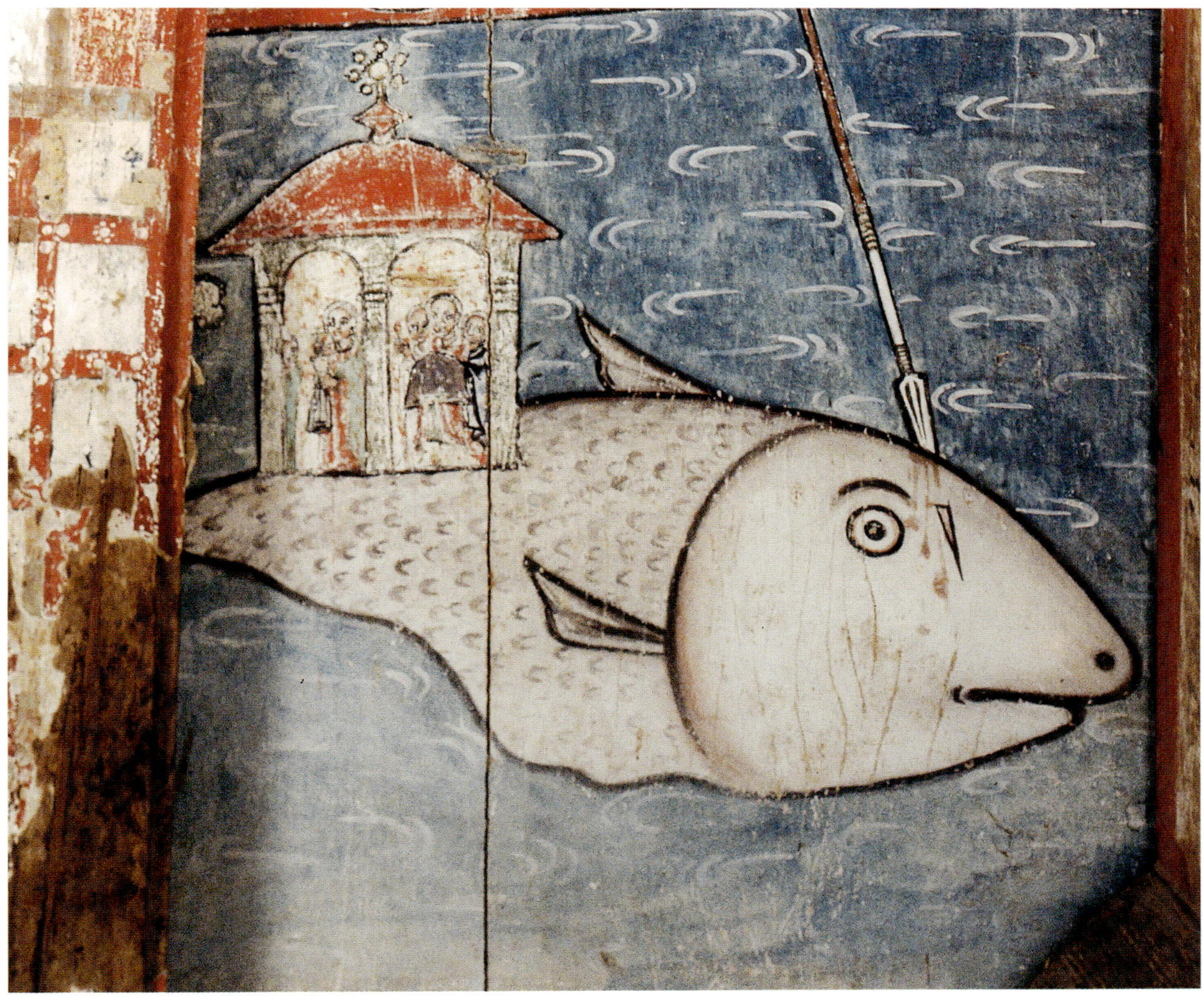

The attention to reality becomes more evident, and although the paintings on the whole are of a high artistic level, sometimes this goes against formal, stylistical and compositional inventiveness (fig. 153).

The depiction of fabric becomes even brighter and more ornate at Nārgā Śellāsē, towards mid-18th century, where it reaches an almost rococo exhibition of preciousness and its policromy—no longer opaque—shows the delicacy of pastel tones. The *sfumato* of the uncovered parts of the body (face, hands, ankles) accentuates and moulds the delicacy of the modelling (fig. 155).

Therefore, while the iconography of the archangel guarding the *maqdas* remains the same for centuries, the way he is depicted radically changes, under the most direct artistic influences of the countries with which Ethiopia entertained relationships. The result is an assimilation of a wide variety of influences into Ethiopian culture and sensitivity: the Qwarā or *qwareñña* style, so called after the area where Empress Mentewwāb, who commissioned the most important buildings of the time, came from.

"... luxury is a specific trait. The painters of this epoch liked to wrap their figures in garments overabundant with brocades and embroideries, similar tho those worn by the Neguś and the princes" (LEROY, p. 35). Reading the list of linen of the monastery of Nārgā Śellāsē one finds "brocades, capturing the eye", damasks, Persian and Chinese fabrics.[1]

In the imposing triforate door which takes up the largest part of the western side of the *maqdas* of Nārgā Śellāsē, the archangel Michael is portrayed on the left leaf. In the middle there is the crossing of the Red Sea and on the right the part devoted to the archangel Gabriel repeates the miracle of the church built on an isle, dangerously balanced upon the back of a sort of sea

[1] An inventory of what is left of the old textile equipment of the churches, kept in the "house of the treasure" would be very interesting.

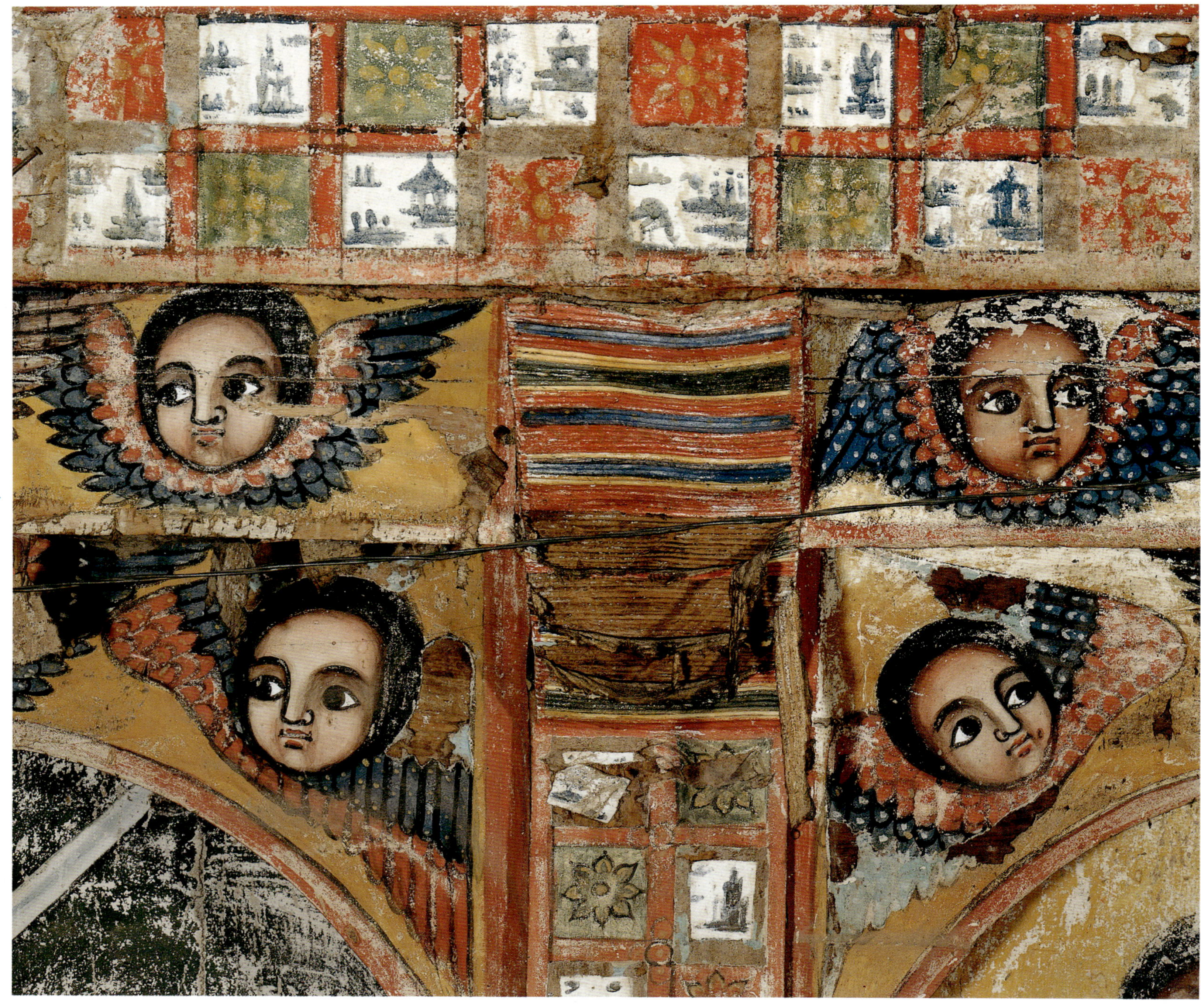

monster represented as a huge fish (fig. 157). A group of cherubs hover in the air above. Only the external frame of the *trifora* and the two central body pillars, outlined in red, are decorated with a chequard pattern. In the small squares, arranged in a double line, stars patterns alternate with landscapes and naturalistic and everyday life scenes, sketched with quick brushstrokes of azure on a white background, to convey the effect of almost real *azulejos*. Moreover, each of the four sides of the *maqdas* has a decorative band, similar to the border of an Oriental carpet, more precisely a Chinese-like one, because of the flower motifs arranged in a meander shape. Even considering only these decorative bands, the primary sources of the *qwareñña* style are obvious: Ethiopia itself, but also Portugal, the Orient and others.

In the Ethiopian tradition—a conservative one—the cycles of paintings which completely cover the *maqdas* are arranged according to quite constant canons (Cf. HABTA MĀRYĀM WAR-

158. Cherubs hover over the entrance of the *maqdas* amongst decorated frames (detail of the leafs of the west door).

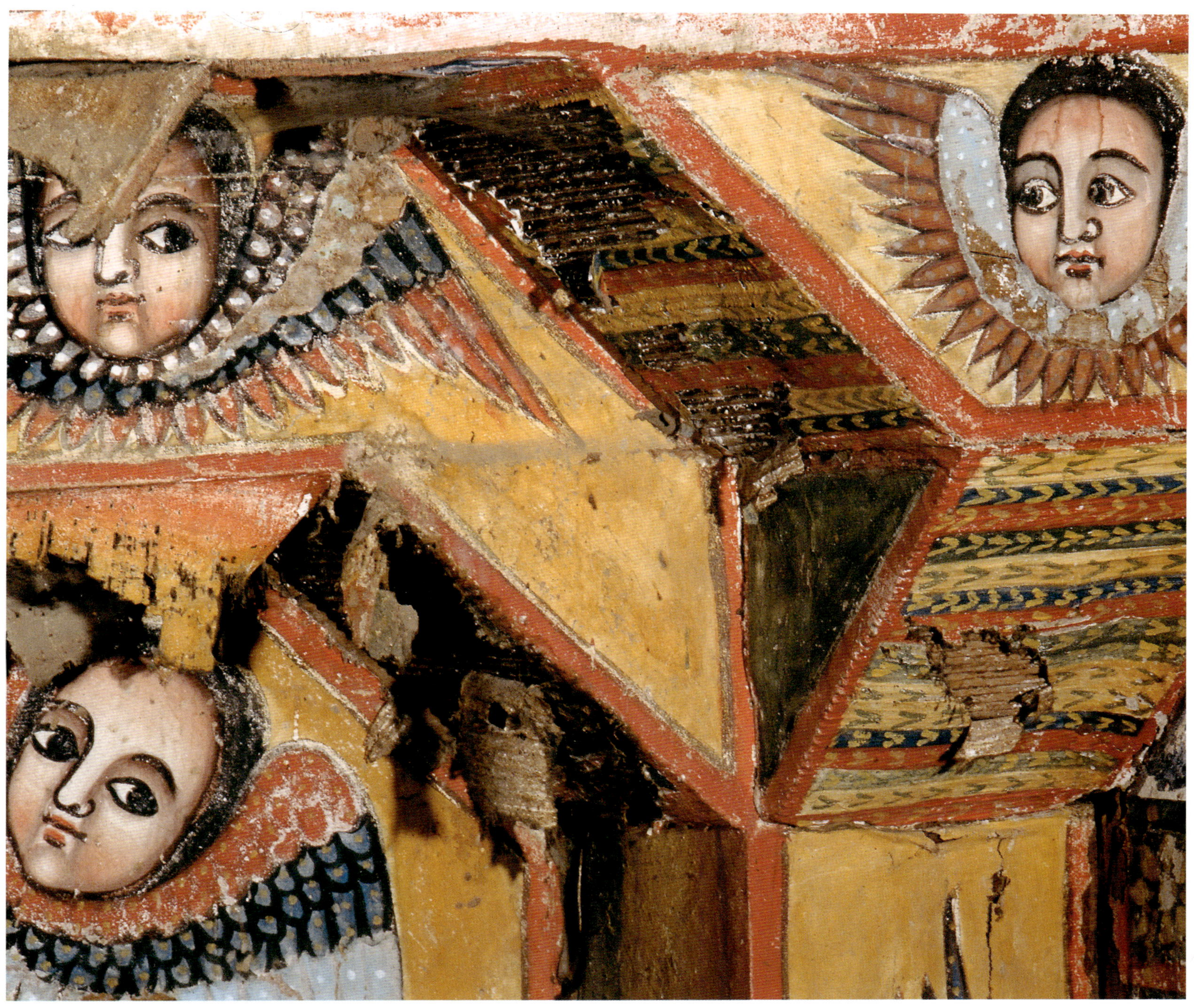

159. Each facet shows a cherub (detail of the west door).

QENAH, JÄGER, STAUDE), obviously linked to symbolic and didactic contents. Nārgā Śellāsē is no exception. Only the eastern side of the *maqdas*, where episodes in the life of Jesus and his miracles are painted, seems to recall more recent representational canons, since the theme is not treated in the same way on the correspondent walls of the churches of Dabra Sinā at Gorgorā and of Abbā Antonios in Gondar (17th century), where the four 'Just Kings', David, Solomon, Hezekiah and Josiah tower.

On the other sides of the *maqdas* the depiction does not differ from the themes as already developed on the same sides in the above-mentioned churches, although some accepted variations are introduced, either by means of integration or suppression of one or other episode of the cycle.

The west wall of the *maqdas*—the most important from the liturgical point of view—picks up again the theme of the Redemption (from the Annunciation to the Resurrection, up to the

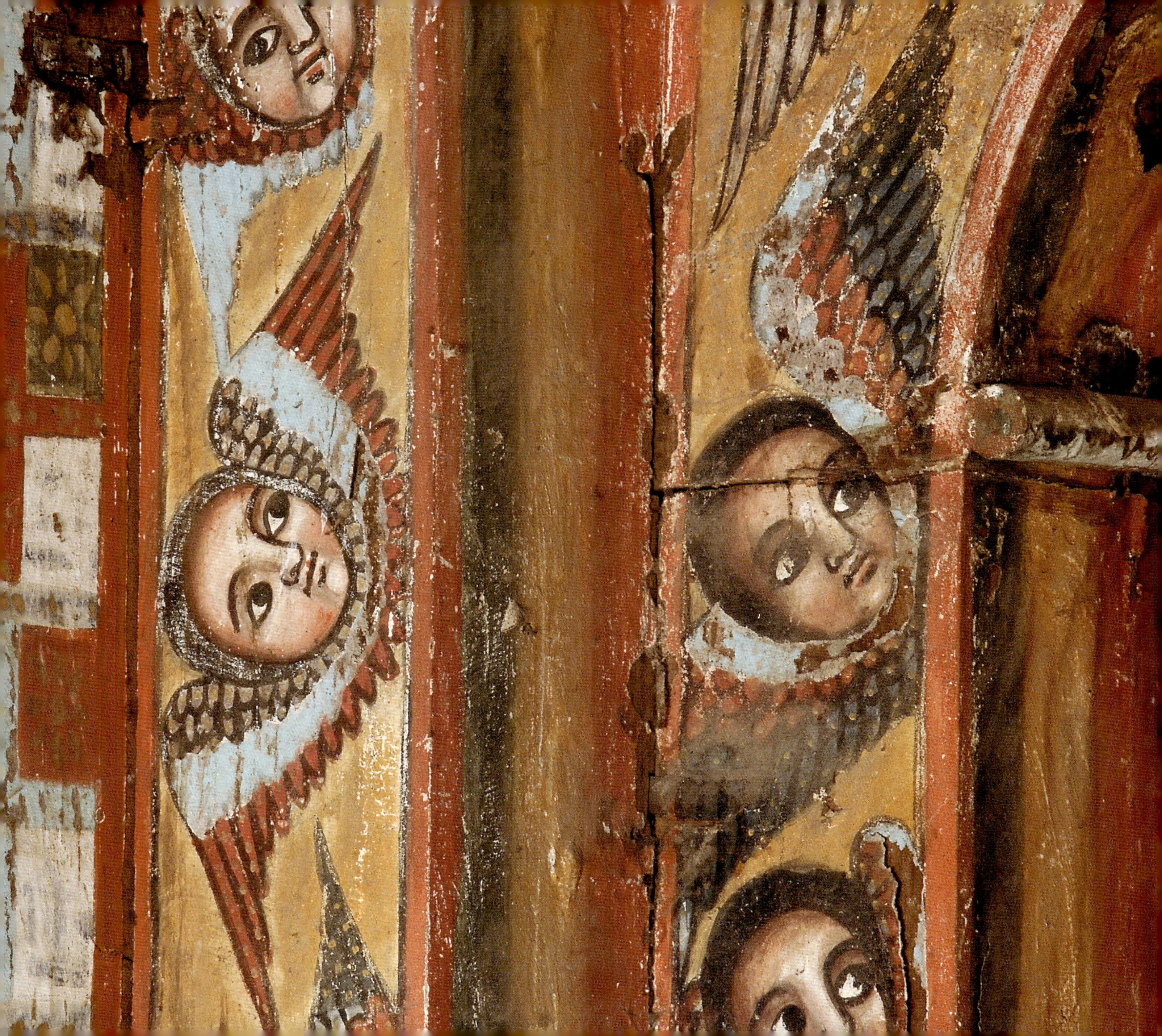

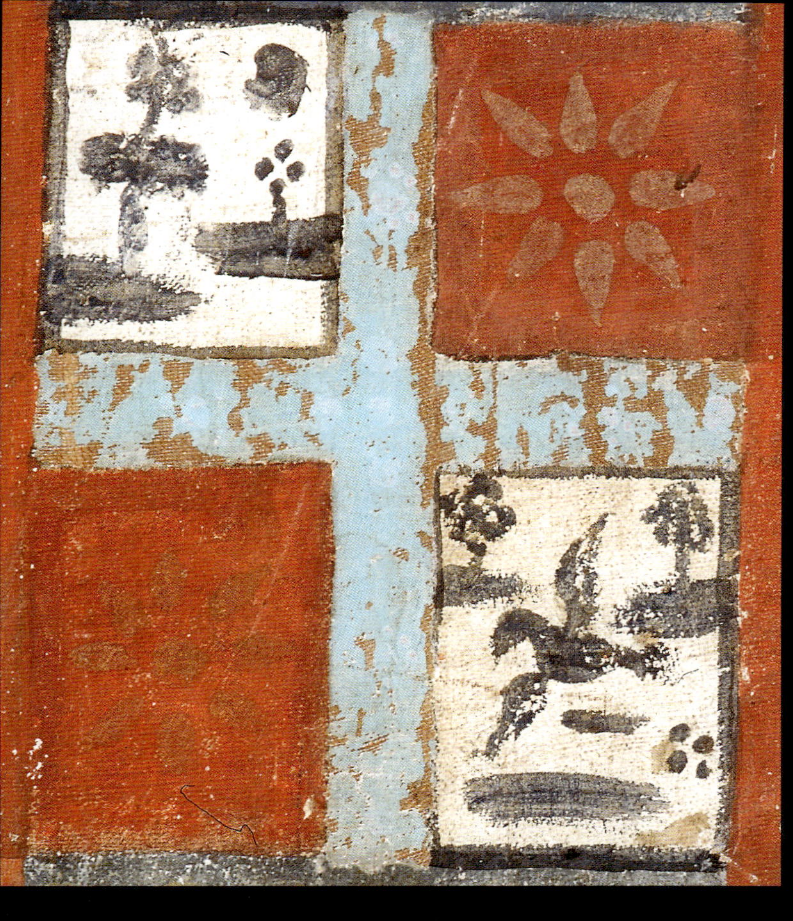
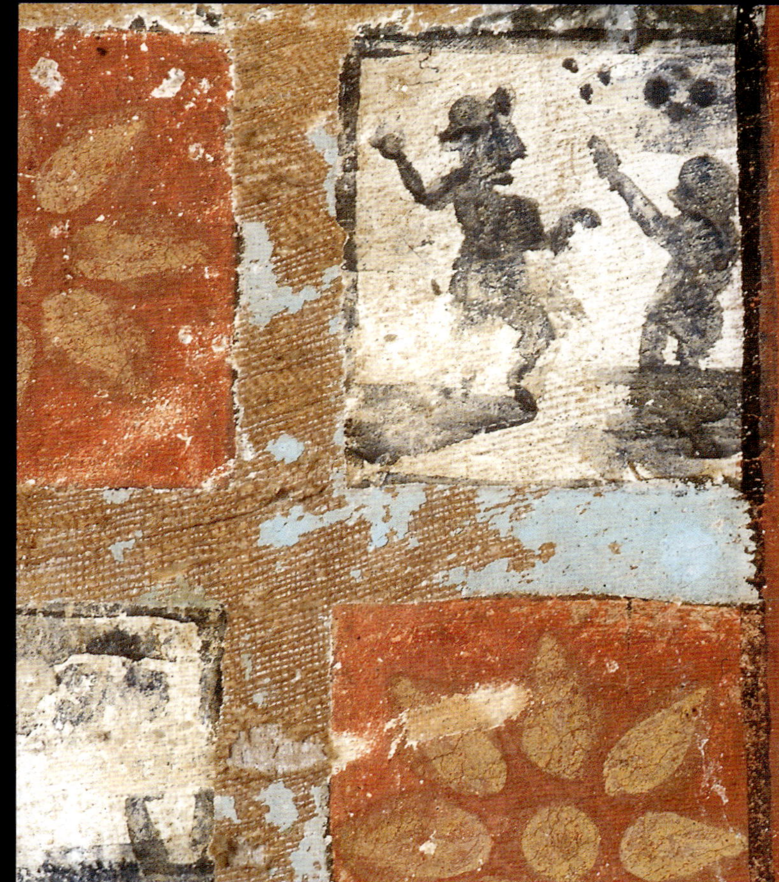
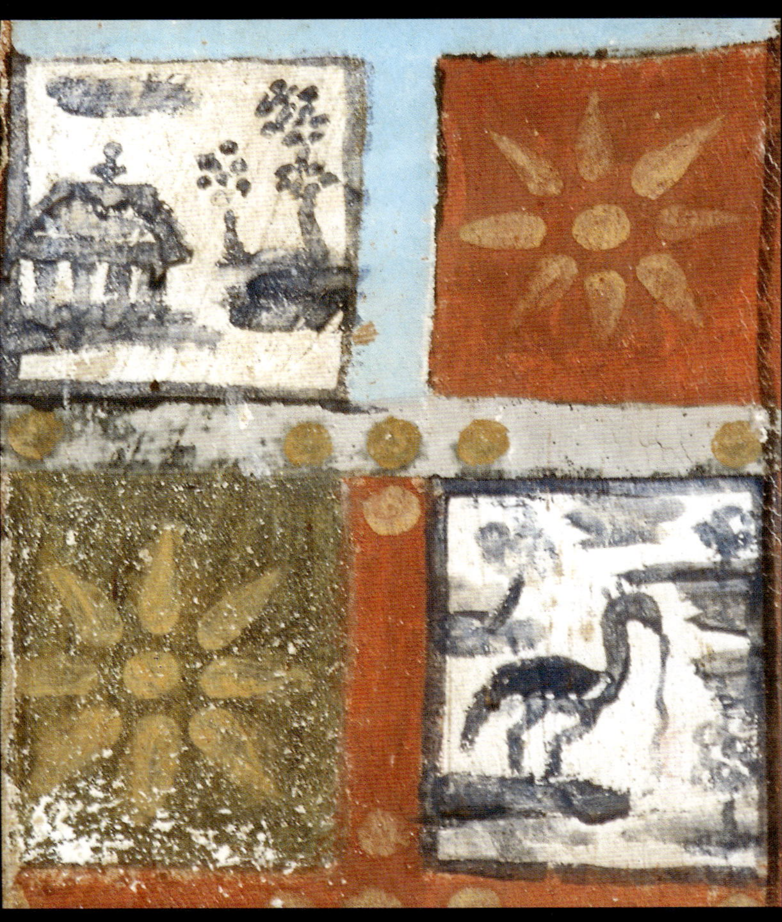
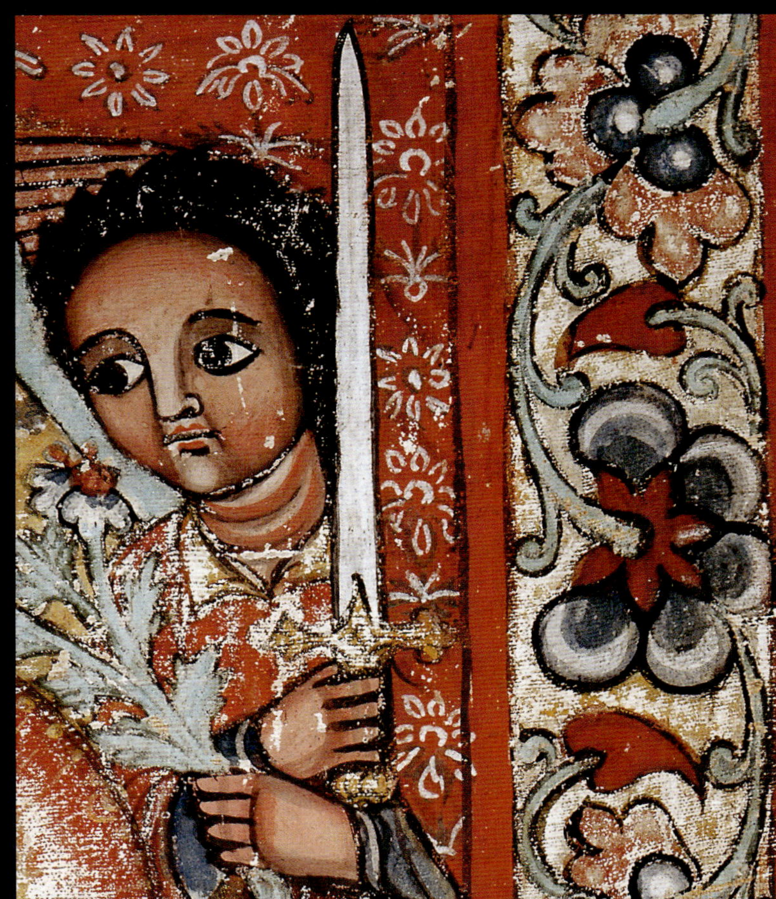

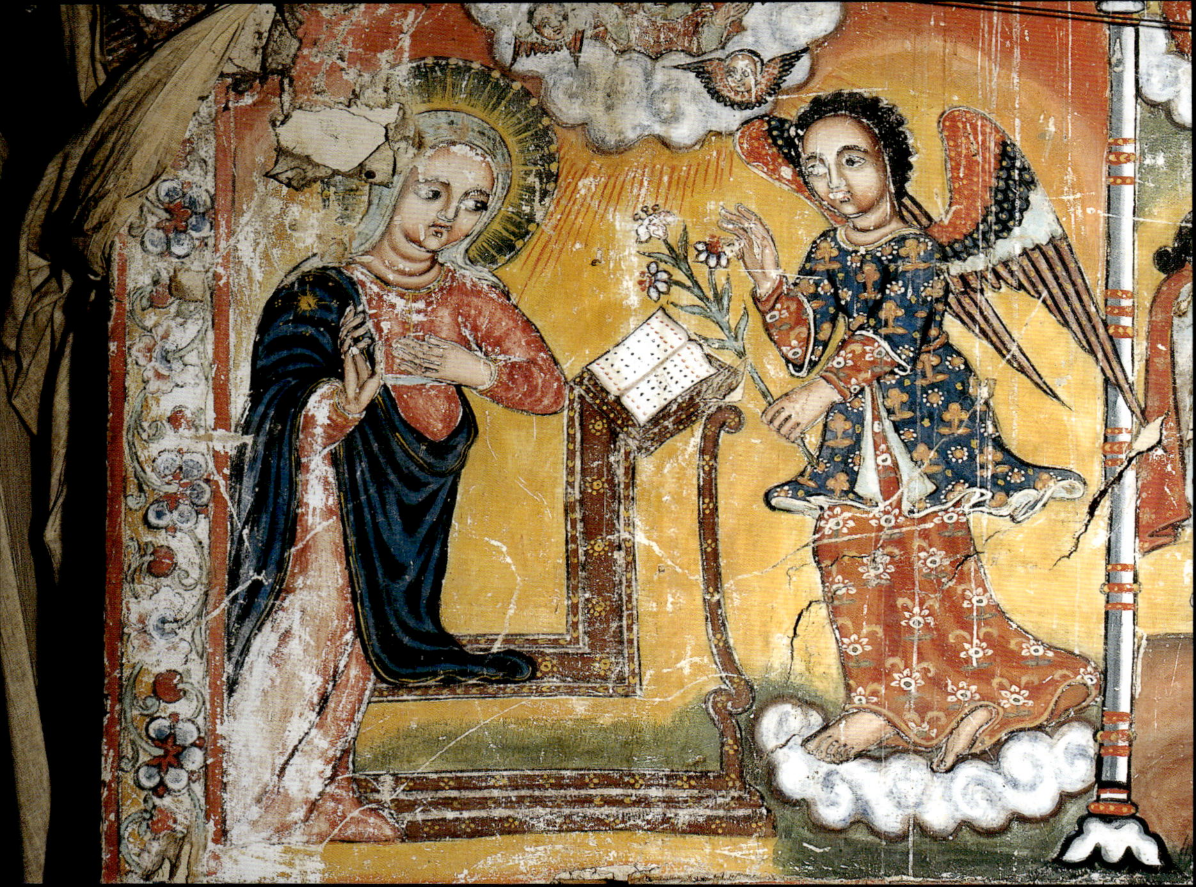

165. West wall of the *maqdas*: the Announciation.

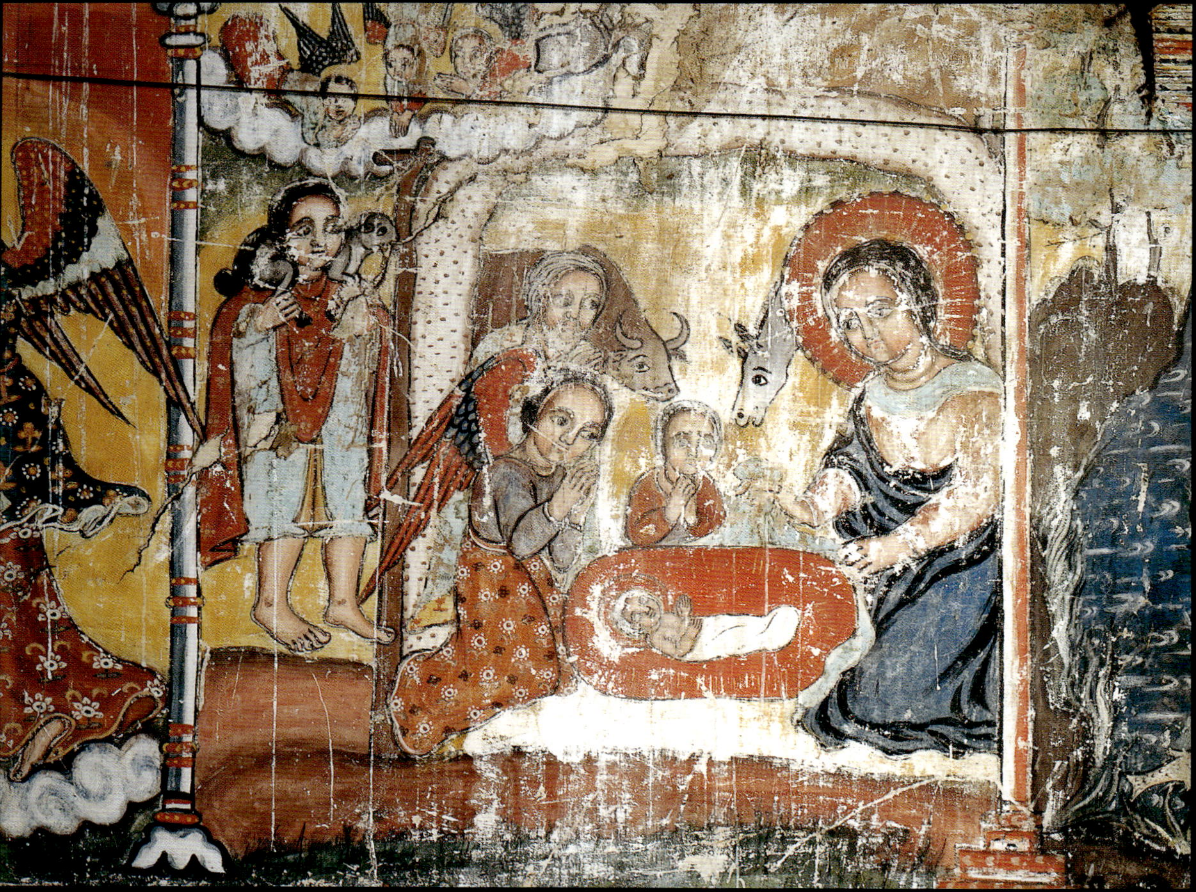

166. West wall of the *maqdas*: the Nativity.

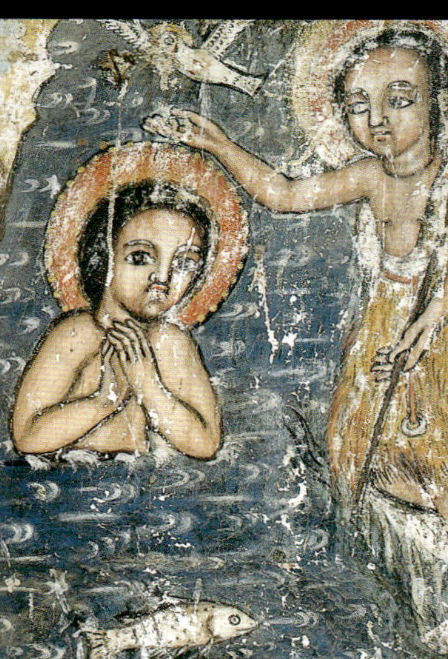

167. West wall of the *maqdas*: Christ's Baptism, detail.

169. West wall of the *maqdas*: Jesus in the garden of Gethsemane

170. West wall of the *maqdas*: Saint George kills the dragon.

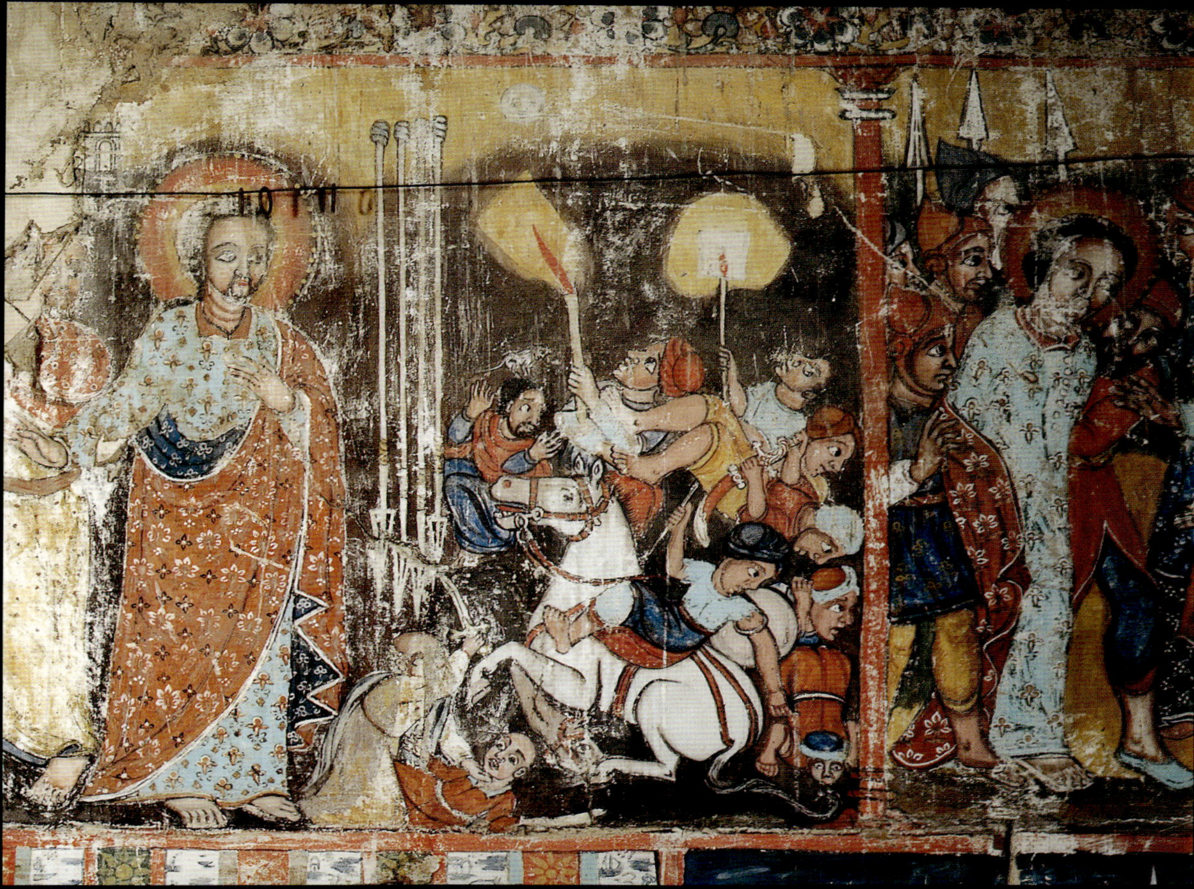

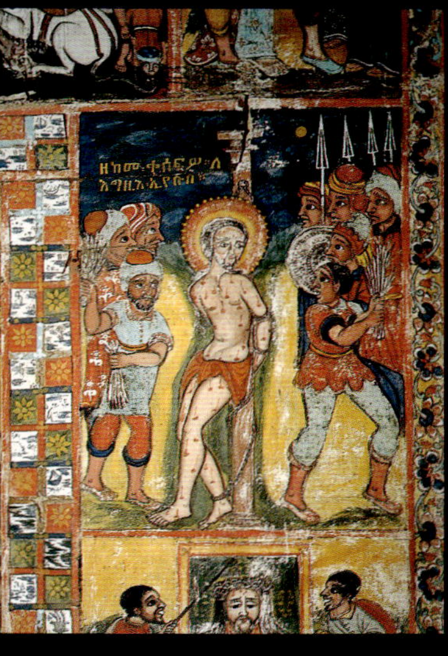

168. West wall of the *maqdas*: Christ's Flagellation.

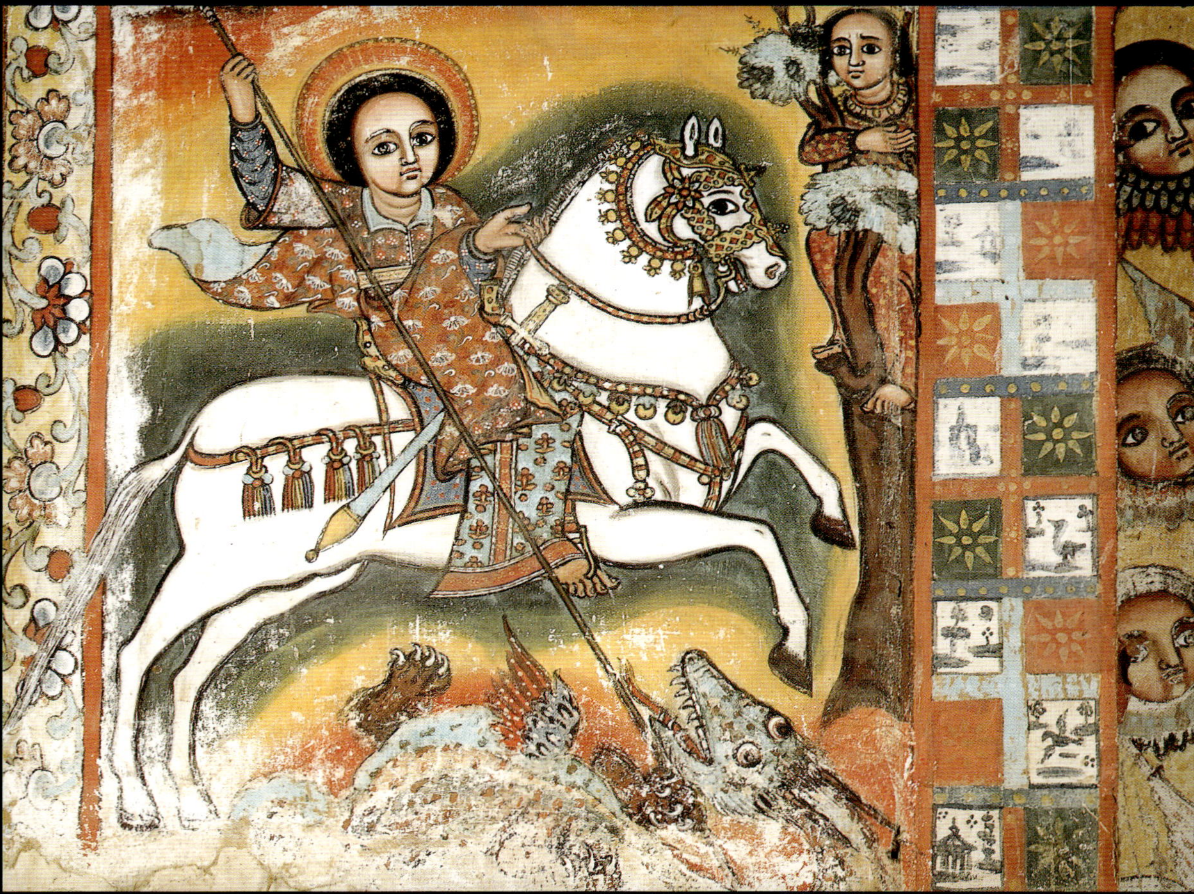

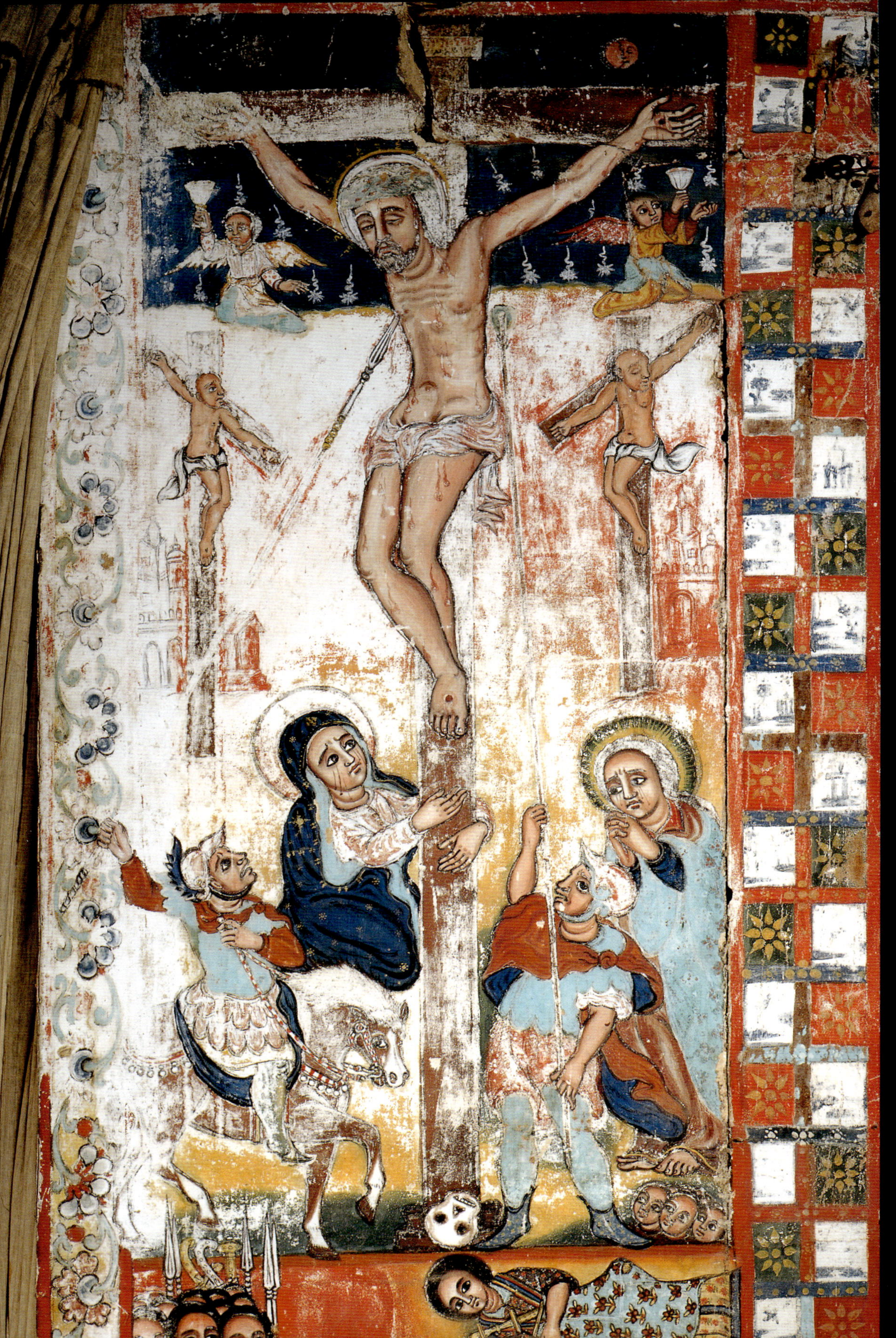

171. West wall
the Crucifixion

172. West wall of the *maqdas*: the Pact of the Alliance (*Kidāna Meḥrat*).

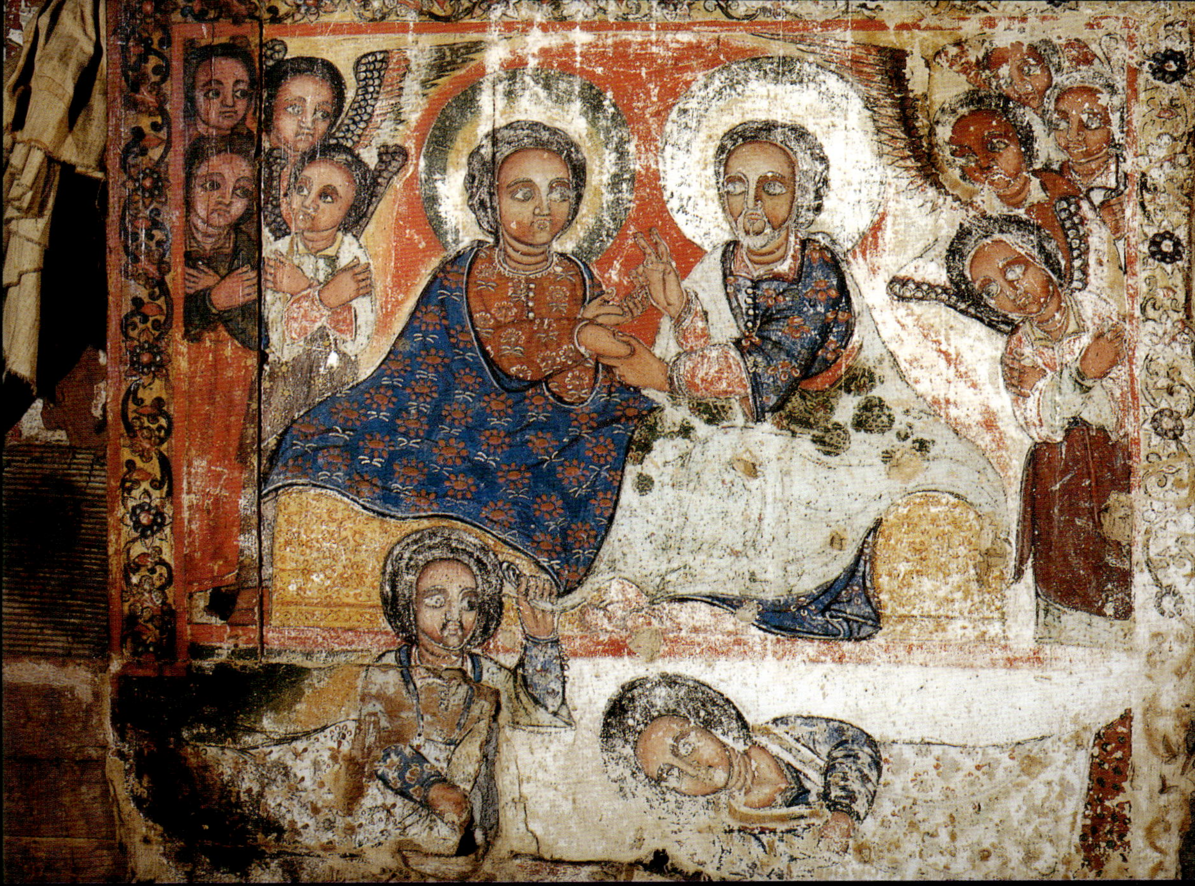

173. West wall of the *maqdas*: the Coronation with thorns.

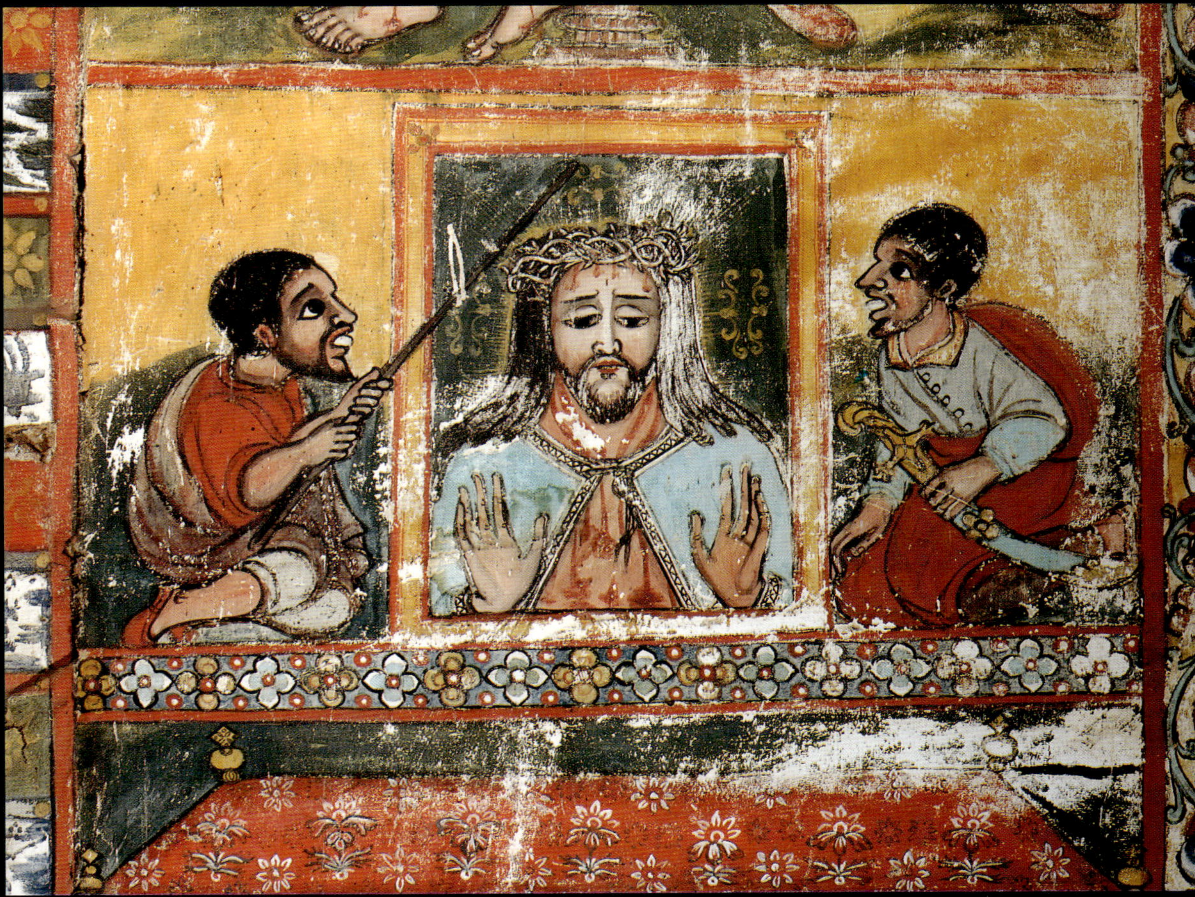

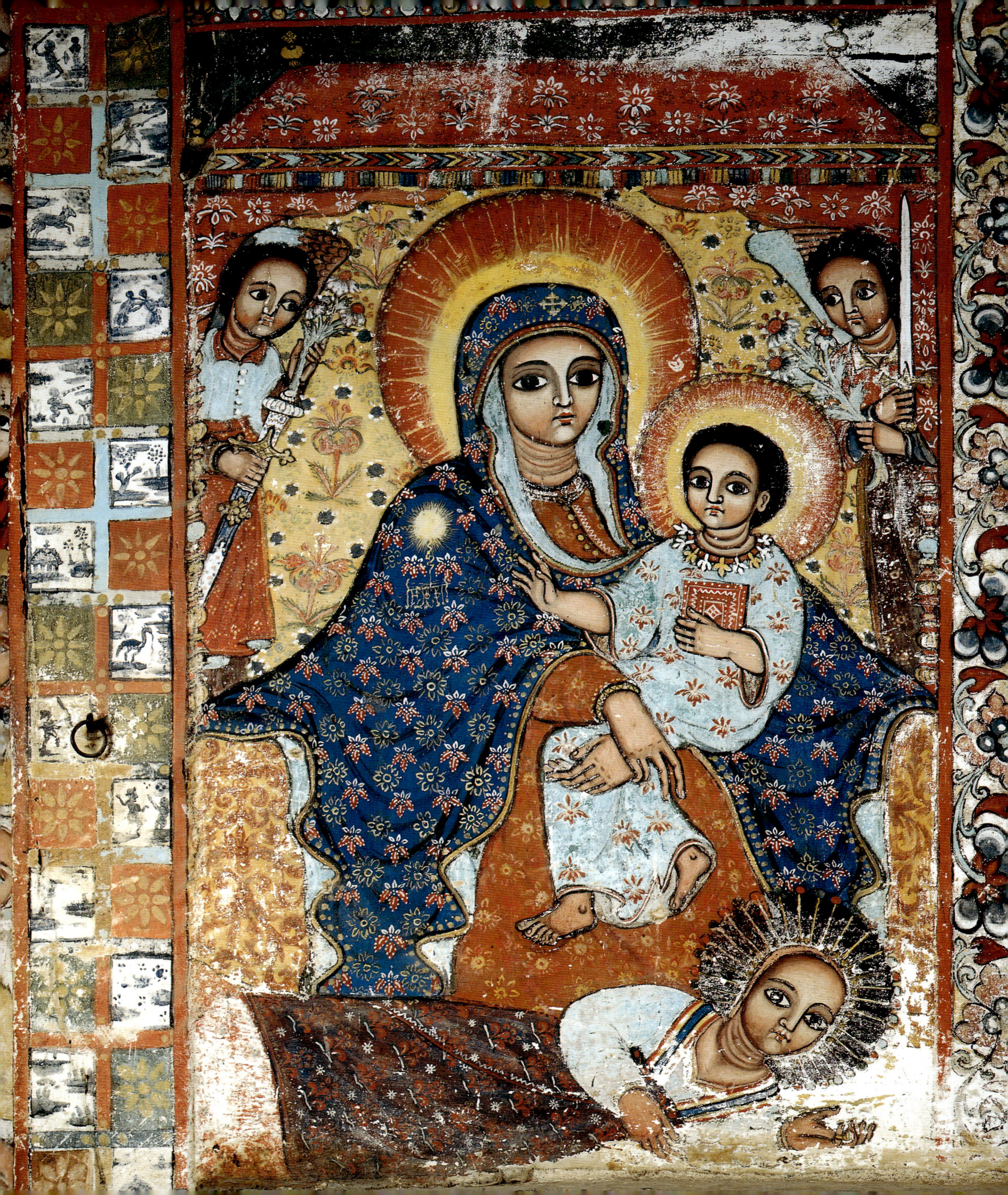

175. Tambour corresponding to the west wall of the *maqdas*: The Holy Trinity.

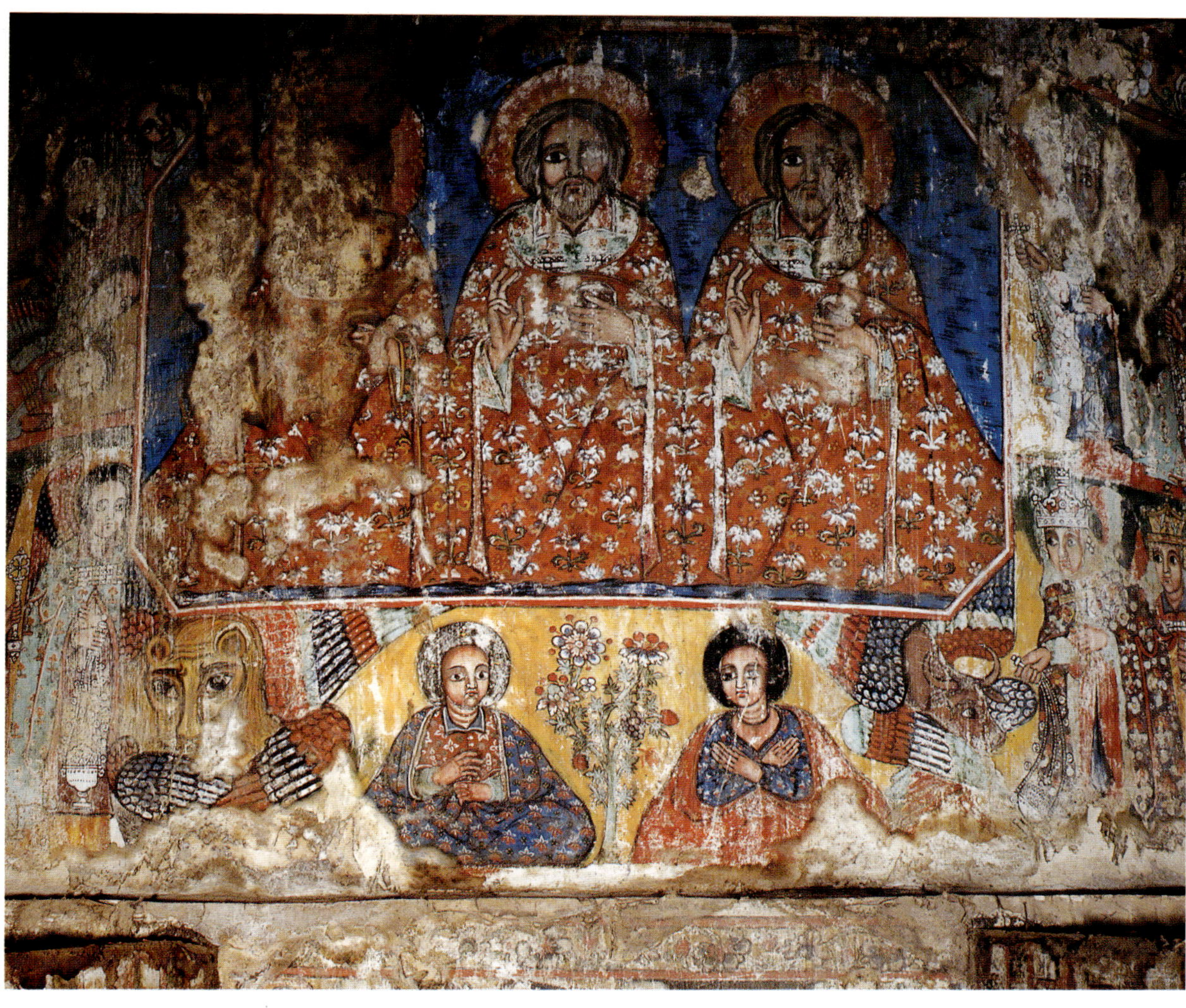

[2] *kidāna meḥrat* in which, according to Ethiopian tradition, God promises Mary that those who invoke him in the name of the Virgin will be pardoned.

174. West wall of the *maqdas*: Virgin with Child and Queen Mentewwāb, offerering.

Descent into hell and the Covenant)[2] and, as is typical, at the sides of the portal there are depictions of the patron saints of Ethiopian Christianity: St. George and the Virgin (fig. 143).

The south face of the *maqdas*, facing the part of the *qeddest* reserved for women, illustrates themes from the life of Mary (fig. 145). Meanwhile on the opposite, north-facing side, which overlooks the area reserved for men, there is a procession of warriors saints and martyrs, some on rearing horses (fig. 144).

A sort of celestial region is created by the themes represented on the tambour as compared with the more "terrestrial" character of the cube of the *maqdas*, confirming a general obedience to the canons traditionally used if not actually precribed. At Nārgā, however, as in other churches of the same period, the eastern side of the tambour has depictions of Christ's Ascension, in accordance with the themes represented in the lower area of the corresponding side of the *maqdas* (fig. 142).

The ordering in sequence of the painted scenes is usually obtained by a simple squaring of the surfaces created between the openings in the sides of the *maqdas* and their edges. At Nārgā this is carried out mainly in a pre-determined way, according to an overall plan drawing on a logic of composition and continuity in the repetition and in the alignement with the doorframes. In other instances a haphazard arrangement seems to prevail, limited only by the dimensional requirements of each single scene.

The skirting is divided using the same criteria, whilst the tambour is decorated with a continuous ring of paintings which celebrate with various technical devices the main themes of the corresponding paintings on the wall below.

The lower part of the paintings of the *maqdas*, more than others, has always been subject to

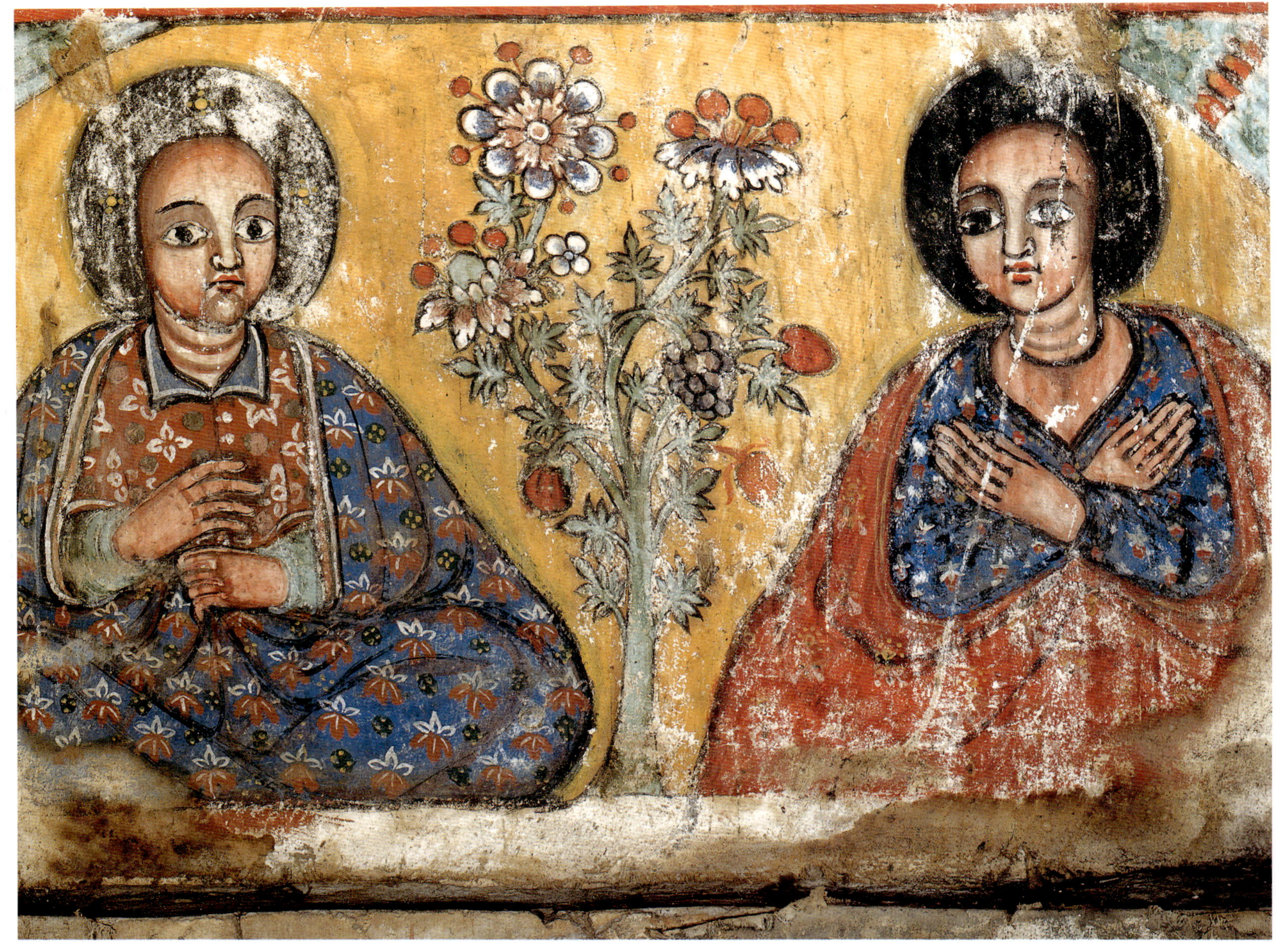

176. Tambour corresponding to the west wall of the *maqdas*: Adam and Eve.

wear, caused by the presence of devotees. At Nārgā Śellāsē the skirting, the lower section of the scenes above and the jambs, shutters and doors, have had their paintings all but obliterated up to the height of a man. This damage has led to the need for later repainting of these areas, except on the west side, where the sacredness of the main entrance to the *maqdas* imposed a greater respect. The painting on the upper parts, on the other hand, has been subject to extensive damage caused by the seepage of water through the roof. Sheets have been roughly hung above these works in an attempt to protect them from the droppings of birds which have entered the *qeddest*. Although they are often in a bad state of repair, these works have nonetheless remained unaltered since they were first executed.

The re-working and the substitute re-painting of the frescoes on the lower part of the *maqdas* must date to a later period—by at least some decades— than the decorative layout of the church, which is documented as belonging to, and traditionally ascribed to, the mid 18th century. Despite this, it would seem that we cannot attribute the original decorative layout to one particular school or a single stylistic conception, let alone one artist. Rather, the whole seems to be the result of a uniting of different artists, each with his own individual stylistic traits. The

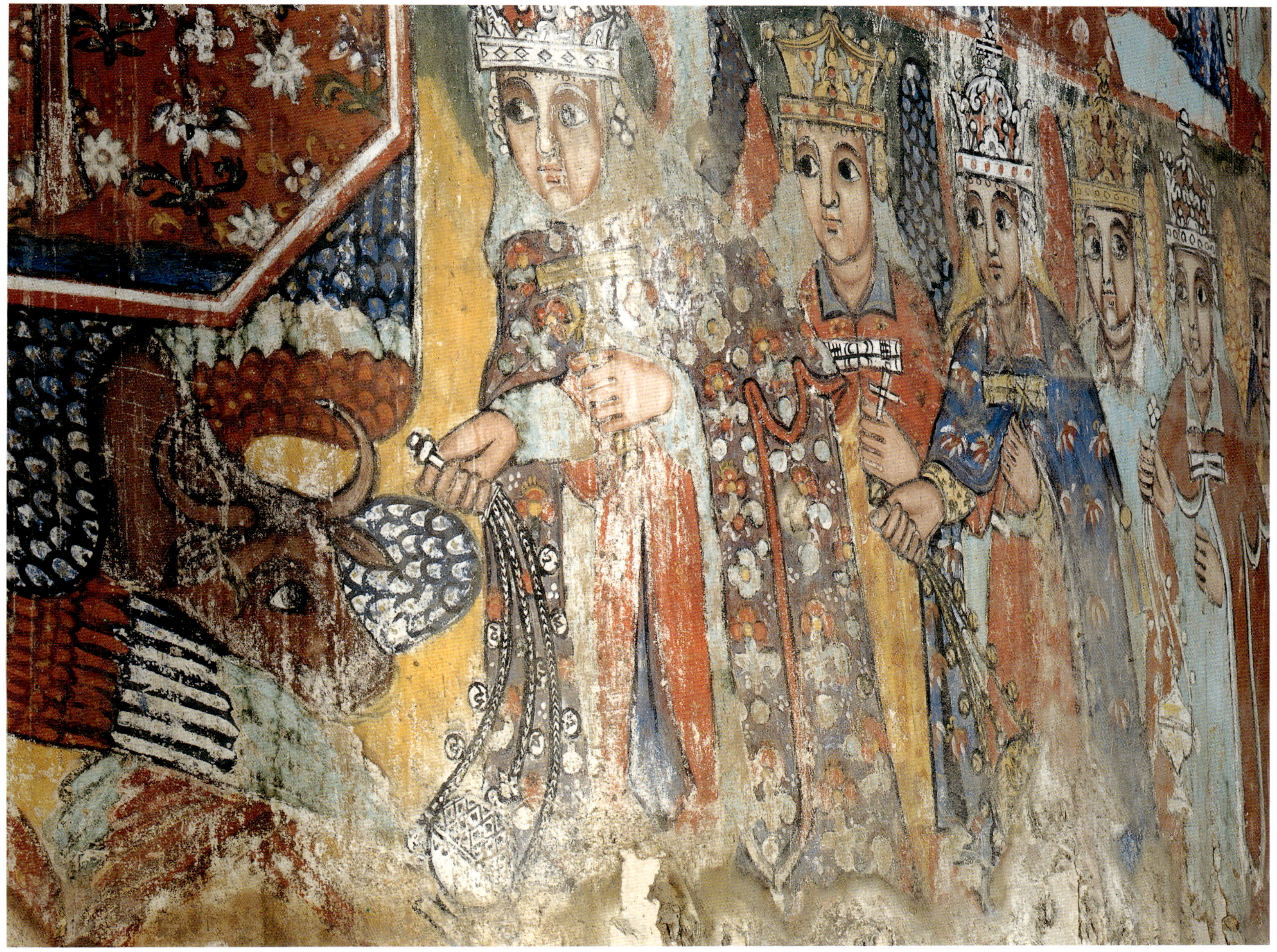

177. Tambour corresponding to the west wall of the *maqdas*: a host of heavenly priests.

impression is that a new tendency within the structure of the *bottega* had developed. Whereas traditionally the artists of the *bottega* worked coherently and homogeneously in the production of a work, here it seems that there was more space for personal expression and artistic individuality. The concept of the *bottega*, that cradle for the formation of a stylistic identity linked to tradition and teaching, has given way in favour of single characterizations in which free expression has been allowed. The unity of the whole is expressed and assured only in conceptual terms: the organization of pictorial cycles which are thematically individuated on the various walls of the *maqdas*. This is a characteristic for which Nārgā Śellāsē church stands out in respect to most other churches, in which there is generally a stylistic coherence of pictorial decoration in all parts of the building, regardless of differences in the superfetations.

The church of Nārgā Śellāsē is dotted with innovative ideas regarding the decoration of the walls, such as the setting of certain scenes inside improbable porticos, or the band high on the west wall, where thin little stylized columns provide illusory support for the frieze above. The various scenes occupying the different bays demonstrate a conception of space previously unseen in Ethiopian wall painting (even if already present, with completely different charac-

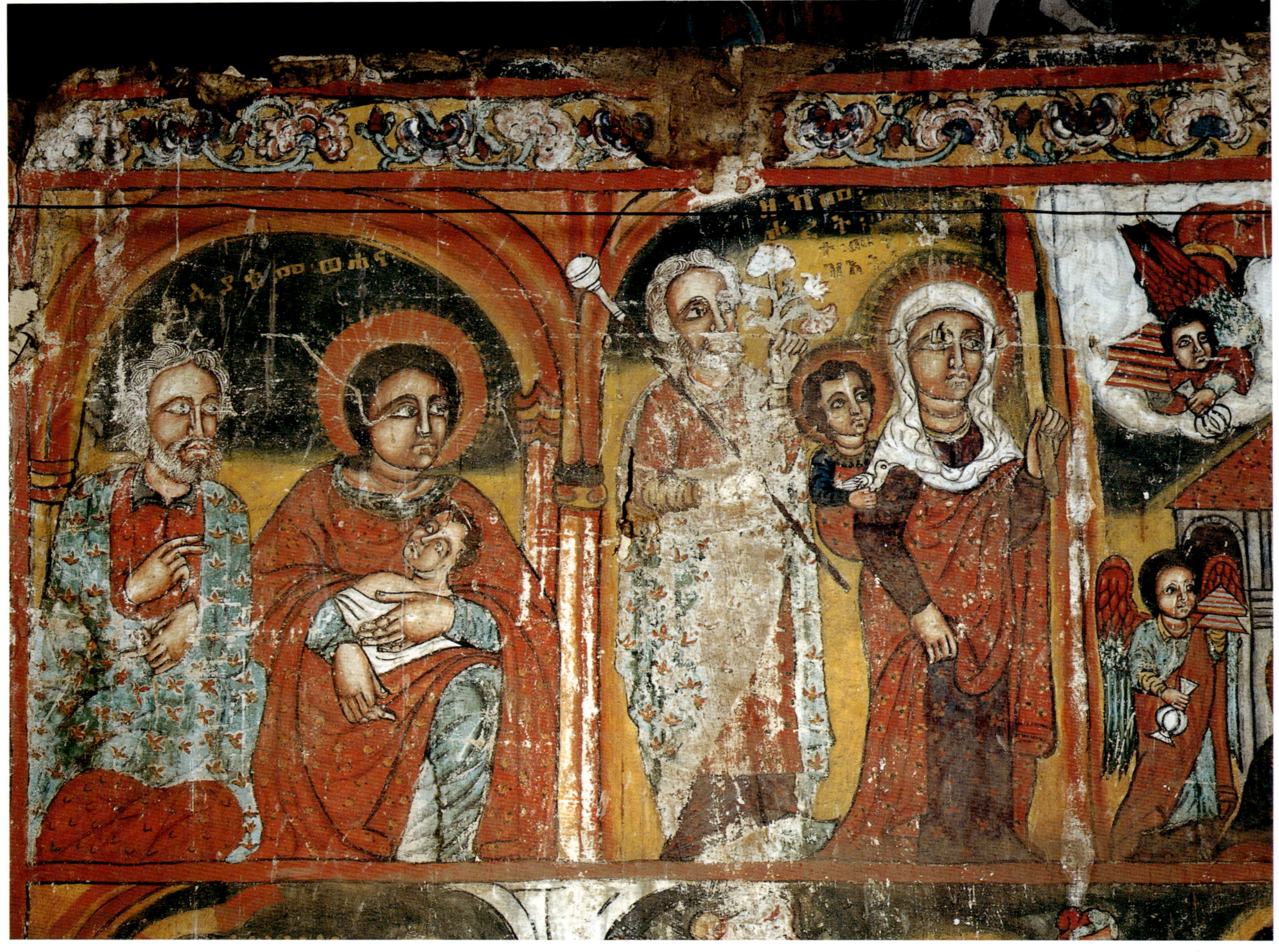

178. South wall of the *maqdas*: Saint Joachim and Saint Anna, Mary's parents, and the child Mary who is brought to the Temple of Jerusalem.

teristics, in the illustration of manuscipts). The sequences are completely independent, as though obeying only the representative exigencies of each single scene, each one of which rates as an individual work in itself.

On the projecting part of the south wall the episodes in the life of Mary are depicted high up, and in an illusory double-rowed portico, as in the one where Herod orders the death of the babies and further on, in the 'Slaughter of the Innocents', where parts of figures extend into the foreground, overlapping the pillars of the portico. In other scenes there are architectural features, similarly porticoed, painted in the background: the Temple of Jerusalem represented in the second scene of the first band below the tambour is a clear reference to the church of Nārgā Śellāsē itself. The depiction, however, does not fully convey the desired effect. The result is uncertain due to a conflict with the idea of portraying figures which still indulges in varying their sizes according to hierarchical importance rather than their positioning in the painting, which was a frequently used device. A certain overall unity is created by the coherent distribution of warm ochre tones (colouring the plane in which the figures are posed or their backgrop), green (upper areas), and a prevalence of reds, blues, and azures in the clothes. Traditional canons are still used in the treatment of

179. South wall of the *maqdas*: Zachary and other priests of the Temple.

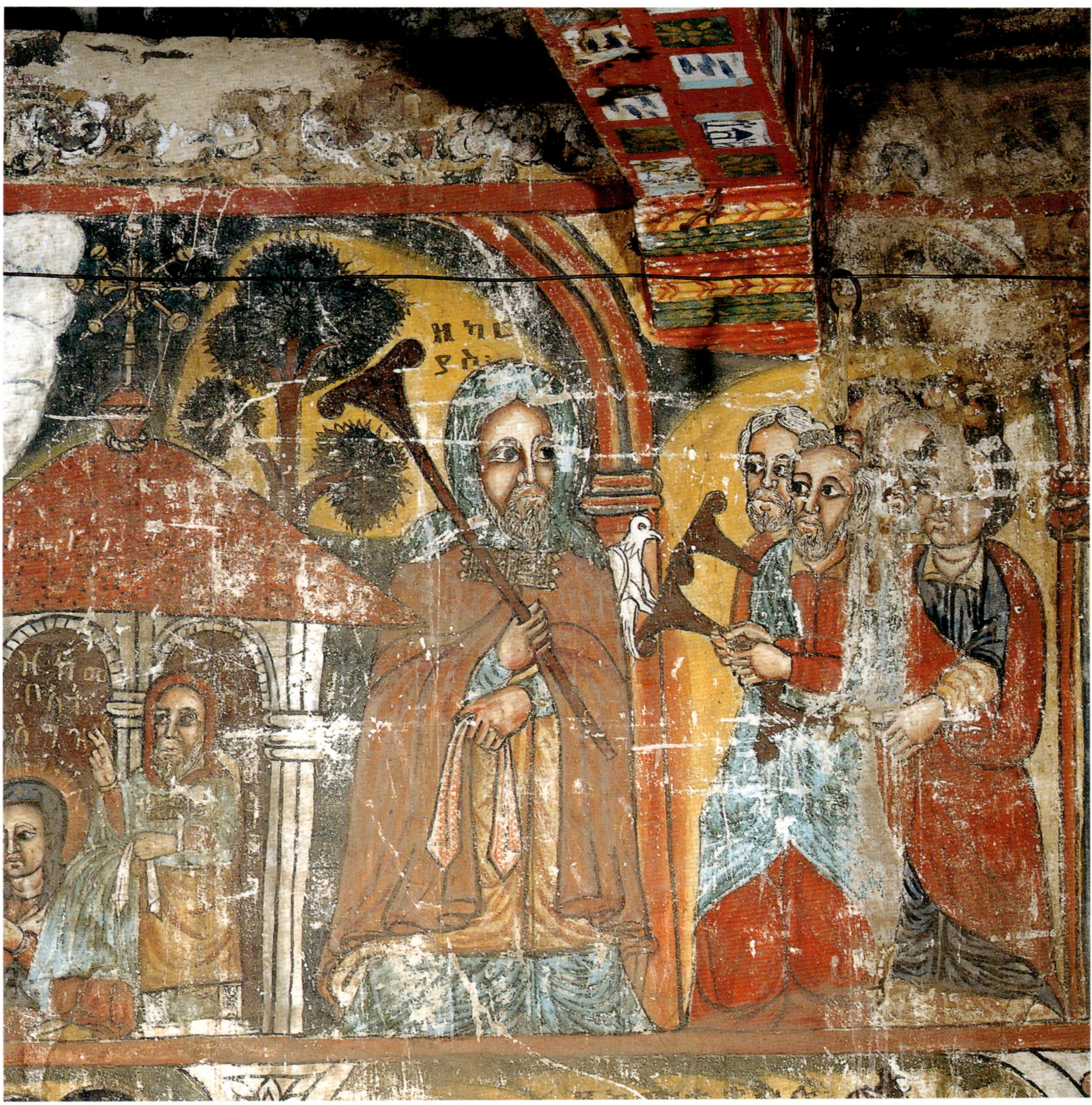

these garments, where the purely decorative motifs are superimposed on the mannerist linearism of the folds in the material.

The painter of this type of pseudo-portico is recognizable also in the characteristic depiction of the faces, where the eyebrows slope markedly down to the outside corners of the eyes, sometimes graphically joined to the outline of the jawbone (fig. 188). This feature is to be found, also, in the figures painted on the tambour above, in particular in the Apparition of Mary, who is painted exageratedly large, enthroned amongst rich Chinese drapes in an arched niche. Also the work of the same artist is the Flight into Egypt, painted on the first square to the left of the door (fig. 182). His workmanship can even be traced in the remaining original hovering cherubs on the high parts of the jambs.

The Adoration of the Magi is painted on, and unites, the two bands along which the story is told, which are separed into two, again only at the right corner of the wall (fig. 185).

More than elsewhere, it is in the lower band—seprated by a red strip decorated with flowers which look as though they are printed—that a different syntax gathers in a single frame various moments, where the areas above and below are not spatial dimensions but rather are just spaces used for an efficacious illustration of the events portrayed, hence, the ascending diagonal

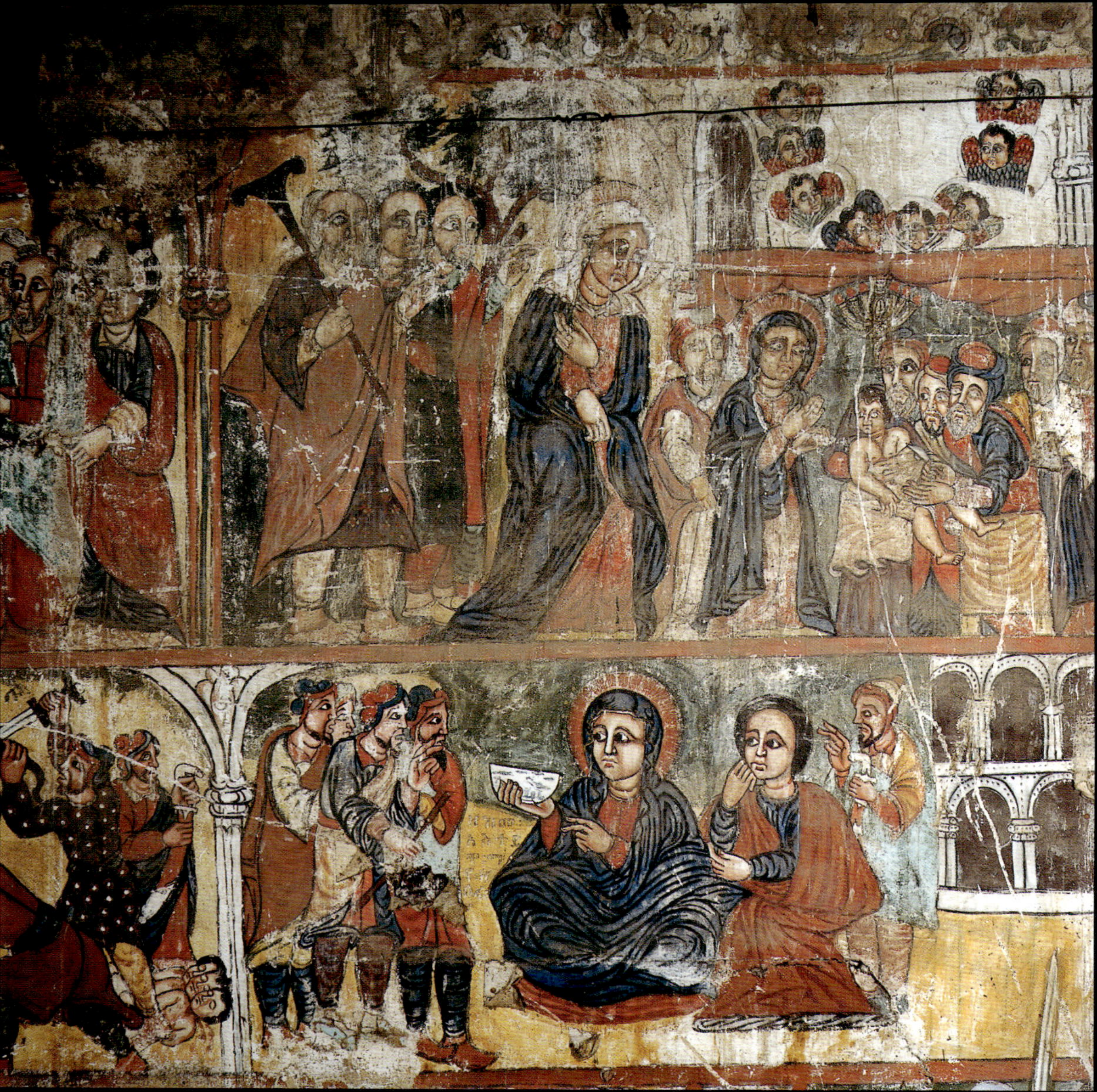

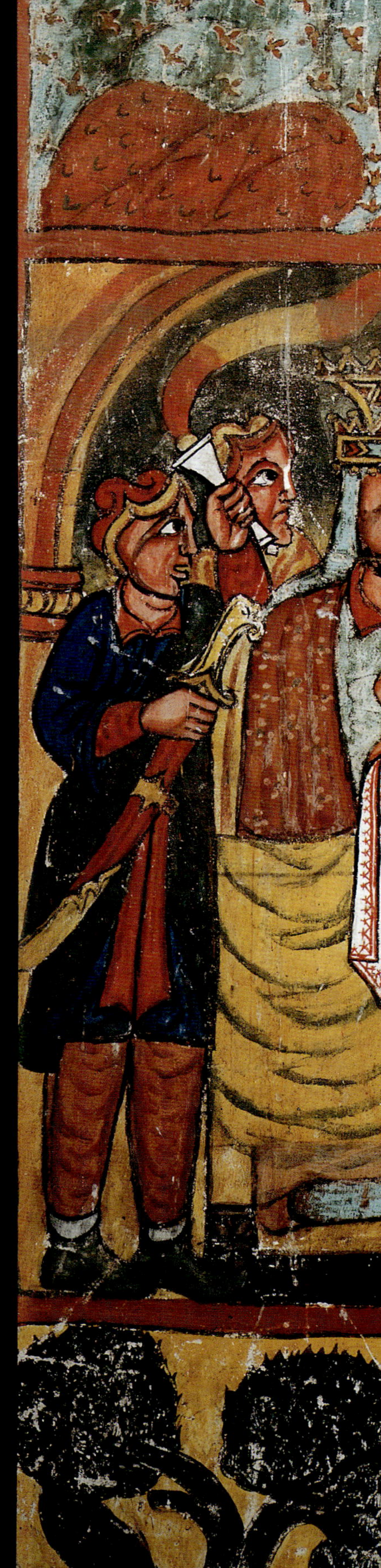

180. South wall of the *maqdas*: Jesus' Circumcision (top); the test of the 'water of malediction' (bottom).

181. South wall of the *maqdas*: Herod orders the Slaughter of the Innocents (left); Herod's town-crier (right).

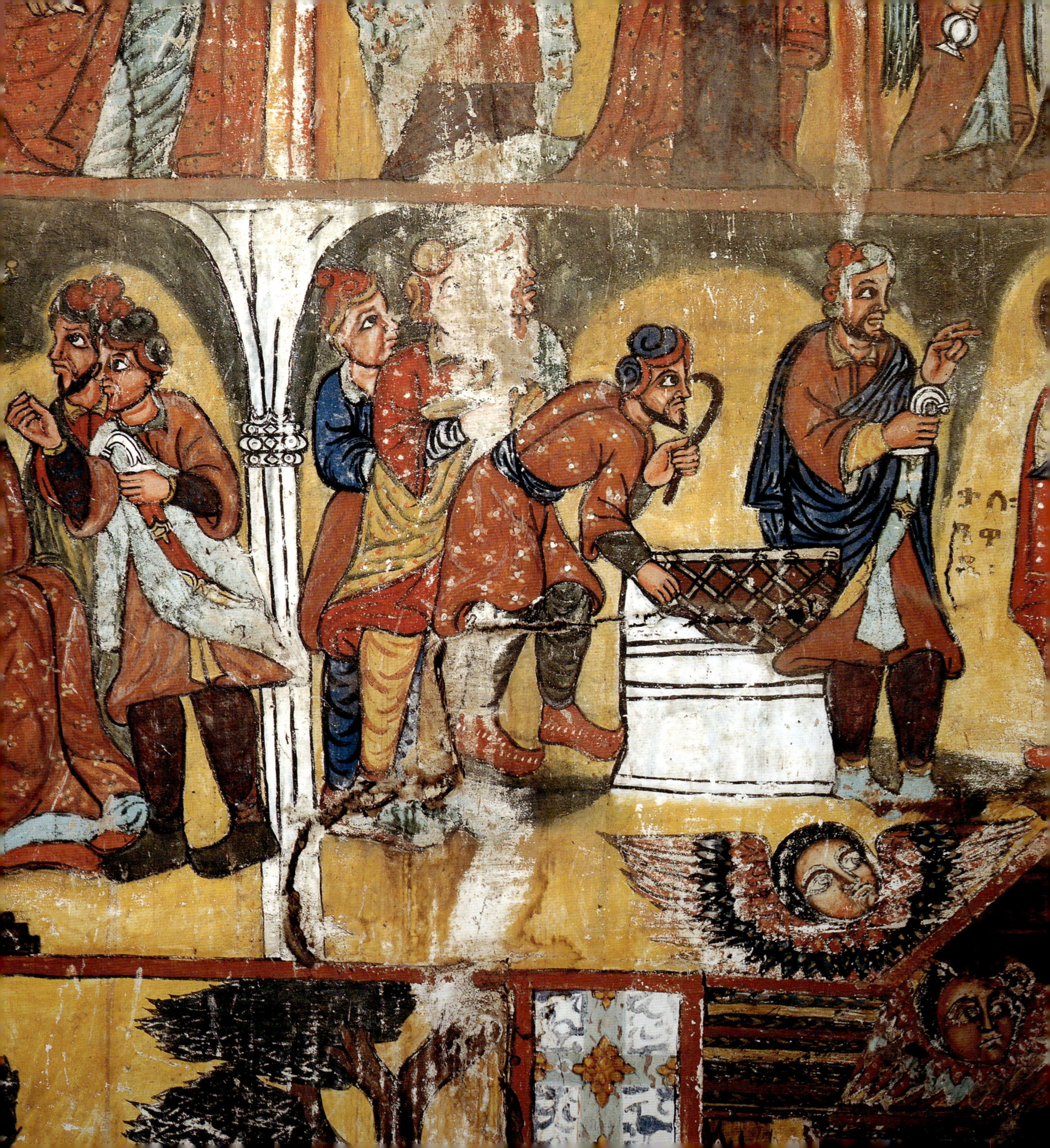

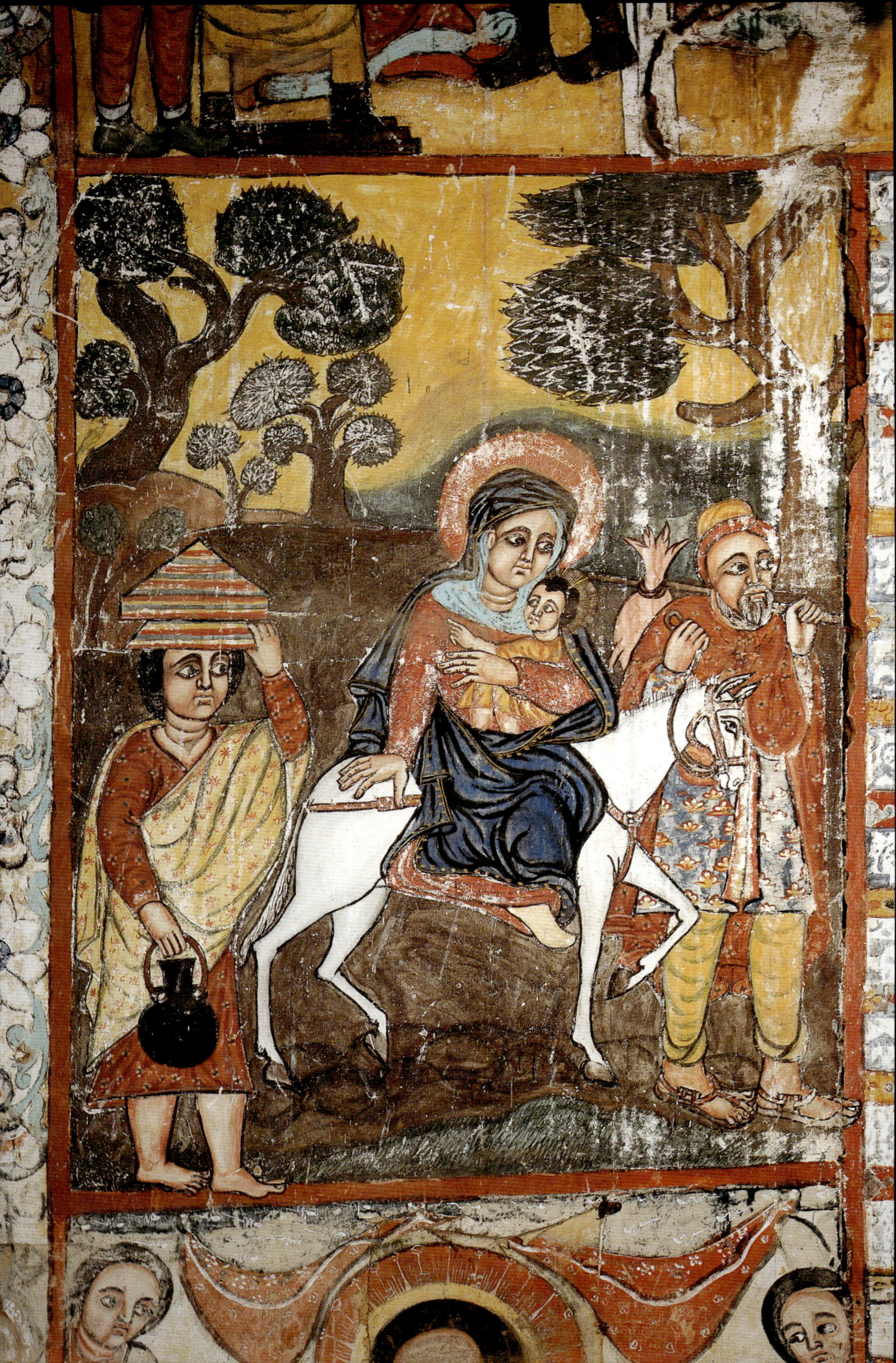

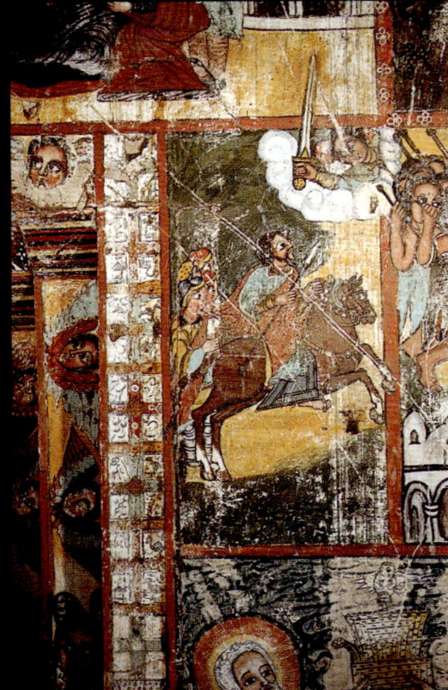

182. South wall of the *maqdas*: the Holy Family flees into Egypt.

183. South wall of the *maqdas*: the legend of Saint Gigar.

184. South wall of the *maqdas*: the legend of Saint Gigar.

185. South wall of the *maqdas*: the Adoration of the Magi.

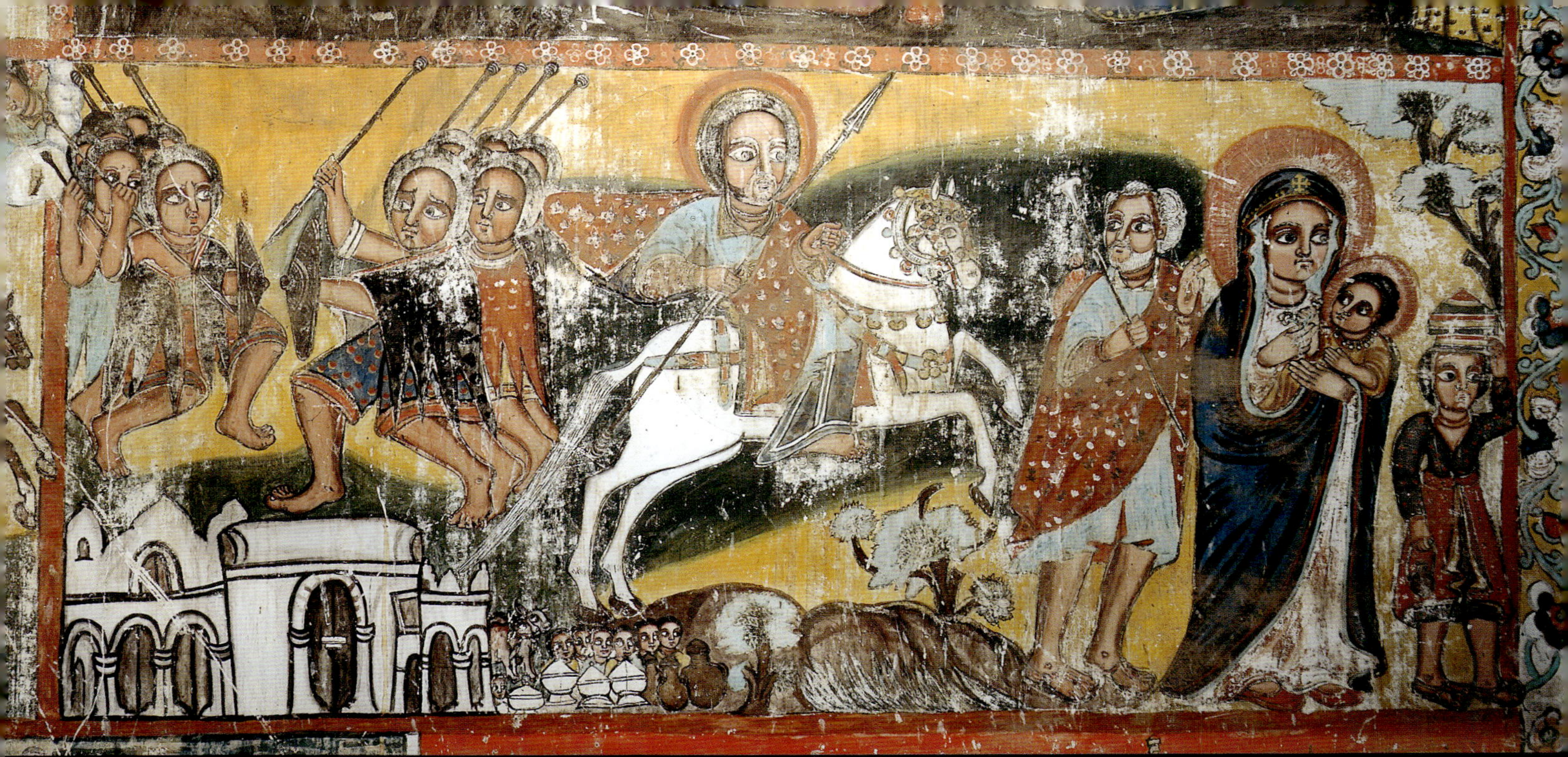

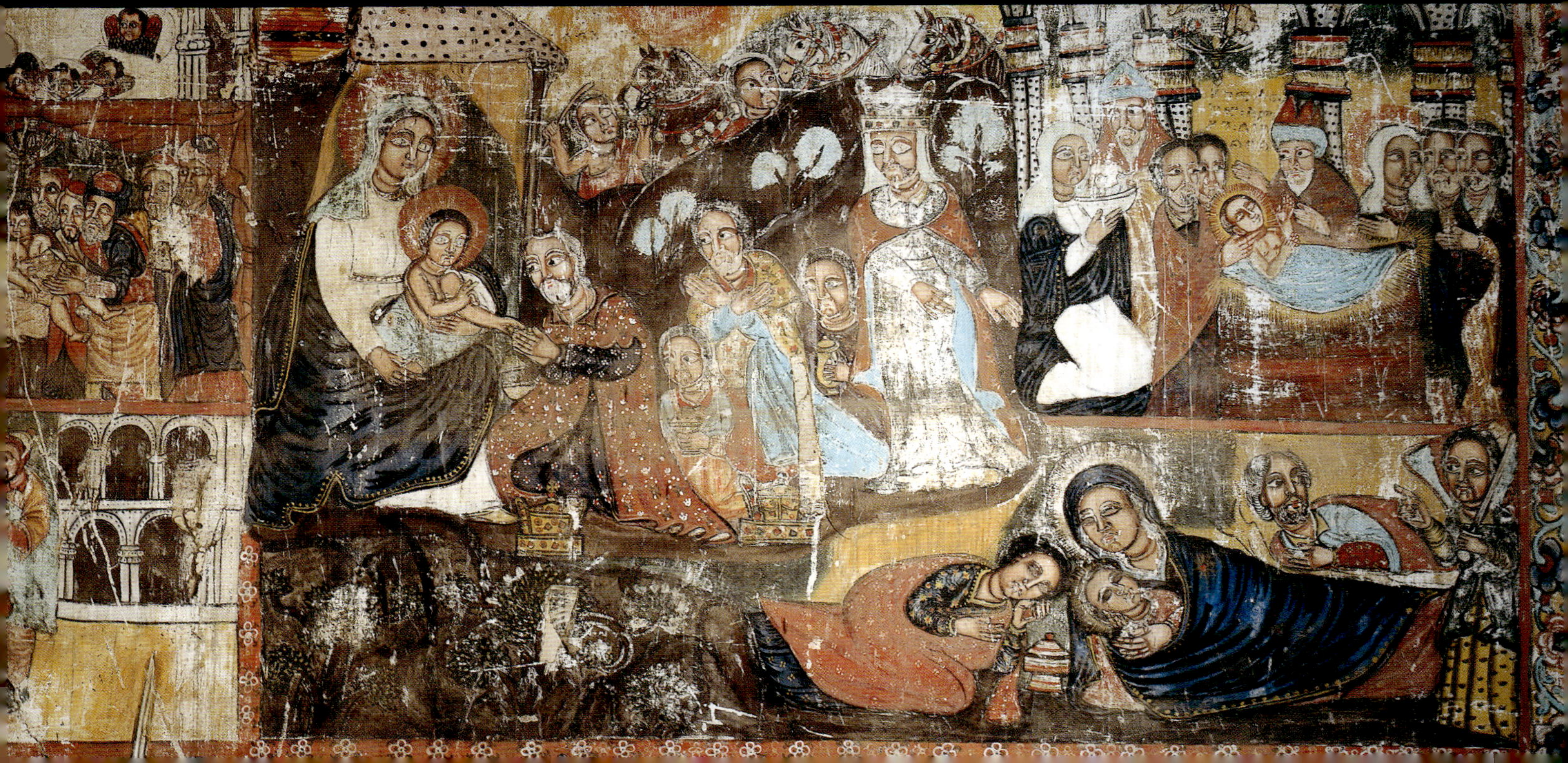

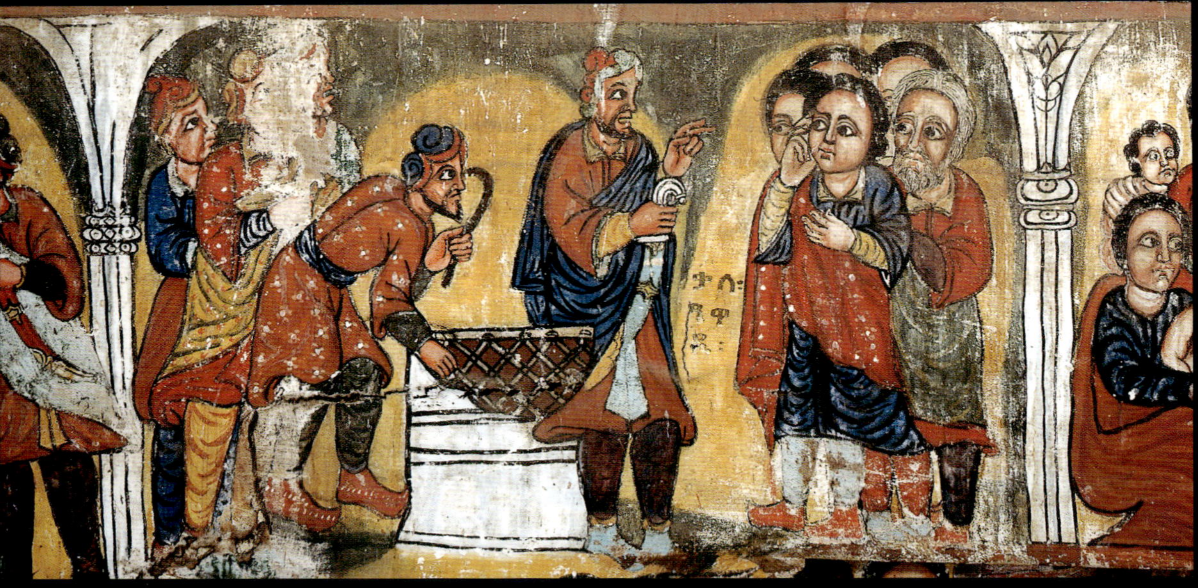

186. South wall of the *maqdas*: Herod's town-crier.

187. South wall of the *maqdas*: the Slaughter of the Innocents.

188. South wall of the *maqdas*: the Slaughter of the Innocents (detail).

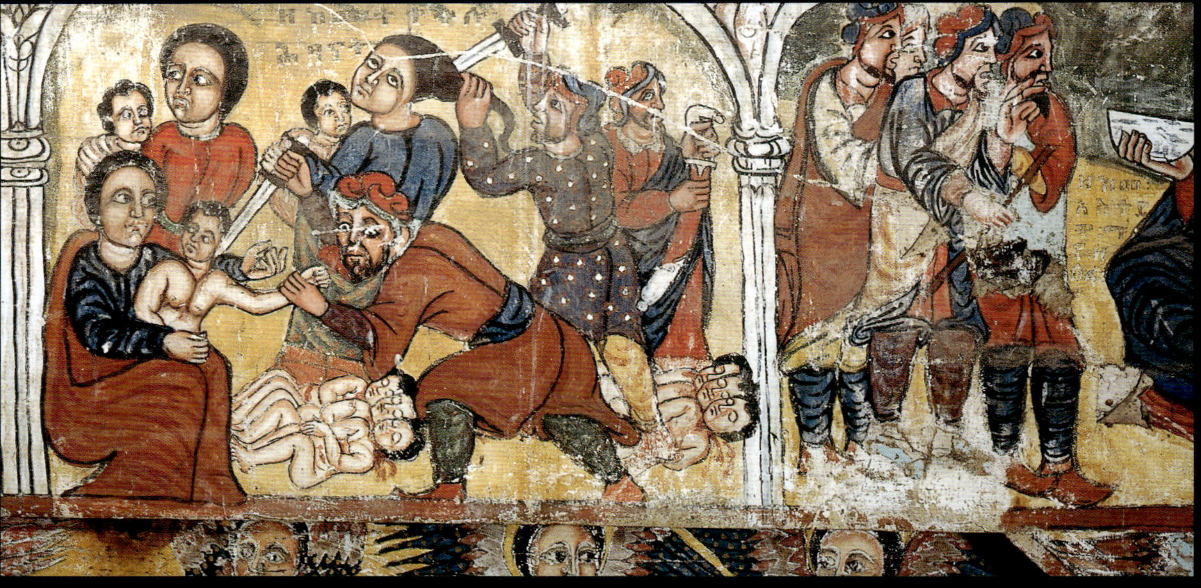

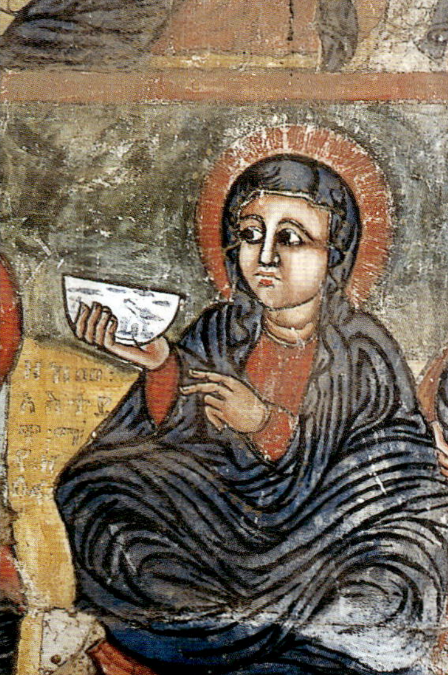

189. South wall of the *maqdas*: the test of the 'water of malediction' (detail).

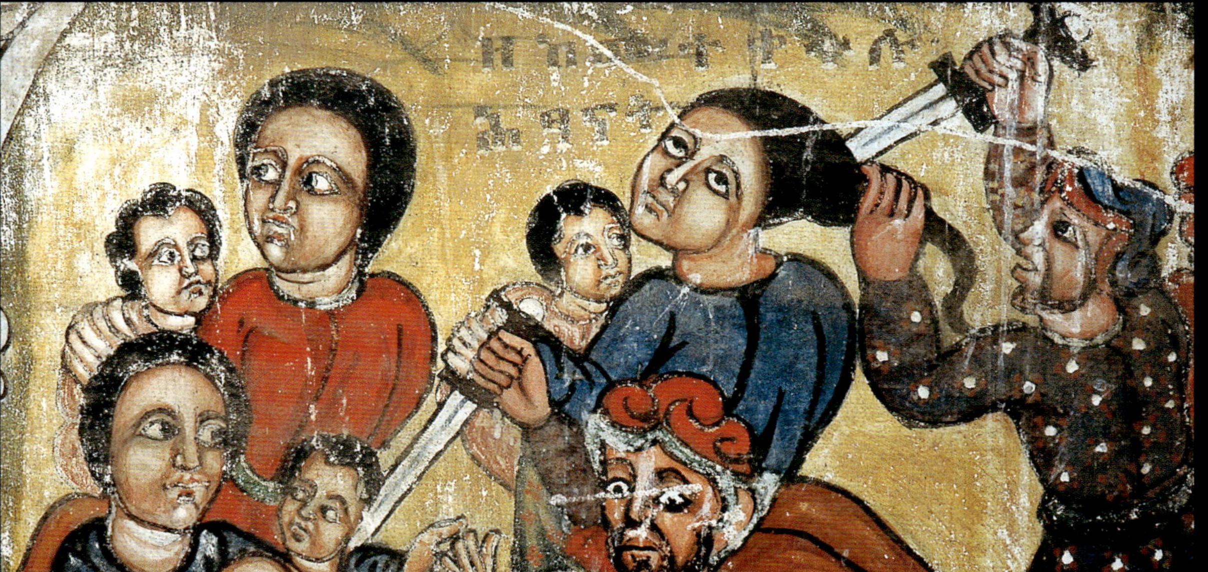

190. South wall of the *maqdas*: the legend of Saint Gigar (detail).

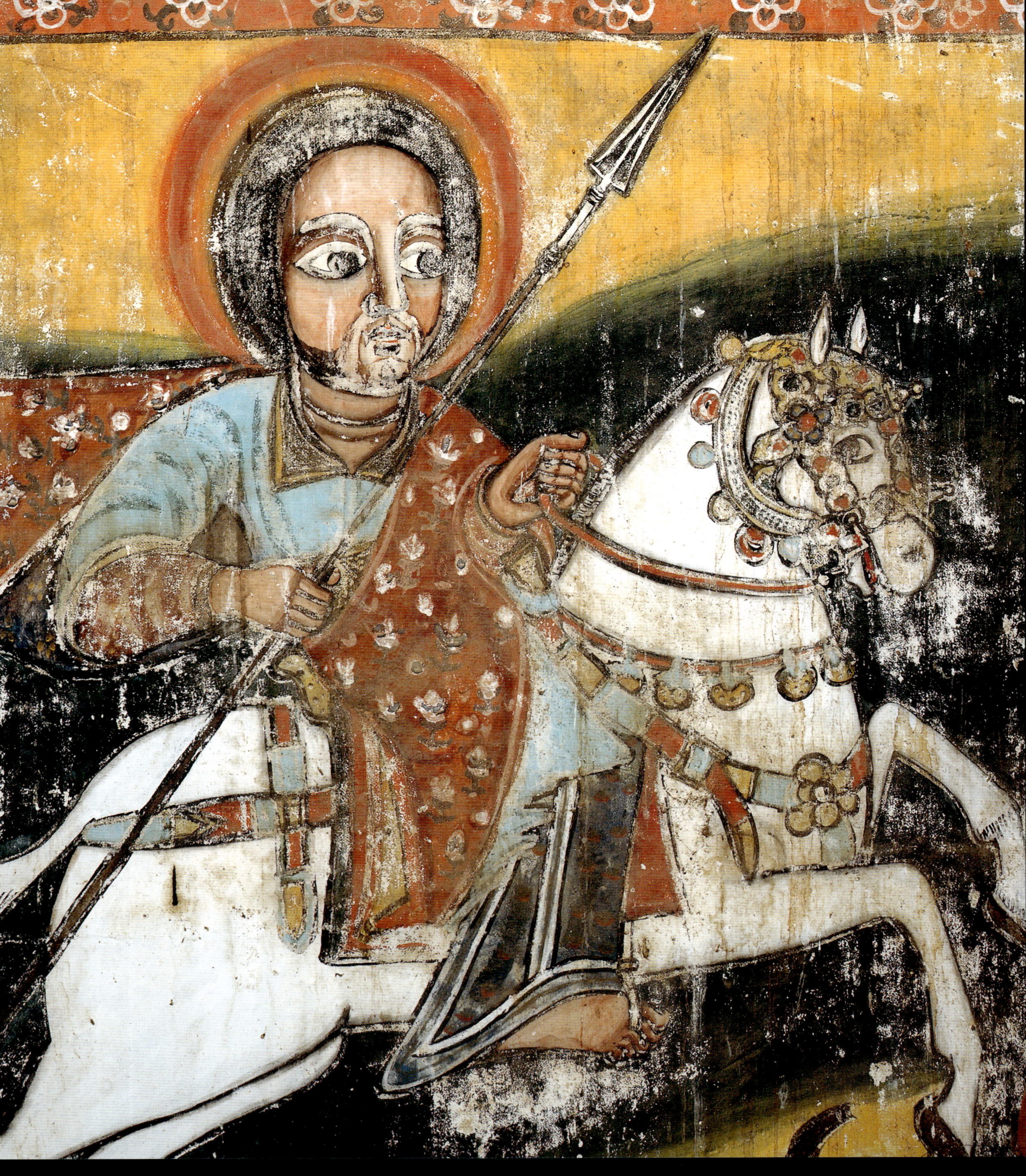

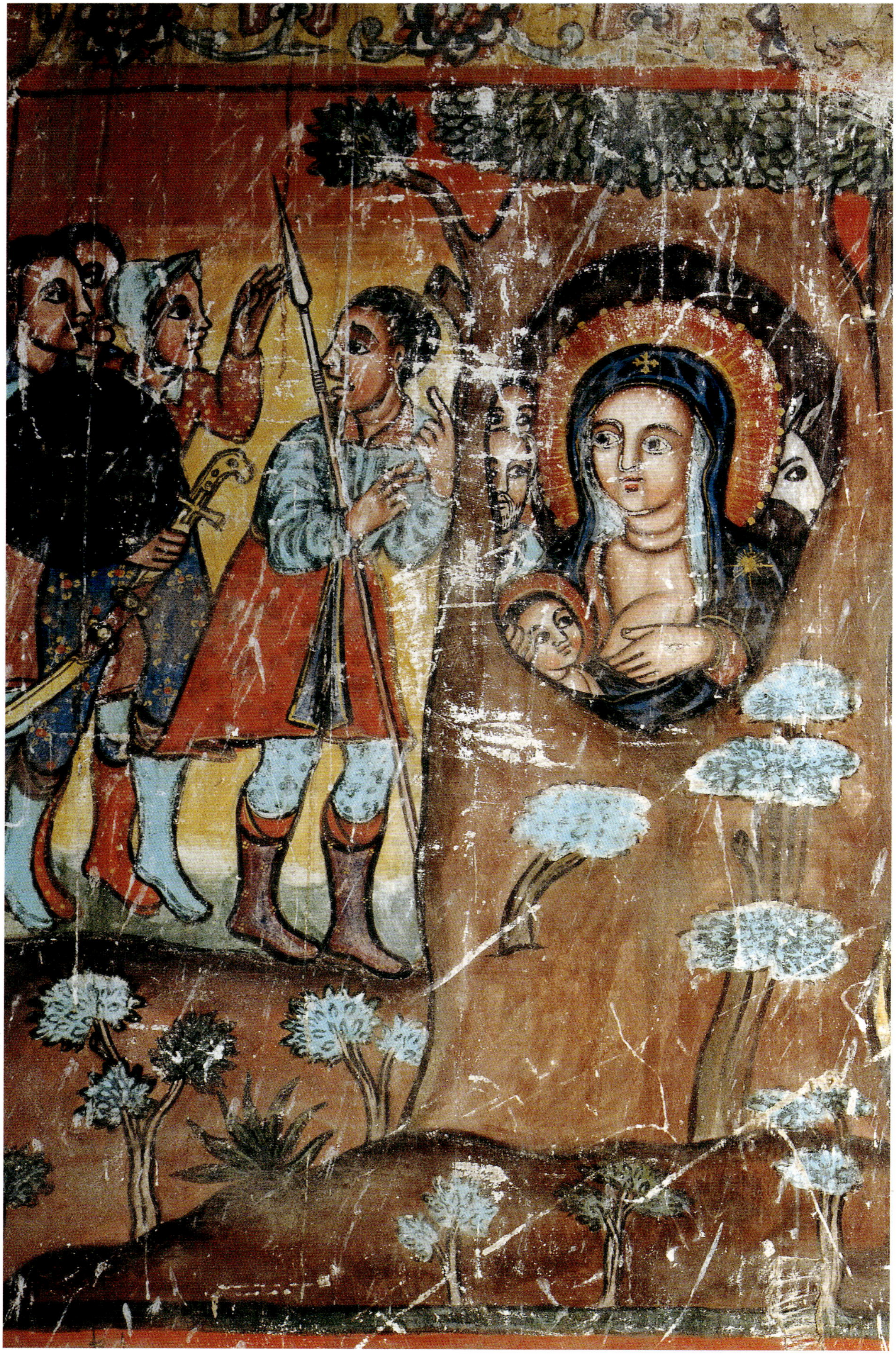

191. East wall of the *maqdas*: a tree opens its trunk offering shelter to the Holy Family.

192. East wall of the *maqdas*: the Virgin prays and an angel brings food and drink to the Holy Family.

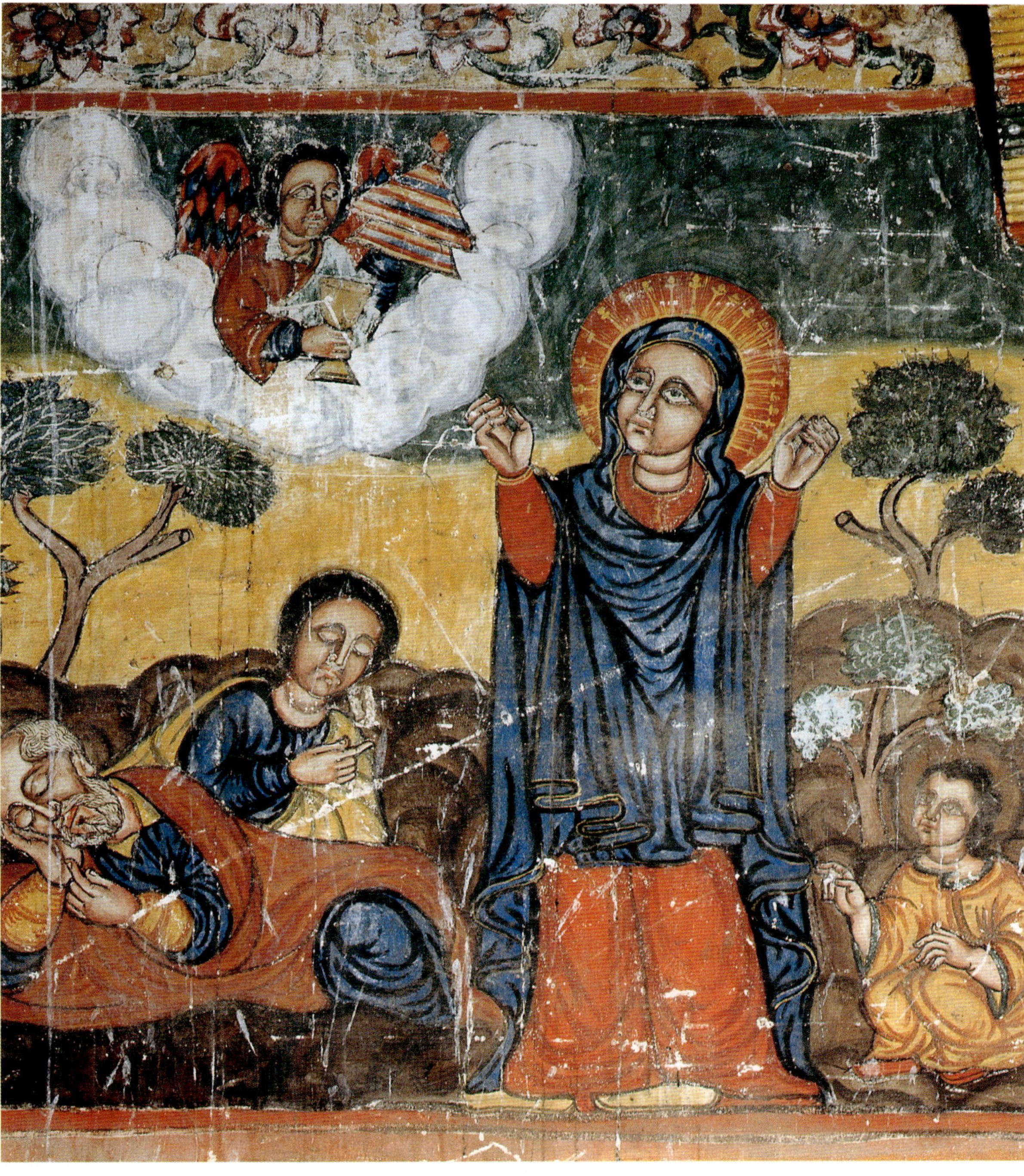

painted in the background with a green aura from which Gigar bursts forth (fig. 184). The "printed" red strip and the angel's sword, brandished menacingly against Herod on his rearing horse stretches into the band above and out of the frame (fig. 183). It is therefore possible to hypothesize on this being a later addition to the painting. This hypothesis is supported by syntactical and stylistic differences, such as in the depiction of faces, in the restless figures glancing behind, and in the actual landscape.

The upper part of the east wall of the *maqdas* is divided into two and framed by a band of floral motifs. Above are depicted various themes from the Flight into Egypt, and below some of Jesus' miracles. At first sight the division of the scenes seems casual and not linked to an overall design: one scene overlaps, breaking the line of the frame of the adjacent ones, and only four of the ten scenes are alligned evenly. This may be evidence of later intervention on a largely integral design, which altered the symmetry of the

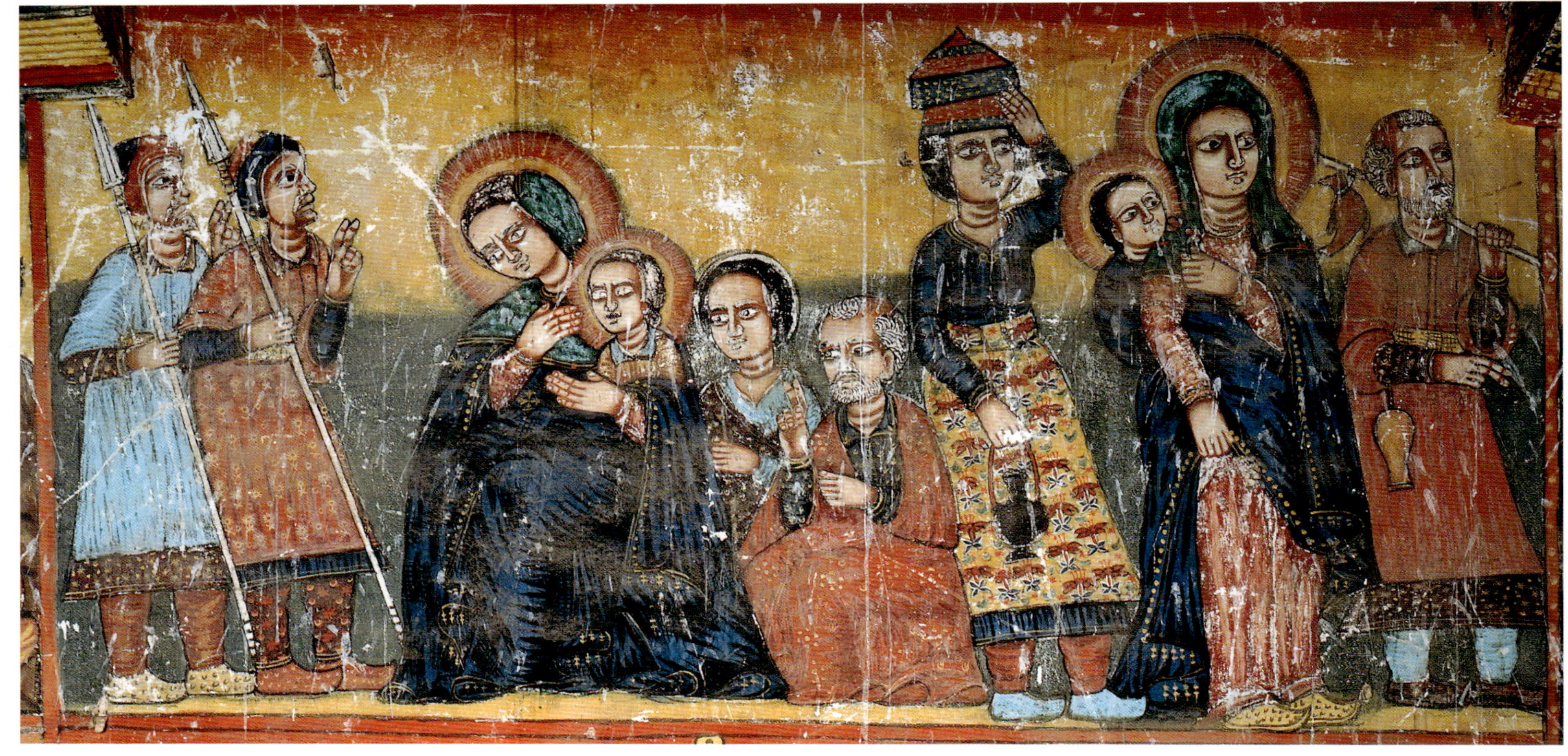

193. East wall of the *maqdas*: the Flight into Egypt.

façade. The individual scenes are broad, with the same stylistic traits as the painting which covers most of the south side (fig. 142).

Meanwhile, the work of the east wall certainly seems to be that most influenced by European paintings, above all in the scene depicting the *Virgo lactans*. Here the faces do not automatically reproduce the characteristic stereotypes of Ethiopian painting: the drapery is given body by contrasts of light and shade; the area depicted has a true sense of perspective, from the nursing Virgin in the foreground to a city in the background which resembles Gondar, whilst in between the story proceeds naturalistically with a saddled horse at pasture, intent on grazing (figs. 198-200). It could be that this is the actual work of a foreign hand, such is the stylistic contrast with the surrounding paintings. It could be the source of teaching which in the tambour manifests itself in an arrangement of the drapery more attentive to reality, given movement without mannerist graphics but, rather, with methods that come from abroad (fig. 196).

This work could be the result of a fascination with the exotic, which infused the Imperial Court of Gondar, which at Lake Tana gathered the fruit of European influences as well as those from the East and the Far East. These contributions from afar were not absorbed passively, but consciously assimilated into local identity and tradition.

Along the bands of the north wall of the *maqdas* elegant horses, sorrel, grey, white and black, some rearing, some walking, procede richly caparisoned. Their profiles stand out clear and vibrant, with refined linearism against ochre, green and red auras. The horses are stamping on dragons and strange beings as they are led by sacred knights recognizable only by their identifying symbols. Their capes in the wind, the knights are shaking their spears and have been painted in three-quarte face (in the Ethiopian painting only the evil men are drawn in profile) (fig. 144).

On the right of the door, there are two other horsemen, St. Fāsiladas and a king, who are mounting two steeds European style (with the whole foot in the stirrup, not just the big toe). The two horses stand still, wearing rich ankle bands, covered with a precious saddle-cloth down to their hocks. They have no plasticity at

194. East wall of the *maqdas*: Jesus' Temptations.

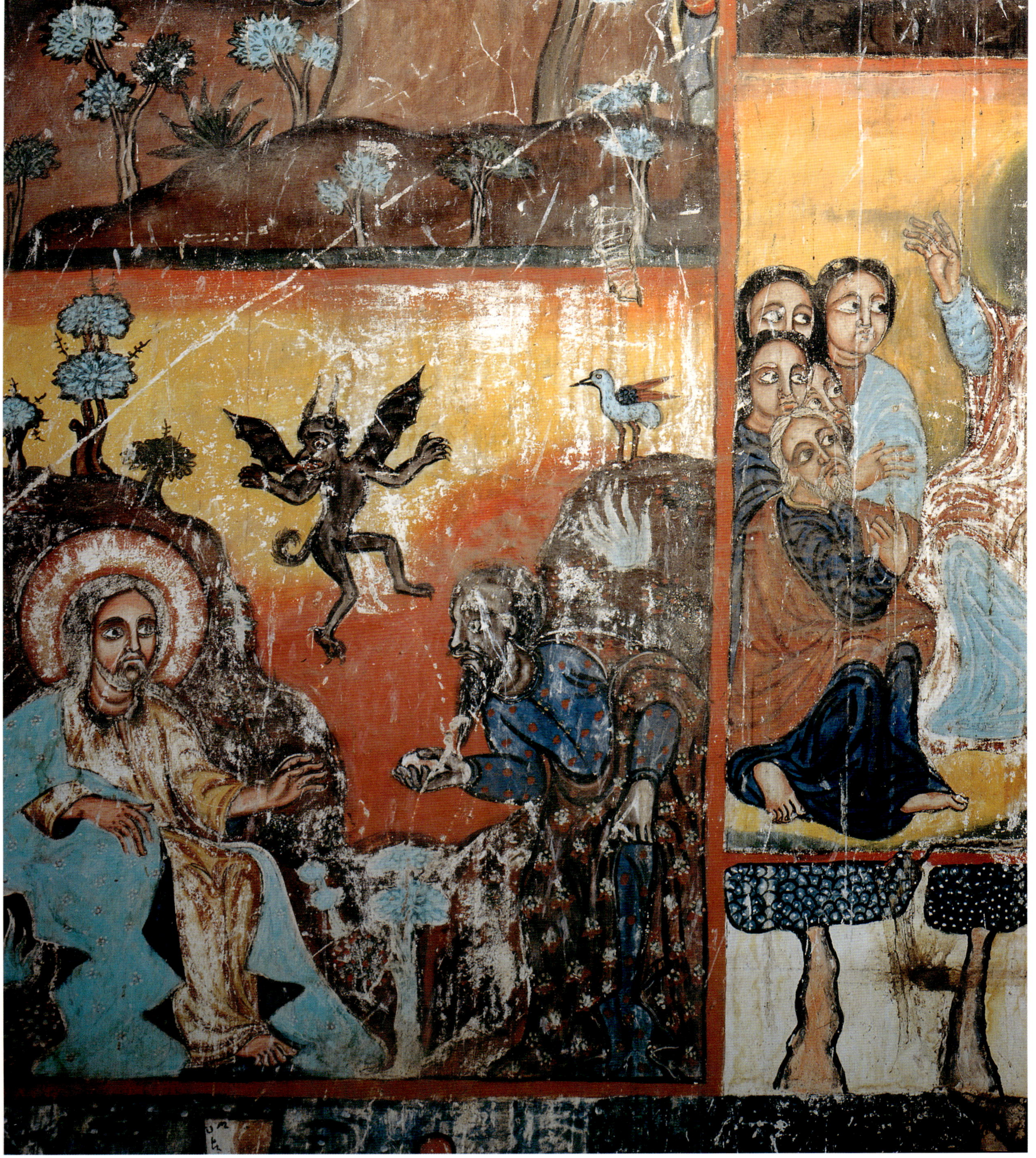

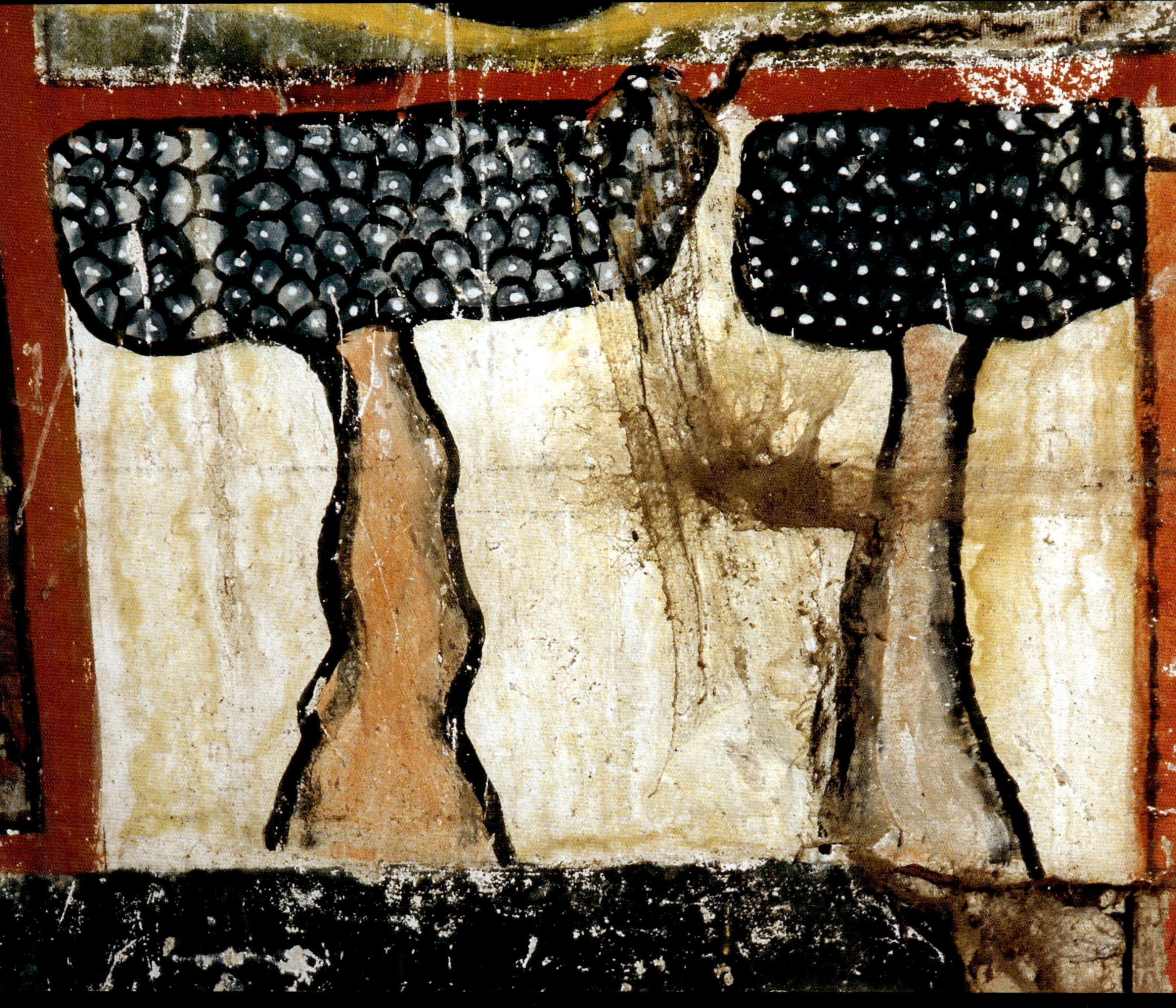

195. East wall of the *maqdas*: decorative detail with two trees in a panel.

196. Tambour on the east wall of the *maqdas*: Jesus' Ascension to heaven with angels playing.

197. East wall of the *maqdas*: Resurrection of Jairus' daughter.

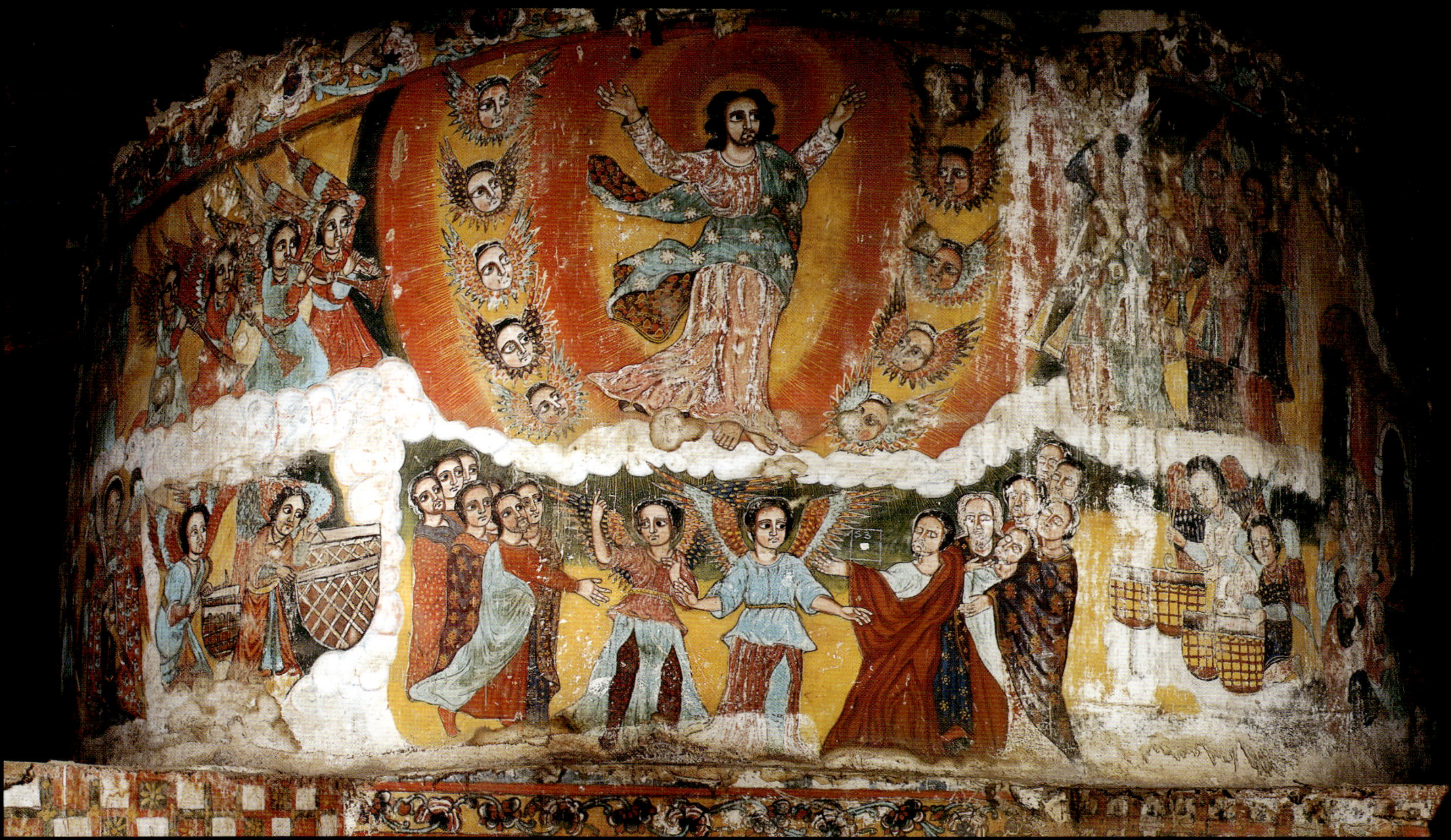

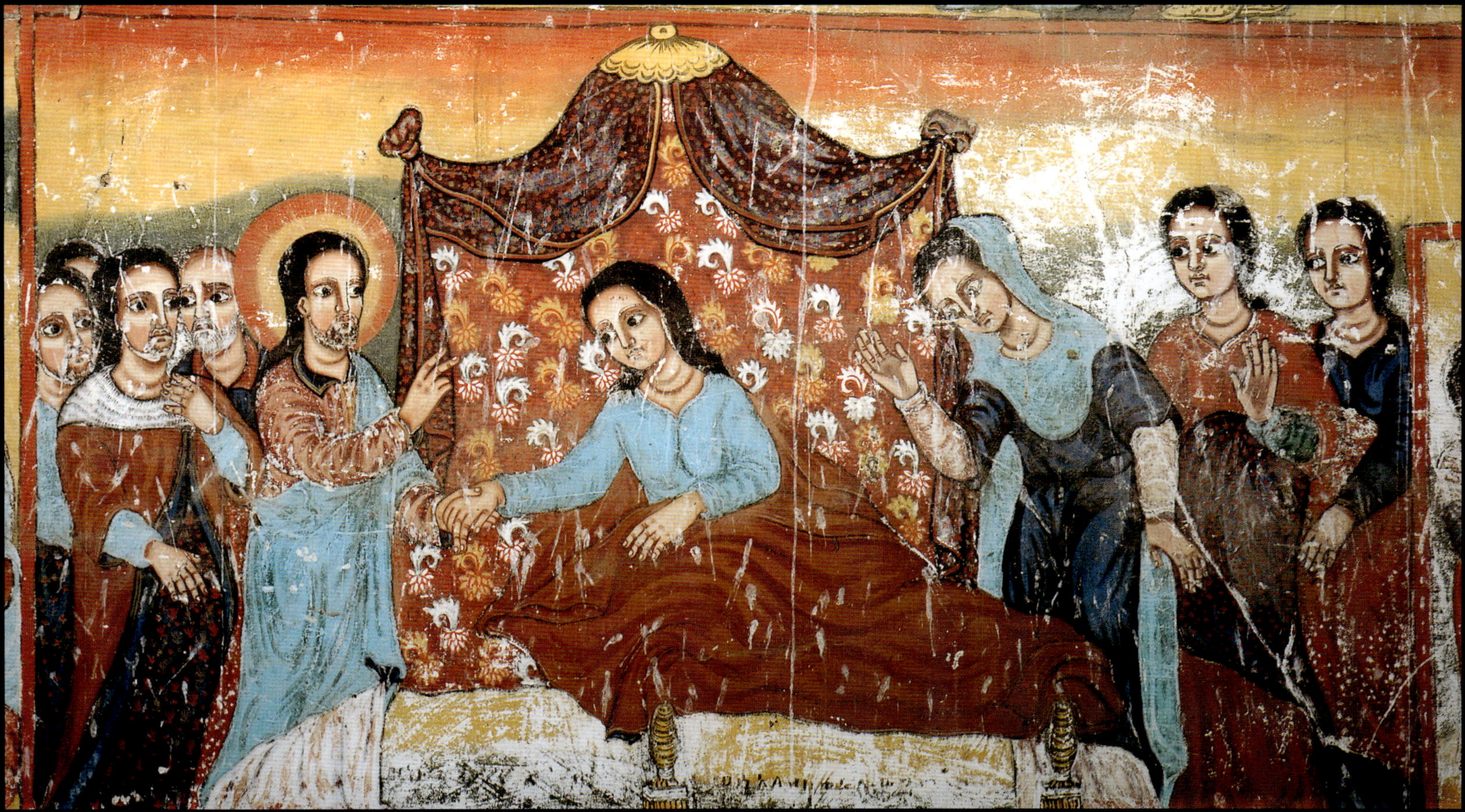

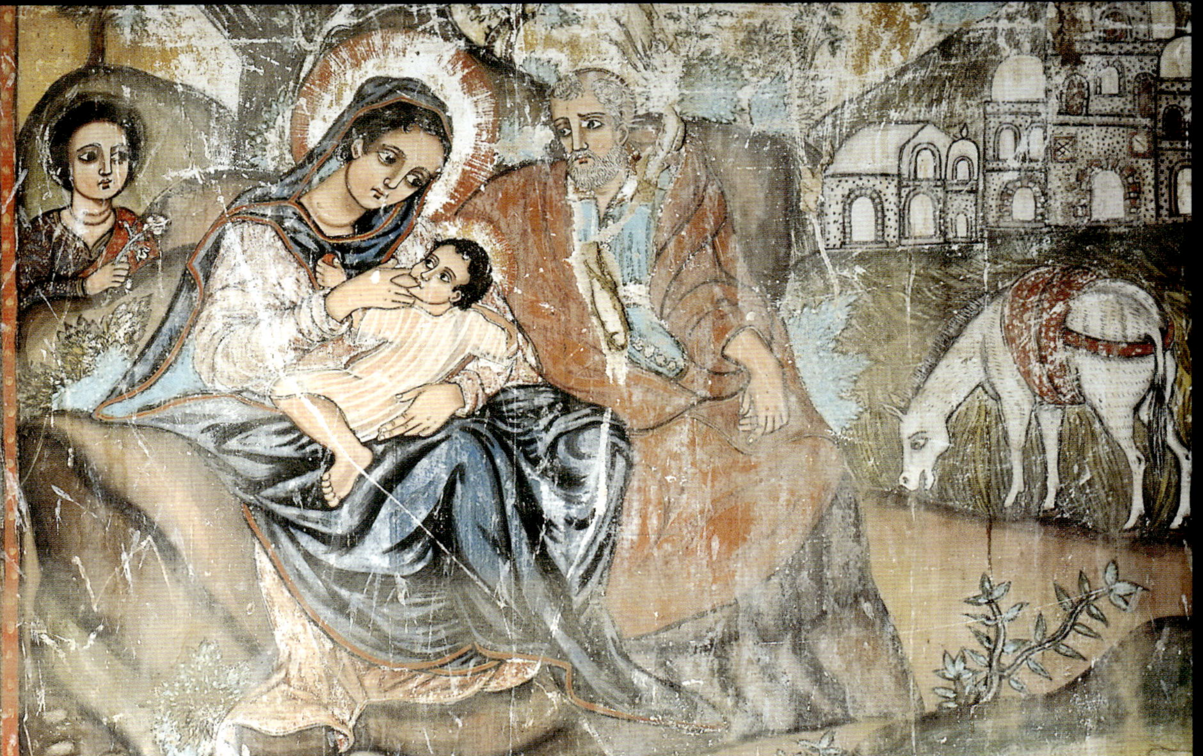

198. East wall of the *maqdas*: *Virgo lactans* during the Flight into Egypt (detail).

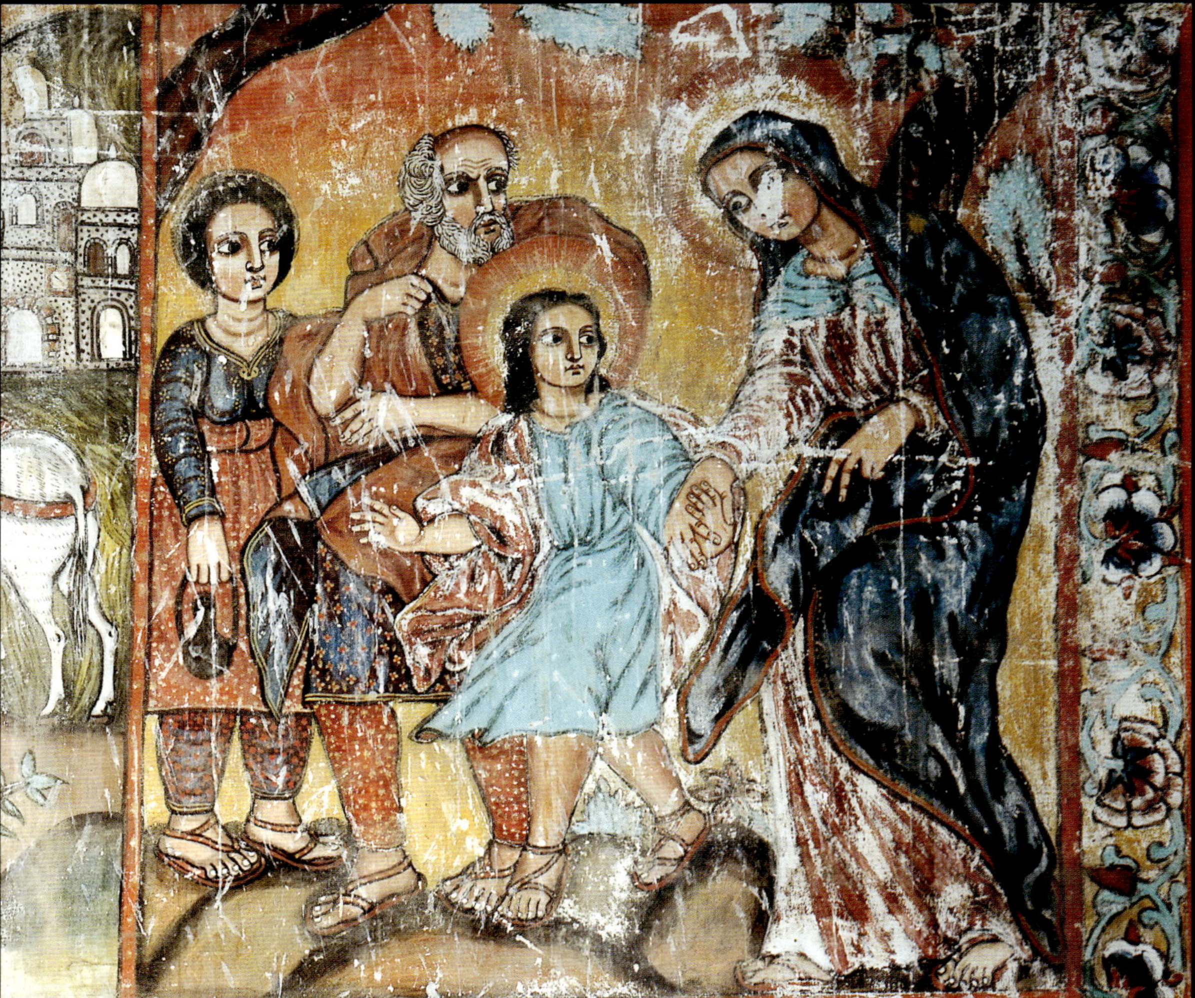

199. East wall of the *maqdas*: The Holy Family returns from Egypt

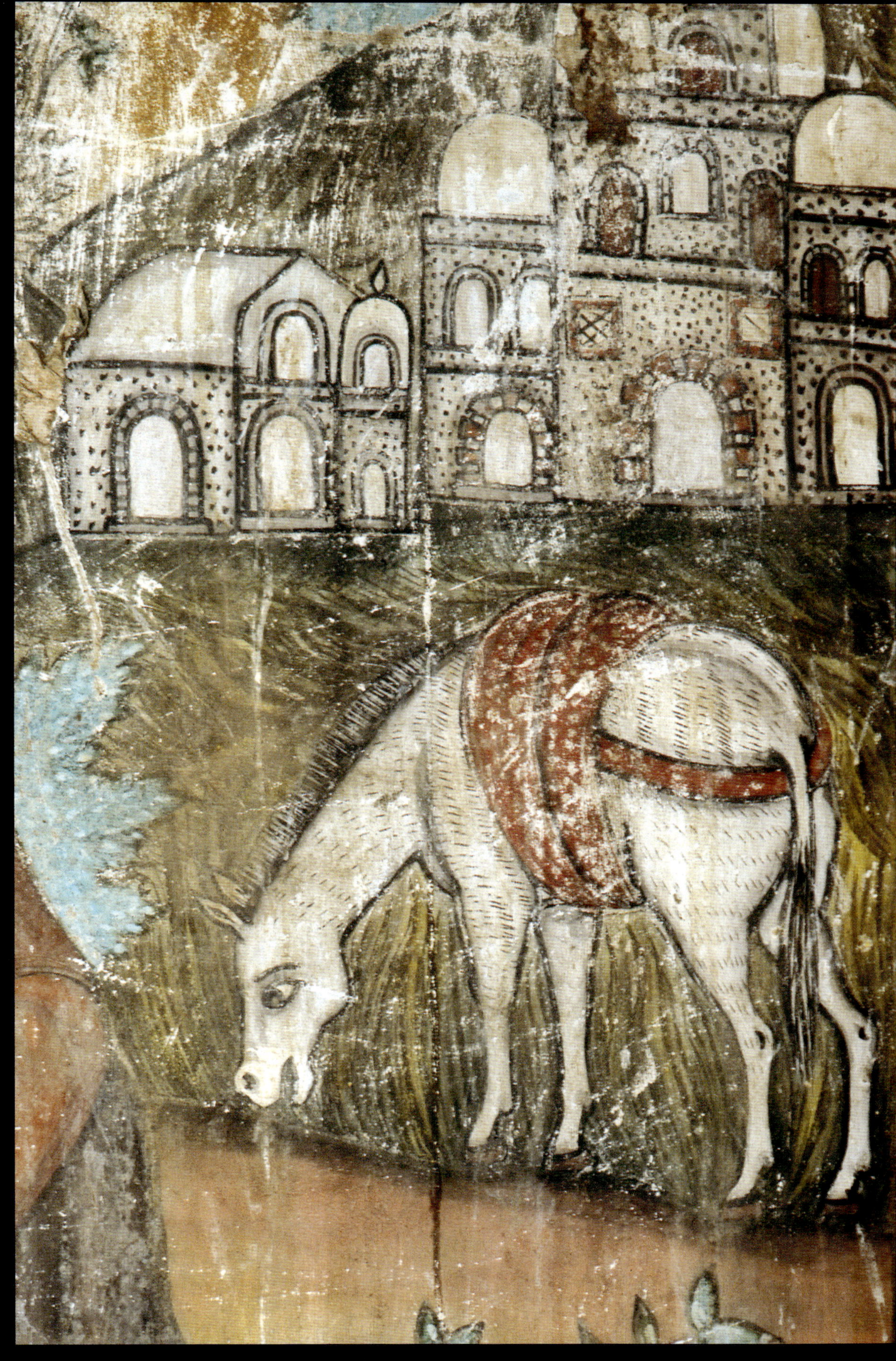

200. East wall of the *maqdas*:
a quadruped grazes in the background
to a city whose architecure is the same
as that of Gondar.

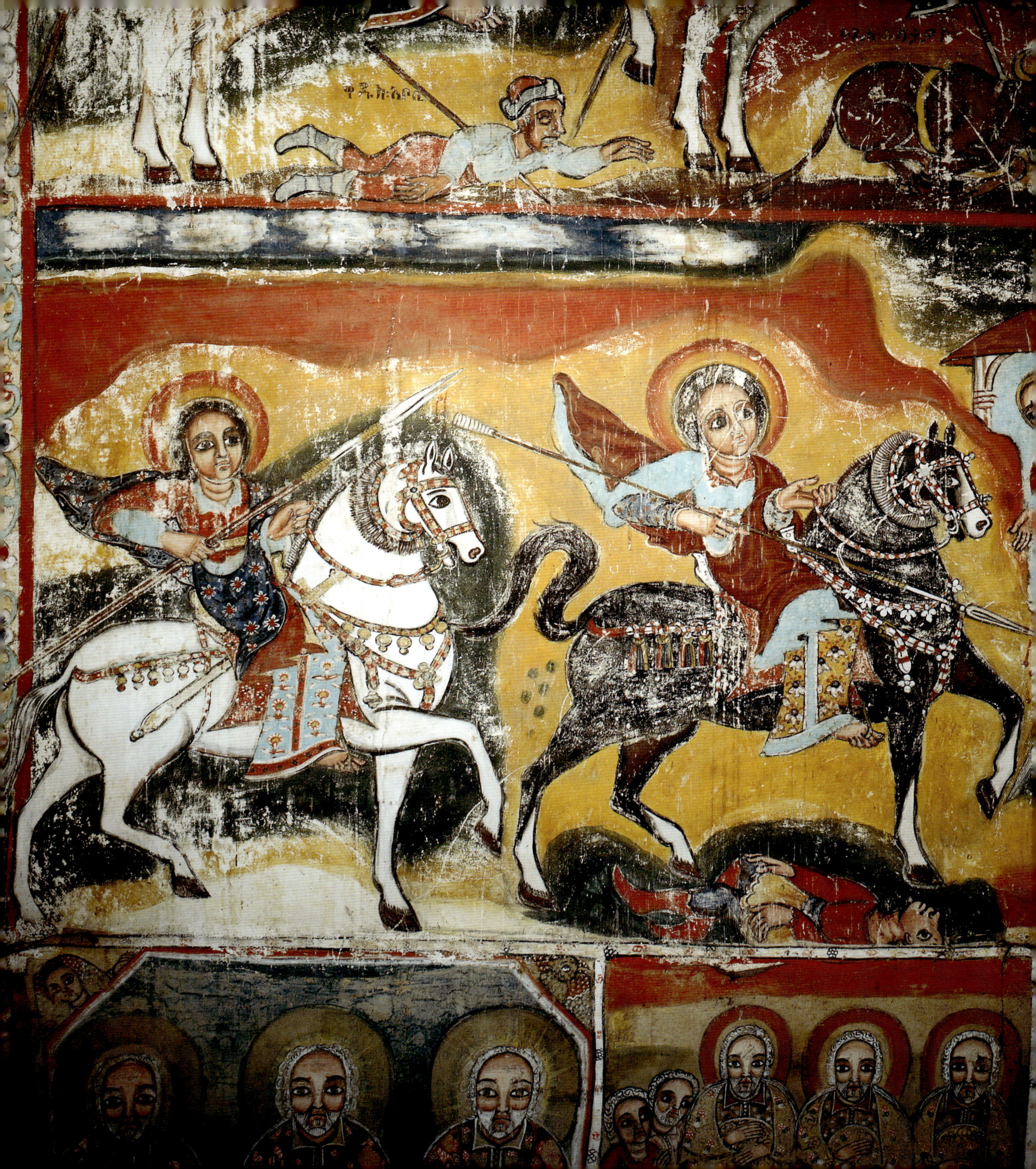

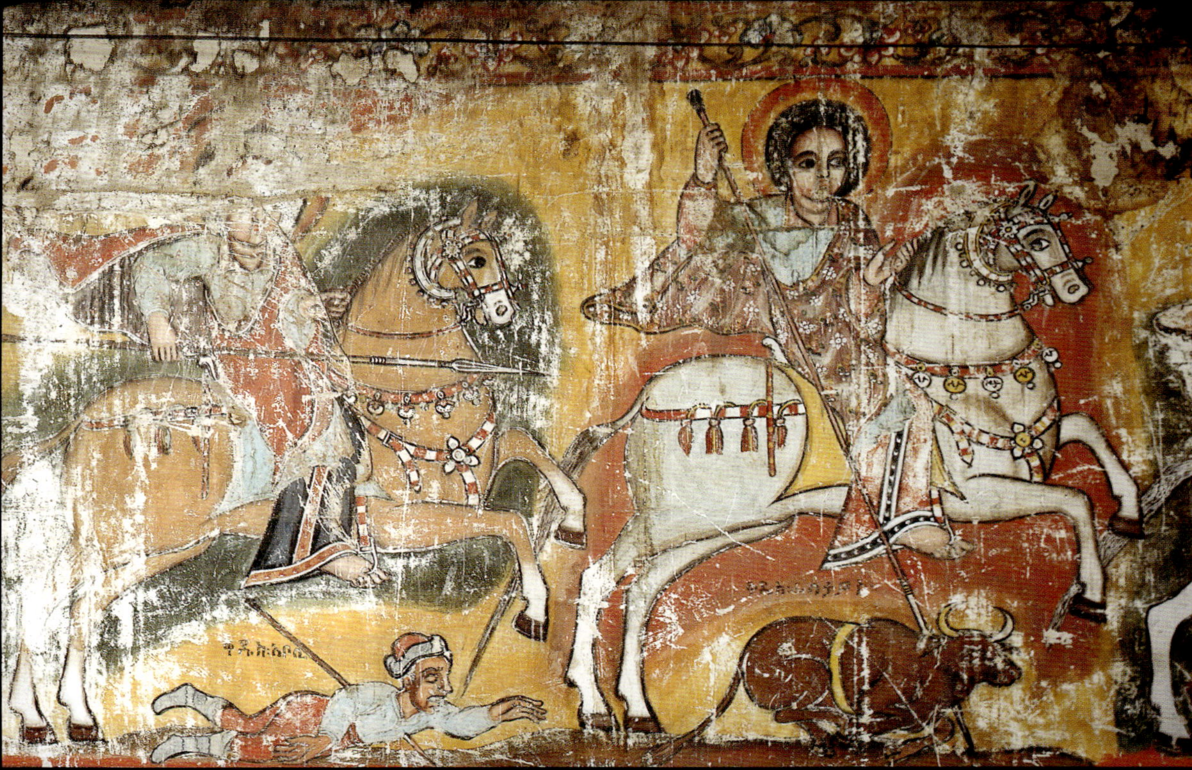

201. North wall of the *maqdas*: Theodore the Egyptian and Mercury, saints on horseback.

202. North wall of the *maqdas*: Aboli and Philoteus, saints on horseback.

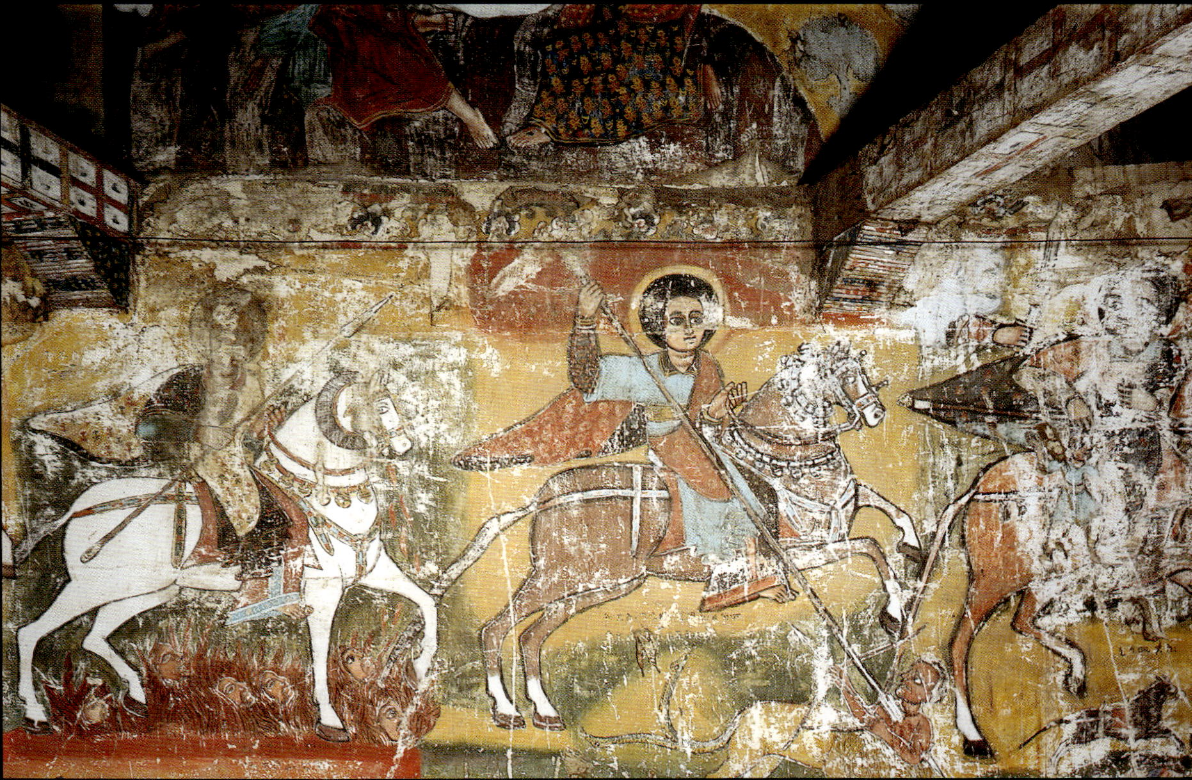

203. North wall of the *maqdas*: Menna (?) and Claude (?), saints on horseback.

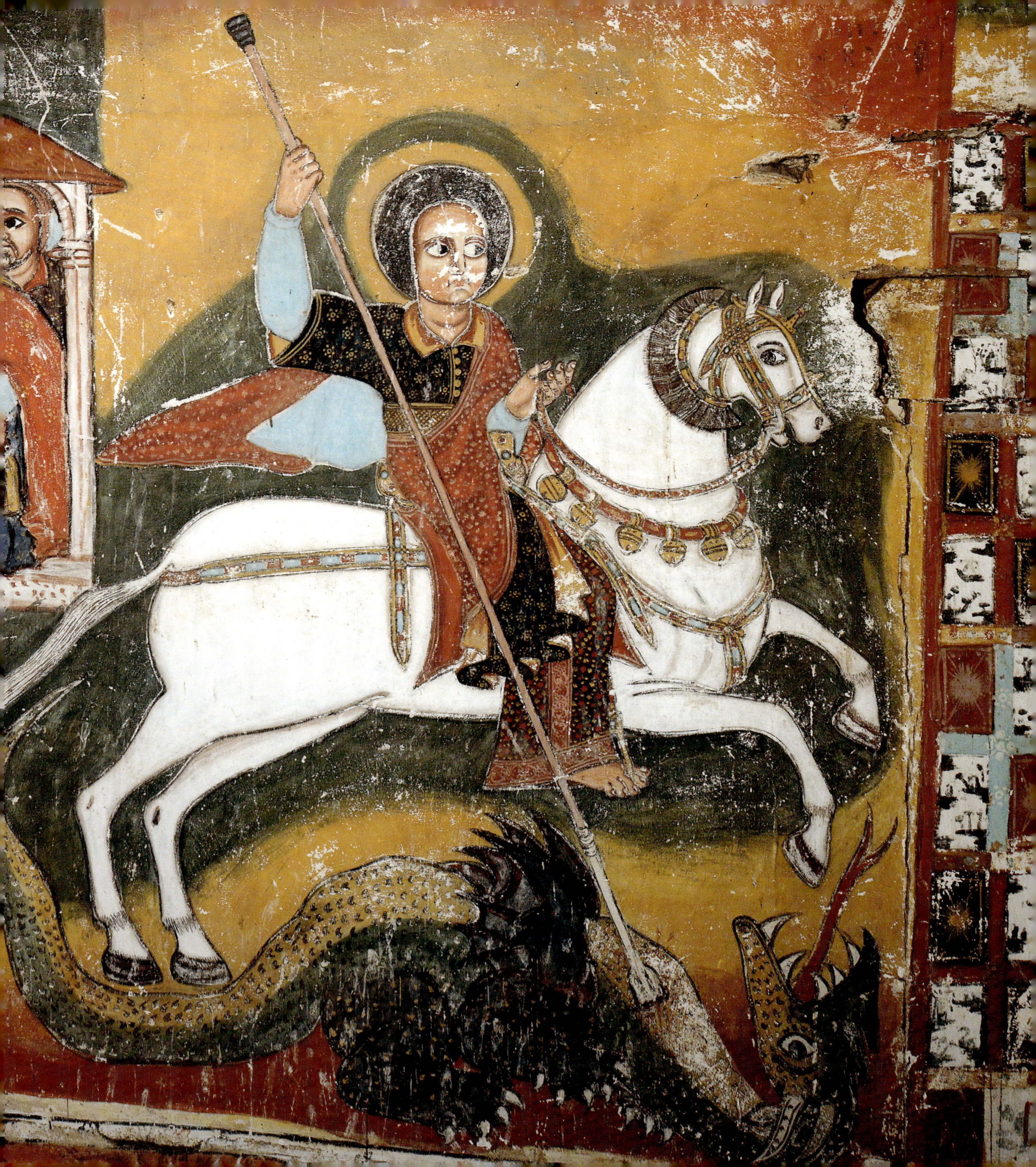

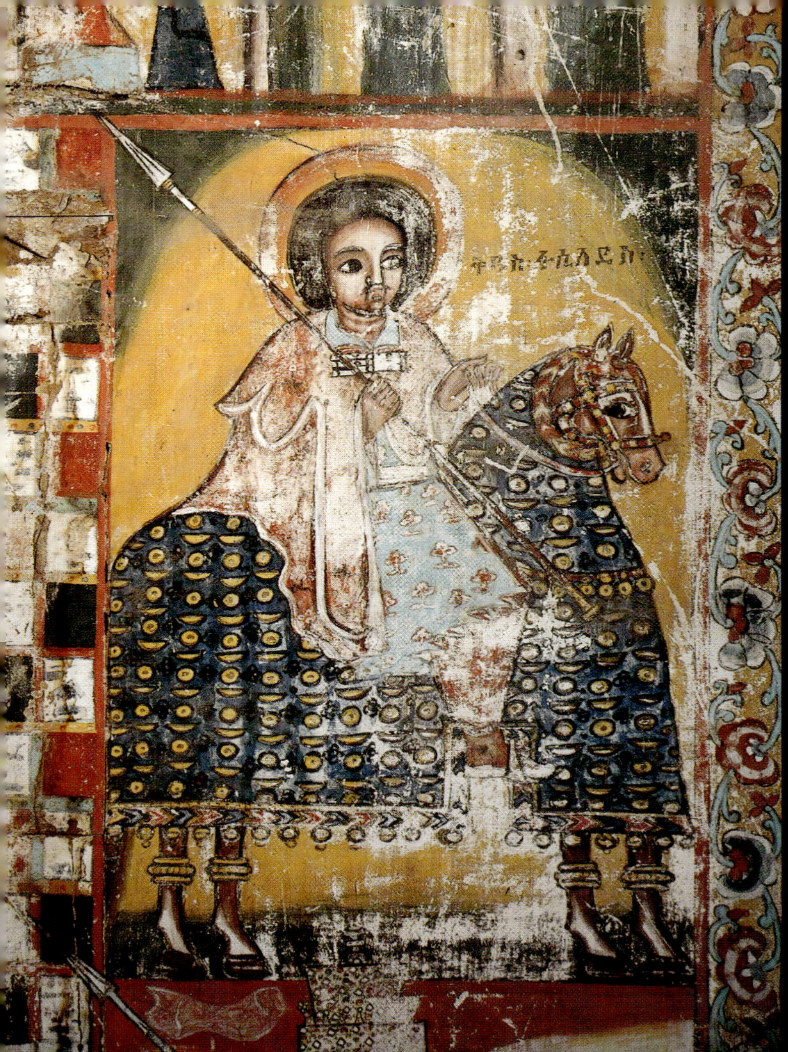

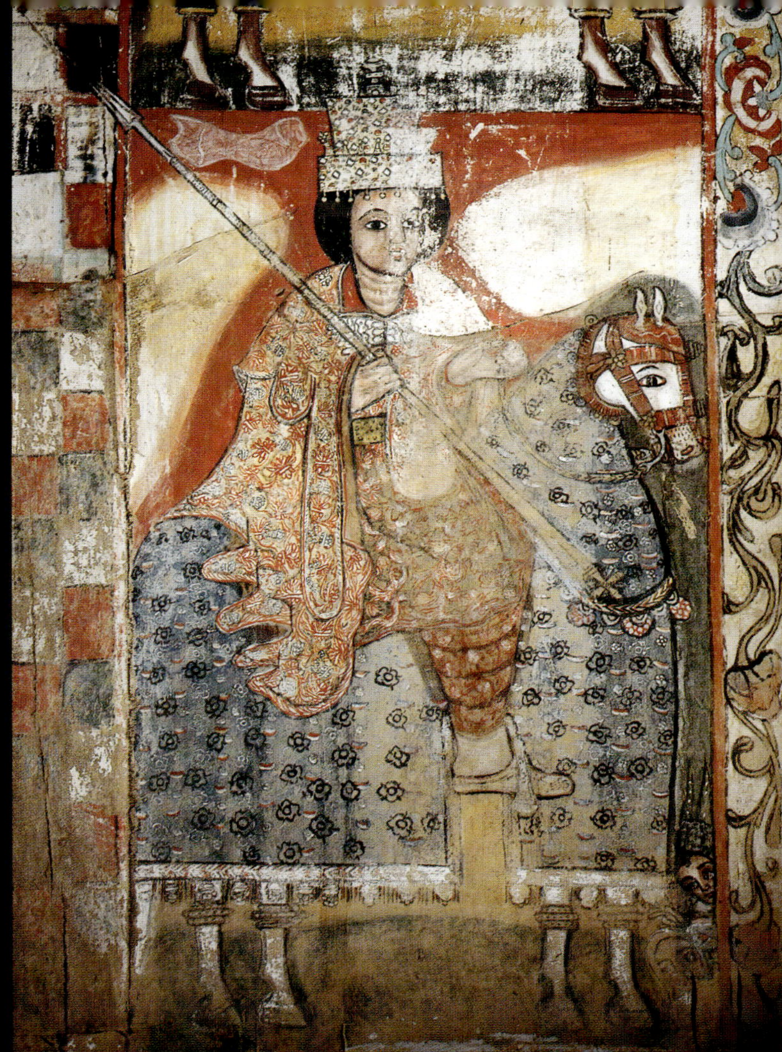

204. North wall of the *maqdas*:
Saint George

205. North wall of the *maqdas*:
Qeddus Fāsiladas, Saint Basilides

206. North wall of the *maqdas*:
Saint George, the king of saints

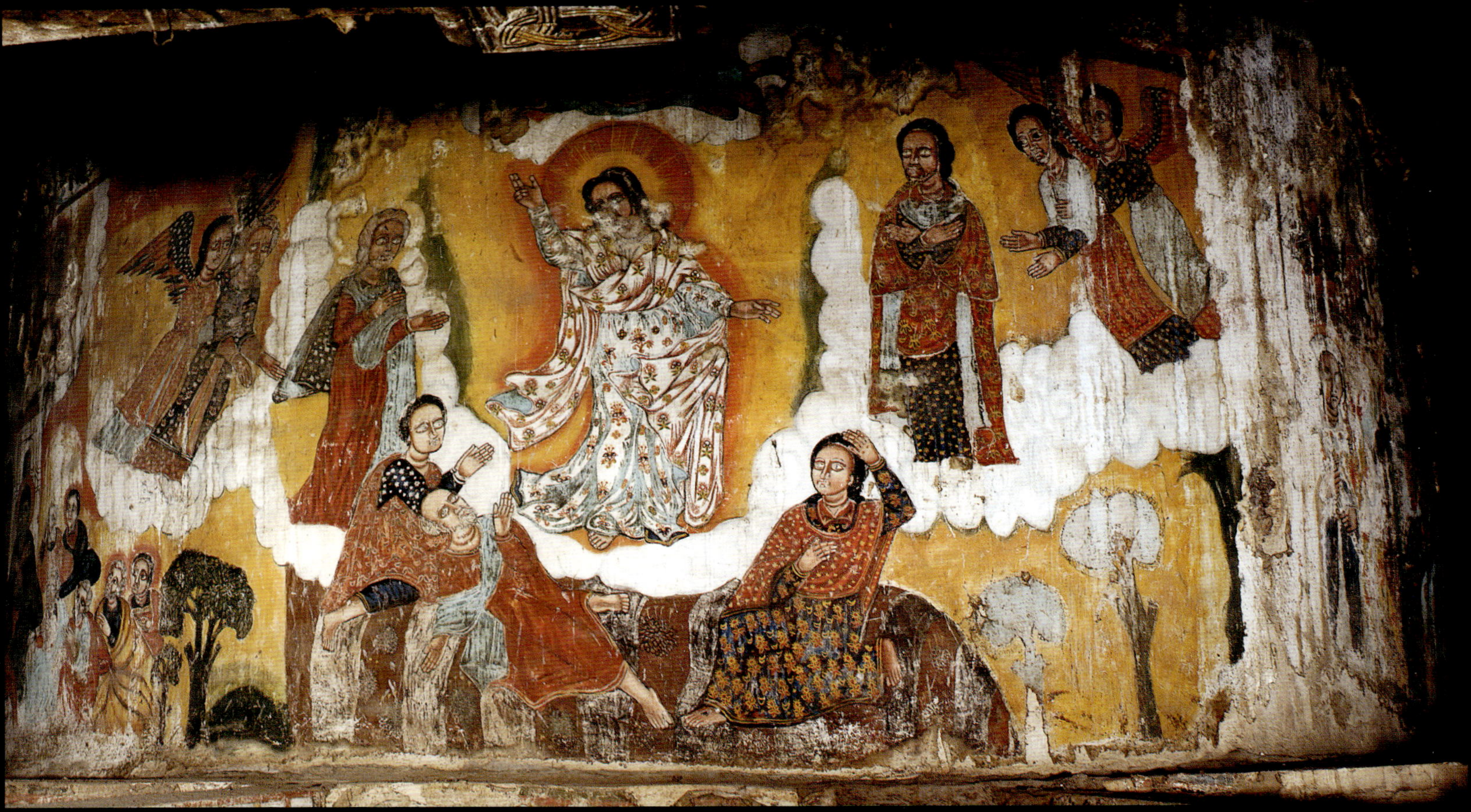

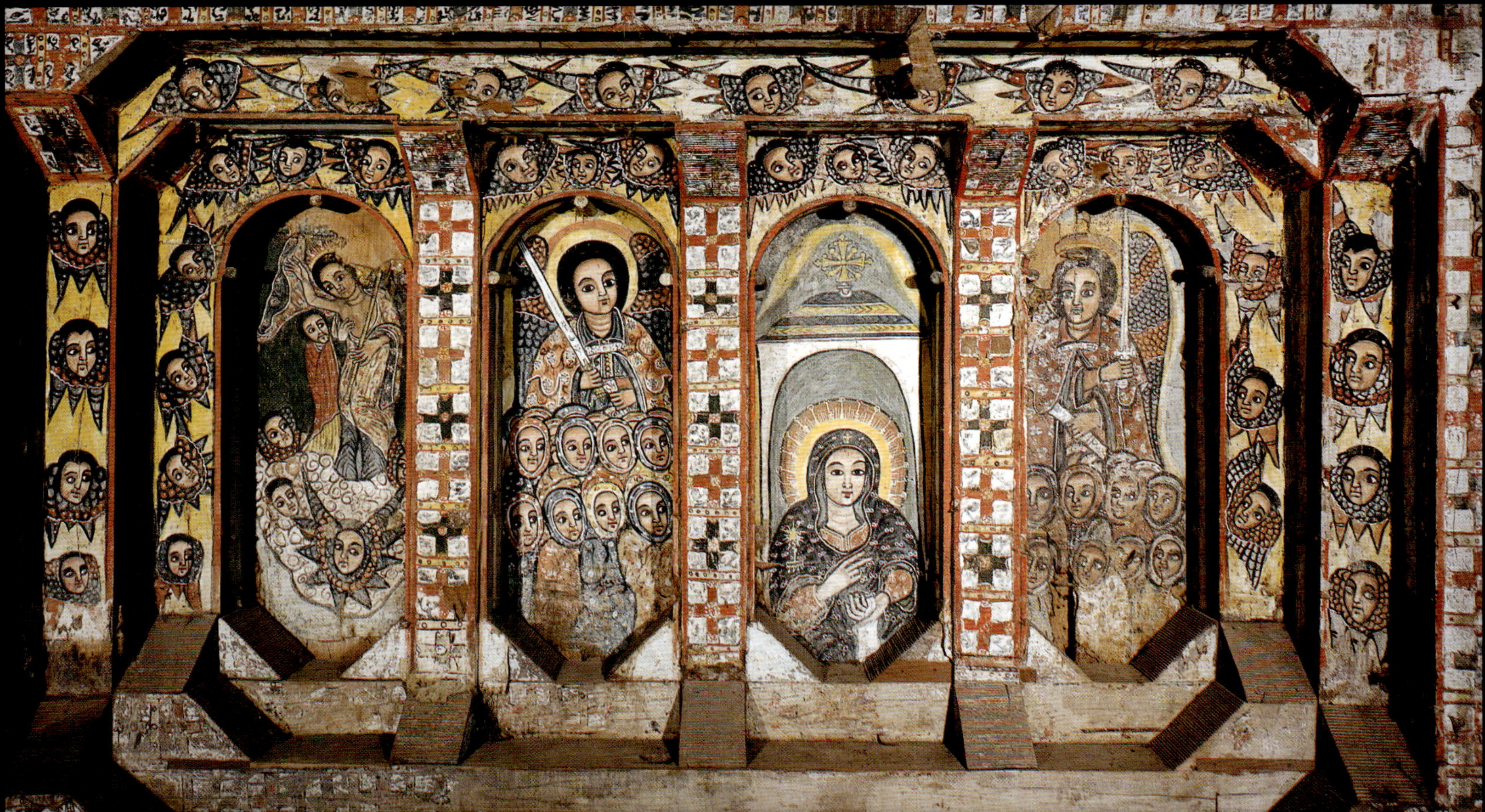

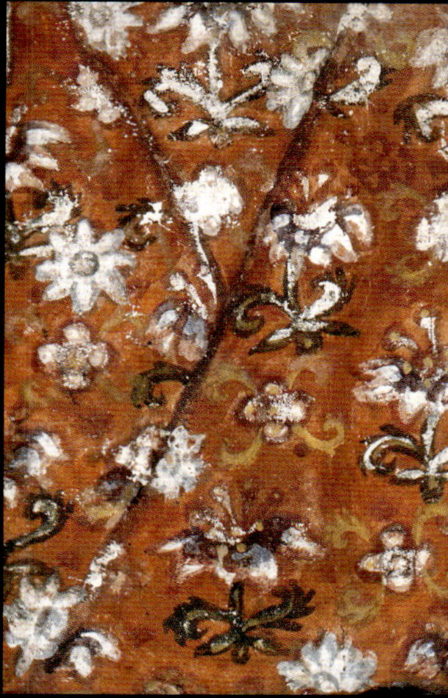

209. North wall of the *maqdas*: detail of the precious vestments of the Holy Trinity.

210. West wall of the *maqdas*: the Virgin with Child (detail).

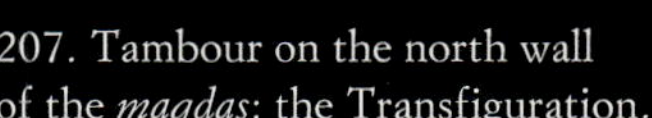

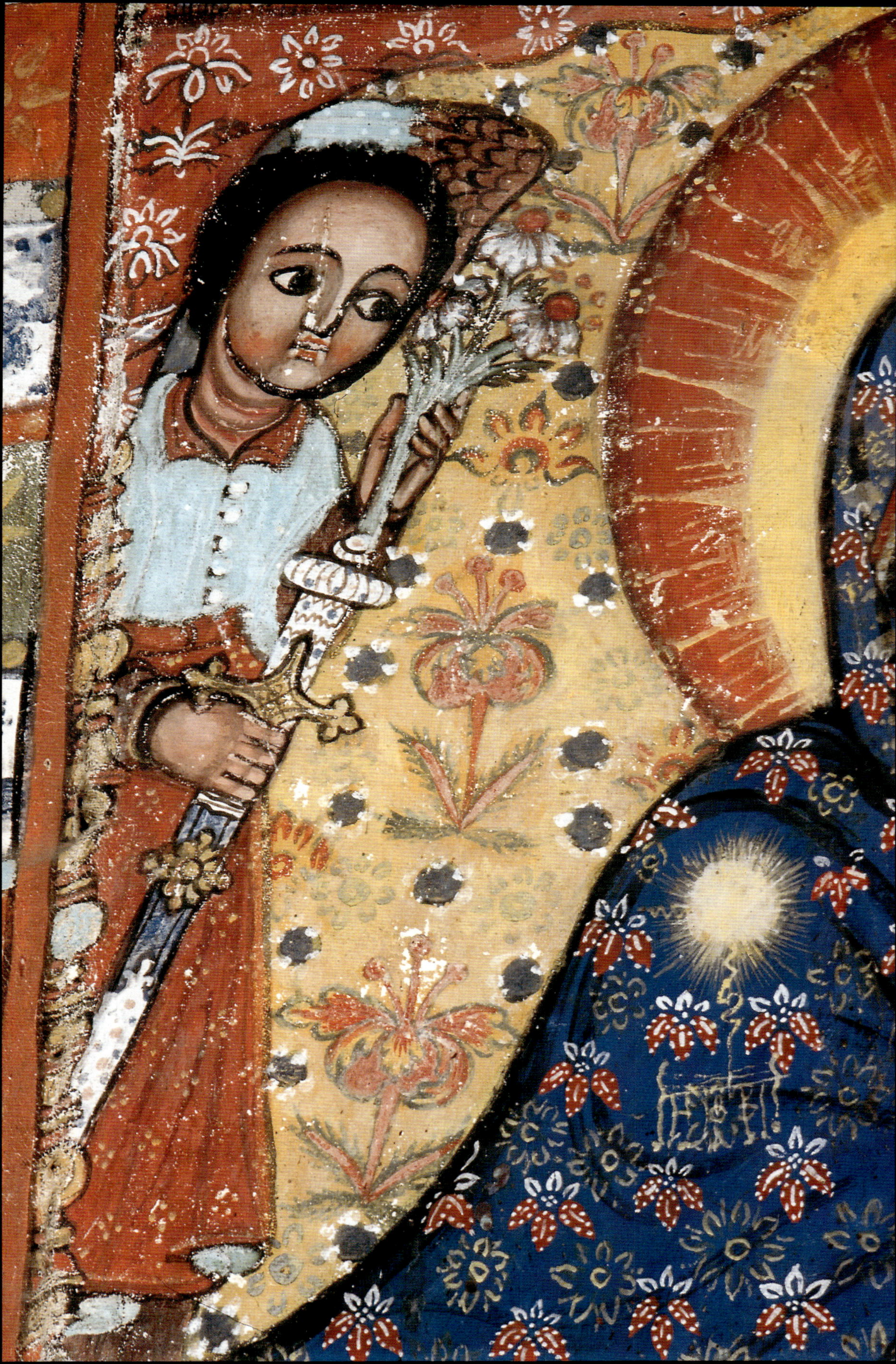

207. Tambour on the north wall of the *maqdas*: the Transfiguration.

208. East wall of the *maqdas*: the quadriforate window with Jeus appearing to his disciple Thomas and the Archangels Michael and Gabriel, with the believers, turning towards the Virgin.

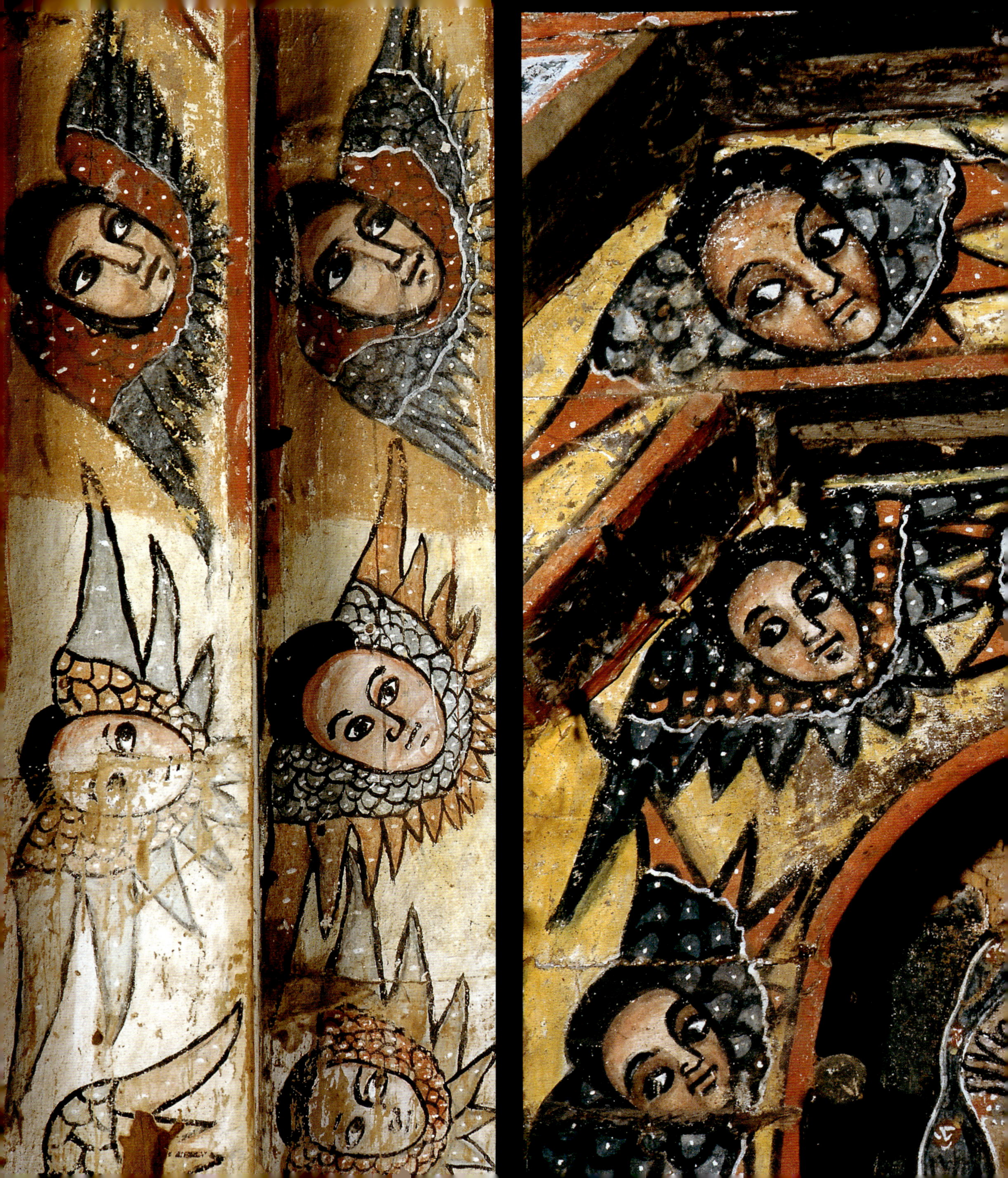

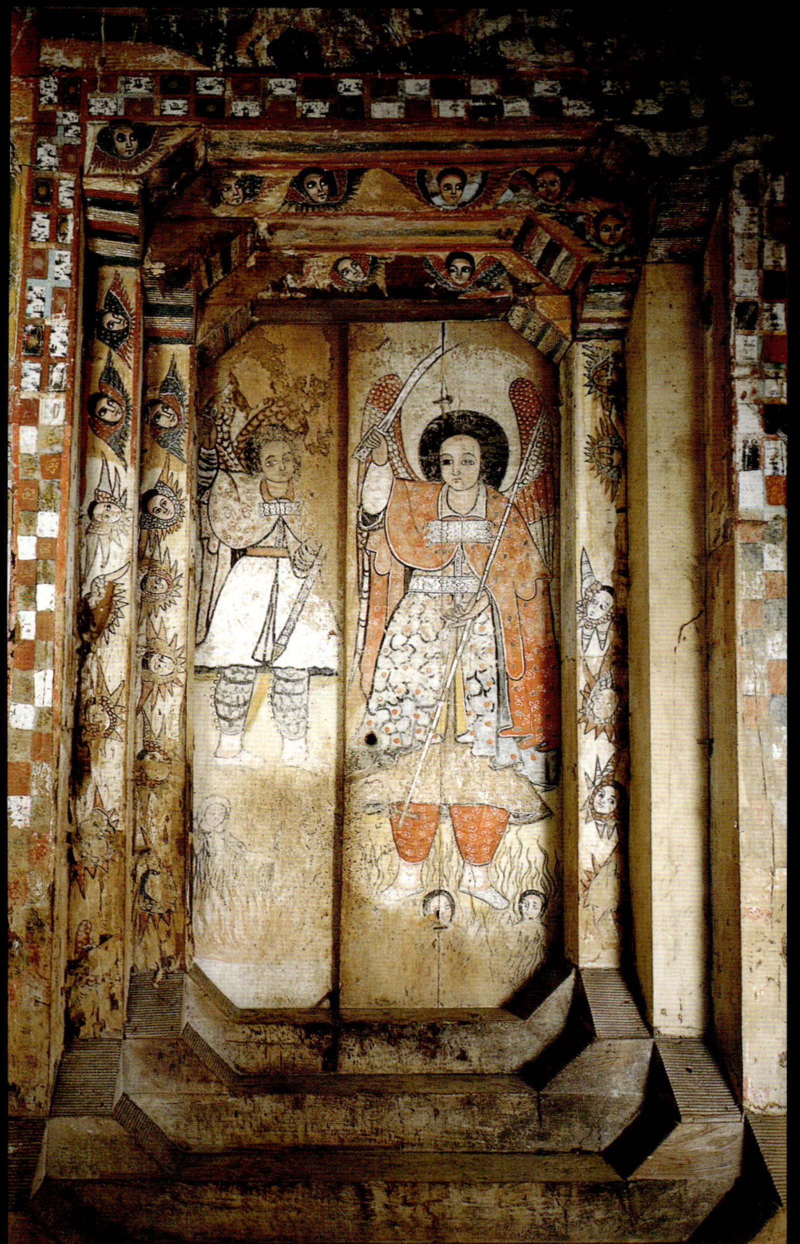

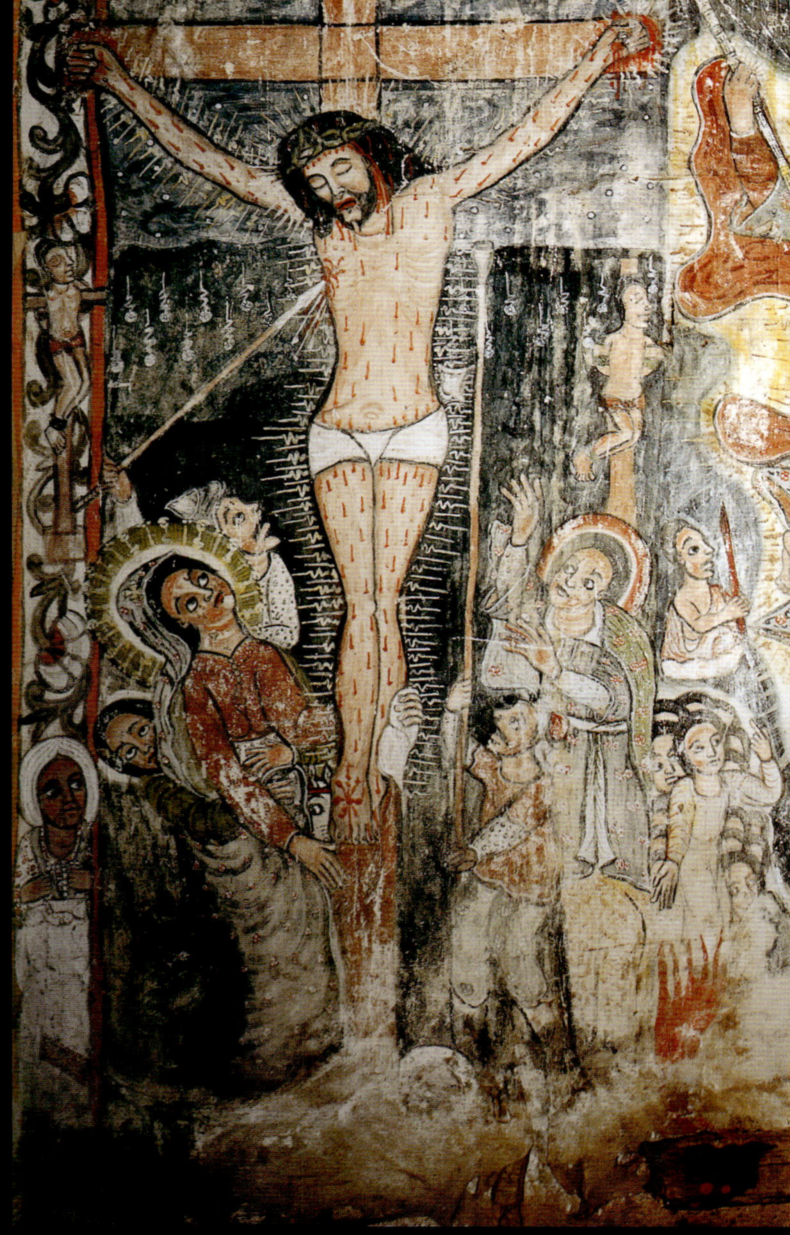

211. North wall of the *maqdas*: detail of the door. Note the stylistical difference of the cherubs in the bottom part.

212. East wall of the *maqdas*: detail of the quadrifora.

213. North wall of the *maqdas*: the door, with Saint Mchael and the Archangel Saint Gabriel who frees the three kids from the burning furnace.

214. East wall of the *maqdas*: the Crucifixion.

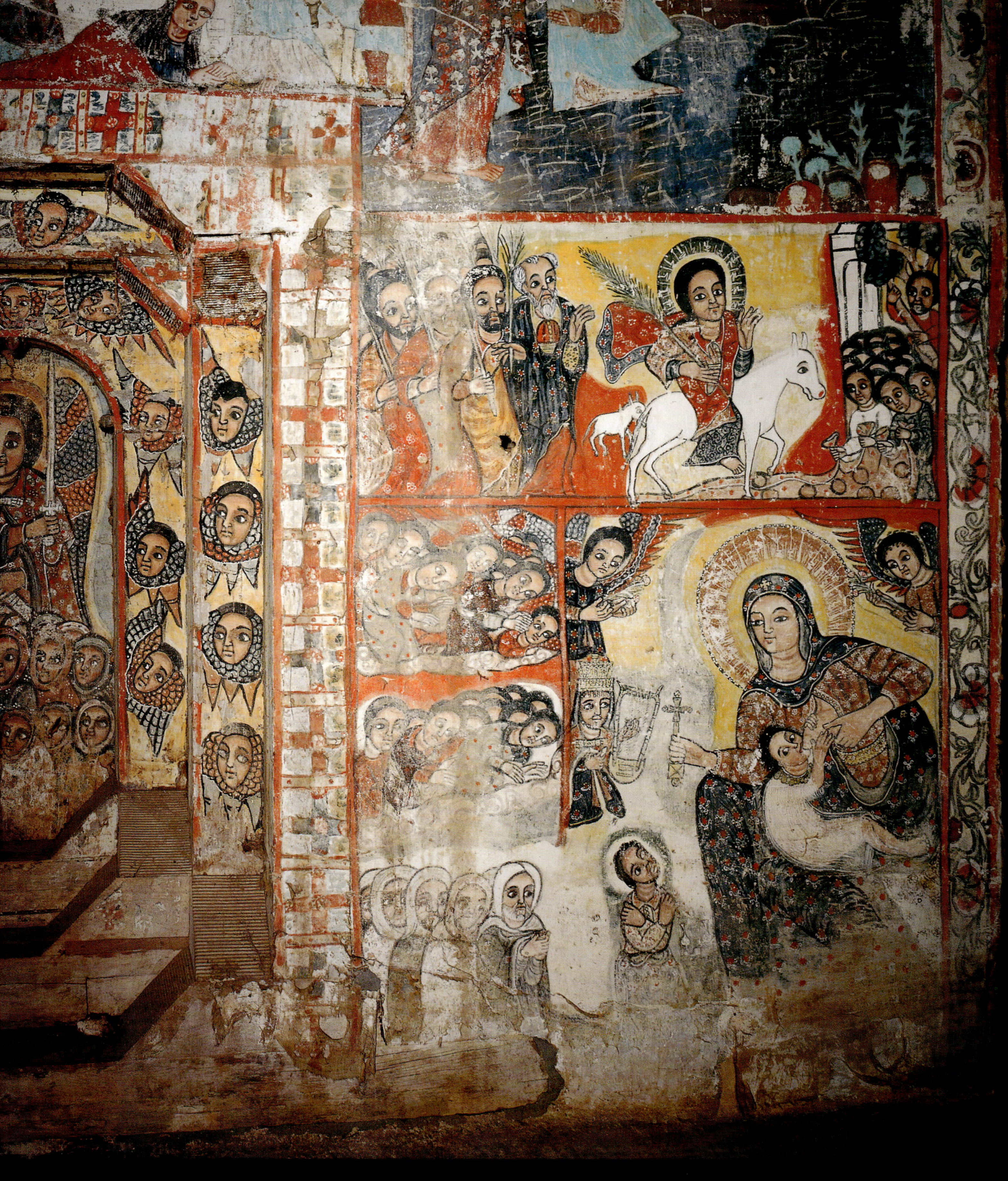

215. East wall of the *maqdas*: the triumphant entrance of the Messiah into Jerusalem and (bottom) Michael, Gabriel, David with his harp, saints and monks worship the *Virgo lactans*.

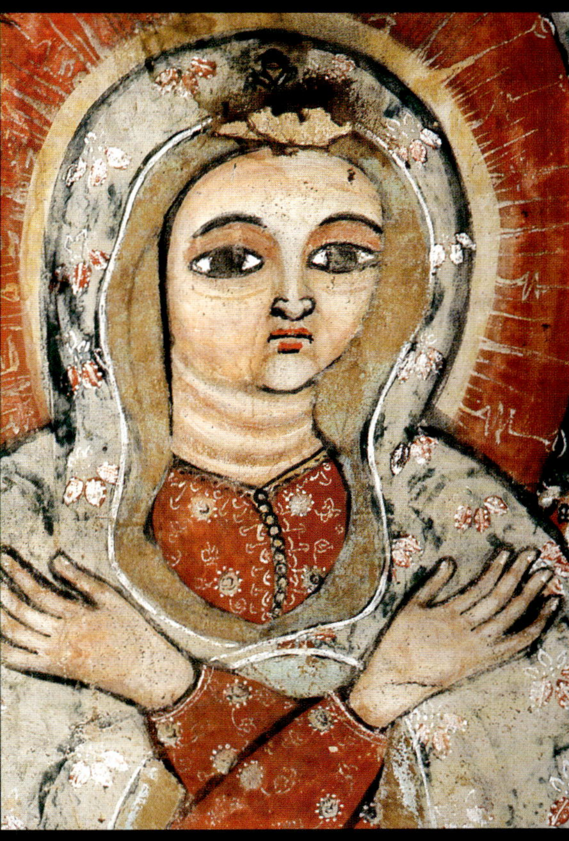

216. South wall of the *maqdas*: the Coronation of the Virgin (detail).

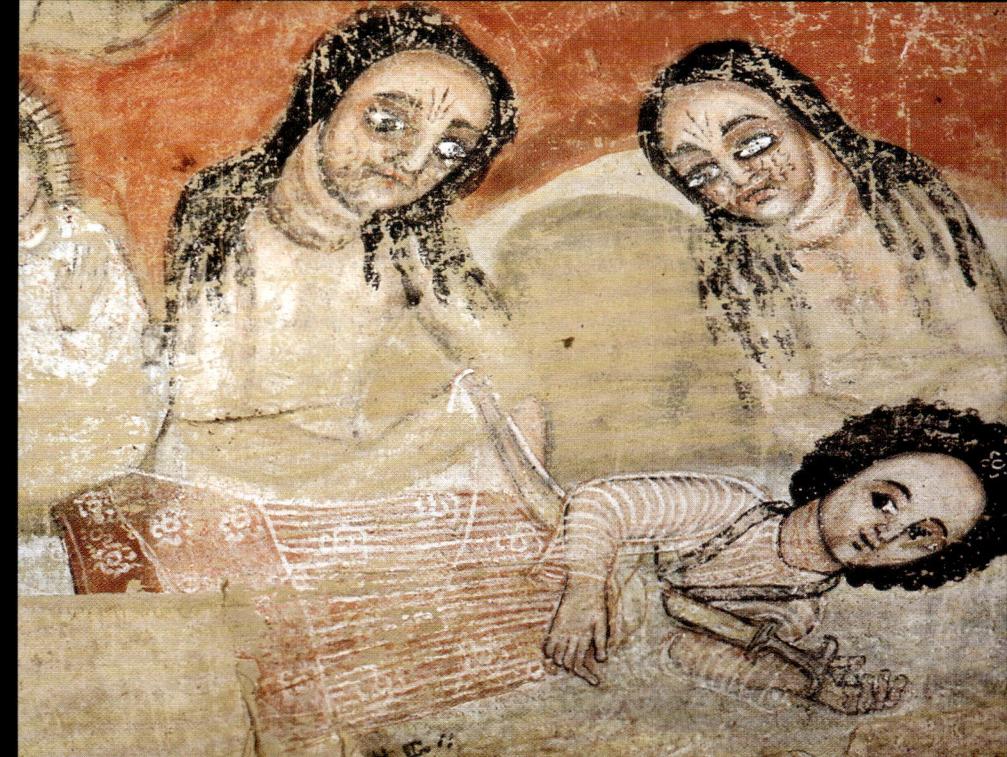

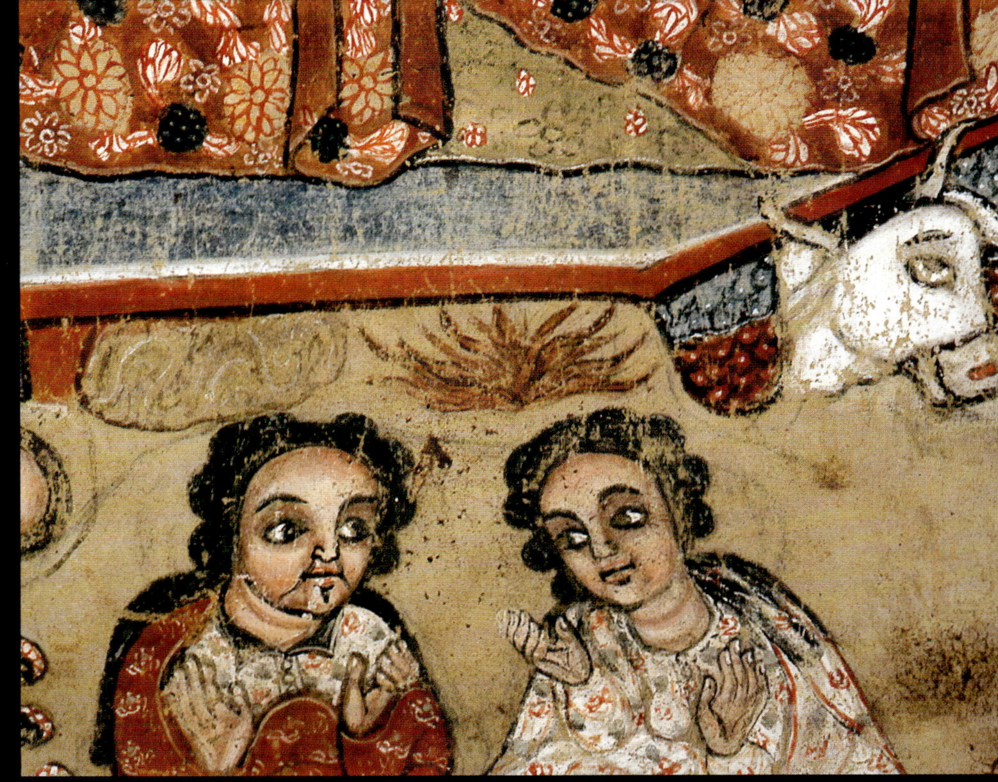

217. North wall of the *maqdas*: an offerer prostrate under the image of Adam and Eve, naked after original sin.

218. North wall of the *maqdas*: Adam and Eve, dressed, in the Eartly Paradise before the original sin prior to their committing original sin, placed under a panel supported by a heavenly

all, made totally flat by the repetitive and minute pattern of the fabric (figs. 205-206). Up higher in the Transfiguration, amongst "ambient" small clouds, Christ's hanging white tunic is disarranged and given a sense of movement by quick folds, marked in blue (fig. 207). Once again different and sometimes contrasting stylistic components come into play, juxtapposed on the same wall.

The tour of the *maqdas* thus returns to the starting point, on the west wall, which is also the best preserved—there are no gaps or re-makings— and the most hieratical with its composed axiality, and the most vivid thanks to its precious decoration. The Holy Trinity is placed so as to dominate the "heavenly" area of the tambour, according to the typical iconography which encloses and unifies three people surrounded by the four hermetical heavenly animals of the Apocalypse (fig. 175). Immediately below there is Man: Adam and Eve—portrayed in the style of a Moghul artist— sitting in an oriental fashion around the tree of life.

The thin little columns which divide the episodes are painted with a certain sense of symmetry and rest on the majestic and sumptuous triforate portal. Where the story's consequentiality allows it, these columns are substituted with different architectural elements, such as a bundle of spears pointing downwards, vertically, so as to repropose the compositional rhythm of the background (fig. 169). The sequence unfolds with extreme attention to the chracterization of the theme, ranging from an almost baroque Annuciation to the night-piece showing the capturing of Jesus, passing from the brightest and placid serenity to the most disquiet and shadowy dramaticality. Therefore the band does not present that homogenous quality which has already been observed elsewhere. Its dominant tones are always different, and on the whole it seems more free and inventive, notwithstanding a certain fixity in the iconography.

Apart from the very refined and magnificent preciousness of the fabric, this seems almost a style different from that of the other walls: the *sfumato* becomes more delicate and sweetens facial expressions, while the picturesqueness of the figures is accentuated by the flowery *qwarañña* style, and by the bright colours of a more varied palette (figs. 209-210).

The painting seems to be all coeval, although in one image one component of the Ethiopian art of the period prevails, while in another depiction it is another aspect which holds sway. Characteristics of this painting are: the native and spontaneous efficaciousness of the depiction— as in the scene with the Pharaoh's troops submersed in water, where the butts of their rifles appear on the surface, amongst the hair of the drowned—; the preciosity and the posture of the figures themselves (illuminating with regards to the exchanges with Islamic culture and the countries around the Indian Ocean); the constant reference to an iconography derived from the West (ranging from the Annunciation to the Crowning with thorns). Anyway, everything is fused into a unitarian artistic taste, which is not just Ethiopian and neither purely European, nor totally oriental, Islamic or Moghul. It is a synthesis, a synergy, rather than a mere juxtaposition of influences. The study of the single components does not explain fully the overall fascination of this artistic invention. It may help to understand its genesis but not to appreciate the results, which pertain to a different category, that of art itself.

Such high quality does not find an equal in the re-made paintings of the the lower parts of the *maqdas,* in substitution for consumed ones. Observing the four-light window on the east side of the *maqdas*, the more accentuated schematicism in the decoration of the ouline strikes us, especially when compared to that on the west portal: the drawing is similar, but here the heavier cross-shaped sections prevail on the sequence of *azulejos*, which are painted in a more summary way (fig. 208). Even the cherubs are brusquely stylized, their small wings ending with acute triangular points, which are almost merely sketched in the lower parts of the north and south doors of the *maqdas (figs. 211-212).* Since we have the original cherubs up higher, this is evidence of a re-painting which took place at least after a few decades. Even the frames around each single section change colour, varying—with few exceptions—from red to white. The style becomes different. The range of colours changes: green and azures disappear, while ochres—more tenuous and colder—reds, pinks and blues prevail. A certain type of gestuality also becomes typical, such as in the white zig-zag parts of the halos, which are also used for the aura surrounding the body of the crucified Christ which is portrayed to the right of the window on the east wall (figs. 214-216). Also the outline band is different from the one above; they share the same decorative motif with meandering vegetation, but here one of the thieves is crucified amongst the shoots and the hand of Christ reaches over it, without any spatial plan. Pure lack of constraint! A comparison with the correspondant scene to the left of the portal on the west wall makes patent this new calligraphism, which is accentuated by the red drops of blood which run all along the body of Christ and punctuate it. The iconography is the same, but the pictorial rendering is completely different.

Another typical feature is the way in which the Virgin turns her head: lifted upwards and exaggeratedly bowed in an innatural position, in the same way as the devotee standing at the feet of the *Virgo lactans* on the opposite corner of the same wall (fig. 215). Yet, above there is an opposite, European-oriented, interpretation of the same scene.

Some identifying characteristics of a later—and, for certain aspects, more naive—school seem therefore recognizable. The painting becomes quicker, more synthetic, reaching almost cartoon-like connotations, although sometimes being extremely skillful, expressive and effective. In the lower part of the north side and along the south, east and west sides of the *maqdas* on the skirting, where the figures are little more then outlined, tiny drawings cover the clothing and the palette is reduced to the minimum, with red auras usually marking the upper part of the sections (figs. 217-218). A different approach can certainly be seen in the scenes held to be thematically more significant according to a hierarchy of values—for example in the Coronation of the Virgin on the south wall—as against others whose presence is practically due only to the descriptive and didactic logic of the pictorial cycle.

No documentary evidence is known of in regard to the dating of the re-painting of the lower parts of the *maqdas* at Nārgā Śellāsē—except for a vague *post quem* reference—. Neither have simple stylistic comparisons with the sometimes very high quality pictorial cycles in the Lake Tana region or in Gondar itself, which are ascribable to the second half of the 18th or the beginning of the 19th century, furnished clear confirmation to date. This is due to their, up to now, relatively summary documentation. The diachronous developement of Ethiopian wall painting is a subject in which there is still ample space for research and deeper study. It is to be hoped that this gap can be filled before other treasures disappear due to indifference. It should be the aim of this research that men cooperate in saving these works of art and that all is not left to the providence of God, glory be to Him.

The Narrative Cycle

Osvaldo Raineri

Foreword

The criteria followed in the description of these paintings[1] are basically reduced to the simple enunciation, with an appropriate *Title* for each individual scene with the addition of an eventual *Caption*— both the text and its translation— in the few cases in which there is one on the paintings. I thought it was useful to accompany the *Titles* relating to the panels with a short text including the narration of the individual scenes represented in the paintings. These narrations are mainly taken from the Holy Scripture, from which the great majority of the depictions draw their inspiration while, for the paintings recalling the traditional history of the Ethiopian Church, the texts are taken from the holy texts used by the Church itself, in which the stories can be found.

The type and the arrangement of the paintings of our *maqdas* basically correspond to the canons reported by *Habta Māryām Warqenah* (*ivi*, p. 273), about the recurrent themes in the pictorial decoration of Ethiopian churches. In fact, as far as the *tambour* is concerned, we find always the same subjects reproduced on both sides, such as: "On the east side: The Ascension; on the west side: the Holy Trinity; on the north side: the Transfiguration; on the south side: Mary appears in the Egyptian monastery of Metmaq" (*ibidem*, p. 273, 5). Also the recurrent episodes on the door of the western wall are identical: Saint Michael, the Egyptians swept away from the Red Sea during the Exodus, Saint Gabriel and the miracle of the church built on an isle (*ibidem*, p. 273, 6). The same can be said about the main narrative sequences depicted in the paintings on the four walls: 1) east: episodes of the life of Jesus and his miracles (*ibidem*, p. 273, 1); 2) west: birth, baptism, passion, death and resurrection of Jesus; Virgin and Child; Saint George (*ibidem*, p. 273, 2); 3) north: the martyr saints (*ibidem*, p. 273, 3); 4) south: the life of the Virgin Mary, from her birth to her coronation in Heaven (*HABTA MĀRYĀM WARQENAH*, p. 273, 4; CHOJNACKI, pp. 171-215 – Stories from the life of Mary, pp. 250-332 – The Sleeping and the Assumption of the Virgin, and pp. 333-373 – The crowned Virgin and her Coronation).

Obviously, apart from the above-mentioned, which follows the rules usually applied in the pictorial decoration of Ethiopian churches, the *maqdas* of Nārgā Śellāsē also includes paintings of other subjects, those which were dearer to the devotion of the believers and which can often be found in the various expressions of Ethiopian art. On the façades in fact, we can see: 1) east: scenes depicting the Holy Family's Flight into Egypt (HAMMERSCHMIDT-JÄGER, pp. 18-19; CHOJNACKI, pp. 39-99); Saint Yared (HAMMERSCHMIDT-JÄGER, p. 28); Costantine convenes the council of Nicaea (the painting, on whose interpretation I am still uncertain, seems to me quite unusual in Ethiopian art); Samuel of Wāldebbā, Gabra Manfas Qeddus, Takla Haymānot (HAMMERSCHMIDT-JÄGER, p. 26); the Nine Saints (STAUDE, p. 199); 2) west: the Pact of Mercy (HAMMERSCHMIDT-JÄGER, p. 18; STAUDE p. 213); 3) north: scenes from the Old Testament (HAMMERSCHMIDT-JÄGER, p. 23), concerning Abraham, Moses, Adam and Eve (CHOJNACKI, pp. 474-476), Isaac, Jacob, the three kids in the furnace (CHOJNACKI, pp. 117, 177, 195).

It seems evident, even to a less expert eye, that the paintings were made by different artists at different epochs, a fact which might also be responsible for the lack of logical connection in the order of the scenes. For example, on the north wall, one notes how the representation of the episode of the "Water of malediction" which Mary was forced to drink, comes after the "Slaughter of the Innocents", while the evoked fact is directly related to the conception of Jesus and therefore precedes his birth. There are also characters and scenes which are repeatedly depicted, such as the Holy Trinity, the Virgin, and Saint George. The fact can be easily explained since they are personages which lay at the heart of Ethiopian devotion, and which are consequently the first which the "supplicants" asked for, in order to obtain their protection. Moreover, the Virgin is worshipped with many different names and many are the episodes taken from her life, derived not only from the Gospels, but especially from the abundant apocryphal literature.

I did not manage either to interpret all of the painted scenes, especially those which have been remarkably damaged by time, or to give an exact name to every personage such as, for example, the "Warrior saints on their horses", which did not have a caption. In such cases I did not want to avoid a possible interpretation, which I therefore suggested, even though followed by a question mark.

In the following detailed description of the paintings on the walls of the *maqdas*, the order proposed by the above-mentioned Habta Māryām Worqenah has been strictly followed: east-west-north-south (*HABTA MĀRYĀM WARQENAH*, p. 273).

[1] My reading and interpretation of the paintings on the *maqdas* of the church of Nārgā Śellāsē, has been based uniquely on photogrpahic documentation, since I could not go there, as I had originally planned. I listened attentively to architect Mario Di Salvo, who visited the church many times, personally supervising the whole of the photographical survey. Moreover, Eric Godet has been of great help, in always being available for clarifying some of my doubts. I wish to thank both scolars for their kindness.
Biblical quotations relating to the scenes in the pictorical eydes are taken from the King James version of the Holy Bible.

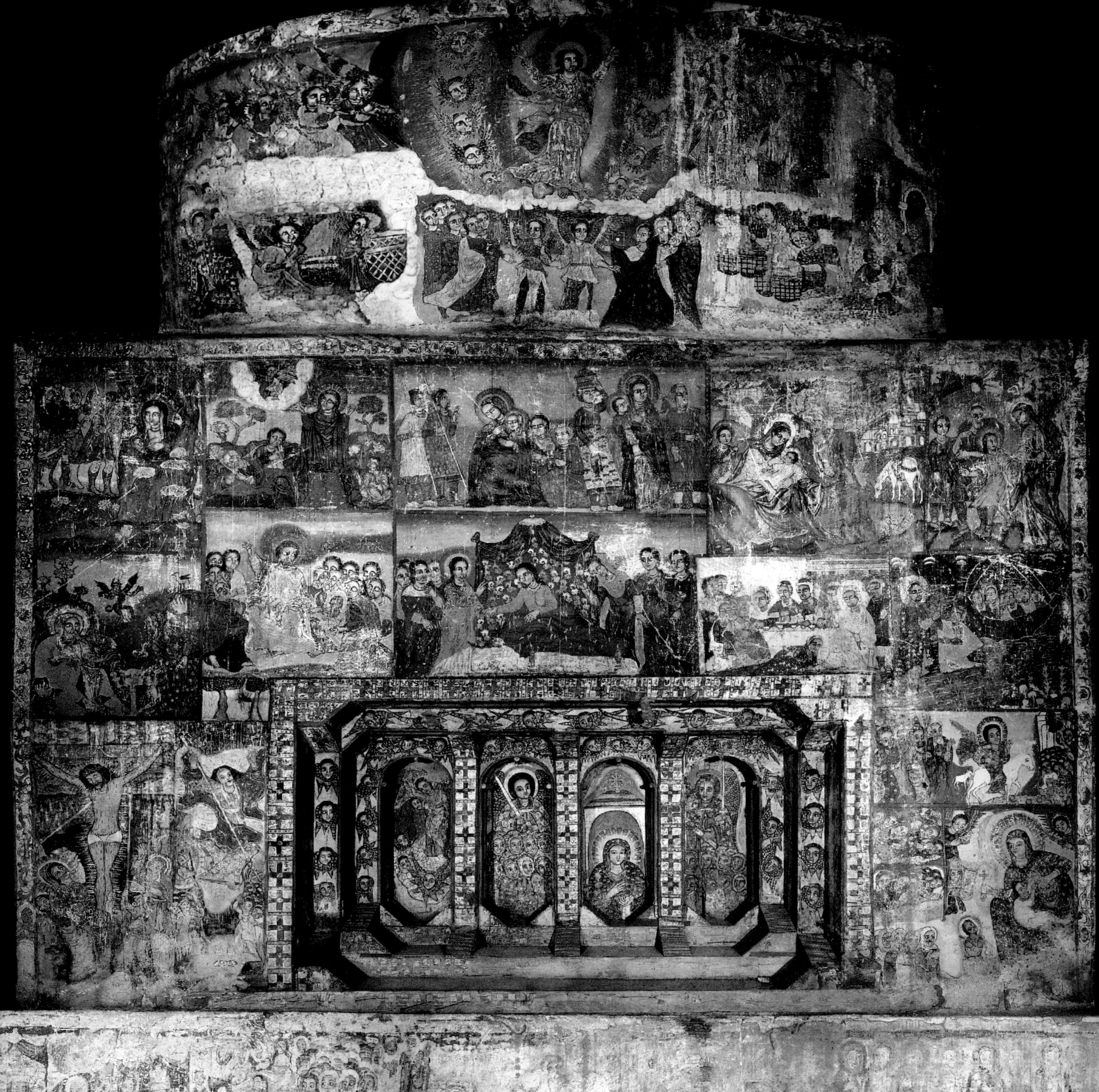

East Wall

Tambour

Ascension of Jesus to Heaven and Angels Playing
"When they therefore were come together, they asked of him, saying, Lord, wilt thou at this time restore again the kingdom to Israel? And he said unto them, It is not for you to know the times or the seasons, which the Father hath put in his own power. But ye shall receive power, after that the Holy Ghost is come upon you: and ye shall be witnesses unto me both in Jerusalem, and in all Judaea, and in Samaria and unto the uttermost part of the earth.
And when he had spoken these things, while they beheld, he was taken up; and a cloud received him out of their sight. And while they looked steadfastly towards heaven as he went up, behold, two men stood by them in white apparel; which also said, Ye men of Galilee, why stand ye gazing up into heaven? this same Jesus, which is taken up from you into heaven, shall so come in like manner as ye have seen him go into heaven" (The Acts 1, 6-11).

First band under the tambour

1. *The Flight into Egypt: a Tree Opens Its Trunk and Shelters the Holy Family*
A miracle reported by the legends around the vicissitudes which the Holy Family had to face during the Flight into Egypt. While Herod's soldiers, who were looking for the baby Jesus, are almost on the verge of capturing him, with no escape left to the fugitives, suddenly a tree opens up its trunk in a cavern shape: here Jesus, Joseph and Mary take shelter, well hidden from their persecutors (HAMMERSCHMIDT-JÄGER, p. 18).

2. *The Flight into Egypt: Having Nothing to Eat, the Virgin Prays and an Angel from Heaven Brings her Food and Drink*

3. *The Flight into Egypt: during the Journey, they Arrived at a Desert where there were Bandits*
(*Patrologia Orientalis*, 12, 1917, pp. 69-73; RAINERI 1998, ms. 72, pp. 518-520).

4. Virgo lactans *during the Flight into Egypt: in the Background an Egyptian Town which Resembles Gondar*

5. *Return of the Holy Family from Egypt*
"An angel of the Lord appeareth in a dream to Joseph in Egypt, saying, Arise and take the young child and his mother, and go into the land of Israel: for they are dead which sought the young child's life" (St. Matthew 2, 20).

Second band under the tambour

1. *Jesus' Temptations*
"Then was Jesus led up of the spirit into the wilderness to be tempted of the devil. And when he had fasted forty days and forty nights, he was afterward an hungred. And when the tempter came to him, he said, If thou be the Son of God, command that these stones be made bread. But he answered and said, It is written, Man shall not live by bread alone, but every word that proceedeth out of the mouth of God. Then the devil taketh him up into the holy city, and setteth him on a pinnacle of the temple. And saith unto him, If thou be the Son of God, cast thyself down: for it is written, He shall give his angels charge concerning thee: and in their hands they shall bear thee up, lest at any time thou dash thy foot against a stone. Jesus said unto him, It is written again, Thou shalt not tempt the Lord thy God. Again, the devil taketh him up into an exceeding high mountain, and sheweth him all the kingdoms of the world, and the glory of them; and saith unto him, All these things will I give thee, if thou wilt fall down and worship me. Then saith Jesus unto him, Get thee hence, Satan: for it is written, Thou shalt worship the Lord thy God, and him only shalt thou serve. Then the devil leaveth him, and, behold, angels came and ministered unto him" (St. Matthew 4, 1-11).

2. *Jesus Teaches the Apostles*
"And when he had called unto him his twelve disciples, he gave them power against unclean spirits, to cast them out, and to heal all manner of sickness and all manner of disease" (St. Matthew 10, 1).

3. *Resurrection of Jairus' Daughter*
"And, behold, there cometh one of the rulers of the synagogue, Jairus by name; and when he saw him, he fell at his feet. And besought him greatly, saying, My little daughter lieth at the point of death: I pray thee, come and lay thy hands on her, that she may be healed; and she shall live. And Jesus went with him; and much people followed him, and thronged him [...] While he yet spake, there came from the ruler of the synagogue's house certain which said, Thy daughter is dead: why troublest thou the Master any further? As soon as Jesus heard the word that was spoken, he saith unto the ruler of the synagogue, be not afraid, only believe. And he suffered no man to follow him, save Peter, and James, and John the brother of James. And he cometh to the house of the ruler of the synagogue, and seeth the tumult, and them that wept and wailed greatly. And when he was come in, he saith unto them, Why make ye this ado, and weep? the damsel is not dead, but sleepeth. And they laughed him to scorn. But when he had put them all out, he taketh the father and the mother of the damsel, and them that were with him, and entereth in where the damsel was lying. And he took the damsel by the hand, and said unto her, Talitha cumi;

which is, being interpreted, Damsel, I say unto thee, arise. And straightway the damsel arose, and walked; for she was of the age of twelve years. And they were astonished with a great astonishment. And he charged them straitly that no man should know it; and commanded that something should be given her to eat" (St. Mark 5, 21-24.35-43).

4. *The Supper at Bethany: Mary Anoints Jesus' Feet*
"Then Jesus six days before the passover came to Bethany, where Lazarus was which had been dead, whom he raised from the dead. There they made him a supper; and Martha served: but Lazarus was one of them that sat at the table with him. Then took Mary a pound of ointment of spikenard, very costly, and anointed the feet of Jesus, and wiped his feet with her hair: and the house was filled with the odour of the ointment. Then saith one of the disciples, Judas Icariot, Simon's son, which should betray him, Why was not this ointment sold for three hundred pence, and given to the poor? This he said, not that he cared for the poor; but because he was a thief, and had the bag, and bare what was put therein. Then said Jesus, Let her alone: against the day of my burying hath she kept this. For the poor always ye have with you; but me ye have not always" (St. John 12, 1-8).

5. *Jesus Walks on the Water*
"And in the fourth watch of the night Jesus went unto them, walking on the sea. And when the disciples saw him walking on the sea, they were troubled, saying, It is a spirit; and they cried out for fear. But straightway Jesus spoke unto them, saying, Be of good cheer; it is I; be not afraid. And Peter answered him and said, Lord, if it be thou, bid me come unto thee on the water. And he said, Come. And when Peter was come down out of the ship, he walked on the water, to go to Jesus. But when he saw the wind boisterous, he was afraid; and beginning to sink, he cried, saying, Lord, save me. And immediately Jesus stretched forth his hand, and caught him, and said unto him, O thou of little faith, wherefore didst thou doubt? And when they were come into the ship, the wind ceased" (St. Matthew 14, 25-32).

On the right of the 'window': First band

Triumphant Entrance of the Messiah into Jerusalem
"And the disciples went, and did as Jesus commanded them, and brought the ass, and the colt, and put on them their clothes, and they set him thereon. And a very great multitude spread their garments in the way; others cut down branches from the trees, and strawed them in the way. And the multitudes that went before, and that followed, cried, saying, Hosanna to the son of David: Blessed is he that cometh in the name of the Lord; Hosanna in the highest. And when he was come into Jerusalem, all the city was moved, saying, Who is this? And the multitude said, This is Jesus the prophet of Nazareth of Galilee" (St. Matthew 21, 6-11).

Second band

Virgo lactans*: Michael and Gabriel, David with the Harp, Saints and Monks Worship Mary*

At the left of the 'window'

1. *Death of Jesus: the two Thieves, the three Marys, John, Longinus with a Spear Pierces Jesus' Side and the Soldier Holds up the Sponge with the Vinegar*
"Then came the soldiers, and brake the legs of the first, and of the other which was crucified with him. But when they came to Jesus, and saw he was dead already, they brake not his legs: but one of the soldiers with a spear pierced his side, and forthwith came there out blood and water. And he that saw it bare record, and his record is true: and he knoweth that he said true, that ye might believe. For these things were done, that the scripture should be fulfilled, A bone of him shall not be broken. And again another scripture saith, They shall look on him whom they pierced" (St. John 19, 32-37).

2. *The Descent of Jesus to the Underworld and the Liberation of the Souls of the just from the Old Testament: at the bottom Satan.*
"Jesus Christ has subdued us, and brought us closer to his Father. Having come, after descending in the *sceol*, he subtracted the soul of the dead in order to get life back. Death, who saw him descending in the flesh, was mistaken about him and judged him of the same species of those which he used to devour; and divining in him the beauty of holiness, cried out loud: "Who is this who, disguised as a man subject to my dominion, beat me? Who is this whom has been given the flesh, which is under my sovereignity, in order to bring me to perdition? Who is this, covered with earth, whilst being heavenly? Who is this, born in corruption, whilst he is incorruptable? Who is this, extraneous to my law? Who is this who takes what is mine? Who is this who fights against death with the power of flames? Who is this who won victory over darkness? Who is this new glory whose apparition prevented me from doing what I want? Who is this, without sin, who is dead? Who is this who, with the intensity of his light, blinded darkness, and does not let me command over my followers, but takes up to heaven all the souls which have been given to me? Who is this glory who prevents the corruption of flesh? Who is this who cannot be touched? What is the inscrutable glory surrounding him? That is why I perish and I have nobody to corrupt amongst his men" (RAINERI 1981).

"Window"

1. *Jesus's Apparition to his Disciple Thomas*
"But Thomas, one of the twelve, called Didymus, was not with them when Jesus came. The other disciples therefore said unto him, We have seen the Lord. But he said unto them, Except I shall see in his hands the print of the nails, and put my finger into the place of the nails, and thrust my hand into his side, I will not believe. And after eight days again his disciples were within, and Thomas with them: then came Jesus, the doors being shut, and stood in the midst, and said, Peace be unto you. Then saith he to Thomas, Reach hither thy finger, and behold my hands; and reach hither thy hand, and thrust it into my side: and be not faithless, but believing. And Thomas answered, and said unto him, My Lord and my God. Jesus saith unto him, Thomas, because thou hast seen me, thou hast believed: blessed are they that have not seen, and yet have believed" (St. John 20, 24-29).

2. *The Archangel Saint Michael and some Believers Turned Towards the Virgin Who Is Standing in the Centre*

3. *The Virgin Mary Holding a Mappula with her Left Hand*

4. *The Archangel Saint Gabriel and some Believers Turned Towards the Virgin who is Standing in the Centre*

Socle

1. *Saint Yared the Hymnist and the King Gabra Masqal*
"On the 11th of *genbot* (11th of May) Yared the hymnist, who was almost a seraphim, died. He belonged to the family of Abbā Gideon, a priest of the church of Axum, which was the first Ethiopian church to be built [...].
In those days the office was not chanted at full voice [...]. The saint created chants for each moment of the liturgical year: for the summer and the winter, the spring and the autumn, the feasts and the Sundays, those of the angels and the prophets, the martyrs and the just, in three different modes, which are: *ge'ez, 'ezel, arārāy*. On these three modes niether the words of men nor the voice of birds and animals prevailed. One day, while Saint Yared was singing at the feet of King Gabra Masqual the latter, who was totally entranced by the saint's voice, accidentally stuck his iron staff into Yared's foot, and much blood spilled. The saint did not realize what had happened until he finished his chant. When the king saw what he had done, he was dismayed by it, took the staff from Yared's foot and told him: 'Ask me whatever you want as a price for your blood which has been shed.' The saint answered him: 'Swear that you will not refuse me it.' Once the king swore, Saint Yared said: 'Let me go, so that I can become a monk.' [...]. Later on he

went to Samen desert and there he lived fasting and praying. He tormented his body severely and there he spent his life, then he died in peace" (*Patrologia Orientalis*, 47, 1997, pp. 242-245).

2. *Costantine Convened the Council of Nicae (?)*
"On the 22nd of *miyāzyā* (27th of April), the saint father Abbā Alexander, the 19th Patriarch of Alexandria, died. [...] When he became the Patriarch, the chiefs of the people came and asked him to receive Arius, but he refused and renewed the excommunication. [...] Then he chased Arius off, together with all those who believed in his evil faith. Arius went to see Emperor Constantine, slandered the saint and told him: 'Abbā Alexander unjustly excommunicated me.' For him, Constantine convened the holy council of the 318 in the city of Nicae and this father (Alexander) guided the council. He fought against Arius and revealed his heresy with words short in their expression and magnificent in their greatness [...]. He held the seat of Saint Mark the Evangelist for sixteen years and died in peace" (*Patrologia Orientalis*, 46, 1995, pp. 556-561).

3. *Saint Samuel of Wāldebbā*
"On the 12th of *tāḫśāś* (18th of December), Abbā Samuel of Wāldebbā died. His father's name was Stephen and his mother's Amata Māryām (Servant of Mary). They came from an honorable family, and this saint was born in Axum. When he grew up, he was taught from church books. Later on, when his father and mother both died, he went to Debra Bankol to see Abbā Madḫanina Egzi' (Christ is Our Saviour), and became a monk [...] Lions, leopards and all sorts of ferocious beasts came to him, knelt before him and licked the dust at his feet [...] The lions went through his cave like rams; sometimes he measured their bodies, others he incised their sores and pulled their thorns [...] Later on, when his time came, the archangel Michael came to him, transported him on his wings and showed him all the glory of the heavenly Jerusalem and brought him before God's throne [...] Then he returned to his poor bed, explained what he had seen to his disciples and died in peace" (*Patrologia Orientalis*, 15, 1927, pp. 195-199).

4. *Saint Gebra Manfas Qeddus*
On the 30th of *maggābit* (5th of April) Saint Gabra Manfas Qeddus (Servant of the Holy Spirit), star of the desert, is commemorated. He came from the city of Nahisa, in southern Egypt. Gabra Manfas Qeddus lived naked in the desert, covered only by his hairs, hair and beard, amongst lions and leopards. Every day he healed many sick people from every type of illness but, unable to take his popularity, he secluded himself in a hidden place on the right bank of the Nile and devoted himself to fasting, praying, to vigils and prostrations. He ate only fruits, roots and herbs. The Lord then ordered him to go to Ethiopia, where he was taken on a heavenly wain by the angel Gabriel, with a retinue of lions and leopards. He established himself on the shores of Lake Zuquala, from where he saw all the other regions of Ethiopia from above and beseeched the Lord for mercy for the sins of its inhabitants. The whole of his body was consumed, his blood dripped into the lake and his bones became crystal-like, until the Lord gave him back his previous appearance. One day three holy monks, Samuel, Ansasa and Benjamin went with their lions and see Gabra Manfas Qeddus, whose lions, however, devoured the visitors' beasts. They were brought back to life by the saint, who gave them back to their owners. When Gabra Manfas Qeddus fell ill, many solitarary beings came and visited him, until he died a holy death, accompanied by thunder and lightening" (*Patrologia Orientalis*, 46, 1994, pp. 441-467; *Encyclopedia*, coll. 991-994).

5. *Saint Takla Haymānot (?)*
On the 24th of *naḫasē* (31st of August) the doctor of the world, our father Takla Haymānot (Plant of the faith) died. His father was called Ṣaggā Za'ab (Grace of the Father), and his mother Egzi' Ḫārayā (Chosen by the Lord). Ṣaggā Za'ab came from a family of priests who illuminated Ethiopia with their faith. His wife Egzi' Ḫārayā was sterile. For this reason they were always sad and they prayed to God for a son. An angel of God appeared to them and announced that they were to give birth to a son, whose famed justice would stretch to the ends of the world. When he was born, there was much joy in the house of his father and mother and amongst all his relatives. The day that he became part of the Church, they called him Feśśeḥa Ṣeyon (Joy of Zion). He was brought up in the Holy Spirit and in the power of wisdom: he performed many miracles and prodigies, so many that all who saw and listened to him marvelled. Then he was brought to the bishop Abbā Cyril, so that he made him a deacon, then went back to his country. Later on, once he became a priest, he started to preach the Gospels in all the land of Shoa. One day he baptized about 12,300 people. He destroyed all the sanctuaries where idols were worshipped and felled their sacred woods, so that all the demons living there ran away. In Damot he converted many pagan priests and witch doctors. Then in his cave he built a sort of cage in which he placed iron spikes which surrounded him on all sides, so that he could not lean against them. He stood there for seven years, for so long that his leg eventually broke. He carried on for four years without eating nor drinking at all. For some time he had a terrible illness, and died in peace when he was very old, living to the age of 99 years, 10 months and 10 days. He was buried in his cave with great honour and glory" (*Patrologia Orientalis*, 9, 1913, pp. 377-383).

6. *The Nine Saints*
The Nine Saints form part of three groups which, together with that of the *Ṣādqān* (the Justs) and one made of single saints, came from the West and, according to Ethiopian tradition, spread Christianity in the country during the 5th and the 6th centuries. The Nine Saints, in particular, lived and operated in the wide Tigrē area which is south of Mareb. Their names were: "Za-Micaèl Aragâwi, Ieshàc or Garimâ, Pantaleuòn from Ròm or Romià; Licanòs of Questentenià (Constantinople); Iem'atà of Cosiàt; Tsehmà of Antioch; Gubà of Chilcheià; Aftsé of Esià; and Alêf of Cheserià: this last one is sometimes substituted with an 'Ots'" (CONTI ROSSINI 1928, p. 158 ss.).

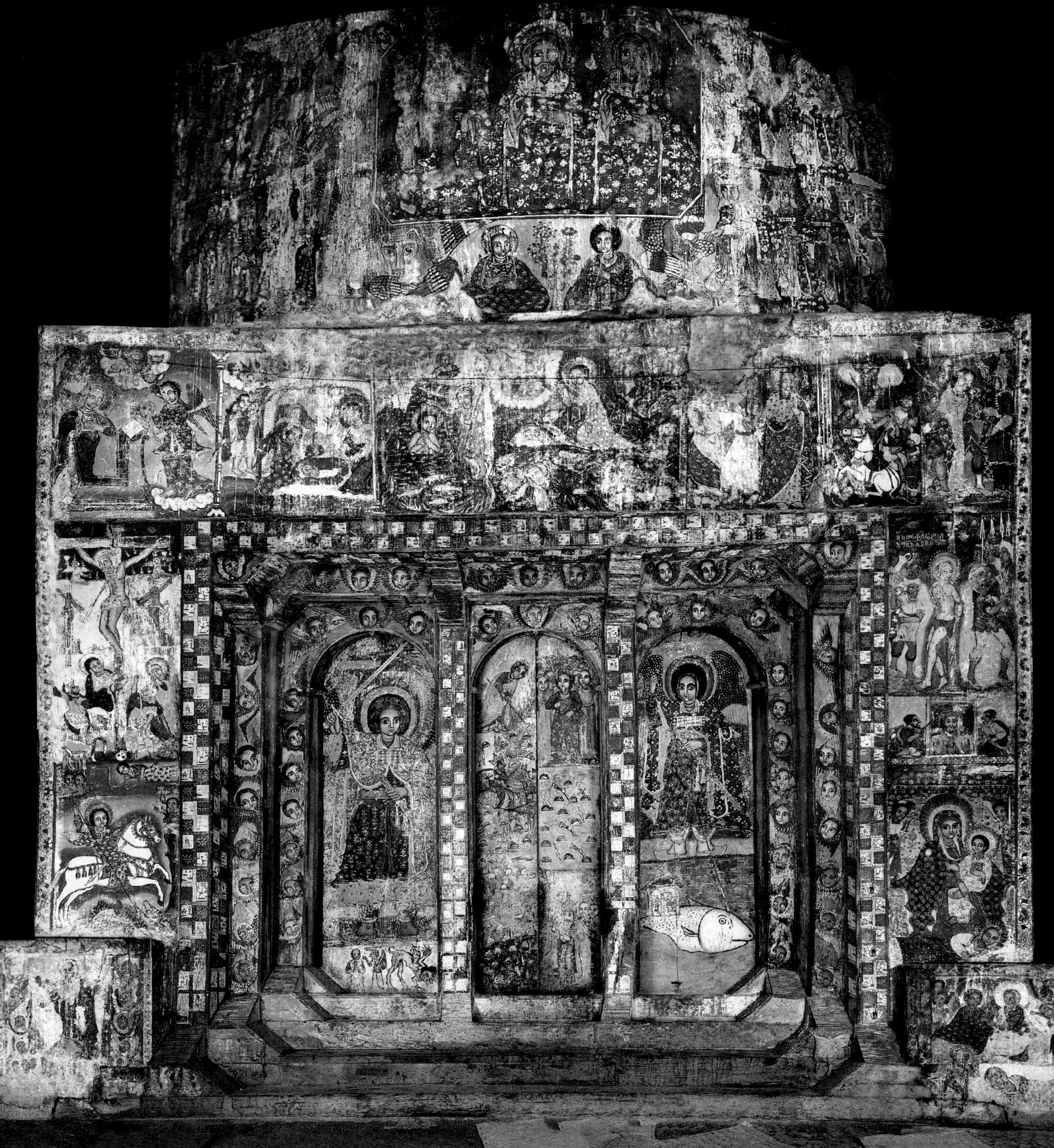

West Wall

Tambour

A. *The Holy Trinity of Father, Son and Holy Ghost* (CHOJNACKI, pp. 101-170).
The Holy Trinity Is Glorified in Unity and Trinity
The Lord God says: "I am the God of Abraham, and the God of Isaac and the God of Jacob" (Exodus 3, 6; St. Matthew 22, 32); by repeating 'God' three times, He expressed the 'Trinity', whilst by saying 'I am', he disclosed the 'Unity'. In Isaiah's vision (6, 1-3), the Seraphims around God's throne, repeat unceasingly: "Holy, holy, holy, is the Lord of hosts: the whole earth is full of his glory." The thrice repeated 'Holy' refers to the mystery of the Holy Trinity, while the expression 'his glory' confirms its unity.
Saint John of Antioch affirms that the Holy Trinity is 'Three in people and One in divinity.' Saint Basil of Caesarea declares that the Holy Trinity is "One in Three and Three in One" (*Short History*, pp. 24-27).

B. *The Four Heavenly Animals* depicted on the four corners of the painting of the Holy Trinity.
"Also out of the midst thereof came the likeness of four living creatures. And this was their appearance; they had the likeness of a man. And every one had four faces, and every one had four wings [...] As for the likeness of their faces, they four had the face of a man, and the face of a lion, on the right side: and they four had the face of an ox on the left side; they four also had the face of an eagle" (Ezekiel 1, 5-11).
"And before the throne there was a sea of glass like unto crystal: and in the midst of the throne, and round about the throne, were four beasts full of eyes before and behind. And the first beast was like a lion, and the second beast like a calf, and the third beast had a face as a man, and the fourth beast was like a flying eagle. And the four beasts had each of them six wings about him; and they were full of eyes within: and they rest not day and night, saying, Holy, holy, holy, Lord God Almighty, which was, and is, and is to come" (Revelation 4, 6-8).

C. *Adam and Eve, and the Tree of Life between Them* depicted at the bottom of the painting of the Holy Trinity

D. *The Twenty-four Heavenly Priests and the Censer-Swingers* portrayed on the right and the left of the Holy Trinity (Revelation 4, 4; 5, 6-8).

Band above the door

1. *Annunciation of Jesus's Birth*
"And in the sixth month the angel Gabriel was sent from God unto a city of Galilee, named Nazareth, to a virgin espoused to a man whose name was Joseph, of the house of David; and the virgin's name was Mary. And the angel came in unto her, and said, Hail, thou that art highly favoured, the Lord is with thee: blessed art thou among women. And when she saw him, she was troubled at his saying, and cast in her mind what manner of salutation this should be. And the angel said unto her, Fear not, Mary: for thou hast found favour with God. And, behold, thou shalt conceive in thy womb, and bring forth a son, and shalt call his name Jesus. He shall be great, and shall be called the Son of the Highest [...] Then said Mary unto the angel, How shall this be, seeing I know not a man? And the angel answered and said unto her, The Holy Ghost shall come upon thee, and the power of the Highest shall overshadow thee: therefore also that holy thing which shall be born of thee shall be called the Son of God [...] And Mary said, Behold the handmaid of the Lord; be it unto me according to thy word. And the angel departed from her" (St. Luke 1, 26-38).

2. *The Birth of Jesus*
"And it came to pass in those days, that went out a decree from Caesar Augustus, that all the world should be taxed [...] And all went to be taxed, every one into his own city. And Joseph also went up from Galilee, out of the city of Nazareth, into Judia, unto the city of David, which is called Bethlehem; (because he was of the house and lineage of David:) to be taxed with Mary his espoused wife, being great with child. And so it was, that, while they were there, the days were accomplished that she should be delivered. And she brought forth her firstborn son, and wrapped him in swaddling clothes, and laid him in a manger; because there was no room for them in the inn" (St. Luke 2, 1-7).

3. *Baptism of Jesus*
"Then cometh Jesus from Galilee to Jordan unto John, to be baptized of him. But John forbad him, saying, I have need to be baptized of thee, and comest thou to me? And Jesus answering said unto him, Suffer it to be so now: for thus it becometh us to fulfil all righteousness. Then he suffered him. And Jesus, when he was baptized, went up straightway out of the water: and, lo, the heavens were opened unto him, and he saw the Spirit of God descending like a dove, and lighting upon him: and lo a voice from heaven, saying, This is my beloved Son, in whom I am well pleased" (St. Matthew 3, 13-17).

4. *Oration of Jesus on the Mount of Olives*
"And he came out, and went, as he was wont, to the mount of Olives; and his disciples also followed him. And when he was at the place, he said unto them, Pray that ye enter not into temptation. And he was withdrawn from them about a stone's cast, and kneeled down, and prayed. Saying, Father, if thou be willing, remove this cup from me: nevertheless not my will, but thine, be done. And there appeared an angel unto him from heaven, strength-

ening him. And being in an agony he prayed more earnestly: and his sweat was as it were great drops of blood falling down to the ground. And when he rose up from prayer, and was come to his disciples, he found them sleeping for sorrow. And said unto them, Why sleep ye? rise and pray, lest ye enter into temptation" (St. Luke 22, 39-46).

5. *Jesus in the Garden of Gethsemane*
"When Jesus had spoken these words, he went forth with his disciples over the brook of Cedron, where was a garden, into the which he entered, and his disciples. And Judas also, which betrayed him, knew the place: for Jesus ofttimes resorted thither with his disciples. Judas then, having received a band of men and officers from the chief priests and Pharisees, cometh thither with lanterns and torches and weapons" (St. John 18, 1-3).

6. *Jesus is Caught*
"Jesus therefore, knowing all things that should come upon him, went forth, and said unto them, Whom seek ye? They answered him, Jesus of Nazareth. Jesus said unto them, I am he. And Judas also, which betrayed him, stood with them. As soon as he had said unto them, I am he, they went backward, and fell to the ground. Then asked he them again, Whom seek ye? And they said, Jesus of Nazareth. Jesus answered, I have told you that I am he: if therefore ye seek me, let these go their way: That the saying might be fulfilled, which he spake, Of them which thou gavest me have I lost none. Then Simon Peter having a sword drew it, and smote the high priest's servant, and cut off his right ear. The servant's name was Malchus. Then said Jesus unto Peter, Put up thy sword into the sheath: the cup which my Father hath given me, shall I not drink it?" (St. John 18, 4-11).

7. *Jesus is Struck*
"And when he had thus spoken, one of the officers which stood by struck Jesus with the palm of his hand, saying, Answerest thou the high priest so?" (St. John 18, 22).

To the left of the door

1. *The Flagellation*
with the caption: *Zakama qasafewwo la'egzi'ena Iyasus*
(How our Lord Jesus was scourged)
"When Pilate saw that he could prevail nothing, but that rather a tumult was made, he took water, and washed his hands before the multitude, saying, I am innocent of the blood of this just person: see ye to it. Then answered all the people, and said, His blood be on us, and on our children. Then released he Barabbas unto them: and when he had scourged Jesus, he delivered him to be crucified" (St. Matthew 27, 24-26).

2. *The Heathens Hit the Image in the Painting Which Portrays Jesus being Smote on the Head*
(CHOJNACKI, pp. 405-407: *Kwer'ata re'esu)*, as in the past the Jews had scourged the Redeemer
"Then the soldiers of the governor took Jesus into the common hall, and gathered unto him the whole band of soldiers. And they stripped him, and put on him a scarlet robe. And when they had platted a crown of thorns, they put it upon his head, and a reed in his right hand: and they bowed at the knee before him, and mocked him, saying, Hail, King of the Jews! And they spit upon him, and took the reed, and smote him on the head. And after that they had mocked him, they took the robe off him, and put his own rainment on him, and led him away to crucify him" (St. Matthew 27, 27-31).

To the left of the door

Jesus Dies on the Cross, While Two Angels Gather in Chalices the Blood Dripping from His Hands
"And he bearing his cross went forth into a place called the place of a skull, which is called in the Hebrew Golgotha: where they crucified him, and two other with him, on either side one, and Jesus in the midst. [...] Now there stood by the cross of Jesus his mother, and his mother's sister, Mary the wife of Cleophas, and Mary Magdalene. When Jesus therefore saw his mother, and the disciple standing by, whom he loved, he saith unto his mother, Woman, behold thy son! Then saith he to the disciple, Behold thy mother! And from that hour that disciple took her unto his own home. [...] But when they came to Jesus, and saw that he was dead already, they brake not his legs: but one of the soldiers with a spear pierced his side, and forthwith came there out blood and water" (St. John 19, 17-34).
Below, laying, the supplicant King 'Iyāsu (1730-1755).

Door

A. on the left
The Archangel St. Michael Frees a Soul from the Power of Devil

B. in the middle
The Crossing of the Red Sea
a) left leaf: *Moses Stretches out His Hand over the Water, which Carries Away the Egyptians*
b) right leaf, at the top:
Mary, Moses' Sister, Sings with the Other Jewish Women;
c) right leaf, at the bottom:
Aaron and the Jews
"And the Lord said unto Moses, Wherefore criest thou unto me? speak unto the children of Israel, that they go forward: but lift thou up thy rod, and stretch out thine hand over the sea, and divide it: and the children of Israel shall go on dry ground through the midst of the sea [...] And Moses stretched out his hand over the sea; and the Lord caused the sea to go back by a strong east wind all that night, and made the sea dry land, and the waters were divided. And the children of Israel went into the midst of the sea upon the dry ground; and the waters were a wall unto them on their right hand, and on their left. And the Egyptians pursued, and went in after them to the midst of the sea, even all Pharaoh's horses, his chariots, and his horsemen [...] And Moses stretched forth his hand over the sea, and the sea returned to his strength when the morning appeared; and the Egyptians fled against it; and the Lord overthrew the Egyptians in the midst of the sea. And the waters returned, and covered the chariots, and the horseman, and all the host of Pharaoh that came into the sea after them; there remained not so much as one of them. But the children of Israel walked upon dry land in the midst of the sea; and the waters were a wall unto them on their right hand, and on their left. Thus the Lord saved Israel that day out of the hand of the Egyptians; and Israel saw the Egyptians dead upon the sea shore" (Exodus 14, 15-30).

C. on the right
The Church of Saint Raphael is Built on an Island
"On the 3rd of *pāguemēn* (9th of September) the glorious archangel Saint Raphael is celebrated [...], together with the dedication of his church, which was built on an island, outside the city walls of Alexandria, when Abbā Teophilus was the Patriarch; and the prodigy which there took place [...] The saint Abbā Teophilus had many churches built, amongst which the one on an island, which is outside the city of Alexandria, in honour of the glorious archangel Raphael. The Patriarch Abbā Teophilus completed its building and consacrated it on the very day of the saint's commemoration. While the believers were praying, the church started to shake, it split in two and collapsed; they discovered that it had been built on the back of a monster on which sand had accumulated and conferred it some stableness. When men trod on it, Satan shook the monster in order to destroy the church. The believers and the patriarch cried out, prayed to Our Lord Jesus Christ who interceded with the glorious archangel Saint Raphael. God Almighty sent the glorious archangel Raphael and took pity upon the sons of man. (Raphael) impaled the monster on his spear, telling him: 'Our Lord commands that you stay still and do not move from here.' The sea monster stood still and did not move. Many miracles and prodigies, as well as important recoveries of the sick, took place in this church. The church remained as it was, until the caliphs came to power; then the church was destroyed and the sea monster started to move. Again the sea roughened and swallowed many of those were there" (*Patrologia Orientalis*, 9, 1913, pp. 440-442).

At the left of the door: second panel

Saint George, the Dragon and the Maiden from Beirut
In Cappadocia there was a city whose king and inhabitants worshipped idols. Near the city there was a large pond from whence a huge dragon used to emerge and kill the locals. Consequently, the population complained to the king, threatening to destroy the town unless he did something against the terrible disgrace which had struck them. The king then decided to offer every day a young child to the hungry dragon, so that the monster did not devour his subjects; he would even give his own daughter as the next victim.
But one day Saint Geroge passed through the area to water his horse and, entering the pond, the martyr saw the royal maiden sitting there. He asked her what she was doing, she told him the truth and told him that her father and all his subjects worshipped Jupiter, Mercury and Apollo. When he heard her story, the martyr declared that those deities were false ones, and explained to her Christ's doctrine. He finally asked God for a sign, so that people believed that He was the only true God.
Then a roar of water was heard and the monster emerged from the pond. But the saint, after he had crossed, evoked our Lord Jesus Christ and the dragon was calmed. The saint then asked the princess for the laces which tied her hair and used them to tie the monster down and finally consigned it to her who, exultant, brought it to the city. Then George explained the truths of faith, saying that if they had believed in Christ, they would have killed the dragon. They all immediately converted to Christianity, and the saint thrust his spear into the monster's jaws and beheaded it with his sword (RAINERI 1996, pp. 98-99).

At the right of the window: third band

Virgin with Child and the Angels Michael and Gabriel
According to tradition, the beautiful girl laying at the Virgin's feet is Queen Walatta Giyorgis, also known as Mentewwāb: 1730-1755 (JÄGER, p. 70; LEROY, pp. 35, 58 and plate XL; HELFRITZ, p. 188, CHOJNACKI, p. 282).

Socle at the left of the door
Jesus' Descent to the Underworld

Socle at the right of the door
Mary, the Pact of Mercy and Two Supplicants
According to Ethiopian tradition, the Lord allowed Mary a "Pact of Mercy" (*Kidāna Meḥrat*), according to which all those who, under certain circumstances, invoked her, were to be forgiven. It was the Redeemer's mother who actually asked her Son to show his clemency towards those who invoked Him through her.
"The mother of Our Lord Jesus Christ beseeched him, saying, 'Oh, my Lord Jesus Christ, Son of God Almighty, who does as he pleases both in heaven and on the earth, forgive the creatures which your hand created and every soul who celebrates your name! Bless, Lord, those places where feasts in my honour will take place! Accept my supplication and bless thy people and the kings which you have anointed, who offer sacrifice to You in my name!' Our Lord Jesus Christ answered thus: 'I have bestowed it upon you. Rejoice because henceforth both I and the Holy Ghost have conferred on you all the grace of power; and all who will remember or invoke thy name will niether perish nor become lost either in this world or the other, but on the contrary will find grace with My Fahter who is in heaven'" (CERULLI 1957, pp. 53-57).

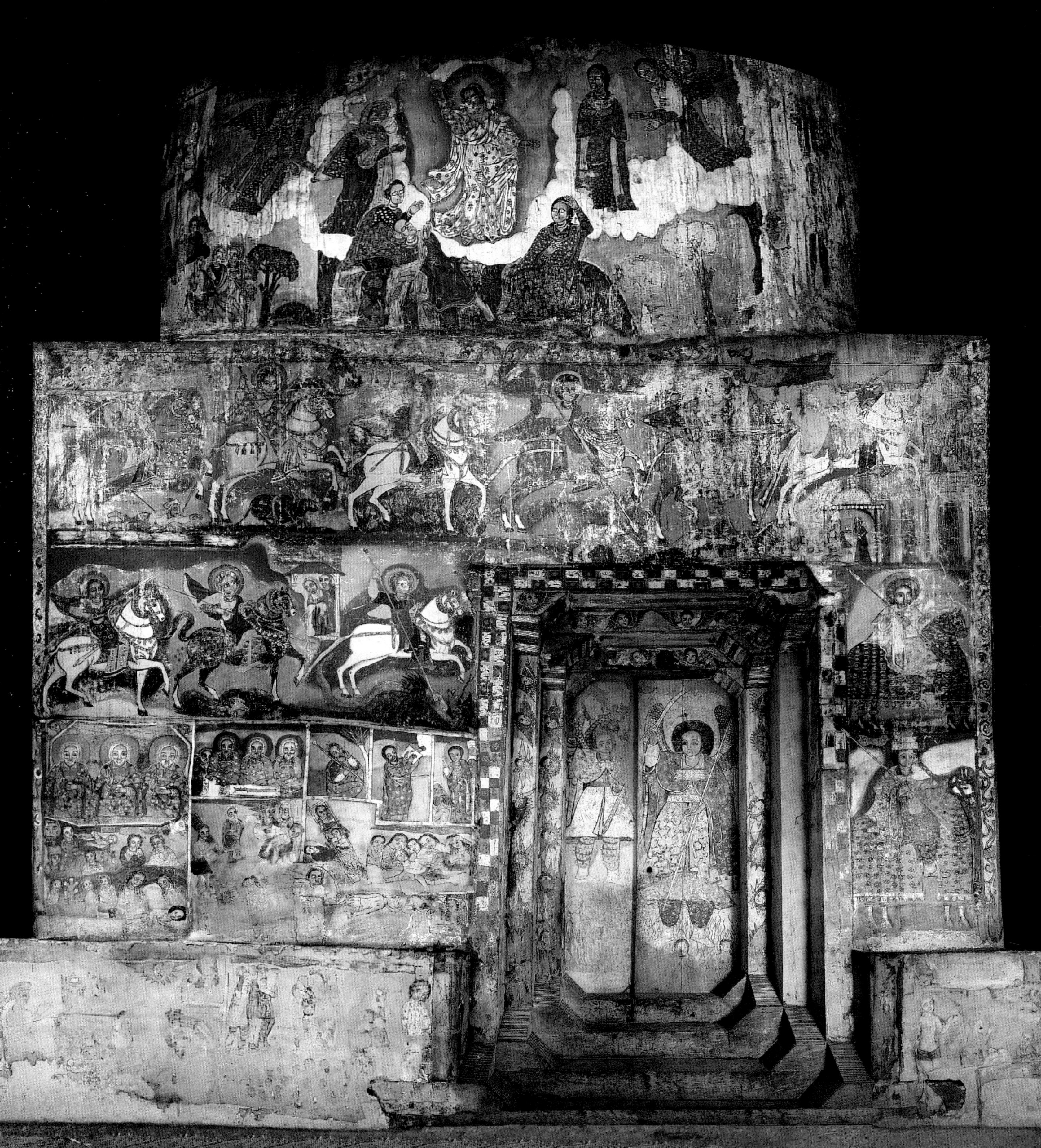

North Wall

Tambour

Christ's Transfiguration
(CHOJNACKI, pp. 117, 195, 383)
"And after six days Jesus taketh Peter, James, and John his brother, and bringeth them up into an high mountain apart. And was transfigured before them: and his face did shine as the sun, and his raiment was white as the light. And, behold, there appeared unto them Moses and Elias talking with him. Then answered Peter, and said unto Jesus, Lord, it is good for us to be here: if thou wilt, let us make here three tabernacles; one for thee, and one for Moses, and one for Elias. While he yet spake, behold, a bright cloud overshadowed them: and behold a voice out of the cloud, which said, This is my beloved Son, in whom I am well pleased; hear ye him. And when the disciples heard it, they fell on their face, and were sore afraid. And Jesus came and touched them, and said, Arise, and be not afraid. And when they had lifted up their eyes, they saw no man, save Jesus only" (St. Matthew 17, 1-8).

First band below the tambour

Knight Saints (RAINERI 1996)
1. *Aboli*
caption: *Qeddus Aboli*
(Saint Aboli)
Saint Aboli, martyr, son of Just, is commemorated on the 1st of *naḥasē* (7th of August). Back from a war in Antioch, this saint found out that Diocletian had renegned Christ and re-established the cult of the idols. The Emperor tried with all means to convince him to adore them, but he did not succeeded. Later Diocletian sent Just, his wife Teoclia and their son Aboli to Egypt, to meet Armenius, the judge of the city of Alexandria, so that he might persuade them to sacrifice to the deities. Aboli proclaimed his Christian faith before the judge, who condemned him to horrible tortures: to be burnt, to the wheel, to have his extremities cut off, to be thrown to the lions, but the Lord always rescued him and made him survive.
However, the result was that the judge became even more angry with the saint and ordered that he had to suffer more tortures: yet, since they were all to no avail, he had his head cut off with a sword, and Aboli became a martyr. His body rests in the convent of Handaq, outside Cairo (RAINERI 1996, pp. 61-64).

2. *Philoteus*
caption: *Filātāwos* (Philoteus)
Saint Philoteus, who is commemorated on the 16th of *ṭerr* (21st of January), was from Antioch, and his ancestors worshipped a bull called Maragd. When he was ten years old, his parents instructed him to worhip the bull, but he refused to obey. When the Lord saw the child's integrity, he sent him his angel, and disclosed to him the mystery of God, from the creation of the world to the incarnation of Our Lord Jesus Christ. One day his parents decided to give a party for his friends and asked their son to offer incense to Magdad, but Philoteus ordered that the bull be killed and burnt. His fame thus reached the pagan emperor Diocletian, who commanded that Philoteus was brought unto him. He ordered him to burn incense in honour of Apollo, but the saint cheated and promised that he was going to adore Apollo. Diocletian ordered that Apollo was brought in, together with 70 idols and 70 priests, but immediately the earth opened up and swallowed the idols and their priests.
As far as Philoteus is concerned, since the emperor became tired of torturing him, he was beheaded and thus received the crown of martyrdom (RAINERI 1996, pp. 86-87).

3. *Menna* (?)
Saint Menna, whose martyrdom is commemorated on the 15th of *ḫedār* (21st of November), was the son of Eudoxus of Nikiu. Whilst still an adolescent he lost both his parents. Appointed governor instead of his father, was beheaded because, refusing to abjure his Christian faith, he did not obey Diocletian's order to worship the idols. From his body, which was carried into a boat by the believers, fire burst forth which consumed some sea monsters. He was then buried near Alexandria and, at the time of the Emperors Arcadius and Honorius, due to the prodigious healings which took place by using the water of a pond which was close to his tomb, a beautiful church dedicated to him was built, where people from all countries used to come and recover from all types of illness (RAINERI 1996, pp. 106-108).

4. *Claude* (?)
On the 11th of *sanē* (5th of June) Saint Claude, martyr, died. He came from a royal family, since his father was the brother of Numerianus, Roman Emperor. When a war started between the people from Quez and the Armenians, saint Claudius marched against them, won, then went to Antioch where he found out that the Emperor Diocletian had abjured Our Lord Jesus Christ and served the idols.
The emperor, who was unable to lead Claude to idolatry, wrote a message to Arian, the governor of Andenaw, telling him to convince the saint with all means or, and in the case that he refused, to behead him. Arian pleaded with Claudius by saying these words: "Oh my lord Claudius, do not disobey the emperor's orders!". To which the saint replied: "I have not been sent to you to be seduced by your discourse, but for you to do what the emperor ordered". And thus they spoke to each other, until Arian became angry and ran through the saint with a javelin. Claude died instantly and received the crown of martyrdom. His body rests in the city of Asyut (RAINERI 1996, pp. 72-73).

5. *Saint Sisinnius* (?)
Saint Sisinnius, son of Sosipatrus, was martyred on the 26th of *miyāzyā* (1st of May). The Emperor Diocletian sent him to Nicomedia, where he was baptized. Later on, when he went back to Antioch, he discovered that his sister had given birth to a monstrous son because Satan had possessed her, and by magic she could take either the form of a bird or a dragon. When Saint Sisinnius saw it, he took his spear and killed both his sister and her son, because he was Satan's son. He also killed her husband and her father-in-law, because

they were witch-doctors. One day Saint Sisinnius was in a temple of the idols: he ordered them, for Christ's power, to descend to hell, and all of a sudden the earth opened its mouth and swallowed them. For this reason he was denounced to the emperor, who condemned him first to cruel torments, and later to death (RAINERI 1996, pp. 124-126).

6. *Marmenham (?)*
On the 14th of *tāḫśāś* (20th of December) Saint Marmenham, his sister Sarah and their forty servants were martyred. His father was King Ator, a pagan, while his mother was a Christian. The monk Matthew miraculously cured Marmenham of leprosy and later baptized both the saint, his sister and their servants. When he found out that they had embraced Christianity, Ator, who could not dissuade them from their faith, had them beheaded and ordered their bodies to be burnt. The Lord, however, hid their mortal spoils. Due to the intervention of Marmenham's mother, the monk Matthew first freed the King from Satan and later baptized him and all the city population and ordered that a church dedicated to the Virgin was built and their wealth was distributed amongst the poor. The mother of the martyred brother and sister then had tombs built where her children and their servants could receive a worthy burial (RAINERI 1996, pp. 100-103).

Second band, at the left of the door

1. *Theodore the Egyptian* (?)
On the 20th of *ḥamlē* (7th of July) Saint Theodore, a great general, was martyred. His father, John, came from Seteb in northern Egypt, and married the daughter of a judge of Antioch, with whom he had Theodore. When his mother, who was still a pagan, wanted to bring him to the idols' temple and teach him her religion, his father would not allow it, so she became angry with her husband and sent him away. Little Theodore stayed with is mother, whilst his father, John, prayed unceasingly to God that his son might find the path of justice. Saint Theodore grew up, went to see an archbishop who baptized him and was appointed general by the emperor. At Awkitos there was a great snake, to which great honours were payed and to which every day two men were offered as his meal. Theodore, on his horse, turned his eyes towards the east and prayed, then ran the serpent through with his spear and killed him. For this he was accused and the emperor, tired of inflicting tortures on him, ordered that he be beheaded. His body is kept in the monastery of Seteb, his father's city (RAINERI 1996, pp. 130-133).

2. *Saint Mercury Kills Julian the Apostate*
top right
Saint Basil of Caesarea
Saint Mercury the Martyr, whose feast occurs on the 25th of *ḫedār* (29th of November), came from Asletes. One day, while Mercury's father and grandfather were hunting, they met two men with dog's heads, who devoured the grandfather, while his father was saved by the intervention of an angel, who tamed the monsters and brought them back to town. When Mercury was born, both his parents, who were still pagan, and the men with dog's heads, who obeyed to the father of the saint—who in the meantime had been appointed commander of the army—, converted to Christianity. When his father died, Mercury took his place and served Emperor Decius, who persecuted him, however, because he did not want to adore the idols, and for this he received the palm of martyrdom.
Amongst the numerous miracles attributed to the saint, a famous one is the murder of Julian the Apostate. Julian, after reneguing Christ, imprisoned Saint Basil of Caesarea, who, together with his followers, invoked Saint Mercury's intervention against the Apostate. God listened to him and sent Mercury the martyr, who ran his spear through Julian's head (RAINERI 1996, pp. 109-118).

3. *Saint George Kills the Dragon*

Second band, at the right of the door

Saint Basilides
caption: *Qeddus Fāsiladas*
(Saint Basilides)
On the 11th of *maskaram* (18th of September), Saint Basilides, the father of Antiochian kings, became a martyr. He was a general of the Roman Emperor Numerianus, who had married Basilides's sister, mother to Iustus, Claudius and Abadir. As for Basilides, he had two sons, Eusebius and Macarius. Iustus and Eusebius both took part in a war and then went back to Antioch, where Emperor Adrianus worshipped the idols. They wanted to kill him and set Iustus on the throne. The project was blocked by Saint Basilides, who told everybody of his willingness to have his blood shed for Christ. The saint therefore suffered numerous cruel tortures and his limbs were lacerated with pointed iron aculei. Basilides died, but Our Lord brought him back to life, intact and without wounds (RAINERI 1996, pp. 68-70).

Third band, at the right of the door

Saint George King of the Saints
(HAMMERSCHMIDT-JÄGER, p. 24, fig. 28)
On the 27th of *miyāzyā* (1st of May) the martyrdom of Saint George of Lydda is celebrated. He was son of Anastasius, who came from Cappadocia, and of Teopista, a Palestinian. When George was twenty years old, Emperor Dodianos appointed him to the office previously held by his father, who had just died. Even though the Emperor worshipped the idols and obliged everybody to do the same, Saint George professed his faith in Christ before him. Dodianos then tried to make the saint submit both with promises and tortures, but he did not succeed. Because of the tortures which were inflicted on him, George reached death three times, and each time Our Lord brought him back to life. Having experienced enormous cruelty, he was finally brought to the Emperor, who was in the company of seventy kings, seated on their seventy thrones: they ordered him to make the thrones blossom and produce fruits. George prayed to Our Lord and immediately the thrones blossomed and put forth fruits. However, since the saint persevered in his faith, the Emperor ordered that he be beheaded. George took it with joy and prayed to the Lord that fire would come down from heaven to destroy the 70 kings and that the persecutions against the Christians would cease. Immediately fire descended from heaven and burnt the 70 kings. The saint was beheaded and his body was brought to Lydda, where it was buried in a church built in his honour (RAINERI 1996, pp. 92-95).

Third band, at the left of the door

1. *The Holy Trinity and the Four Heavenly Animals*

2. *God Appears to Abraham at Mamre Oak Forest*
"And the Lord appeared unto him in the plains of Mamre: and he sat in the tent door in the heat of the day; and he lift up his eyes and looked, and, lo, three men stood by him: and when he saw them, he ran to meet them from the tent door, and bowed himself towards the ground. And said, My Lord, if now I have found favour in thy sight, pass not away, I pray thee, from thy servant: Let a little water, I pray you, be fetched, and wash your feet, and rest yourselves under the tree: and I will fetch a morsel of bread, and comfort ye your hearts; after that ye shall pass on: for therefore are ye come to your servant. And they said So do, as thou hast said [...] and he stood by them under the tree, and they did eat" (Genesis 18, 1-8).

3. *Moses' Calling*
"Now Moses kept the flock of Jethro his father in law, the priest of Midian: and he led the flock to the backside of the desert, and came to the mountain of God, even to Horeb. And the angel of the Lord appeared unto him in a flame of fire out of the midst of a bush: and he looked, and, behold, the bush burned with fire, and the bush was not consumed. And Moses said, I will now turn aside, and see this great sight, why the bush is not burnt. And when the Lord saw that he turned aside to see, God called unto him out of the midst of the bush, and said, Moses, Moses. And he said, Here I am. And he said, Draw not nigh hither: put off thy shoes from off thy feet, for the place whereon thou standest is holy ground. Moreover he said, I am the God of Abraham, the God of Isaac, and the God of Jacob" (Exodus 3, 1-6).

4. *On Mount Sinai Moses Receives Two Tables of the Law from God*
"And the Lord said unto Moses, Come up to me into the mount, and be there: and I will give thee tables of stone, and a law, and commandments which I have written; that thou mayest teach them. And Moses rose up, and his minister Joshua: and Moses went up into the mount of God [...] And he gave unto Moses, when he had made an end of communing with him upon mount Sinai, two tables of testimony, tables of stone, written with the finger of God" (Exodus 24, 12-13; 31, 18).

Fourth band, at the left of the door

1a. *The Creation of Eve*
"And the Lord God caused a deep sleep to fall upon Adam, and he slept: and he took one of his ribs, and closed up the flesh instead thereof; and the rib, which the Lord God had taken from man, made he a woman, and brought her unto the man. And Adam said, This is now bone of my bones, and flesh of my flesh: she shall be called Woman, because she was taken out of Man" (Genesis 2, 21-23).

1b. *Adam and Eve, Still Uncorrupted, Dressed, in the Earthly Paradise*

1c. *God Talks to Adam and Eve, Naked, after They Have Sinned*
(cf. Genesis 3, 9-22).
At the bottom of the paintings is portrayed a supplicant.

2. *The Sacrifice of Isaac*
"[...] so they went both of them together. And they came to the place which God had told him of; and Abraham built an altar there, and laid the wood in order, and bound Isaac his son, and laid him on the altar upon the wood. And Abraham stretched forth his hand, and took the kinfe to slay his son. And the angel of the Lord called unto him out of heaven, and said, Abraham, Abraham, and he said: Here am I. And he said, Lay not thine hand upon the lad, neither do thou any thing unto him: for now I know that thou fearest God, seeing thou hast not withheld thy son, thine only son from me. And Abraham lifted up his eyes, and looked, and behold behind him a ram caught in a thicket by his horns: and Abraham went and took the ram, and offered him up for a burnt offering in the stead of his son" (Genesis 22, 8-13).

3a. *Jacob's Vision at Betel*
"And Jacob went out of from Beersheba, and went toward Haran. And he lighted upon a certain place, and tarried there all night, because the sun was set; and he took the stones of that place, and put them for his pillows, and lay down in that place to sleep. And he dreamed, and behold a ladder set up on the earth, and the top of it reached to heaven: and behold the angels of God ascending and descending on it. And, behold, the Lord stood above it, and said, I am the Lord God of Abraham thy fahter, and the God of Isaac: the land whereon thou liest, to thee will I give it, and to thy seed; and thy seed shall be as the dust of the earth, and thou shalt spread abroad to the west, and to the east, and to the north, and to the south: and in thee and in thy seed shall all the families of the earth be blessed" (Genesis 28, 10-14).

3b-c. *Death and Burial of Jacob*
"And [Jacob] charged them, and said unto them, I am to be gathered unto my people: bury me with my fathers in the cave that is in the field of Ephron the Hittite, in the cave that is in the field of Machpelah, which is before Mamre, in the land of Canaan, which Abraham bought with the field of Ephron the Hittite for a possession of a burying-place. There they buried Abraham and Sarah his wife; there they buried Isaac and Rebekah his wife; and there I buried Leah. The purchase of the field and of the cave that is therein was from the children of Heth. And when Jacob had made an end of commanding his sons, he gathered up his feet into the bed, and yielded up the ghost, and was gathered unto his people" (Genesis 49, 29-33).

Socle, at the left of the door

1. *Decollation of John the Baptist*
at the top right is portrayed the
Winged Head of the Saint
"But when Herod's birthday was kept, the daughter of Herodias danced before them, and pleased Herod. Whereupon he promised with an oath to give her whatsoever she would ask. And she, being before instructed of her mother, said, Give me here John Baptist's head in a charger. And the king was sorry: nevertheless for the oath's sake, and them which sat with him at meat, he commanded it to be given her. And he sent, and beheaded John in the prison. And his head was brought in a charger, and given to the damsel: and she brought it to her mother. And the disciples came, and took up the body, and buried it, and went and told Jesus" (St. Matthew 14, 6-12; cf. St. Mark 6, 14-29; St. Luke 9, 7-9; 3, 19-20).

2. *The Stoning of Saint Stephen*
"When they heard these things, they were cut to the heart, and they gnashed on him with their teeth. But he, being full of the Holy Ghost, looked up steadfastly into heaven, and saw the glory of God, and Jesus standing on the right hand of God. And said, Behold, I see the heavens opened, and the Son of man standing on the right hand of God. Then they cried out with a loud voice, and stopped their ears, and ran upon him with one accord, and cast him out of the city, and stoned him: and the witnesses laid down their clothes at a young man's feet, whose name was Saul. And they stoned Stephen, calling upon God, and saying, Lord Jesus, receive my spirit. And he kneeled down, and cried with a loud voice, Lord, lay not this sin to their charge. And when he had said this, he fell asleep. And Saul was consenting unto his death" (The Acts 7, 54-60).

3. *Martyrdom of the Saints Quiricus and Julith*
When Alexander was the governor, on the15th of *ṭerr* (20th of January) Saint Quiricus and his mother Julith became martyrs. The governor asked Julith to sacrifice to the gods, unless she wanted to die suffering cruel torments. She replied: "If you want to do so, send someone in town to look for a three year old boy; he will tell us whom we must worship." The governor sent someone to look for him, and they found the boy, whose name was Quiricus. The governor asked him: "What is your name?" The boy answered "I am A Christian and my baptismal name is Quiricus." The governor told him: "Sacrifice to the gods, so that I may honour you and give you some money." The boy answered: "Get away from me, you servant of Satan and enemy of justice." When he heard that, the governor became furious and ordered that he be taken away and given 50 slashes, until his blood ran like water. When Julith saw her son's constancy, she thanked God. The governor then ordered that a boiling cauldron be brought and the two thrown into it. When Julith saw it, she was filled with fear. Her son prayed, and God Almighty conferred on her a divine power so that when she entered into the cauldron with her son, nothing happened and they came out unburnt. The governor then ordered that they were put into a torture machine, to pull them with ropes, so that their bodies were lacerated until the angel of God came and saved them. Since he could nothing against them, the governor ordered that their necks be cut with a sword (RAINERI 1996, pp. 119-122).

Socle, at the right of the door

The Martyrdom of Saint Ripsima

Ripsima lived at the time of Tiridates of Armenia, a pagan king. She was the daughter of Theodore, a priest who, when she was twelve years old, promised her to a man of her same social level. Talmiwos, one of Tiridates's high officers and a cruel persecutor of the Christians, sends her to the royal palace, where she is imprisoned and suffers various tortures because of her faith. Ripsima is also thrown into the fire but, at the contact with her body, it changes into dew. Tiridates offers to marry her, under the condition that she becomes a pagan, so that he can produce an heir to the throne. The saint who does not give in to the king's enticements and turns down all allurements with jewels and rich clothes, predicts to Tiridates a Christian future for Armenia. In order to marry her, the king is even ready to let her keep her Christian faith. But the girl still turns down the king's proposal and, after having healed many martyrs, she is finally beheaded on the 6th of *tāḫśāś* (12th of December). From the neck of the beheaded saint blood and milk sprang out (CERULLI 1968, pp. 215-218).

Door

left leaf
Saint Michael

right leaf
The Archangel Saint Gabriel Releases the Three Youths From the Burning Furnace
"Then Nebuchadnezzar the king was astonied, and rose up in haste, and spake, and said unto his counsellors, Did not we cast three men bound into the midst of the fire? They answered and said unto the king, True, O King. He answered and said, Lo, I see four men loose, walking in the midst of the fire, and theu have no hurt; and the form of the forth is like the Son of God. Then Nebuchadnezzar came near to the mouth of the burning fiery furnace, and spake, and said, Shadrach, Meshach and Abednego, ye servants of the most high God, come forth, and come hither. Then Shadrach, Meshach and Abednego, came forth in the midst of the fire. And [they] [...] saw thse men, upon whose bodies the fire had no power [...] Nebuchadnezzar spake, and said, Blessed be the God of Shadrach, Meshach, and Abednego, who hath sent his angel, and delivered his servants..." (Daniel 3, 24-28).

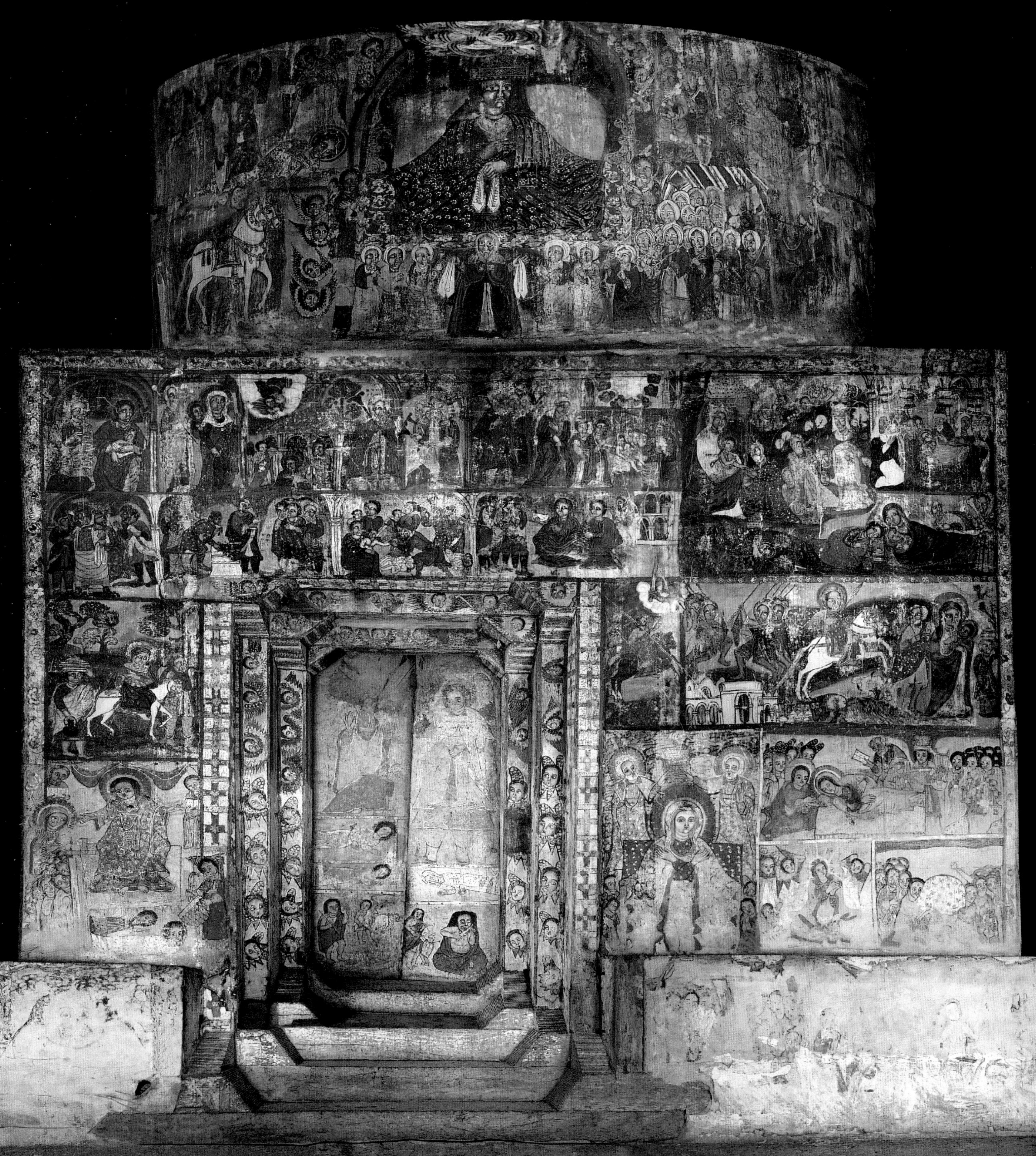

South Wall

Tambour

Mary's Apparition in the Egyptian Monastery of Metmaq
On the 21st of *genbot* (26th of May), a feast is celebrated to honour the apparition of the Virgin Mary at Dabra Metmaq. The Virgin appeared seated in a circle, above a light, in the church built in her honour. She was surrounded by a divine light and around her, casting shadows on her, there were the Seraphims who stood upright, holding the thuribles and prostrating themselves before the greatness of her realm. Each time they bent, they praised her, saying: "God the Father looked down at the earth from heaven and did not find anyone like you. He sent his only son and he was born to you." The martyrs also were there, according to their orders, mounted on white horses. Also the assembly of the prophets and the just came; they prostrated themselves and filed before her. Also the innocents slaughtered by Herod came, played before her and smiled. When the people assembled came there, they were filled with joy: it seemd to them that they were in heaven. When they decided to return home, they prostrated themselves before her and took their leave. She gave them the benediction with her fingers and they left (*Patrologia Orientalis*, 47, 1997, pp. 306-309).

Under the tambour: first band

1. *Saints Joachim and Ann, Mary's Parents*
caption: *Iyāqēm wa-Ḥannā*
(Joachim and Ann)

2. *The Child Mary is Brought to the Temple of Jerusalem*
caption: *Zakama ḥorat westa bēta maqdas* (How she went to the temple)

3. *Mary In the Temple*
a) *Angels Bring Food From Heaven and They Serve It to Mary*
caption: *Zakama bo'at egze'tena*
(How Our Lady entered)
b) *Zacharias and Other Priests of the Temple*
caption: *Zakāryās* (Zacharias)
On the 3rd of *tāḫśāś* (9th of December) the Presentation of the Virgin Mary to the temple of Jerusalem is celebrated, which took place when she was three years old. In fact, she had been given over to the Lord. Her mother Ann, who had no other child, became very sad, and so did her husband Joachim. The Lord heard their cries. Ann, the mother of the Holy Virgin, made this vow to the Lord: she said that the fruit which He gave her, she would consacrate to Him. When she had the baby, she raised her for three years at home, then took her to the Lord's temple so that she stayed with the virgins. Mary stayed in the temple for twelve years, she received her food from the hands of angels, until Our Lord Jesus Christ came into the world, born of her (*Patrologia Orientalis*, 15, 1927, pp. 569-570).

4. *Jesus' Circumcision*
"And when eight days were accomplished for the circumcising of the child, his name was called Jesus, which was so named of the angel before he was conceived in the womb" (St. Luke 2, 21).

5a. *Adoration of the Magi*
"When they had heard the king, they departed; and, lo, the star, which they saw in the east, went before them, till it came and stood over where the young child was. When they saw the star, they rejoiced with exceeding great joy. And when they were come into the house, they saw the young child with Mary his mother, and fell down, and worshipped him: and when they had opened their treasures, they presented unto him gifts; gold, and frankincense, and myrrh. And being warned of God in a dream that they should not return to Herod, they departed into their own country another way" (St. Matthew 2, 9-12).

5b. *Jesus is Presented in the Temple and Old Simeon Meets Him*
"And when the days of her purification according to the law of Moses were accomplished, they brought him to Jerusalem, to present him to the Lord [...] And, behold, there was a man in Jerusalem, whose name was Simeon; and the same man was just and devout, waiting for the consolation of Israel: and the Holy Ghost was upon him. And it was revealed unto him by the Holy Ghost, that he should not see death, before he hath seen the Lord's Christ. And he came by the Spirit into the temple: and when the parents brought in the child jesus, to do for him after the custom of the law, then took him up in his arms, and blessed God, and said ..." (St. Luke 2, 22-28).

5c. *Joseph's Dream*
"And when they were departed, behold, the angel of the Lord appeareth to Joseph in a dream, saying, Arise, and take the young child and his mother, and flee into Egypt, and be thou there until I bring thee word: for Herod will seek the young child to destroy him" (St. Matthew 2, 13).

Second band

1. *Herod Orders the Slaughter of the Children of Bethlehem*

2. *Herod's Town Crier*
caption: *Qāla 'āwādi*
(Proclamation of the town crier)

3. *The Slaughter of the Innocents*
caption: *Zakama katalu ḥeṣānāt*
(How the children were killed)
"Then Herod, when he saw that he was mocked of the wise men, was exceedingly wroth, and sent forth, and slew all the children that were in Bethlehem, and in all the coasts thereof " (Matthew 2, 16-17).

4. *Jesus's Conception and the Trial of the Water*

of Malediction Which the Elders Made Mary Drink
The news of his conception spread all over the land of Israel: they said that the Virgin Mary was pregnant. The Jews reported the fact to their priests who discussed the news. One of them said: "She must drink the water of malediction out of the little basin which the Lord showed to Moses His servant. Because every woman of Israel who has fornicated will be obliged to drink this water. Her womb will open up and tear apart and she will die immediately.
After she drank, her face lit and shone like the sunlight. From her clothes luminous lightning spread. When the Jews saw this great miracle, they bent and prostrated themselves at the feet of Our Lady Mary, and numerous hordes of people believed that in her womb the Word had been conceived. This was Mary's first miracle, when she conceived Our saviour, without the seal of her virginity being violated (*Patrologia Orientalis*, 12, 1917, pp. 28-32; Numbers 5, 11 onwards).

First panel at the left of the door

The Holy Family's Flight into Egypt
"When he (Joseph) arose, he took the young child and his mother by night, and departed into Egypt: and was there until the death of Herod: that it might be fulfilled which was spoken of the Lord by the prophet, saying, Out of Egypt have I called my son" (St. Matthew 2, 14-15).

First band at the right of the door

1-2. *Saint Gigar*
The figure of Saint Gigar belongs to the legends arising around Herod's persecution and his attempts to find Mary, Joseph, and the child Jesus in order to kill them. Before the Flight into Egypt, the Holy Family found refuge in the desert of Lebanon, but Herod found this out and went with his soldiers to catch the fugitives. Mary, her husband and the child are benevolently helped by Domitian and Gigar, an influential Syrian magistrate. For this, Gigar was arrested and Herod, after having inflicted on him terrible tortures, had him beheaded. From Gigar's severed neck milk, water and blood spurted out and in the place where his head fell a spring appeared. When Herod, who had been told about the miracle, went to the spring of miraculous water, he saw the martyr coming towards him, on a horse of white fire, holding a spear which seemed to be of fire in his hand, accompanied by those who had been martyred before him, all on horses like his. Gigar grasped Herod and struck him thrice, and then disappeared (RAINERI 1996, pp. 89-91).

Second and third band at the left of the door

1. *Dormitio Mariae*
"Our Lord Jesus Christ arrived on a cloud, surrounded by many angels. He entered the place where Mary was. Jesus and Michael chanted psalms together, and at the beginning they stood still before the internal room. When Our Saviour entered to see Mary, everybody greeted him. Then also Mary greeted him and opened her mouth with the blessing: "I bless him who spoke to me..." Once she had said that, she finished her duty, without turning her face away from the Lord. He took her soul and entrusted it to Michael. It was wrapped up in a shroud, whose glory is impossible to hide (*ASSUMPTION*, p. 435).

2-3. *The Virgin's Funerals*
"Then Our Saviour said to Peter: "Take Mary's body out. Hurry and leave from the east side of the city. There you will find a new sepulchre. Lay her body down there and take care of it, as I ordered you [...] Peter, the other disciples and the three virgins prepared Mary's body and laid it on a bed [...] The disciples started away, bringing with them the bed with Mary, and Peter sang: "When Israel left Egypt, Alleluhiah." The Lord and the angels walked at the sides of the bed, chanting unseen (*ASSUMPTION*, p. 436).

4. *Coronation of the Virgin*
"*Mary in the Third Heaven*. – Then the Lord turned towards a two-winged seraphim and nodded to him. The seraphim left two words, which nobody can understand. Then a numerous throng of angels came in, bringing a throne, pure and full of inexplicable glory. There were myriads of angels around, each on his own throne. They told us: "Go on the earth and preach what you have just seen." They brought another throne for Mary. Around her there were ten thousand angels and three virgins. She sat down and went up into Paradise. They stopped there, in the third heaven, and they chanted..." (*ASSUMPTION*, p. 449-450).

Second panel at the left of the door
Mary Pleads the Pact of Mercy from Christ and two Supplicants

Socle at the left of the door
Satan

Socle at the right of the door
The Martyrdom of Saint Ripsima (?)

Door

Scenes Portraying 'Mary's Miracles' with Supplicants
especially, on the right leaf, bottom:
The Virgin Mary and the Cannibal of Qemer
In the city of Qemer lived a Christian who, however, was a great sinner, because he ate human flesh. The cannibal, after he had already devoured his friends and relatives, also ate his wife and his two sons. One day the cannibal gave some water to a thirsty leper, only because he had asked for it in the name of Mary. When this sinner died, the angels of darkenss came to take his soul to hell, but the Virgin Mary pleaded with her Son Jesus on his behalf. Jesus asked her if the sinner, while he was alive, had done anything for her, and she answered: "He gave, in my name, some water for a thirsty man to drink." Then Jesus, for that one work of mercy which the dead cannibal had performed, saved his soul, which was carried to heaven by the angels of light (BUDGE 1923, pp. 94-96; HAMMERSCHMIDT-JÄGER, pp. 21-22, fig. 27).

Appendix

The Story of Nārgā (Zēnā Nārgā)

edited by *Osvaldo Raineri*

[p. 237] We are writing the story of the devotion of our King Iyāsu [1730-1755] and of our Queen Walatta Giyorgis, since their devotion brought us great joy, because there has not been another king like Iyāsu, except Constantine, and no queen like Walatta Giyorgis, except Helen. In fact they resemble each other and their love was really one, one their advice and one their devotion. As far as their good qualities are concerned, we will not list them all; however, God willing, we will report some of them. In fact, without God's help, not only would we not be able to tell these things concerning Him and his cult, but we also could not say anything about what concerns mankind. In our present task, we truly hope that God may help us.

[I. *Foundation and Building of the Church and the Monastery of Nārgā*]

Let us go back to where we started. One day, the king and the queen were discussing the clemency and mercy which God had shown them, and they said to each other: "What could we do to repay Jesus for everything that He has done for us?" They were surprised and they did not know what to do and they asked each other's opinion, until the queen mother had a great idea. She said: "Oh, my son, we will build a sanctuary for the Lord, so that there God's Lamb, who was sacrificed on Mount Calvary for all the sinners, can be sacrificed, because every day a sacrifice will be unceasingly offered." And the king, her son, answered her: "Oh, mother, you have thought well, well suggested and well said. So be it as you have said." That queen of queens then said to her son, the king of kings: "If that is the way it has to be, my son, then I will leave and go to look for a place where the sanctuary of God will be built. But you stay here until I return and guard the capital [p. 238] of your kingdom, and pray to the Lord so that he protects you from Satan's tricks. Remember me in your prayers, so that I might come back in peace and in good health." And with these loving words this queen of queens took leave of her beloved son, the king of kings, and he let her go with glory and honour, but very sad and afflicted because he was parting from her. There was a reason for him not to leave together with his mother: in fact that eighth year [of his reign —1737-38] was a year of troubles. And if he had left together with his mother the poor would have lost any hope of [receiving] justice through the pronouncement of Solomon's language, while the oppressors would have exulted and rejoiced at the king's absence from the capital of the kingdom and would have showed the poor the violence of their arrogance.

For this reason the king stayed in his palace with his army, to protect the poor, while she left and went with her garrison and servants and her councellors and her officers to find the place where the sanctuary of the Lord was going to be built. And she went along the shore of the lake, westwards, leaving that lake which is called Tana to her left, and she arrived at the city of Leğomi, then turned eastward and saw far away the Daq region, and sailed on the lake in a fragile Ethiopian boat called a *tānkuā*, since on Ethiopian lakes there are not strong boats as those sailing on the Mediterranean. This was quite an extraordinary thing, because the queen was quite delicate, having grown up amongst comforts and she did not know the fatigues of the sea. To tell the truth, the waves of the lake frightened her very much, since from the time of her childhood to that very day she had never crossed even a small river, not to mention a great lake, but she had seen water only when she had asked for it in the basin for her ablutions. That day, instead, on the shore of the lake, she neither was scared by the waves nor feared them; on the contrary, she jumped on the boat like a calf which, in the evening, finds his mother which he had left in the morning [p. 239]. And she seated herself on that fragile boat, so that God could show how pleased He was with her, and started to sail on the fragile boat in the direction which she had decided in advance, while the boatmen carried her. During that period the lake was calm and flat, and was not perturbed as usual. When later on men quite renowned for their learning remembered this fact, it seemed to them that the angels led her, as they had led her glorious father, the Star of the Desert, Abbā Eustachius, when he crossed the Mediterranean on his coat.

In this way she reached the place she was determined to arrive at, and there, between Leğomi and Daq, she found four islands; however, when she arrived where the islands were, it was midday. She alighted from the fragile boat, visited those islands and found them wild and uncultivated, while beads of sweat ran all along her body because, as we already said, it was midday. And it was a true miracle that she, a young lady and the queen of Ethiopian believers, could wander from an uncultivated place to another and from one deserted place to another, while the midday sun was suffocating her and drops of sweat ran all along her body, without her being bothered by it. It seemed to me that God's love surrounded her, so that the drops of sweat ran all along her body because it burnt for all that time in her soul, like the green wood, when it is put on the fire, and the fire, consuming it all around, makes moisture come out from everywhere, from every limb. Indeed, when this queen set her soul to God's love and it burnt with the fire of it, she poured out and exuded drops of sweat from her whole body. And if it had not been so, she would not have been able to wander around on the four islands at midday, but she would have panted and fainted, because this queen was a delicate woman, not used to the sun's heat [p. 240] and she had seen the sun shining only through the windows of her palace.

There is one more proof of this fact: indeed, when she was struck by the ardour of the sun, she could have kept her umbrella over her head to protect herself from the sun's heat, or she could have found relief in the shadow of a thicket, because those islands were wild and uncultivated, and no man had ever entered there to cut down a tree with the strength of his axe, since the world was created. And the islands were inhabited by terrible beasts and evil snakes which terrorized the people.

However, the day when the queen crossed the land of those islands, exclaiming and saying: "Where is it, and where can it be found, and who knows the place for the sanctuary of the Lord, where his Lamb, who takes away the sins of the world, will be sacrificed?", those beasts and snakes were troubled and frightened and fled, because they saw the sword in the hand of the angel protecting the queen, which was giving forth flames like a fire. Then the angel chose for her an island in the middle of the four, and whispered to her soul's ear and said: "Here God's sanctuary will be built." Then she went to the middle of that isle and looked eastward and westward, northward and southward, just as the angel showed her; however, even though the angel pointed it out to her, the queen did not neglect to seek for her councellors' and officers' advice, because she was humble. She called her councellors and officers and asked for their advice, showed them the place where God's sanctuary had to be built, and together they all told her: "Oh, queen, this place where you are is the apt one for building the sanctuary of the Holy Trinity." Then she started to clear the wild earth and the brushwood, and found [p. 241] the place beautiful and suitable for a church to be built, and rejoiced, as Helen had cleared the hill of the Golgota, searching the wood of the glorious cross which the Jews had buried. When she found it she rejoiced, exactly like her, because in all her works she was a second Helen. Then the queen called carpenters and masons and gave them much gold and silver and exquisite food and told them: "Build a church for me, in honour of the Holy Trinity; Father, Son and Holy Ghost!" She recommended to them that they be not negligent when building the church and told them: "I pray you not to worry if the material that I give you for building this church runs out: rather, you should be more concerned that my time does not finish without my having completed this church, since the human being is made for death and for the sepulchre. Do not worry for the scarcity of material, because the Lord will not leave you to run short of the goods of this world. I will always send you the material which you will need in order to build the church of the Holy Trinity." Then those carpeners and masons told her: "Be it as you said, Oh queen (who sits) on the throne of David, be it as you command, our lady of all women, be it as you wish, beloved by men and angels."

Later they started to build the church, while the queen rose and went back to her city, and arrived in peace and good health where her son was, and they met in happiness and peace, and the queen told the king her son what had happened, from the beginning to the end. And they pleasantly entertained themselves with spiritual discourses. And the building of the sanctuary in honour of the Holy Trinity was finished: it was beautiful to behold and marvellous to the good-hearted, and there they summoned priests so that they sacrificed the Lamb, Christ, and they chanted a new chant.

[(p. 242) II. *The Church's and the Monastery's Endowment* - a) *Lands*]

Later on they took care of keeping the priests and they gave them: the land of Anṣo, which belonged to the Wellāğ, the land of Bad which belonged to Yetu and Dagbāsā, and the land of Qualalā which belonged to Amata Iyasus, who had no children, and the land of Tākudeb which belonged to Walatta Pāwlos, who had no children and the land of Daq, which belonged to the *bažirondoč*, and the lands of Aylā and of Damimā which was theirs [of the king and the queen].

For the church's needs: the land of Robit which belonged to Amata Iyasus, who had no children; the land of Resta Māryām, the land of Enkeš, the land of Wanžeṭā, which was theirs [of the king and the queen].

Later on they called the Metropolite, who was *abuna* Yoḥannes [1746-1762], and the abbot of Dabra Libānos, who was abbā Eustachius, and all the doctors of the church, and said: "All this we offer to the Lord." And those clergymen answered: "Well done! God will be thankful for it." And the priests, protected by the Gospel and supported by the cross, proclaimed excommunicated anyone who would have ravaged that area of the church, so that it could not be transpasssed by the believers, and the king and the queen ordered that a town crier spread the news in the camp. He went and announced, through a proclamation, the news of the holy church and once this was heard, cries of exultation and joy arose from the camp.

[b) *Books*]

After this, they took care of the church books, and gave as a gift: two copies of Gospels, two copies of the Faith of the Fathers (*Hāymānota abaw*), two copies of the Absolution (*Fetḥat*), two Mass-books (*Qeddāsē*), the Book of the Synaxis (*Senkessār*) which is read all through the year, the Book of Mary's miracles (*Ta'ammera Māryām*), the Book of Christ's miracles (*Ta'ammera Iyasus*), a copy of the New Testament (without the Gospels, called *Ḥaddisāt*), the Book of the Collection of Effigies (*Gubā'ē malke'*), the Book of the Hours (*Sa'ātāt*), the Book of Psalms (*Dāwit*), the Book of the Holy Week's Acts (*Gebra ḥemāmāt*), the Book of the Collection of Salutations (*Arkē*); the Book of the Kings' Legislation (*Fetḥa nagaśt*), the Book of Spiritual Medicine (*Faws manfasāwi*) [p. 243] which were all included in only one volume; the Book of Anthony's Disciple(*Rade'a Enṭonyos*), the Book of Captions (*Didesqelyā*), the Book of the Church's Organization (*Śer'āta bēta krestiyān*), the Book of the Pact (*Kidān*), the Ritual of the Entrance of the Holy Stone in the Sanctuary (*Ser'ātā la-tābot gizē tebawe' bēta maqdas*), the Book of the Ritual of the Oil of the Sick (*Qandil*), the Book of the Ritual of Baptism (*Ṭemqata krestennā*); the Book of the Ritual of the Baptism of Repentance (*Qēder*), the Book of the Ritual of Marriage (*Taklil*) which were all included in only one volume; the Book of the 47 Prophets (*Nabiyāt*), of which, however, three were missing: Judith, the Jubilees (*Kufālē*) and the Chronicles (*Ḥeṣuṣān*). Plus four books included in only one volume, which were: the Minor Prophets, Jeremiah, the Chronicles and the Maccabees.

The Book of the Kings' Glory (*Kebra nagaśt*), the Book of John Madabbār (the Bishop of Nikiu, called *Yoḥannes Madabbār*), the Book of Jesus' Explanation (*Fekkarē Iyasus*), the Book of Mary's Apocalypse (*Rā'eya Māryām*), the Book of the Phisiologist (*Fisālgos*), the Book of the Story of Alexander (*Zēnāhu la-Eskender*), the Book of Giyorgis Walda Amid (called al-Makīn), Epiphanius' Treatise on the Holy Trinity (*Śellus qeddus za-fakarā Epifānyos*), the Collection of letters of Abgar, King of Edessa (to Christ, called *Aqāryos neguśa Roḥa*), Saint Ephraim's Book on Our Redeemer's Passion (*Qeddus Efrēm za-darasa ba'enta ḥemāmātihu la-Madḥen*), the Book on the thief and the angel by James of Serug (*Yā'eqob za-Śerug za-darasa be'enta fayātāwi wa-mal'ak*); the Book by James of Nisibi (which is also known as Afraate, called *Yā'qob za-Neṣebin*), the Sybil's Book (*Sābēlā*), which were all included in only one volume. The Book of Chants, that is, Yārēd's hymns and antiphones (*Degguā*), the Book of Psalms and Chants (*Me'erāf*), the Book of Gabriel's Homilies and of the Four Heavenly Beasts (called *Dersāna Gabre'ēl wa-4 ensesā*), the Book of the Synod (*Sinodos*), the Book of George's Acts (*Gadla Giyorgis*), John Chrysostom's Book (*Yoḥannes Afa worq*); Cyril's Book (*Qērlos*), Epiphanius' Book (*Epifānyos*), which were all included in only one volume.

[c) *Vestments*

After doing all this, they also took care [of donating] the priests' paraments, which they were to wear when they sacrificed the Lamb of mercy, Christ, since they knew that priests need paraments when they celebrate the holy mysteries and when they teach the Gospels, and on that occasion they become heavenly and the church itself becomes heavenly. They brought from their houses and they donated to the sanctuary of the Holy Trinity these brocade fabrics [p. 244], which capture the eyes. And the number of brocades [was thus]: two white damask cowls, *zāfām* [with grains; for translational notes here and *passim* cf. EURINGER I, pp. 296-297 e II, p. 131] and with hoods; one violet damask, *zāfām*, brocaded; one yellow cowl of Chinese fabric, *zāfām*, with a hood; two azure cowls, *zāfām*, brocaded, with hoods; one azure cowl of Persian fabric, *zāfām*, with a hood; one red cowl of Chinese fabric, with a hood; one red cowl of Chinese fabric, brocaded, with a hood; a hyacinth cowl of Chinese fabric, *zāfām*, with a hood; one green cowl of Chinese fabric, with a hood; one red damask cowl of Chinese fabric, *zāfām*.

They also donated tight sleeved albs: three green damask albs, *zāfām*; two green albs of Chinese fabric, *zāfām*; one green alb of Chinese fabric, brocaded; two azure albs of Chinese fabric, *zāfām*; three hyacinth albs in Chinese fabric, *zāfām*; one red alb in Chinese fabric, *zāfām*.

They also donated albs with large sleeves, called *melote*: one azure, *zāfām*, in Chinese fabric; one azure, *zāfām*, of damask; one hyacinth, *zāfām*, of Chinese fabric; two hyacinth ones, of Chinese fabric, brocaded; one red, *zāfām*, of Chinese fabric; one red, *zāfām*, of damask; one violet-red, *zāfām*, of Chinese fabric; one hyacinth, *zāfām*, of damask; one green, *zāfām*, of Chinese fabric; one red of Chinese fabric; one black, of Persian fabric, with a fringe embroidered in various colours.

And they donated trousers: one red pair, of Chinese fabric; two red pairs, *zāfām*, in Chinese fabric; two red pairs, brocaded; four green pairs, *ḥeṭyā*; one azure pair, of Chinese fabric, brocaded.

One red woolen cloak; one black cloak, of muslin, *zāfām*; one black cloth to use as a curtain for the altar; eleven pieces of silk; eighteen silk cuts for the everyday chasubles; two silver *morasas*; four red coverings for the crosses; one thin black cloth for covering the great paten; three thin red cloths for covering the crown.

[d) *Church Ornaments*]

Besides donating these vestments, they also donated: eight golden and silver crowns, one of which was much bigger and more beautiful than the others, because it was very bright and it was also a copy of the royal crown. And the priests [p. 245] would have worn these crowns when they entered God's sanctuary, because it is proper that priests are completely attired.

Indeed the king and the queen did so because they had the knowledge and they knew that the Lord was going to adorn them with the purple of light and the crown of glory, that is, with the glory of His divinity. What else remains for us to tell of? In fact we are not capable of reporting what this king and this queen did for the Lord; however, we will report, using our insufficient capability, the little which the Almighty allowed us the power to report, and we will witness that they had sent, and gave to, those priests: three great crosses with decorated poles, a silver one and two golden ones; and three small crosses, of the type which priests carry, with no poles, a golden one and a silver one, and another golden one with which the Superior blesses the monks' cap of his disciples when he teaches them the angels' path which is purity.

This is indeed what this king and this queen did, because the infamy of the cross of the God of mercy who was crucified for them and shed his blood on the cross always afflicted them. Moreover, they brought and donated nine silver, copper and iron censers; more specifically, two silver ones, four copper ones, three iron ones.

Then when the doctors, the disciples of the Holy Ghost, reveal the mysteries of the Scripture and interpret these objects in a mystical way, because they use them as symbols, they say: the censer is the symbol of the Virgin Mary; the embers which are put into the censer are the symbol of the Son of God, who incarnated from her; while the perfume of the incense is the symbol of the Holy Spirit who purified this pure [Virgin]; finally, the smoke coming out of it is the symbol of the saints' prayer, ascending towards heaven.

[p. 246] Moreover, they had sent and donated two great patens, which were wrought we know not how, because they were not made in our country, but beyond, in the country of the wise [Europe]; a silver paten and a golden one; a silver chalice and a golden one, and more, poles for crosses and brocaded vestments. The doctors also give a mystical explanation to all [the symbols] of these objects, in accordance with what they learnt from their master, the Holy Ghost: the large paten is the image of Jerusalem, while the smaller one, which is placed in the middle of the large one, is the symbol of Mount Calvary where Our saviour was crucified. As the Scripture say: "And he worked salvation in the midst of the earth." [Psalm 74, 12]. In fact Mount Calvary is in the centre of Jerusalem, the paten in the middle of the larger paten which is the victim. Then there is the bread which we see in the paten, which is not bread of this earth, but Our Saviour who was crucified on Mount Calvary in order to save the world. However, before the priest consacrates it, it is still bread, while, after the priest has consacrated it, it is no more as it was previously: rather, it becomes the fire of divinity. The same applies to the wine which is poured into the chalice. According to what one of the doctors of the church said: "The chalice is the symbol of His death, as Our Lord said: 'Ye shall drink indeed my cup.' [St. Matthew 20, 23] And therefore, just as His blood was found in his death for saving the world, so now His blood is in this chalice." As for the cross-shaped spoon which we now see in the hands of the priest to draw Our Lord's blood for the believers, before Isaiah saw it in the hands of the Seraphim, so that we did not dare to touch his blood with our hands, so that even the prophet did not dare to touch the charcoal of the altar, but instead the angel gave it to him with firetongs. Then the linen, those on the large paten of the sacrifice, [are symbols of those which] Joseph and Nicodemus, who knew the prophecy, brought and used to wrap up the corpse of the Emmanuel, Our Lord, who died for us and was buried. The king and the queen brought and donated also: two jugs of water to be used in the house of the sacrifice, and two [p. 247] copper basins with their accessories, and one pyx of an unkwown colour, but which seems emerald to us, with everything that goes with it, for solemn occasions. And two crystal chalices, of an unknown colour, in which the deacon prepares the wine of Our Saviour's blood, before the priest consacrates it; and a silver strainer for filtering it. And also a great bell which calls even from a distance those who are far away; and two small bells, one for the time of the Mass, the other for the week of passion of Our Redeemer. They also brought and donated: two signs of honour both for the monastery and the abbot, that are, the cross-shaped sphere (*Sandaq*) with brocade and decorated poles, so that, through these objects, this monastery would be known as the king's and queen's monastery. They also offered two umbrellas with their accessories, one for the sanctuary and the other for the abbot.

[e) *Carpets and Curtains*

They also took care of the church's ornaments, since they did not avoid taking the trouble of caring for what is the Lord's. They therefore brought and donated: a purple tablecloth which has to be put on the throne of the sacred stone (or *Tābot*, that is, on the altar) when the Lamb of God is sacrificed for life and redemption by the priest; and 20 carpets, and 48 embroidered carpets, and 47 carpets which had a smaller value. If we put them all together and count them, it comes to 95 all together, which served both for the interior and the outside of the church. They also donated two field tents which were to be used for the church.

[III. *Eulogy of the Royal Founders*]

Listen, father and brothers, sons of the Jordan [that is, of Baptism], you who the Lord, in His mercy, has called and gathered in the king and queen's camp, since this very city, the kings of the Christians, as well as the [p. 248] books which are here kept and the upright masters who live in this city, have a righteous faith. Moreover, in this place every need both of the body and the soul can be satisfied. If I question my soul and ask it: "Why did this king and this queen struggle and take so much pain in doing all this?" Then promptly it answers, in a quite angry and upset tone: "You fool, who do not recognize your hope: your heart hardened and your greatest love is someone else's wealth. Listen to what I tell you and do not be foolish, because foolishness is your custom. Indeed, this king and this queen did their very best and took pain not without reaons, but because they knew their hope." And if you ask me: "What is their hope?", I will answer: "As He made them kings of an earthly kingdom, in the same way He will make them kings in the heavenly kingdom, like their ancestor David reigned both here and in the other world." In fact, it is not wealth which causes an angry judgement, bur rather the lack of discernement; neither does poverty lead to a merciful judgement, while a good discernement brings this, as the Scripture say: "He does not take piety on the poor just because he is poor, if he is not pleased with him." Also Lazarus did not obtain Our Lord's glory because he was poor, but rather by virtue of his great patience and goodness; and Nun [Syracides 46, 1], the rich, did not receive the infamy of the demons because of his wealth, but rather for his lack of pity and for the harshness of his heart towards the poor, because he did not do as the Scripture say: "Blessed is he that considereth the poor" [Psalm 41, 2]. Also the father's father, Abraham, even though the land with all that comes with it was in his hands, said: "I am a stranger" [Genesis 23, 4]. Knowing that his hope was in heaven, he considered himself as one of the poor and he did not rely upon his wealth. Also Job did not give up hope when he lost both his children and his wealth, but instead he said: "The Lord gave, and the Lord hath taken away." [Job 1, 21], and bore everything with great patience. If, instead [p. 249] he had lost hope in heaven and placed it instead in his wealth, he would not have spoken so, but on the contrary he would have complained with his Creator because of this, that is, love for wealth. As for this king and this queen, there is nothing more to be done to obtain the heavenly kingdom, because they did not rely upon the richness of their kingdom which is of this earth, but they placed their hope in heaven, and their thought was there. Indeed, they knew the words which Our Saviour uttered in the days of his reincarnation: "Lay not up for yourselves treasures upon earth [...] But lay up for yourselves treasures in heaven [...] For where your treasure is, there will your heart be also." [St. Matthew 6, 19-21].

And as they built Our Saviour's sanctuary in remembrance of his suffering on the cross, which lasted from Thursday evening to Friday evening, and they brought there the sacred stone (*Tābot*) which is dedicated to him, so is for him: in fact he owns a sanctuary which is the heavenly Jerusalem, which he built and opened with his suffering, after that man, the sinner, had shut it with a strong bolt, that is, the concupiscence of sin; there he will let them in. And as they did not discriminate the small from the big, the rich from the poor, while they were gathering in that sanctuary the children of the Jordan, their mother, [that is, Baptism], in the same way he will not make distinctions amongst prophets and apostles, the just and martyrs, virgins, monks and orthodox kings when he will gather them in the heavenly Jerusalem, but he will make them all enter, with the previous ones, in this sanctuary, according to what they hoped for. And in the same way that, on the same occasion, they had fed and satiated the poor in his name, so he will feed and satiate them with heavenly bread, which is the eternal joy of seeing his face, as the prohet said: "In thy presence is fulness of joy" [Psalm 16, 11]. And as under this circumstance they gave water to the thirsty, so that unadulterated wine which is eternal life, as the Scripture said: "Out of his belly [p. 250] shall flow rivers of living water" [St. John 7, 38]; and as he says: "If any man thirst, let him come unto me, and drink" [St. John 7, 37].

And as on that occasion they clothed the naked, in the same way, he will cloth them with uncorruptible garments, that is, the light of baptism which comes out from his pure chest, as the Scripture said: "We will wear the garments which he took from us and made his own!" [Cf. I Corinthians, 5, 1-5; Romans 13, 14; Colossians 3, 10]. And as in that time they welcomed many foreigners, in the same way he will welcome them into his house together with his beloved ones, and they will rest in eternal love, as he says to his belivers: "They shall sit down with Abraham, and Isaac, and Jacob in the kingdom of heaven" [St. Matthew 8, 11]. And as under that circumstance they visited many convicts in the name of the Saviour, in the same way he, in his mercy, will bring them with him in the day of reward and condemnation, while he stays on the right, as he says: "And he shall set the sheep on his right hand" [St. Matthew 25, 33]. In fact this king and this queen are tame sheep. And as under that circumstance they went to visit the captives and made the weight of their trial lighter and freed them from their shackles, in the same way he will alleviate the weight of their trial and free them from their sins' bonds, in the same way he will bestow on them peace, and allow them to stay with him, as the Scripture say: "I have no pleasure in the death of the wicked; but that the wicked turn from his way and live" [Ezekiel 33, 11]. Oh Dabra Esrā'ēl [monastery of Israel], we thank the Lord who has built you, because in you he carried out every aspect of our King Iyāsu and our Queen Walatta Giyorgis' work and faith, and we glorify him, because He chose you for us and us for you. Oh Dabra Esrā'ēl, tell us then: where have you been, since the world was created, until now? And if you say: "I am an island which is in the middle of the lake, from the very beginning up until now," [then I will ask you:] "If it was so, why neither David, King of Israel, nor Constantine, the just, the youth of the glorious cross did not find you?" If really you did hide from those [p. 251] kings and you have disclosed your presence in the middle of the great lake to King Iyāsu and to Queen Walatta Giyorgis, we admit that you love Iyāsu and Walatta Giyorgis, who love both His body and His soul. Oh King Iyāsu, blessed are you and blessed is your mother, the queen. Oh Queen, Walatta Giyorgis, blessed are you and blessed is your son, the king. Because to you has been revealed what was not revealed to the ancients and to you has been done what was not previously done.

And now, my lords, may God bless you and make your days longer for repentance, and forgive your sins and accept your alms and finally, on the day of the Judgement, may he place you to his right together with his blessed sheep, because you are tame sheep. And may He chase away from you the goats on his left and, when the time for resurrection comes, that you may resurrect in the glory of resurrection, because you have imitated him in bringing the cross. And may He chase from you the resurrection of condemnation, because you did not follow the path of vengeance, and may He, as

He gave you the kingdom of the earth, give you the kingdom of heaven. And may He allow that the earthly kingship does not leave your house, the royal crown may not slip down from your children's heads, nor your descendancy step down from the royal throne, no other king may reign over Ethiopia, your country, instead of your sons and your sons' sons, nor may He let another master enter your house, except your children and your children's children, nor may He grant another king your crown and your throne, but only to your sons and your sons' sons. And may He send you the angel of mercy and clemency, so that he may help you in the works both of the body and the soul, and as you have lived in the right faith, so may He sustain you in until the end, and as you have loved many poor people, may he love you. Because you [p. 252] have not sought the kingdom of this earth, but the kingdom of heaven, your abode, and whilst seeking it, you have also been given this kingdom of all the earth, as Our Lord said: "But seek ye first the kingdom of God, and his righteousness: and all these things shall be added unto you" [St. Matthew 6, 33]. Moreover, you have transferred the wealth of the kingdom of the earth to the kingdom of heaven, and may He free you from all enemies both of your body and your soul. May the Lord bless all the governors and the armies under your command, that they did not divert from your will, and, as a reward for their submisson, may He grant them the kingdom of heaven, and may He reveal both to them and to you the judgement of Solomon, your ancestor (father). May Our Saviour preserve the servants of your house, and my he free your from any tribulation that you might fear. Amen. Our Lord who art in heaven.

[IV. *Ecclesiastical Regulations*]

In the name of the Father, the Son and the Holy Ghost, one God. We list the priests and the psalmists' directors who gathered in the sanctuary of the Holy Trinity which was built at Dabra Esrā'ēl, Nārgā. Nārgā means "honey"; the honey does not remain alone while it is in its original place, the beehive, but the bees swarm around it, while tasting the sweetness of the blessing which the Lord granted them. Also this monastery does not remain alone, but those who behold God, each one with his own time, swarm around it, while they taste the sweetness of the goodness he did for them, as King David said: "O taste and see that the Lord is good: blessed is the man that trusteth in him" [Psalm 34, 8]. For this reason they call it Dabra Esrā'ēl, because Israel means "Those who behold God".

Now [p. 253] we begin the list of the priests who gathered in this sanctuary, one after the other, according to the place they took with respect to the altar, according to the vocation of love and peace [Ephesians 4, 1-3], while we say: Mal'aka Esrā'ēl, *mamher* abbā Benyās of Dabra Warq, abbā Isaiah of ṣelālo, abbā Kenfa Masqal of Guanğ, abbā Adarā Giyorgis of Denğ, *afa mamher* abbā Walda Giyorgis of Dabra Warq; these are the ones who stay on the right [of the altar] during [the month of] *maskaram*. Abbā Adarā Giyorgis of Ṭārā, abbā Germā of Dabsān, abbā Giuseppe of Guanğ, abbā Lessāna Krestos of Guanğ, abbā Aklog of Guanğ: these instead are the priests in *ṭeqemt*. *Maggābē kāhnāt* abbā Batra Giyorgis of Dabsān, abbā Awdokyos of Ṭārā, abbā Germā of Dabra Demāḥ, Akālu of Ṣadā, abbā Adarā Mikā'ēl of Adāgāt: and these are the priests in *ḫedār*. Abbā Iyāsu of Adāgāt, abbā Eusebius of Adāgāt, abbā Walda Gabra Manfas Qeddus of Ṣelālo, abbā Takla Māryām of Dabra Warq, abbā Yāred of Adāgāt: and those are the priests of *tāḫśāś*. Severianus of Guanğ, abbā Takla Mikā'ēl of Dabra Warq, abbā Awkātēwos of Tāmrē, Taddeo of Gāšolā, abbā Takla Śellāsē of Ṭārā: in *ṭerr*. These are the ones which stay and serve at the right of the altar of the eloquent Lamb, while he says: "He that hath seen me hath seen the Father" [St. John 14, 9]; he says, moreover: "I and my Father are one" [St. John10, 30], and was sacrificed on Mount Calvary to save the world.

We are still writing, not leaving out anything, because our King Iyāsu, lover of God, and our Queen Walatta Giyorgis, lover of God, commanded that we write: *mamher* abbā Walda Yonā of Guanğ, *nabiya Esrā'ēl* abbā Walda Gabrēl of Dabra Warq, abbā Azaza Ab, *mamher* Maśwā'eta Krestos of Guanğ, abbā Abacuc of Dabra Warq: these are the priests on the left side in [p. 254] *maskaram*. Abbā Marteyānos of Dabra Warq, abbā Arka Dengel of Dabra Warq, abbā Walda Yoḥannes of Dabra Warq, abbā Mardocheus of Adāgāt, abbā Askāl di Denğ: priests during *ṭeqemt*. Quiricus of Qomā, abbā Mangeśta Ab of Dabsān, Walda Ewosṭātēwos of Dāwā, abbā Qāla 'Āwādi of Dabra Warq, abbā Ṣaḥaya Ledā of Dabra Ṭārā: the *ḫedār* priests. Abbā Walda Ewosṭātēwos of Gāšolā, abbā Awkātēwos of Ṭārā, abbā Cyriac of Guanğ, abbā Oryo of Marṭula Māryām, Kidāna Māryām: the *tāḫśāś* priests. Oryo of Ambā, abbā Amḫā Pēṭros, *abēto* Talāfinos of Dabra Warq, *abēto* Walda Rufā'ēl of Marṭula Māryām, abbā Sinodā of Dabra Warq: the *ṭerr* priests. These are the ones who stay and serve at the left of the altar of the eloquent Lamb, while he said: "for I am not come to call the righteous, but sinners to repentance" [St. Matthew 9, 13], and he taught this: that he would sacrifice himself on Mount Calvary to save the world.

[*V. The Hebdomadaries*]

We will also list [the ministers] hebdomadories of Our Lord Jesus Christ's body and blood: *abuna* John, metropolit [1746-1762] of Ethiopia, *aṣē* Adyām Sagad, *aṣē* Iyo'ab, *liqta danāgel* Walatta Qeddusān, that is, Enkuaya, *bitwaddad* Walda Le'ul, *mamher* abbā Stephen of Adāgāt, *mal'aka ṣaḥay mamher* abbā Theodore of Ṣelālo, *dağ azmāč* Walda Gabre'ēl, that is, Guašu, *liqa monakosāt* abbā A'eyenta Krestos di Wāfā, *mamher* Alexander, *mamher* Josiah of Denğ, Fālēq of Guanğ, *ṣawārē salām* abbā Ḥenṣā Giyorgis of Ṭārā, abbā Ba'eda Māryām of Guanğ, *dağ azmāč* Aboladis, that is, Danē Māmmo, *dağ azmāč* Eusebio, *gerā azmāč* Yemāna Krestos, *abēto* Walda Mikā'ēl, *abēto* Gabra Ḥeywat [p. 255], *abēto* Gabra Madḫen, abbā Abraham of Dabsān, abbā Adarā Giyorgis of Dabra Warq, *abēto* Yā'eqob, *abēto* Ḥiruta Śellāsē, *liqa le'uqān* abbā Akāla Masqal, abbā Śenna Egzi' of Qomā, *dağ azmāč* Zawalda Māryām, that is, Yamāryām Bāryā of Ayo, abbā Samuel of Dabra Warq, George of Denğ, *asāllāfi*

Manbara Krestos, that is, Aškar Yābbo Bāryā, Marmehenām of Dabra Warq, Amda Mikā'ēl of Wāfā, abbā Zamanfas Qeddus of Denğ, *wayzaro* Śāhela Śellāsē, abbā Asāf of Guanğ, Ḫāyla Dengel of Ṣelālo, Śarṣa Dengel of Enaganā, abbā Walda Abib of Guanğ, abbā Sunotyos of Adāgāt, Iyorām of Denğ, abbā Abdeyu of Ṣelālo, abbā Ḫāylu of Ṣelālo, Mangeśta Ab of Guanğ, abbā Walda Kiros of Ṣelālo, abbā Latṣun di Adāgāt, abbā Eusebius of Tāmrē, *abēto* Kenfa Mikā'ēl of Esther, Habta Śellāsē of Esther, abbā Walda Mikā'ēl of Adāgāt, *wayzaro* Walatta Śellāsē of Helena, Ṣegē Śellāsē of Helena, Walda Mikā'ēl of Adāgāt, Walda Śellāsē of Weglo, Zekro, *ṣamāqi za-yamān*. These are they who stand and officiate at the right of the altar and each day sacrifice this lamb who was once sacrificed on Mount Calvary to save the world.

We shall also list [the ministers] ebdomadaries of the body and blood of Our Lord Jesus Christ: *yetēgē* Berhān Mogasā, *wayzaro* Walatta Esrā'ēl, *abēto* Ḫāyla Iyasus, *wayzaro* Helen, *wayzaro* Esther, *wayzaro* Walatta Iyasus, *abēto* Aṣqu, *abēto* Ḫāylu, the sons of the Royal Family, *'āqābē sa'āt* Job, *dağ azmāč* Walda Ewosṭātēwos who was *warañña*, *asāllāfi* Kenfa Masqal, abbā Tasfā Giyorgis of Ṣelālo, *dağ azmāč* Takla Hāymānot who was Gētā, *bālābārās* Eusinius, that is [p. 256] Ešatē, *dağ azmāč* Cyriac, *aba monakosāt* abbā Jeremy of Ṭārā, *afa neguś wa-negeśt abēto* Armāsqos, *abēto* Ḫāyla Mikā'ēl, *ṣaḥafē maṣāḥeft* Akāla Qāl of Qomā, Sutu'ēl of Dabra Warq, *yašālaqā* Claudius, that is, Māmmo of Ešatē, *yašālaqā* Zawalda Māryām, that is Yamāryām Bāryā, *mal'aka gannat* abbā Walda Yoḥannes, *abēto* Arka Śellus of Dabsān, abbā Dionysius of Dabra Warq, Gabra Dengel of Dabra Wark, abbā John of Ṣarābē, *gabaza kāhenāt* abbā Arka Mar'āwi of Dabra Demāḥ, abbā Mēlyos of Guanğ, abbā Theodotus of Dabra Warq, abbā Qāynān of Guanğ, abbā Ḫaliba Wangēl of Arahunā, *abēto* Ḫāyla Giyorgis, *abēto* Ḫenṣā Kessos, *abēto* Absalon, 'Āṣma Giyorgis, that is, Ḫanāṣi Teku, Walda Ṣeyon of Feṭqā, abbā 'Āṣma Giyorgis, that is, Bāntihun, Abel of Dabra Warq, abbā Walda Le'ul of Dabsān, abbā Kidāna Wald of Guanğ, abbā Takla Egzi' of Adāgāt, abbā Walda Ewosṭātēwos of Ǧabarā, abbā Walda Rufā'ēl, abbā Gabra Ḫeywat of Guanğ, abbā Asāf of Dabra Warq, Walda Le'ul of Andābēt, abbā Śarṣa Ewosṭātēwos of Dabra Warq, *yašālaqā* Yābbo Bāryā, Mā'eqaba Egzi' of Dabra Warq, Zekro, *ṣamāqi za-ṣagām*. These are they who stand and celebrate at the right of the altar, and each day sacrifice this lamb which was once sacrificed on Mount Calvary to save the world.

We also write the names of the keepers of the sanctuary of the Lord: *azāži* Ḫiruta Śellāsē, Walda Yoḥannes, Walda Iyasus, *belāttēn gētā* Peter, Kenfa Masqal and Kenfu di Guarguarā, *abēto* Ḫāyla Śellāsē, Zekerē and Gabra Śellus, *belāttēn gētā* Joseph, that is, Teku, Ḫāyla Śellāsē and Gabra Śellāsē, *abēto* Gabra [p. 257] Krestos, Gabra Amlāk and Stephen, Walda Aragāwi, Qebreyāl and Abdeyu, abbā Isaiah, Rāgew and Kidāna Māryām, *anṭeraññā* Kenfu, Walda Gabrēl and Walda Yoḥannes, Walda Ab and Kidāna Wald, Walda Gabre'ēl, Ephrem and Serapion, *asāllāfi* Tadlā, that is, Aškar Nač.o, Zawga Dengel and Kefla Giyorgis, Tersita Dengel of Ṣadā, Māryām Wadad, that is, Zawalda Māryām.

We now list these keepers of the sanctuary of the Lord according to their turn and their duties: Walda Ab, Kidāna Wald, Kefla Giyorgis and Walda Yoḥannes of Ǧabarā prepared the Eucharistic sacrifice from the beginning to the end of the year. Ephraim and Serapion always rang the bell and drew water for the sacrifice and fixed the baldachin in the day when the feast was celebrated, according to their turn. Stephen, Kenfa Masqal, Kidāna Māryām, Gabra Śellus and Zekra Māryām played the horn the day when the feast was celebrated and brought the incense embers to the priest who swings the censer, and read David's Psalter, from the beginning to the end, with their own section, when the priests gathered for the meal commemorating the king and the queen, according to their turn. *Azzāži* Ḫiruta Śellāsē, Walda Yoḥannes, Walda Iyasus and *belāttēn gētā* Peter guarded the sanctuary of the Lord in *maskaram*. *Abēto* Ḫāyla Śellāsē, Gabra Amlāk and [Stephen], *belāttēn gētā* Joseph, that is, Teku did the same in *ṭeqemt*; *abēto* Gabra Krestos, Ḫāyla Śellāsē and Gabra Śellāsē, Walda Aragāwi did the same in *ḫedār*; abbā Isaiah, Qebreyāl and Abdeyu, *anṭeraññā* Kenfu did the same in *tāḫśāś*; [Kidāna Māryām], Rāgew and Walda Gabrēl of Danda and Tersita Dengel of Ṣadā did the same in *ṭerr*. Abbā Adarā of Dabra Warq, in collaboration with Stephen for the embers of incense in *maskaram*; and abbā Theodotus together with Kenfa [p. 258] Masqal for the incense embers in *eqemt*; and abbā Gabra Ḫeywat of Guanğ, aided by Gabra Amlāk for the incense embers in *ḫedār*, and abbā Mēlyos with the collaboration of Kidāna Māryām for the incense embers in *tāḫśāś*; and abbā Latṣun with the collaboration of Zekra Māryām in *ṭerr*.

They cense each at his own time and they intercede with Our God according the Ordinary of the disciples' intercession and the Ordinary of the litanies of the Three Hundreds (eighteen Fathers of Nicea) and the Ordinary of the *za-yenaggeś* by Yārēd, the master of the holy psalmody, at the time of the*wāzēmā* and of the *mawaddes* and of the morning lauds and of the *aryām* and of the *ṣoma degguā* and of the *mehellā*, according to their turn. May the God of mercy be merciful to us and, being patient, may He not make his rage last any longer. Amen! Our father who art in heaven.

Fālēq, Yā'eqob, on the right; Walda Ewosṭātēwos of Ǧabarā, *abēto* 'Āṣqu, *abēto* Ḫāylu, royal princes, on the left, having as their assistants Māryām Wadad, that is, Zawalda Māryām in *maskaram*. *Aṣē* Iyo'as, *abēto* Kenfa Mikā'ēl of Esther, Takla Ewosṭātēwos, on the right; *dağ azmāč warañña* Bāntihun, Kidānu, on the left, with the help of Māryām Wadad, that is, Zawalda Māryām, in the month of*ṭeqemt*. *Dağ azmāč* Guašu, Walda Abib, Sunotyos, on the right; Ḫanāṣi Teku, Śarṣa Dengel, Mangeśta Ab, on the left, with the collaboration of Zawga Dengel: in the month of *ḫedār*; *gerā azmāč* Yemānē, *abēto* Walda Mikā'ēl, abbā Walda Mikā'ēl of Adāgāt, on the right;

wayzaro Walatta Iyasus, Abraham, Walda Le'ul, on the left, with the help of Walda Gabrēl, in the [month of] *tāḫśāś*; Eusebius of Tāmrē, Ḫabta Śellāsē of Esther, Ṣegē Śellāsē of Helen, on the right; *abēto* Ḫāyla Mikā'ēl, Ḫalibu, Abel, on the right, with the help of Walda Gabrel, in the month of *ṭerr*. They say day and night prayers, every day of the year, with the exception of Pentecost and the nine feasts of [p. 259] Our Lord, Saturday and Sunday, and the Feast of Our Lady Mary, the Mother of God, and the feast of the Angels, and the Feast of the Apostles and the Feast of the martyrs and the Feast of the Holy Monks, where the priests sing the chant of Yāred, the priest of the new regulations, each according to their position and to ther turn. As for the compline prayer, they will not forget [it] on Saturdays and Sundays, since this is prescribed in the book by our abbā George, master of the faith. May their prayers and their blessing be with our King Iyāsu and with his mother, Queen Walatta Giyorgis, for ever and ever, Amen! Our Father who art in heaven.

Abbā Samuel in *maskaram*, Walda Yoḥannes in *ṭeqemt*, abbā Śarṣa Ewosṭātēwos of Dabra Warq in *ḫedār*, Marmehnām of Dabra Warq in *tāḫśāś*, Sutu'ēl of Ṣelālo in *ṭerr*: They will read David's Psaltery, from the beginning to the end, with their own section, every day, each according to their turn; and the abbot who will be elected, when the time comes, he will read St. John's Gospel and the Book of the "Fillet of Justification" and the Homily of the "Passage of the soul", for the soul of our King Iyāsu and of our Queen Walatta Giyorgis. May the Lord have mercy and take pity on them, and may He allow them much time for repentance. Amen! Our Father who art in heaven.

Aṣē Adyām Sagad, *mamher* Alexander, *mamher* Josiah, *abēto* Gabra Ḥeywat, George of Denǧ, on the right; *yetēgē* Berhān Mogasā, *aqābē sa'āt* Job, abbā Jeremy, *abēto* Armāsqos, abbā John, *asāllāfi* Kenfu, Ešatē Māmmo, on the left, in the month of *maskaram*. *Abuna* John, *bitwaddad* Walda Le'ul, abbā Akāla Masqal, abbā Ba'eda Māryām, 'Āmdu, *wayzaro* Śāhela Śellāsē, on the right; *wayzaro* Walatta Esrā'ēl, *mal'aka gannat* Walda Yoḥannes, abbā Dionysius, Gabra Dengel, Gabra Madḫen, Walda Ṣeyon, of the right: in the month of [p. 260] *ṭeqemt*. *Mamher* Theodore, abbā A'eyenta Krestos of Wāfā, abbā Śenna Egzi', abbā Asāf, *Abēto* Ḫiruta Śellāsē, on the right; *wayzaro* Helen, *wayzaro* Ester, *abēto* Ḫenṣā Krestos, *abēto* Absalon, abbā Tasfā, Akāla Qāl of Qomā, abbā Gabra Giyorgis, on the left: in the month *ḫedār*. *Tāllāq emmabētē wayzaro* Walatta Śellāsē of Helen, Danē Māmmo, abbā Zamanfas Qeddus, abbā Abdeyu, Ḫāyla Dengel, on the right; *dağ azmāč* Gētā, *dağ azmāč* Cyriac, abbā 'Ārka Mar'āwi, *abēto* Arka Śellus, abbā Qāynān, abbā Walda Rufā'ēl, on the left: in the month of *tāḫśāś*; *dağ azmāč* Eusebius, abbā Ḫenṣā Giyorgis, Walda Kiros, on the right side; *mamher* Stephan, *bālāmbārās* Ešatē, *abēto* Ḫāylu, *abēto* Yamāryām Bāryā, Yābbo Bāryā, abbā Takla Egzi', abbā Walda Le'ul, Mā'eqaba Egzi': in the month of *ṭerr*.

May the prayer and the blessing of these elected priests, harps of the Church, be with our King Iyāsu, lover of God, and with our Queen Walatta Giyorgis, lover of God, for ever and ever. Our father who art in heaven.

'Āsbē, Walda Malakot, Alpheus, Gabārē, Takla Hāymānot, Kidānu will make the whip of cords crack when the horn plays on the day of the celebration of the feast, and when the abbot of the monastery comes out to visit the priests' residence, and they will draw water for the plants of the church and they will take care of the monastery's field and they will clean the church according to their turn. As for the payment for their work, it is only the land [of the island] of Daq, and they do not have other territories. For this reason we have not numbered them together with the priests, when we described, one after the other, their duties. The insignia of the celebration of the feast and of the abbot, that is, the cross-shaped globe with the pole and the brocade beneath will be carried by the following three people: Raphael, Walda Le'ul, Nabiya Le'ul, according to their turn. The payment for their work is as the one for those who make the whip with cords crack.

Short Glossary

aba monakosāt: 'the monks' father'
abba: deferential title applied to all clergy in general
abēto: title applied exclusively to the princes of the Royal Family
abuna: 'our father'; title applied specifically to the metropolite, also used for the other bishops and high prelates
afa mamher: 'the master's mouth'; the subsitute, the abbot's vicar, prior of Dabra Esrā'ēl (Nārgā)
afa neguś wa-negeśt: 'The King's and Queen's mouth'; master of ceremonies
anṭeraññā: goldsmith
'āqābē sa'āt: 'guardian (keeper) of the hours'; the king's councellor; position occupied in Gondar by an abbot of Dabra Meṭmaq
aryām: one of the modes of the plain-chant
asāllāfi: cup-bearer, with the charge of pouring hydromel during banquets
aṣē: His Majesty (the King)
azāž: 'he who commands, supervisor'; the substitute, the abbot's vicar; prior of Dabra Esrā'ēl
azzāži: judge of the Supreme Court; title of the sons of the princesses of the Royal Family, to whom the king attributed this position
bālāmbārās: 'commander of an amba'
bažirond: the King's treasurer, keeper of the wealth of the Royal Family
belāttēn gētā: a sort of Prime Minister of the Royal Family
bēta krestiyān: 'the house of the Christians'; church
bētaleḥēm: 'Bethelem, or House of the bread'; place near the church where the eucharists are prepared
bitwaddad: Councellor of the kingdom
dabtarā: cantors of liturgical chants
dağ azmāč: 'commmander of the door'; a sort of court general
dağğa salām: 'the door of the peace'; place near the church where the priests, after the liturgy, eat the *makfalt*
ečagē: title of the abbot of Dabra Libānos monastery
endā ta'ammer: 'the place of miracles'; the *qeddest*, that is, the central part of the church
gabaza kāhenāt: 'the priests' administrator'
genbot: the ninth month of the year (6th May -4th June)
gerā azmāč: 'commmander of the left', military commander
ḥamlē: the eleventh month of the year (5th July-3rd August)
ḥedār: the third month of the year (8th November-7th December)
ḥetyā: a type of fabric
liqa le'uqān: 'chief of the hebdomadaries'
liqa monakosāt: 'the monks' chief'
liqta danāgel: 'the virgins' superioress', that is, the nuns' superioress
magābit: seventh month of the year (7th March-5th April)
maggābē kāhnāt: 'the priests' treasurer'
makfalt: 'repartition'; agape or bread eaten by the priests after the liturgy
mal'aka gannat: 'angel of the paradise'; abbot of the monastery of St. Michael in Gondar
mal'aka ṣaḥay: 'angel of the sun'; abbot of Dabra Berhān in Gondar
mamher: 'master'; abbot, a clergyman renowned for his learning
manbar: 'throne'; the altar on which the *tābot* is placed
maqdas: 'sanctuary'; the part of the church where the liturgy is celebrated
maqomyā: ceremonial stick, which the cantors use to beat out the rhythm and to lean on
maskaram: the first month of the year (9th September-8th October)
mawaddes: the Sunday mass
meḥellā: supplication, rogation
miyāzyā: the eight month of the year(6th April-5th May)
morasas: a type of fabric
nabiya Esrā'ēl: 'prophet of Israel'
naḥasē: the twelfth month of the year (4th August-2th September)
qañ azmāč: 'commander of the right', army officer
qeddest: 'saint'; the central part of the church
qeddesta qeddusān: 'saint of saints'; a square room, in the middle of the *maqdas*, where the *tābot* is placed
pāguemēn: the thirteenth month of the year (3rd September-8th September)
qenē māḥlēt: the part of the church where the liturgical chants are sung
rās: military and political chief, the supreme charge after the king
ṣaḥafē maṣāḥeft: 'writer of books'; court chronicler

ṣamaqi za-ṣagām: 'left cup-bearer'
ṣamaqi za-yamān: 'right cup-bearer'
ṣānāṣel: sistrum, musical instrument used for playing the sacred chant
sandaq: globe surmounted by a cross or imperial globe
sanē: the tenth month of the year (5th June-4th July)
ṣawārē salām: 'bringer of peace'
ṣoma deggʷā: liturgical book containing the hymns and the antiphons used during the celebrations of Lent
tābot: 'ark'; sacred stone
tāḫśāś: the fourth month of the year (8th December-7th January)
tāllāq emmabētē: Her Majesty the lady of the house; title of the Mother Queen
tānkuā: raft, small boat made with papyrus
ṭeqemt: the second month of the year (9th October-7th November)
ṭerr: the fifth month of the year (7th January-5th February)
warañña: 'narrator', 'boaster'; pretender, rebel
wayzaro: princess; lady
wāzēmā: the Vesper service of solemn feasts, chanted on the vigil
wellāğ: mulatto
yakātit: the sixth month of the year (6th February-7th March)
yašālaqā: 'commander of a thousand'
yetēgē: 'Her Majesty (the Queen)'
za-yenaggeś: 'he who reigns'; characterizes the intercession-type of prayers.

	Nome delle lettere	Trascri-zione	1° a	2° u	3° i	4° ā	5° ē	6° ĕ	7° o	
1.	*hoy*	h	ሀ	ሁ	ሂ	ሃ	ሄ	ህ	ሆ	h
2.	*lāw*	l	ለ	ሉ	ሊ	ላ	ሌ	ል	ሎ	l
3.	*ḥawt*	ḥ	ሐ	ሑ	ሒ	ሓ	ሔ	ሕ	ሖ	ḥ
4.	*māy*	m	መ	ሙ	ሚ	ማ	ሜ	ም	ሞ	m
5.	*śawt*	ś	ሠ	ሡ	ሢ	ሣ	ሤ	ሥ	ሦ	ś
6.	*rēʾēs*	r	ረ	ሩ	ሪ	ራ	ሬ	ር	ሮ	r
7.	*sāt*	s	ሰ	ሱ	ሲ	ሳ	ሴ	ስ	ሶ	s
8.	*qāf*	q	ቀ	ቁ	ቂ	ቃ	ቄ	ቅ	ቆ	
9.	*bēt*	b	በ	ቡ	ቢ	ባ	ቤ	ብ	ቦ	b
10.	*tāw*	t	ተ	ቱ	ቲ	ታ	ቴ	ት	ቶ	t
11.	*ḫarm*	ḫ	ኀ	ኁ	ኂ	ኃ	ኄ	ኅ	ኆ	ḫ
12.	*nahās*	n	ነ	ኑ	ኒ	ና	ኔ	ን	ኖ	n
13.	*alĕf*	ʾ	አ	ኡ	ኢ	ኣ	ኤ	እ	ኦ	ʾ
14.	*kāf*	k	ከ	ኩ	ኪ	ካ	ኬ	ክ	ኮ	k
15.	*wāwē*	w	ወ	ዉ	ዊ	ዋ	ዌ	ው	ዎ	w
16.	*ʿayn*	ʿ	ዐ	ዑ	ዒ	ዓ	ዔ	ዕ	ዖ	ʿ
17.	*zay*	z	ዘ	ዙ	ዚ	ዛ	ዜ	ዝ	ዞ	z
18.	*yaman*	y	የ	ዩ	ዪ	ያ	ዬ	ይ	ዮ	y
19.	*dant*	d	ደ	ዱ	ዲ	ዳ	ዴ	ድ	ዶ	d
20.	*gamĕl*	g	ገ	ጉ	ጊ	ጋ	ጌ	ግ	ጎ	g
21.	*ṭāyt*	ṭ	ጠ	ጡ	ጢ	ጣ	ጤ	ጥ	ጦ	ṭ
22.	*p̣āyt*	p̣	ጰ	ጱ	ጲ	ጳ	ጴ	ጵ	ጶ	p̣
23.	*ṣaday*	ṣ	ጸ	ጹ	ጺ	ጻ	ጼ	ጽ	ጾ	ṣ
24.	*ṣ̱app̣ā*	ṣ̱	ፀ	ፁ	ፂ	ፃ	ፄ	ፅ	ፆ	ṣ̱
25.	*af*	f	ፈ	ፉ	ፊ	ፋ	ፌ	ፍ	ፎ	f
26.	*p̂ēsā*	p	ፐ	ፑ	ፒ	ፓ	ፔ	ፕ	ፖ	ṗ

Translation-table from ethiopian alphabet into Latin characters (from Carlo Conti Rossini, *Grammatica elementare della lingua etiopica*, Roma 1967).

Bibliography

ALVAREZ = Francisco Alvarez, *Viaggio nella Ethiopia al Prete Ianni*, in Giovan Battista Ramusio, *Navigazioni e viaggi*, Turin 1979.

ANFRAY = F. Anfray, *Les anciens éthiopiens*, Paris 1990.

ANNEQUIN 1965 I = G. Annequin, "Adadi-Maryam (ou Anfar-Maryam) Choa §V.B di Cronique archéoligique (1960-1964)", *Annales d'Ethiopie*, VI, Paris 1976, pp. 13-16.

ANNEQUIN 1965 II = G. Annequin, "Eglise de Barié-Guemb, §V.C.3 di Cronique archéologique (1960-1964)", *Annales d'Ethiopie*, VI, Paris 1976, pp. 17-22.

ANNEQUIN 1975 = G. Annequin, "Tresors meconnus d'une Thebaide a l'abandon", *Les dossier de l'archèologie*, n. 8, January-February 1975, pp. 81-115.

ANNEQUIN 1976 = G. Annequin, "De quand datent l'église actuelle de Dabra Behran Sellase de Gondar et son ensemble de peintures?", *Annales d'Ethiopie*, X, Paris 1976, pp. 215-226.

ASSUNZIONE = Il Libro del Riposo etiopico, *Gli Apocrifi del Nuovo Testamento* , edited by Mario Erbetta, voll. I/1-2. *Vangeli* I/2: *Infanzia e passione di Cristo - Assunzione di Maria*, Casale Monferrato 1981, Marietti, pp. 421-456.

BACHMANN = *IV. König Iyāsē II. und der Königin Mutter Walatta Giyorgis Verdienste um die Erbarung des* Maqdasa Śellus Qeddus (Nach dem Berliner Mscr. or. fol. 595, ff. 168 sgg.), *Aethiopische Lesenstücke. Inedita aethiopica für den Gebrauch in Universitäts-Vorlesungen herausgegeben von* Dr. Johannes Bachmann, Leipzig 1893, J.C. Hinrichs'sche Buchhandlung , pp. 13-19.

BIANCHI BARRIVIERA = L. Bianchi Barriviera, *Le chiese in roccia di Lalibela e di altre chiese del Lasta*, Rome 1963.

BRUCE = *Voyage en Nubie et en Abyssinie, entrepris pour découvrir les sources du Nil, Pendant les années 1768, 1769, 1770, 1771, 1772 & 1773,* edited by M. James Bruce, translation from the English by M. Castera, tome IV, Paris 1791, Hôtel de Thou, Rue des Poitvins,.

BUDGE 1923 = *One hundred & ten Miracles of our Lady Mary translated from Ethiopic Manuscripts for the most part in the British Museum, with extracts from some ancient European versions, and Illustrations from the paintings in Manuscripts by Ethiopian Artists, by Sir E.A. Wallis Budge...*, London 1923.

BUDGE 1928 = E.A. Wallis Budge, *The Book of the Saints of the Ethiopian Church*, voll. I-IV, Cambridge 1928.

BUDGE 1933 = E.A. Wallis Budge, *Legends of Our Lady Mary the Perprtual Virgin and Her Mother Ḥannā*, Oxford-London 1933.

CATALDI = G. Cataldi, *Introduzione allo studio dell'abitazione umana*, Florence 1989.

CERULLI 1943 = E. Cerulli, *Il Libro etiopico dei Miracoli di Maria e le sue fonti nelle letterature del Medio Evo latino*, Rome 1943.

CERULLI 1957 = E. Cerulli, La festa etiopica del Patto di Misericordia e le sue fonti nel greco "Liber de Transitu" e nel racconto latino dei Cinque Dolori di Maria, in "'Silloge Bizantina'" in onore di Silvio Giuseppe Mercati, *Studi Bizantini e Neoellenici*, 9, Rome 1957, pp. 53-71.

CERULLI 1968 = E. Cerulli, *La letteratura etiopica. Con un saggio sull'Oriente Cristiano*, Milan 1968.

CHOJNACKI = S. Chojnacki, "Major Themes in Ethiopian Painting: Indigenous Developments, the Influence of Foreign Models and Their Adaptation From the 13th to the 19th Century", (*Äthiopistische Forschungen*, vol. 10), Wiesbaden 1983, Steiner.

CONTI ROSSINI 1928 = C. Conti Rossini, *Storia d'Etiopia*, Bergamo 1928.

CONTI ROSSINI 1937 = C. Conti Rossini, *Etiopia e genti d'Etiopia*, Florence 1937.

DAE III = *Deutsche Aksum-Expedition*, (Herausgegeben von der Generalverwaltung der königlichen Museen zu Berlin, vol. III). *Profan- und Kulturbauten Nordabessiniens aus älterer und neurer Zeit* von Theodor von Lüptke, unter Mitwirkung von Enno Littmann und Daniel Krencker, mit 11 Tafeln und 281 Textabbildungen, Berlin 1913, Druck und Verlag von Georg Reiner.

DAINELLI 1938 = G. Dainelli, *Missione di studio al Lago Tana*, Rome 1938.

DAINELLI 1939 = G. Dainelli, *La regione del Lago Tana*, with 174 previously unpublished illustrations and a map, Mondadori, Milan 1939.

DE CHAMPEAUX = G. De Champeaux, S. Sterckx, *I simboli del medioevo*, Milan 1992.

DE CONTENSON = H. de Contenson, Les fouilles à Haoulti-Melazo en 1958, *Annales d'Ethiopie*, IV, Paris 1961, pp. 39-60.

DI LAURO 1936[1] = R. Di Lauro, *Le terre del lago Tsana. Possibilità economiche attuali del nord-ovest etiopico*. Under the auspices of the Fascist Colonial Office, Rome-XIV, Società Italiana Arti Grafiche, Rome 1936.

DI LAURO 1936[2] = R. Di Lauro, *Tre anni a Gondar*, Milan 1936.

DORESSE = J. Doresse, *Histoire sommaire de la Corne orientale d'Afrique*, Paris 1971.

ENCICLOPEDIA = *Enciclopedia dei Santi. Le Chiese Orientali* (Bibliotheca Sanctorum Orientalium), vol. I (A-Gio), Città Nuova Editrice, Rome 1998.

ESTEVES PEREIRA = F.M. Esteves Pereira, *Vida do Abba Samuel do Mosteiro do Kalamon*. Versão ethiopica, Lisbon 1894.

ETHIOPIAN = *The Ethiopian Orthodox Tewahedo Church. Faith, Order of Worship and Ecumenical Relations*. This Book was published in line with the current effort being made by His Holiness Abune Paulos I Patriarch of Ethiopia to accelerate the progress of the Church. 2nd Edition. *Publisher*: Tensae publishing House, Addis Ababa, July 1996 (Amharic-English).

EURINGER I-II = "Die Geschichte von Nārgā. Ein Kapitel aus der abessinischen Kulturgeschichte des 18. Jahrhunderts", Übersetzt und erläutert von Sebastian Euringer, in *Zeitschrift für Semitistik und verwandte Gebiete*, 9, 1934, 3/4, pp. 280-311 [= I]; 10, 1935, pp. 105-162 [= II].

FETḤA NAGAŚT = *"Fetḥa Nagaśt" o "Legislazione dei Re". Codice ecclesiastico e civile di Abissinia*, translated and annotated by Ignazio Guidi, Rome 1899.

GARBINI = G. Garbini, *Siro-palestinesi: antichi centri e tradizioni*, in *Enciclopedia Universale dell'Arte*, vol. XII, Venice-Rome 1972, col. 582.

GERSTER = G. Gerster, *L'arte etiopica. Chiese nella roccia*, Milan 1970.

GUÉNON = R. Guénon, *La Grande Triade*, Milan 1980.

GUIDA = *Guida dell'Africa Orientale Italiana*, CTI, Milan 1938.

GUIDI 1896 = I. Guidi, "Sopra due degli 'Aethiopische Lesenstücke' del Dr. Bachmann", in *Zeitschrift für Assyrologie und varwandte Gebiete*, 11 (1896-97), pp. 401-416.

GUIDI 1932 = I. Guidi, *Storia della letteratura etiopica*, Rome 1932.

HABTA MĀRYĀM WARQENAH = *Liqa śelṭānāt* Habta Māryām Warqenah, *Ṭentāwi ya-Ityop.yā śer'āta temhert* [= The classical teaching structure in Ethiopia], Addis Ababā, Berhānennā Salām, 40th year of the reign of the Emperor Hāyla Śellāsē I = A.D. 1970-71).

HAMMERSCHMIDT-JÄGER = E.Hammerschmidt e O.A. Jäger, *Illuminierte äthiopische Handschriften* (Verzeichnis der Orientalischen Handschriften in Deutschland, Band XV), Franz Steiner Verlag GMBH, Wiesbaden 1968.

HELFRITZ = H. Helfritz, *Äthiopien - Kunst im Verborgenen. Ein Reisebegleiter ins älteste Kulturland Afrikas*, Verlag M. DuMont Schauberg, Köln 1974.

JÄGER = O.A. Jäger, *Antiquities of North Ethiopia. A guide*, Stuttgart 1965.

KAMMERER = A. Kammerer, *Essai sur l'histoire antique d'Abyssinie*, Paris 1926.

LEROY = J. Leroy, *La pittura etiopica durante il medioevo e sotto la dinastia di Gondar*, Electa, Milan 1964.

LUDOLF 1681 = Ludolfus Jobus, *Historia Aethiopica, sive Brevis & succincta descriptio Regni Habessinorum*, Francofurti ad Moenum 1681.

LUDOLF 1691 = Ludolfus Jobus, *Ad suam Historiam Aethiopicam antahac editam Commentarius*, Francofurti ad Moenum 1691.

MILANESI = M. Milanesi, "I regni del Prete Gianni", in *Storie di viaggiatori italiani. Africa*, Milan 1986, pp. 42-55.

MONNERET DE VILLARD 1935 = U. Monneret De Villard, "Un tipo di chiesa abissina", abstract from *Africa italiana*, vol. 6, July-December 1935, nn. 3-4, pp. 1-9.

MONNERET DE VILLARD 1942 = U. Monneret De Villard, "La coronazione della Vergine in Abissinia", in *La Bibliofilia*, 44, 1942, pp. 167-175.

MONNERET DE VILLARD 1947 = U. Monneret De Villard, "La Madonna di S. Maria Maggiore e l'illustrazione di Maria in Abissinia", *Annali Lateranensi. Pubblicazione del Pontificio Museo Missionario Etnologico*, vol. 9, 1947, Città del Vaticano, pp. 9-90.

MONTI DELLA CORTE = A. Monti della Corte, *I castelli di Gondar*, Rome 1938.

MORDINI = A. Mordini, "La chiesa di Aramò (con considerazioni sulla datatzione dei monumenti d'arte religiosa etiopica)", *Rassegna di studi etiopici*, XV (1959), Rome 1960, pp. 39-54.

NAGARA MĀRYĀM = *Nagara Māryām (ba'amāreññā)* [The stories of M (in Amharic)], Addis Ababā, *ḫedār 5 qan 1961 'ā. m.* [15 novembre 1968], ba-Tasfā Mātamiyā bēt tāttama [Tasfā].

PANKHURST = S. Pankhurst, *Ethiopia. A Cultural History*, Essex 1955.

PÉTRIDÈS = S. Pierre Pétridès, *Le livre d'or de la dynastie salomonienne d'Ethiopie*, Paris 1964.

PHILIPPSON 1997 = D.W. Philippson, *The monuments of Aksum*, Addis Abeba 1997.

PHILIPPSON 1998 = D.W. Philippson, *Ancient Ethiopia. Aksum: Its Antecedents and Successors*, London 1998.

POLLERA 1926 = A. Pollera, *Lo stato etiopico e la sua chiesa*, Rome-Milan 1926.

POLLERA 1935 = A. Pollera, *Storie, leggende e favole del paese dei Negus*, Florence 1935.

RAFFRAY 1876 = A. Raffray, *Abyssinie*, Paris 1876.

RAFFRAY 1900 = A. Raffray, *L'Abissinia*, Milan 1900.

RAINERI 1981 = O. Raineri, "La 'Dottrina degli Arcani' (temherta ḫebu'āt) del Messale Etiopico Vaticano", *Ephemerides Liturgicae*, 95/6 (1981), pp. 550-555.

RAINERI 1996 = O. Raineri, *Santi guerrieri a cavallo, Tele etiopiche / Warrior Saints on Horseback, Ethiopian Paintings*, Ferrari Edizioni, Clusone (Bg) 1996.

RAINERI 1998 = O. Raineri, "Inventario dei manoscritti etiopici "Raineri" della Biblioteca Vaticana', in *Collectanea in honorem Rev.mi Patris Leonardi E. Boyle, O.P., septuagesimum quintum annum feliciter complens*, "Miscellanea Bibliothecae Apostolicae Vaticanae", VI (Studi e Testi 385), Città del Vaticano 1998, pp. 485-548.

RAVA = M. Rava, *Al lago Tsana (Il Mar profondo d'Etiopia). Relazione del viaggio compiuto dalla Missione Tancredi, per incarico della Reale Società Geografica*, Reale Società Geografica, Rome 1913.

SERGEW HABLE SELLASIE = S. Hable Sellassie, *Ancient and medieval ethiopian history to 1270*, Addis Ababa 1972.

SHORT HISTORY = *A Short History, Faith and Order of the Ethiopian Orthodox Tewahedo Church*. Published by the Ethiopian Orthodox Tewahedo Church Holy Synod, Printed by Tensae Zegoubae Printing Press, Addis Ababa, Ethiopia, First Edition, 1983 (Amharic-English).

SCERRATO = U. Scerrato, *Sasànidi centri e correnti*, in *Enciclopedia Universale dell'Arte*, vol. XII, Venice-Rome 1972.

SELIS = C. Selis, *Les Syriens orthodoxes et catholiques*, Brussels 1988.

STAUDE = W. Staude, "Études sur la décoration picturale des églises d'Abbā Antonios de Gondar et Dabra Sinā de Gorgora", *Annales d'Éthiopie*, 3, 1959, pp. 185-250.

TEDESCO ZAMMARANO = V. Tedesco Zammarano, *Da Adua al Lago Tana. Alle sorgenti del Nilo Azzurro*, Milan 1936.

TUCCI = G. Tucci, *Teoria e pratica del mandala*, Rome 1969.

VIGONI = P. Vigoni, *Abissinia. Giornale di Viaggio*, Milan 1881.

ZĒNĀ NĀRGĀ = I. Guidi, Il *Zēnā Nārgā* ('The story of Nārgā'), *Rendiconti dell'Accademia Nazionale dei Lincei*, vol. 14, 1905, pp. 233-267.

Index of names and place-names

The index does not include the names and the place-names mentioned in the Appendix.
(*) Denotes churches, monasteries and other religious buildings.